The ISS Directory of Overseas Schools

1997 – 1998

The Comprehensive Guide to K–12 American and International Schools Worldwide

Fees and other data are accurate as reported to ISS by the individual schools as of July 1, 1997. Readers are advised to obtain updated information from the individual schools. Maps are representational and intended for general orientation only. Country information was obtained from *The World Almanac and Book of Facts 1997.*

Published in 1981

Seventeenth edition in August 1997

ISBN 0-913663-14-X paperback

Distributed by Peterson's, PO Box 2123, Princeton, New Jersey 08543-2123, U.S.A.; telephones: (1)(800)338-3282, (1)(609)243-9111

Cost: $34.95 plus postage and handling charge of $6.75 domestic and $13.50 international

Cover: Suzanne Garfield Graphic Design, Hopewell Twp., New Jersey

International Schools Services, Inc.

PO Box 5910, Princeton, New Jersey 08543, U.S.A.

Telephone: 609.452.0990

Facsimile: 609.452.2690

E-mail: iss@iss.edu

http://www.iss.edu

CONTENTS

School Additions, Deletions & Changes

Additions

Bosnia & Herzegovina
QSI International School of Bosnia & Herzegovina, page 38

Cambodia
International School Cambodia, page 56

Honduras
Escuela Bilingue Santa Barbara, page 162
Discovery School, page 166

Hong Kong
Canadian International School, page 168
Carmel School, page 168

Indonesia
Hope International School, page 197

Korea
Indianhead School, page 254

Macedonia
American School, Macedonia, page 272

Nigeria
American International School of Abuja, page 317
The International Foreign Residents School of Eket, page 318

Qatar
The Learning Center, page 359

Singapore
International School Singapore, page 374

Taiwan
Lincoln American School, page 428

Thailand
Ake Panya International School, page 441

United States of America
Chinese American International School, page 479

Uzbekistan
The Tashkent Ulugbek International School, page 493

Deletions

Colombia
Marymount

Italy
Panterra American School

Japan
St. Joseph International School

Mozambique
American International School of Mozambique

The Netherlands
Beverweert International School

Panama
Escuela Las Palmas

Thailand
International School of Siam
Nakorn Payap International School

Country Name Change

The American School of Kinshasa of the country formerly known as Zaire can now be found under The Congo, Democratic Republic of.

ISS SERVICES

For 41 years, International Schools Services has been an integral part of the international education community, providing a broad range of services to schools throughout the world. Founded in 1955 as a not-for-profit educational organization, ISS provides support services to American and international schools. Over the years, hundreds of international schools, as well as many multinational corporations, have sought the services of ISS. In turn, ISS has expanded and evolved in response to the requirements of the schools and the international communities overseas.

Among the ISS services sought by multinational corporations are the establishment and operation of schools for their expatriate American/international communities and the consultation ISS provides regarding the educational needs of the dependents of overseas employees.

American and international schools around the world solicit the services of ISS to:

- ❑ recruit the best possible administrative and teaching staff
- ❑ procure and deliver quality school supplies at the best rates possible
- ❑ plan and implement school facilities
- ❑ plan and implement personnel, accounting, and benefit programs
- ❑ keep abreast of the most recent developments in U.S. education
- ❑ research and implement new programs
- ❑ consult on day-to-day operations, curriculum, and long-range planning
- ❑ operate U.S. foundations established by overseas schools

A range of services

Many people know ISS through one or another of its services, but few know the full extent of its activities. What follows are descriptions of the many services ISS offers to the international education community. If you would like more information on any of the following services, unless otherwise noted, please contact: ISS, PO Box 5910, Princeton, NJ 08543 U.S.A.; phone: 609.452.0990; fax: 609.452.2690; e-mail: iss@iss.edu; web: http://www.iss.edu.

School Management and Consulting

When American and multinational corporations set up operations abroad, an employee community often follows. If an American or international school is nearby, most of the expatriate children enroll there. When the company is located in a remote area, however, it must establish its own educational facility. At this point, the company often calls upon ISS to establish and operate a company school in accordance with the highest professional standards. In such situations, ISS handles staffing, personnel management, curriculum, community relations, supplies, and all other aspects of the operation.

At present, ISS operates such schools for companies in Asia, Africa, Europe, and Latin America.

Administrator Search

The Administrator Search department collaborates with school governing boards seeking chief school officers, and with current school heads searching for principals. This service exists to expedite the recruiting process and to ensure that outstanding candidates are notified and interviewed to produce the best possible match. Drawing on its experience of 40 years working with international schools, ISS provides personalized service, experience, and expertise that guarantees satisfaction.

Educational Staffing/IRC

Since 1955, ISS has placed well over 12,000 teachers and administrators in international schools. Utilizing state-of-the-art recruitment technology and a personalized screening approach tailored to each school's needs, ISS is able to present the most qualified teaching and administrative candidates for service in international schools around the world. In addition to continuous year-round recruitment, ISS hosts three International Recruitment Centers (IRCs) in the United States each year. The IRCs provide recruiting administrators with direct electronic access to candidate data and on-site interviewing of experienced, highly qualified teaching and administrative candidates. Candidates must have an active file with ISS to attend a recruitment center.

School & University Supply

This program provides a complete procurement system for overseas schools and universities. Offering over 20 years' experience and utilizing state-of-the-art procurement technology, our supply program delivers efficient, cost-effective, reliable, and on-time service. The service presently purchases for over 200 schools worldwide. Any commodity that a school might need, be it a pencil or a computer system, a textbook or a complete library, can be procured and shipped according to specific needs.

Technology Support

As a value-added supplement to the school supply program, ISS provides a consultation service that helps schools make informed purchasing decisions. ISS has a variety of contacts with professional experts in technology and can provide support on subjects such as networking, library automation, CD ROM resources, laserdisc technology, computer integration in curriculum, computer facility design, the Internet, and other forms of telecommunications.

International Technology Center (ITC)

ISS further enhances its technology support service by holding an annual technology conference. This four-day workshop on the latest technology in education is attended by over 200 U.S. and overseas educators each year. Topics range from computer integration throughout the curriculum, to multi-media with Hyperstudio, to the World Wide Web and Internet. Hands-on workshops, informative discussions, and tours of state-of-the-art educational facilities are all part of the ITC experience.

Healthcare Supply

Through an extensive network of suppliers and the expertise of our Healthcare Supply staff, this new program provides a comprehensive procurement and delivery system for teaching hospitals around the world.

Facility Planning and Interior Design

ISS has brought together professional consulting companies with previous overseas experience to provide international schools with a comprehensive and economical facility planning service. This team can help with any of the steps of planning or implementation within a project or can deliver a completely planned, built, and supplied facility. Major services available include the development of a master plan, detailed educational specifications, architectural and interior designs, and procurement and installation of equipment.

Foundations Management

For over a quarter of a century, ISS has helped to provide the U.S. support that overseas schools need to establish and/or maintain IRS-recognized, U.S.-based foundations. A foundation can enable tax-deductible support from corporations, individuals, and grant-giving foundations; allow professional staff to participate in U.S. Social Security, Medicare, healthcare and retirement programs (such as TIAA/CREF); and provide for U.S.-based payroll processing with direct-wire banking in U.S. dollars or a foreign currency. Currently, ISS is assisting foundations for both small and large schools on all continents.

Financial Management

The ISS accounting department, using a computerized system specifically designed to meet the needs of overseas schools, offers business and accounting consulting services to overseas schools. This unique service includes customized payroll processing, processing payroll benefits and reports, bookkeeping, cash management, ledger maintenance, invoicing, and preparation of quarterly financial statements.

Publications

In addition to *The ISS Directory of Overseas Schools*, ISS publishes a newspaper, ***NewsLinks***, distributed five times a year to schools, individuals, and companies interested in overseas education. Advertising space is available in both publications, and subscriptions to ***NewsLinks*** are available for $20 per year. For more information, please contact: Anne Schlessinger, Advertising Representative, ISS, PO Box 5910, Princeton, NJ 08543-5910 U.S.A.; phone: 609.452.0990; fax: 609.452.2690; e-mail: aschlessinger@iss.edu.

To order your copy of the 1997–98 *ISS Directory*, please send $34.95 plus shipping and handling charges of $6.75 per book domestic or $13.50 per book international to Peterson's Inc., Department ISS97, 202 Carnegie Center, PO Box 2123, Princeton, NJ 08543-2123 U.S.A. Or call 800.338.3282 (within the U.S.), 609.243.9111 (outside the U.S.).

USER'S GUIDE

The schools in the *ISS Directory* are primarily American and/or international with an English-language curriculum. They are arranged alphabetically, first by country, then city or town, and finally by school name. Isolated schools in rural areas are listed under the town nearest them. Schools in the suburbs of large cities are usually listed under the name of the city rather than that of the suburb. At the end of each country, there may be short entries for certain schools. These schools did not supply enough information to warrant a full-length entry. These "one-liners," as they are called, are in alphabetical order by city after the full-length entries in each country.

School addresses: Street addresses often differ from mailing addresses. When they are specifically given, use the mailing address for correspondence. This will save you time and money, particularly when mail originates within the United States and the mailing address is also within the United States, as in the case of the U.S. Department of State, APO, and FPO addresses.

APO and FPO are U.S. military mail services with strict regulations. No personal name may appear in an APO or FPO address. Instead, use the title of the chief school officer, followed by the address. U.S. Department of State addresses may include personal names.

Telephone numbers: Schools that can be dialed directly from the United States are listed with the country and city codes in parentheses (or only the country code if that is all that is needed), followed by the telephone number. If you are using the AT&T long-distance phone system, dial the international access code 011 before dialing any overseas number, except for Caribbean/Atlantic islands with an 809 area code. For these, dial 1, followed by the area code and phone number as you would for any call within the United States.

"No direct dial" means you need operator assistance to reach the number. To call from countries other than the United States, follow local procedures. To call the United States from abroad, use the local international access code followed by 1 (the U.S. country code), then the area code, and finally the phone number.

Multiple numbers are listed for schools that report them. Dissimilar numbers are indicated by a slash (444789/444802) and consecutive numbers by a dash (444789–91). For information on rates, codes, and time differences, call AT&T International Information Service, toll-free: 1-800-331-1140.

Facsimile, telex, cable, e-mail, and web: Facsimile numbers are listed with the country and then city code, followed by the school's number. Telex numbers are listed with the appropriate 3-digit area code, then the school's number, followed by the answerback. Cables can be sent to a school's name and address if no cable code is listed. For assistance with telexes and cables, call Western Union toll-free at 1-800-325-6000. All e-mail addresses listed in this directory are formatted for the Internet, unless otherwise noted. E-mail and web site addresses (or URLs) are in appendices in the back of this publication.

Chief school officer: The name and title of the head of the school is listed first, followed by the names of academic division heads and other administrative staff as reported to us. We can list a maximum of 5 school officials in each listing. The chief school officers are listed alphabetically in an appendix of this book.

Teaching staff: The number of both full and part-time teaching staff members are listed.

Nationalities of teaching staff and nationalities of student body: In most cases, both teaching staff and students are defined by four nationality groups: United States, United Kingdom, host country, and "other" nationalities.

Grade levels: Grades are listed in terms used by the schools themselves, usually as "grades," sometimes as English "forms," and occasionally as "ages." Forms 1 through 6 normally correspond to grades 7 through 12. The following abbreviations are used: N for nursery (usually 3- to 4-year-olds); preK for prekindergarten; K for kindergarten (usually 5- to 6-year-olds); preP for preprimary; R for reception; and preS for preschool.

Enrollment and capacity: In most cases, grade-level enrollments are given, followed by a total enrollment figure. Capacity figures are arranged in the same way.

Teacher/student ratio: This figure indicates the average number of students for each teacher. When a school did not indicate a teacher/student ratio, the following calculation was used: the total student enrollment is divided by the number of full-time staff plus half the number of part-time staff. The quotient is then rounded to the nearest whole number. For example, for a school with 187 students, 12 full-time, and 3 part-time teachers, the equation is 187 divided by 13.5. The quotient is 13.85 which rounds up to 14; therefore, the teacher/student ratio is 1/14.

Boarding facilities: Schools which offer boarding services are identified within their entries and in an appendix at the end of the *Directory*.

Tuition: Most tuition figures are given in U.S. dollars, indicated by a dollar sign. When a school reports its tuition in the currency of the host country, the first figure is marked with a double asterisk and the unit of currency is noted at the bottom of the entry. Succeeding tuition figures are also reported in the host currency.

Other fees: School charges other than tuition are listed. As above, host-country currency is noted with a double asterisk.

School year: Most schools in the Northern Hemisphere are in session from September to June, in the Southern Hemisphere from March to December.

Year founded: The oldest school listed is Hvitfeldtska Gymnasiet in Göteborg, Sweden, founded in 1647.

Type of school: Individual schools have identified themselves as falling within the following categories: coeducational, boys only, girls only, boarding, day, company-sponsored, church-related, proprietary, private nonprofit.

School government: Most overseas schools are governed by a board of directors or the host country's equivalent, a company, religious organization, or individual proprietor. Sponsors or operators are listed when reported.

Accredited by: Accreditation is not mandatory, but many overseas schools elect to go through the voluntary process of evaluation and accreditation by private accrediting associations and may report this in *The ISS Directory* as either a completed activity or one still in process. Other schools may list the host-national ministry of education or another official body as the accrediting agency. U.S. private accrediting associations are listed in an appendix.

Regional organization(s): Many schools are members of regional organizations. Schools that reported membership will have the names of these organizations listed here. Information about the regional organizations is listed in an appendix of this book.

Curriculum: Each school in the *ISS Directory* has an English-language curriculum, either alone or in combination with a host-national curriculum. Some offer the International Baccalaureate program (IB), a two-year course of study recognized by many colleges and universities throughout the world. The International Baccalaureate Middle Years program is IBMYP. Further explanation and a list of the schools offering the IB program are found in an appendix of this volume. ISCP stands for the International Schools' Curriculum Project. AP is the abbreviation for Advanced Placement.

Languages of instruction: This is included only if the language of instruction is English in combination with one or more other languages. No listing within this category means that instruction is in English only.

Languages taught: This lists the languages offered within the curriculum.

Staff specialists, special programs, special curricular, and extracurricular activities: This category lists specialists and offerings outside the main academic curriculum.

Tests: A key to the tests given by American and British international schools is included in an appendix at the back of *The ISS Directory*.

Percentage of graduates attending college and the colleges they attend: Secondary schools were asked to list five colleges or universities recently attended by their graduates.

Location, campus, library, and facilities: These brief descriptions are intended to convey the physical resources of a school.

LIST OF SCHOOLS

International School Resource Guide

Use this guide to make your school's purchasing decisions. Schools that purchase their supplies through ISS receive special discounts. Contact Gloria Petro, Director of School & University Supply at gpetro@iss.edu for more information.

Adirondack Direct *page A17*
Address: The Adirondack Bldg., 31-01 Vernon Blvd., Long Island City, NY 11106
Telephone: (718)204-4500 Facsimile: (718)204-4554
E-mail: adiron@gap.net Web: http://www.adirondack.thomasregister.com

Baker Taylor *page A17*
Address: P.O. Box 734, Somerville, NJ 08876-0734 USA
Telephone: (908)429-4074 Facsimile: (908)429-4037
E-mail: intlsale@baker-taylor.e-mail.com

Chelsea House Publishers *page A10*
Contact: Vince Spinella, International Sales Director
Address: 1974 Sproul Road, Suite 400, Broomall, PA 19008-0914
Telephone: (800)362-9786 Facsimile: (610)359-1439
E-mail: Sales@ChelseaHouse.com

Clements & Company *page A12*
Address: 1660 L Street, NW, 9th Floor, Washington, DC 20036
Telephone:(202)872-0060 or (800)872-0067 Facsimile: (202)466-9064
E-mail: info@clements.com

Collegeboard/Expan The Comphrensive Guidance Admission Network *page A22*
Facsimile: (212)213-4351 E-mail: expan@collegeboard.org
Web: http://www.collegeboard.org

The College of New Jersey *page A18*
Contact: The Office of International Studies
Address: CN 4700, Hillwood Lakes, Trenton, NJ 08650-4700
Telephone: (609)771-2596 Facsimile: (609)637-5124
E-mail: internat@tcnj.edu

Cornell University Summer College *page A12*
Address: Box 269, B20 Day Hall, Ithaca, NY 14853
Telephone: (607)255-6203 Facsimile: (607)255-8942
E-mail: sc@sce.cornell.edu Web: http://www.sce.cornell.edu/SC/

Dakota Sports *page A8*
Address: PO Box 88710, Sioux Falls, SD 57105
Telephone: (605)332.2131 Facsimile: (605)332-8642
E-mail: daksport@iw.net

Delta Education *page A16*
Address: 401 North Michigan Avenue, Suite 1200, Chicago, IL 60611
Telephone: (312)840-8584 Facsimile: (312)755-0690
E-mail: Tguet@aol.com

ECIS *page A27*
Contact: T. Michael Maybury
Address: 21 Lavant Street, Petersfield GU32 3EL, UK
Telephone: (44)(1730)268244 Facsimile:(44)(1730)267914
E-mail: ecis@ecis.org Web: http://www.ecis.org

The Educational Register *page A25*
Address: 224 Claredon Street, Suite 237, Boston MA 02116
Telephone: (617)536-0100 Facsimile: (617)536-8098
E-mail: register@vincentcurtis.com

FlagHouse *page A20*
Address: 601 Flaghouse Drive, Dept. #900928, Hasbruck Heights, NJ 07604
Telephone: (800)793-7000; local (201)288-7600
Facsimile: (800)793-7922; local (201)288-7887
E-mail: info@flaghouse.com

Gopher Sport *page A15*
Contact: Vicky Pete, International Account Representative
Address: 2929 West Park Dr., PO Box 998, Owatonna, MN 55060
Telephone:(507)451-7470 Facsimile: (507)451-4755
E-mail: GopherSport@LL.net

Great Source Education Group *page A8*
Contact: Debbie Secrist
Address: 181 Ballardvale Street, Wilmington, MA 01887 USA
Telephone: (508)661-1471 Facsimile: (508)661-1335
Web: http://www.greatsource.com

J.L. Hammett *inside back cover*
Contact: David Shepard
Address: Hammett Place, PO Box 859057, Braintree, MA 02185-9057
Telephone: (617)848-1000 ext. 168 Facsimile: (617)843-4901
E-mail: dave.shepard@hammett.com Web: http://www.hammett.com

Harcourt Brace Intl. Education Group *page A7*
Address: 6277 Sea Harbor Drive, Orlando, FL 32887, USA
Telephone: (407)345-3800 Facsimile: (407)352-3395
E-mail: international@harcourtbrace.com

Houghton Mifflin Company *page A15*
Address: 13400 Midway Road, Dallas, TX 75244-5165
Telephone: (972)980-1100 Facsimile: (972)980-6814 Web: http://eduplace.com

Living Abroad Magazine *page A31*
Address: 32 Nassau Street, Princeton, NJ 08542 USA
Telephone: (609)924-9302 Facsimile: (609)924-7844
E-mail: info@livingabroad.com

McDougall Littell *page A14*
Contact: International Coordinator
Address: PO Box 1667, Evanston, IL 60204-9906
Telephone:(847)869-3230, 3207 Facsimile: (847)424-3433
E-mail:rosemary_train@hmco.com E-mail: janice_nelson@hmco.com

McGraw-Hill *inside front cover*
Contact: International Department
Address: 1221 Avenue of Americas, New York, NY 10020-1095
Telephone: (212)512-3641 Facsimile: (212)512-2186

National Audio Visual Supply *page A21*
Address: Route 121 East, PO Box 116, Grafton, VT 05146-0116
Telephone: (802)869-6500 Facsimile: (802)869-6565
Web: http://www.web.com/~natav/

NTC/Contemporary Publishing Company *page A14*
Contact: Jim Schmelzer, Director of International Sales
Address: 4255 W. Touhy Ave. Lincolnwood, IL 60646-1975 USA
Telephone: (847)679-5500 Facsimile: (847)679-2494
E-mail: ntcpub@tribune.com

Optical Access International *page A22*
Address: 500 West Cummings, Woburn, MA 01801
Telephone:(617)937-3910 Facsimile: (617)937-3950
E-mail: sales@oai.com Web: http://www.oai.com

Rand McNally *page A19*
Contact: Educational Publishing Division
Adress: PO Box 1906, Skokie, IL 60076-8906
Telephone: (847)329-8100 Facsimile: (847)329-1985

Scholastic International *page A21*
Address: 555 Broadway, New York, NY 10012
Telephone:(212)343-4688 Facsimile: (212)343-4714
Web: http://Scholastic.com

School Specialty *page A12*
Contact: Janet Wendland
Address: 3525 South Ninth Street, PO Box 1547, Salina, KS 67402-1547 USA
Telephone: (913)827-0451 Facsimile: (913)827-3726
E-mail: schspec@tri.net Web: http://www.tri.net/~schspec

Scott Foresman Addison Wesley *page A13*
Address: 1 Jacob Way, Reading, MA 01867
Telephone: (1)(617)944-3700 ext. 5190 Facsimile: (1)(617)942-2829
E-mail: intorder@aw.com Web: http://www.sf.aw.com

Simon & Schuster Intl. School Division *page A29 & back cover*
Address: 160 Gould Street, Needham, MA 02194
Telephone: (617)455-1850 Facsimile: (617)455-1220
E-mail: first name_last name@trenhall.com Web: http://www.phschool.com

Social Studies School Services *page A8*
Address: 10200 Jefferson Blvd., PO Box 802, Culver City, CA 90232-0802
Telephone: (310)839-2436 Facsimile: (310)839-2249
E-mail: access@SocialStudies.com Web: http://SocialStudies.com

Steck-Vaughn Company *page A9*
Contact: Robert F. Sheridan, Director of International Sales
Address: PO Box 26015, Austin, TX 78755
Telephone: (512)343-8227 Facsimile: (512)795-3699
Web: http://www.steck-vaughn.com

TIAA-CREF *page A11*
Address: 730 3rd Avenue, New York, NY 10017
Telephone: (800)842-2776
Web: http://www.tiaa-cref.org

University of Maryland System *page A10*
Contact: International Programs (PDP)
Address: University Boulevard at Adelphi Road, College Park, MD 20742-1644
Telephone: (301)985-7442 Facsimile: (301)985-7959
E-mail: gradpdp@nova.umuc.edu

VIRCO *page A23*
Contact: Cheryl Rogers
Address: PO Box 5000, Hwy. 65 South, Conway, AR 72033
Telephone: (501)450-1106 Facsimile: (501)450-1170
E-mail: 73324.210@compuserve.com Web: http://www.virco-mfg.com

VWR Scientific Products / Sargent Welch *page A20*
Address: 3000 Hadley Road, South Plainfiled, NJ 07080 USA
Telephone: (908)412-7726 Facsimile: (908)757-0313
E-mail: cnevins@vwrsp.com Web: http://www.sargentwelch.com

World of Reading, Ltd. *page A6*
Address: PO Box 13092, Atlanta, GA 30324-0092
Telephone: (800)729-3703; (404)233-4042 Facsimile: (404)237-5511
E-mail: polyglot@wor.com Web: http://www.wor.com

HARCOURT BRACE
Dedicated to education around the world.
(and cyberspace, too)
Visit us at http://www.harcourtbrace.com on the Internet.
HARCOURT BRACE INTERNATIONAL EDUCATION GROUP
6277 Sea Harbor Drive • Orlando, FL 32887 • U.S.A. • Tel: 407-345-3800 • Fax: 407-352-3395 • E-mail: international@harcourtbrace.com
HARCOURT BRACE
Harcourt Brace School Publishers
Holt, Rinehart and Winston
Harcourt Brace Educational Measurement
Harcourt Brace Trade Division
BROWN-ROA

Independent School Guide

Canadian International School (Singapore) *page A37*
Contact: Registrar
5 Toh Tuck Road, Singapore 596679
Telephone: (65)467-1732 Facsimile: (65)467-1729
E-mail: CIS5@Cdn-Intl.edu.sg Web: http://www.Cdn-Intl.edu.sg

The Ethel Walker School *page A38*
Contact: Director of Admission
Address: Simsbury, CT 06070
Telephone: (860)408-4200 Facsimile: (860)408-4201

The Masters School *page A37*
Contact: Director of Admission
Address: 49 Clinton Ave., Dobbs Ferry, NY 10522
Telephone: (914)693-1400 ext. 215

Ojai Valley School *page A39*
Contact: Director of Admission
Address: 723 El Paseo Rd., Ojai, CA 93023
Telephone: (800)433-4687; (805)646-1423
Web: http://www.ovs.org

The Putney School *page A38*
Contact: Director of Admission
Address: Elm Lea Farm, Putney, VT 05346
Telephone: (802)387-6219
E-mail: admissions@putney.com Web: http://www.putney.com

Southwestern Academy *page A38*
Contact: Director of Admission
2800 Monterey Road, San Marino, CA 91108-1780 USA
Telephone: (818)799-5010 Facsimile: (818)799-0407

St. Margaret's School *page A39*
Contact: Director of Admission
PO Box 158, Tappahannock, VA 22560
Telephone: (804)443-3357
E-mail: admit@sms-va.com Web: http://www.sms-va.com

The Williston Northampton School *page A40*
Contact: Director of Admission
Address: 19 Payson Ave., Easthampton, MA 01027
Telephone: (413)529-3241 Facsimile: (413)527-9494
E-mail: admissions@williston.com Web: http://www.williston.com

THE OVERSEAS SCHOOLS

ALBANIA

Region: Eastern Europe
Size: 11,100 square miles
Population: 3,249,136
Capital: Tiranë
Telephone code: 355
Currency: lek
Languages: Albanian, Greek

TIRANA

Tirana International School

Phone: (355)(42)27734 **Facsimile:** (355)(42)32222
E-mail: glenn_mosher@tis.tirana.al
U.S. mail: Director, Box A, American Embassy Tirana, APO AE 09624
Director: Glenn H. Mosher
Teaching staff: full-time, 4; part-time, 6; total, 10
Nationalities of teaching staff: U.S., 5; other, 5; total, 10
Grade levels: N – 8
Enrollment: N, 6; K, 8; 1 – 6, 20; 7 – 8, 15; total, 49
Capacity: N, 10; K, 10; 1 – 6, 20; 7 – 8, 20; total, 60
Teacher/student ratio: 1/7
Tuition (annual): N, $2,000; K – 5, $6,900; 6 – 8, $9,200
Other fees: registration*, $100; capital levy, $4,000 deposit or $1,600/year fee; busing, $600/year
School year: September to June

Year founded: 1991. **Type of school:** coed, day, private nonprofit. **Governed by:** appointed board of directors. **Sponsored by:** Quality Schools International. **Regional organizations:** CEESA.

Curriculum/physical plant

Type: U.S. **Staff specialists:** reading, nurse. **Special programs:** intensive English, Albanian studies, Dutch studies. **Special curricular:** art, physical education, computer instruction, library, music. **Extracurricular:** field trips, seasonal music productions, plays, after-school clubs. **Sports:** basketball, field hockey, soccer, track and field, volleyball, roller hockey. **Tests:** CTBS. **Location:** in Tirana on small compound. **Campus:** 1 acre. **Library:** over 1,000 volumes. **Facilities:** 3 buildings, 5 classrooms, computer lab, playing fields, air conditioning.

*Once only fee

ARGENTINA

Region: South America
Size: 1,073,518 square miles
Population: 34,672,997
Capital: Buenos Aires
Telephone code: 54
Currency: peso
Languages: Spanish, Italian, English

BUENOS AIRES

ASOCIACION ESCUELAS LINCOLN

Street address: Andrés Ferreyra 4073, (1636) La Lucila, Buenos Aires, Argentina
Phone: (54)(1)7949400 **Facsimile:** (54)(1)7902117
E-mail: doll_g@lincoln.edu.ar
Superintendent: Gloria J. Doll
Dean of junior college: Raymond McKay
High school principal: Virginia Satterfield
Middle school principal: Linda Parcell
Elementary principal: Thomas Quinn
Business manager: Carlos A Patiño
Teaching staff: full-time, 92; part-time, 14; total, 106
Nationalities of teaching staff: U.S., 31; host, 65; other, 10; total, 106
Grade levels: preK – 12
Enrollment: preK, 51; K, 64; 1 – 5, 305; 6 – 8, 223; 9 – 12, 263; total, 906
Teacher/student ratio: 1/9
Tuition (annual): preK, $3,400; K, $8,550; 1 – 8, $11,650; 9 – 12, $12,550
Other fees (annual): capital levy*, $3,000; busing, $1,100; lunch, $600; matriculation, first year one month tuition and following years half month tuition; construction fee, $2,500
School year: August to June

Year founded: 1936. **Type of school:** coed, day, private nonprofit. **Governed by:** elected board of governors. **Accredited by:** Southern, Argentine Provincial Ministry of Education.

Curriculum

Type: U.S., national, IB, AP. **Languages of instruction:** English, Spanish. **Languages taught:** French, Spanish. **Staff specialists:** reading, computer, counselor, special education, nurse. **Special programs:** ESL, honors sections, SSL. **Special curricular:** art, chorus, band, physical education, computer instruction. **Extracurricular:** drama, yearbook, newspaper, literary magazine, excursions/expeditions, field trips. **Sports:** basketball, field hockey, soccer, softball, swimming, volleyball. **Clubs:** computer, drama, National Honor Society, National Junior Honor Society, student council, French, chorus, band, student lounge. **Tests:** PSAT, SAT, ACT, IB, AP, Iowa. **Graduates attending college:** 95%. **Graduates have attended:** Princeton, Cornell, Duke, Harvard, Tufts.

Physical plant

Location: in northern suburbs, 6 miles from downtown Buenos Aires. **Campus:** 7 acres. **Library:** 27,622 volumes. **Facilities:** 4 buildings, 67 classrooms, auditorium, cafeteria, infirmary, covered play area, tennis court, gymnasium, playing field, 5 science labs, 3 computer labs, swimming pool, air conditioning.

*Once only fee

St. George's College

Street address: Guido 800, 1878 Quilmes, Buenos Aires, Argentina
Phone/facsimile: (54)(1)2573472 – 4 **Facsimile:** (54)(1)2530030
E-mail: info@stgeorge.com.ar
Mail: Casilla de Correo No. 2, 1878 Quilmes, Buenos Aires, Argentina
Headmaster: N. P. O. Green
Teaching staff: full-time, 71; part-time, 12; total, 83
Nationalities of teaching staff: U.K., 11; host, 72; total, 83
Grade levels: K – 12
Enrollment: K, 73; prep, 225; secondary, 307; total, 605
Teacher/student ratio: 1/15
Boarders: boys, 69; girls, 28 **Grades:** 1 – 12 **Program:** planned 5- and 7-day
Tuition, 6 months: prep, $4,926 – 7,014; secondary, $7,854 – 8,268
Tuition and board, 6 months: 1 – 12, $6,600 (for overseas students only)
School year: March to December

Year founded: 1898. **Type of school:** coed, day, boarding, private nonprofit. **Governed by:** elected board of governors. **Accredited by:** Headmaster's Conference.

Curriculum

Type: U.K., national, IB, IBMYP. **Languages of instruction:** English, Spanish. **Languages taught:** French. **Staff specialists:** math, counselor, learning disabilities, nurse. **Special programs:** ESL. **Special curricular:** art, physical education, computer instruction, vocational, music. **Extracurricular:** drama, gymnastics, dance, computers, yearbook, literary magazine, excursions/expeditions, field trips, sports. **Tests:** PSAT, SAT, ACT, TOEFL, IB, IGCSE, IBMYP, Argentine Bachillerato. **Graduates attending college:** 95%. **Graduates have attended:** Dartmouth, Princeton, Columbia, Pennsylvania, Lafayette.

Physical plant

Location: in suburban area, 20 kilometers south of Buenos Aires center. **Campus:** 54 acres. **Library:** 9,000 volumes. **Facilities:** 15 buildings, 29 classrooms, cafeteria, infirmary, 11 playing fields, 4 science labs, 2 swimming pools, shooting range, all-weather surface for basketball, tennis, hockey, soccer, volleyball.

St. John's School

Street address: Pueyrredon 1499, 1641 Acassuso, Buenos Aires, Argentina
Phone: (54)(1)7923944/7927764 **Facsimile:** (54)(1)7925282
Headmaster: John Harrison
Teaching staff: full-time, 50; part-time, 75; total, 125
Nationalities of teaching staff: U.K., 6; host, 119; total, 125
Grade levels: N – 12
Enrollment: N – preK, 80; K, 40; 1 – 6, 360; 7 – 9, 180; 10 – 12, 130; total, 790
Nationalities of student body: U.K., 8; host, 750; other, 32; total, 790
Teacher/student ratio: 1/9
Tuition (annual): N – preK, $2,200; K – 6, $4,800; 7 – 12, $6,000
School year: February to December

Year founded: 1950. **Type of school:** coed, day, private nonprofit. **Governed by:** appointed and elected board.

Curriculum/physical plant

Type: U.K., IB. **Languages of instruction:** English, Spanish. **Staff specialists:** reading, math, computer, speech/hearing, counselor, psychologist, nurse. **Special programs:** independent study. **Special curricular:** art, physical education, computer instruction, vocational. **Extracurricular:** gymnastics, dance, choral music, yearbook, newspaper, photography, excursions/expeditions, field trips. **Sports:** athletics, hockey, rugby, soccer. **Tests:** IB, GCSE. **Graduates attending college:** 95%. **Graduates have attended:** Harvard, U. of San Andres, U. of Buenos Aires, Technological U. of Buenos Aires, Catholic U. of Buenos Aires. **Location:** in suburban area of Buenos Aires. **Campuses (3):** 25 acres. **Facilities:** cafeteria, infirmary, tennis court, playing field, science lab, computer lab, library.

BUENOS AIRES

Colegio San Marcos

Street address: Jorges Miles 153, 1842 Monte Grande, Buenos Aires, Argentina
Phone: (54)(1)2964215/2901261 **Facsimile:** (54)(1)2901261
Headmistress: Susana R. Raffo

St. Andrew's Scots School

Street address: Rawson 2759, Olivos, Buenos Aires, Argentina
Phone: (54)(1)7908032 – 3 **Facsimile:** (54)(1)7998318
Mail: R.S. Peña 691, 1636-Olivos, Buenos Aires, Argentina
Headmaster: A. G. F. Fisher

St. Catherine's Moorlands

Street address: Carbajal 3250, 1426 Buenos Aires, Argentina
Phone: (54)(1)5522973/5524353/5528572 **Facsimile:** (54)(1)5544113
E-mail: 104767.1611@compuserve.com or 104767.1576@compuserve.com
Principal: Mabel M. Manzitti

ARMENIA

Region: Eastern Europe
Size: 11,500 square miles
Population: 3,463,574
Capital: Yerevan
Telephone code: 374
Currency: dram
Language: Armenian

YEREVAN

QSI International School of Yerevan

Phone/facsimile: (374)(2)151438 **E-mail:** qsi@arminco.com
Mail: c/o American Embassy, Yerevan, Dept. of State, Washington, DC 20521-7020
Director: James T. Billings
Teaching staff: full-time, 3; part-time, 3; total, 6
Nationalities of teaching staff: U.S., 4; other, 2; total, 6
Grade levels: K – 8
Enrollment: K, 2; 1 – 6, 8; 7 – 8, 2; total, 12
Nationalities of student body: U.S., 5; other, 7; total, 12
Teacher/student ratio: 1/2
Tuition (annual): K – 5, $7,900; 6 – 8, $10,200
Other fees: registration*, $100; capital levy, $4,000 deposit or $1,600/year fee
School year: September to June

Year founded: 1995. **Type of school:** coed, day, private nonprofit. **Governed by:** appointed board of directors. **Sponsored by:** Quality Schools International. **Regional organizations:** CEESA.

Curriculum/physical plant

Type: U.S. **Special programs:** ESL. **Special curricular:** art, physical education, computer instruction. **Extracurricular:** drama, excursions/expeditions, field trips. **Location:** close to center of Yerevan, near U.S. Embassy and the American U. of Armenia. **Facilities:** 2 classrooms, multipurpose hall, nearby playing field.

*Once only fee

ARUBA

Region: Dutch Caribbean
Size: 75 square miles
Population: 68,000
Capital: Oranjestad

Telephone code: 297
Currency: florin
Languages: Papiamento, Dutch, English, Spanish

SEROE COLORADO

International School of Aruba

Phone: (297)(8)45365 **Facsimile:** (297)(8)47341
E-mail: intschool@setarnet.aw
Mail: Seroe Colorado, Aruba, Dutch Caribbean
Headmaster: Jerry C. McGee, Ed.D.
Guidance counselor: Richard Hurt
Teaching staff: total, 23
Grade levels: preK – 12
Enrollment: preK – K, 24; 1 – 5, 60; 6 – 8, 36; 9 – 12, 50; total, 170
Teacher/student ratio: 1/7
Tuition (annual): preK (full day), $4,000; K, $5,150; 1 – 5, $7,100; 6 – 8, $7,700; 9 – 12, $8,600
Other fees (annual): registration, $550; new student enrollment*, $550
School year: August to June

Year founded: 1985. **Type of school:** coed, day, private nonprofit. **Governed by:** self-perpetuating foundation board. **Accredited by:** New England, ECIS. **Regional organizations:** AASSA, ECIS, AAIE, A/OS.

Curriculum/physical plant

Type: U.S., international, AP. **Languages taught:** Spanish (K – 12); Dutch (1 – 12). **Staff specialists:** reading, computer, guidance counselor, librarian. **Special programs:** IBM Writing-to-Read. **Special curricular:** art, physical education, computer instruction, journalism. **Extracurricular:** drama, computers, yearbook, newspaper, excursions/expeditions, field trips, Model UN. **Sports:** basketball, soccer, softball, tennis, track and field, volleyball. **Tests:** PSAT, Iowa, TAP. **Location:** in suburban area, 5 minutes from the nearest town. **Campus:** 20 acres. **Facilities:** 3 buildings, 19 classrooms, 2 playing fields, 3 science labs, computer lab, multipurpose room, AV equipment, air conditioning.

*Once only fee

AUSTRALIA

Region: Pacific Ocean
Size: 2,966,200 square miles
Population: 18,260,863
Capital: Canberra
Telephone code: 61
Currency: Australian dollar
Languages: English, aboriginal languages

CORIO

Geelong Grammar School

Street address: 50 Biddlecombe Avenue, Corio, Victoria, Australia 3214
Phone: (61)(352)739257 **Facsimile:** (61)(352)756151
E-mail: simonl@ggscorio.vic.edu.au
Principal: Lister Hannah
Deputy principal/head of pastoral care: Sean Burke
Head of studies: Rob Wakefield
Business manager: Andrew Patterson
Teaching staff: full-time, 158; part-time, 18; total, 176
Grade levels: N – 12
Enrollment: preK – K, 185; 1 – 6, 416; 7 – 9, 464; 10 – 12, 621; total, 1,686
Teacher/student ratio: 1/9
Tuition (annual): $4,420 – 10,200
Other fees (annual): registration*, 50**; boarding, $10,860 – 11,400; books, 200; music
School year: February to December

Year founded: 1855. **Type of school:** coed, day, boarding, church-related. **Governed by:** appointed and elected school board.

Curriculum

Type: Victorian Certificate of Education. **Languages taught:** French, German, Japanese, Mandarin. **Staff specialists:** reading, math, speech/hearing, counselor, psychologist, learning disabilities, nurse. **Special programs:** ESL, remedial. **Special curricular:** art, band, physical education, computer instruction, vocational, choir, equestrian program. **Extracurricular:** drama, gymnastics, dance, choral and instrumental music, computers, yearbook, literary magazine, photography, excursions/expeditions, field trips. **Sports:** athletics, badminton, cricket, hockey, netball, rugby, soccer, softball, swimming, tennis, rowing, horseback riding, surfing, bushwalking, rock climbing, scuba diving, Australian rules football. **Clubs:** wetlands landcare, cooking, music, band. **Tests:** Victorian Certificate of Education. **Graduates attending college:** 100%. **Graduates have attended:** Melbourne U., Harvard, Monash, Sydney, Adelaide.

Physical plant

Location: in picturesque, semi-rural area overlooking Corio Bay, 10 kilometers from Geelong. **Campuses (4):** 1,300 acres. **Libraries (6):** 110,000 volumes. **Facilities:** 210 buildings, 100 classrooms, 4 auditoriums, 18 tennis courts, 4 gymnasiums, 4 science labs, 7 computer labs, 3 swimming pools, boarding facilities.

*Once only fee **Australian dollar

KILMORE

The Kilmore International School

Street address: 40 White Street, Kilmore 3764, Victoria, Australia
Phone: (61)(57)822211 **Facsimile:** (61)(57)822525
E-mail: kilmorei@hyperlink.net.au
Mail: PO Box 163, Kilmore 3764, Australia
Principal: Stewart Finn
IB coordinator: Arumugum Naidoo
Business manager: Ray Wittmer
Teaching staff: full-time, 17; part-time, 10; total, 27
Nationalities of teaching staff: U.K., 2; host, 14; other, 11; total, 27
Grade levels: 7 – 12
Enrollment: 7 – 9, 31; 10 – 12, 129; total, 160
Nationalities of student body: host, 36; other, 124; total, 160
Teacher/student ratio: 1/7
Boarders: boys, 109; girls, 38 **Grades:** 7 – 12 **Program:** planned 7-day
Tuition (annual): 7 – 8, 7,500**; 9 – 10, 11,000; 11, 11,500; 12, 12,000
Other fees (annual): registration*, 50**; boarding, 9,000; administration, 850; tutorial, 3,500
School year: February to mid-December

Year founded: 1990. **Type of school:** coed, day, boarding, proprietary. **Governed by:** appointed board of directors.

Curriculum/physical plant

Type: IB. **Languages taught:** Japanese, Chinese, Indonesian, Korean, Thai. **Staff specialists:** math, computer. **Special programs:** ESL, independent study. **Special curricular:** art, physical education, computer instruction. **Extracurricular:** drama, dance, instrumental music, computers, newspaper, excursions/expeditions, field trips. **Sports:** badminton, basketball, soccer, volleyball. **Tests:** IB. **Graduates attending college:** 90%. **Location:** small town in the countryside, 60 kilometers from Melbourne. **Campus:** 12 acres. **Library:** 2,500 volumes. **Facilities:** 4 buildings, 16 classrooms, auditorium, cafeteria, 2 tennis courts, 2 playing fields, 6 science labs, computer lab, current boarding facilities are being expanded.

*Once only fee **Australian dollar

AUSTRIA

Region: Europe
Size: 32,378 square miles
Population: 8,023,244
Capital: Vienna
Telephone code: 43
Currency: schilling
Language: German

KAPRUN

International School Kaprun

Phone/facsimile: (43)(6547)7106
Mail: Postfach 47, 5710 Kaprun, Austria
U.S. mail: 6681 Stone-Brook Drive, Clifton, VA 22024, U.S.A.
Principal: David Feltham
Vice-principal (curricular): Judit Feltham
Grade levels: 1 – 13
Tuition and board (annual): 15,750**
Other fees: registration*, 50**; uniform, 500; deposit, 500 (refundable)
School year: September through June

Year founded: 1996. **Type of school:** coed, company-sponsored. **Governed by:** appointed and elected board. **Accredited by:** ASAI (in process).

Curriculum/physical plant

Type: U.S./U.K. **Languages taught:** English, French, German, Italian, Yugoslavian. **Staff specialists:** reading, math, counselor, learning disabilities, sports trainers. **Special curricular:** art, physical education, computer instruction, vocational. **Extracurricular:** drama, gymnastics, dance, instrumental music, computers, photography, field trips. **Sports:** athletics, hockey, soccer, ski racing, snowboarding, sailing, canoeing, climbing, rafting, paragliding, cross-country skiing. **Tests:** SAT, A-level GCE, GCSE, IGCSE. **Location:** in rural setting, 45 minutes from Salzburg. **Campuses (2):** 2 acres. **Library:** 2,000 volumes. **Facilities:** 2 buildings, cafeteria, gymnasium, science lab, many nearby indoor and outdoor tennis courts and playing fields, boarding facilities.

*Once only fee **Pound sterling

SALZBURG

American International School Salzburg

Street address: Moosstrasse 106, A-5020 Salzburg, Austria
Phone: (43)(662)824617 – 8 **Facsimile:** (43)(662)824555
Principal: Paul McLean
Teaching staff: full-time, 15; part-time, 12; total, 27
Nationalities of teaching staff: U.S., 20; host, 4; other, 3; total, 27
Grade levels: 7 – 12, postgraduate
Enrollment: total, 130
Nationalities of student body: U.S., 50; other, 80; total, 130
Boarders: boys, 60; girls, 60 **Grades:** 7 – 12, PG **Program:** planned 7-day
Tuition and fees (annual): 120,000** (day); 225,000 (boarding)
Other fees: registration*, 500**
School year: September to May

Year founded: 1976. **Type of school:** coed, day, boarding, private nonprofit. **Governed by:** board of directors. **Accredited by:** Middle States, Austrian Ministry of Education. **Regional organizations:** ECIS, CEESA (associate member).

Curriculum

Type: IB, American college preparatory, AP. **Languages taught:** French, Spanish, German. **Special programs:** ESL, honors sections, independent study, international curriculum. **Special curricular:** art, chorus, physical education, computer instruction. **Extracurricular:** drama, dance, choral and instrumental music, computers, yearbook, newspaper, photography, excursions/expeditions, field trips. **Sports:** aerobics, basketball, bowling, dance, skiing, soccer, squash, swimming, tennis, volleyball, horseback riding, body-building, golf, rock climbing. **Clubs:** chess, debating, student council, Model UN, language. **Tests:** PSAT, SAT, ACT, TOEFL, IB, AP. **Graduates attending college:** 95%. **Graduates have attended:** Princeton, Dartmouth, Stanford, UCLA, Harvard.

Physical plant

Location: in residential suburb of Salzburg. **Campus:** 6 acres. **Library:** 10,000 volumes. **Facilities:** 16 classrooms, cafeteria, science lab, computer lab, lounge, photo lab, art room, separate fully supervised dormitory facilities for boys and girls, physical-education facilities (off campus).

*Once only fee **Austrian schilling

VIENNA

AMERICAN INTERNATIONAL SCHOOL

Street address: Salmanndorfer Strasse 47, A-1190 Vienna, Austria
Phone: (43)(1)40132 **Facsimile:** (43)(1)401325 **E-mail:** director@ais.at
Director: Dr. Richard Spradling
Upper school principal: Dr. Alan Benson
Middle school principal: Michael Colaianni
Lower school principal: Herman Glass
Business manager: Dietrich Probst
Teaching staff: full-time, 79; part-time, 18; total, 97
Nationalities of teaching staff: U.S., 64; U.K., 6; host, 9; other, 18; total, 97
Grade levels: N – 13
Enrollment: N – preK, 16; K, 38; 1 – 6, 327; 7 – 9, 171; 10 – 12, 215; 13, 7; total, 774
Nationalities of student body: U.S., 265; U.K., 20; host, 143; other, 346; total, 774
Capacity: N – preK, 16; K, 40; 1 – 6, 345; 7 – 9, 210; 10 – 12, 225; 13, 5; total, 841
Teacher/student ratio: 1/8
Tuition (annual): N – preK, 67,000**; K, 111,600; 1 – 5, 124,000; 6 – 11, 138,100; 12 – 13, 140,900
Other fees (annual): registration*, 2,000**; busing, 7,200 – 7,950; lunch, 6,850; matriculation*, 4,000
School year: August to June

Year founded: 1959. **Type of school:** coed, day, private nonprofit, college preparatory. **Governed by:** elected executive board. **Accredited by:** Middle States, Austrian Ministry of Education.

Curriculum

Type: U.S., IB, AP, Austrian Matura. **Languages taught:** French, German. **Staff specialists:** reading, math, computer, counselor, learning disabilities, nurse. **Special programs:** ESL. **Special curricular:** art, physical education, computer instruction, choral and instrumental music. **Extracurricular:** drama, gymnastics, dance, computers, yearbook, newspaper, literary magazine, photography, excursions/expeditions, field trips. **Sports:** baseball, basketball, soccer, softball, swimming, tennis, track and field, volleyball. **Clubs:** National Honor Society, speech and debate. **Tests:** PSAT, SAT, TOEFL, IB, AP, Iowa. **Graduates attending college:** 90%. **Graduates have attended:** U. of Vienna, Brown, U. of Pennsylvania, Tufts, Macalester.

Physical plant

Location: on edge of Vienna Woods. **Campus:** 15 acres. **Library:** 20,000 volumes. **Facilities:** building complex, 63 classrooms, auditorium, cafeteria, 2 tennis courts, 2 gymnasiums, playing field, 5 science labs, 3 computer labs.

*Once only fee **Austrian schilling

Danube International School

Street address: Gudrun Strasse 184, A-1100 Vienna, Austria
Phone: (43)(1)6030246 **Facsimile:** (43)(1)6030248
Director: Peter Harding
Secondary school principal: Alan Honeyman
Middle school coordinator: Sally Brunner
Elementary school coordinator: Sally Gunter
Business manager: Wolfgang Alber
Teaching staff: full-time, 26; part-time, 7; total, 33
Nationalities of teaching staff: U.S., 3; U.K., 18; host, 3; other, 9; total, 33
Grade levels: K – 12
Enrollment: K, 19; reception, 17; 1 – 4, 69; 5 – 8, 89; 9 – 12, 88; total, 282
Nationalities of student body: U.S., 18; U.K., 19; host, 102; other, 143; total, 282
Teacher/student ratio: 1/10
Tuition (annual): K (half day), 52,500**; K (full day), 74,000; R, 103,500; 1 – 4, 108,500; 5, 112,500; 6 – 8, 128,000; 9 – 10, 136,500; 11 – 12, 141,500
Other fees: registration*, 6,000**
School year: late August through late June

Year founded: 1992. **Type of school:** coed, day, proprietary. **Governed and sponsored by:** owners. **Accredited by:** Austrian Ministry of Education.

Curriculum/physical plant

Type: IB, IGCSE, ISCP. **Languages taught:** French, German. **Special programs:** ESL. **Special curricular:** art, chorus, physical education, drama, dance. **Extracurricular:** choral and instrumental music, yearbook, excursions/expeditions, field trips, theater, ballet, student council. **Sports:** basketball, soccer, swimming, tennis, volleyball. **Tests:** SAT, TOEFL, IB, IGCSE. **Graduates attending college:** 80%. **Graduates have attended:** U. of Bath, U. of Hull, U. of Manchester, U. of London, U. of Vienna. **Location:** city building next to a park with sports field and playground. **Libraries (2):** 6,500 volumes. **Facilities:** 21 classrooms, cafeteria, infirmary, 2 science labs, computer lab, drama studio.

*Once only fee **Austrian schilling

Vienna Christian School

Street address: Kreilplatz 1/2, A-1190 Vienna, Austria
Phone: (43)(1)3188211 **Facsimile:** (43)(1)31882114
E-mail: 100337.1501@compuserve.com
Director: Phillip Paden
Principal: Nancy Deibert
Counselor: Everett Peterson
Business manager: Ron Avery
Teaching staff: full-time, 22; part-time, 20; total, 42
Nationalities of teaching staff: U.S., 30; U.K., 3; host, 3; other, 6; total, 42
Grade levels: 1 – 12
Enrollment: 1 – 6, 57; 7 – 9, 42; 10 – 12, 36; total, 135
Nationalities of student body: U.S., 57; U.K., 10; host, 5; other, 63; total, 135
Teacher/student ratio: 1/7
Tuition (annual): 1 – 5, $6,200; 6 – 12, $7,200

Other fees (annual): registration, $200; caution fee (returnable), $100
School year: September through June

Year founded: 1986. **Type of school:** coed, church-related, private nonprofit.

Curriculum/physical plant

Type: U.S., AP. **Languages taught:** German. **Staff specialists:** counselor, learning disabilities. **Special programs:** ESL. **Special curricular:** art, chorus, band, physical education, computer instruction. **Extracurricular:** drama, yearbook. **Tests:** SAT, AP, Stanford. **Graduates attending college:** 75%. **Graduates have attended:** Wesleyan U., Pepperdine U., Liberty U., Wheaton College, U.S. Air Force Academy. **Library:** 5,000 volumes. **Location:** rented floor of building in city. **Facilities:** auditorium, science lab, computer lab.

Vienna International School

Street address: Strasse der Menschenrechte 1, A-1220 Vienna, Austria
Phone: (43)(1)2035595 **Facsimile:** (43)(1)2030366 **E-mail:** info@vis.ac.at
Web: http://www.vis.ac.at
Director: David Toze
Head, secondary school: Malcolm Davis
Head, primary school: Anne Poenisch
Teaching staff: full-time, 124; part-time, 6; total, 130
Nationalities of teaching staff: U.S., 15; U.K., 65; host, 17; other, 33; total, 130
Grade levels: K – 13
Enrollment: K, 100; 1 – 6, 588; 7 – 9, 300; 10 – 12, 303; 13, 95; total, 1,386
Nationalities of student body: U.S., 96; U.K., 160; host, 428; other, 702; total, 1386
Teacher/student ratio: 1/11
Tuition (annual, 1996 – 97 figures): K (half day), $3,486; K, $5,976; 1 – 6, $7,805 – 8,062; 7 – 9, $9,639 – 9,724; 10 – 13, $10,499 – 10,672
Other fees (annual, 1996 – 97 figures): registration*, $492; busing, $1,041; lunch, $620 – 868; refundable security deposit, $328
School year: August to June

Year founded: 1978 (English School 1955). **Type of school:** coed, day, private nonprofit. **Governed by:** elected board of governors. **Accredited by:** Austrian Ministry of Education, ECIS.

Curriculum

Type: IB, IBMYP, ISCP. **Languages taught:** French, Spanish, German. **Staff specialists:** math, computer, counselor, psychologist, learning disabilities, nurse. **Special programs:** ESL, special educational needs. **Special curricular:** art, chorus, band, physical education, computer instruction. **Extracurricular:** drama, gymnastics, dance, choral and instrumental music, computers, yearbook, newspaper, photography, excursions/expeditions, field trips, tap-dancing. **Sports:** basketball, cricket, field hockey, gymnastics, softball, swimming, table tennis, tennis, volleyball, association football, athletics (field and track), skiing, skating, rugby. **Clubs:** chess, scouts, Scrabble, knitting, martial arts, collecting. **Tests:** PSAT, SAT, TOEFL, IB. **Graduates attending college:** 90%. **Graduates have attended:** Cambridge U., London U., Princeton, Harvard, Oxford U.

Physical plant

Location: in suburban setting, 15 minutes by underground from city center. **Campus:** 10.5 acres. **Facilities:** 1 building, 77 classrooms, auditorium, cafeteria, 2 tennis courts, 5 gymnasiums, 2 playing fields, 7 science labs, 2 computer labs, library, art and music areas, outdoor amphitheater, ecology area.

*Once only fee

AZERBAIJAN

Region: Eastern Europe
Size: 33,400 square miles
Population: 7,676,953
Capital: Baku
Telephone code: 994
Currency: manat
Languages: Azeri, Armenian, Russian

BAKU

Baku International School†

Phone: (994)(12)906352 **E-mail:** qsi@bis.baku.az
Mail: c/o U.S. Embassy Baku, Dept. of State, Washington, DC 20521-7050
Director: Margaret Davis, Ph.D.
Teaching staff: full-time, 2; part-time, 6; total, 8
Nationalities of teaching staff: U.S., 4; host, 4; total, 8
Grade levels: N – 9
Enrollment: N, 2; K, 1; 1 – 6, 22; 7 – 9, 0; total, 25
Teacher/student ratio: 1/6
Tuition (annual): N, $2,000; K – 5, $7,900; 6 – 9, $10,200
Other fees (annual): registration*, $100; capital levy, $4,000/deposit or $1,600/year fee
School year: September to June

Year founded: 1994. **Type of school:** coed, day, private nonprofit. **Governed by:** appointed board of directors. **Sponsored by:** Quality Schools International. **Regional organizations:** CEESA.

Curriculum/physical plant

Type: U.S. **Special programs:** ESL. **Special curricular:** art, computer instruction, physical education. **Extracurricular:** drama, excursions/expeditions, field trips, science club. **Sports:** basketball, soccer, track and field, volleyball. **Location:** center of Baku. **Facilities:** rented building with 3 classrooms, 2 adjacent portable classrooms, access to sports complex.

*Once only fee †formerly QSI International School Baku

BAHRAIN

Region: Middle East
Size: 268 square miles
Population: 590,042
Capital: Manama
Telephone code: 973
Currency: dinar
Languages: Arabic, Farsi, Urdu, English

ISA TOWN

BAHRAIN BAYAN SCHOOL

Street address: Isa Town 841, Road 4111, Bldg. Block 230, Bahrain
Phone: (973)682227 **Facsimile:** (973)780019
E-mail: bayan@batelco.com.bh
Mail: PO Box 32411, Isa Town, Bahrain
Director general: Nabil Sukhun
Secondary principal: Omer Troyer
Elementary principal: Dorothy Loveland
Registrar: Maha Tadros
Business manager: Samar Nabhan
Teaching staff: full-time, 109; part-time, 3; total, 112
Nationalities of teaching staff: U.S., 24; U.K., 13; host, 40; other, 35; total, 112
Grade levels: N – 12
Enrollment: N – preK, 110; K, 74; 1 – 5, 382; 6 – 12, 331; total, 897
Nationalities of student body: host, 829; other, 68; total, 897
Capacity: N – preK, 100; K, 65; 1 – 5, 375; 6 – 9, 265; 10 – 12, 225; total, 1,030
Teacher/student ratio: 1/10
Tuition (annual): N, $2,515; K/1, $3,175; K/2 – grade 5, $3,835; 6 – 12, $4,315
Other fees (annual): registration*, $135; books, $105 – 160
School year: September through June

Year founded: 1982. **Type of school:** coed, day, private nonprofit. **Governed by:** board of trustees. **Accredited by:** Middle States (K – 8 only; 9 – 12 in process).

Curriculum/physical plant

Type: U.S., national, IB. **Languages of instruction:** English, Arabic. **Languages taught:** French. **Staff specialists:** reading, math, computer, learning disabilities, nurse. **Special programs:** ESL, remedial. **Special curricular:** art, physical education, computer instruction, music. **Extracurricular:** drama, gymnastics, instrumental music, computers, yearbook, newspaper, excursions/expeditions, various sports. **Clubs:** student councils, social service, science, environmental. **Tests:** PSAT, SAT, TOEFL, IB. **Location:** in suburban area. **Campus:** 10 acres. **Library:** 18,000 volumes. **Facilities:** 6 buildings, 46 classrooms, infirmary, covered play area, tennis court, gymnasium, 3 playing fields, 3 science labs, 3 computer labs, assembly hall, 3 art rooms, 2 music rooms.

*Once only fee

MANAMA

BAHRAIN SCHOOL

Phone: (973)727828 **Facsimile:** (973)725714/728583
Mail: PO Box 934, Juffair, State of Bahrain, Arabian Gulf
U.S. mail: (no personal name) PSC 451, FPO AE 09834-5200
Principal: Carl Albrecht
Assistant principals: Kathryn Forystek, Jennifer Halley
Deputy head: Trevor Burt
Teaching staff: full-time, 69; part-time, 4; total, 73
Nationalities of teaching staff: U.S., 66; U.K., 1; host, 1; other, 5; total, 73
Grade levels: K – 12
Enrollment: K, 23; 1 – 6, 325; 7 – 9, 185; 10 – 12, 319; total, 852
Nationalities of student body: U.S., 382; U.K., 15; host, 163; other, 292; total, 852
Capacity: total, 1,200
Teacher/student ratio: 1/12
Boarders: boys, 60; girls, 60
Tuition (annual): K, $5,478; 1 – 6, $10,956; 7 – 8, $11,532; 9 – 12, $12,110
Other fees (annual): boarding, 3,410**; building levy, 430
School year: September to June

Year founded: 1968. **Type of school:** coed, day, boarding. **Governed by:** U.S. Department of Defense Dependents Schools (educators must apply through DoDDS). **Sponsored by:** U.S. government. **Accredited by:** North Central. **Regional organizations:** ECIS.

Curriculum

Type: U.S., national, IB, AP. **Languages taught:** French, Spanish, German, Arabic. **Staff specialists:** reading, computer, counselor, learning disabilities, nurse, music, enrichment. **Special programs:** ESL, learning disabilities, enrichment. **Special curricular:** art, chorus, band, physical education, computer instruction, vocational. **Extracurricular:** yearbook, Brain Bowl, choral and instrumental music, drama, elementary choir and band, field trips/workshops; MathCounts, Model UN, Science and Junior Science Day, sports. **Clubs:** chess, computer, literary magazine, National Honor Society, National Junior Honor Society, student council, Arabic, Beta, photo/video, service. **Tests:** PSAT, ACT, IB, AP, GCSE, SAT I, SAT II, CTBS, TOEFL, American High School Mathematics Exam. **Graduates attending college:** 90%. **Graduates have attended:** Boston U., Brown, Georgetown, Harvard, Princeton.

Physical plant

Location: 5 minutes from downtown Manama. **Campus:** 25 acres. **Library:** 33,000 volumes, CD-ROMs, Internet. **Facilities:** 12 buildings, 60 classrooms, auditorium, cafeteria, gymnasium, 4 playing fields, 8 science labs, 5 computer labs, swimming pool, AV equipment, lighted tennis courts, 2 squash courts, track, water treatment facility, home economics room, technology center, video-telecommunication center, air conditioning.

**Bahraini dinar

IBN KHULDOON NATIONAL SCHOOL

Phone: (973)682451/780661 **Facsimile:** (973)689028
E-mail: iknsnet@batelco.com.bh
Mail: PO Box 20511, Manama, Bahrain
President: Samir J. Chammaa
Principal secondary: Robert Schaub
Principal elementary: Ghada Bou Zeineddine
Business manager: Hassan Radhi
Teaching staff: full-time, 96; total, 96
Nationalities of teaching staff: U.S., 28; host, 21; other, 47; total, 96
Grade levels: K – 12
Enrollment: K, 160; 1 – 6, 520; 7 – 9, 265; 10 – 12, 225; total, 1,170
Nationalities of student body: host, 1,110; other, 60; total, 1,170
Capacity: K, 160; 1 – 6, 520; 7 – 9, 260; 10 – 12, 240; total, 1,180
Teacher/student ratio: 1/12
Tuition (annual): K, 1,200**; 1 – 6, 1,450; 7 – 9, 1,650; 10 – 12, 2,100
Other fees (annual): registration*, 100**; lunch, 60 (K – 6)
School year: September through June

Year founded: 1983. **Type of school:** coed, day, private nonprofit. **Governed by:** elected board of trustees. **Accredited by:** Middle States.

Curriculum/physical plant

Type: U.S., national syllabi in Arabic, Islamic, and social studies, IB. **Languages of instruction:** English, Arabic. **Languages taught:** English, French, Arabic. **Staff specialists:** reading, computer, nurse. **Special programs:** ESL. **Special curricular:** art, physical education, computer instruction. **Extracurricular:** drama, gymnastics, computers, yearbook, newspaper, literary magazine, photography, excursions/expeditions, field trips, choral music, band. **Sports:** badminton, basketball, soccer, tennis, volleyball. **Clubs:** chess, painting, social service, science and technology, photography. **Tests:** PSAT, SAT, IB. **Location:** in suburban area, 12 kilometers from Manama. **Campus:** 10 acres. **Library:** 24,000 volumes. **Facilities:** 6 buildings, 78 classrooms, infirmary, 4 covered play areas, 2 tennis courts, 2 gymnasiums, 3 playing fields, 4 science labs, 2 computer labs, 3 art rooms, 3 music rooms.

*Once only fee **Bahraini dinar

BANGLADESH

Region: South Asia
Size: 56,977 square miles
Population: 123,062,800
Capital: Dhaka
Telephone code: 880
Currency: taka
Languages: Bangla, English

DHAKA

AMERICAN INTERNATIONAL SCHOOL/DHAKA

Street address: United Nations Road, Baridhara, Dhaka, Bangladesh
Phone: (880)(2)882452/882860/882414/884750 **Facsimile:** (880)(2)883175
E-mail: admin@aisd.pradeshta.net
U.S. mail: American Embassy (AIS/D), Dhaka, Bangladesh, Dept. of State, Washington, DC 20521-6120
Superintendent: David Cramer, Ed.D.
Secondary principal: David Shawver, Ph.D.
Elementary principal: Richard Sands
Business manager: Raquibul Husain
Teaching staff: full-time, 50; part-time, 22; total, 72
Nationalities of teaching staff: U.S., 46; U.K., 3; host, 5; other, 18; total, 72
Grade levels: preK – 12
Enrollment: preK, 39; K, 40; 1 – 5, 210; 6 – 8, 126; 9 – 12, 127; total, 542
Nationalities of student body: U.S., 106; host, 66; other, 370; total, 542
Teacher/student ratio: 1/9
Tuition (annual): preK, $2,950; K – 4, $7,350; 5, $7,550; 6 – 8, $8,750 – 9,000; 9 – 12, $9,200 – 9,800
Other fees (annual): lunch card, 6,000 – 9,300**; application*, $750; ESL surcharge; capital fee: preK, $400; K – 3, $1,000; 4 – 12, $1,300
School year: August to June

Year founded: 1972. **Type of school:** coed, day, private nonprofit. **Governed by:** elected board from parent community. **Accredited by:** Middle States, ECIS. **Regional organizations:** NESA, SAISA.

Curriculum/physical plant

Type: U.S., AP. **Languages taught:** French, Spanish. **Staff specialists:** computer, nurse, remedial center, ESL, elementary guidance, secondary guidance. **Special programs:** ESL. **Special curricular:** art, chorus, band, physical education, computer instruction. **Extracurricular:** drama, gymnastics, choral music, computers, yearbook, excursions/expeditions, field trips, sports. **Tests:** SSAT, PSAT, CTP. **Graduates have attended:** Brown, Cambridge, Harvard, McGill, U. of Pennsylvania. **Location:** in residential area of Dhaka. **Campus:** 4.5 acres. **Library:** 25,000 volumes. **Facilities:** 2 buildings, 50 classrooms, auditorium, cafeteria, infirmary, 2 gymnasiums, playing field, 4 science labs, 2 computer labs, swimming pool, air conditioning.

*Once only fee **Bangladesh taka

BELARUS

Region: Eastern Europe
Size: 80,153 square miles
Population: 10,415,973
Capital: Minsk
Telephone code: 375
Currency: Belarusian ruble
Languages: Belarusian, Russian

MINSK

Minsk International School

Phone/facsimile: (375)(172)343035 **E-mail:** mis@brc.minsk.by
Mail: c/o American Embassy Minsk, Dept. of State, Washington, DC 20521-7010
Director: Ron Frnka
Teaching staff: full-time, 4; part-time, 6; total, 10
Nationalities of teaching staff: U.S., 5; host, 4; other, 1; total, 10
Grade levels: K – 12
Enrollment: K, 0; 1 – 12, 26; total, 26
Capacity: K, 10; 1 – 12, 60; total, 70
Teacher/student ratio: 1/4
Tuition: K, $6,900; 1 – 12, $9,200
Other fees: registration*, $100; capital levy, $4,000 deposit or $1,600/year fee
School year: September to June

Year founded: 1993. **Type of school:** coed, day, private nonprofit. **Governed by:** appointed board of directors. **Sponsored by:** Quality Schools International. **Regional organizations:** CEESA, ECIS.

Curriculum/physical plant

Type: U.S. **Languages taught:** Russian, Hindi. **Special programs:** ESL, independent study. **Special curricular:** art, computer instruction, Russian instruction, woodshop, journalism class which publishes school newspaper, swimming, field trips. **Location:** Minsk. **Facilities:** rented portion of public school, 5 classrooms, computer lab.

*Once only fee

BELGIUM

Region: Europe
Size: 11,787 square miles
Population: 10,170,241
Capital: Brussels
Telephone code: 32
Currency: franc
Languages: Flemish (Dutch), French, German

ANTWERP

Antwerp International School

Street address: Veltwijcklaan 180, 2180 Ekeren/Antwerp, Belgium
Phone: (32)(3)5439300 **Facsimile:** (32)(3)5418201
E-mail: 101352.1676@compuserve.com
Headmaster: Robert F. Schaecher
Secondary school principal: René De Mol
Elementary school principal: Keith Boniface
Director of development: Christopher Massi
Business manager: Theo Van Limbergen
Teaching staff: full-time, 59; part-time, 16; total, 75
Nationalities of teaching staff: U.S., 37; U.K., 14; host, 10; other, 14; total, 75
Grade levels: preschool – 12
Enrollment: preS – preK, 60; K, 40; 1 – 6, 250; 7 – 9, 150; 10 – 12, 90; total, 590
Nationalities of student body: U.S., 150; U.K., 113; host, 25; other, 302; total, 590
Tuition (annual): preschool, 120,000**; preK, 163,000; K, 418,000; 1 – 5, 460,000; 6, 471,000; 7 – 8, 517,000; 9 – 12, 548,000
Other fees (annual): application*, 25,000**/family; busing 68,000 – 79,000
School year: August to June

Year founded: 1967. **Type of school:** coed, day, private nonprofit. **Governed by:** elected board of directors. **Accredited by:** New England, ECIS.

Curriculum/physical plant

Type: U.S., IB, IGCSE, AP. **Languages taught:** French, German, Dutch. **Staff specialists:** computer. **Special programs:** ESL, remedial, EFL. **Special curricular:** art, music, computer, study skills, life skills, Theory of Knowledge, physical education. **Extracurricular:** computers, yearbook, newspaper, art, choir, typing, word processing, Model UN, environmental concerns, sports, creative writing, business education, field week. **Sports:** basketball, soccer, swimming, tennis, track and field, volleyball, racquet sports. **Clubs:** student council, Model NATO, speech and debate, scouts, music lessons. **Tests:** PSAT, SAT, ACT, TOEFL, IB, AP, GCSE, CTP - II. **Graduates attending college:** 95%. **Graduates have attended:** Stanford, Princeton, Villanova, Radford, Harvard. **Location:** in suburban area, 10 kilometers from Antwerp. **Campus:** 5 – 7 acres. **Library:** 15,000 volumes. **Facilities:** 5 buildings, 35 classrooms, cafeteria, infirmary, gymnasium, playing field, 3 science labs, 3 computer labs, early childhood center, fine arts center.

*Once only fee **Belgian franc

EEC International School

Street address: Jacob Jordaensstraat 77, 2018 Antwerp, Belgium
Phone: (32)(3)2185431 **Facsimile:** (32)(3)2185868
E-mail: eurunia@eunet.be
Director: Mr. F. X. Nieberding
Teaching staff: full-time, 21; part-time, 8; total, 29
Nationalities of teaching staff: U.S., 1; U.K., 9; host, 9; other, 10; total, 29
Grade levels: preK – 12
Enrollment: preK, 10; K, 10; 1 – 12, 180; total, 200
Nationalities of student body: U.S., 12; U.K., 33; host, 46; other, 109; total, 200
Capacity: preK, 20; K, 20; 1 – 6, 70; 7 – 9, 70; 10 – 12, 100; total, 280
Teacher/student ratio: 1/8
Boarders: boys, 14; girls, 20 **Grades:** 7 – 12 **Program:** planned 5-day
Tuition (annual): preK – K, 120,000**; prep, 140,000; 1, 150,000; 2, 160,000; 3 – 4, 180,000; 5 – 6, 200,000; 7 – 8, 275,000; 9 – 12, 320,000; IGCSE O-levels, 320,000; GCE A-levels, 390,000
Other fees (annual): boarding, 280,000**; books, approximately 5,000; application*, 15,000
School year: September to June

Year founded: 1979. **Type of school:** coed, day, boarding, proprietary. **Governed by:** appointed board of governors. **Sponsored by:** American European Educational Association.

Curriculum

Type: U.S., U.K. **Languages taught:** French, Spanish, German, Dutch. **Staff specialists:** reading, math, computer, speech/hearing, counselor, psychologist, learning disabilities. **Special curricular:** art, physical education, computer instruction. **Extracurricular:** drama, dance, computers, excursions/expeditions, field trips, karate, arts and crafts, ski trip, fashion show. **Sports:** badminton, baseball, basketball, gymnastics, hockey, netball, soccer, squash, volleyball, handball, racquetball, korfball, physical fitness, jazz, aerobics, ping-pong. **Tests:** PSAT, SAT, TOEFL, A-level GCE, IGCSE. **Graduates attending college:** 97%.

Physical plant

Location: in Antwerp, on a quiet street near park. **Campus:** 2.5 acres. **Facilities:** 3 buildings, 25 classrooms, cafeteria, 2 covered play areas, gymnasium, 2 science labs, 3 computer labs, AV equipment, fitness center, boarding facilities.

*Once only fee **Belgian franc

BRUSSELS

THE BRITISH SCHOOL OF BRUSSELS

Street address: Leuvensesteenweg 19, 3080 Tervuren, Belgium
Phone: (32)(2)7674700 **Facsimile:** (32)(2)7678070
Principal (senior section): Jennifer Bray
Deputy principal (junior section): Peter Saunders
Deputy principal (infant section): Carol Walker
Teaching staff: full-time, 78; part-time, 24; total, 102
Nationalities of teaching staff: U.K., 88; host, 6; other, 8; total, 102
Grade levels: K – 13
Enrollment: K, 33; reception, 32; 1 – 6, 379; 7 – 9, 221; 10 – 12, 212; 13, 68; total, 945
Nationalities of student body: U.S., 14; U.K., 725; host, 13; other, 193; total, 945
Capacity: K, 40; reception, 40; 1 – 6, 435; 7 – 9, 240; 10 – 12, 240; 13, 80; total, 1,075
Teacher/student ratio: 1/11
Tuition (annual): K, 125,000**; reception, 239,000; 1 – 2, 498,000; 3 – 6, 503,000; 7, 575,000; 8 – 9, 611,000; 10 – 11, 635,000; 12 – 13, 648,000
Other fees (annual): registration*, 20,000**, first child; 10,000, subsequent children; busing, 66,000
School year: September to July

Year founded: 1969. **Type of school:** coed, day. **Governed by:** board of trustees. **Regional organizations:** HMC, ECIS, COBISEC.

Curriculum/physical plant

Type: U.K. **Languages taught:** French, Spanish, German, Dutch. **Staff specialists:** math, counselor, psychologist, nurse, art, music, physical education, English, science, technology, geography, history. **Special programs:** ESL, remedial. **Extracurricular:** drama, gymnastics, dance, excursions/expeditions, field trips, choral and instrumental music. **Sports:** athletics, badminton, basketball, football, hockey, rugby, squash, swimming, tennis. **Tests:** A-level GCE, GCSE, end of Keystage testing. **Graduates have attended:** Oxford, Cambridge, London, Manchester, Sussex. **Location:** 15 kilometers from center of Brussels. **Campus:** 50,000 square meters. **Library:** 60,000 volumes. **Facilities:** auditorium, infirmary, 3 gymnasiums, 4 playing fields, 8 science labs, 4 computer labs, 2 covered and 4 open tennis courts.

*Once only fee **Belgian franc

Brussels' English Primary School S.P.R.L.

Street address: 23 Avenue Franklin Roosevelt, Brussels 1050, Belgium
Phone: (32)(2)6484311 **Facsimile:** (32)(2)6872968 **E-mail:** info@beps.com
Web: http://www.beps.com
Director: Charles A. Gellar
Headmistress: Julia Beverley
Teaching staff: full-time, 17; part-time, 6; total, 23
Nationalities of teaching staff: U.S., 2; U.K., 14; host, 2; other, 5; total, 23
Grade levels: N – 6
Enrollment: N – preK, 20; K, 24; 1 – 6, 136; total: 180
Nationalities of student body: U.S., 22; U.K., 27; host, 27; other, 104; total, 180
Tuition (annual): N – K (half day), 130,000**, (full day) 212,000; 1 – 3, 337,000; 4 – 6, 364,000
Other fees (annual): registration*, 10,000**; busing, 86,000 (optional); lunch, 2,800; refundable deposit, 20,000; trips, 2,000 – 8,000
School year: September through June

Year founded: 1972. **Type of school:** coed, day, proprietary. **Governed by:** director elected by company shareholders. **Regional organizations:** ECIS, CESSIB.

Curriculum/physical plant

Type: international. **Languages taught:** French. **Staff specialists:** computer, physical education, ballet. **Special programs:** ESL, remedial. **Special curricular:** swimming, woodwork. **Extracurricular:** instrumental music, computers, literary magazine, excursions/expeditions, field trips. **Sports:** swimming. **Tests:** Common Entrance Exam (U.K.). **Location:** 5 kilometers from center of Brussels, opposite large park and U. of Brussels. **Campus:** 2,000 square meters. **Library:** 8,000 volumes. **Facilities:** 2 buildings, 15 classrooms, playing field, science lab, nearby tennis courts and swimming pool.

*Once only fee **Belgian franc

The City International School, Brussels

Street address: Boulevard Louis Schmidt 101-103, Brussels B-1040, Belgium
Phone: (32)(2)7344413 **Facsimile:** (32)(2)7333233
Director: François Xavier Nieberding
Superintendent: P. Van Landeghem
Headteacher: G. Aston
Teaching staff: full-time, 17; part-time, 14; total, 31
Nationalities of teaching staff: U.K., 18; host, 5; other, 8; total, 31
Enrollment: preK – 6, 95; 7 – 12, 73; total, 168
Tuition (annual): preK – K, 189,000**; reception – 3, 231,000; primary 4 – 6, 252,000; secondary 1 – 7, 357,000 – 420,000; A-level, 462,000
Other fees: registration, 15,000**
School year: September to June

Year founded: 1985. **Type of school:** coed, day, proprietary. **Governed by:** appointed board of governors. **Sponsored by:** American European Educational Association.

**Belgian franc

THE INTERNATIONAL SCHOOL OF BRUSSELS

Street address: Kattenberg 19, B-1170 Brussels, Belgium
Phone: (322)6614211 **Facsimile:** (322)6614200 **E-mail:** admissions@isb.be
Director: Richard P. Hall
High school head: Walther Hetzer
Middle school head: Malcolm Cromarty
Elementary school head: Eric Klauda
Early childhood center head: Madeleine Maceda Heide
Teaching staff: full-time, 106; part-time, 23; total, 129
Nationalities of teaching staff: U.S., 39; U.K., 32; host, 26; other, 32; total, 129
Grade levels: N – 13
Enrollment: N – preK, 72; K, 56; 1 – 6, 450; 7 – 9, 294; 10 – 13, 336; special education, 6; total, 1,214
Nationalities of student body: U.S., 494; U.K., 79; host, 40; other, 601; total, 1,214
Teacher/student ratio: 1/10
Tuition (annual): N (morning), 168,000**; N – preK (full day), 288,000; K, 548,000; 1 – 2, 597,000; 3 – 6, 610,000; 7 – 9, 688,000; 10 – 13, 713,000
Other fees (annual): application*: N – preK, 10,000**, K – 13, 35,000; busing, 71,000; capital building surcharge, 30,500; lunch (optional), 165/each
School year: September through June

Year founded: 1951. **Type of school:** coed, day. **Governed by:** appointed board of trustees. **Accredited by:** Middle States, ECIS.

Curriculum

Type: U.S., IB, AP. **Languages taught:** French, Spanish, German, IB Language A in Japanese, Swedish, English, French. **Staff specialists:** computer, speech/hearing, counselor, psychologist, learning disabilities, nurse. **Special programs:** ESL, remedial, special education. **Special curricular:** art, chorus, band, physical education, computer instruction, drama, chamber choir, orchestra, jazz band. **Extracurricular:** drama, gymnastics, computers, yearbook, newspaper, literary magazine, excursions/expeditions, field trips, choral and instrumental music, National Honor Society, forensics and debate, Model UN, film literature, technical theater. **Sports:** baseball, basketball, cross-country, field hockey, football, rugby, soccer, softball, swimming, tennis, track and field, volleyball. **Tests:** SSAT, PSAT, SAT, ACT, TOEFL, IB, AP, Iowa. **Graduates attending college:** 93%. **Graduates have attended:** Princeton, Wellesley, MIT, Stanford, Brown.

Physical plant

Location: beautiful wooded campus in residential area of southeast Brussels, approximately 8 kilometers from center city. **Campus:** 40 acres. **Libraries:** 70,000 volumes. **Facilities:** 8 buildings, 87 classrooms, 3 cafeterias, infirmary, 2 tennis courts, 2 gymnasiums, 3 playing fields, 11 science labs, 3 computer labs, theater, AV equipment.

*Once only fee **Belgian franc

LIMAL

B.E.P.S. 2 – Limal International School

Street address: 13 Rue Léon Deladrière, 1300 Limal, Belgium
Phone: (32)(10)417227 **Facsimile:** (32)(2)6872968 **E-mail:** info@beps.com
Web: http://www.beps.com
Director: Charles A. Gellar
Headmistress: Henny de Waal
Teaching staff: full-time, 7; part-time, 4; total, 11
Nationalities of teaching staff: U.S., 1; U.K., 7; host, 2; other, 1; total, 11
Grade levels: N – 6
Enrollment: total, 90
Nationalities of student body: U.K., 45; host, 8; other, 37; total, 90
Teacher/student ratio: 1/8
Tuition (annual): N – preK (half day), 155,000**, (full day) 253,000; 1 – 4, 375,000; 5 – 6, 401,000; special provisions for non-company parents
Other fees (annual): busing, 84,000** (optional); lunch, 2,250; enrollment, 10,000; refundable deposit, 20,000; trips, 2,000 – 8,000
School year: September through June

Year founded: 1992. **Type of school:** coed, day, proprietary. **Governed by:** director elected by company shareholders. **Regional organizations:** ECIS, CESSIB.

Curriculum/physical plant

Type: international. **Languages taught:** French. **Special programs:** remedial, EFL. **Special curricular:** woodwork. **Extracurricular:** pony-riding club. **Sports:** swimming. **Tests:** Common Entrance Exam (U.K.). **Location:** 30 kilometers south of Brussels, in a rural setting of gardens and woodlands, with pet animals. **Campus:** 9 acres. **Library:** 3,000 volumes. **Facilities:** 4 buildings, theater, specially designed preschool building, children's museum, 2 playgrounds, sports field.

**Belgian franc

WATERLOO

St. John's International School

Street address: Drève Richelle 146, Waterloo 1410, Belgium
Phone: (32)(2)3520610 **Facsimile:** (32)(2)3520620/30
E-mail: 72233.3322@compuserve.com
Superintendent: Sr. Barbara Hughes, F.C.J.
Secondary school principal: Dennis McCann
Elementary school principal: Sr. Beatrice Molyneux, F.C.J.
Business manager: Richard Katherman
Teaching staff: full-time, 89; part-time, 24; total, 113
Nationalities of teaching staff: U.S., 25; U.K., 43; host, 27; other, 18; total, 113
Grade levels: N – 13

Enrollment: N – preK, 60; K, 60; 1 – 5, 373; 6 – 8, 215; 9 – 12, 242; 13, 5; total, 955
Nationalities of student body: U.S., 384; U.K., 163; host, 33; other, 375; total, 955
Teacher/student ratio: 1/9
Tuition: N, 154,500**; K, 524,500; 1 – 2, 577,000; 3 – 4, 586,000; 5, 594,500; 6 – 8, 681,500; 9 – 13, 689,000
Other fees (annual): busing: N – K, 63,675**; 1 – 13, 70,750; registration: N, 10,000; K – 13, 35,000
School year: September to June

Year founded: 1964. **Type of school:** coed, day, private nonprofit. **Governed by:** Conseil d'administration (nonprofit organization) and advisory board. **Sponsored by:** Faithful Companions of Jesus. **Accredited by:** Middle States, ECIS.

Curriculum

Type: U.S., U.K., IB, AP. **Languages taught:** French (all students, N – 12); Spanish, German (optional); Dutch, Swedish (IB). **Staff specialists:** counselor, psychologist, learning disabilities, nurse, information technology. **Special programs:** ESL, honors sections, remedial. **Special curricular:** art, chorus, band, physical education, drama, ensemble, dance, photography, ceramics, film/video, religion, information technology, swimming (K – 7). **Extracurricular:** drama, gymnastics, choral and instrumental music, yearbook, newspaper, literary magazine, excursions/expeditions, field trips, chess, ballet, puppetry, video. **Sports:** baseball, basketball, cross-country, soccer, softball, swimming, tennis, track and field, volleyball. **Clubs:** debating, Model UN, Model NATO, International Schools Theater Association, foreign language. **Tests:** SSAT, PSAT, SAT, TOEFL, IB, AP, IGCSE, Iowa. **Graduates attending college:** 95%. **Graduates have attended:** Duke, MIT, Harvard, Tufts, Oxford.

Physical plant

Location: pleasant residential suburb, 12 miles from Brussels. **Libraries (2):** 30,000 volumes. **Facilities:** 7 buildings, 44 classrooms, auditorium, 2 cafeterias, infirmary, 3 tennis courts, 2 gymnasiums, playing field, 6 science labs, 3 computer labs, local swimming pool, arts building (including gallery), 2 music rooms, recreation areas, boarding with local families as required.

*Once only fee **Belgian franc

BENIN

Region: West Africa
Size: 43,500 square miles
Population: 5,709,529
Capitals: Porto-Novo
Telephone code: 229
Currency: CFA franc
Languages: French, Fon, Yoruba

COTONOU

Brilliant Stars International School

Street address: Lot 123 Residence-Ouest, Cotonou, Benin
Phone: (229)302079 **Facsimile:** (229)313701/313809
Mail: BP 04-919, Cotonou, Benin
Director: Blanche Moyaert
Teaching staff: full-time, 6; part-time, 5; total, 11
Nationalities of teaching staff: U.S., 1; host, 4; other, 6; total, 11
Grade levels: N – 8
Enrollment: N, 14; K, 10; 1 – 8, 26; total, 50
Nationalities of student body: U.S., 9; other, 41; total, 50
Capacity: N, 30; K, 15; 1 – 8, 60; total, 105
Teacher/student ratio: 1/6
Tuition (annual): N – K, $1,900; 1 – 8, $3,800
Other fees: registration, $350
School year: September to June

Year founded: 1986. **Type of school:** coed, day, private nonprofit. **Regional organizations:** ECIS, AISA.

Curriculum/physical plant

Type: U.S. **Languages taught:** English, French. **Special programs:** ESL, independent study. **Special curricular:** physical education, computer instruction. **Location:** in residential green oasis, 200 meters from the U.S. Embassy in Cotonou. **Library:** 3,000 volumes. **Facilities:** 2 buildings, 9 classrooms, 2 tennis courts, computers, shaded garden with playground.

BERMUDA

Region: Western Atlantic
Size: 20.6 square miles
Population: 62,100
Capital: Hamilton
Telephone code: 441
Currency: Bermudian dollar
Language: English

HAMILTON

The Bermuda High School for Girls

Street address: 27 Richmond Road, Pembroke HM08, Bermuda
Phone: (1)(441)2956153 **Facsimile:** (1)(441)2952754
Principal: Eleanor W. Kingsbury
Deputy head and head of primary department: Lorna Andersen
Registrar: Diane Gordon
Teaching staff: full-time, 52; part-time, 10; total, 62
Grade levels: 1 – 12 (British)
Enrollment: total, 635
Teacher/student ratio: 1/12
Tuition (annual): $7,710
School year: September through June

Year founded: 1894. **Type of school:** girls, day, private nonprofit. **Governed by:** Bermuda High School Association.

Curriculum/physical plant

Type: U.K. **Languages taught:** English, French, Spanish, Latin. **Staff specialists:** reading, dance, drama, art, music. **Special curricular:** art, physical education, computer instruction, drama, dance. **Extracurricular:** drama, gymnastics, dance, yearbook, photography, field trips, choral and instrumental music, Duke of Edinburgh scheme. **Sports:** cross-country, field hockey, netball, soccer, softball, swimming, track and field, volleyball. **Tests:** PSAT, SAT, GCSE, IGCSE, CAT, DAT. **Graduates have attended:** all major Canadian, U.K., and U.S. universities. **Location:** in Hamilton. **Campus:** 5 acres. **Facilities:** 5 buildings, auditorium, gymnasium, playing field, 3 science labs, 2 computer labs, 2 libraries, playground, music center, dance studio.

Bermuda Institute of Seventh-day Adventists

Street address: 234 Middle Road, Southampton SN 04, Bermuda
Phone: (1)(441)2381566 **Facsimile:** (1)(441)2381309 **E-mail:** svholder@ibl.bm
Mail: PO Box SN 114, Southampton SN BX, Bermuda
Principal: Sheila Holder
Vice-principal/registrar: Kathleen Wilson-Allers
Head of library: Belvina Barnes
Head of computer services: Clinton Gittens
Teaching staff: full-time, 36; part-time, 3; total, 39
Nationalities of teaching staff: U.S., 11; host, 21; other, 7; total, 39
Grade levels: K – 12
Enrollment: K – 6, 263; 7 – 9, 153; 10 – 12, 78; total, 494
Nationalities of student body: U.S., 44; host, 436; other, 14; total, 494
Capacity: K, 45; 1 – 6, 265; 7 – 9, 120; 10 – 12, 120; total, 550
Teacher/student ratio: 1/22
Tuition (annual): K – 6, $4,350; 7 – 8, $4,840 – 4,940; 9 – 11, $5,600; 12, $5,700
Other fees: registration*, $30
School year: August to June

Year founded: 1907. **Type of school:** coed, day, church-related, private nonprofit. **Governed by:** appointed and elected school board. **Sponsored by:** Seventh-day Adventist Church. **Accredited by:** NAD Board of Regents.

Curriculum/physical plant

Type: U.S., national. **Languages taught:** French. **Staff specialists:** counselor, special education, nurse. **Special programs:** honors sections. **Special curricular:** chorus, band, physical education, computer instruction, vocational. **Extracurricular:** drama, computers, yearbook, newspaper, excursions/expeditions, field trips, choral and instrumental music, sports, Big Brother/Big Sister. **Clubs:** language, science. **Tests:** PSAT, ACT, Iowa, DAT, CAT. **Graduates attending college:** 90%. **Graduates have attended:** Andrews U., Atlantic Union College, Oakwood College. **Location:** in suburban area, 5 miles from the city of Hamilton. **Campus:** 7 acres. **Library:** 12,461 volumes. **Facilities:** 4 buildings, 25 classrooms, cafeteria, infirmary, 2 playing fields, science lab, computer lab.

*Once only fee

Mount Saint Agnes Academy

Street address: 99 Dundonald Street West, Hamilton, Bermuda
Phone: (1)(441)2924134 **Facsimile:** (1)(441)2957265 **E-mail:** msa@ibl.bm
Mail: PO Box HM 1004, Hamilton HM DX, Bermuda
High school principal: Sr. Judith Marie Rollo
Elementary school principal: Sr. Dolores Sullivan
Teaching staff: full-time, 33; part-time, 1; total, 34
Grade levels: K – 12
Enrollment: K, 35; 1 – 6, 222; 7 – 9, 177; 10 – 12, 118; total, 552
Teacher/student ratio: 1/16
Tuition (annual): K – 6, 4,360**; 7 – 8, 5,185; 9 – 12, 5,665
Other fees (annual): registration*, 500**; books, 100; P.E. uniform, $30
School year: September to June

Year founded: 1890. **Type of school:** coed, day, church-related. **Governed by:** appointed and elected board of governors. **Sponsored by:** Roman Catholic Diocese. **Accredited by:** Bermuda Department of Education.

Curriculum/physical plant

Type: U.S. **Languages taught:** French, Spanish. **Staff specialists:** reading, counselor. **Special programs:** remedial. **Special curricular:** art, chorus, band, physical education, computer instruction. **Extracurricular:** drama, computers, yearbook, newspaper, literary magazine, excursions/expeditions, field trips, choral and instrumental music. **Sports:** basketball, rugby, soccer, softball, volleyball. **Clubs:** computer, debating, folksinging, yearbook. **Tests:** PSAT, SAT. **Graduates attending college:** 85 – 90%. **Graduates have attended:** Wellesley, Boston College, Penn State, U. of Western Ontario, Queens (Ontario). **Location:** on island. **Campus:** 1.5 acres. **Library:** 18,000 volumes. **Facilities:** 1 building, 25 classrooms, auditorium, gymnasium, science lab, 2 computer labs.

*Once only fee **Bermudian dollar

Saltus Grammar School

Phone: (1)(441)2926177 **Facsimile:** (1)(441)2954977
Mail: PO Box HM 2224, Hamilton HM JX, Bermuda
Headmaster: Trevor Rowell
Teaching staff: full-time, 63; part-time, 4; total, 67
Nationalities of teaching staff: U.K., 37; host, 28; other, 2; total, 67
Grade levels: K – 12
Enrollment: K, 75; 1 – 6, 444; 7 – 9, 223; 10 – 12, 185; total, 927
Capacity: K, 75; 1 – 6, 450; 7 – 9, 225; 10 – 12, 220; total, 970
Teacher/student ratio: 1/14
Tuition (annual): $7,020
Other fees (annual): books, $130; refundable deposit, $600
School year: September through June

Year founded: 1888. **Type of school:** coed, day. **Governed by:** appointed trustees.

Curriculum/physical plant

Type: U.K., U.S. in grade 12, AP. **Languages taught:** French, Spanish. **Staff specialists:** reading, counselor. **Special curricular:** art, physical education, computer instruction, vocational, choir. **Extracurricular:** drama, gymnastics, dance, instrumental music, computers, yearbook, newspaper, photography. **Sports:** basketball, cricket, hockey, netball, rugby, soccer, squash, swimming, tennis, volleyball, sailing, running, cycling. **Tests:** PSAT, SAT, ACT, AP, GCSE. **Graduates have attended:** Queens, Yale, Princeton, Brown, MIT. **Location:** 5 minutes from city center. **Facilities:** 9 buildings, 40 classrooms, auditorium, cafeteria, covered play area, gymnasium, playing field, swimming pool, science labs, computer center, darkroom, administration center, music center, arts and crafts center.

BOLIVIA

Region: South America
Size: 424,164 square miles
Population: 7,165,257
Capitals: Sucre(judicial)
La Paz(administrative)
Telephone code: 591
Currency: boliviano
Languages: Spanish, Quechua, Aymara

COCHABAMBA

American International School of Bolivia

Street address: Avenida Cerveceria Taquina to Malteria Linde turn-off, Cochabamba, Bolivia
Phone: (591)(42)88577 **Facsimile:** (591)(42)88576
E-mail: aisb@llajta.nrc.bolnet.bo
Mail: Casilla 5309, Cochabamba, Bolivia
U.S. mail: (no personal name) Superintendent, AIS/B U.S. Embassy, LaPaz, Bolivia, APO Miami 34032
Superintendent: Dennis Smith
Teaching staff: full-time, 21; total, 21
Nationalities of teaching staff: U.S., 15; host, 3; other, 3; total, 21
Grade levels: preK – 12
Enrollment: total, 235
Teacher/student ratio: 1/10
Boarders: boys, 5; girls, 3 **Grades:** preK – 12
Tuition (annual): preK, $1,000; K, $1,500; 1 – 4, $3,500; 5 – 8, $3,750; 9 – 12, $4,000
Other fees (annual): registration, $100 – 400; boarding, $4,850; busing, $250; admission, $2,000 (installments option); plus Bolivian taxes
School year: mid-August to June

Year founded: 1993. **Type of school:** coed, day, boarding, private nonprofit. **Governed by:** permanently vested board of directors. **Sponsored by:** private donations. **Accredited by:** Southern, Bolivian Ministry of Education. **Regional organizations:** AASSA, AAIE, ECIS, IBO.

Curriculum/physical plant

Type: U.S., national, IB, AP. **Languages taught:** French, Spanish, German, Dutch, Italian, Portuguese. **Staff specialists:** counselor, learning disabilities, librarian, resource. **Special programs:** ESL, independent study, learning disabilities. **Special curricular:** Model UN, creative expression, studio art, home economics, computer programming, community service. **Extracurricular:** karate, driver's education, trekking, publications, National Honor Society, student council, Classrooms Without Walls. **Sports:** basketball, soccer, softball, swimming, tennis, track and field, volleyball. **Graduates attending college:** 100%. **Campus:** 12 acres. **Library:** 10,000 volumes, 500 CD ROMs. **Facilities:** 7 buildings, cafeteria, tennis court, playing field, science lab, computer lab, swimming pool.

Cochabamba Cooperative School

Street address: Avenida Circunvalacion, Cochabamba, Bolivia
Phone: (591)(42)32643/98761 **Facsimile:** (591)(42)32906
Mail: Casilla 1395, Cochabamba, Bolivia
U.S. mail: (no personal name) CCS, U.S. Embassy, La Paz, APO AA 34032
Director: John Byers
High school principal: Josette Antaki
Elementary school principal: Teresa Brantley
Teaching staff: full-time, 33; total, 33
Nationalities of teaching staff: U.S., 20; host, 10; other, 3; total, 33
Grade levels: preK – 12
Enrollment: total, 362
Nationalities of student body: U.S., 54; host, 272; other, 36; total, 362
Capacity: total, 450
Teacher/student ratio: 1/11
Tuition (annual): preK, $1,000; K, $1,400; 1 – 6, $2,050; 7 – 12, $2,600
Other fees (annual): registration, $100 – 260; insurance, $15; busing, $160; entrance*, $500
School year: August to June

Year founded: 1958. **Type of school:** coed, day, private nonprofit. **Governed by:** elected board of directors. **Sponsored by:** parents. **Accredited by:** Southern, Bolivian Ministry of Education.

Curriculum/physical plant

Type: U.S., national, AP. **Languages taught:** French, Spanish, German. **Staff specialists:** counselor, librarian, resource. **Special programs:** ESL, independent study. **Special curricular:** art, chorus, physical education, computer instruction, community service. **Extracurricular:** choral music, computers, yearbook, newspaper, literary magazine, excursions/expeditions, student council, National Honor Society. **Sports:** basketball, soccer, track and field, volleyball. **Tests:** PSAT, SAT, ACT, TOEFL, Iowa. **Graduates attending college:** 85%. **Graduates have attended:** Penn State, Texas A&M, MIT, Harvard, U. of California at Berkeley. **Location:** on northeast side of city. **Campus:** 11 acres. **Library:** 16,000 volumes. **Facilities:** 8 buildings, 38 classrooms, cafeteria, 2 playing fields, science lab, computer lab, AV equipment, playground.

*Once only fee

LA PAZ

AMERICAN COOPERATIVE SCHOOL

Street address: Calle Las Kantutas y Calle 10, Calacoto, La Paz, Bolivia
Phone: (591)(2)792302/794750 **Facsimile:** (591)(2)797218
E-mail: acs@megalink.com
Mail: (no personal name) c/o U.S. Embassy, La Paz, APO AA 34032
U.S. mail: Suite LA-390, 6964 NW 50th Street, Miami, FL 33166-5632
Superintendent: Dennis Sheehan, Ph.D.
Secondary school principal: Donald Mercer
Elementary school principal: Gail Van Adelsberg
Teaching staff: full-time, 54; part-time, 3; total, 57
Nationalities of teaching staff: U.S., 44; host, 11; other, 2; total, 57
Grade levels: preK – 12
Enrollment: preK, 20; K, 33; 1 – 6, 237; 7 – 9, 139; 10 – 12, 147; total, 576
Nationalities of student body: U.S., 168; host, 305; other, 103; total, 576
Capacity: preK, 22; K, 54; 1 – 6, 250; 7 – 9, 140; 10 – 12, 150; total, 616
Teacher/student ratio: 1/11
Tuition (annual): preK – K, $3,620; 1 – 5, $5,150; 6 – 12, $5,330
Other fees (annual): capital levy*, $1,500; busing, $470
School year: August to May

Year founded: 1955. **Type of school:** coed, day, private nonprofit. **Governed by:** elected board of directors. **Accredited by:** Southern.

Curriculum/physical plant

Type: U.S., AP. **Languages taught:** French, Spanish. **Staff specialists:** reading, computer, counselor, learning disabilities, nurse. **Special programs:** ESL, independent study, correspondence, remedial. **Special curricular:** art, chorus, band, physical education, computer instruction. **Extracurricular:** drama, gymnastics, instrumental music, yearbook, literary magazine, photography, excursions/expeditions, field trips. **Sports:** basketball, soccer, swimming, track and field, volleyball. **Clubs:** computer, service organizations. **Tests:** SSAT, PSAT, SAT, ACT, AP, Iowa. **Graduates attending college:** 95%. **Graduates have attended:** Notre Dame, Dartmouth, Georgetown U., U. of Miami, MIT. **Location:** in residential area, 4 miles from La Paz. **Campus:** 7 acres. **Library:** 12,000 volumes. **Facilities:** 9 buildings, auditorium, cafeteria, infirmary, 2 covered play areas, 2 tennis courts, gymnasium, playing field, 2 science labs, computer lab, swimming pool, 2 racquetball courts, sauna, weightroom.

*Once only fee

SANTA CRUZ

SANTA CRUZ CHRISTIAN LEARNING CENTER

Street address: Km. 6-1/2 Carretera a Cochabamba, Santa Cruz, Bolivia
Phone: (591)(3)526666 **Facsimile:** (591)(3)526667
E-mail: learning.center@mail.scbbs-bo.com
Web: http://www.scclc.org/
Mail: Cajon 4049, Santa Cruz, Bolivia
Director: Thomas Hilgeman
High school principal: Virginia Swartzendruber
Elementary principal: Billie Sue Dunn
Business manager: Florence Monteith
Teaching staff: total, 26
Nationalities of teaching staff: U.S., 21; host, 3; other, 2; total, 26
Grade levels: preK – 12
Enrollment: preK, 10; K, 12; 1 – 6, 95; 7 – 9, 49; 10 – 12, 28; total, 194
Nationalities of student body: U.S., 98; U.K., 3; host, 54; other, 39; total, 194
Capacity: preK, 12; K, 18; 1 – 6, 120; 7 – 9, 60; 10 – 12, 40; total, 250
Teacher/student ratio: 1/7
Tuition (annual): preK – K, $865; 1 – 6, $1,735; 7 – 12, $1,905 (2nd and 3rd child discount available)
Other fees (annual): registration, $225; busing, $30/month; student activity, $75; capital*, $1,000/family
School year: August to May

Year founded: 1977. **Type of school:** coed, day, church-related. **Governed by:** Gospel Missionary Union, South America Mission, World Gospel Mission. **Accredited by:** Bolivian government, ACSI.

Curriculum/physical plant

Type: U.S. **Languages taught:** English, Spanish. **Staff specialists:** speech/hearing, nurse, special education/learning disabilities. **Special programs:** honors sections. **Special curricular:** art, physical education, computer instruction, yearbook, newspaper. **Extracurricular:** drama, gymnastics, field trips, art/science fair, field day, spelling/math competitions, interschool competitions, student social organization. **Sports:** basketball, soccer, volleyball. **Tests:** PSAT, SAT, ACT, Stanford, GRE (testing center). **Graduates attending college:** 98%. **Graduates have attended:** American U., Boston U., Kansas State U., George Mason U., Grace Bible College. **Location:** in suburb, 7 kilometers from center of Santa Cruz. **Campus:** 2.5 hectares. **Library:** 10,000 volumes. **Facilities:** 8 buildings, 20 classrooms, 2 playing fields, 2 science labs, computer lab, gymnasium/multipurpose building, kitchen, partial air conditioning, nearby boarding facilities operated by World Gospel Mission.

*Once only fee

Santa Cruz Cooperative School

Street address: Calle Barcelona No. 1, Santa Cruz, Bolivia
Phone: (591)(3)530808 **Facsimile:** (591)(3)526993
E-mail: students@datacom-bo.net
Mail: Casilla 753, Santa Cruz, Bolivia
U.S. mail: (no personal name) SCCS, U.S. Embassy–Santa Cruz, Bolivia, APO AA 34032
Director: David Deuel
Secondary principal: Bryn Gabriel
Elementary principal: Susan Zapata
Head of library: Kathy Hemmat
Teaching staff: full-time, 47; part-time, 4; total, 51
Nationalities of teaching staff: U.S., 27; host, 18; other, 6; total, 51
Grade levels: preK – 12
Enrollment: preK, 35; K, 51; 1 – 6, 300; 7 – 9, 122; 10 – 12, 105; total, 613
Nationalities of student body: U.S., 80; host, 433; other, 100; total, 613
Capacity: preK, 50; K, 50; 1 – 6, 300; 7 – 9, 150; 10 – 12, 150; total, 700
Teacher/student ratio: 1/14
Tuition (annual): preK, $1,960; K, $2,932; 1 – 6, $3,221; 7 – 12, $3,709
Other fees (annual): capital levy*, $4,000/family; busing, $350
School year: August to June

Year founded: 1959. **Type of school:** coed, day, parent cooperative. **Governed by:** elected board of directors. **Accredited by:** Bolivian Ministry of Education, Southern. **Regional organizations:** AASSA.

Curriculum

Type: U.S., AP. **Languages taught:** French, Spanish. **Staff specialists:** computer, counselor, nurse, librarian. **Special programs:** ESL, independent study, correspondence. **Special curricular:** art, chorus, physical education, computer instruction, debating, drama, economics, ecology, dance, photography. **Extracurricular:** drama, computers, yearbook, newspaper, literary magazine, photography, field trips, choral music, cheerleading. **Sports:** basketball, soccer, track and field, volleyball. **Tests:** PSAT, SAT, ACT, TOEFL, AP, Iowa. **Graduates attending college:** 98%. **Graduates have attended:** Georgetown, U. of Texas, Harvard, William and Mary, MIT.

Physical plant

Location: 2 miles from center city. **Campus:** 10 acres. **Library:** 10,000 volumes. **Facilities:** 5 buildings, 36 classrooms, cafeteria, covered play area, 2 tennis courts, 2 playing fields, 2 science labs, 2 computer labs, gymnasium/auditorium, AV area, teachers' workroom/lounge.

*Once only fee

BOSNIA AND HERZEGOVINA

Region: Europe
Size: 19,741 square miles
Population: 2,656,240
Capital: Sarajevo
Telephone code: 387
Currency: new dinar
Languages: Serbo-Croatian

SARAJEVO

QSI International School of Bosnia and Herzegovina

U.S. mail: c/o American Embassy Sarajevo, Dept. of State, Washington, DC 70521-7130
Teaching staff: full-time, 2; total, 2
Nationalities of teaching staff: U.S., 2; total, 2
Grade levels: K – 8
Capacity: K, 10; 1 – 6, 20; 7 – 8, 10; total, 40
Tuition (annual): K – 5, $6,900; 6 – 8, $9,200
Other fees: registration*, $100; capital levy, $4,000 deposit or $1,600/year fee
School year: September to June

Year founded: 1997. **Type of school:** coed, day, private nonprofit. **Governed by:** appointed board of directors. **Sponsored by:** Quality Schools International. **Regional organizations:** CEESA.

Curriculum/physical plant

Type: U.S., national. **Special programs:** ESL. **Special curricular:** computers, physical education.

*Once only fee

BOTSWANA

Region: Southern Africa
Size: 224,607 square miles
Population: 1,477,630
Capital: Gaborone
Telephone code: 267
Currency: pula
Languages: English, Setswana

GABORONE

Legae Academy

Street address: Plot 19893, Phase 2, Extension 12, Gaborone West, Gaborone, Botswana
Phone/facsimile: (267)324313/324333
Mail: PO Box 750, Mogoditshane, Botswana
Principal: W. S. Grisdale
Vice principal: V. Bunjun
Business manager: M. T. Rubadiri
Teaching staff: full-time, 33; total, 33
Nationalities of teaching staff: U.S., 2; U.K., 7; host, 3; other, 21; total, 33
Grade levels: 7 – 11
Enrollment: 7 – 9, 350; 10 – 11, 200; total, 550
Nationalities of student body: U.S., 5; U.K., 20; host, 400; other, 125; total, 550
Capacity: 7 – 9, 350; 10 – 11, 250; total, 600
Teacher/student ratio: 1/16
Tuition (annual): nationals, 7,900**; expatriates, 9,300
Other fees: registration*, 50**
School year: January to December

Year founded: 1992. **Type of school:** coed, proprietary. **Governed by:** appointed board of directors. **Accredited by:** Botswana Ministry of Education, U. of Cambridge Examiners. **Regional organizations:** AISA.

Curriculum/physical plant

Type: U.K., national. **Languages taught:** English, French, Setswana. **Staff specialists:** math, computer, counselor, nurse. **Special programs:** remedial. **Special curricular:** art, physical education, computer instruction, fashion and fabric. **Extracurricular:** drama, dance, computers, yearbook, excursions/expeditions, field trips. **Sports:** athletics, cricket, netball, soccer, softball, volleyball. **Clubs:** chess, debating, geography, mathematics, table tennis, French. **Tests:** Cambridge. **Location:** in city. **Facilities:** 10 buildings, 14 classrooms, infirmary, playing field, 2 science labs, 2 computer labs, swimming pool, library, weather station, agricultural area, 2 art studios.

*Once only fee **Botswana pula

Maru a Pula School

Street address: Maru a Pula Way, Gaborone, Botswana
Phone: (267)312953 **Facsimile:** (267)373338 **E-mail:** pua@aztec.co.za
Mail: Private Bag 0045, Gaborone, Botswana
Principal: Malcolm H. McKenzie
Deputy principals: John O'Brien, Alan Wilson, Chris Madeley
Directors of studies: Guy Walker, Sheila Case
Bursar: Greta Steele
Teaching staff: full-time, 44; part-time, 6; total, 50
Nationalities of teaching staff: U.S., 4; U.K., 17; host, 8; other, 21; total, 50
Grade levels: 8 – A-level
Enrollment: 8 – 9, 188; 10 – 12, 297; A-level, 58; total, 543
Teacher/student ratio: 1/12
Boarders: boys, 70; girls, 74 **Grades:** 8 – A-level **Program:** planned 7-day
Tuition (annual): 12,000**
Other fees (annual): registration*, 50**; boarding, 8,400; lunch, 320/term
School year: January to December

Year founded: 1972. **Type of school:** coed, day, boarding, private nonprofit. **Governed by:** elected Council of Maru a Pula. **Accredited by:** Botswana Ministry of Education.

Curriculum/physical plant

Type: U.K., AP. **Languages taught:** French, Setswana. **Staff specialists:** computer, nurse, guidance counselor. **Special programs:** honors sections. **Special curricular:** art, computer instruction. **Extracurricular:** drama, dance, instrumental music, computers, yearbook. **Sports:** athletics, basketball, netball, soccer, softball, swimming, tennis, volleyball. **Clubs:** chess, debating, bridge, sewing, cooking, library, social service, service projects within the school. **Tests:** A-level GCE, O-level GCE. **Graduates attending college:** 85%. **Graduates have attended:** U. of Pennsylvania, Middlebury, Stanford, Oxford, Cambridge. **Location:** in suburbs. **Campus:** 50 acres. **Library:** 15,000 volumes. **Facilities:** 35 buildings, 26 classrooms, auditorium, cafeteria, infirmary, 2 tennis courts, 2 playing fields, 6 science labs, computer lab, AV center, boarding in shared cubicles, 34 faculty houses.

*Once only fee **Botswana pula

Northside Primary School

Street address: Tshekedi Crescent, Gaborone, Botswana
Phone: (267)352440 **Facsimile:** (267)353573
Mail: PO Box 897, Gaborone, Botswana
Headmistress: Margaret Dixon-Warren
Deputy head: Mandy Watson
Teaching staff: full-time, 27; part-time, 2; total, 29
Nationalities of teaching staff: U.K., 14; host, 1; other, 14; total, 29
Grade levels: K – 7
Enrollment: K, 50; 1 – 6, 343; 7, 29; total, 422
Nationalities of student body: U.S., 14; U.K., 91; host, 93; other, 224; total, 422
Teacher/student ratio: 1/13
Tuition (annual): 10,050**

Other fees: registration*, 100**; capital levy*, 1,050
School year: January through December

Year founded: 1974. **Type of school:** coed, day, private nonprofit. **Governed by:** elected school council. **Sponsored by:** corporation. **Accredited by:** ECIS.

Curriculum/physical plant

Type: U.K., national. **Languages taught:** French, Setswana. **Staff specialists:** computer, librarian, music, physical education, science, special needs. **Special programs:** remedial, acceleration, specific learning problems. **Extracurricular:** drama, gymnastics, dance, choir, orchestra, chess, guitar, flute violin, recorder. **Sports:** badminton, basketball, cricket, netball, soccer, swimming, table tennis, tennis, traditional dancing, primary hockey, judo. **Clubs:** computer, Cub Scouts, Brownies. **Location:** in attractive suburb. **Campus:** 7 acres. **Library:** 10,000 volumes. **Facilities:** 16 classrooms, 2 tennis courts, gymnasium, playing field, science lab, computer lab, swimming pool, all-purpose hall with stage, PTA kitchen, uniform shop, music room, French room, 2 Setswana language rooms, computer and printer in every classroom.

*Once only fee **Botswana pula

Westwood School

Phone: (267)306736 **Facsimile:** (267)306734 **E-mail:** westwood@info.bw
Mail: PO Box 2446, Gaborone, Botswana
Principal: Robert F. Sylvester
Head of secondary programs: Wilma G. Matheson
Teaching staff: full-time, 39; total, 39
Nationalities of teaching staff: U.S., 6; U.K., 6; host, 6; other, 21; total, 39
Grade levels: K – 11
Enrollment: K, 40; 1 – 6, 270; 7 – 11, 167; total, 477
Nationalities of student body: U.S., 36; U.K., 44; host, 100; other, 297; total, 477
Teacher/student ratio: 1/12
Tuition (annual): K – 6, $4,933; 7 – 11, $5,800
School year: January to December

Year founded: 1988. **Type of school:** coed, day. **Governed by:** appointed and elected private school board. **Sponsored by:** diplomatic/corporation. **Accredited by:** New England. **Regional organizations:** AISA, ECIS.

Curriculum/physical plant

Type: U.S., U.K. **Languages taught:** French, Setswana. **Staff specialists:** reading, math, learning disabilities, nurse. **Special programs:** ESL, remedial, American studies. **Special curricular:** art, physical education, vocational, information technology. **Extracurricular:** drama, choral music, computers, literary magazine, photography, excursions/expeditions, field trips. **Sports:** basketball, cricket, soccer, softball, swimming, tennis, track and field, volleyball. **Clubs:** chess, musical instruments, history, aerobics, stamp collecting, conservation, science, photography. **Tests:** ITBS, Botswana National Exams. **Location:** in Gaborone. **Campus:** 12 acres. **Library:** 12,000 volumes. **Facilities:** 12 buildings, 27 classrooms, auditorium, infirmary, 5 playing fields, science labs, swimming pool, tennis courts, research lab, air conditioning.

BRAZIL

Region: South America
Size: 3,286,500 square miles
Population: 162,661,214
Capital: Brasilia
Telephone code: 55
Currency: real
Languages: Portuguese, English Spanish, French

BELEM

AMAZON VALLEY ACADEMY

Phone: (55)(91)2352166 **Facsimile:** (55)(91)2352906 (voice, then fax)
E-mail: miceb@amazon.com.br
Mail: Caixa Postal 13030, Agencia Nazare, 66.040-970 Belem, Para Brazil
Principal: Ken Trough
Vice-principals: Ellen Johnson, Beat Müller
Teaching staff: full-time, 13; part-time, 2; total, 15
Nationalities of teaching staff: U.S., 13; host, 1; other, 1; total, 15
Grade levels: K – 12
Enrollment: K – 6, 39; 7 – 9, 10; 10 – 12, 8; total, 57
Nationalities of student body: U.S., 29; other, 28; total, 57
Capacity: total, 160
Teacher/student ratio: 1/3
Tuition (annual): K, $2,500; 1 – 9, $4,116; 10 – 12, $5,136
School year: August to June

Year founded: 1957. **Type of school:** coed, day. **Governed by:** elected local mission board. **Sponsored by:** UFM International. **Accredited by:** Southern.

Curriculum/physical plant

Type: U.S., U.K., German/Swiss (grades 1 – 9). **Languages of instruction:** English, German. **Languages taught:** German, Portuguese. **Special curricular:** chorus, physical education, computer instruction. **Extracurricular:** drama, yearbook, photography, field trips. **Sports:** basketball, soccer, swimming, volleyball. **Tests:** PSAT, SAT, ACT, AP, GCSE, Stanford. **Graduates attending college:** 95%. **Graduates have attended:** Wheaton, Biola, Hardin-Simmons, Georgia Tech, Aberdeen (Scotland). **Location:** 3 kilometers outside city. **Campus:** 22 acres. **Libraries:** 15,000 volumes (English and German). **Facilities:** auditorium, tennis court, gymnasium, 2 playing fields, swimming pool, air conditioned science lab, computer lab.

BELO HORIZONTE

Escola Americana de Belo Horizonte

Street address: Av. Dom Joao VI, 3002-Buritis, Belo Horizonte, Minas Gerais, Brazil
Phone: (55)(31)3786700 **Facsimile:** (55)(31)3786878
E-mail: amschool.eabh@metalink.com.br
Mail: Caixa Postal 2.501, 30.161 Belo Horizonte, Minas Gerais, Brazil
U.S. mail: (no personal name) Director, ASBH, Unit 3505, APO AA 34030
Director: Dr. Keith Costello
Assistant director: Gary Walker
Teaching staff: full-time, 17; part-time, 7; total, 24
Nationalities of teaching staff: U.S., 15; host, 9; total, 24
Grade levels: preK – 12
Enrollment: preK, 26; K, 12; 1 – 6, 75; 7 – 9, 38; 10 – 12, 15; total, 166
Nationalities of student body: U.S., 18; host, 100; other, 48; total, 166
Capacity: preK, 21; K, 21; 1 – 6, 80; 7 – 9, 45; 10 – 12, 45; total, 212
Teacher/student ratio: 1/7
Tuition (annual): preK – 6, $9,090; 7 – 12, $10,850
Other fees: registration*, $2,500
School year: August to June

Year founded: 1956. **Type of school:** coed, day, private nonprofit. **Governed by:** elected board of governors. **Sponsored by:** association of parents. **Accredited by:** Southern.

Curriculum/physical plant

Type: U.S., IB (Brazilian), AP. **Languages taught:** Portuguese, French, Spanish. **Staff specialists:** counselor. **Special curricular:** physical education, computer instruction. **Extracurricular:** drama, computers, yearbook. **Sports:** basketball, soccer, volleyball. **Tests:** PSAT, SAT, IB, AP, Iowa. **Graduates attending college:** 90%. **Graduates have attended:** Stanford, Keio U. (Tokyo), U. of Southern California, Stetson U., U. of Florida. **Location:** in suburban area, 20 kilometers from city center. **Campus:** 26,000 square meters. **Library:** 10,000 volumes. **Facilities:** 6 buildings, 14 classrooms, cafeteria, infirmary, gymnasium, 2 playing fields, science lab, computer lab, AV equipment.

*Once only fee

BRASILIA

American School of Brasilia

Street address: Avenida L-2 Sul, SGAS Q-605-E, Brasilia, DF, Brazil
Phone: (55)(61)4433237 **Facsimile:** (55)(61)2444303
E-mail: rwerner@bus.eabdf.br **Web:** http://www.eabdf.br
U.S. mail: (no personal name) Headmaster, Unit 3500, APO AA 34030
Headmaster: Robert Werner
Secondary school principal: John Gates
Elementary school principal: Shirley Gregory
Director of guidance: David A. Topham
Teaching staff: full-time, 65; total, 65
Nationalities of teaching staff: U.S., 40; host, 20; other, 5; total, 65
Grade levels: preK – 12
Enrollment: preK – 6, 380; 7 – 12, 290; total, 670
Nationalities of student body: U.S., 100; host, 405; other, 165; total, 670
Teacher/student ratio: 1/11
Tuition (annual): preK – 6, $8,000; 7 – 12, $10,000
Other fees: registration*, $3,500
School year: August to June

Year founded: 1964. **Type of school:** coed, day. **Governed by:** elected board of directors. **Accredited by:** Southern. **Regional organizations:** AASSA, AASB.

Curriculum/physical plant

Type: U.S., AP. **Languages of instruction:** English, Portuguese. **Languages taught:** English, French, Portuguese. **Staff specialists:** reading, counselor, learning disabilities, nurse, gifted. **Special programs:** ESL, optimal match. **Special curricular:** art, chorus, physical education, computer instruction, instrumental music. **Extracurricular:** drama, computers, yearbook, photography, field trips. **Sports:** basketball, soccer, softball, volleyball, Brazilian salao. **Organizations:** National Honor Society, National Junior Honor Society, student council. **Tests:** SSAT, PSAT, SAT, ACT, AP, Iowa, DAT. **Graduates attending college:** 90%. **Graduates have attended:** Cornell, U. of Pennsylvania, Brown, Harvard, West Point. **Location:** 5 minutes from downtown area. **Campus:** 7 acres. **Libraries (2):** 18,000 volumes. **Facilities:** 5 buildings, 40 classrooms, cafeteria, infirmary, tennis court, gymnasium, playing field, 4 science labs, 2 computer labs, air conditioning.

*Once only fee

CAMPINAS

Escola Americana de Campinas

Street address: Rua Cajamar 35, 13093-230, Chacara de Barra, Campinas, Sao Paulo, Brazil
Phone: (55)(19)2517377 **Facsimile:** (55)(19)2532321
E-mail: 2146993@mcimail.com
Mail: PO Box 1183, 13001-970, Campinas, SP, Brazil
Superintendent: David E. Cardenas
High school principal: Paul Olson
Elementary principal: Debbie Murphy
Teaching staff: full-time, 30; part-time, 8; total, 38
Nationalities of teaching staff: U.S., 13; host, 25; total, 38
Grade levels: preK – 12
Enrollment: preK, 67; K, 36; 1 – 6, 177; 7 – 9, 66; 10 – 12, 51; total, 397
Capacity: preK, 36; K, 36; 1 – 6, 205; 7 – 9, 75; 10 – 12, 75; total, 427
Teacher/student ratio: 1/9
Tuition (annual): preK – K, $6,290; 1 – 6, $8,390; 7 – 12, $10,360
Other fees (annual): registration*, $2,000; busing, $1,200
School year: August to June

Year founded: 1957. **Type of school:** coed, day, private nonprofit. **Governed by:** elected board of directors. **Accredited by:** Southern.

Curriculum/physical plant

Type: U.S., Brazilian, IB, AP. **Languages of instruction:** English, Portuguese. **Languages taught:** French, Portuguese. **Staff specialists:** computer, counselor, psychologist, learning disabilities, gifted, marketing and admissions. **Special programs:** honors sections, independent study, remedial, gifted. **Special curricular:** art, physical education, computer instruction, music. **Extracurricular:** computers, yearbook, newspaper, literary magazine, field trips. **Sports:** basketball, softball, volleyball, indoor soccer, outdoor soccer, golf, track, ballet. **Tests:** PSAT, SAT, ACT, IB, AP, Iowa. **Graduates attending college:** 100%. **Graduates have attended:** Yale, MIT, Vassar, Cornell, Princeton. **Location:** 10 minutes from center of Campinas, 1 hour from São Paulo. **Campus:** 14 acres. **Library:** 15,000 volumes. **Facilities:** 7 buildings, 35 classrooms, auditorium, tennis court, gymnasium, 2 playing fields, 2 science labs, 2 computer labs.

*Once only fee

CURITIBA

International School of Curitiba

Street address: Av. Des. Hugo Simas 1800, Bom Retiro, Curitiba, Parana, Brazil 80520-250
Phone: (55)(41)3386611 **Facsimile:** (55)(41)3386782
E-mail: isc@eic.arauc.br **Web:** http://www.eic.arauc.br
Mail: PO Box 7004, Curitiba, PR, Brazil, 80011-970
Director: Edward F. Pisani, Ed.D.
Assistant director: Ana Lucia de Albuquerque Schulhan
Head of library: Jussara Kanashiro
Head of computer services/business manager: Carla Jacobs
Teaching staff: full-time, 20; part-time, 8; total, 28
Nationalities of teaching staff: U.S., 6; host, 14; other, 8; total, 28
Grade levels: preK – 12
Enrollment: preK, 20; K, 20; 1 – 6, 130; 7 – 9, 35; 10 – 12, 35; total, 240
Nationalities of student body: U.S., 34; host, 145; other, 61; total, 240
Teacher/student ratio: 1/10
Tuition (annual): preK – 6, $7,300; 7 – 12, $8,300
Other fees: registration, K – 6, $570; 7 – 12, $650; capital endowment: K, $500; 1 – 12, $2,000
School year: August to June

Year founded: 1959. **Type of school:** coed, day, private nonprofit. **Governed by:** elected association of families via board of directors. **Sponsored by:** association of parents. **Accredited by:** Southern. **Regional organizations:** AASB, AASSA, AAIE, IBO.

Curriculum/physical plant

Type: U.S., IB. **Languages of instruction:** English, Portuguese. **Languages taught:** French, Swedish. **Staff specialists:** computer, counselor. **Special programs:** ESL, independent study, remedial, college-prep seminar. **Special curricular:** art, physical education, computer instruction, music. **Extracurricular:** computers, yearbook, excursions/expeditions, field trips, judo. **Sports:** basketball, volleyball, full-field soccer. **Tests:** PSAT, SAT, IB, Iowa. **Graduates attending college:** 95%. **Graduates have attended:** Kansas State, U. of Arizona, Bradley U., Duquesne, U. of Central Florida. **Location:** in Curitiba. **Campus:** 7,000 square meters. **Facilities:** 5 buildings, 19 classrooms, cafeteria, gymnasium, science lab, computer lab, 2 libraries, 3 courts, 2 soccer fields, video room, all-purpose room, art room.

PORTO ALEGRE

Pan American School of Porto Alegre

Street address: Rua João Paetzel 440, Porto Alegre, RS, Brazil 91.330-280
Phone/facsimile: (55)(51)3345866 **E-mail:** paspoa@portoweb.com.br
Director: Priscilla Abel
Business manager: Sérgio Nunes
Teaching staff: full-time, 4; part-time, 6; total, 10
Nationalities of teaching staff: U.S., 4; host, 4; other, 2; total, 10
Grade levels: preK – 6
Enrollment: preK, 24; K, 11; 1 – 6, 25; total, 60
Nationalities of student body: U.S., 5; host, 38; other, 17; total, 60
Teacher/student ratio: 1/10
Tuition (annual): preK, $3,480; K – 6, $7,536
Other fees (annual): registration, $348; development fee, $232
School year: August to June

Year founded: 1966. **Type of school:** coed, day, private nonprofit. **Governed by:** elected board of directors. **Sponsored by:** Association of PAS. **Accredited by:** MEC, Southern.

Curriculum/physical plant

Type: U.S. **Languages of instruction:** English, Portuguese. **Languages taught:** Portuguese. **Staff specialists:** computer, counselor. **Special curricular:** physical education, computer instruction. **Extracurricular:** computers, newspaper, field trips, soccer. **Tests:** PSAT, SAT, Iowa. **Location:** in city of Porto Alegre. **Library:** 5,000 volumes. **Facilities:** 1 building, 12 classrooms, cafeteria, science lab, basketball court.

RECIFE

American School of Recife

Street address: Rua Sá e Souza, 408, Boa Viagem, 51030-060 Recife – PE, Brazil
Phone: (55)(81)3414716/4621502 **Facsimile:** (55)(81)3410142
E-mail: ear@elogica.com.br
U.S. mail: (no personal name) c/o U.S. Consulate – Recife, APO AA, Unit 3503, 34030
Superintendent: Helen Ruth VanDerVeer Gueiros
Principal: Martha Luhrs Viegas
Portuguese coordinator: Ester Correa
Business manager: Fernanda Teodoro
Teaching staff: full-time, 32; part-time, 6; total, 38
Nationalities of teaching staff: U.S., 13; host, 20; other, 5; total, 38
Grade levels: preK – 12

Enrollment: preK, 31; K, 29; 1 – 5, 153; 6 – 8, 81; 9 – 12, 62; total, 356
Nationalities of student body: U.S., 40; host, 256; other, 60; total, 356
Capacity: preK, 40; K, 40; 1 – 5, 150; 6 – 8, 75; 9 – 12, 80; total, 385
Teacher/student ratio: 1/10
Tuition (annual): preK – K, $4,947; 1 – 5, $6,135; 6 – 12, $7,082
Other fees (annual): registration*, $120; capital levy*, $2,000; re-registration, $61; books and materials, $576
School year: August to June

Year founded: 1966. **Type of school:** coed, day, private nonprofit. **Governed by:** elected board of directors. **Accredited by:** Southern.

Curriculum/physical plant

Type: U.S., national university requirements. **Languages taught:** French, Portuguese. **Staff specialists:** math, computer, nurse, guidance counselor. **Special programs:** ESL, independent study, remedial. **Special curricular:** art, physical education, computer instruction, Model UN. **Extracurricular:** drama, Math Counts, Odyssey of the Mind, calligraphy, woodcraft. **Sports:** basketball, soccer, volleyball. **Tests:** PSAT, SAT, ACT, TOEFL, Iowa, SLEP, ESL, reading. **Graduates attending college:** 100%. **Graduates have attended:** Texas A&M, Georgetown, Duke, Boston U., Southern Illinois. **Location:** in suburban area adjacent to city. **Campus:** 8.5 acres. **Library:** 12,000 volumes. **Facilities:** 8 buildings, 24 classrooms, covered play area, science lab, AV room, canteen, partial air conditioning.

*Once only fee

RIO DE JANEIRO

Escola Americana do Rio de Janeiro

Street address: 132 Estrada da Gávea, 22451-260 Rio de Janeiro, Brazil
Phone: (55)(21)2590330/2594807 **Facsimile:** (55)(21)2594722
E-mail: dennis@uninet.com.br
Headmaster: Dennis Klumpp
High school principal: Thomas Connolly
Middle school principal: Michael Groeninger
Elementary school principal: Robert Woods
Early childhood coordinator: Suely Pecanha
Teaching staff: full-time, 107; part-time, 8; total, 115
Nationalities of teaching staff: U.S., 43; host, 62; other, 10; total, 115
Grade levels: preK – 12
Enrollment: preK, 157; K, 60; 1 – 5, 365; 6 – 8, 225; 9 – 12, 223; total, 1,030
Nationalities of student body: U.S., 250; U.K., 15; host, 605; other, 160; total, 1030
Capacity: preK, 150; K, 60; 1 – 5, 410; 6 – 8, 240; 9 – 12, 255; total, 1,115
Teacher/student ratio: 1/9
Tuition (annual): preK – K, $12,230; 1 – 5, $12,940; 6 – 8, $13,930; 9 – 12, $15,850

Other fees: capital levy*, $3,000
School year: August through June

Year founded: 1937. **Type of school:** coed, day, private nonprofit. **Governed by:** appointed board of directors. **Sponsored by:** community. **Accredited by:** Southern. **Regional organizations:** AASB, AASSA, AAIE, ECIS.

Curriculum

Type: U.S., IB, AP. **Languages taught:** French, German, Portuguese. **Staff specialists:** computer, counselor, psychologist, learning disabilities, nurse, high capacity/high potential. **Special programs:** ESL. **Special curricular:** art, band, physical education, computer instruction. **Extracurricular:** drama, dance, instrumental music, computers, yearbook, newspaper, excursions/expeditions, field trips, National Honor Society. **Sports:** basketball, soccer, softball, track and field, volleyball, handball. **Tests:** PSAT, SAT, ACT, IB, AP, Iowa. **Graduates attending college:** 100%. **Graduates have attended:** Boston U., Georgetown, Cornell, Stanford, Duke.

Physical plant

Location: in suburban area, 8 kilometers west of city. **Campus:** 16.5 acres. **Library:** 38,000 volumes. **Facilities:** 9 buildings, 75 classrooms, auditorium, cafeteria, infirmary, 3 covered play areas, gymnasium, playing field, 8 science labs, 3 computer labs, swimming pool, band room.

*Once only fee

SALVADOR

Pan American School of Bahia

Street address: Loteamento Patamares s/n, Salvador, Bahia, Brazil
Phone: (55)(71)3679099 **Facsimile:** (55)(71)3679090
E-mail: epaba@svn.com.br
Mail: Caixa Postal 231, 40.001/970-Salvador, Bahia, Brazil
U.S. mail: (no personal name) American Consular Agency PAS, Salvador, Brazil, APO Miami 34030
Superintendent: Mary Jo Heatherington, Ph.D.
Academic directors: Joanne Lalumiere, Lenise Sampaio, Susan Miller
Teaching staff: full-time, 33; part-time, 4; total, 37
Nationalities of teaching staff: U.S., 20; host, 17; total, 37
Grade levels: preK – 12
Enrollment: preK – K, 78; 1 – 6, 181; 7 – 9, 72; 10 – 12, 45; total, 376
Teacher/student ratio: 1/10
Tuition (annual): preK – K, $4,990; 1 – 6, $6,811; 7 – 12, $7,722
Other fees (annual): registration*, $2,000; capital levy*, $6,500; busing, $1,100; ESL, $1,848
School year: August through June

Year founded: 1960. **Type of school:** coed, day, private nonprofit. **Governed by:** elected board of directors. **Accredited by:** Southern. **Regional organizations:** AASB, AASSA.

Curriculum/physical plant

Type: U.S., national college entrance. **Languages of instruction:** English, Portuguese. **Languages taught:** Portuguese. **Staff specialists:** computer, counselor, nurse, art, music. **Special programs:** ESL. **Special curricular:** art, physical education, computer instruction. **Extracurricular:** computers, yearbook, field trips, National Honor Society. **Sports:** basketball, soccer, swimming, volleyball. **Tests:** SSAT, PSAT, SAT, Iowa. **Graduates attending college:** 100%. **Graduates have attended:** Boston U., Lisbon U., Michigan State, Mackenzie U., Macalester College. **Location:** near beach, 15 minutes from downtown Salvador. **Library:** 15,000 volumes. **Facilities:** 2 buildings, 29 classrooms, cafeteria, infirmary, covered play area, gymnasium, playing field, 2 science labs, computer lab, swimming pool.

*Once only fee

SAO PAULO

Associacao Escola Graduada de Sao Paulo

Street address: Av. Presidente Giovanni Gronchi, 4710, Sao Paulo, Brazil
Phone: (55)(11)8422499 **Facsimile:** (55)(11)8429358
E-mail: graded@eagle.aegsp.br **Web:** http://www.aegsp.br
Mail: Caixa Postal 7432, 05724-002 Sao Paulo, SP, Brazil
Superintendent: David Tully
Principal, high school: Timothy Carr
Principal, middle school: Sherry McClelland
Principal, elementary school: Paige Geiger
Principal, pre-primary school: Vera Giusti
Teaching staff: full-time, 115; part-time, 4; total, 119
Nationalities of teaching staff: U.S., 54; host, 58; other, 7; total, 119
Grade levels: N – 12
Enrollment: N – preK, 91; K, 89; 1 – 5, 413; 6 – 8, 239; 9 – 12, 314; total, 1,146
Nationalities of student body: U.S., 422; host, 480; other, 244; total, 1,146
Teacher/student ratio: 1/10
Tuition (annual): (estimated) N – preK, $10,507; K– 5, $15,404; 6 – 8, $19,285; 9 – 12, $22,228
Other fees (annual): registration*, $300; busing, $2,460; entrance*, $5,000
School year: August to June

Year founded: 1920. **Type of school:** coed, day, private nonprofit. **Governed by:** appointed board of directors. **Sponsored by:** American Chamber of Commerce. **Accredited by:** Southern, Sao Paulo State Council of Education.

Curriculum

Type: U.S., national, IB, AP. **Languages taught:** French, Spanish, Portuguese. **Staff specialists:** computer, counselor, nurse, art, music. **Special programs:** ESL. **Special curricular:** art, physical education, computer instruction, journalism, photography. **Extracurricular:** drama, yearbook, literary magazine, excursions/expeditions, field trips. **Sports:** basketball, soccer, softball, tennis, volleyball. **Clubs:** chess, Cub Scouts, National Honor Society, student council, thespian. **Tests:** SSAT, PSAT, SAT, ACT, IB, AP, Iowa. **Graduates attending college:** 98%. **Graduates have attended:** Colgate, Brown, Harvard, Smith, Yale.

Physical plant

Location: mainly residential, fast-developing suburban area within city limits of Sao Paulo. **Campus:** 16 acres. **Library:** 50,000 volumes. **Facilities:** 12 buildings, 75 classrooms, auditorium, cafeteria, infirmary, covered play area, 6 tennis courts, 2 gymnasiums, 2 playing fields, 6 science labs, 3 computer labs, graphics department, AV center.

*Once only fee

CHAPEL (ESCOLA MARIA IMACULADA)

Street address: Rua Vigário João de Pontes 537, 04748-000 Sao Paulo, SP, Brazil
Phone: (55)(11)2477455/2477007 **Facsimile:** (55)(11)5217763
Mail: Caixa Postal 21293, Brooklin 04602-970, Sao Paulo, SP, Brazil
Superintendent: Gerald C. Gates
High school principal: John Ciallelo
Lower school principal: Deborah Ann Martin
Brazilian program director: Lizete Marostega
Business manager: Peter F. Curran
Teaching staff: full-time, 64; part-time, 6; total, 70
Nationalities of teaching staff: U.S., 28; U.K., 1; host, 38; other, 3; total, 70
Grade levels: N – 12
Enrollment: N – preK, 70; K, 50; 1 – 6, 300; 7 – 9, 140; 10 – 12, 140; total, 700
Nationalities of student body: U.S., 140; host, 350; other, 210; total, 700
Teacher/student ratio: 1/10
Tuition (annual): N – preK, $6,000; K – 6, $10,000; 7 – 12, $14,000
Other fees (annual): registration, $2,300; books, $370
School year: August to June

Year founded: 1947. **Type of school:** coed, day, church-related, private nonprofit. **Governed by:** appointed advisory council. **Sponsored by:** Oblates of Mary Immaculate. **Accredited by:** Southern.

Curriculum/physical plant

Type: U.S., national, IB. **Languages of instruction:** English, Portuguese. **Languages taught:** French, Spanish. **Staff specialists:** reading, computer, counselor, nurse. **Special programs:** ESL, honors sections, independent study, remedial. **Special curricular:** art, physical education, computer instruction. **Extracurricular:** drama, gymnastics, computers, yearbook, newspaper, literary magazine, excursions/expeditions, field trips. **Sports:** basketball, soccer, tennis, track and field, volleyball, handball, indoor soccer, Olympic gym. **Clubs:** computer, National Honor Society, student council, arts & crafts, scouting, retreats, first aid, CPR. **Tests:** PSAT, SAT, ACT, TOEFL, IB, AP, Stanford, MAT, Otis-Lennon, DAT. **Graduates attending college:** 82%. **Graduates have attended:** Brown, Boston U., MIT, Cornell, Tufts. **Location:** in residential suburb of Sao Paulo. **Campus:** 4 acres. **Library:** 21,000 volumes. **Facilities:** 3 buildings, 45 classrooms, auditorium, cafeteria, infirmary, covered play area, 2 tennis courts, gymnasium, playing field, 2 science labs, computer lab, AV room, playgrounds.

Pan American Christian Academy

Street address: Rua Cassio de Campos Nogueira 393, Sao Paulo, SP 04829-310, Brazil
Phone: (55)(11)5209655/5209167 **Facsimile:** (55)(11)5209591
E-mail: paca@opus.com.br **Web:** http://www.opus.com.br/~paca/
Director: Michael Epp
High school coordinator: Robin Rugg
Elementary school coordinator: Claudia Limpic
Head of library: Sue Spoelhof
Teaching staff: full-time, 24; part-time, 13; total, 37
Nationalities of teaching staff: U.S., 26; host, 9; other, 2; total, 37
Grade levels: K – 12
Enrollment: K, 21; 1 – 6, 136; 7 – 9, 70; 10 – 12, 73; total, 300
Nationalities of student body: U.S., 107; host, 159; other, 34; total, 300
Teacher/student ratio: 1/10
Tuition (annual): K – 5, $5,000; 6 – 8, $6,000; 9 – 12, $7,750
Other fees: registration*, $600; books, $200 (annually); academic development: K – 8, $10; 9 – 12, $20 (monthly)
School year: August to June

Year founded: 1959. **Type of school:** coed, day, private nonprofit, evangelical Christian. **Governed by:** appointed board of directors. **Accredited by:** Southern, Brazilian Ministry of Education and Culture. **Regional organizations:** AASSA, AASB, ACSI.

Curriculum/physical plant

Type: U.S., national, AP. **Languages of instruction:** English, Portuguese. **Staff specialists:** counselor, learning disabilities. **Special curricular:** art, chorus, computer instruction, physical education (includes swimming), accounting, typing, speech, anatomy & physiology, knowledge bowl. **Extracurricular:** drama, instrumental music, field trips, independent study through Nebraska U., choir. **Sports:** basketball, cheerleading, soccer, softball, swimming, track and field, volleyball, indoor soccer. **Clubs:** National Honor Society, pep club. **Tests:** PSAT, SAT, ACT, TOEFL, Iowa. **Graduates attending college:** 95%. **Graduates have attended:** Wheaton College, Biola U., Johns Hopkins, Boston U., U. of Sao Paulo. **Location:** near Guarapiranga lake in southwestern part of city. **Campus:** 7.5 acres. **Library:** 10,000 volumes. **Facilities:** 5 buildings, 20 classrooms, cafeteria, gymnasium, playing field, science lab, computer lab, swimming pool, AV equipment, learning lab, administrative block, multipurpose room, playgrounds, teacher housing complex, 2 outside courts.

*Once only fee

BULGARIA

Region: Europe
Size: 42,855 square miles
Population: 8,612,757
Capital: Sofia
Telephone code: 359
Currency: lev
Language: Bulgarian

SOFIA

American College of Sofia

Street address: Floyd Black Lane, Sofia 1799, Bulgaria
Phone: (359)(2)762918 **Facsimile:** (359)(2)803943 **E-mail:** acs@sf.cit.bg
U.S. phone: (1)(212)3192453
Mail: PO Box 873, Sofia 1000, Bulgaria
U.S. mail: Director, American College of Sofia, 850 Third Avenue, 18th floor, New York, NY 10022, U.S.A.
Director: Lou Perske
Deputy director: Maria Shoteva
Business manager: Daniela Peneva
Teaching staff: full-time, 57; part-time, 6; total, 63
Nationalities of teaching staff: U.S., 17; host, 46; total, 63
Grade levels: prep ESL and 9 – 12
Enrollment: total, 515
Nationalities of student body: host, 490; other, 25; total, 515
Capacity: total, 540
Teacher/student ratio: 1/10
Tuition (annual): $4,000 (Bulgarian); $8,900 (international)
School year: September to June

Year founded: 1860s, closed 1942 – 1992, and reopened 1992. **Type of school:** coed, day, private nonprofit. **Governed by:** elected board of trustees. **Sponsored by:** Sofia-American Schools, Inc. **Regional organizations:** ECIS.

Curriculum/physical plant

Type: U.S., national. **Languages taught:** French, Spanish, German, Bulgarian. **Staff specialists:** computer, nurse. **Special programs:** ESL. **Special curricular:** art, chorus, physical education, computer instruction, creative writing, extensive list of elective courses. **Extracurricular:** drama, dance, choral and instrumental music, computers, newspaper, sports. **Clubs:** art, dance, student newspaper, music, tennis, language and culture. **Location:** at base of 6,000 foot mountain on outskirts of capital city. **Campus:** 50 acres. **Facilities:** 6 academic and 6 residential buildings, auditorium, cafeteria, infirmary, tennis court, playing field, science lab, computer lab, library.

Anglo-American School

Street address: U.S. Embassy, 1 Suborna, 1000 Sofia, Bulgaria
Phone/facsimile: (359)(2)778484 **Facsimile:** (359)(2)773411
U.S. mail: c/o U.S. Embassy (Sofia, Bulgaria), Dept. of State, Washington, DC 20521-5740
Director: Brian Garton
Teaching staff: full-time, 15; part-time, 7; total, 22
Nationalities of teaching staff: U.S., 12; U.K., 7; host, 2; other, 1; total, 22
Grade levels: preK – 8
Enrollment: preK, 20; K, 15; 1 – 8, 100; total, 135
Nationalities of student body: U.S., 32; U.K., 15; host, 11; other, 77; total, 135
Capacity: preK, 15; K, 15; 1 – 6, 112; 7 – 8, 36; total, 178
Teacher/student ratio: 1/10
Tuition (annual): preK – 8, $9,500
Other fees (annual): registration*, $600; busing, $950; capital levy: $1,500 (new student), $1,000 (returning student)
School year: August to June

Year founded: 1967. **Type of school:** coed, day. **Governed by:** board appointed by U.S. and British ambassadors, plus representative of PTO. **Accredited by:** New England, ECIS.

Curriculum/physical plant

Type: U.S. **Languages taught:** French. **Staff specialists:** reading, computer, art, ESL, librarian, music, physical education. **Extracurricular:** choral music, computers, newspaper, excursions/expeditions, field trips. **Sports:** skiing, swimming, volleyball, skating. **Tests:** SAT. **Location:** in suburb on American College campus. **Library:** 7,000 volumes. **Facilities:** 14 classrooms, large playground.

*Once only fee

BURKINA FASO

Region: West Africa
Size: 105,946 square miles
Population: 10,623,323
Capital: Ouagadougou
Telephone code: 226
Currency: CFA franc
Languages: French, Sudanic tribal languages

OUAGADOUGOU

International School of Ouagadougou

Street address: Secteur 13 (Zogona 1) No. 612, Rue 13.22, Ouagadougou, Burkina Faso
Phone: (226)362143 **Facsimile:** (226)362228 **Telex:** 9855290 BF
Mail: 01 BP 35, Ouagadougou 01, Burkina Faso
U.S. mail: U.S. Embassy Ouagadougou (I.S.O.), Dept. of State, Washington, DC 20521-2440
Director: Steven Asp–Schussheim
Teaching staff: full-time, 9; part-time, 11; total, 20
Nationalities of teaching staff: U.S., 11; other, 9; total, 20
Grade levels: preK – 9 (10 – 12 tutorial correspondence)
Enrollment: preK, 9; K, 6; 1 – 5, 49; 6 – 9, 33; 10 – 12, 3; total, 100
Nationalities of student body: U.S., 18; other, 82; total, 100
Teacher/student ratio: 1/10
Tuition (annual): preK, $2,850; K, $7,220; 1 – 2, $8,500; 3 – 4, $9,125; 5 – 9, $9,450; 10 – 12, $9,800
Other fees (annual): capital levy, $1,000 per year for a maximum of 3 years; ESL, $1,200; PE uniform, $20; optional lunch service and school supplies
School year: late August to June

Year founded: 1976. **Type of school:** coed, day, private nonprofit. **Governed by:** elected school board. **Accredited by:** Middle States. **Regional organizations:** AISA.

Curriculum/physical plant

Type: U.S., IBMYP. **Languages taught:** French, English. **Special curricular:** art, physical education, computer instruction, Burkina culture, choral music, recorder. **Extracurricular:** drama, dance, computers, yearbook, field trips, magazine, school-to-school exchange program, academic olympics, MathCounts, community service, scouts. **Sports:** aerobics, soccer, softball, swimming, tennis, volleyball, Tae Kwon Do, floor hockey. **Clubs:** chess, Bible. **Tests:** PSAT, SAT, Iowa. **Location:** in residential area of Ouagadougou. **Campus:** 5 acres. **Library:** 8,000 volumes. **Facilities:** 9 buildings, 14 classrooms, tennis courts, science lab, computer lab, softball/soccer field, swimming pool, squash court, snack bar, French and ESL instruction rooms, art/music/Burkina culture room, AV room, basketball court, student center/lunch service, air conditioning.

CAMBODIA

Region: South Asia
Size: 70,238 square miles
Population: 10,861,218
Capital: Phnom Penh
Telephone code: 855
Currency: riel
Languages: Khmer, French

PHNOM PENH

INTERNATIONAL SCHOOL CAMBODIA

Phone: (855)(23)367367 **Facsimile:** (855)(23)363120
Mail: 11, Street 310, Boeng Keng Kang 1, Chamcarmon, Phnom Penh, Cambodia
Superintendent: David E. Eaton
Counselor/admissions: Joseph LaMelza
Head of library: Joyce Carroll
Business manager: Amporn Sirichindakul
Teaching staff: full-time, 17; part-time, 1; total, 18
Nationalities of teaching staff: U.S., 14; U.K., 1; host, 1; other, 2; total, 18
Grade levels: preK – 12
Enrollment: preK, 10; K, 10; 1 – 6, 60; 7 – 9, 35; 10 – 12, 5; total, 120
Nationalities of student body: U.S., 25; U.K., 15; host, 12; other, 68; total, 120
Teacher/student ratio: 1/7
Tuition (annual): preK, $4,500; K – 5, $6,200; 6 – 12, $7,400
Other fees: registration*, $1,500; capital levy, one-time (refundable) assessment fee, $5,000, or annual fee (non-refundable), $1,200; ESL, $1,800 or $1,200
School year: August to June

Year founded: 1997. **Type of school:** coed, day, company-sponsored, private nonprofit. **Governed by:** appointed volunteer board of trustees. **Sponsored by:** Northbridge Communities, Ltd. **Accredited by:** Western (in process). **Regional organizations:** EARCOS, SEATCCO.

Curriculum/physical plant

Type: U.S. **Languages taught:** French, Khmer (Cambodian). **Staff specialists:** reading, math, computer, speech/hearing, counselor, learning disabilities. **Special programs:** ESL, independent study. **Special curricular:** art, chorus, physical education, computer instruction. **Extracurricular:** drama, dance, choral music, computers, yearbook, newspaper, excursions/expeditions, field trips. **Sports:** baseball, basketball, soccer, softball, swimming. **Clubs:** computer, student council, science, math. **Tests:** Iowa, entrance/placement battery. **Location:** part of a 150-acre planned community near the airport, 3 miles from Phnom Penh. **Campus:** 17 acres. **Library:** 7,000 volumes. **Facilities:** 14 classrooms, auditorium, cafeteria, infirmary, 3 tennis courts, gymnasium, 2 playing fields, 2 science labs, 2 computer labs, swimming pool, 2 ESL/resource rooms; music and art rooms, air conditioning.

*Once only fee

INTERNATIONAL SCHOOL OF PHNOM PENH – CAMBODIA

Phone: (855)(23)360507/361002 **Facsimile:** (855)(23)360041
E-mail: ispp@uni.fi
Mail: PO Box 138, Phnom Penh, Cambodia
Director: Michael Francis
Principal: Ann Greve
Business manager: Joyce Copple
Teaching staff: full-time, 17; part-time, 27; total, 44
Nationalities of teaching staff: U.S., 9; host, 5; other, 30; total, 44
Grade levels: preK – 12
Enrollment: preK, 22; K, 24; 1 – 6, 157; 7 – 12, 77; total, 280
Nationalities of student body: U.S., 59; U.K., 54; other, 167; total, 280
Teacher/student ratio: 1/10
Tuition (annual): preK, $3,300; K, $5,200; 1 – 6, $5,600; 7 – 12, $6,500
Other fees (annual): registration, $750; enrollment*, $1,500; ESL, $800
School year: August to June

Year founded: 1989. **Type of school:** coed, day, private nonprofit. **Governed by:** elected board of directors. **Accredited by:** Western (in process). **Regional organizations:** EARCOS.

Curriculum/physical plant

Type: U.S., international. **Languages taught:** French, Khmer. **Staff specialists:** reading, math. **Special programs:** ESL. **Special curricular:** art, chorus, physical education. **Extracurricular:** excursions/expeditions, field trips, clubs, ballet, karate. **Location:** in Phnom Penh. **Facilities:** 8 buildings, 26 classrooms, 2 science labs, 2 computer labs, swimming pool, media center/library, art room, outdoor cafeteria, access to sports stadium, outdoor basketball/volleyball court.

*Once only fee

CAMEROON

Region: West Africa
Size: 183,569 square miles
Population: 14,261,557
Capital: Yaoundé
Telephone code: 237
Currency: CFA franc
Languages: English, French, numerous African groups

DOUALA

American School of Douala

Street address: 39, Rue des Palmiers, Douala, Cameroon
Phone: (237)421437 **Facsimile:** (237)427790
Mail: BP 1909, Douala, Cameroon, West Africa
U.S. mail: Administrative Officer (ASD), Dept. of State–Yaounde, Washington, DC 20521-2520
Administrator: Ken Jarman
Teaching staff: full-time, 9; part-time, 4; total, 13
Nationalities of teaching staff: U.S., 5; U.K., 1; other, 7; total, 13
Grade levels: preK – 8
Enrollment: preK, 13; K, 13; 1 – 6, 46; 7 – 8, 3; total, 75
Nationalities of student body: U.S., 13; host, 15; other, 47; total, 75
Capacity: preK, 20; K, 10; 1 – 6, 60; 7 – 8, 20; total, 110
Teacher/student ratio: 1/9
Tuition: preK, $3,360; K, $5,040; 1 – 8, $7,560
Other fees (annual): registration*, $400; annual entry fee, $180
School year: September to June

Year founded: 1978. **Type of school:** coed, day, private nonprofit. **Governed by:** elected school board. **Regional organizations:** ECIS, AISA.

Curriculum/physical plant

Type: U.S. **Languages taught:** French. **Staff specialists:** speech therapist. **Special programs:** ESL, limited remedial. **Special curricular:** art, physical education, computer instruction, music, Cameroonian culture. **Extracurricular:** yearbook, excursions/expeditions, field trips, musical drama, modern dance, African dance, crafts. **Sports:** basketball, soccer, volleyball, mountain climbing. **Clubs:** computer, game, scouting. **Tests:** Iowa, COGAT. **Location:** in residential area of Douala. **Campus:** 1.5 acres. **Library:** 8,000 volumes, CD ROM. **Facilities:** 1 building (4 portables), 13 classrooms, 2 playing fields, science lab, computer lab, art room, basketball court, air conditioning.

*Once only fee

YAOUNDE

American School of Yaounde

Phone: (237)230421/229465 **Facsimile:** (237)236011
E-mail: asoy@camfido.gn.apc.org
Mail: BP 7475, Yaounde, Cameroon
U.S. mail: Director, Dept. of State–Yaounde, Washington, DC 20521-2520
Director: Areta Williams
Administrative assistant: Valerie Ngolle
Business manager: Bettina Wiesmann
Teaching staff: full-time, 20; part-time, 1; total, 21
Nationalities of teaching staff: U.S., 11; U.K., 1; host, 4; other, 5; total, 21
Grade levels: preK – 10
Enrollment: preK, 19; K, 4; 1 – 5, 67; 6 – 10, 42; total, 132
Nationalities of student body: U.S., 65; U.K., 3; host, 17; other, 47; total, 132
Capacity: preK, 54; K, 18; 1 – 5, 100; 6 – 10, 90; total, 262
Teacher/student ratio: 1/7
Tuition (annual): preK, $1,860; K, $6,390; 1 – 5, $8,040; 6 – 10, $8,450
Other fees (annual): registration*: preK, $60; K – 10, $250; busing, $1,250; computer use fee (grades 4 – 10), $50; ESL, $1,000
School year: August to June

Year founded: 1964. **Type of school:** coed, day, private nonprofit. **Governed by:** elected board of directors. **Accredited by:** Middle States. **Regional organizations:** AISA, ECIS (associate member).

Curriculum/physical plant

Type: U.S. **Languages taught:** French. **Staff specialists:** computer, librarian, physical education. **Special programs:** ESL, limited remedial. **Special curricular:** physical education, computer instruction, swimming. **Extracurricular:** drama, computers, yearbook, excursions/expeditions, field trips, art, choir, music. **Sports:** basketball, soccer, softball, swimming, tennis, volleyball, Tae Kwon Do, mountain climbing. **Clubs:** Boy Scouts, Girl Scouts, National Junior Honor Society, student council, French, knowledge bowl. **Tests:** SSAT, Iowa, CogAT, TAP. **Location:** in city. **Campus:** 10 acres. **Library:** 14,000 volumes. **Facilities:** 6 buildings, 19 classrooms, 4 tennis courts, playing field, science lab, computer lab, swimming pool, Big Toys playground, basketball/volleyball court.

*Once only fee

CANADA

Region: North America
Size: 3,849,674 square miles
Population: 28,820,671
Capital: Ottawa
Telephone code: 1
Currency: Canadian dollar
Languages: English, French

VICTORIA, BRITISH COLUMBIA

LESTER B. PEARSON COLLEGE OF THE PACIFIC

Street address: Pearson College Drive, Victoria, British Columbia, Canada
Phone: (1)(250)3912411 **Facsimile:** (1)(250)3912412
Mail: RR #1, Victoria, British Columbia, Canada V9C 4H7
President: Peter D. Bavinton
Director of studies: Marc Abrioux
IB coordinator: Narendra Mehrotra
Teaching staff: full-time, 20; part-time, 4; total, 24
Nationalities of teaching staff: host, 20; other, 4; total, 24
Grade levels: IB (grades 12 – 13)
Enrollment: total, 200
Nationalities of student body: U.S., 6; host, 57; other, 137; total, 200
Capacity: total, 200
Teacher/student ratio: 1/9
Boarders: boys, 100; girls, 104 **Grades:** 12 – 13 **Program:** planned 7-day
Tuition: all attend on scholarships
School year: September to May

Year founded: 1974. **Type of school:** coed, boarding, nonprofit. **Governed by:** elected board of trustees.

Curriculum

Type: IB. **Languages of instruction:** English, French, Spanish. **Languages taught:** French, Spanish, German, Japanese, Chinese. **Staff specialists:** counselor, nurse. **Special programs:** ESL, international affairs. **Special curricular:** art, computer instruction, choir. **Extracurricular:** drama, dance, instrumental music, computers, yearbook, newspaper, photography, excursions/expeditions, field trips, ham radio club. **Organizations:** land search and rescue, sea, forestry, humanitarian, firefighting. **Tests:** SAT, ACT, TOEFL, IB. **Graduates attending college:** 98%.

Physical plant

Location: on forested seafront, 18 miles west of the city of Victoria. **Campus:** 80 acres. **Library:** 20,000 volumes. **Facilities:** 20 buildings, 15 classrooms, auditorium, cafeteria, infirmary, 2 tennis courts, playing field, 4 science labs, computer lab, swimming pool, 5 residence buildings.

CHILE

Region: South America
Size: 292,135 square miles
Population: 14,333,258
Capital: Santiago
Telephone code: 56
Currency: peso
Language: Spanish

ANTOFAGASTA

THE ANTOFAGASTA INTERNATIONAL SCHOOL

Street address: Subida de la Quebrada 590, Antofagasta, Chile
Phone: (56)(55)242342 **Facsimile:** (56)(55)246198 **E-mail:** ais@reuna.cl
Principal: Laurel A. Peterson
Teaching staff: full-time, 11; part-time, 2; total, 13
Nationalities of teaching staff: U.S., 3; host, 4; Canadian, 5; other, 1; total, 13
Grade levels: K – 8 (9 – 12 correspondence)
Enrollment: K, 8; 1 – 6, 46; 7 – 8, 13; 9 – 12, 15; total, 82
Teacher/student ratio: 1/6
Tuition (annual): $9,000
School year: February through December

Year founded: 1994. **Type of school:** coed, day, company-sponsored. **Governed by:** Compania Minera Zaldivar. **Operated by:** International Schools Services, Princeton, New Jersey.

Curriculum/physical plant

Type: North American. **Languages taught:** French, Spanish. **Special curricular:** physical education, computer instruction. **Extracurricular:** yearbook, excursions/ expeditions, field trips. **Location:** in converted villa overlooking Pacific coast, 5 kilometers from Antofagasta, and one campus in central Antofagasta. **Facilities:** 2 buildings, 8 classrooms, science lab, computer lab, 2 libraries.

CONCEPCION

ST. JOHN'S SCHOOL

Street address: Pedro de Valdivia 1711, Concepcion, Chile
Phone: (56)(41)331044 **Facsimile:** (56)(41)340809
E-mail: stjohns@arauco.reuna.cl
Mail: Casilla 284, Concepcion, Chile
Headmaster: Christopher Pugh
Academic head: Patricia Artigues
Business manager: Victor Pino
Teaching staff: full-time, 74; part-time, 12; total, 86

Nationalities of teaching staff: U.K., 6; host, 80; total, 86
Grade levels: preK – 12
Enrollment: preK, 70; K, 70; 1 – 6, 450; 7 – 9, 260; 10 – 12, 250; total, 1,100
Nationalities of student body: U.S., 5; U.K., 18; host, 1,069; other, 8; total, 1,100
Capacity: preK, 90; K, 90; 1 – 6, 540; 7 – 9, 270; 10 – 12, 270; total, 1,260
Teacher/student ratio: 1/14
Tuition (annual): 900,000**
Other fees (annual): registration, 50,000**; busing, 60,000
School year: March to December

Year founded: 1942. **Type of school:** coed, day, private nonprofit. **Governed by:** elected board of governors.

Curriculum/physical plant

Type: national, IB. **Languages of instruction:** English, Spanish. **Languages taught:** English, Spanish. **Staff specialists:** reading, math, computer, counselor, learning disabilities, nurse. **Special programs:** remedial. **Special curricular:** art, chorus, physical education, computer instruction, vocational. **Extracurricular:** drama, gymnastics, dance, choral and instrumental music, computers, yearbook, literary magazine, photography, excursions/expeditions. **Sports:** athletics, basketball, football, hockey, rugby, volleyball. **Tests:** IB, IGCSE. **Graduates attending college:** 95%. **Graduates have attended:** U. de Concepcion, U. de Chile, U. de Santiago. **Location:** in suburban area, 3 kilometers from Concepcion. **Facilities:** 8 buildings, 45 classrooms, cafeteria, tennis court, gymnasium, playing field, science lab, computer lab, Internet.

**Chilean peso

SANTIAGO

The Grange School S.A.

Street address: Principe de Gales 6154, Santiago, Chile
Phone: (56)(2)2771181 **Facsimile:** (56)(2)2770946
E-mail: sinclair@grange.cl **Web:** http://www.grange.cl
Mail: Casilla 218, Correo 12, Santiago, Chile
Headmaster: John Mackenzie
Deputy head: James Cowan
Head, senior school: Donald MacAulay
Business manager: Ronald G. Brown
Teaching staff: full-time, 115; part-time, 10; total, 125
Nationalities of teaching staff: U.K., 10; host, 115; total, 125
Grade levels: preK – 12
Enrollment: preK, 120; K, 120; 1 – 6, 730; 7 – 9, 375; 10 – 12, 375; total, 1,720
Teacher/student ratio: 1/14
Tuition (annual): preK – K, $1,594; 1 – 12, $2,114
Other fees (annual): registration, $30; insurance, $44; lunch, $400
School year: March to December

Year founded: 1928. **Type of school:** coed, day, private nonprofit. **Governed by:** board of directors. **Accredited by:** Chilean Ministry of Education.

Curriculum

Type: national, IB. **Languages of instruction:** English, Spanish. **Languages taught:** French. **Staff specialists:** reading, math, computer, counselor, psychologist, learning disabilities, nurse. **Special programs:** ESL, remedial. **Special curricular:** art, chorus, band, physical education, computer instruction, vocational. **Extracurricular:** drama, gymnastics, dance, choral and instrumental music, computers, yearbook, literary magazine, photography, excursions/expeditions. **Sports:** basketball, football, hockey, rugby, table tennis, tennis, volleyball, karate. **Clubs:** chess, computer, arts & crafts, philately, social service, journalism, outdoor pursuits, technical drawing. **Tests:** IB, Chilean universities' entrance exams, O-levels Cambridge. **Graduates attending college:** 80%. **Graduates have attended:** Texas A&M, Utah State, U. of California at Berkeley, Cambridge, Vassar.

Physical plant

Location: 6 kilometers from city center. **Campus:** 8 hectares. **Library:** 14,500 volumes. **Facilities:** 16 buildings, 94 classrooms, auditorium, cafeteria, infirmary, 2 gymnasiums, 4 science labs, 3 computer labs, playing fields, creative arts building, new media center.

The International Preparatory School

Phone: (56)(2)2151094/2153783 **Facsimile:** (56)(2)2153843
E-mail: inschool@inet.macland.cl
Mail: Pastor Fernandez 16001-El Arrayan, Lo Barnechea, Santiago, Chile
Headmistress: Lesley Easton Allen
Curriculum coordinator: Pamela Thomson
Financial administrator: Carlos Willson
Teaching staff: full-time, 19; part-time, 8; total, 27
Nationalities of teaching staff: U.S., 1; U.K., 11; host, 4; other, 11; total, 27
Grade levels: preK – 12
Enrollment: preK – K2, 44; 1 – 5, 57; 6 – 9, 40; 10 – 12, 14; total, 155
Nationalities of student body: U.S., 31; U.K., 40; host, 8; other, 76; total, 155
Teacher/student ratio: 1/5
Tuition (annual): preK – K, $5,900; 1 – 4, $6,600; 5 – 6, $7,300; 7 – 12, $7,600
Other fees (annual): incorporation*, $6,500; book rental and materials, $500; matriculation, $380
School year: March to December (summer school in January)

Year founded: 1975. **Type of school:** coed, day. **Governed by:** private governing body. **Accredited by:** ECIS.

Curriculum

Type: U.K./U.S. AP. **Languages taught:** French, Spanish. **Staff specialists:** reading, math, speech/hearing, counselor, psychologist, learning disabilities, resource. **Special programs:** ESL, independent study, correspondence, remedial. **Special curricular:** art, physical education, computer instruction. **Extracurricular:** drama, gymnastics, dance, instrumental music, newspaper, scouts, horseback riding.

Sports: athletics, baseball, football, tennis. **Clubs:** chess, ecology, table tennis, animal, backgammon, book. **Tests:** Common Entrance examinations to independent and public schools, Bristol Achievement Tests, IGCSE-recognized center, U. of Cambridge A levels. **Graduates have attended:** U. of Cambridge, Hull U., Berkeley, Catholic U. Chile, Sherbourne.

Physical plant

Location: El Arrayan, at foot of mountain. **Campus:** 14,000 square meters. **Library:** 18,500 volumes. **Facilities:** auditorium, computer lab, access to 4 tennis courts, mini-golf, extensive multipurpose sports and football field, use of swimming pool.

*Once only fee

The International School Nido de Aguilas

Street address: Camino Nido de Aguilas 14515, 10 Barnechea, Santiago, Chile
Phone: (56)(2)2166842 **Facsimile:** (56)(2)2167603 **E-mail:** mail@nido.cl
Mail: Casilla 16211 – Correo 9, Santiago, Chile
Headmaster: Clifford H. Strommen, Ed.D.
High school principal: Joseph McDonald
Chilean director: Renan Muñoz
Middle school principal: Lynn Roberts
Elementary school principal: Charles Prince
Teaching staff: full-time, 91; part-time, 3; total, 94
Nationalities of teaching staff: U.S., 34; U.K., 2; host, 51; other, 7; total, 94
Grade levels: preK – 12
Enrollment: preK, 44; K, 142; 1 – 6, 430; 7 – 12, 415; total, 1,031
Nationalities of student body: U.S., 302; U.K., 15; host, 331; other, 383; total, 1,031
Teacher/student ratio: 1/11
Tuition (annual): preK, $1,700; K, $6,900; 1 – 5, $7,600; 6 – 12, $7,800
Other fees (annual): registration, $480; capital levy*, $7,200; busing, $700; lunch, $350
School year: August to December, February to July

Year founded: 1934. **Type of school:** coed, day. **Governed by:** board of directors. **Accredited by:** Southern, Chilean Ministry. **Regional organizations:** AAIE, AASSA.

Curriculum

Type: U.S., national, IB. **Languages taught:** French, Spanish. **Staff specialists:** reading, psychologist, learning disabilities, nurse, ESL, gifted and talented, counselors. **Special programs:** ESL, minor disabilities, reading, summer school. **Special curricular:** art, chorus, band, physical education, computer instruction, orchestra. **Extracurricular:** drama, choral and instrumental music, yearbook, literary magazine, sports, outdoor, handicrafts, student interest groups, Suzuki strings. **Sports:** basketball, soccer, softball, tennis, track and field, volleyball. **Tests:** SSAT, PSAT, SAT, ACT, TOEFL, IB, Iowa, PAA (Chile). **Graduates attending college:** 97%. **Graduates have attended:** Brown, MIT, U. of Southern California, Purdue, U. of Chile.

Physical plant

Location: in rural Santiago suburb at the foot of the Andes mountains. **Library:** 19,000 volumes. **Facilities:** 8 buildings, 65 classrooms, cafeteria, infirmary, 4 tennis courts, 4 playing fields, 6 science labs, 3 computer labs, gymnasium/auditorium, 2 art labs, band room, music room.

*Once only fee

LINCOLN INTERNATIONAL ACADEMY

Street address: Camino San Antonio 55, Lo Barnechea, Santiago, Chile
Phone: (56)(2)2171907/2424128 **Facsimile:** (56)(2)2151080
Mail: Casilla 20.000, Correo 20, Santiago, Chile
Director/principal of primary levels: Verónica Caroca, Ed.D.
Principal of upper levels: Guacolda Espinace
Principal of elementary levels: Verónica Roa
Business manager: Paz Suarez
Teaching staff: full-time, 40; part-time, 10; total, 50
Nationalities of teaching staff: host, 48; other, 2; total, 50
Grade levels: preK – 12
Enrollment: preK, 19; K, 47; 1 – 6, 249; 7 – 9, 88; 10 – 12, 68; total, 471
Capacity: preK, 50; K, 50; 1 – 6, 300; 7 – 9, 125; 10 – 12, 75; total, 600
Teacher/student ratio: 1/9
Tuition (annual): preK – K, $3,000; 1 – 12, $3,240
Other fees (annual): registration, $92; capital levy*, $1,528
School year: March to December

Year founded: 1976. **Type of school:** coed, day, proprietary. **Governed by:** appointed board. **Accredited by:** Chilean Ministry of Education, Southern (in process).

Curriculum/physical plant

Type: U.S., national. **Languages of instruction:** English, Spanish. **Languages taught:** French, grades 5 – 9; Latin, grades 7 – 12. **Staff specialists:** math, computer, counselor, psychologist, nurse. **Special curricular:** art, chorus, physical education, computer instruction. **Extracurricular:** drama, gymnastics, dance, choral music, computers, yearbook, excursions/expeditions, field trips, Suzuki strings. **Sports:** basketball, soccer, volleyball, handball. **Graduates attending college:** 99%. **Graduates have attended:** U. of Chile, Catholic U. (Chile), U. Diego Portales, U. of Texas, U. of Oxford. **Location:** northeast edge of city, near Andes mountains. **Campus:** 2.5 acres. **Library:** over 7,000 volumes. **Facilities:** 12 buildings, 26 classrooms, infirmary, gymnasium, playing field, 2 science labs, computer lab, art and music rooms.

*Once only fee

Santiago College

Street address: Los Leones 584, Santiago, Chile
Phone: (56)(2)2321813 **Facsimile:** (56)(2)2320755
E-mail: admiss@scollege.cl
Mail: Casilla 130-D, Santiago 9, Chile
Headmistress: Elisabeth Fox
Upper school principal: Richard Minutoli
Middle school principal: Annabella Farba
Lower school principal: Lorna Prado
Teaching staff: full-time, 73; part-time, 95; total, 168
Nationalities of teaching staff: U.S., 7; host, 152; other, 9; total, 168
Grade levels: preK – 12
Enrollment: preK, 132; K, 134; 1 – 6, 783; 7 – 9, 389; 10 – 12, 415; total, 1,853
Nationalities of student body: U.S., 81; host, 1,658; other, 114; total, 1,853
Teacher/student ratio: 1/16
Tuition (annual): $3,765
Other fees (annual): registration, $65; insurance, $60; lunch, $3.00/each; books, $95; additional costs, $315; initial registration*, $2,075
School year: March to December

Year founded: 1880. **Type of school:** coed, day. **Governed by:** appointed board of trustees, New York. **Sponsored by:** local board, Santiago, Chile. **Accredited by:** Southern. **Regional organizations:** ECIS, AASSA.

Curriculum

Type: North American, national, IB. **Languages of instruction:** English (preK – 9), Spanish (10 – 12). **Languages taught:** English, French. **Staff specialists:** reading, counselor, psychologist, librarian. **Special curricular:** art, chorus, physical education, computer instruction. **Extracurricular:** computers, field trips, chess, chorus, band, ceramics, science club, cooking, musical group, drama (English and Spanish), French, journalism, piano, glass painting, violin, social service. **Sports:** athletics, basketball, hockey, rugby, soccer, volleyball, handball. **Tests:** PSAT, IB, Iowa. **Graduates attending college:** 97%. **Graduates have attended:** U. de Chile, Catholic U., U. de Santiago, Catholic U. of Valparaiso, U.S. universities.

Physical plant

Location: in Santiago. **Campuses (2):** 147,710 square meters. **Library:** 35,000 volumes. **Facilities:** 11 buildings, 98 classrooms, 4 auditoriums, cafeteria, infirmary, covered play area, 3 gymnasiums, 4 playing fields, 8 science labs, 3 computer labs.

*Once only fee

CHINA

Region: Asia
Size: 3,696,100 square miles
Population: 1,210,004,956
Capital: Beijing
Telephone code: 86
Currency: yuan
Languages: Mandarin, Yue, Wu, Hakka, Minbei, Minnan, Xiang, Gan

BEIJING

THE INTERNATIONAL SCHOOL OF BEIJING

Street address: Building #7, Lido Complex, Ji Chang Road, Jiang Tai Road, Beijing 100004, People's Republic of China
Phone: (86)(10)64377119 **Facsimile:** (86)(10)64376989
E-mail: isb-info@isb.bj.edu.cn **Telex:** 71622701 AMEMB CN
U.S. mail: (no personal name) ISB American Embassy—Beijing, PSC 461, Box 50, FPO AP 96521-0002 (no more than 2 lbs.)
Director: Alex Horsley
High school principal: Brian Atkins
Middle school principal: Marilyn Holladay
Elementary principal: Larry Lawson, Ed.D.
Manager of business affairs: Peter Taylor
Teaching staff: full-time, 101; part-time, 12; total, 113
Nationalities of teaching staff: U.S., 75; U.K., 6; other, 32; total, 113
Grade levels: preK – 12
Enrollment: preK, 20; K, 55; 1 – 5, 410; 6 – 8, 270; 9 – 12, 295; total, 1,050
Nationalities of student body: U.S., 400; other, 650; total, 1,050
Capacity: preK, 24; K, 80; 1 – 5, 530; 6 – 8, 330; 9 – 12, 396; total, 1,360
Teacher/student ratio: 1/10
Tuition (annual): preK, $8,000; K – 5, $12,650; 6 – 8, $13,550; 9 – 12, $14,950
Other fees (annual): capital, $3,300; building*, $15,000 (refundable)
School year: August to June

Year founded: 1980. **Type of school:** coed, day. **Governed by:** appointed and elected school board. **Sponsored by:** the embassies of the U.S., Australia, New Zealand, and Canada. **Accredited by:** Western. **Regional organizations:** AAIE, EARCOS, ECIS.

Curriculum/physical plant

Type: U.S., IB. **Languages taught:** French, Chinese. **Staff specialists:** computer, nurse, art, music, counselors, resource, ESOL. **Special programs:** China studies. **Special curricular:** art, physical education, computer instruction, drama, journalism. **Extracurricular:** gymnastics, computers, yearbook, excursions/expeditions, field trips, Model UN, vocal and instrumental music. **Sports:** basketball, soccer, volleyball. **Clubs:** student council, scouting. **Tests:** SSAT, SAT, IB, TAP, ITBS. **Location:** on Lido Hotel Ltd. compound, on leased Chinese government land; and at nearby satellite building, 5 kilometers from downtown Beijing, and 14 kilometers from Capital airport. **Campus:** 6 acres. **Library:** 22,000 volumes. **Facilities:** 13 buildings, 62 classrooms, infirmary, 3 gymnasiums, 4 science labs, 4 computer labs, 3 art rooms, 2,000 square meter play/sports area, 6 music rooms, learning media center, multipurpose room with stage, 16 language rooms, 10 resource and ESL rooms, 2 food-serving kitchens.

*Once only fee

Western Academy of Beijing

Phone: (86)(10)64375935 **Facsimile:** (86)(10)64375936
E-mail: ian@wab.hk.net
Mail: PO Box 8547 Chaoyang Qu, Beijing 100015, People's Republic of China
Director: Ian Rysdale
Lower school principal: Neil Hugo
Business manager: Leelian Ong
Teaching staff: full-time, 34; part-time, 8; total, 42
Nationalities of teaching staff: U.S., 10; U.K., 12; host, 4; other, 16; total, 42
Grade levels: N – 8
Enrollment: N, 50; K, 40; 1 – 6, 250; 7, 40; 8, 20; total, 400
Nationalities of student body: U.S., 60; U.K., 40; other, 300; total, 400
Capacity: N, 40; K, 40; 1 – 6, 300; 7, 20; 8, 20; total, 420
Tuition (annual): N, $7,100; K – 5, $4,200; 6 – 8, $11,900
Other fees (annual): registration*, $200; capital levy, $750 – 2,500; busing, $600
School year: September to June

Year founded: 1994. **Type of school:** coed, private nonprofit. **Governed by:** appointed and elected board of governors. **Regional organizations:** ECIS, EARCOS.

Curriculum/physical plant

Type: ISCP. **Languages taught:** French, Mandarin. **Staff specialists:** computer, nurse, ESL. **Special programs:** ESL. **Special curricular:** art, physical education, computer instruction, music. **Extracurricular:** drama, gymnastics, dance, choral and instrumental music, computers, newspaper, excursions/expeditions, field trips. **Sports:** basketball, rugby, soccer, softball. **Location:** in suburban area, 20 minutes from Beijing. **Library:** 15,000 volumes. **Facilities:** 3 buildings, 15 classrooms, gymnasium, playing field, 2 science labs, 2 computer labs, 2 play areas, partial air conditioning.

*Once only fee

GUANGZHOU

American International School of Guangzhou†

Street address: #55 Hua Yang Street, Ti Yu Road E., Tianhe District, 510620 Guangzhou, People's Republic of China
Phone: (86)(20)87580001 **Facsimile:** (86)(20)87580002
E-mail: asg@gitie.guangzhou.gd.cn
Director: Dr. Nancy Stephan
Principal: Pat Meyer

Teaching staff: full-time, 25; part-time, 2; total, 27
Nationalities of teaching staff: U.S., 18; other, 9; total, 27
Grade levels: K – 12
Enrollment: K, 32; 1 – 6, 141; 9 – 12, 32; total, 205
Nationalities of student body: U.S., 45; other, 160; total, 205
Teacher/student ratio: 1/8
Tuition (annual): $13,000
Other fees (annual): registration, $500 (deducted from tuition); expansion assessment, $2,000; ESL, $1,400 – 2,400
School year: August through June

Year founded: 1981. **Type of school:** coed, day. **Governed by:** elected board. **Sponsored by:** American Consulate. **Accredited by:** Western. **Regional organizations:** EARCOS.

Curriculum/physical plant

Type: U.S. **Languages taught:** English, French, Spanish, Mandarin. **Special programs:** ESL. **Special curricular:** art, physical education, music, Chinese culture. **Extracurricular:** computers, excursions/expeditions, field trips, various after-school activities. **Sports:** swimming, tennis. **Tests:** Iowa, Gates-MacGinitie. **Location:** in Guangzhou. **Campus:** school occupies purpose-built facility within new greenery complex (residential expatriate village). **Library:** 10,000 volumes. **Facilities:** 18 classrooms, tennis court, swimming pool, AV equipment, playground, multipurpose gymnasium air conditioning.

†formerly the American School of Guangzhou

PANYU

Clifford School

Street address: Clifford Estates (Panyu) Ltd., Panyu, Guangdong Province, 511495 People's Republic of China
Phone: (86)(20)84711441 **Facsimile:** (86)(20)84713667
Director/principal: James E. Veitch
Teaching staff: full-time, 80; part-time, 14; total, 94
Grade levels: K – 6
Enrollment: K – 6, 492
Nationalities of student body: U.S., 5; other, 487; total, 492
Teacher/student ratio: 1/15
Boarders: boys, 160; girls, 160 **Grades:** K – 6 **Program:** planned 6-day
Tuition (annual): K – 6, 39,500**
Other fees (annual): registration, 5,000**; boarding, 9,800; miscellaneous, 19,000
School year: August to June

Year founded: 1995. **Type of school:** coed, day, boarding, private nonprofit. **Governed by:** appointed board. **Sponsored by:** Clifford Estates (Panyu) Ltd. **Regional organizations:** EARCOS, CERCOS. **Associated with:** International Schools Services, Princeton, New Jersey.

Curriculum/physical plant

Type: U.S. **Languages taught:** Mandarin. **Staff specialists:** computer, nurse. **Special programs:** ESL. **Special curricular:** art, physical education, computer instruction. **Extracurricular:** dance, field trips. **Location:** suburban setting in the rolling hills of Panyu, Guangdong. **Facilities:** 7 buildings, auditorium, 2 cafeterias, 2 infirmaries, 4 tennis courts, playing field, science labs, 2 computer labs, swimming pool, library, air conditioning, boarding facilities.

**renmibi

SHANGHAI

Shanghai American School

Street address: 50 Ji Di Lu, Zhudi Town, Minhang District, Shanghai, People's Republic of China 201106
Phone: (86)(21)62211445 **Facsimile:** (86)(21)62211269
E-mail: shaamsch@public.sta.net.cn **Web:** http://www.sasch.org
U.S. mail: Shanghai American School, c/o American Consulate General, PSC 461, Box 200, FPO AP 96521-0002
Superintendent: Ronald I. Montgomery
Assistant superintendent for instruction: Dr. Robin Leveillee
Middle school principal: Douglas Otjen
Elementary principals: Victoria Montgomery, Deborah Karmozyn
Director of development: Dr. Robert Horn
Teaching staff: full-time, 85; total, 85
Nationalities of teaching staff: U.S., 67; U.K., 2; host, 4; other, 12; total, 85
Grade levels: preK – 12
Enrollment: preK, 45; K, 60; 1 – 5, 355; 6 – 8, 230; 9 – 12, 210; total, 900
Nationalities of student body: U.S., 306; other, 594; total, 900
Teacher/student ratio: 1/11
Tuition (annual): preK, $10,500; K – 5, $11,500; 6 – 8, $12,000; 9 – 12, $13,000
Other fees: registration*, $250; capital levy*, $6,000
School year: September to June

Year founded: 1980. **Type of school:** coed, day, private nonprofit. **Governed by:** elected board of management. **Sponsored by:** American Consulate General. **Accredited by:** Western. **Regional organizations:** EARCOS, CERCOS, CHIMCOS.

Curriculum/physical plant

Type: U.S., AP. **Languages taught:** French, Spanish, Chinese. **Special curricular:** art, physical education, computer instruction, drama, choral music, Chinese language and culture classes, yearbook, newspaper, field trips, athletics, Model UN, instrumental music. **Tests:** PSAT, SAT, TOEFL, AP, Iowa. **Graduates attending college:** 100%. **Location:** West campus: 7 kilometers west of Honqiao International airport. East campus: in the Hua Xia District of Pudong. **Campus:** 3.8 acres. **Library:** 16,000 volumes. **Facilities:** new building, 55 classrooms, cafeteria, infirmary, gymnasium, science lab, library, track and field, air conditioning.

*Once only fee

Yew Chung Shanghai International School†

Street address: 11 Shui Cheng Lu, Shanghai, People's Republic of China
Phone: (86)(21)62423243 **Facsimile:** (86)(21)62427331
E-mail: ycsis@public.sta.net.cn
Co-principals: Barbara Markland, Roy Markland, Zhang Hong
Teaching staff: total, 76
Nationalities of teaching staff: U.K., 4; host, 32; other, 40; total, 76
Grade levels: preK – 8
Enrollment: preK, 97; K, 96; 1 – 8, 435; total, 628
Nationalities of student body: U.K., 60; U.S./Canada, 105; other, 463; total, 628
Capacity: K – 1, 380; 2 – 8, 570; total 950
Teacher/student ratio: 1/9
School year: September to July

Year founded: 1993. **Type of school:** coed, day, private nonprofit. **Governed by:** appointed board of directors. **Sponsored by:** Yew Chung Education Foundation.

Curriculum/physical plant

Type: UK-based international. **Languages taught:** Mandarin. **Staff specialists:** computer, music, EFL, doctor. **Special programs:** ESL, Chinese as a Foreign Language. **Special curricular:** art, physical education, computer instruction. **Extracurricular:** dance, choral music, computers, yearbook, field trips, sports, excursions. **Clubs:** calligraphy, Chinese brush painting. **Location:** near Honqiao International Airport. **Libraries:** 12,500 volumes. **Facilities:** 2 campuses, 2 buildings, 47 classrooms, 2 auditoriums, cafeteria, infirmary, computer lab, air conditioning.

†The Yew Chung Education Foundation also has schools in Hong Kong and Beijing

SHEKOU

Shekou International School

Phone: (86)(755)6693669 **Facsimile:** (86)(755)6674099
E-mail: bwerber2@compuserve.com
Mail: c/o Amoco Orient Petroleum Company, 15th floor, Chiwan Petroleum Building, Chiwan, Shenzhen, 5/8068 People's Republic of China
U.S. mail: SIS, Expatriate-China, PO Box 4381, Houston, TX 77210, U.S.A.
Director: Bruce Werber
Teaching staff: full-time, 15; part-time, 1; total, 16
Nationalities of teaching staff: U.S./Canada, 15; host, 1; total, 16
Grade levels: K – 8 (grade 9 via U. of Nebraska special program)
Enrollment: K, 22; 1 – 6, 68; 7 – 8, 20; total, 110
Nationalities of student body: U.S., 80; other, 30; total, 110
Capacity: K, 16; 1 – 8, 120; total, 136
Teacher/student ratio: 1/7
Tuition (annual): K – 8, $16,000
Other fees: capital levy*, $7,500; ESL testing, $450
School year: August to June

Year founded: 1988. **Type of school:** coed, day, company-sponsored. **Sponsored by:** international oil companies. **Operated by:** International Schools Services, Princeton, New Jersey. **Regional organizations:** EARCOS, SEATCCO.

Curriculum/physical plant

Type: U.S. **Languages taught:** Mandarin. **Special curricular:** art, physical education, computer instruction, Chinese language and culture, music. **Extracurricular:** computers, yearbook, newspaper, field trips, soccer, swimming, crafts, basketball. **Tests:** California. **Location:** in Shekou, 1 hour from Hong Kong by Hovercraft. **Library:** 5,000 volumes. **Facilities:** 15 classrooms, science lab, computer lab, swimming pool, playing fields, multipurpose room, air conditioning.

*Once only fee

TIANJIN

TEDA INTERNATIONAL SCHOOL, TIANJIN BRANCH

Street address: 6 Mu Nan Dao, He Ping District, Tianjin 300050, People's Republic of China
Phone: (86)(22)3114772 **Facsimile:** (86)(22)3312263
E-mail: tist@public.tpt.tj.cn
Principal: Eric Larson
ESOL program: Sara Goering, Doreen Lew-Larson
Teaching staff: full-time, 16; total, 16
Nationalities of teaching staff: U.S., 10; host, 3; other, 3; total, 16
Grade levels: N – 8
Enrollment: N – preK, 32; K – 8, 108; total, 140
Nationalities of student body: U.S., 20; other, 120; total, 140
Teacher/student ratio: 1/9
Tuition (annual): N – preK, $6,000; K – 7, $9,500
Other fees (annual): registration, $200; capital levy, $1,000 – 2,000
School year: September to mid-June

Year founded: 1994. **Type of school:** coed, day, private nonprofit. **Governed by:** board of governors.

Curriculum/physical plant

Languages taught: Chinese. **Staff specialists:** speech/hearing. **Special programs:** ESL. **Special curricular:** art, physical education, computer instruction, music. **Location:** new building in older neighborhood. **Campus:** .25 acre. **Library:** 4,900 volumes. **Facilities:** 12 classrooms, auditorium, art room, air conditioning.

Tianjin International School

Street address: Xing Guo School, Xi Yuan Road, Ti Yuan Bei, He Xi District, Tianjin 300061, People's Republic of China
Phone: (86)28353200 **Facsimile:** (86)28352455 **E-mail:** tmis@public.tpt.tj.cn
Superintendent: Gregg A. Vossler
Teaching staff: full-time, 24; part-time, 8; total, 32
Nationalities of teaching staff: U.S., 18; other, 14; total, 32
Grade levels: K – 12
Enrollment: K, 13; 1 – 6, 102; 7 – 9, 46; 10 – 12, 16; ESL, 25; total, 202
Nationalities of student body: U.S., 40; other, 162; total, 202
Capacity: K, 18; 1 – 6, 64; 7 – 9, 27; 10 – 12, 27; total, 136
Teacher/student ratio: 1/8
Tuition (annual): K – 12, $9,950 – 10,500
Other fees (annual): registration, $200; capital levy, $2,000
School year: late August to June

Year founded: 1986. **Type of school:** coed, day, private nonprofit. **Governed by:** appointed school committee. **Sponsored by:** MTI Education Foundation, Inc. **Accredited by:** Western. **Regional organizations:** EARCOS.

Curriculum/physical plant

Type: U.S. **Languages taught:** Chinese. **Staff specialists:** computer, counselor, doctor on call. **Special programs:** ESL. **Special curricular:** art, chorus, physical education, computer instruction. **Extracurricular:** drama, choral music, computers, yearbook, excursions/expeditions, orchestra. **Sports:** basketball, soccer, volleyball. **Tests:** PSAT, SAT, Stanford. **Graduates attending college:** 98%. **Graduates have attended:** Trinity College, U. of North Carolina, Baylor, Bethel College, Houghton College. **Location:** in city. **Library:** 5,000 volumes. **Facilities:** 2 buildings, 18 classrooms, auditorium, playing field, science lab, computer lab. MTI Education Foundation, Inc. also has schools in Qingdao and Chengdu.

COLOMBIA

Region: South America
Size: 440,762 square miles
Population: 36,813,161
Capital: Bogota
Telephone code: 57
Currency: peso
Language: Spanish

BARRANQUILLA

Colegio Albania

Phone: (57)(53)505804/505648 **Facsimile:** (57)(55)776899
Mail: Apartado Aereo 52-499, Barranquilla, Colombia
U.S. mail: Colegio Albania c/o Intercor, PO Box 02-5573, Miami, FL 33102-5573, U.S.A.
Director: Bryan K. Lewallen
Teaching staff: full-time, 73; total, 73
Nationalities of teaching staff: U.S., 16; host, 57; total, 73
Grade levels: preK – 11
Enrollment: preK, 55; K, 52; T, 78; 1 – 4, 234; 5 – 8, 233; 9 – 11, 150; total, 802
Nationalities of student body: U.S., 4; host, 794; other, 4; total, 802
Capacity: preK, 92; K, 92; 1 – 6, 475; 7 – 9, 225; 10 – 11, 100; total, 984
Teacher/student ratio: 1/11 (preK – 2); 1/22 (grades 3 – 11)
School year: August to June

Year founded: 1983. **Type of school:** coed, day, company-sponsored. **Governed by:** elected school advisory board. **Sponsored by:** Intercor-FECEN. **Accredited by:** Southern, Colombian Ministry of Education. **Regional organizations:** AAIE, ACCAS, Tri-Assoc.

Curriculum

Type: U.S., national. **Languages of instruction:** English, Spanish. **Languages taught:** English, Spanish. **Staff specialists:** computer, learning disabilities, nurse, 3 counselors. **Special programs:** ESL, computer. **Special curricular:** art, computer instruction, vocational. **Extracurricular:** drama, dance, computers, newspaper, excursions/expeditions, field trips, orchestra. **Sports:** baseball, basketball, bowling, soccer, swimming, tennis, volleyball, racquetball, cycling, roller skating, aerobics. **Tests:** SAT, TOEFL, Iowa.

Physical plant

Location: at coal-mining camp, 1-hour company-plane flight from Barranquilla, 1.5 hours by highway to state capital. **Campus:** 10 acres. **Libraries (2):** 15,000 volumes. **Facilities:** auditorium, infirmary, 4 playing fields, 3 science labs, 2 computer labs, 2 swimming pools, air conditioning.

Colegio Karl C. Parrish

Street address: Kilometro 2 Carretera Antigua a Puerto Colombia, Barranquilla, Colombia
Phone: (57)(53)598789/598972 **Facsimile:** (57)(53)598828
E-mail: kcparrish@rnd.net.co
Mail: Apartado Aereo 52962, Barranquilla, Colombia
Director: Michael Farr, Ph.D.
High school principal: Betty Scalise
Elementary school principal: Hectalina Donado
Teaching staff: full-time, 51; total, 51
Grade levels: N – 12
Enrollment: N – preK, 112; K, 58; 1 – 5, 278; 6 – 8, 174; 9 – 12, 185; total, 807
Nationalities of student body: U.S., 56; host, 739; other, 12; total, 807
Capacity: N – preK, 56; K, 60; 1 – 6, 360; 7 – 9, 180; 10 – 12, 180; total, 836
Teacher/student ratio: 1/25
Tuition (annual): N – K, $1,380; 1 – 5, $1,638; 6 – 8, $1,842; 9 – 11, $1,926; 12, $1,998
Other fees: registration*, N – 12, $4,000
School year: August to June

Year founded: 1938. **Type of school:** coed, day, private nonprofit. **Governed by:** board of directors appointed by board of trustees. **Accredited by:** Southern, Colombian Ministry of Education. **Regional organizations:** AAIE, ACCAS, Tri-Assoc.

Curriculum

Type: U.S., national. **Languages of instruction:** English, Spanish. **Languages taught:** English, Spanish. **Staff specialists:** reading, computer, counselor, psychologist. **Special programs:** ESL, remedial reading, learning disabilities. **Special curricular:** art, physical education, computer instruction, vocational, folklore band. **Extracurricular:** gymnastics, computers, yearbook, newspaper, photography, field trips, music. **Sports:** baseball, basketball, soccer, volleyball. **Organizations:** National Honor Society, student council. **Tests:** SSAT, PSAT, SAT, ACT, TOEFL, Iowa. **Graduates attending college:** 100%. **Graduates have attended:** Tulane, Dartmouth, Brown, Georgia Institute of Technology, U. of Pennsylvania.

Physical plant

Location: in suburban area, 2 kilometers from Barranquilla. **Campus:** 18.78 acres. **Library:** 25,000 volumes. **Facilities:** 8 buildings, 35 classrooms, 2 tennis courts, gymnasium, 2 playing fields, 2 science labs, 2 computer labs, swimming pool, air conditioning.

*Once only fee

BOGOTA

Colegio Nueva Granada

Street address: K 2 Este #70-20, Bogota, Colombia
Phone: (57)(1)2355350 **Facsimile:** (57)(1)2113720
E-mail: sngrana@col.telecom.com.co
Mail: A.A. 51339, Bogota, Colombia
U.S. mail: 6964 NW 50th Street, Suite 8258, Miami, FL 33166-5632, U.S.A.
Director: Dr. Barry L. McCombs
High school principal: Donald Groves, Ed.D.
Bachillerato director: Carlos Bernal
Student services director: Annie Acevedo
Instructional technology coordinator: Timothy Beach
Teaching staff: full-time, 145; part-time, 6; total, 151
Nationalities of teaching staff: U.S., 67; U.K., 2; host, 72; other, 10; total, 151
Grade levels: preK – 12
Enrollment: preK, 80; K, 105; 1 – 6, 660; 7 – 9, 330; 10 – 12, 320; total, 1,495
Teacher/student ratio: 1/10
Tuition (annual): preK – K, $4,370; 1 – 3, $4,300; 4 – 5, $4,450; 6, $4,670; 7, $4,820; 8, $4,970; 9, $5,040; 10, $5,190; 11, $5,260; 12, $5,340
Other fees: registration, preK – K, $8,000; 1 – 5, $8,750; 6 – 11, $9,250; 12, $4,750; registration*: preK – K, $5,000; 1 – 5, $5,500; 6 – 11, $6,000; 12, $3,500
School year: late August through June

Year founded: 1938. **Type of school:** coed, day, private nonprofit. **Governed by:** elected board of directors. **Accredited by:** Southern, Colombian Ministry of Education. **Regional organizations:** AAIE, ACCAS, Tri-Assoc.

Curriculum/physical plant

Type: U.S., national, AP. **Languages of instruction:** English, Spanish. **Languages taught:** English, French, Spanish. **Staff specialists:** computer, counselor, psychologist, learning disabilities, nurse. **Special programs:** honors sections, independent study, remedial, gifted. **Special curricular:** art, chorus, band, physical education, computer instruction, debating, drama, speech. **Extracurricular:** drama, gymnastics, choral and instrumental music, computers, yearbook, newspaper, photography, excursions/ expeditions, field trips, Model UN . **Sports:** baseball, basketball, soccer, softball, track and field, volleyball. **Tests:** PSAT, SAT, ACT, AP, DAT, ITBS, LSI, COGAT. **Graduates attending college:** 96%. **Graduates have attended:** Tufts, Georgetown, U. of Pennsylvania, Boston U., Stanford. **Location:** on wooded hillside overlooking Bogota. **Campus:** 18 acres. **Libraries (2):** 30,000 volumes. **Facilities:** 12 buildings, 74 classrooms, cafeteria, infirmary, covered play area, 2 tennis courts, 2 gymnasiums, 12 playing fields, 9 science labs, 2 computer labs, theater, soccer field, weight-lifting room.

*Once only fee

BUCARAMANGA

COLEGIO PANAMERICANO

Street address: Calle 34 #8-73, Canaveral Alto, Bucaramanga, Santander, Colombia
Phone/facsimile: (57)(76)387336
Mail: Apartado Aereo 522, Bucaramanga, Colombia
Director: Dale Swall
Secondary school principal: Patricia Marshall
Teaching staff: full-time, 50; total, 50
Nationalities of teaching staff: U.S., 2; Canada, 10; other, 38; total, 50
Grade levels: preK – 11
Enrollment: preK, 67; K, 43; 1 – 6, 184; 7 – 9, 73; 10 – 11, 66; total, 494
Nationalities of student body: U.S., 16; other, 478; total, 494
Capacity: preK, 85; K, 50; 1 – 6, 200; 7 – 9, 75; 10 – 12, 75; total, 485
Teacher/student ratio: 1/10
Tuition (annual): K, $950; 1 – 6, $2,300; 7 – 9, $2,500; 10 – 12, $2,700
Other fees (annual): registration*, $547; insurance, $50; busing, $340; lunch, $399
School year: February to November

Year founded: 1963. **Type of school:** coed, day. **Governed by:** elected board of directors. **Accredited by:** Colombian Ministerio. **Regional organizations:** ACCAS.

Curriculum/physical plant

Type: U.S., national. **Languages of instruction:** English, Spanish. **Languages taught:** English, French, Spanish. **Staff specialists:** counselor. **Special programs:** ESL. **Extracurricular:** drama, dance, computers, newspaper, photography, excursions/expeditions, field trips, scouting. **Sports:** basketball, soccer, volleyball. **Tests:** PSAT, SAT. **Graduates attending college:** 90%. **Graduates have attended:** U. of Florida, U. of Alabama, Florida State. **Location:** 5 miles south of Bucaramanga. **Facilities:** cafeteria, covered play area, playing field, science lab, computer lab, new library.

*Once only fee

CALI

COLEGIO BOLIVAR

Street address: Calle 5 #122-21, Cali, Valle, Colombia
Phone: (57)(2)5552039 **Facsimile:** (57)(2)5552041
Mail: Apartado Aereo 26300, Cali, Colombia
Director: Martin Felton, Ph.D.
Secondary school principal: Robert McCarthy
Middle school principal: Raquel Cruz
Primary principal: Joe Nagy

Pre-primary principal: Rosemary Palencia
Teaching staff: full-time, 102; part-time, 4; total, 106
Nationalities of teaching staff: U.S./Canadian, 40; host, 60; other, 6; total, 106
Grade levels: preK – 12
Enrollment: pre-primary, 288; primary, 358; middle, 263; secondary, 298; total, 1,207
Teacher/student ratio: 1/12
Tuition (annual): pre-primary – primary, $3,600; middle, $4,100; secondary, $4,800
Other fees (annual): registration, $160; busing, $350; entrance donation*, $7,500
School year: September to June

Year founded: 1948. **Type of school:** coed, day. **Governed by:** bondholding companies, appointed board of directors. **Accredited by:** Southern, Colombian Ministry of Education. **Regional organizations:** AAIE, ACCAS, Tri-Assoc.

Curriculum

Type: U.S., national, AP. **Languages of instruction:** English, Spanish. **Languages taught:** Spanish. **Staff specialists:** reading, counselor, learning disabilities, nurse. **Special programs:** ESL, honors sections. **Special curricular:** art, chorus, physical education, computer instruction, vocational. **Extracurricular:** drama, gymnastics, dance, choral and instrumental music, computers, yearbook, newspaper, literary magazine, photography, excursions/expeditions, field trips, sports, Boy Scouts, Girl Scouts. **Tests:** PSAT, SAT, ACT, Stanford, Iowa, Otis-Lennon, Strong-Campbell. **Graduates attending college:** 95%. **Graduates have attended:** Brandeis, Boston U., Harvard, Brown, Georgetown.

Physical plant

Location: in rural area, 10 miles from city center. **Campus:** 21 acres. **Library:** 20,000 volumes. **Facilities:** 10 buildings, 60 classrooms, auditorium, cafeteria, infirmary, covered play area, gymnasium, 3 playing fields, 9 science labs, computer lab, swimming pool, AV equipment.

*Once only fee

CARTAGENA

Colegio Jorge Washington

Street address: Carrera 1a, No. 12-120, Bocagrande, Cartagena, Colombia
Phone: (57)(5)6653136/6654035 **Facsimile:** (57)(5)6656447
Mail: Apartado Aereo 2899, Cartagena, Colombia
Director: Conrad Pholar
High school principal: Joan Galdi
Elementary school principal: Miriam Angulo
Head of library: Linda Bradford
Head of computer services: Eduardo Vera
Teaching staff: full-time, 52; part-time, 8; total, 60

Nationalities of teaching staff: U.S., 24; host, 28; other, 8; total, 60
Grade levels: preK – 12
Enrollment: preK, 41; K, 41; 1 – 6, 262; 7 – 9, 112; 10 – 12, 96; total, 552
Nationalities of student body: U.S., 28; U.K., 5; host, 499; other, 20; total, 552
Capacity: preK, 41; K, 41; 1 – 6, 264; 7 – 9, 132; 10 – 12, 132; total, 610
Teacher/student ratio: 1/10
Tuition (annual): $3,500
Other fees (annual): registration, $250; entrance*, $7,000
School year: August to June

Year founded: 1952. **Type of school:** coed, day, private nonprofit. **Governed by:** elected board of directors. **Accredited by:** Southern. **Regional organizations:** AASSA, ACCAS, Tri-Assoc.

Curriculum/physical plant

Type: U.S., national. **Languages of instruction:** English, Spanish. **Languages taught:** English, Spanish. **Staff specialists:** math, computer, psychologist. **Special programs:** remedial. **Special curricular:** physical education, computer instruction. **Extracurricular:** drama, computers, yearbook, newspaper, excursions/expeditions. **Tests:** PSAT, SAT, TOEFL, Iowa. **Graduates attending college:** 100%. **Graduates have attended:** Georgia Tech, Duke, U. of South Carolina, Georgetown, Texas A&M. **Location:** on oceanfront within Cartagena city limits. **Campus:** 2 acres. **Library:** 10,000 volumes. **Facilities:** 4 buildings, 20 classrooms, cafeteria, tennis court, playing field, science lab, computer lab, air conditioning.

*Once only fee

MANIZALES

Colegio Granadino

Phone: (57)(68)745774/741454/745884 **Facsimile:** (57)(68)746066
E-mail: granadino@emtelsa.com.co
Mail: Apartado Aereo 2138, Manizales, Colombia
Director: Gonzalo Arango
Secondary principal: Silvia L. Spaggiari
Elementary principal: David L. Pruner
Head of library: Constanza Maria Gonzalez
Teaching staff: full-time, 45; part-time, 5; total, 50
Nationalities of teaching staff: U.S., 2; host, 36; other, 12; total, 50
Grade levels: N – 12
Enrollment: N, 31; preK, 37; K, 34; 1 – 5, 205; 6 – 12, 237; total, 544
Nationalities of student body: U.S., 11; host, 528; other, 52; total, 544
Teacher/student ratio: 1/10
Tuition (annual): K – T, $2,098; 1 – 5, $2,255; 6 – 12, $2,674
Other fees (annual): registration*, $3,440; busing, $470; lunch, $581; books, $260
School year: mid-August through late June

Year founded: 1980. **Type of school:** coed, day, private nonprofit, university preparatory, non-denominational. **Governed by:** appointed board of directors, school director. **Accredited by:** Colombian Ministry, Southern (in process). **Regional organizations:** ACCAS.

Curriculum/physical plant

Type: U.S., national, AP. **Languages of instruction:** English, Spanish. **Staff specialists:** math, computer, counselor, psychologist, learning disabilities, instrumental music. **Special programs:** ESL, SSL, reinforcement. **Special curricular:** art, chorus, physical education, computer instruction, music, seminars, research, field trips. **Extracurricular:** drama, gymnastics, dance, choral music, computers, yearbook, newspaper, scouts, reading club, painting, cooking, judo, skating, sports teams, ceramics. **Sports:** basketball, soccer, softball, track and field, volleyball. **Clubs:** National Honor Society, yearbook, student councils. **Tests:** PSAT, SAT, TOEFL, ICFES. **Location:** 5 miles from Manizales. **Campus:** 21 acres. **Library:** 8,500 volumes. **Facilities:** 9 buildings, 40 classrooms, 2 auditoriums, cafeteria, 8 playing fields, 2 computer labs, AV room.

*Once only fee

MEDELLIN

The Columbus School

Street address: Calle 78B #72A-220, Medellin, Colombia
Phone: (57)(4)4415151 **Facsimile:** (57)(4)4417744
E-mail: columbus@inter.net.co
Mail: Apartado Aereo 5225, Medellin, Colombia
Superintendent: John K. Schober, Ph.D.
High school principal: Mike Cooper
Elementary school principal: Jeff Jurkovac
Teaching staff: full-time, 92; part-time, 4; total, 96
Nationalities of teaching staff: U.S., 43; host, 34; other, 19; total, 96
Grade levels: N – 12
Enrollment: N – preK, 100; K, 110; 1 – 5, 475; 6 – 8, 235; 9 – 12, 280; total, 1,200
Teacher/student ratio: 1/12
Tuition (annual): N – K, $3,700; 1 – 5, $3,800; 6 – 8, $3,150; 9 – 12, $4,000
Other fees (annual): registration, $125; capital levy*, $3,000; busing, $300; books, $60
School year: August to June

Year founded: 1947. **Type of school:** coed, day, private nonprofit. **Governed by:** elected board of directors. **Accredited by:** Southern. **Regional organizations:** ACCAS, Tri-Assoc.

Curriculum/physical plant

Type: binational (U.S./national). **Languages of instruction:** English, Spanish. **Languages taught:** French. **Staff specialists:** reading, math, counselor, learning disabilities. **Special programs:** ESL, honors sections. **Special curricular:** physical education, computer instruction. **Extracurricular:** drama, gymnastics, choral music, computers, yearbook, newspaper. **Sports:** basketball, soccer, volleyball. **Tests:** PSAT, SAT, ACT, TOEFL, Iowa. **Graduates attending college:** 95%. **Graduates have attended:** Stanford, Johns Hopkins, Emory, Loyola, U. of Miami. **Location:** on mountainside, 3 miles northwest of center city. **Campus:** 10 acres. **Library:** 15,000 volumes. **Facilities:** 7 buildings, 60 classrooms, cafeteria, gymnasium, computer lab, playing fields, science labs. A new 45-acre site is planned for the near future.

*Once only fee

THE CONGO, DEMOCRATIC REPUBLIC OF†

Region: Central Africa
Size: 905,354 square miles
Population: 46,498,539
Capital: Kinshasa
Telephone code: 243
Currency: new zaire
Languages: French, Kongo, Luba, Mongo, Rwanda, others

KINSHASA

THE AMERICAN SCHOOL OF KINSHASA (TASOK)

Street address: Route de Matadi, Ngaliema, Kinshasa, Democratic Republic of The Congo
Phone: (243)(88)46619 **Facsimile:** (243)(88)41161
E-mail: tasok-teachers@maf.org
U.S. mail: TASOK-Kinshasa (via TTM), c/o Panalpiha World Transport, Building 743-Zone Brucargo, 1931 Zaventem-Brussels, Belgium
Superintendent: Ronald C. Brown
Principal: Larry Cummins
Teaching staff: full-time, 19; part-time, 4; total, 23
Grade levels: preK – 12
Enrollment: total, 207
Nationalities of student body: U.S., 60; host, 12; other, 135; total, 207
Capacity: preK, 20; K, 40; 1 – 6, 300; 7 – 9, 135; 10 – 12, 190; total, 685
Teacher/student ratio: 1/9
Tuition (annual): preK – K, $3,000; 1 – 6, $6,500; 7 – 8, $7,200; 9 – 10, $8,900; 11 – 12, $9,400
Other fees: registration*, $1,500; ESL*, $1,200
School year: August to June

Year founded: 1961. **Type of school:** coed, day. **Governed by:** school board elected by parent assembly. **Accredited by:** Middle States. **Regional organizations:** ECIS, AISA.

Curriculum/physical plant

Type: U.S. **Languages taught:** French. **Special programs:** ESL. **Special curricular:** art, physical education, computer instruction, music. **Extracurricular:** drama, computers, yearbook, excursions/expeditions, field trips. **Sports:** basketball, soccer, softball, swimming, track and field, volleyball. **Clubs:** cheerleaders, student government. **Tests:** PSAT, SAT. **Graduates attending college:** 90%. **Graduates have attended:** Yale, Grinnell, Seattle Pacific, Wheaton, Michigan State. **Location:** 10 kilometers from the center of Kinshasa. **Campus:** 42 acres. **Library:** 20,000 volumes. **Facilities:** 22 buildings, 40 classrooms, tennis court, 2 playing fields, 2 science labs, computer lab, swimming pool, multipurpose room, air conditioning.

*Once only fee †formerly Zaire

CONGO, REPUBLIC OF

Region: Africa
Size: 132,047 square miles
Population: 2,527,841
Capital: Brazzaville

Telephone code: 242
Currency: CFA franc
Languages: French, Lingala, Kikongo

BRAZZAVILLE

INTERNATIONAL SCHOOL OF BRAZZAVILLE

Street address: 5 Bd. Lyautey, Brazzaville, Congo
Phone: (242)837529
Mail: B.P. 2039, Brazzaville, Congo
Administrator: Kamal Zein, Ph.D.
Teaching staff: full-time, 4; part-time, 3; total, 7
Nationalities of teaching staff: U.S., 2; U.K., 1; host, 2; other, 2; total, 7
Grade levels: K – 12
Enrollment: K, 1; 1 – 6, 18; 7 – 9, 7; 10 – 12, 1; total, 27
Nationalities of student body: U.S., 10; other, 17; total, 27
Teacher/student ratio: 1/7
Tuition (annual): K – 8, $5,500; 9 – 12, $7,200
Other fees: registration*, $100
School year: September to June

Year founded: 1992. **Type of school:** coed, day, private nonprofit. **Governed by:** elected board of directors. **Operated by:** Children's International Foundation.

Curriculum/physical plant

Type: U.S., U.K. **Languages taught:** French. **Special programs:** correspondence. **Special curricular:** art. **Extracurricular:** choral music, field trips. **Location:** cozy two-story building in city. **Library:** 2,000 volumes. **Facilities:** 1 building, 3 classrooms, small volleyball/soccer field.

*Once only fee **1996–97 listing**

COSTA RICA

Region: Central America
Size: 19,730 square miles
Population: 3,463,083
Capital: San José
Telephone code: 506
Currency: colon
Language: Spanish

SAN JOSÉ

THE AMERICAN INTERNATIONAL SCHOOL OF COSTA RICA†

Street address: Bosques De Dona Rosa, Ciudad Cariari, San José, Costa Rica
Phone: (506)2390376 **Facsimile:** (506)2390625 **E-mail:** aiscr@cra.ed.cr
Mail: Apartado 4941, San José 1000, Costa Rica
Director: Lawrence D. Lyons
High school principal: John B. Brown
Elementary principal: Moni Guth
Teaching staff: full-time, 40; total, 40
Grade levels: preK – 12
Enrollment: preK, 12; K, 10; 1 – 6, 98; 7 – 9, 74; 10 – 12, 80; total, 274
Nationalities of student body: U.S., 110; host, 69; other, 95; total, 274
Capacity: preK, 16; K, 16; 1 – 6, 120; 7 – 9, 90; 10 – 12, 90; total, 332
Teacher/student ratio: 1/7
Tuition (annual): preK, $2,000; K – 12, $5,150
Other fees (annual): registration*, $50; busing, $880; matriculation fee*, $1,000; building fund, $600 for 3 years; PTA, $40
School year: August to June

Year founded: 1970. **Type of school:** coed, day, private nonprofit. **Governed by:** elected board of directors. **Accredited by:** Southern. **Regional organizations:** AAIE, AASCA, Tri-Assoc.

Curriculum/physical plant

Type: U.S., AP. **Languages of instruction:** English, Spanish (one lesson daily). **Languages taught:** English, French, Spanish. **Staff specialists:** math, computer, counselor, nurse, AV. **Special programs:** ESL, independent study, remedial, tutoring, learning disabilities (K – 12), enrichment, optimal match. **Special curricular:** art, physical education, computer instruction, introduction to music. **Extracurricular:** drama, gymnastics, computers, yearbook, newspaper, photography, excursions/expeditions, field trips. **Tests:** PSAT, SAT, ACT, TOEFL, AP, Iowa, MAT. **Graduates attending college:** 90%. **Location:** adjacent to Cariari Country Club, 10 miles from San José. **Library:** 19,000 volumes. **Facilities:** 33 classrooms, cafeteria, infirmary, covered play area, gymnasium, 2 playing fields, 2 science labs, 2 computer labs.

*Once only fee †formerly Costa Rica Academy

Anglo American School

Street address: Calle 37, Av. Central, San José, Costa Rica
Phone: (506)2251723/2251729 **Facsimile:** (506)2347813
Mail: Apartado 3188, 1000 San José, Costa Rica
Principal: Elsa Pérez Góngora
Head of library: Lucia Jiménez
Head of computer services: Anabelle Vargas
Teaching staff: full-time, 40; total, 40
Nationalities of teaching staff: host, 40; total, 40
Grade levels: preK – 6
Enrollment: preK – K, 280; 1 – 6, 550; total, 830
Teacher/student ratio: 1/19
Tuition (annual): $1,475
Other fees: registration, $50/year; busing, $25/month; entrance*, $60; book rental, $12/month
School year: February to December

Year founded: 1949. **Type of school:** coed, day, proprietary.

Curriculum/physical plant

Type: U.S., national. **Languages of instruction:** English, Spanish. **Languages taught:** English. **Special curricular:** art, band, physical education, music, religion. **Extracurricular:** yearbook, excursions/expeditions. **Clubs:** computer, chorus, soccer, basketball, cheerleaders, volleyball, painting. **Location:** in San José. **Campus:** 1 acre. **Library:** 1,500 volumes. **Facilities:** 1 building, 30 classrooms, (2 with computers), 3 playing fields, auditorium/gymnasium, multiple-use room, preschool yard, outdoor classroom.

*Once only fee

The Country Day School

Phone: (506)2898406 **Facsimile:** (506)2282076
Mail: Apartado 8-6170, 1000 San José, Costa Rica
U.S. mail: Acct. 191, PO Box 025216, Miami, FL 33102-5216, U.S.A.
Director: Gunther Brandt
Business director: Woodson C. Brown
High school principal: F. Larue Goldfinch
Middle school principal: Paul Maxfield
Elementary school principal: William Large
Teaching staff: full-time, 62; part-time, 23; total, 85
Nationalities of teaching staff: U.S., 33; host, 41; other, 11; total, 85
Grade levels: preK – 12
Enrollment: preK, 39; K – 3, 253; 4 – 5, 110; 6 – 8, 146; 9 – 12, 152; total, 700
Nationalities of student body: U.S., 280; host, 280; other, 140; total, 700
Teacher/student ratio: 1/10
Tuition (annual): preK (half day), $1,832; K – prep (half day), $2,680; K – prep (full day), $3,995; 1 – 12, $5,390
Other fees: matriculation, $475
School year: August to June

Year founded: 1963. **Type of school:** coed, day, proprietary. **Accredited by:** Costa Rican Ministry of Education, Southern. **Regional organizations:** AASCA, Tri-Assoc.

Curriculum

Type: U.S., AP. **Languages taught:** French, Spanish. **Staff specialists:** computer, nurse, learning specialist. **Special programs:** ESL, SSL, advanced placement courses, honor courses, resource. **Special curricular:** art, chorus, band, computer instruction, violin, orchestra. **Extracurricular:** drama, dance, choral and instrumental music, yearbook, newspaper, photography, field trips, computer. **Sports:** basketball, soccer, swimming, volleyball. **Clubs:** chess, drama, international, anthropology, social service, bridge. **Tests:** PSAT, SAT, ACT, TOEFL, AP, Iowa, Achievement Tests. **Graduates attending college:** 99%. **Graduates have attended:** Brown, Yale, Columbia, Trinity College Dublin, Harvard.

Physical plant

Location: in town of Escazú, 10 minutes from San Jose. **Campus:** 8 acres. **Library:** 22,500 volumes. **Facilities:** 9 buildings, 52 classrooms, 2 infirmaries, covered play area, gymnasium, 2 playing fields, 2 science labs, 3 computer labs, swimming pool, 2 art rooms, photography lab, band room, cafeteria/auditorium.

LINCOLN SCHOOL

Phone: (506)2357733 **Facsimile:** (506)2361706
E-mail: director@ns.lincoln.ed.cr **Web:** http://www.lincoln.ed.cr
Mail: PO Box 1919, San José, Costa Rica
U.S. mail: PO Box 025216, Miami, FL 33102-5216, U.S.A.
Director: Jack Delman
High school principal: Joseph Dunham
Elementary school principal: Iris Prada-Mora
Teaching staff: full-time, 106; total, 106
Nationalities of teaching staff: U.S., 44; host, 62; total, 106
Grade levels: preK – 12
Enrollment: preK, 72; K, 70; preparatory, 78; 1 – 5, 434; 6 – 8, 273; 9 – 12, 386; total, 1,313
Teacher/student ratio: 1/13
Tuition (annual): preK – K, $2,500; prep – 3, $2,808; 4 – 6, $3,119; 7 – 12, $3,420
Other fees (annual): registration, $45; insurance, $5; busing, $400; enrollment*, $1,000/family; various fees, $150
School year: February to December

Year founded: 1945. **Type of school:** coed, day, private nonprofit. **Accredited by:** Southern, Costa Rican Ministry of Education. **Regional organizations:** AAIE, AASCA, Tri-Assoc.

Curriculum

Type: U.S., national, IB. **Languages of instruction:** English, Spanish. **Languages taught:** English, French, Spanish. **Staff specialists:** reading, math, computer, counselor, psychologist, learning disabilities, nurse, ESL. **Special programs:** honors sections, independent study, honors thesis, university level math, computer. **Special**

curricular: art, chorus, band, physical education, computer instruction. **Extracurricular:** drama, gymnastics, choral and instrumental music, yearbook, newspaper, excursions/expeditions, field trips, Model UN, Math Counts, NASA space camp, presidential classroom. **Sports:** basketball, soccer, softball, volleyball, flag football, cheerleaders. **Clubs:** chess, National Honor Society, National Junior Honor Society, community service, ecology, French, Tae Kwon Do, ceramics, photography, literary magazine. **Tests:** PSAT, SAT, ACT, TOEFL, Iowa, Slingerland Screening. **Graduates attending college:** 98%. **Graduates have attended:** Harvard, Swarthmore, Dartmouth, Brown, MIT.

Physical plant

Location: in suburb, Moravia. **Campus:** 9 acres. **Facilities:** 25 buildings, 77 classrooms, cafeteria, infirmary, gymnasium, 2 playing fields, 3 science labs, 4 computer labs, 2 libraries.

*Once only fee

MARIAN BAKER SCHOOL

Phone: (506)2733426/2733204 **Facsimile:** (506)2734609
E-mail: mbschool@sol.racsa.co.cr
Mail: Apartado 4269-1000, San José, Costa Rica
Director: Linda A. Niehaus
Elementary principal: Sofia Solis
Business manager: Bonnie Heigold
Teaching staff: full-time, 29; part-time, 1; total, 30
Nationalities of teaching staff: U.S., 12; host, 14; other, 4; total, 30
Grade levels: preK – 12
Enrollment: total, 203
Nationalities of student body: U.S., 53; host, 65; other, 85; total, 203
Teacher/student ratio: 1/7
Tuition (annual): preK, $2,500; K – 5, $4,600; 6 – 12, $5,300
Other fees (annual): registration, $450; busing; insurance, books, and class photo included in tuition
School year: August to June

Year founded: 1984. **Type of school:** coed, day, proprietary. **Governed by:** school owners and board of directors. **Accredited by:** Costa Rican Ministry of Education, Southern. **Regional organizations:** AASCA, Tri-Assoc.

Curriculum/physical plant

Type: U.S., AP. **Languages taught:** Spanish. **Staff specialists:** computer, counselor, special education. **Special programs:** ESL, SSL. **Special curricular:** art, band, physical education, computer instruction. **Extracurricular:** drama, instrumental music, yearbook, excursions/expeditions, field trips, science club. **Sports:** basketball, soccer, volleyball, ultimate frisbee. **Tests:** PSAT, SAT, TOEFL, AP, Iowa. **Graduates attending college:** 100%. **Graduates have attended:** U. of San Diego, U. of Costa Rica, William and Mary, Harvard, Wheaton. **Location:** beautiful, wooded area in hills northeast of San José, 4 kilometers from San Pedro. **Campus:** 4 acres. **Library:** 8,000 volumes. **Facilities:** 3 buildings, 29 classrooms, auditorium, cafeteria, gymnasium, playing field, science lab, computer lab.

CÔTE D'IVOIRE

Region: West Africa
Size: 124,504 square miles
Population: 14,762,445
Capitals: Yamoussoukro (official), Abidjan (de facto)
Telephone code: 225
Currency: CFA franc
Languages: French, Dioula

ABIDJAN

INTERNATIONAL COMMUNITY SCHOOL OF ABIDJAN

Phone: (225)471152 **Facsimile:** (225)471996
E-mail: 75204.1313@compuserve.com
Mail: 06 BP 544, Abidjan 06, Côte d'Ivoire, West Africa
Director: Larry Jones
Deputy director: Robert Walbridge
Upper school principal: David Pera
Lower school principal: Diana Bartley
Teaching staff: full-time, 47; part-time, 1; total, 48
Nationalities of teaching staff: U.S., 29; U.K., 1; host, 8; other, 10; total, 48
Grade levels: K – 12
Enrollment: K, 18; 1 – 5, 185; 6 – 8, 110; 9 – 12, 110; total, 423
Nationalities of student body: U.S., 137; U.K., 17; host, 5; other, 264; total, 423
Capacity: K, 30; 1 – 5, 212; 6 – 8, 120; 9 – 12, 105; total, 467
Teacher/student ratio: 1/9
Tuition (annual): K, $8,410; 1 – 5, $8,820; 6 – 8, $10,520; 9 – 12, $10,770
Other fees (annual): registration, $621 ($207 credited toward tuition); capital development*, $3,570
School year: August to June

Year founded: 1972. **Type of school:** coed, day, private nonprofit. **Governed by:** elected board of directors. **Sponsored by:** U.S. Embassy. **Accredited by:** Middle States (K – 12), ECIS (7 – 12). **Regional organizations:** AAIE, ECIS, AISA.

Curriculum

Type: U.S., AP. **Languages taught:** French. **Staff specialists:** counselor, nurse. **Special programs:** ESOL, reception. **Special curricular:** art, physical education, computer instruction, music, health. **Extracurricular:** computers, yearbook, field trips, student government, other clubs. **Sports:** basketball, soccer, swimming, volleyball, intramurals. **Tests:** PSAT, ACT, TOEFL, AP, Iowa, SAT I & II, Test of Achievement and Proficiency, PLAN. **Graduates attending college:** 98%. **Graduates have attended:** U. of Pennsylvania, Michigan State U., Morehouse College, Oberlin College, Spelman College.

Physical plant

Location: Riviera III, a residential area on the outskirts of Abidjan. **Campus:** 13 acres. **Library:** 10,000 volumes. **Facilities:** middle school complex, 37 classrooms containing 3 science labs, 2 computer labs, language and special services rooms, music room, art room, and an infirmary, plus a regulation-size soccer/football pitch, 400-meter track, softball field, air conditioning.

*Once only fee

CROATIA

Region: Europe
Size: 21,889 square miles
Population: 5,004,112
Capital: Zagreb
Telephone code: 385
Currency: kuna
Language: Croatian

ZAGREB

THE AMERICAN SCHOOL OF ZAGREB

Street address: 45/1B Zelenga, 41000 Zagreb, Croatia
Phone: (385)(1)4578109/07 **Facsimile:** (385)(1)4578203
U.S. mail: c/o Dept. of State, Washington, DC 20520-5080
Director: Robert Morrison
Teaching staff: full-time, 9; total, 9
Nationalities of teaching staff: U.S., 5; other, 4; total, 9
Grade levels: K – 8
Enrollment: K, 11; 1 – 6, 61; 7 – 8, 13; total, 85
Nationalities of student body: U.S., 19; U.K., 12; other, 54; total, 85
Capacity: K, 10; 1 – 6, 60; 7 – 8, 15; total, 85
Teacher/student ratio: 1/12
Tuition (annual): $8,000
Other fees: building, $1,000/family
School year: August to June

Year founded: 1966. **Type of school:** coed, day, private nonprofit. **Governed by:** elected school board. **Accredited by:** Middle States.

Curriculum/physical plant

Type: U.S. **Special curricular:** art, physical education, computer instruction. **Extracurricular:** computers, yearbook, newspaper, field trips, cooking. **Tests:** SAT, TOEFL, GRE, GMAT, ITBS. **Location:** in suburban area. **Library:** 4,300 volumes. **Facilities:** 9 classrooms, 2 computer labs, rented gymnasium, public playing field.

CUBA

Region: Western Atlantic
Size: 42,804 square miles
Population: 10,951,334
Capital: Havana
Telephone code: 537
Currency: peso
Language: Spanish

HAVANA

International School of Havana

Street address: #315 18th Street & 5th Avenue, Miramar, Havana, Cuba
Phone: (537)242540/242818/242960 **Facsimile:** (537)242723
U.K. mail: c/o FCO (Havana), King Charles Street, London SW1A2AH, England
U.S. mail: ISH c/o USINT (Havana), Dept. of State, Washington, DC 20521-3200
Principal: Dr. Adrienne Hunter
Teaching staff: full-time, 20; total, 20
Nationalities of teaching staff: host, 19; Canada, 1; total, 20
Grade levels: N – 11
Enrollment: N, 35; K – 5, 80; 6 – 8, 20; 9 – 11, 15; total, 150
Nationalities of student body: U.S., 20; U.K., 10; other, 120; total, 150
Capacity: N, 33; K – 5, 75; 6 – 8, 35; 9 – 12, 30; total, 173
Teacher/student ratio: 1/7
Tuition (annual): N, $1,200 (half day), $1,800 (full day); K – 6, $3,400; 7 – 12, $3,750 (UNL students, $2,880)
Other fees (annual): registration*, $60; busing, $360; supplementary classes, $10 per hour
School year: September to June

Year founded: 1965. **Type of school:** coed, day, private nonprofit. **Governed by:** patronage (board of governors) of 12 ambassadors.

Curriculum/physical plant

Type: U.S., U.K., O-level. **Languages taught:** French, Spanish. **Special programs:** ESL, correspondence. **Extracurricular:** field trips, interschool sports. **Clubs:** computer, drama, yearbook, handicrafts, basketball, football. **Tests:** SAT, TOEFL, Cambridge EFL certificates. **Location:** in residential suburb, 2 blocks from sea. **Library:** 7,000 volumes. **Facilities:** 2 buildings, 15 classrooms, science lab, computer lab, playground.

*Once only fee

CURAÇAO†

Region: West Indies
Size: 171 square miles
Capital: Willemstad
Telephone code: 599
Currency: guilder
Languages: Dutch, Papiamento, English, Spanish

WILLEMSTAD

INTERNATIONAL SCHOOL OF CURAÇAO

Street address: Koninginnelaan, Emmastad, Netherlands Antilles,
Phone: (599)(9)7373633 **Facsimile:** (599)(9)7373142 **E-mail:** livy@cura.net
Mail: PO Box 3090, Curaçao, Netherlands Antilles
Director: Dr. Livingston Merchant
Deputy director: Brian Travers
Business manager: Emma Van Delden
Teaching staff: full-time, 29; part-time, 4; total, 33
Grade levels: preK – 12
Enrollment: preK, 19; K, 26; 1 – 5, 92; 6 – 9, 92; 10 – 12, 60; total, 289
Nationalities of student body: U.S., 18; host, 58; other, 213; total, 289
Capacity: preK, 48; K, 24; 1 – 5, 144; 6 – 8, 80; 9 – 12, 104; total, 400
Teacher/student ratio: 1/10
Tuition (annual): preK, $3,164; K – 5, $5,235; 6 – 9, $5,865; 10 – 12, $6,712
Other fees (annual): registration: preK, $556; K – 12, $835; capital levy*, $420; expansion, $85
School year: August to June

Year founded: 1971. **Type of school:** coed, day, private nonprofit. **Governed by:** board of directors. **Accredited by:** Southern.

Curriculum/physical plant

Type: U.S., IB, AP. **Languages taught:** Spanish, Dutch. **Staff specialists:** computer, counselor, college placement officer. **Special programs:** ESL, learning resource. **Special curricular:** art, physical education, computer instruction, music, Model UN. **Extracurricular:** extensive activities including crafts, sports, arts, music, Dutch, French, Spanish, and English. **Sports:** basketball, softball, volleyball, flag football, floor hockey, team handball. **Organizations:** National Honor Society, National Junior Honor Society. **Tests:** PSAT, SAT, ACT, AP, Iowa, ERB writing. **Graduates attending college:** 85%. **Location:** in suburban area, 5 kilometers from Willemstad. **Campus:** 40 acres. **Library:** 10,000 volumes. **Facilities:** 8 buildings, 24 classrooms, science lab, computer lab, media resource room, 3 playgrounds, air conditioning.

*Once only fee †Curaçao is part of Netherlands Antilles

CYPRUS

Region: Middle East
Size: 3,572 square miles
Population: 744,609
Capital: Nicosia
Telephone code: 357
Currency: pound
Languages: Greek, Turkish, English

LARNACA

AMERICAN ACADEMY LARNACA, CYPRUS

Street address: Gregory Afxentiou Avenue, Larnaca, Cyprus
Phone: (357)(46)52046/57206 **Facsimile:** (357)(46)51046
Mail: PO Box 112, 6301 Larnaca, Cyprus
Principal: Graham Watson
Assistant principals: M. Pambou, A. Ellinas, D. Koumandaris
Teaching staff: full-time, 51; part-time, 14; total, 65
Nationalities of teaching staff: U.K., 5; host, 57; other, 3; total, 65
Grade levels: 1 – 13
Enrollment: 1 – 6, 143; 7 – 9, 385; 10 – 12, 359; 13, 125; total, 1,012
Capacity: 1 – 6, 300; 7 – 9, 440; 10 – 12, 420; 13, 120; total, 1,280
Teacher/student ratio: 1/17
Tuition (annual): 1 – 6, $2,400; 7 – 9, $2,800; 10 – 12, $2,950; 13, $3,150
Other fees (annual): books, $454 (average)
School year: September to June

Year founded: 1908. **Type of school:** coed, day, private nonprofit. **Governed by:** elected body of governors from the alumni of the school.

Curriculum

Type: U.S., U.K. **Languages taught:** English, French, German, Greek. **Staff specialists:** counselor. **Special curricular:** art, physical education, computer instruction. **Extracurricular:** drama, dance, computers, yearbook, newspaper, excursions/expeditions, field trips. **Sports:** basketball, football, hockey, softball, tennis, volleyball. **Clubs:** debating, French, science, folklore, folk-dancing, economics and current affairs, literary, cultural. **Tests:** SAT, TOEFL, GCSE, O- and A-level GCE, Achievement Tests. **Graduates attending college:** 65%. **Graduates have attended:** Oxford, Manchester, Sheffield, Yale, Cornell.

Physical plant

Location: in center city. **Campus:** 8 acres. **Library:** 5,000 volumes. **Facilities:** 3 buildings, 50 classrooms, auditorium, 6 science labs, computer lab, medical room, tennis, basketball and volleyball courts, football pitch.

LIMASSOL

Logos School of English Education

Street address: 33-35 Yialousa Street, 3501 Limassol, Cyprus
Phone: (357)(5)336061/336650 **Facsimile:** (357)(5)33557
E-mail: pr@logos.ac.cy **Web:** http://www.logos.ac.cy
Mail: PO Box 1075, 3501 Limassol, Cyprus
Principal: Peter Ross
Assistant principals: John Ross, Demitris Tsoulloftas
Teaching staff: full-time, 18; part-time, 2; total, 20
Nationalities of teaching staff: U.K., 8; host, 7; other, 5; total, 20
Grade levels: 1 – 13
Enrollment: total, 200
Teacher/student ratio: 1/10
Boarders: boys, 15
Tuition (annual): 1 – 6, $2,486; 7 – 9, $2,910; 10 – 13, $3,163
Other fees (annual): registration, $100 (day), $200 (boarding); boarding, $6,920; books, $290; advanced level surcharge per subject

Year founded: 1973. **Type of school:** coed, day, boarding. **Governed by:** appointed board of directors.

Curriculum/physical plant

Type: U.K., Cambridge U.-approved IGCSE. **Languages taught:** French, Arabic, Greek. **Special curricular:** physical education, biology, chemistry, physics, history, geography. **Extracurricular:** drama, computers. **Tests:** SAT, TOEFL, IGCSE, O- and A-level GCE, English Graded Tests. **Location:** in city. **Campus:** 3 acres. **Facilities:** auditorium, cafeteria, covered play area, tennis court, playing field, computer lab, library, science labs.

NICOSIA

The American Academy Nicosia

Street address: 3A Michael Paridis, Nicosia, Cyprus
Phone: (357)(2)462886 **Facsimile:** (357)(2)466290
Mail: PO Box 1967, Nicosia, Cyprus
Principal: Christo Psiloinis
Assistant principals: Mary Psiloinis, Jovanna Xenophontos, Maria Iacovidou
Teaching staff: full-time, 34; part-time, 19; total, 53
Nationalities of teaching staff: U.S., 1; host, 50; other, 2; total, 53
Grade levels: 1 – 13
Enrollment: 1 – 6, 109; 7 – 9, 173; 10 – 12, 252; 13, 97; total, 631
Nationalities of student body: U.S., 2; U.K., 1; host, 512; other, 116; total, 631
Teacher/student ratio: 1/11

Tuition (annual): 1 – 6, 1,150**; 7, 1,200; 8, 1,250; 9, 1,300; 10, 1,400; 11, 1,500; 12, 1,600; 13, 1,700
Other fees (annual): registration*, 50**; insurance, 2.50; books, 130 – 150; uniform, 100
School year: September through June

Year founded: 1922. **Type of school:** coed, day, private nonprofit. **Governed by:** elected board of directors. **Accredited by:** Ministry of Education, Cyprus.

Curriculum/physical plant

Type: U.S., U.K., AP. **Languages taught:** French, Greek. **Staff specialists:** reading, math, computer, speech/hearing, counselor, nurse. **Special programs:** remedial, special language. **Special curricular:** art, chorus, band, physical education, computer instruction, photography, orchestra, guitar, UNESCO, cultural. **Extracurricular:** drama, gymnastics, dance, choral and instrumental music, computers, yearbook. **Sports:** badminton, basketball, football, volleyball, olympic gym, scouts, St. John ambulance. **Tests:** TOEFL, A- and O-level GCE. **Graduates attending college:** 80%. **Graduates have attended:** Oxford, London U. **Location:** in city. **Library:** 20,000 volumes. **Facilities:** 44 classrooms, 2 auditoriums, cafeteria, infirmary, covered play area, 2 playing fields, 4 science labs, 2 computer labs.

*Once only fee **Cypriot pound

American International School in Cyprus

Street address: 11 Kassos Street, Nicosia, Cyprus
Phone: (357)(2)316345 **Facsimile:** (357)(2)316549 **E-mail:** aisc@aisc.ac.cy
Mail: PO Box 3847, Nicosia, Cyprus
Superintendent: Walid Abushakra
Secondary principal/counselor: Joanna Ramos
IB director: Patricia Eriksson
Activities director: Arno Morales
Teaching staff: full-time, 38; total, 38
Nationalities of teaching staff: U.S., 21; U.K., 6; host, 5; other, 6; total, 38
Grade levels: K – 12
Enrollment: K, 16; 1 – 5, 63; 6 – 8, 50; 9 – 12, 86; total, 215
Nationalities of student body: U.S., 65; U.K., 5; host, 19; other, 126; total, 215
Capacity: K, 36; 1 – 5, 75; 6 – 8, 100; 9 – 12, 100; total, 311
Teacher/student ratio: 1/10
Boarders: boys and girls **Grades:** 8 – 12 **Program:** planned 5- and 7-day in a separate dorm facility
Tuition (annual): K4, 1,475**; K5, 2150; 1 – 5, 2,940; 6 – 8, 3,360; 9 – 12, 4,200
Other fees (annual): registration*, 100**; boarding, 4,200 (exclusive of day school fees); busing, 290 (optional); building surcharge (new students only), 700; ESL, 160 – 800; learning center, 275 – 1,375; lunch; IB
School year: September to June

Year founded: 1987. **Type of school:** coed, day, boarding, private. **Accredited by:** Middle States, Cyprus Education Ministry. **Regional organizations:** AAIE, NESA.

Curriculum/physical plant

Type: U.S., IB, AP. **Languages taught:** French, Spanish, Modern Greek. **Staff specialists:** reading, math, computer, counselor, learning disabilities, nurse. **Special programs:** ESL, independent study, resource room, outdoor education. **Special curricular:** art, physical education, computer instruction, music. **Extracurricular:** drama, gymnastics, computers, yearbook, newspaper, literary magazine, photography. **Sports:** basketball, soccer, swimming, track and field, volleyball, various intramural activities. **Tests:** PSAT, SAT, ACT, TOEFL, AP, Iowa, Gates-MacGinitie. **Location:** overlooking Nicosia. **Campus:** 4 acres. **Library:** 10,000 volumes. **Facilities:** 3 buildings, 32 classrooms, auditorium, 2 cafeterias, infirmary, covered play area, 2 tennis courts, playing field, 2 science labs, 3 computer labs, swimming pool, AV equipment, recreation room, video rooms, playground, air conditioning.

*Once only fee **Cypriot pound

THE GRAMMAR SCHOOL

Street address: Anthoupolis Highway, Nicosia, Cyprus
Phone: (357)(2)621744 **Facsimile:** (357)(2)623044
Mail: PO Box 2262, Nicosia, Cyprus
Director general: Akis Gregoriou
Headmaster: Vassos Hajiyerou
Headmistress: Marina Koni
Teaching staff: full-time, 62; total, 62
Nationalities of teaching staff: host, 62; total, 62
Grade levels: first class (ages 12 – 13) – seventh class (ages 18 – 19)
Enrollment: total, 970
Nationalities of student body: U.S., 25; U.K., 100; host, 800; other, 45; total, 970
Capacity: total, 1,100
Teacher/student ratio: 1/15

Year founded: 1963. **Type of school:** coed, day, proprietary. **Governed by:** board of directors. **Accredited by:** Cyprus government.

Curriculum/physical plant

Type: U.S., U.K., AP. **Languages of instruction:** English, Greek. **Languages taught:** English, French, Greek. **Staff specialists:** reading, math, computer, counselor, psychologist, nurse. **Special curricular:** art, chorus, physical education, computer instruction. **Extracurricular:** drama, gymnastics, dance, choral music, computers, yearbook, newspaper, photography, excursions/expeditions, field trips. **Sports:** basketball, volleyball, handball. **Clubs:** chess, drama, debate, science, environment, flower arrangement, radio, music. **Tests:** SAT, TOEFL, A-level GCE, GCSE, LCCI. **Graduates attending college:** 75%. **Graduates have attended:** Harvard, New School for Social Research, Yale, Cambridge, Oxford. **Location:** in suburban area. **Library:** 10,000 volumes. **Facilities:** 7 buildings, 40 classrooms, auditorium, tennis court, gymnasium, playing field, swimming pool, 3 science labs, computer lab, AV hall, music hall, central heating.

PAPHOS

The International School of Paphos

Street address: 22-26 Ellados Avenue, Paphos, Cyprus
Phone: (357)(6)232236 **Facsimile:** (357)(6)242541
Mail: PO Box 2018, Paphos, Cyprus
Headmaster: Dr. L. Olynpiou
Managing director/administrator: Antonis Frangos
Teaching staff: full-time, 19; part-time, 1; total, 20
Nationalities of teaching staff: U.K., 5; host, 12; other, 3; total, 20
Grade levels: K – form 6
Enrollment: total, 170
Teacher/student ratio: 1/9
Tuition (annual): K, 726**; reception, 1,110; infants, 1,329; junior 1 – 2, 1,590; junior 3 – prep, 1,638; forms 1 – 2, 1,800; form 3, 1,896; forms 4 – 6, 1,974
Other fees (annual): boarding, 3,114** (ages 11 – 18); enrollment*, $150
School year: September to June

Year founded: 1988. **Type of school:** coed, day, boarding, private nonprofit. **Governed by:** elected board of directors. **Accredited by:** government of Cyprus.

Curriculum

Type: U.K., AP. **Languages of instruction:** English, Greek. **Languages taught:** English, French, German, Russian, Greek. **Staff specialists:** reading couselor. **Special curricular:** art, physical education, computer instruction. **Extracurricular:** drama, gymnastics, dance, choral music, computers, yearbook, newspaper, excursions/expeditions, field trips. **Sports:** basketball, hockey, netball, swimming, tennis, volleyball, diving, sailing, football (U.K.). **Clubs:** computer, debating. **Tests:** PSAT, SAT, TOEFL, AP, A-level GCE, GCSE, O-level GCE. **Graduates have attended:** universities of Warwick, Wolverhampton, Bristol, Birmingham in the U.K., American U. of Beirut, Lebanon.

Physical plant

Location: just outside maintown in residential/rural area. **Campus:** 6 acres. **Library:** 3,200 volumes. **Facilities:** 5 buildings, 15 classrooms, 2 auditoriums, covered play area, 2 science labs, computer lab, AV facilities.

*Once only fee **Cypriot pound

CZECH REPUBLIC

Region: Europe
Size: 30,450 square miles
Population: 10,321,120
Capital: Prague
Telephone code: 420
Currency: koruna
Languages: Czech, Slovak

PRAGUE

INTERNATIONAL SCHOOL OF PRAGUE

Street address: Nebusicka 700, Prague 6, Czech Republic
Phone: (420)(2)90049514 **Facsimile:** (420)(2)601209849
E-mail: ispmail@isprague.anet.cz
Mail: c/o U.S. Embassy, Trziste 15, 118 01 Prague, Czech Republic
U.S. mail: c/o U.S. Embassy (Prague, Czech Republic), Dept. of State, Washington, DC 20521-5630
Director: David W. Buck
Deputy director/middle school principal: Dr. Ken Vogel
High school principal: Olen Kalkus
Elementary school principal: Anne Ross
Business manager: James Kerrigan
Teaching staff: full-time, 55; part-time, 10; total, 65
Nationalities of teaching staff: U.S., 50; host, 3; other, 12; total, 65
Enrollment: preK, 48; K, 38; 1 – 5, 225; 6 – 8, 115; 9 – 12, 150; total, 576
Nationalities of student body: U.S., 130; U.K., 25; host, 30; other, 391; total, 576
Tuition (annual): preK, $4,300 (half-day); K – 5, $9,300; 6 – 8, $9,800; 9 – 12, $10,300
Other fees (annual): registration*, $500; building levy, $2,500
School year: August to June

Year founded: 1948. **Type of school:** coed, day. **Governed by:** appointed/elected school board. **Accredited by:** Middle States, ECIS (in process). **Regional organizations:** AAIE, ECIS, CEESA, ELMLE, ISCP.

Curriculum/physical plant

Type: U.S., IB. **Languages taught:** French, Spanish, German. **Staff specialists:** computer, art, ESL, music, physical education. **Extracurricular:** drama, dance, computers, yearbook, newspaper, literary magazine, music, student council, choir, athletics, Model UN. **Clubs:** Boy Scouts, Girl Scouts, environmental, cooking, Amnesty International, model congress, sports, arts and crafts, hiking, sewing, excursions. **Tests:** PSAT, SAT, IB, ERB. **Graduates attending college:** 95%. **Graduates have attended:** Bryn Mawr, Duke, Johns Hopkins, U. of Virginia, U. of Texas (Austin). **Location:** village of Nebusice at the outskirts of Prague's residential area, connected by public transportation to downtown areas. **Library:** 30,000 volumes, state-of-the-art technology. **Facilities:** cafeteria, 4 tennis courts, 2 gymnasiums, playing field, 4 science labs, 2 computer labs, theater, soccer field, playgrounds and picnic areas.

*Once only fee

DENMARK

Region: Europe
Size: 16,639 square miles
Population: 5,249,632
Capital: Copenhagen
Telephone code: 45
Currency: krone
Language: Danish

COPENHAGEN

COPENHAGEN INTERNATIONAL SCHOOL

Street address: Hellerupvej 22-26, 2900 Hellerup, Denmark
Phone: (45)(39)403303 **Facsimile:** (45)(39)612230
Director: Dr. Kenneth J. Wrye
Senior school principal: John Kruk
Middle school prinicipal: Kim Krekel
Primary school principal: Dr. Thomas Walters
Administration manager: John Lind Jans
Teaching staff: full-time, 58; part-time, 6; total, 64
Nationalities of teaching staff: U.S., 25; U.K., 20; host, 10; other, 9; total, 64
Grade levels: preK – 12
Enrollment: preK, 20; K, 18; 1 – 6, 179; 7 – 10, 131; 11 – 12, 87; total, 435
Teacher/student ratio: 1/7
Tuition (annual): preK, 52,000**; K – 6, 37,900; 7 – 9, 42,000; 10 – 12, 77,850
Other fees (annual): registration*, 4,100**; busing, 14,500 – 18,500; application*, 1,550; ESL*, 4,400 – 9,900
School year: August to June

Year founded: 1963. **Type of school:** self-owning, independent. **Governed by:** eleven-member board. **Accredited by:** ECIS, New England.

Curriculum/physical plant

Type: IB, IBMYP, international, ISCP. **Languages taught:** English, French, German, Swedish, Danish, Finnish, Norwegian. **Staff specialists:** high school counselor, two librarians. **Special programs:** ESL. **Special curricular:** writing in all subjects, house system. **Extracurricular:** drama, computers, yearbook, charity, ballet, journalism, art, sports, music, Model UN, math club. **Graduates attending college:** 95%. **Graduates have attended:** MIT, Columbia, Stanford, London School of Economics, Cambridge. **Location:** suburban Copenhagen (north), 15 minutes from center city, with easy access to greater Copenhagen by train or bus. **Facilities:** 2 gymnasiums, 4 science labs, 2 computer labs, library, outdoor play areas.

*Once only fee **Danish krone

DOMINICAN REPUBLIC

Region: Caribbean
Size: 18,704 square miles
Population: 8,088,881
Capital: Santo Domingo
Telephone code: 809
Currency: peso
Language: Spanish

JARABACOA

Escuela Caribe (Caribe – Vista School)

Street address: Pinar Quemado, Jarabacoa, Dominican Republic
Phone: (1)(809)5742760 **Facsimile:** (1)(809)5742917
E-mail: e.caribe@codetel.net.do **U.S. facsimile:** (1)(800)3334009
U.S. mail: c/o New Horizons Ministries, Roads 1000 South at 350 East, Marion, IN 46953, U.S.A.
Principal: Gloria Satchell
Business manager: Taty Hernandez
Grade levels: 8 – 12
Enrollment: 8 – 9, 14; 10 – 12, 34; total, 48
Nationalities of student body: U.S., 48; total, 48
Capacity: total, 48
Boarders: boys, 36; girls, 12 **Grades:** 8 – 12 **Program:** planned 7-day
Tuition: $1,700 – 3,200 per month, based on income
School year: year round

Year founded: 1971. **Type of school:** coed, boarding, private nonprofit, evangelical, behavior modification/therapeutic education. **Governed by:** elected board of directors. **Sponsored by:** New Horizons Ministries. **Accredited by:** Association of Christian Schools International (ACSI).

Curriculum/physical plant

Type: U.S. **Languages taught:** Spanish. **Staff specialists:** counselor, psychologist, special education teacher. **Special programs:** independent study, correspondence, remedial. **Special curricular:** chorus, physical education, computer instruction, instruments. **Extracurricular:** choral and instrumental music, computers, yearbook, excursions/expeditions, field trips, student achievement club, student committee, community service projects. **Tests:** SAT, Stanford, DATA. **Graduates attending college:** 30%. **Graduates have attended:** Westmont, Indiana Wesleyan, Pensacola Christian, Taylor, Azusa Pacific. **Location:** in the beautiful highlands near Jarabacoa. **Campus:** 30 acres. **Library:** 3,000 volumes. **Facilities:** 10 buildings, 5 classrooms, 2 playing fields, computer lab, basketball court, AV equipment, vocational shop, 4 student boarding houses.

LA ROMANA

ABRAHAM LINCOLN SCHOOL

Phone: (1)(809)6877787 ext. 1284 **Facsimile:** (1)(809)6879740
Mail: Central Romana Corporation, La Romana, Dominican Republic
U.S. mail: ALS c/o Americas Export Corporation, 626 North Dixie Highway, West Palm Beach, FL 33401, U.S.A.
Headmaster: Harry Magee
Deputy head teacher: Alan Wood
Head of primary school: Teresa Dodkin
Teaching staff: full-time, 38; total, 38
Nationalities of teaching staff: U.S., 2; U.K., 24; host, 12; total, 38
Grade levels: preK – 12
Enrollment: preK, 36; K, 36; 1 – 6, 200; 7 – 9, 100; 10 – 12, 68; total, 440
Teacher/student ratio: 1/12
Tuition (annual): 65,000**
School year: September to June

Year founded: 1917. **Type of school:** coed, day, company-sponsored. **Governed by:** board of governors. **Sponsored by:** Central Romana Corporation. **Accredited by:** Department of Education of Dominican Republic.

Curriculum/physical plant

Type: U.K., national. **Languages of instruction:** English, Spanish. **Languages taught:** French. **Special programs:** remedial. **Special curricular:** art, chorus, physical education, computer instruction. **Extracurricular:** drama, dance, choral music, computers, literary magazine, photography, field trips. **Sports:** basketball, soccer, softball, volleyball, golf. **Clubs:** chess, natural history, photography, ceramics, gymnastics. **Tests:** SAT, TOEFL. **Graduates attending college:** 90%. **Graduates have attended:** Wisconsin, Babson, Columbia, Notre Dame, Louisiana State U. **Location:** 1 mile from city of La Romana, overlooking Caribbean Sea. **Library:** 15,000 volumes. **Facilities:** 7 buildings, 28 classrooms, auditorium, 3 science labs, computer lab, softball field, soccer field, volleyball/basketball court, air conditioning.

**Dominican peso

SANTIAGO

SANTIAGO CHRISTIAN SCHOOL

Street address: Km. 5.5 Autopista Duarte, Santiago, Dominican Republic
Phone: (1)(809)5820447 **Facsimile:** (1)(809)5814613
E-mail: c.school@codetel.net.do
Mail: Apartado 62, Santiago, Dominican Republic
U.S. mail: PO Box 5600, Ft. Lauderdale, FL 33340, U.S.A.
Director: Richard York
Secondary principal: Sandra Gonzales

Teaching staff: full-time, 33; part-time, 12; total, 45
Nationalities of teaching staff: U.S., 29; host, 16; total, 45
Grade levels: preK – 12
Enrollment: preK, 45; K, 34; 1 – 6, 200; 7 – 9, 75; 10 – 12, 66; total, 420
Nationalities of student body: U.S., 193; host, 200; other, 27; total, 420
Teacher/student ratio: 1/11
Tuition (annual): preK – K, $1,600; 1 – 6, $2,150; 7 – 9, $2,460; 10 – 12, $3,190
Other fees: capital levy*, $1,500
School year: September to June

Year founded: 1968. **Type of school:** coed, church-related. **Governed by:** appointed board of directors. **Accredited by:** Southern.

Curriculum/physical plant

Type: U.S. **Languages taught:** Spanish. **Staff specialists:** reading, computer, nurse, music. **Special curricular:** art, physical education, computer instruction. **Extracurricular:** drama, yearbook, newspaper, field trips, National Honor Society, young life, student council. **Sports:** baseball, basketball, soccer, volleyball. **Tests:** PSAT, SAT, Stanford. **Graduates attending college:** 90%. **Graduates have attended:** U. of Michigan, Ohio State U., State U. of New York, U. of Miami. **Location:** in rural area, 5 kilometers from Santiago. **Campus:** 11 acres. **Library:** 7,000 volumes. **Facilities:** 4 buildings, 26 classrooms, cafeteria, playing field, science lab, computer lab.

*Once only fee

SANTO DOMINGO

The Carol Morgan School of Santo Domingo

Street address: Ave. Sarasota esq. Nunez de Caceres, Santo Domingo, Dominican Republic
Phone: (1)(809)5378080 **Facsimile:** (1)(809)5339222
E-mail: headmaster@cms.edu.do **Web:** http://www.cms.edu.do
Mail: Apartado 1169, Santo Domingo, Dominican Republic
U.S. mail: (no personal name) The Carol Morgan School of Santo Domingo, EPS-P-2379, PO Box 02-5261, Miami, FL 33102-5261, U.S.A.
Headmaster: Dr. Ralph Jahr
Secondary school principal: Harold Fleetham
Middle school principal: Roger Bicksler
Elementary school principal: Dr. Frank Jennings
Business manager: Rebeca Paiewonsky
Teaching staff: full-time, 84; total, 84
Nationalities of teaching staff: U.S., 55; host, 18; other, 11; total, 84
Grade levels: preK – 12
Enrollment: preK, 51; K, 63; 1 – 5, 305; 6 – 8, 162; 9 – 12, 220; total, 801
Nationalities of student body: U.S., 150; host, 560; other, 91; total, 801
Tuition (annual): preK, $3,000; K, $3,846; 1, $4,962; 2 – 3, $5,077; 4 – 5, $5,538; 6, $5,821; 7 – 8, $6,107; 9 – 12, $6,654

Other fees: enrollment*: 1 – 5, $2,143; 6 – 8, $2,500; 9 – 12, $2,857
School year: August to June

Year founded: 1933. **Type of school:** coed, day. **Governed by:** elected board of directors. **Accredited by:** Southern. **Regional organizations:** ACCAS, Tri-Assoc.

Curriculum/physical plant

Type: U.S., AP. **Languages taught:** Spanish. **Staff specialists:** computer, counselor, nurse. **Special programs:** ESL. **Special curricular:** art, chorus, band, physical education, computer instruction, drama, creative writing. **Extracurricular:** drama, yearbook, newspaper, literary magazine, interscholastic and intramural athletics, various clubs. **Tests:** SSAT, PSAT, SAT, ACT, AP, Iowa, MAT, ACH. **Graduates attending college:** 95%. **Graduates have attended:** Stanford, U. of Pennsylvania, Smith, U. of Texas, MIT. **Location:** in city. **Campus:** 12 acres. **Library:** 20,000 volumes. **Facilities:** 8 buildings, 53 classrooms, cafeteria, infirmary, gymnasium, 3 playing fields, 3 computer labs, science building with 6 laboratories.

*Once only fee

ECUADOR

Region: South America
Size: 105,037 square miles
Population: 11,466,291
Capital: Quito
Telephone code: 593
Currency: sucre
Languages: Spanish, Quechuan, Other Amerindian

GUAYAQUIL

Colegio Americano de Guayaquil

Street address: Avda. Juan Tanca Marengo, Km. 6-1/2, Guayaquil, Ecuador
Phone: (593)(4)255503 **Facsimile:** (593)(4)250453
E-mail: amschool@telconet.net
Mail: Apartado 09-01-3304, Guayaquil, Ecuador
U.S. mail: Air Center 1452, 2898 NW 79 Ave., Miami, FL 33152-1053, U.S.A.
Director general: Robert E. Thompson
High school principal: Irene Secaira
Elementary school principal: Nancy Rohde
Preschool principal: Maria Elena Pin
Head of computer services: Luis Costales
Teaching staff: full-time, 118; part-time, 17; total, 135
Grade levels: N – 12
Enrollment: N – K, 266; 1 – 6, 750; 7 – 12, 684; total, 1,700
Teacher/student ratio: 1/15
Tuition (annual): N – K, $1,575; 1 – 6, $1,638; 7 – 12, $1,752
Other fees (annual): computer, $80; IB, 7 – 9, $46; 10 – 12, $203
School year: April to January

Year founded: 1942. **Type of school:** coed, day, private nonprofit, nonsectarian, bilingual, bicultural. **Governed by:** elected board of directors. **Sponsored by:** school board. **Accredited by:** Southern (in process). **Regional organizations:** Andean Association of IB Schools, AASSA.

Curriculum/physical plant

Type: U.S., national, IB. **Languages of instruction:** English, Spanish. **Staff specialists:** computer, counselors, ESL, librarians, IB-MYP coordinator, IB coordinator, curriculum coordinator, 2 school physicians. **Special programs:** business education. **Special curricular:** art, physical education, computer instruction, music. **Extracurricular:** gymnastics, yearbook, chorus, chess, debate, student council. **Sports:** baseball, basketball, football, swimming, volleyball, roller blade hockey. **Tests:** PSAT, TOEFL, IB, CTBS, TAP, SLEP. **Graduates attending college:** 95%. **Graduates have attended:** Catholic U., Polytechnical U., Brookdale College, UCLA, Carnegie-Mellon. **Location:** North Guayaquil. **Campus:** 30 acres. **Library:** 9,000 volumes. **Facilities:** 20 buildings, 70 classrooms, auditorium, 2 infirmaries, 3 science labs, 4 computer labs, 2 football fields, baseball field, weight room.

Inter-American Academy

Street address: Km. 10-1/2 via a la Costa, Guayaquil, Ecuador
Phone: (593)(4)870448 **Facsimile:** (593)(4)873358
E-mail: admin@acig.k12.ec **Web:** http://www.acig.k12.ec
Mail: PO Box 09-06-209-U, Guayaquil, Ecuador
U.S. mail: Inter-American Academy, Suite 8227, 6964 NW 50th Street, Miami, FL 33166-5632, U.S.A.
Executive director: Raymond Marshall
Secondary school principal: Michael Dale
Elementary school principal: Amalfis Meija
Accountant: Humberto Acosta
Teaching staff: full-time, 31; total, 31
Nationalities of teaching staff: U.S., 18; host, 5; other, 8; total, 31
Grade levels: preK – 12
Enrollment: preK, 16; K, 14; 1 – 6, 145; 7 – 9, 73; 10 – 12, 72; total, 320
Nationalities of student body: U.S., 67; host, 105; other, 148; total, 320
Tuition (annual): preK, $4,150; K, $4,750; 1 – 8, $5,720; 9 – 12, $6,260
Other fees (annual): capital levy*, $1,500; ELC, $792; ESL, $234; application, $50
School year: August to May

Year founded: 1979. **Type of school:** coed, day. **Governed by:** elected board of directors. **Accredited by:** Southern, Ecuadorean Ministry of Education. **Regional organizations:** AAIE, AASSA.

Curriculum/physical plant

Type: U.S., IB, AP. **Languages taught:** French, Spanish. **Staff specialists:** counselor. **Special programs:** ESL. **Special curricular:** art, physical education, computer instruction, music. **Extracurricular:** drama, computers, yearbook, newspaper, literary magazine, photography, excursions/expeditions, National Honor Society, student council. **Tests:** PSAT, ACT, TOEFL, IB, MAT, SAT I, SAT II, GRE. **Graduates attending college:** 99%. **Graduates have attended:** U. of Miami, U. of British Columbia, William & Mary, Purdue, Boston College. **Location:** in Puerto Azul, a suburb of Guayaquil. **Campus:** 28,000 square meters. **Library:** 10,000 volumes. **Facilities:** 10 buildings, 32 classrooms, cafeteria, tennis court, 2 playing fields, science lab, computer labs, video room.

*Once only fee

QUITO

ALLIANCE ACADEMY

Street address: Villalengua 789, Quito, Ecuador
Phone: (593)(2)466985 **Facsimile:** (593)(2)440350 **E-mail:** alliance@hcjb.org.ec
Mail: Casilla 17-11-06186, Quito, Ecuador
Director: Daniel J. Egeler, Ph.D.
Secondary school principal: Timothy Wilbanks, Ed.D.
Elementary school principal: Timothy Sheppard
Teaching staff: full-time, 37; part-time, 22; total, 59
Nationalities of teaching staff: U.S., 48; host, 8; other, 3; total, 59
Grade levels: preK – 12
Enrollment: preK, 24; K, 19; 1 – 6, 162; 7 – 8, 80; 9 – 12, 184; total, 469
Nationalities of student body: U.S., 261; host, 75; other, 133; total, 469
Capacity: preK, 24; K, 40; 1 – 6, 240; 6 – 8, 120; 9 – 12, 240; total, 664
Teacher/student ratio: 1/8
Boarders: boys, 41; girls, 23 **Grades:** 1 – 12 **Program:** planned 7-day
Tuition (annual): pre-K – K, $2,550; 1 – 6, $5,100; 7 – 8, $5,500; 9 – 12, $5,900
Other fees (annual): insurance, $16; activities, $8.50; yearbook, $30
School year: August to June

Year founded: 1929. **Type of school:** coed, day, boarding, church-related. **Governed by:** elected and appointed school board. **Sponsored by:** Christian and Missionary Alliance. **Accredited by:** Southern, ACSI. **Regional organizations:** AASSA.

Curriculum

Type: U.S., AP. **Languages taught:** French, Spanish. **Staff specialists:** reading, computer, learning disabilities, nurse, counselors. **Special programs:** ESL, educational therapy. **Special curricular:** art, chorus, band, physical education, computer instruction, home economics, woodshop, photography, journalism, pre-vocational education. **Extracurricular:** drama, gymnastics, choral and instrumental music, computers, yearbook, newspaper, photography, field trips. **Sports:** basketball, soccer, track and field, volleyball, intramural sports. **Clubs:** National Honor Society, student council, music ensemble, Christian Service Organization, mountain-climbing, garden, video. **Tests:** PSAT, SAT, ACT, TOEFL, AP, Stanford, OVIS. **Graduates attending college:** 95%. **Graduates have attended:** Wheaton College, California Polytechnical Institute, Bethel College, Notre Dame, U. of Pennsylvania.

Physical plant

Location: in northern section of Quito. **Campus:** 5 acres. **Library:** 32,000 volumes. **Facilities:** 8 buildings, 50 classrooms, auditorium, infirmary, covered play area, tennis court, gymnasium, 2 playing fields, 3 science labs, 3 computer labs, 5 associated dormitories.

American School of Quito

Street address: Carcelén, Quito, Ecuador
Phone: (593)(2)472974 – 5 **Facsimile:** (593)(2)472972
E-mail: pponce@uio.satnet.net
Mail: PO Box 1701157, Quito, Ecuador
U.S. mail: (no personal name) Director, ASQ, c/o U.S. Embassy Quito, Unit 5372-Box 004, APO AA Miami 34039
Director: Pilar Ponce
Director of international program: Susan Barba
High school director: Irma de Serrano
Elementary principal: Susana Hervas
Secondary English coordinator: Susan Davalos
Teaching staff: full-time, 262; total, 262
Nationalities of teaching staff: U.S., 54; host, 174; other, 34; total, 262
Grade levels: K – 12
Enrollment: K – 6, 1,261; 7 – 12, 1,128; total, 2,389
Teacher/student ratio: 1/10
Tuition (annual): international section: K, $2,450; 1 – 6, $4,300; 7 – 12, $4,400; national section: K – 3, $1,992; 4 – 6, $1,807; 7 – 12, $1,944
Other fees (annual): registration, $200; capital levy*, $200; insurance, $13; busing, $300; books and materials, $215; equipment, $300
School year: September to June

Year founded: 1939. **Type of school:** coed, day, private nonprofit, bilingual. **Governed by:** elected board of administration. **Accredited by:** Southern, Ecuadorean Ministry of Education. **Regional organizations:** AAIE, ACCAS, AASSA, Tri-Assoc.

Curriculum

Type: U.S., national, IB. **Languages taught:** English, Spanish. **Staff specialists:** nurse, counselors, psychologists, medical doctor, pediatrician. **Special programs:** ESL, honors sections, learning disabilities. **Extracurricular:** drama, computers, newspaper, literary magazine, field trips, book club, mathematics, physics, English, Model UN. **Sports:** baseball, basketball, hockey, soccer, track and field, volleyball, ping-pong, Olympic gymnastics. **Clubs:** Girl Scouts, National Honor Society, Model UN, ecology, journalism, music, ceramics, flower and garden, video, theater and drama, forensics. **Tests:** PSAT, SAT, TOEFL, IB, Iowa. **Graduates attending college:** 99%. **Graduates have attended:** Cornell, Carnegie-Mellon, Brown, Yale, Wellesley.

Physical plant

Location: in suburban area, 17 kilometers north of city. **Campus:** 22 acres. **Libraries:** 29,300 volumes. **Facilities:** 14 buildings, 110 classrooms, auditorium, infirmary, gymnasium, 7 playing fields, 8 science labs, 5 computer labs, 2 snack bars, 3 AV rooms, language lab, track and stadium, multipurpose coliseum.

*Once only fee

Cotopaxi Academy
American International School

Street address: De las Higuerillas y Alondras (Monteserrin), Quito, Ecuador
Phone: (593)(2)433602/434976 **Facsimile:** (593)(2)445195
E-mail: director@cotopaxi.k12.ec
Mail: PO Box 17-01-199, Quito, Ecuador
U.S. mail: (no personal name) c/o American Embassy Quito (Coto), Unit 5373, APO AA 34039-3420
Superintendent: Donald Wise, Ph.D.
High school principal: Richard McBee
Middle school principal: Dale Hill
Elementary school principal: Monica Medina-Olds, Ed.D.
Registrar: Paola T. Pereira
Teaching staff: full-time, 91; part-time, 10; total, 101
Nationalities of teaching staff: U.S., 70; host, 17; other, 14; total, 101
Grade levels: preK – 12
Enrollment: preK – K, 131; 1 – 5, 304; 6 – 8, 176; 9 – 12, 193; total, 804
Teacher/student ratio: 1/8
Tuition (annual): preK, $3,010; K, $5,770; 1 – 2, $6,080; 3 – 5, $6,240; 6 – 8, $7,170; 9 – 12, $7,690
Other fees (annual): registration*, $150 (returning students), $250 (new students); capital levy*, $2,500; busing, $400 – 500
School year: August to June

Year founded: 1959. **Type of school:** coed, day, private nonprofit. **Governed by:** elected board of directors. **Accredited by:** Southern. **Regional organizations:** AASSA.

Curriculum/physical plant

Type: U.S., IB. **Languages taught:** Spanish, French. **Staff specialists:** reading, math, computer, psychologist, learning disabilities, nurse, counselors. **Special programs:** ESL, honors sections, remedial. **Special curricular:** art, band, physical education, computer instruction, orchestra, glee club. **Extracurricular:** drama, dance, choral and instrumental music, computers, yearbook, newspaper, photography, excursions/expeditions, field trips, Model UN. **Sports:** basketball, volleyball, soccer, softball. **Clubs:** honor society, student council, cheerleaders, outing clubs, social action. **Tests:** PSAT, SAT, ACT, TOEFL, IB, MAT, Otis-Lennon. **Graduates attending college:** 90%. **Graduates have attended:** Harvard, Brown, Virginia Tech, U. of Pennsylvania, Cornell. **Location:** in city. **Campus:** 7 hectares. **Libraries:** 32,000 volumes. **Facilities:** 80 classrooms, auditorium, 2 cafeterias, infirmary, gymnasium, 2 playing fields, 3 computer labs, swimming pool, music complex, 4 art rooms.

*Once only fee

EGYPT

Region: Africa
Size: 385,229 square miles
Population: 63,575,107
Capital: Cairo
Telephone code: 20
Currency: pound
Languages: Arabic, English, French

ALEXANDRIA

Schutz American School

Street address: 51 Schutz Street, Alexandria, Egypt
Phone: (20)(3)5701435/5712205 **Facsimile:** (20)(3)5710229
E-mail: 103375.1022@compuserve.com
Mail: PO Box 1000, Alexandria, Egypt
Headmaster: Lawrence Pattee, Ph.D.
Assistant headmaster: Ronald Walters
Teaching staff: full-time, 28; part-time, 2; total, 30
Nationalities of teaching staff: U.S., 17; host, 7; other, 6; total, 30
Grade levels: N – 12
Enrollment: N – preK, 19; K, 10; 1 – 6, 93; 7 – 9, 48; 10 – 12, 45; total, 215
Nationalities of student body: U.S., 59; host, 61; other, 95; total, 215
Capacity: N – preK, 15; K, 15; 1 – 6, 100; 7 – 9, 60; 10 – 12, 60; total, 250
Teacher/student ratio: 1/7
Tuition (annual): N, $3,650; K, $6,810; 1 – 4, $8,020; 5 – 8, $8,260; 9 – 12, $8,740
Other fees: registration*, $1,030
School year: September to June

Year founded: 1924. **Type of school:** coed, day, private nonprofit. **Governed by:** local board. **Accredited by:** ECIS, New England. **Regional organizations:** AAIE, ECIS, NESA.

Curriculum/physical plant

Type: U.S., AP. **Languages taught:** French, Spanish, Arabic. **Staff specialists:** computer, nurse, ESL. **Special programs:** ESL. **Special curricular:** art, computer instruction, music. **Extracurricular:** drama, computers, yearbook, newspaper, athletics, academic games. **Tests:** PSAT, SAT, TOEFL, AP, ITBS. **Graduates attending college:** 95%. **Location:** in residential area of Alexandria. **Campuses (2):** 3 acres. **Libraries (2):** 20,000 volumes. **Facilities:** 7 buildings, 20 classrooms, auditorium, cafeteria, 2 infirmaries, tennis court, playing field, 2 science labs, 2 computer labs, swimming pool, snack bar.

*Once only fee

CAIRO

The American International School in Egypt

Street address: Ismailia Road–Ahmed Orabi Zone, Cairo, Egypt
Phone: (20)(2)4770044 **Facsimile:** (20)(2)4770055
E-mail: ais@powermail.intouch.com
Mail: PO Box 8090, Masaken Nasr City 11371, Cairo, Egypt
Chairman/superintendent: Walid Abushakra
Associate superintendent: Dr. Guy Lott, Jr.
Chief operating officer: Wahib Girgis
High school principal: Glen Hadlock, Ed.D.
Business manager: Mamdouh Mazhar
Teaching staff: full-time, 90; total, 90
Nationalities of teaching staff: U.S., 76; host, 14; total, 90
Grade levels: preK – 12
Enrollment: preK, 20; K, 40; 1 – 6, 310; 7 – 9, 200; 10 – 12, 190; total, 760
Nationalities of student body: U.S., 110; U.K., 12; host, 390; other, 248; total, 760
Capacity: preK, 40; K, 80; 1 – 6, 310; 7 – 9, 370; 10 – 12, 400; total, 1,200
Teacher/student ratio: 1/8
Tuition (annual): preK – K, $4,400; 1 – 4, $5,500; 5 – 8, $6,500; 9 – 12, $6,750
Other fees (annual): busing, $800; building fund*, $1,500
School year: September to June

Year founded: 1990. **Type of school:** coed, day. **Accredited by:** Middle States, Egyptian Ministry of Education. **Regional organizations:** AAIE, ECIS, NESA.

Curriculum/physical plant

Type: U.S., IB. **Languages taught:** English, French, Arabic. **Staff specialists:** computer, counselor, nurse, special education. **Special programs:** ESL, honors sections. **Special curricular:** art, chorus, band, physical education, computer instruction, Model UN. **Extracurricular:** drama, choral and instrumental music, computers, yearbook, newspaper, excursions/expeditions, field trips, National Honor Society. **Sports:** basketball, soccer, tennis, track and field, volleyball, intramurals. **Clubs:** chess, computer, drama, science, French, intramurals, running, aerobics. **Tests:** PSAT, SAT, TOEFL, IB. **Graduates attending college:** 100%. **Location:** in pollution-free suburban northeast Cairo. **Campus:** 12 acres. **Library:** 20,000 volumes. **Facilities:** 2 buildings, 90 classrooms, auditorium, cafeteria, infirmary, gymnasium, 6 science labs, 3 computer labs, large playing fields, state-of-the-art media center, air conditioning.

*Once only fee

British International School, Cairo

Street address: Imara el Yemani Street, Zamalek, Cairo, Egypt
Phone: (20)(2)3406674/3415959 **Facsimile:** (20)(2)3414168
Mail: PO Box 137, Gezira, Cairo, Egypt
Principal: Alun Cooper
Head of seniors: Anthony Lindoe
Head of primary: Jeremy Long
Teaching staff: full-time, 46; part-time, 4; total, 50
Nationalities of teaching staff: U.K., 36; other, 14; total, 50
Grade levels: kindergarten (ages 3 – 4); primary (ages 4 – 11); seniors (ages 11 – 18)
Enrollment: kindergarten, 30; primary, 320; seniors, 200; total, 550
Teacher/student ratio: 1/11
Tuition (annual): kindergarten, 2,100**; primary, 4,260; seniors, 5,055; IB, 5,490
Other fees: registration*, 100**; admission*: primary, 1,420; seniors, 1,685; IB, 1,830; supply fund*, 700
School year: September to June

Year founded: 1976. **Type of school:** coed, day, private nonprofit. **Governed by:** board of directors. **Regional organizations:** ECIS.

Curriculum/physical plant

Type: U.K., IB, GCSE. **Languages taught:** French, Spanish, German, Arabic. **Staff specialists:** reading, computer, counselor, nurse, librarian. **Special curricular:** art, chorus, physical education, computer instruction. **Extracurricular:** drama, gymnastics, dance, computers, yearbook, field trips. **Sports:** athletics, badminton, basketball, dance, gymnastics, netball, soccer, swimming, table tennis, tennis, volleyball, Tae Kwon Do. **Clubs:** chess, Brownies, Guides, Bookworms, Cubs. **Tests:** IB, GCSE. **Graduates attending college:** 80%. **Graduates have attended:** Oxford U., Cambridge U., London School of Economics, Toronto U., Sorbonne. **Location:** in Zamalek, a multinational residential area on an island in Cairo. **Libraries:** 10,000 volumes. **Facilities:** 1 building, 30 classrooms, auditorium, infirmary, 2 covered play areas, 2 gymnasiums, 3 playing fields, 3 science labs, computer lab, AV-aids room.

*Once only fee **Pound sterling

Cairo American College

Street address: 1 Midan Digla, Maadi, Cairo, Egypt 11431
Phone: (20)(2)3529244/3529393 **Facsimile:** (20)(2)3523057
E-mail: bhetzel@tc.cac.edu.eg
Mail: PO Box 39, Maadi, Cairo, Egypt 11431
U.S. mail: (no personal name) Superintendent, CAC, c/o American Embassy, Unit 64900-Box 21, APO AE 09839-4900
Superintendent: Dr. Robert Hetzel
Assistant superintendent: Dr. Gordon Anderson
High school principal: Dr. Paul Chmelik
Middle school principal: Douglas Joy
Elementary school principal: Sandy Smith
Teaching staff: full-time, 149; part-time, 18; total, 167
Nationalities of teaching staff: U.S., 127; U.K., 4; host, 15; other, 21; total, 167
Grade levels: K – 12
Enrollment: K, 78; 1 – 5, 449; 6 – 8, 330; 9 – 12, 475; total, 1,332
Nationalities of student body: U.S., 733; U.K., 28; host, 177; other, 394; total, 1,332
Capacity: K, 75; 1 – 5, 475; 6 – 8, 360; 9 – 12, 520; total, 1,430
Teacher/student ratio: 1/8
Tuition (annual): K – 5, $9,120; 6 – 8, $9,370; 9 – 12, $9,120
Other fees (annual): registration, $2,475; busing, $1,340; capital equipment, $930; ESL $2,730; building and construction, $210; AP and IB tests
School year: August to June

Year founded: 1945. **Type of school:** coed, day, private nonprofit. **Governed by:** appointed and elected board of directors. **Accredited by:** Middle States. **Regional organizations:** NESA, AISA.

Curriculum

Type: U.S., IB, AP. **Languages taught:** French, Spanish, Arabic. **Staff specialists:** reading, math, computer, counselor, psychologist, nurse, speech/language, learning resource. **Special programs:** ESL, academic tutorial. **Special curricular:** chorus, band, physical education, computer instruction, fine and applied arts, business education. **Co-curricular:** drama, instrumental music, literary magazine, Model UN, Close Up, math, speech and debate, student council, National Honor Society, Arabic, French, Spanish, World Rights, community service, International Club, Quill and Scroll, Future Business Leaders, middle school intramural program, elementary after-school activities program. **Sports:** badminton, baseball, basketball, cheerleading, cross-country, soccer, softball, swimming, tennis, track and field, volleyball, wrestling. **Tests:** SSAT, PSAT, SAT I and II, ACT, TOEFL, IB, AP, ITBS. **Graduates attending college:** 95%. **Graduates have attended:** American U. in Cairo, Wesleyan, Oberlin, Duke, Brown.

Physical plant

Location: in Maadi, a residential suburb near River Nile about 6 miles south of Cairo. **Campus:** 11 acres. **Library:** 63,000 volumes; 7,000 AV materials. **Facilities:** 12 buildings, over 126 classrooms, auditorium, gymnasium, 2 playing fields, 12 science labs, 6 computer labs, swimming pool, health clinic, tennis courts, media center, industrial arts building, 400-meter all-weather track, air conditioning.

EL SALVADOR

Region: Central America
Size: 8,124 square miles
Population: 5,828,987
Capital: San Salvador
Telephone code: 503
Currency: colon
Language: Spanish

SAN SALVADOR

AMERICAN SCHOOL OF EL SALVADOR

Street address: Final Calle La Mascota #3, Colonia La Mascota, San Salvador, El Salvador
Phone: (503)2234353 **Facsimile:** (503)2790337 **E-mail:** wscotti@trojans.edu.sv
Mail: PO Box (01) 35, San Salvador, El Salvador, C.A.
U.S. mail: Superintendent, American School of El Salvador, Unit No. 3123, APO AA 34023
Superintendent: (to be announced)
Secondary school principal: Larry Smith
Middle school principal: Krikor Ghazarian
Elementary school principal: Santiago Guajardo
Teaching staff: full-time, 124; part-time, 2; total, 126
Nationalities of teaching staff: U.S., 58; host, 60; other, 8; total, 126
Grade levels: preK – 12
Enrollment: preK, 88; K, 109; 1 – 6, 544; 6 – 8, 375; 9 – 12, 446; total, 1,562
Nationalities of student body: U.S., 175; host, 1,297; other, 90; total, 1,562
Teacher/student ratio: 1/12
Tuition (annual): preK – K, $3,300; 1 – 12, $3,800
Other fees (annual): registration*, $2,500; activity, $150
School year: August to June

Year founded: 1946. **Type of school:** coed, day. **Governed by:** elected board of directors. **Accredited by:** Southern, Salvadoran Ministry of Education. **Regional organizations:** NAIS, AASCA, Tri-Assoc., AAIE.

Curriculum/physical plant

Type: U.S., AP. **Languages taught:** French, Spanish. **Staff specialists:** reading, math, computer, counselor, learning disabilities, nurse. **Special programs:** honors sections, remedial. **Special curricular:** art, chorus, physical education, computer instruction. **Extracurricular:** drama, dance, choral music, computers, yearbook, newspaper, photography, field trips. **Sports:** basketball, soccer, softball, volleyball, intramurals. **Clubs:** chess, computer, social services, math. **Tests:** SSAT, PSAT, SAT, ACT, TOEFL, Stanford, Iowa. **Graduates attending college:** 99%. **Graduates have attended:** U. of Texas, Texas A&M, Purdue, Harvard, Emory. **Location:** in pleasant residential area, 10 minutes from San Salvador. **Campus:** 40 acres. **Libraries:** 50,000 volumes. **Facilities:** 19 buildings, auditorium, 2 cafeterias, 3 playing fields, 4 science labs, 3 computer labs, 2 health rooms.

*Once only fee **1996–97 listing**

Colegio Internacional de San Salvador

Street address: Calle la Reforma 169, Colonia San Benito, San Salvador, El Salvador
Phone: (503)2241330 **Facsimile:** (503)2237335
Mail: Apartado 05-15, San Salvador, El Salvador
Principal: Chester Stemp
Teaching staff: full-time, 21; part-time, 10; total, 31
Nationalities of teaching staff: U.S., 18; host, 13; total, 31
Grade levels: preK – 12
Enrollment: preK, 24; K, 24; 1 – 6, 144; 7 – 9, 70; 10 – 12, 73; total, 335
Nationalities of student body: U.S., 90; host, 150; other, 95; total, 335
Capacity: preK, 24; K, 24; 1 – 6, 144; 7 – 9, 72; 10 – 12, 72; total, 336
Teacher/student ratio: 1/13
Tuition (annual): preK – K, $2,015; 1 – 9, $2,255; 10 – 12, $2,455
Other fees (annual): registration*, $1,200; books, $50 – 150
School year: August to June

Year founded: 1979. **Type of school:** coed, day, proprietary. **Governed by:** board of owners. **Accredited by:** Salvadoran Ministry of Education, Southern (in process). **Regional organizations:** AASCA, Tri-Assoc.

Curriculum/physical plant

Type: U.S., equivalency to national program optional. **Languages of instruction:** English (80%), Spanish (20%). **Languages taught:** English, French, Spanish. **Staff specialists:** counselor, librarian. **Special programs:** ESL, correspondence, Spanish as a Second Language. **Special curricular:** physical education. **Extracurricular:** drama, yearbook, newspaper, ballet, excursions. **Sports:** basketball, swimming, volleyball, intramurals. **Clubs:** student council, yearbook, newspaper, first-aid. **Tests:** PSAT, SAT, ACT, TOEFL, Iowa. **Graduates attending college:** 95%. **Graduates have attended:** St. Lawrence, William and Mary, San José State, Liberty, Florida International. **Location:** in upper-income residential area. **Campus:** 1 acre. **Library:** 3,000 volumes. **Facilities:** 2 buildings, 17 classrooms, gymnasium, science lab, computer lab, swimming pool.

*Once only fee

SANTA TECLA

Academia Britanica Cuscatleca

Street address: Kilometro 10-1/2 Carretera Santa Tecla, El Salvador
Phone: (503)2282011 **Facsimile:** (503)2282956 **E-mail:** rbraund@es.com.sv
Mail: Apartado Postal 121, Santa Tecla, El Salvador
Headmaster: Ralph Braund
Deputy head: Ian Morris
Director of studies: Brian Martin
Head of library: Nora Huezo
Head of computer services: Silvia Franco

Teaching staff: full-time, 120; part-time, 6; total, 126
Nationalities of teaching staff: U.S., 1; U.K., 30; host, 95; total, 126
Grade levels: preK – 12
Enrollment: preK, 72; K, 92; 1 – 6, 480; 7 – 9, 196; 10 – 12, 183; total, 1,023
Nationalities of student body: U.S., 63; U.K., 12; host, 824; other, 124; total, 1,023
Teacher/student ratio: 1/8
Tuition: preK, $1,568; K, $1,920; 1 – 6, $2,306; 7 – 12, $2,397
Other fees: registration*, $1,400
School year: August to June

Year founded: 1970. **Type of school:** coed, day, private nonprofit. **Governed by:** appointed board of governors. **Accredited by:** ECIS (in process).

Curriculum/physical plant

Type: U.K., national, IB, IGCSE. **Languages of instruction:** English, Spanish. **Languages taught:** English, French, Spanish. **Staff specialists:** nurse. **Special curricular:** art, physical education. **Extracurricular:** drama, choral and instrumental music, computers, newspaper, photography, student council, excursions/expeditions, field trips. **Sports:** basketball, street hockey, soccer, swimming, volleyball. **Tests:** PSAT, SAT, TOEFL, IB, GCSE. **Graduates attending college:** 100%. **Graduates have attended:** Skidmore, Texas A&M, William and Mary, Loyola, Manchester (U.K.). **Location:** in suburban area, one kilomenter from Santa Tecla. **Campus:** 20 acres. **Libraries (2):** 25,000 volumes. **Facilities:** 15 buildings, 75 classrooms, auditorium, 2 cafeterias, infirmary, covered play area, 4 tennis courts, gymnasium, playing field, 5 science labs, 3 computer labs, 2 swimming pools, air conditioning.

*Once only fee

ERITREA

Region: East Africa
Size: 45,300 square miles
Population: 3,909,628
Capital: Asmara
Telephone code: 291
Currency: birr
Languages: Tigrinya, Tigre

ASMARA

Asmara International Community School

Phone: (291)(1)161705 **Facsimile:** (291)(1)122904
Mail: PO Box 4941, Asmara, Eritrea
Director: Hannah McCarthy
Business manager: Neamin Ogbatensae
Teaching staff: full-time, 5; part-time, 3; total, 8
Nationalities of teaching staff: U.S., 2; U.K., 2; other, 4; total, 8
Grade levels: preK – 6
Enrollment: preK, 6; K, 7; 1 – 6, 31; total, 44
Nationalities of student body: U.S., 11; U.K., 3; host, 12; other, 18; total, 44
Teacher/student ratio: 1/6
Tuition (annual): preK – K, $3,500; 1 – 6, $6,400 – 6,900
Other fees (annual): registration, $100
School year: September to June

Year founded: 1994. **Type of school:** coed, day, private nonprofit. **Governed by:** appointed and elected board of governors. **Sponsored by:** International Community School Association of Asmara. **Regional organizations:** AISA.

Curriculum/physical plant

Type: U.S., international. **Languages taught:** French, Tigrinya. **Staff specialists:** computer. **Special programs:** supervision for independent study. **Location:** in Asmara. **Facilities:** 10 classrooms, auditorium, library, office, playground.

ESTONIA

Region: Eastern Europe
Size: 17,462 square miles
Population: 1,459,428
Capital: Tallinn
Telephone code: 372
Currency: kroon
Languages: Estonian, Latvian, Lithuanian, Russian

TALLINN

The International Elementary School of Estonia

Phone: (372)(2)430662 **E-mail:** iese@online.ee
Mail: Lahe #3, Tallinn EE0001, Estonia
Director: Leighton Brunt
Chairman of the board: Martin Dungay
Teaching staff: full-time, 5; part-time, 5; total, 10
Nationalities of teach2ing staff: U.S., 1; host, 2; other, 7; total, 10
Grade levels: preK – 8
Enrollment: preK, 13; K, 5; 1 – 6, 21; 7 – 8, 2; total, 41
Nationalities of student body: U.S., 9; U.K., 5; host, 8; other, 19; total, 41
Capacity: total, 50
Teacher/student ratio: 1/5
Tuition (annual): preK, 3,750**; K, 7,350; 1 – 8, 12,925
School year: September to June

Year founded: 1995. **Type of school:** coed, day, private nonprofit. **Governed by:** elected board of directors.

Curriculum/physical plant

Type: U.S., international. **Languages taught:** Estonian, German. **Special programs:** ESL. **Location:** in older residential neighborhood of central Tallinn, near park and sea. **Facilities:** 2 buildings, 4 classrooms, library.

**Deutsch mark

ETHIOPIA

Region: East Africa
Size: 437,794 square miles
Population: 57,171,662
Capital: Addis Ababa
Telephone code: 251
Currency: birr
Languages: Amharic,Tigrinya, Orominga

ADDIS ABABA

BINGHAM ACADEMY

Phone: (251)(1)791791 **Facsimile:** (251)(1)791783
E-mail: bingham@telecom.net.et
Mail: PO Box 4937, Addis Ababa, Ethiopia
U.S. mail: c/o SIM, PO Box 7900, Charlotte, NC 28241, U.S.A.
Principal: Judy Neil
Teaching staff: full-time, 13; part-time, 8; total, 21
Nationalities of teaching staff: U.S., 13; other, 8; total, 21
Grade levels: K – 8
Enrollment: K, 18; 1 – 6, 132; 7 – 8, 44; total, 194
Nationalities of student body: U.S., 52; U.K., 15; host, 44; other, 83; total, 194
Capacity: K, 18; 1 – 6, 132; 7 – 8, 44; total, 194
Teacher/student ratio: 1/13
Boarders (mission children): girls, 8 **Grades:** 1 – 8 **Program:** planned 5-day
Tuition (annual): K, $2,340; 1 – 6, $3,900; 7 – 8, $4,290
Other fees: testing, 30 – 50**
School year: September to June

Year founded: 1946. **Type of school:** coed, day, boarding, church-related, private nonprofit. **Governed by:** SIM International. **Regional organizations:** AISA.

Curriculum/physical plant

Type: international. **Languages taught:** French, Amharic. **Staff specialists:** computer, nurse, music. **Special curricular:** art, physical education, computer instruction, vocational. **Sports:** soccer, track and field. **Tests:** Stanford. **Graduates attending college:** 95%. **Graduates have attended:** many universities in North America and Europe. **Location:** secluded, wooded setting in Addis Ababa. **Campus:** 8 acres. **Library:** 12,000 volumes. **Facilities:** 9 buildings, 12 classrooms, auditorium, covered play area, tennis court, playing field, science lab, computer lab, small family-style boarding facilities.

**Ethiopian birr

International Community School/Addis Ababa

Phone: (251)(1)711544/710870/711062 **Facsimile:** (251)(1)710722
E-mail: ics@telecom.net.et
Mail: PO Box 70282, Addis Ababa, Ethiopia
Director: Ronald H. Schultz, Ph.D.
High school principal: Frank Walsh
Elementary school principal: Gordon Wiebe, Ph.D.
Teaching staff: full-time, 50; part-time, 1; total, 51
Grade levels: preK – 12
Enrollment: preK, 29; K, 30; 1 – 6, 208; 7 – 9, 105; 10 – 12, 118; total, 490
Nationalities of student body: U.S., 62; host, 119; other, 309; total, 490
Capacity: preK, 50; K, 50; 1 – 6, 250; 7 – 9, 150; 10 – 12, 150; total, 650
Teacher/student ratio: 1/10
Tuition (annual): preK, $3,080; K– 5, $7,441; 6 – 8, $8,403; 9 – 12, $8,641
Other fees (annual): registration, $500; capital levy, $1,500 (new student); $500 (returning student)
School year: August to June

Year founded: 1964. **Type of school:** coed, day. **Governed by:** elected board of governors. **Accredited by:** Middle States. **Regional organizations:** AAIE, ECIS, AISA.

Curriculum/physical plant

Type: U.S., IB, AP. **Languages taught:** French, Spanish, Amharic. **Staff specialists:** computer, counselor, resource. **Special programs:** ESL, independent study, remedial. **Special curricular:** art, band, physical education, computer instruction, drama, Model UN. **Extracurricular:** instrumental music, yearbook, newspaper, excursions/expeditions, magazine, student council. **Sports:** basketball, soccer, softball, swimming, tennis, track and field, volleyball, house intramurals. **Tests:** PSAT, SAT, IB, AP, ITBS, DAT. **Graduates attending college:** 90%. **Graduates have attended:** Columbia, Cornell, MIT, Harvard, Stanford. **Location:** on sloping, terraced land at base of mountains on edge of Addis Ababa. **Campus:** 15 acres. **Library:** 12,000 volumes. **Facilities:** 13 buildings, 27 classrooms, gymnasium, 2 playing fields, 3 science labs, 3 computer labs, 3 outdoor tennis courts, outdoor amphitheater, vocal music room, board room, multi–purpose room, outdoor basketball/volleyball courts.

Sandford English Community School

Phone: (251)(1)552275 **Facsimile:** (251)(1)551945
Mail: PO Box 30056 MA, Addis Ababa, Ethiopia
Headmaster: Michael J. Thompson
Secondary principal: Terry Hamilton
Primary principal: Diane O'Connell
Business manager: Samuel Mengistu
Teaching staff: full-time, 54; part-time, 3; total, 57
Nationalities of teaching staff: U.K., 34; host, 9; other, 14; total, 57
Grade levels: preK – 13
Enrollment: preK, 77; 1 – 6, 326; 7 – 9, 198; 10 – 11, 109; 12 – 13, 27; total, 737

Nationalities of student body: U.S., 26; U.K., 33; host, 348; other, 330; total, 737
Teacher/student ratio: 1/13
Tuition (annual): preK, $2,880; K, $4,230; 1 – 2, $5,100; 3 – 6, $5,340; 7 – 11, $6,390; 12 – 13, $6,720
Other fees (annual): capital levy, $180; admission*, $800
School year: September to July

Year founded: 1946. **Type of school:** coed, day, private nonprofit. **Governed by:** board of parent governors. **Regional organizations:** AISA, ECIS.

Curriculum/physical plant

Type: U.K., IB, IGCSE. **Languages taught:** French, German, Amharic. **Staff specialists:** reading, math, computer, learning disabilities, nurse. **Special programs:** ESL, remedial. **Special curricular:** art, physical education, computer instruction, music. **Extracurricular:** drama, dance, computers, field trips, community service activities. **Sports:** basketball, soccer, swimming, volleyball, track and field. **Tests:** IB, GCSE. **Location:** in suburban area, 4 miles from city center. **Campus:** 30,000 square meters. **Facilities:** 34 classrooms, auditorium, infirmary, gymnasium, 2 playing fields, 5 science labs, 2 computer labs, 3 libraries.

*Once only fee

FIJI

Region: South Pacific
Size: 7,055 square miles
Population: 782,381
Capital: Suva
Telephone code: 679
Currency: Fiji dollar
Languages: English, Fijian, Hindustani

SUVA

International School, Suva

Street address: Siga Road, Laucala Beach Estate, Suva, Fiji
Phone: (679)393300 **Facsimile:** (679)340017
Mail: PO Box 2393, Government Buildings, Suva, Fiji
Director: David Hill
Teaching staff: full-time, 53; total, 53
Nationalities of teaching staff: host, 27; other, 26; total, 53
Grade levels: prep – 12
Enrollment: prep, 40; K – 6, 320; 7 – 9, 190; 10 – 12, 100; total, 650
Capacity: prep, 50; K – 6, 400; 7 – 9, 200; 10 – 12, 100; total, 750
Teacher/student ratio: 1/13
Tuition (annual): prep, 1,836**; K – 6, 1,500 – 1,588; 7 – 9, 2,324 – 2,968; 10 – 12, 3,164
Other fees (annual): registration, 2,151**; capital levy, 350; busing, optional
School year: January to December

Year founded: primary, 1973; secondary, 1979. **Type of school:** coed, day, private nonprofit. **Governed by:** elected board of governors. **Accredited by:** U.K., Fiji, and Australia ministries of education.

Curriculum/physical plant

Type: U.K., national, IB, Australia, New Zealand. **Languages taught:** French, Japanese, Fijian, Hindi. **Staff specialists:** reading, computer. **Special programs:** ESL. **Special curricular:** art, chorus, physical education, computer instruction, vocational, drama. **Extracurricular:** drama, gymnastics, dance, choral music, yearbook, photography, excursions/expeditions, field trips. **Sports:** athletics, basketball, cricket, field hockey, netball, rugby, squash, swimming, tennis. **Tests:** SSAT, PSAT, TOEFL, IB, IGCSE, PAT (New Zealand aptitude tests), Fiji Form 7. **Graduates attending college:** 75%. **Location:** in suburban area, 9 kilometers from city center. **Campus:** 10 acres. **Library:** 12,000 volumes. **Facilities:** 5 buildings, 35 classrooms, 3 science labs, 2 computer labs, woodwork room, home economics room, music room, art/craft room.

**Fiji dollar

FINLAND

Region: Europe
Size: 130,559 square miles
Population: 5,105,230
Capital: Helsinki
Telephone code: 358
Currency: markka
Languages: Finnish, Swedish

HELSINKI

The English School

Street address: Mäntytie 14, 00270 Helsinki, Finland
Phone: (358)(0)904771123 **Facsimile:** (358)(0)904771980
Principal: Biruta Meirans, Ph.D.
Assistant principal: Liisa Kaskinen
Head of library: Marjatta Kurtén
Head of computer services: Heikki Naakka
Teaching staff: full-time, 28; part-time, 3; total, 31
Nationalities of teaching staff: U.S., 6; U.K., 2; host, 21; other, 2; total, 31
Grade levels: preK – 12
Enrollment: preK, 96; 1 – 6, 208; 7 – HS, 153; total, 457
Nationalities of student body: U.S., 5; host, 385; other, 67; total, 457
Capacity: preK, 51; K, 51; 1 – 6, 210; 7 – HS, 190; total, 502
Teacher/student ratio: 1/14
Tuition: 1,000 – 2,000** per semester; foreign pupils, 12,000 per semester, if not residency status
Other fees: registration*, 250**
School year: mid-August to June

Year founded: 1945. **Type of school:** coed, day, private nonprofit. **Governed by:** appointed board of directors. **Accredited by:** Finnish Ministry of Education.

Curriculum/physical plant

Type: U.S., national. **Languages of instruction:** English, Finnish. **Languages taught:** French, Spanish, German, Italian, Russian, Swedish. **Staff specialists:** reading, math, computer, nurse. **Special curricular:** art, chorus, physical education, computer instruction, vocational, drama. **Extracurricular:** choral music, computers, yearbook, photography, excursions/expeditions, field trips. **Sports:** gymnastics, skiing, track and field, skating. **Parent associations:** English School Friends, Alumni-Senior Association. **Graduates attending college:** 100%. **Location:** Helsinki. **Library:** 9,506 volumes. **Facilities:** 18 classrooms, auditorium, cafeteria, gymnasium, science labs, computer lab, handwork and technical handwork rooms, music, performing arts .

*Once only fee **Finnmark

International School of Helsinki

Street address: Selkamerenkatu 11, 00180 Helsinki, Finland
Phone: (358)(9)6866160 **Facsimile:** (358)(9)6856699
E-mail: mainoffice@ish.edu.hel.fi **Web:** http://www.ish.edu.hel.fi
Headmaster: William D. Rose
Teaching staff: full-time, 34; total, 34
Nationalities of teaching staff: U.S., 15; U.K., 7; host, 5; other, 7; total, 34
Grade levels: K – 12
Enrollment: K, 17; 1 – 6, 120; 7 – 9, 107; total, 244
Nationalities of student body: U.S., 49; U.K., 20; host, 68; other, 107; total, 244
Capacity: K, 25; 1 – 6, 150; 7 – 9, 150; total, 325
Teacher/student ratio: 1/8
Tuition (annual): K – 8, $9,260; 9– 12, $9,950
Other fees (annual): registration*, $800; busing, $3,250; lunch, $570
School year: August to June

Year founded: 1963. **Type of school:** coed, day, private nonprofit. **Governed by:** elected board of governors. **Accredited by:** New England, ECIS. **Regional organizations:** ECIS, CEESA.

Curriculum/physical plant

Type: U.S., U.K., IB, IGCSE. **Languages taught:** French, Swedish, Finnish. **Staff specialists:** computer, learning disabilities, nurse, librarian, music, physical education. **Special programs:** ESL, remedial. **Special curricular:** art, chorus, physical education, computer instruction, skiing/skating during winter. **Extracurricular:** field trips, chorus, afterschool club. **Tests:** Iowa, Richmond. **Location:** in center of Helsinki. **Library:** 12,000 volumes. **Facilities:** new, purpose-built, state-of-the-art campus, 25 classrooms, gymnasium, 2 science labs, 2 computer labs, auditorium/cafeteria, art suite with darkroom/kiln, music suite, computer networked, Internet access, school radio and TV channel, satellite TV.

*Once only fee

FRANCE

Region: Europe
Size: 210,026 square miles
Population: 58,040,230
Capital: Paris
Telephone code: 33
Currency: franc
Language: French

BORDEAUX

Bordeaux International School

Street address: 53 Rue de Laseppe, 33000 Bordeaux, France
Phone: (33)(57)870211 **Facsimile:** (33)(56)790047
Director: Christine Cussac
Head, secondary school: Tony Woodcock
Head, primary school: Judith Huguenin
Teaching staff: full-time, 6; part-time, 7; total, 13
Nationalities of teaching staff: U.K., 6; host, 4; other, 3; total, 13
Grade levels: K – 13
Enrollment: K, 4; 1 – 6, 16; 7 – 9, 20; 10 – 12, 20; 13, 7; total, 67
Nationalities of student body: U.S., 10; U.K., 30; host, 12; other, 15; total, 67
Capacity: K, 6; 1 – 6, 20; 7 – 9, 20; 10 – 12, 25; 13, 10; total, 81
Teacher/student ratio: 1/7
Boarders: boys, 6; girls, 7 **Grades:** 5 – 13
Tuition (annual): 1 – 9, 20,000**; 10 – 13, 55,000
Other fees: capital levy*, 2,500**; lunch, 25/day (10 – 13, lunch included in tuition)
School year: September through June

Year founded: 1988. **Type of school:** coed, day, boarding, private nonprofit. **Governed by:** Association Linguistique Culturelle Internationale. **Regional organizations:** ECIS.

Curriculum/physical plant

Type: U.S., U.K., national in primary. **Languages of instruction:** English, French. **Languages taught:** English, French, Spanish. **Special programs:** ESL. **Special curricular:** art, chorus, band, computer instruction. **Extracurricular:** drama, dance, choral and instrumental music, newspaper, excursions/expeditions, field trips. **Clubs:** debating, drama. **Tests:** SAT, ACT, A-level GCE, GCSE. **Graduates attending college:** 90%. **Graduates have attended:** London U.–Kings, Royal Holloway, Cardiff U., Cambridge–Fitzwilliam College, Bristol. **Location:** 5 minutes from city center. **Facilities:** 10 classrooms, cafeteria, covered play area, science lab, computer lab, neighborhood sports facilities, boarding in 2 teacher-run apartments or with French families.

*Once only fee **French franc

LE CHAMBON-SUR-LIGNON

College Lycee Cevenol International

Phone: (33)(71)597252 **Facsimile:** (33)(71)658738 **Cable:** COLCEV
Mail: 43400 Le Chambon-sur-Lignon, France
Head: Lionel Tarlet
Teaching staff: total, 38
Grade levels: 6 – 13, 2-year postgraduate program in international business
Enrollment: total, 400
Nationalities of student body: U.S., 10; host, 290; other, 100; total, 400
Capacity: total, 500
Teacher/student ratio: 1/11
Boarders: boys, 130; girls, 100 **Program:** planned 7-day
Tuition (annual, for foreign students): 6 – 13 (with special French), 9,634**; 6 – 13 (state education), 2,400
Other fees, (annual, for foreign students): registration, 2,460**; boarding, 38,587; medical insurance, 700
School year: September to June; 2 summer sessions

Year founded: 1938. **Type of school:** coed, day, boarding, private nonprofit. **Governed by:** elected board of directors. **Accredited by:** French government. **Regional organizations:** ECIS, ISA.

Curriculum/physical plant

Type: national. **Languages of instruction:** French. **Languages taught:** English, French, Spanish, German, Italian, Latin, Greek. **Special curricular:** art, band, physical education, computer instruction. **Extracurricular:** drama, gymnastics, dance, choral and instrumental music, computers, yearbook. **Sports:** badminton, basketball, soccer, tennis, volleyball, handball, horseback riding. **Tests:** French Baccalaureate. **Location:** in the Cevenne mountains, southwest of Lyon. **Campus:** 40 acres. **Facilities:** 15 buildings, 4 tennis courts, gymnasium, computer lab, language lab.

**French franc

LILLE

Ecole Active Bilingue Jeannine Manuel Ecole Internationale de Lille Metropole

Street address: 418 bis rue Albert Bailly, Marcq-en-Baroeul 59700, France
Phone: (33)(320)659050 **Facsimile:** (33)(320)980641
Headmistress: Mrs. Lux
Grade levels: 6 – 12
Enrollment: total, 400
Nationalities of student body: host, 320; other, 80; total, 400

Boarding capacity: total, 150
Tuition (annual): bilingual classes, 9,720**; international classes, 15,525
Other fees (annual): registration*, 700**; boarding, 45,480; lunch, 6,028

Year founded: 1992. **Type of school:** coed, day, boarding, proprietary. **Governed by:** appointed board of directors. **Sponsored and accredited by:** French Ministry of Education. **Regional organizations:** ECIS, ELSA.

Curriculum/physical plant

Type: national, IB. **Languages of instruction:** English, French. **Languages taught:** English, French, Spanish, German, Italian, Latin. **Extracurricular:** yearbook, newspaper, photography, games, ecology, excursions, field trips, Harvard Model Congress, Model UN. **Sports:** athletics, basketball, football, gymnastics, rugby, swimming, tennis, volleyball. **Tests:** PSAT, SAT, IB, Cambridge certificates. **Facilities:** cafeteria, infirmary, 3 science labs, computer lab, AV equipment, library, access to playing fields and swimming pools.

*Once only fee **French franc

LYON

Cite Scolaire Internationale de Lyon Gerland—Section Anglophone

Street address: 2 place de Montréal, 69007 Lyon, France
Phone: (33)(78)696006 **Facsimile:** (33)(78)696037/696011
Mail: 2 place de Montréal, 69361 Lyon Cedex 07, France
Headmaster: Ivan Delbarre
Assistant headmaster: C. Lebourgeois
Assistant principal: C. Rougon
Elementary head: A. Mattan
Director, Anglophone section: J. F. Larner, D.A.
Teaching staff: full-time, 13; total, 13
Nationalities of teaching staff: U.S., 5; U.K., 8; total, 13
Grade levels: 1 – 12
Enrollment: 1 – 5, 140; 6 – 9, 219; 10 – 12, 101; total, 460
Nationalities of student body: U.S., 30; U.K., 30; host, 300; other, 100; total, 460
Tuition (annual): 7,620**
Other fees (annual): busing, 800**; lunch, 22/each; books, 400 (high school)
School year: September to June

Year founded: 1987. **Type of school:** coed, day, public. **Anglophone section governed by:** elected board. **Sponsored and accredited by:** French Ministry of Education. **Regional organizations:** ECIS.

Curriculum/physical plant

Type: French IB. **Languages of instruction:** English, French (80%). **Languages taught:** Spanish, German, Italian, Japanese, Polish. **Staff specialists:** math, nurse, French as a Foreign Language. **Extracurricular:** drama, yearbook, newspaper, excursions/expeditions, field trips, sports, Model UN. **Tests:** PSAT, SAT, TOEFL, IGCSE, French International Option of Baccalaureate, Cambridge language exams. **Graduates attending college:** 100%. **Graduates have attended:** King's College, Imperial College, McGill, French universities, Harvard. **Location:** on riverfront parkland in Lyon. **Facilities:** 1 building, auditorium, 3 cafeterias, infirmary, 2 gymnasiums, 4 science labs, 3 computer labs, library.

**French franc

MOUGINS

Mougins School

Street address: 615, avenue Maurice Donat, 06251 Mougins, France
Phone: (33)(49)3901547 **Facsimile:** (33)(49)3753140
E-mail: mouginsschool@riviera.fr
Mail: BP 401, 06251 Mougins Cedex, France
Principal: Brian Hickmore
Teaching staff: full-time, 16; part-time, 8; total, 24
Nationalities of teaching staff: U.S., 2; U.K., 17; host, 3; other, 2; total, 24
Grade levels: preK – 12
Enrollment: preK – K, 42; 1 – 5, 58; 6 – 8, 40; 9 – 12, 40; total, 180
Nationalities of student body: U.S., 20; U.K., 61; host, 39; other, 60; total, 180
Capacity: preK – K, 54; 1 – 5, 110; 6 – 8, 66; 9 – 12, 66; total, 296
Teacher/student ratio: 1/9
Tuition (annual): preK – K, 46,000**; 1 – 5, 54,000; 6 – 8, 58,000; 9 – 12, 67,000
Other fees (annual): registration*, 1,000**; administration, 4,000
School year: September through June

Year founded: 1972. **Type of school:** coed, day, private nonprofit. **Governed by:** elected board of directors. **Regional organizations:** ECIS.

Curriculum

Type: U.K. **Languages taught:** English, French, German. **Staff specialists:** reading, math, computer, counselor, nurse. **Special programs:** ESL, advanced GCSE. **Special curricular:** art, physical education, computer instruction, business studies, local studies. **Extracurricular:** drama, gymnastics, dance, computers, yearbook, excursions/expeditions, field trips, music. **Sports:** athletics, baseball, basketball, cross-country, gymnastics, skiing, soccer, tennis, volleyball. **Clubs:** chess, drama, student council, science, orienteering. **Tests:** GCSE, AS and A-level GCE. **Graduates attending college:** 80%. **Graduates have attended:** Bath U., King's College, U. of Massachusetts, Ecole Nationale Supérieure, Toulouse.

Physical plant

Location: Sophia Antipolis multinational high-tech park on the French Riviera, 10 kilometers from Cannes. **Campus:** 5 acres. **Library:** 6,000 volumes. **Facilities:** 7 buildings, 22 classrooms, infirmary, gymnasium, science lab, 2 play areas, access to pool, playing fields, skiing.

*Once only fee **French franc

NEUILLY-SUR-SEINE

Marymount School

Street address: 72, boulevard de la Saussaye, 92200 Neuilly-sur-Seine, France
Phone: (33)(1)46241051 **Facsimile:** (33)(1)46370750
Headmistress: Sr. Genevieve Murphy, RSHM
Teaching staff: full-time, 41; part-time, 10; total, 51
Nationalities of teaching staff: U.S., 13; U.K., 13; host, 7; other, 18; total, 51
Grade levels: preK – 8
Enrollment: preK – K, 70; 1 – 6, 240; 7 – 8, 52; individual learning center, 6; total, 368
Nationalities of student body: U.S., 199; U.K., 22; host, 37; other, 110; total, 368
Capacity: preK – K, 60; 1 – 6, 240; 7 – 8, 52; individual learning center, 7; total 359
Teacher/student ratio: 1/8
Tuition (annual): preK – K, 63,300**; 1 – 3, 72,800; 4 – 5, 73,500; 6, 77,700; 7 – 8, 79,100; ILC, 88,800 – 93,700
Other fees: registration*, 2,000**; new student assessment, 7,500
School year: September to June

Year founded: 1923. **Type of school:** coed, day, church-related. **Governed by:** Religious of the Sacred Heart of Mary. **Accredited by:** Middle States. **Regional organizations:** ECIS.

Curriculum/physical plant

Type: U.S. **Languages taught:** French. **Staff specialists:** reading, math, speech/hearing, learning disabilities, nurse, resource. **Special programs:** ESL, remedial, self-contained special education class. **Special curricular:** art, chorus, physical education, computer instruction. **Extracurricular:** drama, gymnastics, dance, choral and instrumental music, computers, excursions/expeditions, field trips, French theater. **Sports:** basketball, soccer, swimming, tennis, karate. **Tests:** Iowa. **Location:** in western suburb of Paris. **Campus:** 5,115 square meters. **Library:** 9,000 volumes. **Facilities:** 5 buildings, 32 classrooms, auditorium, cafeteria, infirmary, gymnasium, 2 playing fields, science lab, computer lab.

*Once only fee **French franc

NICE

THE AMERICAN INTERNATIONAL SCHOOL

Street address: 15, avenue Claude Debussy, 06200 Nice, France
Phone: (33)(4)93210400 **Facsimile:** (33)(4)93216911
E-mail: 101644.1546@compuserve.com
Headmaster: Robert M. Silvetz, MD
Teaching staff: full-time, 18; part-time, 6; total, 24
Nationalities of teaching staff: U.S., 5; U.K., 12; host, 4; other, 3; total, 24
Grade levels: K – 12
Enrollment: K – 5, 40; 6 – 8, 55; 9 – 12, 65; total, 160
Nationalities of student body: U.S., 40; U.K., 24; host, 8; other, 88; total, 160
Teacher/student ratio: 1/8
Tuition (annual): K – 5, 51,500**; 6 – 8, 57,000; 9 – 12, 66,000
Other fees (annual): busing, 9,000** (average); capital assessment, 6,000
School year: September to June

Year founded: 1977. **Type of school:** coed, day, private nonprofit. **Governed by:** Chamber of Commerce of the Maritime Alps. **Accredited by:** Middle States, ECIS. **Regional organizations:** ECIS.

Curriculum

Type: U.S., U.K., IB, AP. **Languages taught:** French, others available by arrangement. **Special programs:** ESOL, IGCSE. **Special curricular:** art, physical education, computer instruction, drama, music. **Extracurricular:** drama, gymnastics, dance, computers, yearbook, photography, excursions/expeditions, field trips. **Sports:** badminton, basketball, cross-country, soccer, softball, swimming, tennis, track and field, volleyball, floor hockey. **Tests:** SSAT, PSAT, SAT, ACT, TOEFL, IB, AP, IGCSE. **Graduates attending college:** 90%. **Graduates have attended:** Yale, Dartmouth, Princeton, London School of Economics, Amherst.

Physical plant

Location: in suburban area, 5 minutes from Nice airport. **Campus:** 3 acres. **Library:** 5,000 volumes. **Facilities:** 1 building, 24 classrooms, auditorium, cafeteria, infirmary, covered play area, gymnasium, playing field, 2 science labs, computer lab, boarding with local families available in grades 10 – 12.

**French franc

PARIS

American School of Paris

Street address: 41, rue Pasteur, 92216 Saint-Cloud, France
Phone: (33)(1)41128282 **Facsimile:** (33)(1)46022390
Headmaster: Dr. Donald Billingsley
Upper school director: Dr. John Guse
Middle school director: Paul Schackman
Lower school director: Andrew Hill
Teaching staff: full-time, 50; part-time, 21; total, 71
Nationalities of teaching staff: U.S., 41; U.K., 12; host, 13; other, 5; total, 71
Grade levels: preK – 13
Enrollment: preK, 16; K, 23; 1 – 5, 207; 6 – 8, 165; 9 – 12, 252; 13, 3; total, 666
Nationalities of student body: U.S., 318; host, 53; other, 295; total, 666
Teacher/student ratio: 1/11
Tuition (annual): preK, 42,300**; K – 1, 74,300; 2 – 5, 76,200; 6 – 8, 81,400; 9 – 13, 88,600
Other fees (annual): registration*, 3,000**; capital levy*, 16,000; busing, 9,500 – 11,000
School year: September to June

Year founded: 1946. **Type of school:** coed, day, private nonprofit. **Governed by:** appointed and elected board. **Accredited by:** Middle States. **Regional organizations:** AAIE, ECIS, NAIS.

Curriculum

Type: U.S., IB, AP. **Languages taught:** French, Spanish, Dutch, Swedish. **Staff specialists:** learning disabilities, nurse, computer technician, counselors. **Special programs:** honors sections, independent study, remedial, ESOL. **Special curricular:** art, chorus, band, physical education, computer, theater arts, photography, sculpture, architecture. **Extracurricular:** drama, choral and instrumental music, yearbook, newspaper, literary magazine, excursions/expeditions, field trips, Model UN, student government, sports. **Tests:** PSAT, SAT, ACT, IB, AP. **Graduates attending college:** 98%.

Physical plant

Location: in suburban area. **Campus:** 12 acres. **Libraries:** 28,000 volumes. **Facilities:** cafeteria, infirmary, playing field, adventure playground, rehearsal rooms, electronic music studio, music practice rooms, ceramic and art studios, performing arts center, tennis courts, gymnasiums, science labs, computer labs.

*Once only fee **French franc

Ecole Active Bilingue Jeannine Manuel†

Street address: 70, rue du Théâtre, 75015 Paris, France
Phone: (33)(1)44370080 **Facsimile:** (33)(1)45790666
Mail: 70, rue du Théâtre, 75739 Paris Cedex 15, France
Headmistress/business manager: Madame Zeboulon
Teaching staff: full-time, 160; part-time, 72; total, 232
Nationalities of teaching staff: U.S., 4; U.K., 21; host, 201; other, 6; total, 232
Grade levels: preK – Baccalaureate (International and French)
Enrollment: preK, 68; K, 194; 1 – 5, 675; 7 – 9, 691; 10 – 12, 497; total, 2,125
Nationalities of student body: U.S., 151; U.K., 43; host, 1,631; other, 300; total, 2,125
Teacher/student ratio: 1/10
Tuition (annual): preK, 11,004**; K, 14,535; 1 – 5, 15,999 – 21,015; 6 – 13, 17,228 – 26,796
Other fees (annual): registration*, 700**; lunch, 7,905
School year: September through June

Year founded: 1954. **Type of school:** coed, day, proprietary. **Governed by:** appointed board of directors. **Sponsored by:** French Ministry of Education. **Accredited by:** French Ministry of Education, ECIS.

Curriculum/physical plant

Type: national, IB. **Languages of instruction:** English, French. **Languages taught:** French, Spanish, German, Italian, Arabic, Lebanese, Hebrew, Farsi. **Staff specialists:** math, computer, counselor, nurse. **Special programs:** ESL, honors sections. **Special curricular:** art, physical education, computer instruction. **Extracurricular:** drama, gymnastics, dance, computers, yearbook, newspaper, excursions/expeditions, field trips, music. **Sports:** athletics, football, swimming, tennis. **Clubs:** chess, debating, ecology, electronics, theater. **Tests:** PSAT, SAT, TOEFL, IB. **Graduates attending college:** 98%. **Graduates have attended:** Princeton, Yale, Harvard, Vassar, Oxford. **Location:** in heart of city, near Eiffel Tower. **Library:** 9,000 volumes. **Facilities:** auditorium, cafeteria, infirmary, covered play area, gymnasium, playing field, 7 science labs, computer lab, AV equipment.

*Once only fee **French franc †parent school of Ecole Internationale de Lille Metropole

International School of Paris

Street address: primary school: 96 bis rue du Ranelagh, 75016 Paris, France; middle/high school: 6, rue Beethoven, 75016 Paris, France
Phone: primary: (33)(1)42244340; middle/high school: (33)(1)42240954
Facsimile: (33)(1)45271593 **E-mail:** isp@compuserve.com
Web: http://sunsite.unc.edu:80/isp/index.html
Headmaster: Gareth Jones
Principal (primary school): Elizabeth Hickling
Teaching staff: full-time, 45; part-time, 11; total, 56
Grade levels: K – 12
Enrollment: K, 40; 1 – 5, 86; 6 – 8, 54; 9 – 12, 160; total, 340
Nationalities of student body: U.S., 50; U.K., 30; host, 29; other, 231; total, 340
Teacher/student ratio: 1/7

Tuition (annual): K1, 38,000**; K2 – grade 1, 63,800; 2 – 5, 67,500; 6 – 8, 71,000; 9 – 10, 80,000; 11 – 12, 82,400
Other fees (annual): insurance, 150**; busing, 8,500; entry*, 7,000
School year: September to June

Year founded: 1964. **Type of school:** coed, day, private nonprofit. **Governed by:** appointed and elected board of trustees. **Accredited by:** New England, ECIS. **Regional organizations:** ECIS.

Curriculum/physical plant

Type: U.S., U.K., IB, IGCSE. **Languages taught:** English, French, German, Korean, Russian, Japanese, Swedish, to native speakers of these languages. **Staff specialists:** reading, math, computer, counselor, learning disabilities (primary and middle schools). **Special programs:** ESL. **Special curricular:** art, chorus, physical education, computer instruction. **Extracurricular:** drama, gymnastics, computers, yearbook, photography, excursions/expeditions, field trips. **Sports:** basketball, soccer, swimming, table tennis, volleyball, karate, judo. **Clubs:** chess, computer, Model UN. **Tests:** PSAT, IB, ICGSE. **Graduates attending college:** 95%. **Graduates have attended:** Brown, Harvard, Columbia, Oxford, Cambridge. **Location:** in Paris. **Libraries:** 12,000 volumes. **Facilities:** 2 campuses, 3 buildings, 40 classrooms, 2 gymnasiums, 2 science labs, 2 computer labs, access to tennis courts, kinder playground.

*Once only fee **French franc

United Nations Nursery School Association, Paris

Street address: 40, rue Pierre Guerin, 75016 Paris, France
Phone: (33)(1)45272024 **Facsimile:** (33)(1)45242854
Directrice: Brigitte Weill
Grade levels: 2 1/2 – 6 years old
Enrollment: total, 70
Nationalities of student body: U.S., 25; U.K., 4; host, 30; other, 11; total, 70
Tuition: 4,900** part time, per term; 7,900 full day, per term
Other fees (annual): registration*, 1,000**; lunch, 960; membership, 110
School year: September to June

Year founded: 1951. **Type of school:** coed, day, private nonprofit. **Governed by:** elected board. **Accredited by:** French ministries of health and education.

Curriculum/physical plant

Type: U.S., national. **Languages of instruction:** English, French. **Languages taught:** English, French. **Special programs:** English lessons (ages 6–10); summer school (July). **Extracurricular:** excursions/expeditions. **Location:** in Paris. **Campus:** 350 square meters. **Library:** 500 volumes. **Facilities:** 1 building, 4 classrooms, large garden with animals.

*Once only fee **French franc

ST. GERMAIN-EN-LAYE

LYCEE INTERNATIONAL, AMERICAN SECTION†

Phone: (33)(1)34517485 **Facsimile:** (33)(1)30870049
Mail: BP 230, rue du Fer A Cheval, St. Germain-en-Laye 78104 Cedex, France
Director: D. Michael Veitch
Headmaster, Lycée International: Jean-Pierre Maillard
Teaching staff: full-time, 14; part-time, 1; total, 15
Nationalities of teaching staff: U.S., 14; other, 1; total, 15
Grade levels: preK – 12
Enrollment: preK – K, 12; 1 – 5, 212; 6 – 9, 139; 10 – 12, 134; total, 497
Nationalities of student body: U.S., 140; U.K., 16; host, 152; U.S./host, 149; other, 40; total, 497
Tuition (annual): 22,000**, with family reductions available
Other fees (annual): registration, 2,500**; insurance, 60; busing, 500; lunch, 2,500; application, 500
School year: September to early July

Year founded: 1952. **Type of school:** coed, day. **Governed by:** elected parents' board. **Accredited by:** French Ministry of Education. **Regional organizations:** ECIS.

Curriculum/physical plant

Type: U.S., national, IB, AP. **Languages of instruction:** English, French. **Languages taught:** Spanish, German, Dutch, Italian, Russian, Latin. **Staff specialists:** nurse. **Special programs:** French Baccalaureate with American International Option, IB certificates. **Special curricular:** computer instruction. **Extracurricular:** drama, yearbook, literary magazine, field trips, excursions, Model UN, community service. **Sports:** basketball, soccer, tennis, volleyball, judo, horseback riding. **Clubs:** bioethics, ecology. **Tests:** PSAT, SAT, AP, Iowa, French Baccalaureate International Option, CTP III (ERB), IB (certificates only). **Graduates attending college:** 100%. **Graduates have attended:** Columbia, Yale, Duke, Georgetown, King's College (London). **Location:** in suburban area, 20 kilometers from Paris. **Library:** 100,000 volumes. **Facilities:** 5 buildings, auditorium, cafeteria, infirmary, tennis court, gymnasium, playing field, science lab, computer lab, theater.

**French franc †associated schools: Lycee Marcel Roby, Ecole Henri Dunant

VALBONNE

Centre International de Valbonne: International School of Sophia Antipolis

Phone: (33)(4)92965224 **Facsimile:** (33)(4)93652215
E-mail: aseica@riviera.fr
Web: http://www.ibo.org/schools/civ/civ.htm
Mail: CIV-BP 097, 06902 Sophia Antipolis Cedex, France
Head: Laura Mongiat
IB coordinator: Carole Labrousse
College counselor: Judith Guérard
Teaching staff: full-time, 13; part-time, 27; total, 40
Nationalities of teaching staff: U.S., 10; U.K., 8; host, 18; other, 4; total, 40
Grade levels: 1 – 12
Enrollment: 1 – 5, 85; 6 – 9, 327; 10 – 12, 241; total, 653
Nationalities of student body: U.S., 41; U.K., 101; host, 326; other, 185; total, 653
Teacher/student ratio: 1/24
Tuition (annual): 1 – 5, 11,000**; 6 – 9, 9,500; 10 – 12, 11,000 – 44,000
Other fees: boarding, 39,900**/year; busing, 1,300/trimester; lunch, 1,260/trimester; activities and sports card, 900/trimester
School year: September to June

Year founded: 1979. **Type of school:** coed, day, boarding, bilingual. **Governed by:** elected board of governors. **Accredited by:** French Ministry of Education. **Regional organizations:** ECIS.

Curriculum

Type: national, IB. **Languages of instruction:** English, French. **Languages taught:** Spanish, German, Italian, Russian, Arabic. **Special programs:** ESL, intensive French. **Special curricular:** art, physical education, computer instruction. **Extracurricular:** drama, gymnastics, dance, computers, yearbook, photography, excursions/expeditions, field trips, Model UN, theater and film festival visits, chess club. **Sports:** basketball, rugby, skiing, soccer, squash, tennis, track and field, volleyball, judo, sailing. **Tests:** PSAT, TOEFL, IB, SAT I & II, French Baccalaureate International Option, Brevet du College. **Graduates attending college:** 95%. **Graduates have attended:** Cornell, Oxford, Brown, MIT, Sorbonne.

Physical plant

Location: on the French Riviera between Nice (20 km) and Cannes (15 km) in Europe's largest science park (technopolis). **Campus:** 40 acres. **Library:** over 10,000 volumes. **Facilities:** 14 buildings, 70 classrooms, 2 cafeterias, infirmary, 8 tennis courts, gymnasium, 4 playing fields, 6 science labs, computer lab, AV center, theater, 5 boarding pavilions.

**French franc

GABON

Region: Central Africa
Size: 103,347 square miles
Population: 1,192,798
Capital: Libreville
Telephone code: 241
Currency: CFA franc
Languages: French, Bantu dialects

LIBREVILLE

American International School of Libreville

Phone: (241)744556 **Facsimile:** (241)745240
Mail: BP 4000, Libreville, Gabon
U.S. mail: c/o Dept. of State – Libreville, Washington, DC 20521-2270
Director: Frank N. Sawyer, Jr.
Teaching staff: full-time, 4; part-time, 1; total, 5
Nationalities of teaching staff: U.S., 3; other, 2; total, 5
Grade levels: N – 8
Enrollment: N, 12; K – 2, 9; 3 – 5, 8; 6 – 8, 7; total, 36
Nationalities of student body: U.S., 9; other, 27; total, 36
Capacity: N, 12; K, 10; 1 – 5, 25; 6 – 8, 15; total, 52
Teacher/student ratio: 1/7
Tuition (annual): N, 80,000**/month; K, $7,700; 1 – 8, $11,300
School year: August to June

Year founded: 1975. **Type of school:** coed, day, private nonprofit. **Governed by:** appointed board of directors. **Accredited by:** Middle States. **Regional organizations:** AAIE, AISA.

Curriculum/physical plant

Type: U.S. **Languages taught:** French. **Staff specialists:** computer, art, music, physical education. **Special programs:** ESL. **Extracurricular:** field trips, swimming, tennis, judo. **Tests:** SSAT, Iowa. **Location:** in former Marine security guard residence in Quartier Glass. **Campus:** 1/2 acre. **Library:** 5,000 volumes. **Facilities:** 1 building, 10 classrooms, playing field, computer lab, well-equipped playground, air conditioning.

**CFA franc

THE GAMBIA

Region: Western Africa
Size: 4,127 square miles
Population: 1,204,984
Capital: Banjul
Telephone code: 220
Currency: dalasi
Languages: English, Mandinka, Wolof

BANJUL

Banjul American Embassy School

Phone: (220)495920 **Facsimile:** (220)497181
Mail: Box 2596, Serrekunda, The Gambia
U.S. mail: (official mail only) BANJUL-EmbSchool, Washington, DC 20521-2070
Director: James Swetz
Teaching staff: full-time, 8; part-time, 3; total, 11
Nationalities of teaching staff: U.S., 5; U.K., 4; other, 2; total, 11
Grade levels: preK – 9
Enrollment: preK, 6; K, 10; 1 – 6, 39; 7 – 9, 11; total, 66
Nationalities of student body: U.S., 10; U.K., 10; other, 46; total, 66
Capacity: preK, 15; K, 15; 1 – 6, 120; 7 – 8, 30; total, 180
Teacher/student ratio: 1/8
Tuition (annual): preK, $2,200; K – 5, $6,500; 6 – 9, $7,600
Other fees (annual): application, $50; ESL, $1,050; school development*, $850
School year: September to June

Year founded: 1984. **Type of school:** coed, day, private nonprofit. **Governed by:** board of directors. **Sponsored by:** parent association. **Accredited by:** Middle States. **Regional organizations:** AISA.

Curriculum/physical plant

Type: U.S. **Languages taught:** French. **Staff specialists:** computer, art, music, physical education. **Special programs:** ESL. **Special curricular:** school house competitions. **Extracurricular:** drama, field trips, interscholastic sports, sports day, yearbook, student council. **Tests:** Iowa. **Location:** in tourist/residential suburb near Atlantic Ocean, 15 kilometers from Banjul. **Campus:** 3 acres. **Library:** 4,500 volumes. **Facilities:** 4 buildings, 12 classrooms, 2 playing fields, science lab, computer lab, art room, surfaced play area.

*Once only fee

Marina International School

Phone: (220)496631 **Facsimile:** (220)497280
Mail: PO Box 717, Banjul, The Gambia
Acting headteacher: Ms. S. Foster
Teaching staff: full-time, 55; total, 55
Nationalities of teaching staff: U.S., 1; U.K., 3; host, 24; other, 27; total, 55
Grade levels: preK – 13
Enrollment: preK, 59; K, 61; 1 – 13, 644; total, 764
Nationalities of student body: U.S., 1; U.K., 4; host, 722; other, 37; total, 764
Capacity: preK, 52; K, 52; 1 – 13, 646; total, 750
Teacher/student ratio: 1/16
Tuition (annual): preK – 6, 4,200**; 7 – 13, 9,000 (expatriates extra)
Other fees (annual): building fund, 1,100** (per family); uniform, examinations; registration*, 200 – 300; building levy*, 1,000
School year: September to July

Year founded: 1972. **Type of school:** coed, day, private nonprofit. **Governed by:** elected parent/teacher association executive committee.

Curriculum/physical plant

Type: U.K., national, IGCSE, AICE. **Staff specialists:** reading, learning disabilities. **Sports:** football, basketball, athletics, volleyball, rounders. **Tests:** Richmond, PSAT. **Location:** outskirts of Banjul. **Library:** 6,500 volumes. **Facilities:** 15 buildings, 44 classrooms, 2 playing fields, 2 science labs, computer room, 2 libraries, AV equipment.

*Once only fee **Gambian dalasi

GEORGIA

Region: Eastern Europe
Size: 26,900 square miles
Population: 5,219,810
Capital: Tbilisi
Telephone code: 995
Currency: lari
Languages: Georgian, Russian

TBILISI

QSI International School of Tbilisi

Phone: (995)(32)982909 **E-mail:** bev@access.sanet.ge
U.S. mail: c/o American Embassy Tbilisi, Dept. of State, Washington, DC 20521-7060
Director: Beverly McAloon
Teaching staff: full-time, 2; part-time, 6; total, 8
Nationalities of teaching staff: U.S., 3; other, 5; total, 8
Grade levels: N – 12
Enrollment: K, 4; 1 – 6, 9; total, 13
Teacher/student ratio: 1/4
Tuition (annual): N, $5,000; K – 12, $10,200
Other fees: registration*, $100; capital levy, $4,000 deposit or $1,600/year fee
School year: September to June

Year founded: 1995. **Type of school:** coed, day, private nonprofit. **Governed by:** appointed board of directors. **Sponsored by:** Quality Schools International. **Regional organizations:** CEESA.

Curriculum/physical plant

Type: U.S. **Special programs:** ESL. **Special curricular:** art, physical education, music, computer instruction. **Extracurricular:** drama, computers, excursions/expeditions, music productions, special art activities. **Location:** edge of city park in Tbilisi. **Facilities:** housed in portion of host country kindergarten building, library, 3 classrooms, use of gymnasium, dance room, play area.

*Once only fee

GERMANY

Region: Europe
Size: 137,828 square miles
Population: 83,536,115
Capital: Berlin
Telephone code: 49
Currency: mark
Language: German

BERLIN

Berlin British School

Street address: Dickensweg 17-19, 14055 Berlin, Germany
Phone: (49)(30)3042205/3043780 **Facsimile:** (49)(30)3043856
Head teacher: Valerie Aspden
Business manager: Brigitte Hurst
Teaching staff: full-time, 12; part-time, 8; total, 20
Nationalities of teaching staff: U.S., 2; U.K., 16; host, 2; total, 20
Grade levels: N – 8
Enrollment: N – preK, 61; K, 30; 1 – 6, 70; 7 – 9, 15; total, 176
Nationalities of student body: U.S., 10; U.K., 34; host, 40; other, 92; total, 176
Capacity: N – preK, 36; K, 40; 1 – 6, 240; 7 – 9, 40; total, 356
Teacher/student ratio: 1/11
Other fees: busing, 17**/day; lunch, 5/day
School year: September to July

Year founded: 1994. **Type of school:** coed, private nonprofit. **Governed by:** Ingetragener Verein.

Curriculum

Type: U.K. **Languages of instruction:** English. **Languages taught:** German. **Staff specialists:** reading, math, computer, learning disabilities, swimming. **Special programs:** ESL. **Special curricular:** art, chorus, computer instruction, music. **Extracurricular:** drama, gymnastics, choral and instrumental music, art, chess, pottery, piano. **Sports:** basketball, football, ball games, sailing.

Physical plant

Location: conveniently located in suburb of Berlin. **Facilities:** 1 building, 12 classrooms, auditorium, gymnasium, playing field, science lab, library, computers in all classrooms, use of swimming pools, olympic stadium.

**Deutsche mark

International School Berlin—Potsdam

Street address: Heinrich Heine Weg 15, 14476 Neu Fahrland, Berlin, Germany
Phone: (49)(331)27700 **Facsimile:** (49)(331)277020
Headmaster: Matthias Trüper
Teaching staff: full-time, 23; part-time, 11; total, 34
Nationalities of teaching staff: U.S., 5; U.K., 16; host, 5; other, 8; total, 34
Grade levels: K – 12
Enrollment: K, 40; 1 – 6, 80; 7 – 12, 90; total, 210
Nationalities of student body: U.S., 15; host, 70; other, 125; total, 210
Capacity: K, 50; 1 – 6, 175; 7 – 12, 175; total, 400
Teacher/student ratio: 1/8
Tuition (annual): K, 12,600**; 1 – 3, 16,000; 4 – 6, 17,150; 7 – 10, 18,950; 11 – 12, 19,800 (reduction for siblings)
Other fees (annual): registration*, 1,000** (deducted from tuition); capital levy*, 5,000; busing, 1,650
School year: late August through June

Year founded: 1991. **Type of school:** coed, day, private nonprofit. **Governed by:** elected nonprofit association. **Sponsored by:** national and foreign companies; government subsidy. **Accredited by:** State of Brandenburg. **Regional organizations:** ECIS, ISA, ISCP, AGIS.

Curriculum/physical plant

Type: IB, ISCP, IGCSE. **Languages taught:** English, French, German. **Staff specialists:** computer, counselor, ESL. **Special programs:** mother tongue instruction. **Special curricular:** art, computer instruction, student theater, choral and instrumental music, yearbook, newspaper. **Extracurricular:** drama, computers, sailing, environment, rowing. **Sports:** badminton, basketball, hockey, skiing, soccer, swimming, volleyball. **Location:** in residential area, 20 kilometers from downtown Berlin. **Campus:** 120,000 square meters. **Libraries (2):** 12,000 volumes. **Facilities:** 6 buildings, 25 classrooms, cafeteria, gymnasium, playing fields, science labs, computer lab, pottery, wood workshop, theater hall, boat house.

*Once only fee **Deutsche mark

John F. Kennedy School

Street address: Teltower Damm 87-93, 14167 Berlin, Germany
Phone: (49)(30)8072701/8072713 **Facsimile:** (49)(30)8073377
Managing principal: Charles C. Hanna
American high school principal: Darryl E. Hersant, Ph.D.
German high school principal: Uwe Nieguth
German elementary principal: Gudula Lennert
Teaching staff: full-time, 129; part-time, 28; total, 157
Nationalities of teaching staff: U.S., 67; U.K., 2; host, 88; total, 157
Grade levels: K – 13
Enrollment: K, 105; 1 – 6, 618; 7 – 9, 373; 10 – 12, 284; 13, 43; total, 1,423
Nationalities of student body: U.S., 412; host, 828; other, 183; total, 1,423
Capacity: K, 112; 1 – 6, 600; 7 – 9, 350; 10 – 12, 300; 13, 63; total, 1,425

Teacher/student ratio: 1/10
School year: August to July

Year founded: 1960. **Type of school:** coed, day, public. **Governed by:** State of Berlin. **Accredited by:** New England. **Regional organizations:** ECIS.

Curriculum/physical plant

Type: U.S., national, AP. **Languages of instruction:** English, German. **Languages taught:** French, Spanish, Latin. **Staff specialists:** reading, math. **Special curricular:** art, chorus, band, physical education, computer instruction. **Extracurricular:** drama, choral and instrumental music, computers, yearbook, newspaper, literary magazine, excursions/expeditions, field trips. **Sports:** basketball, rugby, soccer, swimming, track and field, volleyball, rowing, wrestling. **Tests:** PSAT, SAT, AP. **Graduates attending college:** 90%. **Graduates have attended:** Georgetown, Tufts, U. of Michigan, Princeton, Stanford. **Location:** in suburban area, 20 minutes from downtown Berlin. **Campus:** 10 acres. **Library:** 50,000 volumes. **Facilities:** 6 buildings, 2 auditoriums, cafeteria, 2 gymnasiums, 3 playing fields, 7 science labs, 3 computer labs.

BONN

Bonn American High School†

Street address: Martin Luther King Strasse 14, 53175 Bonn, Germany
Phone: (49)(228)379234 **Facsimile:** (49)(228)379357
U.S. mail: (no personal name) BAHS, American Embassy Bonn, PSC 117, Box 390, APO AE 09080-0005
Principal: Lavonne K. Tawney
Assistant principal: Sandra Daniels
Guidance counselor: Nanci Trent
Teaching staff: full-time, 28; part-time, 2; total, 30
Nationalities of teaching staff: U.S., 29; other, 1; total, 30
Grade levels: 6 – 12
Enrollment: total, 250
Nationalities of student body: U.S., 105; other, 145; total, 250
Teacher/student ratio: 1/9
Tuition (annual): 6 – 12, $12,500
School year: August to June

Year founded: 1971. **Type of school:** coed, day. **Accredited by:** North Central.

Curriculum

Type: U.S., IB, AP. **Languages taught:** French, German. **Staff specialists:** reading, counselor, learning disabilities, nurse. **Special programs:** ESL, independent study. **Special curricular:** art, chorus, band, physical education, computer instruction, vocational. **Extracurricular:** drama, choral and instrumental music, computers, yearbook, newspaper, literary magazine, photography, excursions/expeditions, field trips. **Sports:** basketball, cross-country, football, soccer, swimming, tennis, track and field, volleyball, wrestling. **Clubs:** drama, National Honor Society, National Junior Honor Society, stamp, swimming, photography, teen, Math Counts, business. **Tests:** PSAT, SAT, ACT, IB, AP. **Graduates attending college:** 90%.

Graduates have attended: Northwestern, Brown, U. of Michigan, Franklin and Marshall, Georgia Institute of Technology.

Physical plant

Location: in Bonn, along the Rhine River, a few minutes' drive to the Parliament. **Campus:** 2 acres. **Library:** over 10,000 volumes. **Facilities:** 25 classrooms, tennis court, gymnasium, playing field, 3 science labs, computer lab, swimming pool, technology center, industrial arts lab, business lab, humanities center, TV studio, AV equipment.

†merging with British International School **1996–97 listing**

Independent Bonn International School e.V.†

Street address: Tulpenbaumweg 42, 53177 Bonn, Germany
Phone: (49)(228)323166 **Facsimile:** (49)(228)323958
Headmaster: P. A. Ward
Teaching staff: full-time, 16; part-time, 6; total, 22
Nationalities of teaching staff: U.K., 19; host, 3; total, 22
Grade levels: preK – 7
Enrollment: preK – K, 66; 1 – 6, 158; 7, 11; total, 235
Nationalities of student body: U.S., 28; U.K., 70; host, 12; other, 125; total, 235
Capacity: preK – K, 48; 1 – 6, 180; 7, 24; total, 252
Teacher/student ratio: 1/13
Tuition: 4,600**/term (3 terms per year)
Other fees: registration*, 850**
School year: September to July

Year founded: 1963. **Type of school:** coed, day, private nonprofit. **Governed by:** appointed and elected governing body. **Regional organizations:** ECIS, COBISEC, AGIS.

Curriculum/physical plant

Type: U.K. **Languages taught:** French, German. **Staff specialists:** math, learning disabilities, art, music, science, English, geography. **Special programs:** ESL, remedial. **Special curricular:** physical education, computer instruction. **Extracurricular:** drama, gymnastics, dance, choral and instrumental music, computers, photography, excursions/expeditions, field trips, bowling. **Sports:** athletics, hockey, volleyball, football (association), handball. **Tests:** GCSE (German only), Common Entrance, Richmond. **Location:** on the Heiderhof, a southern area of Bad Godesberg, 15 minutes from Bonn center. **Campus:** 1 acre. **Library:** 4,000 volumes. **Facilities:** 4 buildings, 24 classrooms, gymnasium, science lab, computer lab, home economics center, multimedia.

*Once only fee **Deutsche mark †formerly British Embassy Preparatory School e.V.

DÜSSELDORF

INTERNATIONAL SCHOOL OF DÜSSELDORF E.V.

Street address: Niederrheinstrasse 336, 40489 Düsseldorf, Germany
Phone: (49)(211)94066 **Facsimile:** (49)(211)4080774
Director: Robert L. Ater
High school principal: Michael Coffey
Middle school principal: Beverly von Zielonka
Elementary school principal: Carol Esposito
Business manager: Dieter Kapteina
Teaching staff: full-time, 72; part-time, 8; total, 80
Nationalities of teaching staff: U.S., 32; U.K., 23; host, 14; other, 11; total, 80
Grade levels: preK – 13
Enrollment: preK, 15; K, 39; 1 – 5, 207; 6 – 8, 144; 9 – 13, 239; total, 644
Capacity: preK, 20; K, 40; 1 – 5, 244; 6 – 8, 198; 9 – 13, 264; total, 766
Teacher/student ratio: 1/8
Tuition (annual): preK, 11,355**; K, 17,475; 1 – 4, 20,635; 5, 20,025; 6 – 8, 22,300; 9 – 10, 23,850; 11 – 13, 26,655
Other fees: registration*, 7,500**
School year: August to June

Year founded: 1968. **Type of school:** coed, day, private nonprofit. **Governed by:** elected board of trustees. **Accredited by:** New England, ECIS. **Regional organizations:** AAIE, ECIS.

Curriculum/physical plant

Type: U.S., IB. **Languages taught:** French, German, Japanese. **Staff specialists:** computer, counselor, learning development. **Special programs:** ESL, learning development. **Special curricular:** art, chorus, physical education, computer instruction, instrumental music. **Extracurricular:** drama, gymnastics, yearbook, newspaper, literary magazine, music, adventure club, French club. **Sports:** basketball, soccer, softball, track and field, volleyball. **Tests:** PSAT, SAT, TOEFL, IB. **Graduates attending college:** 95%. **Graduates have attended:** Duke, Tokyo U., Stanford, Yale, Oxford. **Location:** in affluent suburb, 10 kilometers from Düsseldorf. **Campus:** 7 acres. **Library:** 12,000 volumes. **Facilities:** 5 interconnected buildings, 54 classrooms, auditorium, cafeteria, gymnasium, science labs, computer labs.

*Once only fee **Deutsche mark

FRANKFURT

THE FRANKFURT INTERNATIONAL SCHOOL E.V. & INTERNATIONAL SCHOOL WIESBADEN

Street address: An der Waldlust 15, 61440 Oberursel, Germany
Phone: (49)(6171)2020 **Facsimile:** (49)(6171)202384
E-mail: 100430.2764@compuserve.com **Web:** http://cocos.cocos.de/fis
Headmaster: James E. Buckheit
High school principal: Don Vinge
Middle school principal: Dr. Jorn Brauer
Elementary school principal: Carol Morrow
Business manager: Detlev Siebrecht
Teaching staff: full-time, 158; total, 158
Nationalities of teaching staff: U.S., 63; U.K., 66; host, 12; other, 17; total, 158
Enrollment: playschool, 21; preP – P, 164; 1 – 5, 579; 6 – 8, 346; 9 – 12, 433; total, 1,543
Nationalities of student body: U.S., 532; U.K., 203; host, 170; other, 638; total, 1,543
Tuition (annual): preP – 4, 19,140**; 5, 19,440; 6 – 8, 21,540; 9 – 10, 22,220; 11, 22,680; 12, 23,140; Wiesbaden campus playschool, 15,740 (full day), 7,870 (half day), 5,250 (afternoon program)
Other fees (annual): registration, 250**, 1,000 (new students); busing, 1,640 – 2,460; capital contribution: year 1, 4,000; years 2 – 5, 1,500; Wiesbaden campus, 5 years, 2,000
School year: August to June

Year founded: 1961. **Type of school:** coed, day. **Governed by:** elected and appointed board of trustees. **Accredited by:** ECIS, Middle States. **Regional organizations:** AAIE, ECIS.

Curriculum/physical plant

Type: U.S., U.K., IB. **Languages taught:** French, Spanish, German. **Staff specialists:** librarians, counselors, learning disabilities teachers, nurses. **Special programs:** ESL. **Special curricular:** art, band, physical education, computer instruction, drama, choir, music appreciation, . **Extracurricular:** yearbook, newspaper, literary magazine, field trips, orchestra, band, choir. **Sports:** basketball, cross-country, soccer, swimming, tennis, track and field, volleyball. **Tests:** PSAT, SAT, ACT, TOEFL, IB, IGCE. **Graduates attending college:** 80%. **Graduates have attended:** McGill U., Michigan State U., Oxbridge, Edinburgh, Waseda U. in Japan. **Location:** at foot of Taunus Mountains, 23 kilometers from Frankfurt/Main. **Campus:** 48 hectares. **Library:** 36,000 volumes. **Facilities:** 93 classrooms, auditorium, 2 cafeterias, infirmary, covered play area, 2 tennis courts, 2 gymnasiums, 2 playing fields, 8 science labs, 3 computer labs, playground, A/V center, career center, band and practice rooms, choir room, 2 faculty lounges, central administration building. **Primary campus:** 1 kilometer from main campus; 4 hectares. Library: 4,000 volumes. **Facilities:** 15 classrooms, PE room, indoor play area, cafeteria, playground. **Wiesbaden campus:** 57 kilometers from main campus. **Facilities:** 12 classrooms, library, gymnasium, lunch room, playground.

*Once only fee **Deutsche mark

Internationale Schule Frankfurt-Rhein-Main

Street address: Friedberger Landstr. 358, 60389 Frankfurt, Germany
Phone: (49)(69)9543190 **Facsimile:** (49)(69)95431920 **E-mail:** isfrm@ipf.de
Web: http://www.sabis.com/school-network/isf.htm
Director: Richard D. Long
Secondary coordinator: Mark Weinberg
Primary coordinator: Alison Hermiston
Teaching staff: full-time, 20; part-time, 4; total, 24
Nationalities of teaching staff: U.S., 8; U.K., 1; host, 7; other, 8; total, 24
Grade levels: preK – 9†
Enrollment: preK, 7; K, 24; 1 – 6, 105; 7 – 9, 40; total, 176
Nationalities of student body: U.S., 25; U.K., 10; host, 87; other, 54; total, 176
Teacher/student ratio: 1/8
Tuition (annual): preK – K, 16,770**; 1 – 4, 17,310; 5, 17,820; 6 – 8, 18,360; 9, 18,840
Other fees: registration, entry share purchase, 20,000**
School year: September to June

Year founded: 1995. **Type of school:** coed, day, company-sponsored, proprietary. **Governed by:** appointed board of directors. **Sponsored by:** local government and private industry. **Regional organizations:** ECIS.

Curriculum/physical plant

Type: Sabis School Network. **Languages taught:** French, German. **Staff specialists:** reading, math, computer. **Special programs:** ESL, intensive German. **Special curricular:** art, chorus, physical education, computer instruction. **Extracurricular:** extended day program (8:00 – 18:00) involving fine arts and sports activities, and a 4-week summer program. **Facilities:** temporarily in ex-U.S. military school 2 kilometers from city center; new facility under construction in West Frankfurt for 1,000 students.

*Once only fee **Deutsche mark †adding a grade each year up to 13 in 2001

HAMBURG

International School Hamburg

Street address: Holmbrook 20, 22605 Hamburg, Germany
Phone: (49)(40)8830010 **Facsimile:** (49)(40)8811405
E-mail: 100272.410@compuserve.com
U.S. mail: (no personal name) International School, AmConGen Hamburg, Dept. of State, Washington, DC 20521-5180
Headmaster: Geoffrey Clark
Teaching staff: full-time, 64; part-time, 7; total, 71
Nationalities of teaching staff: U.S., 11; U.K., 37; host, 10; other, 13; total, 71
Grade levels: preK – 12
Enrollment: preK, 36; K, 30; 1 – 6, 206; 7 – 9, 131; 10 – 12, 112; total, 515
Nationalities of student body: U.S., 80; U.K., 60; host, 88; other, 287; total, 515

Capacity: preK, 36; K, 40; 1 – 6, 300; 7 – 9, 180; 10 – 12, 180; total, 736
Teacher/student ratio: 1/7
Tuition (annual): preK, 9,500**; K, 11,900; reception, 14,300; 1 – 2, 17,900; 3 – 5, 18,900; 6 – 8, 20,500; 9 – 10, 21,600; 11 – 12, 22,500
Other fees (annual): registration*, 100**; capital levy*, 5,000; busing, 1,700
School year: August to June

Year founded: 1957. **Type of school:** coed, day. **Governed by:** elected board of trustees. **Accredited by:** ECIS, New England. **Regional organizations:** AAIE, ECIS.

Curriculum/physical plant

Type: U.S., U.K., IB. **Languages taught:** French, German, Japanese. **Staff specialists:** reading, math. **Special programs:** ESL, remedial. **Special curricular:** art, chorus, physical education, computer instruction. **Extracurricular:** drama, gymnastics, choral and instrumental music, computers, yearbook, photography, excursions/expeditions, field trips, Brownies. **Sports:** basketball, soccer, softball, swimming, track and field, volleyball. **Tests:** PSAT, SAT, TOEFL, IB, IGCSE, Stanford. **Graduates attending college:** 90%. **Graduates have attended:** Brown, Cornell, Princeton, Oxford, Cambridge. **Location:** in western suburbs of Hamburg. **Campus:** 3 acres. **Library:** 25,000 volumes. **Facilities:** 2 buildings, 33 classrooms, auditorium, 2 gymnasiums, 5 science labs, computer lab, AV equipment.

*Once only fee **Deutsche mark

MUNICH

Bavarian International School

Street address: Hallbergmooser Str. 5, 85445 Schwaig/Oberding, Germany
Phone: (49)(8122)97220 **Facsimile:** (49)(8122)972211
E-mail: admissions@bis-school.com **Web:** http://www.bis-school.com
Headmaster: Derek Malpass
Admission/development: Uwe Schweneke
Teaching staff: full-time, 34; part-time, 5; total, 39
Grade levels: reception (age 3) – grade 12
Enrollment: total, 350
Nationalities of student body: U.S., 65; U.K., 95; host, 120; other, 70; total, 350
Teacher/student ratio: 1/10
Tuition (annual): preR, 12,638**; R – 5, 14,788; 6 – 8, 17,462; 9 – 12, 18,878
Other fees (annual): registration, 1,000**; entrance*, 6,000; busing, 500 – 3,000
School year: August to June

Year founded: 1991. **Type of school:** coed, day, private nonprofit. **Governed by:** board of directors. **Sponsored by:** Association of Bavarian International School. **Regional organizations:** ECIS.

Curriculum/physical plant

Type: U.S., IB, U.K. (including IGCSE). **Languages taught:** English, French, German. **Special programs:** ESL. **Special curricular:** art, physical education, computer instruction, ski week, summer program. **Extracurricular:** sports, fine arts, global education. **Location:** near Munich International Airport, 35 kilometers north of Munich center. **Facilities:** 15 classrooms, science lab, library, art room, music rooms, computer in every classroom.

*Once only fee **Deutsche mark

Munich International School

Street address: Schloss Buchhof, Percha, 82319 Starnberg, Germany
Phone: (49)(8151)3660 **Facsimile:** (49)(8151)366109
Headmaster: Raymond J. Taylor
Senior school principal: Michael Webster
Senior school associate principal: Anna Wietrzychowska
Middle school principal: Eifion Phillips
Teaching staff: full-time, 103; part-time, 27; total, 130
Nationalities of teaching staff: U.S., 34; U.K., 48; host, 24; other, 24; total, 130
Grade levels: preK – 12
Enrollment: preK, 14; K, 54; 1 – 6, 387; 7 – 9, 196; 10 – 12, 209; total, 860
Nationalities of student body: U.S., 196; U.K., 136; host, 291; other, 237; total, 860
Capacity: preK, 14; K, 54; 1 – 6, 392; 7 – 9, 210; 10 – 12, 210; total, 880
Teacher/student ratio: 1/11
Tuition (annual, 1996 – 97 figures): preK – 5, 15,960**; 6 – 8, 18,660; 9 – 12, 20,090
Other fees (annual): capital levy*, 8,000**, plus 2,000 (2nd year) and 2,000 (3rd year); busing, 890 – 3,500
School year: September through June

Year founded: 1966. **Type of school:** coed, day, private nonprofit. **Governed by:** elected board of directors. **Sponsored by:** Association of MIS. **Accredited by:** New England, ECIS. **Regional organizations:** ECIS, NAIS.

Curriculum

Type: U.S., U.K., IB. **Languages taught:** English, French, German. **Staff specialists:** math, computer, counselor, nurse, art, ESL, music, physical education, drama, remedial. **Special programs:** ESL, remedial. **Special curricular:** art, chorus, physical education, computer instruction, drama, orchestra. **Extracurricular:** drama, gymnastics, dance, choral and instrumental music, computers, yearbook, newspaper, photography, excursions/expeditions, field trips, speech/debate. **Sports:** badminton, basketball, gymnastics, skiing, soccer, squash, swimming, tennis, track and field, volleyball, kayaking. **Clubs:** drama, sports, environmental, scouts. **Tests:** SSAT, PSAT, SAT, TOEFL, IB, A-level GCE, IGCSE. **Graduates attending college:** 95%. **Graduates have attended:** London School of Economics, Cambridge, Yale, MIT, Princeton.

Physical plant

Location: on wooded grounds of Schloss Buchhof, near Lake Starnberg, 20 kilometers south of Munich. **Campus:** 25 acres. **Libraries:** 15,000 volumes. **Facilities:** 5 buildings, 52 classrooms, 3 auditoriums, cafeteria, 3 tennis courts, 3 playing fields, 5 science labs, 3 computer labs, double gymnasium.

*Once only fee **Deutsche mark

STUTTGART

International School of Stuttgart e.V.

Street address: Vaihinger Strasse 28, 70567 Stuttgart 80, Germany
Phone: (49)(711)7189161 **Facsimile:** (49)(711)7189485
Director: Mary Langley
Teaching staff: full-time, 18; part-time, 13; total, 31
Nationalities of teaching staff: U.S., 14; U.K., 5; host, 8; other, 4; total, 31
Grade levels: preK – 10 (expanding high school program 1998 – 99)
Enrollment: preK – K, 30; 1 – 6, 99; 7 – 9, 27; total, 156
Nationalities of student body: U.S., 65; U.K., 13; host, 17; other, 61; total, 156
Capacity: preK – K, 31; 1 – 6, 132; 7 – 9, 67; total, 230
Teacher/student ratio: 1/6
Tuition (annual): PreK, 12,400**; K – 5, 15,700; 6 – 8, 16,450; 9, 17,250
Other fees (annual): registration, 500**; capital levy*, 2,950; busing, 4,600
School year: August to June

Year founded: 1985. **Type of school:** coed, day, private nonprofit. **Governed by:** elected board of directors. **Regional organizations:** ECIS.

Curriculum/physical plant

Type: U.S., U.K. **Languages taught:** German, French. **Staff specialists:** computer, music, physical education, German. **Special programs:** ESL, special needs. **Special curricular:** art, physical education, computer instruction, drama, health. **Extracurricular:** excursions/expeditions, field trips. **Tests:** CTBS 4. **Location:** on two sites (elementary school and middle school) in suburban area close to airport. **Campuses:** elementary: 1 acre; middle school occupies part of large facility belonging to local German high school. **Libraries:** 5,000 volumes. **Facilities:** elementary: 7 classrooms, gymnasium, middle school: 4 classrooms, science lab, sports facilities.

*Once only fee **Deutsche mark

FRANKFURT

Goethe Gymnasium

Street address: Friedrich-Ebert-Anlage 22, 60325 Frankfurt am Main, Germany
Phone: (49)(69)21233525 **Facsimile:** (49)(69)21230717
Principal: Juergen Nessler

GHANA

Region: Western Africa
Size: 92,098 square miles
Population: 17,698,271
Capital: Accra
Telephone code: 233
Currency: cedi
Languages: English, Akan, Moshi-Dagomba, Ewe, Ga

ACCRA

Ghana International School

Street address: Second Circular Road, Cantonments, Accra, Ghana
Phone: (233)(21)777163/773299 **Facsimile:** (233)(21)774379
E-mail: gis@ncs.com.gh or itdept@gis.aau.org
Mail: PO Box 2856, Accra, Ghana
Principal: Judith S. Sawyerr
Deputy principals: David Kodwo Arku, Ebenezer Siebu
Principal, junior mistress: Diana Nyatepe-Coo
Principal, infant mistress: Agnes Asante-Abedi
Teaching staff: full-time, 99; part-time, 6; total, 105
Nationalities of teaching staff: U.S., 9; U.K., 15; host, 60; other, 21; total, 105
Grade levels: N – A-level
Enrollment: N – K, 78; 1 – 6, 517; secondary, 546; total, 1,141
Nationalities of student body: U.S., 60; U.K., 90; host, 500; other, 491; total, 1,141
Teacher/student ratio: 1/11
Tuition (annual): N – K, $2,775; 1 – 6, $3,900; secondary, $5,420 – 6,075
Other fees: admission*, $2,640 – 3,700
School year: September to June

Year founded: 1955. **Type of school:** coed, day, private nonprofit, nonsectarian. **Governed by:** appointed and elected board of governors. **Accredited by:** Ghana Ministry of Education. **Regional organizations:** AISA, ISA.

Curriculum/physical plant

Type: U.K. **Languages taught:** French, Spanish. **Staff specialists:** reading, math, computer, art, ESL, music, physical education, French, Spanish, science. **Special programs:** ESL. **Special curricular:** art, physical education, music, computer studies. **Extracurricular:** drama, choral music, yearbook, newspaper, art, community work. **Sports:** basketball, hockey, soccer, swimming, tennis, volleyball, handball, international sports exchanges. **Clubs:** chess, wildlife, music, community work, Boy Scouts, Girl Guides. **Tests:** SSAT, SAT I & II, A- and O-level GCE. **Graduates attending college:** 90%. **Graduates have attended:** Brown, Georgia Tech, Princeton, U. of London, MIT. **Location:** in pleasant suburban setting, 15 minutes from center city. **Campuses (2):** 10.5 acres. **Libraries:** 17,000 volumes. **Facilities:** 25 buildings, 40 classrooms, 3 covered play areas, 2 tennis courts, 3 playing fields, 4 science labs, basketball courts, film room, language lab, 3 computer labs with multimedia and the internet.

*Once only fee

Lincoln Community School

Street address: No. 196/21, Antebo Road, Abelenkpe, Accra, Ghana
Phone/facsimile: (233)(21)774018 **E-mail:** lincoln@ncs.com.gh
Mail: c/o U.S. Embassy, PO Box 194, Accra, Ghana
U.S. mail: c/o Dept. of State–Accra, Washington, DC 20521-2020
Superintendent: Merry Wade
Teaching staff: full-time, 25; total, 25
Nationalities of teaching staff: U.S., 10; U.K., 4; host, 4; other, 7; total, 25
Grade levels: preK – 12
Enrollment: preK, 48; K, 32; 1 – 6, 125; 7 – 9, 56; 10 – 12, 19; total, 280
Nationalities of student body: U.S., 57; U.K., 34; host, 59; other, 130; total, 280
Teacher/student ratio: 1/11
Tuition (annual): preK, $2,800; K, $3,050; 1 – 12, $6,300
Other fees: registration*, $1,000; capital levy, 10% of annual tuition
School year: August to June

Year founded: 1968. **Type of school:** coed, day, private nonprofit. **Governed by:** elected board of directors. **Accredited by:** government of Ghana, Middle States. **Regional organizations:** AAIE, AISA.

Curriculum/physical plant

Type: U.S. **Languages taught:** French. **Staff specialists:** computer, learning disabilities, media. **Special programs:** ESL. **Special curricular:** art, music, physical education, computer instruction, storytelling. **Extracurricular:** Tae Kwon Do, ballet, tennis, swimming, afterschool activities. **Tests:** Iowa. **Location:** in suburban area. **Campus:** 5 acres. **Library:** 7,500 volumes. **Facilities:** 4 buildings, 12 classrooms, covered play area, 2 playing fields, science lab, computer lab, art room, multipurpose hall/gymnasium, new classroom building and administrative office, air conditioning.

*Once only fee

GREECE

Region: Europe
Size: 50,949 square miles
Population: 10,538,594
Capital: Athens
Telephone code: 30
Currency: drachma
Languages: Greek, English, French

ATHENS

The American College of Greece (Pierce College)

Street address: 6 Gravias Street, 153 42 Aghia Paraskevi, Athens, Greece
Phone: (30)(1)6009800 – 9 **Facsimile:** (30)(1)6009819
President: John S. Bailey, Ed.D.
Vice president for financial affairs/ dean of administration: Anastasia Alexopoulou
Vice president for administrative affairs: Vassilis Protopsaltis
Associate principal/chairman of English department/dean of afternoon program: Olga E. Julius
Lykeiarchis: Irene Psaltidou
Teaching staff: full-time, 99; part-time, 2; total, 101
Nationalities of teaching staff: U.S., 10; host, 83; other, 8; total, 101
Grade levels: 7 – 12
Enrollment: 7 – 9, 570; 10 – 12, 607; total, 1,177
Nationalities of student body: U.S., 33; U.K., 15; host, 1,102; other, 27; total, 1,177
Capacity: 7 – 9, 630; 10 – 12, 630; total, 1,260
Teacher/student ratio: 1/10
Tuition (annual): $4,943
Other fees (annual): registration, $58; busing, $414 – 832
School year: September through June

Year founded: 1875. **Type of school:** coed, day, private nonprofit. **Governed by:** elected board of trustees. **Accredited by:** Greek Ministry of Education.

Curriculum

Type: national. **Languages of instruction:** English, Greek, French, German. **Staff specialists:** computer, psychologist, nurse, career & vocational counselor. **Special programs:** ESL, remedial. **Special curricular:** art, chorus, band, physical education, computer instruction, vocational, orchestra. **Extracurricular:** drama, gymnastics, dance, choral and instrumental music, computers, yearbook, newspaper, literary magazine, photography, excursions/expeditions, field trips, journalism. **Sports:** basketball, soccer, swimming, tennis, track and field, volleyball, handball, ping-pong, Olympic gymnastics. **Clubs:** drama, forensics, biology, mathematics, chemistry, ecology, Greek folk traditions. **Tests:** TOEFL. **Graduates attending college:** 80%. **Graduates have attended:** Princeton, Yale, Brown, U. of Massachusetts at Amherst, Swarthmore.

Physical plant

Location: on side of Mount Hymettus in northern suburb of Athens. **Campus:** 240,000 square meters. **Libraries:** 25,000 volumes. **Facilities:** 10 buildings, 51 classrooms, auditorium, cafeteria, infirmary, covered play area, 8 tennis courts, gymnasium, playing field, 4 science labs, computer lab, media center, AV equipment, amphitheater, language lab, home economics lab, Olympic-size swimming pool, track.

American Community Schools of Athens

Street address: 129 Aghias Paraskevis Street, 152 34 Halandri, Athens, Greece
Phone: (30)(1)6393200 **Facsimile:** (30)(1)6390051
E-mail: acs1@ath.forthnet.gr
Superintendent: Dr. Peter J. Nanos
Director of curriculum, instruction and human resources: Steve Medeiros
High school principal: Judith Drotar
Middle school/elementary principal: Dr. Joyce Adams
Business manager: Vasili Chryssanthakopoulos
Teaching staff: full-time, 69; part-time, 3; total, 72
Nationalities of teaching staff: U.S., 45; host, 17; other, 10; total, 72
Grade levels: preK – 12
Enrollment: preK, 13; K, 21; 1 – 5, 211; 6 – 8, 231; 9 – 12, 469; total, 945
Nationalities of student body: U.S., 440; host, 145; other, 360; total, 945
Teacher/student ratio: 1/12
Tuition (annual): K – 12, 990,000 – 2,149,000**
Other fees (annual): registration*, 175,000**; capital, 50,000; technology, 15,000; IB (initial), 150,000; semester fees: pre-school, 187,500; ESL, 200,000; resource room, 150,000
School year: September to June

Year founded: 1945. **Type of school:** coed, day, private nonprofit. **Governed by:** elected board of education. **Accredited by:** Middle States. **Regional organizations:** AAIE, ECIS, NESA.

Curriculum

Type: U.S., IB, AP. **Languages taught:** French, Spanish, German, Arabic, Greek. **Staff specialists:** reading, math, computer, psychologist, nurse, counselors, business education, resource center. **Special programs:** ESL, honors sections, remedial. **Special curricular:** art, chorus, band, physical education, computer instruction, vocational. **Extracurricular:** drama, gymnastics, dance, choral and instrumental music, computers, yearbook, newspaper, photography, excursions/expeditions, field trips, literary magazines. **Sports:** basketball, cross-country, soccer, softball, tennis, track and field, volleyball, wrestling. **Clubs:** computer, drama, Model UN, French, Spanish, forensics, German, Greek, Arabic, science, photo, booster. **Tests:** SSAT, PSAT, SAT, ACT, TOEFL, IB, AP, CTBS. **Graduates attending college:** 80%. **Graduates have attended:** Harvard, Boston U., U. of California, Cornell, McGill.

Physical plant

Location: 7 miles northeast of downtown Athens. **Campus:** 27,200 square meters. **Library:** 26,800 volumes. **Facilities:** 7 buildings, auditorium, cafeteria, infirmary, 3 tennis courts, gymnasium, 3 playing fields, 8 science labs, 4 computer labs.

*Once only fee **Greek drachma

GREEN HILL INTERNATIONAL SCHOOL

Street address: 31 Afroditis Street, Hellenikon 16777 - Greece
Phone: (30)(1)9640006/9646866 **Facsimile:** (30)(1)9612732
Mail: PO Box 73817, Hellenikon 16710, Greece
Director: M. A. Sbeiti
Principal: Antonia Hapsis
Admissions: Gloria Binteris
Financial: Zeina Sbeiti
Teaching staff: full-time, 17; part-time, 11; total, 28
Nationalities of teaching staff: U.S., 19; host, 6; other, 3; total, 28
Grade levels: preK – 12
Enrollment: preK, 10; K, 11; 1 – 6, 82; 7 – 9, 26; 10 – 12, 36; total, 165
Nationalities of student body: U.S., 61; host, 62; other, 42; total, 165
Teacher/student ratio: 1/8
Tuition (annual): preK – K, $4,000; 1 – 2, $4,600; 3 – 5, $5,000; 6 – 8, $5,400; 9 – 12, $5,900
Other fees (annual): registration, $200 – 400; busing, $750 – 900
School year: September to June

Year founded: 1987. **Type of school:** coed, day, proprietary. **Governed by:** elected board of trustees. **Accredited by:** Greek Ministry of Education. **Regional organizations:** NESA.

Curriculum/physical plant

Type: U.S. **Languages taught:** French, German, Arabic, Greek. **Staff specialists:** computer, speech/hearing, learning disabilities, nurse. **Special curricular:** art, physical education, computer instruction, music, FutureKIDS. **Extracurricular:** drama, gymnastics, instrumental music, computers, yearbook, newspaper, photography, excursions/expeditions, field trips. **Sports:** basketball, soccer, swimming, tennis, volleyball. **Clubs:** languages, sports, environmental, yearbook. **Tests:** SAT, ACT, TOEFL. **Graduates attending college:** 95%. **Graduates have attended:** U. of Laverne, Deree College, U. of California at San Diego, Stanford. **Location:** in suburban area, 15 miles from Athens. **Campuses (3):** 1 acre. **Library:** 9,500 volumes. **Facilities:** 3 buildings, 22 classrooms, covered play area, 3 playing fields.

TASIS HELLENIC INTERNATIONAL SCHOOL IN ATHENS

Street address: Artemidos and Xenias Streets, Kefalari-Kifissia, Athens, Greece
Phone: (30)(1)8081426 **Facsimile:** (30)(1)8018421 **E-mail:** bhani@hol.gr **Web:** http://www.tasis.com
Mail: PO Box 51025, GR-145 10 Kifissia, Greece
U.S. mail: 1640 Wisconsin Ave., NW, Washington, DC 20007, U.S.A.
Director/headmaster: George B. Salimbene
Elementary school principal: Chris Grant–Bear
Academic dean: Chris Tragas
Business manager: Fanis Malakondas
Teaching staff: full-time, 46; part-time, 2; total, 48
Nationalities of teaching staff: U.S., 22; U.K., 8; host, 6; other, 12; total, 48
Grade levels: preK – 12, postgraduate year
Enrollment: preK – 6, 75; 7 – 9, 75; 10 – 12, 200; total, 350
Nationalities of student body: U.S., 90; host, 110; other, 150; total, 350
Teacher/student ratio: 1/7
Tuition (annual): preK – K, 980,000**; 1 – 6, 1,560,000; 7 – 8, 1,795,000; 9 – 12, 1,830,000
Other fees (annual): registration*, 120,000**; boarding, $19,800; busing, 250,000 – 350,000
School year: September to June

Year founded: 1971. **Type of school:** coed, day, boarding, proprietary. **Governed by:** appointed governing board. **Accredited by:** Middle States. **Regional organizations:** AAIE, ECIS, NESA.

Curriculum

Type: U.S., U.K., AP. **Languages taught:** French, Spanish, Arabic, Modern Greek. **Staff specialists:** computer, psychologist, college counselor, learning disabilities. **Special programs:** ESL, honors sections, independent study, remedial (elementary only). **Special curricular:** art, chorus, physical education, computer instruction, drama, yearbook, newspaper, field trips. **Extracurricular:** drama, dance, choral and instrumental music, computers, literary magazine, photography, excursions/expeditions, National Honor Society, student council. **Sports:** basketball, soccer, softball, track and field, volleyball, handball. **Clubs:** musical society, chess/games, French, Spanish, film, environment, Greek dancing. **Tests:** PSAT, SAT, TOEFL, AP, A-level GCE, IGCSE. **Graduates attending college:** 90%. **Graduates have attended:** American U., New York U., Boston U., London School of Economics, Imperial College (London).

Physical plant

Location: in wooded residential suburb, 10 miles north of Athens. **Libraries:** 15,000 volumes. **Facilities:** 2 buildings, 35 classrooms, auditorium, 2 playing fields, 4 science labs, computer lab, snack bar, art studio, darkroom, music room, typing room, 4 changing rooms. **Boarding facilities:** self-contained family-style facilities nearby include student rooms with private bathrooms, dining room, terrace, lounges, swimming pool, basket/volleyball, soccer.

*Once only fee **Greek drachma

THESSALONIKI

Anatolia College

Phone: (30)(31)323711 **Facsimile:** (30)(31)301076
Mail: PO Box 21021, 555 10 Pylea, Thessaloniki, Greece
U.S. mail: 130 Bowdoin Street, Suite 1009, Boston, MA 02108, U.S.A.
President : William W. McGrew, Ed.D.
Vice president and high school administrator: John Gateley
Principal: Patricia Kastritsis
Business manager: Danos Kanellis
Teaching staff: full-time, 83; part-time, 13; total, 96
Nationalities of teaching staff: U.S., 14; U.K., 4; host, 76; other, 2; total, 96
Grade levels: 7 – 12
Enrollment: 7 – 9, 581; 10 – 12, 576; total, 1,157
Tuition (annual): 7 – 12, $3,950
Boarding fees (annual): 7 – 12, $5,200
Other fees:
School year: September to June

Year founded: 1886. **Type of school:** coed, day, boarding, private nonprofit. **Governed and sponsored by:** Trustees of Anatolia College. **Accredited by:** Greek Ministry of Education.

Curriculum/physical plant

Type: U.S., national. **Languages of instruction:** English, Greek. **Staff specialists:** computer, counselor, nurse. **Special programs:** ESL. **Special curricular:** art, chorus, band, physical education, computer instruction. **Extracurricular:** drama, gymnastics, dance, choral and instrumental music, computers, yearbook, newspaper, literary magazine, excursions/expeditions, forensics, many clubs. **Sports:** basketball, soccer, track and field, volleyball, handball. **Tests:** PSAT, SAT, TOEFL, ACH, Michigan, Cambridge, GRE, GMAT. **Graduates attending college:** 70%. **Graduates have attended:** Harvard, Princeton, MIT, Yale, Dartmouth. **Location:** in suburban area, 30 minutes from Thessaloniki. **Campuses (2):** 45 acres. **Library:** 34,000 volumes. **Facilities:** 22 buildings, 72 classrooms, infirmary, covered play area, gymnasium, 3 computer labs, auditoriums, tennis courts, playing fields, science labs, boys' dormitory, girls' dormitory.

Pinewood Schools of Thessaloniki, Greece

Street address: Panorama Highway, Thessaloniki, Greece
Phone: (30)(31)301221 **Facsimile:** (30)(31)323196
Mail: PO Box 21001, 555 10 Pilea, Thessaloniki, Greece
U.S. mail: (no personal name) Pinewood Schools of Thessaloniki, c/o American Consulate General, PSC 108, Box 37, APO AE 09842
Director: Peter B. Baiter
Business manager: Despina Douptsiou
Teaching staff: full-time, 18; part-time, 7; total, 25

Nationalities of teaching staff: U.S., 10; U.K., 4; host, 5; other, 6; total, 25
Grade levels: pre-K – 12
Enrollment: preK, 20; K, 10; 1 – 6, 76; 7 – 9, 53; 10 – 12, 66; total, 225
Nationalities of student body: U.S., 59; U.K., 10; host, 4; other, 152; total, 225
Teacher/student ratio: 1/8
Boarders: boys, 8; girls, 7 **Grades:** 7 – 12 **Program:** planned 5-day
Tuition (annual): preK, $2,000; K, $3,326; 1 – 6, $5,098; 7 – 12, $5,625
Other fees (annual): boarding, $6,000; capital levy*, $600; busing, $1,047; yearbook, $75
School year: September to June

Year founded: 1950. **Type of school:** coed, day, boarding, private nonprofit. **Governed by:** elected Pinewood School Board. **Accredited by:** Middle States. **Regional organizations:** NESA, ECIS.

Curriculum/physical plant

Type: U.S. **Languages taught:** French, Modern Greek (required). **Special programs:** ESL. **Special curricular:** physical education, computer instruction. **Extracurricular:** computers, yearbook, excursions/expeditions, field trips. **Sports:** basketball, soccer, softball, volleyball. **Clubs:** chess, computer, National Honor Society, student council, forensics, guitar. **Tests:** PSAT, SAT, TOEFL. **Graduates attending college:** 75%. **Graduates have attended:** Clark, Wesleyan, Boston U., Cornell, Princeton. **Location:** in suburb overlooking city, 15 – 20 minutes from center of Thessaloniki. **Campus:** 4 acres. **Library:** 22,000 volumes. **Facilities:** 1 building, 16 classrooms, auditorium, gymnasium, 2 playing fields, science lab, computer lab, media center; boarding at neighboring Anatolia College, a coed Greek secondary school.

*Once only fee

ATHENS

Athens College

Street address: Stephanou Delta 15, Palaio Psychico, Attica 154 10, Greece
Phone: (30)(1)6712771 **Facsimile:** (30)(1)6748156 E-mail: acpresoff@hol.gr
Web: http://www.hol.gr/hosted/athens_college/gr.html
Mail: PO Box 65005, 154 10 Palaio Psychico, Greece
U.S. mail: 342 Madison Avenue, Suite 1616, New York, NY 10173 U.S.A.
President: Patricia L. Poteat, Ph.D.

GRENADA

Region: West Indies
Size: 133 square miles
Population: 94,961
Capital: St. George's
Telephone code: 809
Currency: East Caribbean dollar
Languages: English, French patois

ST. GEORGE'S

INTERNATIONAL SCHOOL OF GRENADA

Phone/facsimile: (1)(809)4444785 **E-mail:** isog@caribsurf.com
Mail: PO Box 744, St. George's, Grenada, West Indies
U.S. mail: c/o Administrative Officer, American Embassy Grenada, Dept. of State, Washington, DC 20502
Principal: Stephen L. Slovenz
Teaching staff: full-time, 6; part-time, 4; total, 10
Nationalities of teaching staff: U.S., 4; U.K., 1; host, 3; other, 2; total, 10
Grade levels: preK – 12
Enrollment: preK, 11; K, 2; 1 – 6, 26; 7 – 12, 9; total, 48
Teacher/student ratio: 1/12
Tuition (annual): preK, $1,030 (3 days), $1,373 (5 days); K – 6, $3,433; 7 – 12, $3,731
Other fees (annual): registration, $100; captial assessment, $180
School year: September to June

Year founded: 1984. **Type of school:** coed, day, private nonprofit. **Governed by:** appointed and elected board of directors.

Curriculum/physical plant

Type: U.S. **Languages taught:** French. **Special curricular:** art, physical education, music. **Extracurricular:** field trips, sports. **Clubs:** computer, art, earth. **Tests:** Iowa. **Location:** 2 miles from Lance aux Epines, in True Blue. **Library:** over 1,500 volumes. **Facilities:** 5 classrooms, playing field, pavilion.

GUAM

Region: West Pacific
Size: 210 square miles
Population: 133,152
Capital: Agana
Telephone code: 671
Currency: dollar
Languages: English, Chamorro

TUMON BAY

St. John's School

Street address: 911 Marine Drive, Tumon Bay, Guam 96911
Phone: (671)6465626/6468080 **Facsimile:** (671)6491055
Headmaster: A. Ronald Tooman
Head, upper school: Dale Jenkins, Ed.D.
Head, lower school: Imelda Santos
Teaching staff: full-time, 71; part-time, 3; total, 74
Grade levels: preK – 12
Enrollment: preK, 40; K, 55; 1 – 6, 306; 7 – 9, 171; 10 – 12, 114; total, 686
Teacher/student ratio: 1/9
Tuition (annual): preK – K, $6,285; 1 – 2, $6,790; 3 – 4, $6,972; 5 – 6, $7,155; 7 – 8, $7,879; 9 – 10, $9,022; 11 – 12, $9,147
Other fees (annual): registration, $250; books, $140; capital levy, $500; tuition insurance*, $170 – 650
School year: August to June

Year founded: 1962. **Type of school:** coed, day, church-related, private nonprofit. **Governed by:** board of trustees. **Sponsored by:** Episcopal Church. **Accredited by:** Western. **Regional organizations:** ECIS.

Curriculum/physical plant

Type: U.S., IB. **Languages taught:** French, Spanish, Japanese. **Staff specialists:** reading, math, computer, counselor, nurse. **Special programs:** honors sections. **Special curricular:** art, physical education, computer instruction. **Extracurricular:** drama, computers, yearbook, newspaper, field trips, sports. **Clubs:** National Honor Society, Lettermen. **Tests:** SSAT, PSAT, SAT, IB. **Graduates have attended:** U. of California at Berkeley, Vassar, Harvard, Brown. **Location:** on tropical island. **Campus:** 7.5 acres. **Library:** 25,000 volumes. **Facilities:** new 8-classroom building, 3 science labs, 2 computer labs, air conditioning.

*Once only fee

GUATEMALA

Region: Central America
Size: 42,042 square miles
Population: 11,227,614
Capital: Guatemala City
Telephone code: 502
Currency: quetzal
Languages: Spanish, Mayan languages

GUATEMALA CITY

THE AMERICAN SCHOOL OF GUATEMALA

Street address: 11 Calle 15-79, zone 15, V.H. III, Guatemala City, Guatemala
Phone: (502)3690791 **Facsimile:** (502)3640212 **E-mail:** cagadm@cag.edu.gt
Mail: Apartado Postal No. 83, 01901 Guatemala City, Guatemala
U.S. mail: Director, c/o ASG, U.S. Embassy Guatemala, Unit 3325, APO AA 34024
Director: Barbara Baker Barillas
Secondary school principal: Maria Hirst
Elementary school principal: Sarah Corrie
Teaching staff: full-time, 164; part-time, 25; total, 189
Nationalities of teaching staff: U.S., 30; host, 144; other, 15; total, 189
Grade levels: K – 12
Enrollment: K, 122; 1, 112; 2 – 7, 676; 8 – 10, 329; 11 – 12, 229; total, 1,468
Nationalities of student body: U.S., 182; host, 1,229; other, 57; total, 1,468
Teacher/student ratio: 1/10
Tuition (annual): K – 7, 13,500**; 8 – 12, 15,000
Other fees (annual): registration*, 1,000**; insurance*, 225; busing, 2,000; books/supplies, 1,600; matriculation, 11,000; technology, 360
School year: January to October

Year founded: 1945. **Type of school:** coed, day, private nonprofit. **Governed by:** appointed board of directors. **Sponsored by:** Foundation of the University of the Valley of Guatemala. **Accredited by:** Southern. **Regional organizations:** NAIS, SAIS, AASCA, AAIE, Tri-Assoc.

Curriculum

Type: U.S., national. **Languages of instruction:** English, Spanish. **Languages taught:** French, Spanish, German. **Staff specialists:** reading, computer, learning disabilities, psychologists, counselors. **Special programs:** ESL, honors sections, remedial. **Special curricular:** art, chorus, physical education, computer instruction, orchestra, swimming. **Extracurricular:** drama, gymnastics, dance, choral and instrumental music, computers, yearbook, newspaper, literary magazine, field trips, student association, Honor Society. **Sports:** baseball, basketball, soccer, softball, swimming, track and field, volleyball, water polo. **Tests:** PSAT, SAT, ACT, TOEFL, Stanford (elementary, ninth, and eleventh). **Graduates attending college:** 92%. **Graduates have attended:** U. of Pennsylvania, Texas A&M, MIT, Stanford, Notre Dame.

Physical plant

Location: in residential area on outskirts of Guatemala City, surrounded by gardens and sports fields. **Campus:** 52 acres. **Library:** 29,000 volumes. **Facilities:** 19 buildings, 46 classrooms, auditorium, cafeteria, covered play area, gymnasium, science labs, 2 computer labs, swimming pool, 10 playing fields and courts, Internet access.

*Once only fee **Guatemalan quetzal

Colegio Interamericano

Street address: Boulevard "La Montaña" Finca El Socorro, zona 16, Guatemala City, Guatemala
Phone: (502)(3)641803/641805/641536/641778 **Facsimile:** (502)(3)642002
Mail: Apartado Postal 1681, Guatemala City, Guatemala, C.A.
U.S. mail: 14431 S.W. 168 Terra, Miami, FL 33177, U.S.A.
General director: Lyle J. Loosle
Administrative director: Alberto Montes
High school director: James Gentrup
Elementary director: Olga Renata de Alejos
Preprimary director: Silvia Munoz de Díaz
Teaching staff: full-time, 90; part-time, 1; total, 91
Nationalities of teaching staff: U.S., 12; host, 61; other, 18; total, 91
Grade levels: preK – 13
Enrollment: preK, 68; K, 70; 1 – 6, 525; 7 – 9, 208; 10 – 12, 119; total, 990
Nationalities of student body: U.S., 39; host, 892; other, 59; total, 990
Capacity: preK, 68; K, 70; 1 – 6, 525; 7 – 9, 208; 10 – 12, 119; total, 990
Teacher/student ratio: 1/10
Tuition (annual): preK, $1,300; K, $1,458; 1 – 6, $1,870; 7 – 12, $2,200; 13, $2,457
Other fees (annual): registration, $417; insurance, $17; busing, $468; books, $150
School year: January to October

Year founded: 1975. **Type of school:** coed, private nonprofit. **Sponsored by:** Fundación Educativa. **Accredited by:** Southern.

Curriculum/physical plant

Type: U.S., national. **Languages of instruction:** English, Spanish. **Languages taught:** English, Spanish. **Staff specialists:** reading, math, computer, counselor, psychologist, nurse. **Special curricular:** art, chorus, physical education, computer. **Sports:** gymnastics, soccer, basketball, volleyball, kickball, cheerleaders. **Clubs:** scouts, experiments, baking, music, ecology, mathematics, dance, arts and crafts. **Tests:** SAT, TOEFL, Stanford, MAT. **Graduates attending college:** 100%. **Graduates have attended:** U. Marroquin, U. Del Valle, U. Mariano Galvez, Texas A & M, Perdue. **Location:** in city. **Facilities:** cafeteria, infirmary, 3 tennis courts, 2 science labs, 4 computer labs.

*Once only fee

Colegio Maya
The American International School

Street address: Km. 12-1/2 Carretera a El Salvador, Guatemala City, Guatemala
Phone: (502)6341209/6340649/6346742 **Facsimile:** (502)6340077
E-mail: colmaya@pronet.net.gt
Mail: Apartado Postal 2-C, Guatemala City, Guatemala
U.S. mail: Colegio Maya, Unit 3326-APO AA 34024
Director: Fred Pasquale, Ed.D.
Secondary principal: James Gentrup
Elementary principal: Antonio L. Trujillo
Counselor: Aida Zea
Teaching staff: full-time, 48; total, 48
Nationalities of teaching staff: U.S., 40; host, 8; total, 48
Grade levels: preK – 12
Enrollment: preK – 5, 160; 6 – 8, 92; 9 – 12, 111; total, 363
Teacher/student ratio: 1/8
Tuition (annual): preK, $2,788; K – 12, $5,959
Other fees (annual): registration*, $2,000; busing, $650; incorporation*, $3,000
School year: August to June

Year founded: 1957. **Type of school:** coed, day, private nonprofit. **Governed by:** elected board of directors. **Accredited by:** Southern, Guatemala Ministry of Education. **Regional organizations:** AAIE, AASCA, Tri-Assoc.

Curriculum/physical plant

Type: U.S., AP. **Languages taught:** Spanish. **Staff specialists:** computer, counselor, learning disabilities, nurse. **Special programs:** ESL, independent study. **Special curricular:** art, physical education, computer instruction, vocal music. **Extracurricular:** computers, yearbook, newspaper, field trips, sports. **Clubs:** honor society, student council. **Tests:** PSAT, SAT, ACT, TOEFL, AP. **Graduates attending college:** 95%. **Graduates have attended:** U. of Pennsylvania, MIT, Notre Dame, U. of Florida, Georgetown. **Location:** on rural mountainside, 6 miles from Guatemala City. **Campus:** 12 acres. **Library:** 10,000 volumes. **Facilities:** 8 buildings, 29 classrooms, infirmary, playing field, science lab, computer labs, cafeteria, gymnasium.

*Once only fee

GUINEA

Region: West Africa
Size: 94,926 square miles
Population: 7,411,981
Capital: Conakry
Telephone code: 224
Currency: franc
Languages: French, Peuhl, Malinke

CONAKRY

The International School of Conakry

Phone: (224)472035 **Facsimile:** c/o U.S. Embassy (224)411522
U.S. mail: c/o Dept. of State–Conakry, Washington, DC 20521-2110
Director: James Fisher
Teaching staff: full-time, 6; part-time, 6; total, 12
Nationalities of teaching staff: U.S., 5; other, 7; total, 12
Grade levels: N – 8
Enrollment: N – preK, 14; K, 6; 1 – 6, 37; 7 – 8, 6; total, 63
Capacity: N – preK, 20; K, 10; 1 – 6, 40; 7 – 8, 10; total, 80
Teacher/student ratio: 1/5
Tuition (annual): N – preK, $3,900; K, $7,800; 1 – 8, $10,000
Other fees (annual): registration, $500; building fund* (students of new association members), $1,500
School year: late August to early June

Year founded: 1963. **Type of school:** coed, day. **Governed by:** elected school board. **Sponsored by:** school association. **Accredited by:** Middle States. **Regional organizations:** AAIE, AISA.

Curriculum/physical plant

Type: U.S. **Languages taught:** English, French. **Staff specialists:** reading, art, librarian, music, physical education. **Special programs:** ESL. **Special curricular:** art, music. **Extracurricular:** Saturday sports, Girl Scouts, Boys Club. **Tests:** Iowa. **Location:** in Conakry, district of Matam. **Facilities:** 1 building, 7 classrooms, computer lab, library, shaded play area, oceanfront site, air conditioning.

*Once only fee

GUYANA

Region: South America
Size: 83,044 square miles
Population: 712,091
Capital: Georgetown
Telephone code: 592
Currency: dollar
Languages: English, Amerindian dialects

GEORGETOWN

Georgetown American International School

Street address: 9/10 Delhi Street, Georgetown, Guyana
Phone: (592)(2)61595 **Facsimile:** (592)(2)61459
U.S. mail: c/o Dept. of State, Washington, DC 20521-3170
Director: Thurston Riehl
Teaching staff: full-time, 12; part-time, 6; total, 18
Nationalities of teaching staff: U.S., 2; host, 14; other, 2; total, 18
Grade levels: N – 12
Enrollment: N, 1; K, 6; 1 – 6, 54; 7 – 12, 38; total, 99
Nationalities of student body: U.S., 31; U.K., 7; other, 61; total, 99
Teacher/student ratio: 1/7
Tuition (annual): N – K, $2,463; 1 – 6, $5,180; 7 – 12, $5,280
School year: September to June

Year founded: 1971. **Type of school:** coed, day, private nonprofit. **Governed by:** elected board of directors.

Curriculum/physical plant

Type: U.S. **Languages taught:** French, Spanish. **Special programs:** ESL. **Special curricular:** art, chorus, physical education, computer instruction, music. **Extracurricular:** choral music, yearbook, newspaper, field trips, mini courses. **Tests:** Iowa. **Location:** in suburban Georgetown. **Campus:** 1 acre. **Facilities:** 2 buildings, 12 classrooms, auditorium, science lab, library, air conditioning.

HAITI

Region: Caribbean
Size: 10,695 square miles
Population: 6,731,539
Capital: Port-au-Prince
Telephone code: 509
Currency: gourde
Languages: French, Creole

DESCHAPELLES

Ecole Flamboyant

Phone: (509)381141–2 **Facsimile:** (509)381142 **E-mail:** has-pap@acn.com
Mail: c/o Hopital Albert Schweitzer, PO Box 1744, Port-au-Prince, Haiti
Principal: Kevan Hull
Teaching staff: full-time, 4; total, 4
Nationalities of teaching staff: host, 2; other, 2; total, 4
Grade levels: preK – 8
Enrollment: preK – K, 12; 1 – 5, 3; total, 15
Nationalities of student body: host, 13; other, 27; total, 40
Capacity: total, 30
Teacher/student ratio: 1/4
School year: September to June

Type of school: day, private nonprofit. **Governed by:** Hopital Albert Schweitzer/Grant Foundation. **Sponsored by:** Hopital Albert Schweitzer/ missionary families.

Curriculum/physical plant

Type: U.S., national. **Languages of instruction:** English, French (Haitian). **Languages taught:** English, French. **Special programs:** ESL. **Special curricular:** art, physical education, music. **Extracurricular:** excursions/expeditions, field trips. **Tests:** SAT. **Location:** in Deschapelles, 2.5 hours by car from Port-au-Prince. **Library:** 1,500 volumes. **Facilities:** 2 buildings on the H.A.S. compound, 4 classrooms, tennis court, playing field, swimming pool.

*Once only fee

PETIONVILLE

The Caribbean-American School

Street address: 56, rue Lambert, Petionville, Haiti
Phone: (509)577961
U.S. mail: c/o Lynx Air, PO Box 407139, Ft. Lauderdale, FL 33340, U.S.A.
Director: Ernestine Rochelle Robinson
High school principal/math department head: Maxo Bourdeau
Elementary head: Connie Deroneth

Teaching staff: full-time, 10; total, 10
Nationalities of teaching staff: U.S., 5; host, 5; total, 10
Grade levels: preK – 12
Enrollment: total, 100
Capacity: total, 150
Teacher/student ratio: 1/10
Tuition (annual): preK – 8, $3,000; 9 – 11, $3,300; 12, $3,600
Other fees (annual): registration, $250; lunch, $100/month; books, $250; entrance*, $700/family
School year: September to June

Year founded: 1980. **Type of school:** coed, day, private nonprofit. **Governed by:** board of directors.

Curriculum/physical plant

Type: U.S., AP. **Languages taught:** French, Spanish. **Staff specialists:** reading, math, computer. **Special programs:** ESL, honors sections, independent study. **Special curricular:** art, physical education, computer instruction, music. **Extracurricular:** gymnastics, dance, computers, excursions/expeditions, field trips. **Sports:** aerobics, swimming, tennis, weight lifting. **Tests:** SSAT, PSAT, TOEFL, Iowa, CAT. **Graduates attending college:** 100%. **Graduates have attended:** U. of Florida, Miami-Dade Community College, Pratt Institute, New York U., Howard. **Location:** in suburban area of Port-au-Prince. **Campus:** .5 acre. **Facilities:** 2 buildings, 12 classrooms, cafeteria, playing field, computer lab, music and art rooms, library. Boarding available in Petionville, with transportation provided.

*Once only fee

PORT-AU-PRINCE

Union School

Phone: (509)570207/577434 **Facsimile:** (509)573131
Mail: PO Box 1175, Port-au-Prince, Haiti
U.S. mail: Lynx Air/UNSCH, PO Box 407139, Fort Lauderdale, FL 33340, U.S.A.
Director: Rita Maselli-Boucicaut
Secondary principal: Marie F. Jean-Baptiste
Elementary principal: Jessye M. Bazile
Teaching staff: full-time, 44; part-time, 1; total, 45
Nationalities of teaching staff: U.S., 26; host, 8; other, 11; total, 45
Grade levels: preK – 12
Enrollment: preK – K, 28; 1 – 6, 143; 7 – 12, 212; total, 383
Nationalities of student body: U.S., 222; host, 135; other, 26; total, 383
Teacher/student ratio: 1/10
Tuition (annual): preK, $1,826; K, $2,700; 1 – 6, $4,120; 7 – 8, $4,340; 9 – 12, $4,515
Other fees (annual): registration, $183 (new student), $125 (returning student); family entrance*, $667; student activities, $97; graduation, $100
School year: late August to early June

Year founded: 1919. **Type of school:** coed, day, private nonprofit. **Governed by:** elected board of trustees. **Accredited by:** Southern. **Regional organizations:** AAIE, ACCAS, Tri-Assoc.

Curriculum/physical plant

Type: U.S., AP. **Languages taught:** English, French, Spanish. **Staff specialists:** computer, counselor, learning disabilities, nurse. **Special programs:** ESL, honors sections. **Special curricular:** art, physical education, computer instruction. **Extracurricular:** choral music, computers, yearbook, field trips, student council. **Sports:** basketball, soccer, volleyball. **Clubs:** chess, National Honor Society, service (affiliated with Rotary International), Spanish, French. **Tests:** SSAT, PSAT, SAT, ACT, TOEFL, AP, Iowa. **Graduates attending college:** 90%. **Graduates have attended:** Yale, Duke, Tulane, Georgetown U., Princeton. **Location:** on wooded hillside overlooking the bay of Port-au-Prince. **Campus:** 4 acres. **Library:** 11,000 volumes. **Facilities:** 2 buildings, infirmary, playing field, computer lab, learning resource center.

*Once only fee

HONDURAS

Region: Central America
Size: 43,433 square miles
Population: 5,605,193
Capital: Tegucigalpa

Telephone code: 504
Currency: lempira
Language: Spanish

EL MOCHITO

ESCUELA BILINGUE SANTA BARBARA

Phone: (504)579979 **Facsimile:** (504)579981
Mail: Apartado 342, San Pedro Sula, Honduras
U.S. mail: IMC-SAP Dept. 265, PO Box 52-3900, Miami, FL 33152, U.S.A.
Principal: John P. Leddy
Teaching staff: full-time, 5; total, 5
Nationalities of teaching staff: U.S., 4; host, 1; total, 5
Grade levels: K – 8
Enrollment: K, 4; 1 – 6, 25; 7 – 9, 4; total, 33
Nationalities of student body: U.S., 4; host, 24; other, 6; total, 34
Teacher/student ratio: 1/7

Sponsored by: AMPAC. **Regional organizations:** Association of Bilingual Schools of Honduras.

Curriculum/physical plant

Type: U.S., national. **Languages of instruction:** English, Spanish. **Special curricular:** computer instruction. **Extracurricular:** drama, computers, yearbook, literary magazine, excursions/expeditions, field trips. **Tests:** Iowa. **Location:** at mining camp, 100 kilometers from San Pedro Sula. **Library:** 2,000 volumes. **Facilities:** 1 building, 5 classrooms.

LA CIEBA

Mazapan School

Phone: (504)432716 **Facsimile:** (504)433559 **E-mail:** mazapan@ns.gbm.hn **Web:** http://www.mazapan.stdfruit.hn
U.S. mail: (first class) 6964 NW 50th St., Suite HO-202, Miami, FL 33166-5632, U.S.A.; PO Box 1747, Gulfport, MS 39502, U.S.A.
Superintendent: Helen Austin
High school principal: Phil Jones
Teaching staff: full-time, 22; part-time, 1; total, 23
Nationalities of teaching staff: U.S., 13; host, 10; total, 23
Grade levels: 1 – 12
Enrollment: 1 – 6, 150; 7 – 9, 75; 10 – 12, 75; total, 300
Capacity: 1 – 6, 150; 7 – 9, 75; 10 – 12, 75; total, 300
Teacher/student ratio: 1/13
Tuition (annual): 1 – 12, $2,860
Other fees (annual): registration, $220; capital levy, $1,000
School year: August to June

Year founded: 1928. **Type of school:** coed, day, company-sponsored. **Governed by:** Standard Fruit de Honduras, SA. **Accredited by:** Southern, Honduran Ministry of Education. **Regional organizations:** AASCA Tri-Assoc., AAIE.

Curriculum/physical plant

Type: U.S. **Languages taught:** English, French, Spanish. **Staff specialists:** math, computer, counselor, art, librarian, music, physical education. **Special programs:** correspondence. **Special curricular:** art, chorus, band, physical education, computer instruction, drama, speech, Internet. **Extracurricular:** drama, instrumental music, computers, yearbook, newspaper, photography, excursions/expeditions, island survival. **Sports:** basketball, soccer, softball, volleyball. **Tests:** PSAT, SAT, ACT, TOEFL, Stanford. **Graduates attending college:** 100%. **Graduates have attended:** U.S. Coast Guard Academy, College of William and Mary, U. of Houston, Georgetown, Auburn. **Location:** park-like setting in city. **Campus:** 4 acres. **Library:** 8,000 volumes. **Facilities:** 7 buildings, 16 classrooms, auditorium, 2 playing fields, science lab, computer lab.

SAN PEDRO SULA

Escuela Internacional Sampedrana

Street address: Colonia Gracias a Dios, San Pedro Sula, Cortes, Honduras
Phone: (504)562722 **Facsimile:** (504)561458 **E-mail:** seis@netsys.hn
Web: http://www.netsys.hn/~seis
Mail: Apt. #565, San Pedro Sula, Honduras
Superintendent: Gregory E. Werner
Principals: Martha Thompson, Craig Hoogendoom, Jeanne Rice
Business manager: Mercedes Diaz
Teaching staff: full-time, 85; part-time, 10; total, 95
Grade levels: N – 12
Capacity: N – preK, 131; K, 153; 1 – 6, 453; 7 – 9, 593; 10 – 12, 116; 13, 54; total, 1,500
Teacher/student ratio: 1/18
Other fees (annual): registration, $40; books, $225; gym, $150; land/construction, $500 per family; locker (7 – 12), $15; lab (9 – 12), $100
School year: August to June

Year founded: 1953. **Type of school:** coed, day, private nonprofit. **Governed by:** elected board of directors. **Sponsored by:** Sociedad Educacional Internacional Sampedrana. **Accredited by:** Southern, Honduran Ministry of Education. **Regional organizations:** AAIE, AASCA, Tri-Assoc.

Curriculum/physical plant

Type: U.S., national. **Languages of instruction:** English, Spanish. **Languages taught:** English, Spanish. **Staff specialists:** reading, math, computer, counselor, psychologist, learning disabilities, nurse. **Special programs:** ESL, honors sections, remedial. **Special curricular:** art, band, physical education, computer instruction. **Extracurricular:** drama, instrumental music, computers, yearbook, newspaper, literary magazine, excursions/expeditions, field trips. **Sports:** basketball, soccer, volleyball. **Clubs:** drama, National Honor Society, film society. **Tests:** PSAT, SAT, ACT, TOEFL, Iowa. **Graduates attending college:** 95%. **Graduates have attended:** Citadel, Tufts, Auburn, U. of Pennsylvania, U. of Miami. **Location:** in San Pedro Sula. **Library:** 20,000 volumes. **Facilities:** 2 campuses, 10 buildings, 40 classrooms, gymnasium, 2 playing fields, 2 science labs, 2 computer labs.

TEGUCIGALPA

Academia Los Pinares

Location: Km. 10, Calle Principal, El Hatillo, D.C. Honduras
Phone: (504)218231 **Facsimile:** (504)218586 **E-mail:** apinares@ns.gbm.hn
Mail: Apartado 3250, Tegucigalpa, D.C. Honduras
Superintendent: Gene Smith
High school principal: James Bedford
Elementary principal: Dennis L. Osberg
Host country director: Josué López
Business manager: Ruth De Padilla
Teaching staff: full-time, 41; part-time, 6; total, 47
Nationalities of teaching staff: U.S., 32; U.K., 5; host, 10; total, 47
Grade levels: preK – 12
Enrollment: preK, 46; K, 49; 1 – 6, 314; 7 – 9, 128; 10 – 12, 108; total, 645
Nationalities of student body: U.S., 75; U.K., 14; host, 516; other, 40; total, 645
Capacity: preK, 46; K, 46; 1 – 6, 300; 7 – 9, 150; 10 – 12, 150; total, 692
Teacher/student ratio: 1/13
Tuition (annual): preK, $760; K – 6, $1,030; 7 – 12, $1,240
Other fees (annual): registration*, $120; capital levy*, $350; busing, $200
School year: August to June

Year founded: 1964. **Type of school:** coed, day, church-related, private nonprofit. **Governed by:** elected school board. **Sponsored by:** 5 U.S.-based churches. **Accredited by:** Southern. **Regional organizations:** Association of Bilingual Schools in Honduras.

Curriculum/physical plant

Type: U.S., national. **Languages of instruction:** English, Spanish. **Languages taught:** English, Spanish. **Special curricular:** art, physical education, computer instruction, vocational. **Extracurricular:** choral music, yearbook, newspaper, excursions/expeditions, computer club. **Sports:** basketball, soccer, volleyball. **Tests:** PSAT, SAT, ACT, TOEFL, Iowa. **Graduates attending college:** 95%. **Location:** on plateau, 2,000 feet above city, 5 miles to center of Tegucigalpa. **Campus:** 22 acres. **Facilities:** 4 buildings, 35 classrooms, infirmary, 2 science labs, 2 computer labs, library.

*Once only fee

The American School of Tegucigalpa

Street address: Las Lomas del Guijarro, Tegucigalpa, Honduras
Phone: (504)324696 **Facsimile:** (504)322380
Mail: c/o U.S. Embassy, Tegucigalpa, Honduras
Superintendent: Dr. Don Groves
Director: Linda Duron
High school principal: Liliana F. Jenkins
Elementary principal: Elcenora Martinez
Teaching staff: full-time, 63; total, 63

Nationalities of teaching staff: U.S., 29; U.K., 1; host, 30; other, 3; total, 63
Grade levels: N – 12
Enrollment: N – K, 210; 1 – 6, 420; 7 – 12, 475; total, 1,105
Nationalities of student body: U.S., 168; U.K., 7; host, 744; other, 186; total, 1,105
Capacity: N, 66; K, 66; 1 – 6, 486; 7 – 9, 243; 10 – 12, 243; total, 1,104
Teacher/student ratio: 1/18
Tuition (annual): N – preK, $1,600; K, $2,150; 1 – 6, $2,400; 7 – 12, $2,600
Other fees (annual): busing, $300; initial enrollment*, $5,000
School year: August to June

Year founded: 1946. **Type of school:** coed, day, private nonprofit. **Governed by:** elected board of directors, Sociedad Educacional Interamericana de Tegucigalpa. **Accredited by:** Southern. **Regional organizations:** AASCA, Tri-Assoc.

Curriculum/physical plant

Type: U.S., national. **Languages of instruction:** English, Spanish (1 hour daily). **Languages taught:** English, Spanish. **Staff specialists:** computer, counselor, learning disabilities, nurse. **Special curricular:** chorus, band, physical education, computer instruction. **Extracurricular:** drama, yearbook, field trips, chess, sports. **Clubs:** National Honor Society, community service. **Tests:** PSAT, SAT, ACT, Iowa. **Graduates attending college:** 95%. **Graduates have attended:** Rosemont, Stanford, Duke, William and Mary, U. of Pennsylvania. **Location:** on hilltop overlooking city. **Campus:** 12 acres. **Library:** 12,818 volumes. **Facilities:** 6 buildings, 45 classrooms, auditorium, cafeteria, infirmary, playing field, 4 science labs, 2 computer labs.

*Once only fee

Discovery School

Street address: Calle Tierno Galvan #2884, Tegucigalpa, M.D.C., Honduras, C.A.
Phone: (504)320414
U.S. mail: TGU 00015, PO Box 025387, Miami, FL 33102-5387, U.S.A.
Director: Martha Rubi
Teaching staff: full-time, 7; part-time, 2; total, 9
Nationalities of teaching staff: U.S., 7; host, 2; total, 9
Grade levels: preK – 7
Enrollment: preK, 10; K, 8; 1 – 6, 50; 7, 2; total, 70
Nationalities of student body: U.S., 53; U.K., 3; host, 2; other, 12; total, 70
Teacher/student ratio: 1/9
Tuition (annual): preK, $1,385; K – 7, $3,000
Other fees (annual): registration*, $2,500; busing, $400
School year: late August to mid-June

Year founded: 1994. **Type of school:** coed, day, private nonprofit. **Governed by:** board of directors. **Accredited by:** Southern (in process).

Curriculum/physical plant

Type: U.S. **Languages taught:** Spanish. **Special curricular:** art, physical education. **Tests:** Iowa. **Location:** in three-level building in residential neighborhood of city.

*Once only fee

HONG KONG

Region: East Asia
Size: 415 square miles
Population: 6,300,000
Capital: Hong Kong
Telephone code: 852
Currency: dollar
Languages: Chinese, English

HONG KONG

AMERICAN INTERNATIONAL SCHOOL†

Street address: 123, 125 & 143 Waterloo Road, Kowloon Tong, Hong Kong
Phone: (852)23363812 **Facsimile:** (852)23365276
Headmistress/elementary principal: Rose Ng
High school principal: Linda O'Donnell
Teaching staff: full-time, 31; total, 31
Grade levels: 1 – 12
Enrollment: 1 – 6, 137; 7 – 9, 141; 10 – 12, 177; total, 455
Capacity: total, 500
Teacher/student ratio: 1/15
Tuition (annual): 1 – 3, 59,800**; 4 – 6, 63,250; 7 – 9, 69,000; 10 – 12, 74,750
Other fees (annual): busing, 650 – 1,100**(monthly); books, 1,500 – 2,500; sport and activities, 200; PSAT, 100; application*, 1,000; yearbook, 300
School year: August to June

Year founded: 1986. **Type of school:** coed, day. **Governed by:** appointed board of directors. **Accredited by:** Western.

Curriculum/physical plant

Type: U.S., AP. **Staff specialists:** reading, math, computer, counselor. **Special programs:** ESL. **Special curricular:** art, physical education, computer instruction. **Extracurricular:** drama, instrumental music, computers, yearbook, newspaper, field trips. **Sports:** badminton, hockey, soccer, swimming, tennis, volleyball. **Tests:** PSAT, SAT, TOEFL, AP. **Graduates attending college:** 76%. **Graduates have attended:** Boston U., Stanford, New York U., Kanagawa U., Ritsumeikan U. **Location:** in city. **Facilities:** 3 buildings, 21 classrooms, playing field, 2 science labs, computer lab, swimming pool, 2 multipurpose halls, air conditioning.

*Once only fee **Hong Kong dollar †formerly California International (USA) School

Canadian International School

Street address: 10 Borrett Road, Mid–levels, Hong Kong
Phone: (852)25257088 **Facsimile:** (852)25257579 **E-mail:** cdnis@hklink.net
Principal: Neil P. Johnston
Vice-principal: Alan Dick
Head of library: Annie Lau
Head of computer services: Michael Zambon
Business manager: Gordon Jones
Teaching staff: full-time, 53; part-time, 4; total, 57
Nationalities of teaching staff: U.S., 2; U.K., 1; host, 8; other, 46; total, 57
Grade levels: prep – 11
Enrollment: N – preK, 31; K, 52; 1 – 6, 361; 7 – 9, 112; 10 – 12, 38; total, 594
Nationalities of student body: U.S., 66; U.K., 56; other, 472; total, 594
Tuition (annual): N – preK, $5,553; K – 9, $7,404; 10 – 12, $8,136
Other fees: registration, $120; capital levy, $1,620
School year: late August through June

Year founded: 1991. **Type of school:** coed, private nonprofit. **Governed by:** appointed board of governors. **Regional organizations:** EARCOS, CAIS.

Curriculum

Type: Canadian. **Languages taught:** English, French, Mandarin. **Staff specialists:** occupational therapist. **Special curricular:** art, chorus, band, physical education, computer instruction. **Extracurricular:** drama, gymnastics, dance, choral and instrumental music, computers, yearbook, photography, excursions/ expeditions, field trips. **Sports:** basketball, swimming, floor hockey, hiking, sailing, cycling, Tai Kwon Do. **Clubs:** yearbook, student council, coin and stamp, photography. **Tests:** NSW International Competition, CAT/2.

Physical plant

Location: in city. **Campuses:** 3 temporary campuses, new buildings under construction. **Libraries (3):** 16,000 volumes. **Facilities:** auditorium, cafeteria, infirmary, covered play area, 3 gymnasiums, 2 playing fields, 2 science labs, 2 computer labs, swimming pool, art/music/dance studios, air conditioning.

Carmel School

Street address: One Robinson Place, 70 Robinson Road, Mid-Levels, Hong Kong
Phone: (852)29641600 **Facsimile:** (852)28134121 **E-mail:** carmelhk@netvigator.com
Executive director: Jonathan Cannon
Principal: Elizabeth Carmody
Teaching staff: full-time, 15; part-time, 5; total, 20
Nationalities of teaching staff: U.S., 7; U.K., 4; other, 9; total, 20
Grade levels: N – 4 (adding a grade each year)
Enrollment: N – preK, 48; K, 20; 1 – 4, 48; total, 116
Nationalities of student body: U.S., 52; U.K., 14; other, 50; total, 116
School year: September through June

Year founded: 1991. **Type of school:** coed. **Sponsored by:** Jewish community.

Curriculum/physical plant

Type: U.S. **Languages of instruction:** English, Hebrew. **Languages taught:** English, Hebrew, Mandarin. **Staff specialists:** reading, math, computer, learning disabilities. **Special programs:** ESL. **Special curricular:** physical education, Mandarin. **Extracurricular:** drama, dance. **Tests:** Iowa. **Location:** in city. **Facilities:** 1 building, auditorium, cafeteria, gymnasium, computer lab, swimming pool, air conditioning.

CHINESE INTERNATIONAL SCHOOL

Street address: 1 Hau Yuen Path, Braemar Hill, Hong Kong
Phone: (852)25107288 **Facsimile:** (852)25107488
E-mail: cis_info@cis.edu.hk **Web:** http://www.hk.super.net/~cis
Headmaster: Christopher Berrisford
Head, senior division: Catherine Fleming
Head, junior division: Jaime Roth
Head, infant division: Ann Leddy
Business administration manager: Paul Cabrelli
Teaching staff: full-time, 94; part-time, 9; total, 103
Nationalities of teaching staff: U.S., 25; U.K., 31; host, 8; other, 39; total, 103
Grade levels: preK – 12
Enrollment: preK – 1, 237; 2 – 5, 312; 6 – 8, 321; 9 – 12, 352; total, 1,222
Teacher/student ratio: 1/12
Tuition (annual): preK, 50,460**; K – 5, 66,400; 6 – 12, 80,400
Other fees (annual): capital levy*, 6,000**, debenture at 75,000; books, 2,900 – 4,000; transport (optional), 2,310 – 8,085
School year: September to June

Year founded: 1983. **Type of school:** coed, day, private nonprofit. **Governed by:** Chinese International School Foundation Ltd. **Accredited by:** Western. **Regional organizations:** EARCOS, ECIS.

Curriculum/physical plant

Type: U.K., IB, bilingual. **Languages of instruction:** English, Mandarin. **Languages taught:** French, Mandarin. **Staff specialists:** computer, art, music, physical education, economics, craft, design and technology, science, drama, librarians. **Special programs:** ESL, CSL. **Special curricular:** art, physical education, computer instruction. **Extracurricular:** gymnastics, dance, computers, literary magazine, excursions/expeditions, field trips, ballet, choral and instrumental music, Mandarin. **Sports:** basketball, hockey, netball, rugby, soccer, swimming, table tennis, tennis. **Tests:** SAT, TOEFL, IB, IGCSE. **Graduates attending college:** 100%. **Graduates have attended:** Oxford, University College (London), Cornell, Princeton, U. of California at Berkeley. **Location:** on Hong Kong Island. **Campus:** 2.5 acres. **Library:** 35,000 volumes. **Facilities:** 1 building, 59 classrooms, auditorium, cafeteria, 2 gymnasiums, 5 science labs, 4 computer labs, swimming pool, CDT workshop, language lab, dance studio, air conditioning.

*Once only fee **Hong Kong dollar

Christian Alliance P. C. Lau Memorial International School

Street address: 2 Fu Ning Street, Kowloon City, Hong Kong
Phone: (852)27133733/27133253 **Facsimile:** (852)27604324
E-mail: cais@netvigator.com
Principal: Lionel Sanders
Assistant to principal: Karen Sanders
Business manager: Michael Wong
Teaching staff: full-time, 23; total, 23
Nationalities of teaching staff: U.S., 2; Canadian, 17; other, 4; total, 23
Grade levels: K – 12
Enrollment: K – 6, 161; 7 – 9, 75; 10 - 12, 49; total, 285
Nationalities of student body: U.S., 45; U.K., 10; Canadian, 125; other, 105; total, 285
Teacher/student ratio: 1/12
Tuition (annual): K – 5, $5,600; 6 – 8, $7,200; 9, $7,700; 10 – 12, $8,000
Other fees (annual): registration*, $25; books, $220 – 600
School year: September to June

Year founded: 1992. **Type of school:** coed, church-related. **Operated by:** Kowloon Tong Alliance Church School Management. **Accredited by:** Education Department of Province of Saskatchewan.

Curriculum/physical plant

Type: U.S., Canadian. **Languages taught:** English, French, Mandarin. **Staff specialists:** counselor, psychologist, learning disabilities. **Special programs:** ESL, independent study, correspondence, remedial, learning assistance, individual education plans, K2 and K3 kindergarten. **Special curricular:** art, chorus, band, physical education, computer instruction, orchestra. **Extracurricular:** choral music, computers, yearbook, newspaper, excursions/expeditions. **Sports:** basketball, table tennis, volleyball. **Clubs:** Christian Youth Organization, library, ESL, career. **Tests:** SAT, TOEFL, Canadian Test of Basic Skills. **Graduates attending college:** 66%. **Graduates have attended:** Trinity Western U., Tufts, U. of Victoria. **Location:** Kowloon. **Libraries (2):** 30,000 volumes. **Facilities:** 1 building, 24 classrooms, auditorium, covered play area, playing field, 5 science labs, computer lab, 2 outdoor volleyball and basketball courts, language lab, air conditioning.

*Once only fee

French International School "Victor Segalen"

Street address: 34 Price Road, Jardine's Lookout, Hong Kong
Phone: (852)25776217 **Facsimile:** (852)25779658
Headmaster: Paul Lagriffoul
Deputy principal, French stream: José Lesaulnier
Deputy principal, English stream: Mary Lawton
Teaching staff: full-time, 80; part-time, 17; total, 97
Grade levels: French stream, ages 3 – 18; English stream, ages 4 – 18
Enrollment: K, 149; primary, 487; junior secondary, 247; senior secondary, 132; total, 1,015

Teacher/student ratio: 1/12
Tuition (annual): K, 47,853**; primary, 55,107; forms I – V, 66,141; IB, 83,007
Other fees (annual): registration*, 3,100**; application*, 300;
canteen: K, 4,912; primary, 6,211; secondary, 6,741
School year: September to June

Type of school: coed, day, private nonprofit. **Accredited by:** Hong Kong Education Department.

Curriculum/physical plant

Type: U.K., French, national, IB. **Languages of instruction:** English, French. **Languages taught:** English, French, Spanish, German, Latin, Mandarin. **Staff specialists:** reading, math, computer, counselor, nurse. **Special curricular:** physical education, computer instruction. **Extracurricular:** drama, gymnastics, dance, computers, yearbook, newspaper, field trips, excursions. **Tests:** IB, IGCSE, French Baccalaureate. **Graduates attending college:** 95%. **Location:** in city. **Library:** 14,000 volumes. **Facilities:** 3 buildings, 61 classrooms, auditorium, cafeteria, infirmary, 3 covered play areas, gymnasium, 3 playing fields, 5 science labs, computer labs, swimming pool, air conditioning.

*Once only fee **Hong Kong dollar

Hong Kong International School

Street address: 1 Red Hill Road, Tai Tam, Hong Kong
Phone: (852)28991211 **Facsimile:** (852)28134293
E-mail: cdull@admin.hkis.edu.hk
Head of school: Charles W. Dull
High school principal: James A. Handrich
Middle school principal: Robert Welch
Elementary school principal: Mary Hoff
Early childhood principal: Jan Hall
Teaching staff: full-time, 185; part-time, 23; total, 208
Nationalities of teaching staff: U.S., 136; U.K./host, 37; other, 35; total, 208
Grade levels: preP – 12
Enrollment: preP – 2, 677; 3 – 5, 515; 6 – 8, 588; 9 – 12, 641; total, 2,421
Nationalities of student body: U.S., 1,519; other, 902; total, 2,421
Teacher/student ratio: 1/12
Tuition (annual): preP, 52,580**; K – 5, 105,260; 6 – 8, 110,620; 9 – 11, 121,520; 12, 112,070
Other fees (annual): registration*, 1,500**; capital levy, 12,000;
busing, 6,000 – 12,000; entry*, 15,000
School year: August to June

Year founded: 1966. **Type of school:** coed, day, church-related. **Governed by:** appointed board of managers for Lutheran Church – Missouri Synod. **Accredited by:** Western. **Regional organizations:** EARCOS.

Curriculum

Type: U.S., AP. **Languages taught:** French, Spanish, Mandarin. **Staff specialists:** reading, counselor, psychologist, nurse, resource. **Special programs:** independent study. **Special curricular:** art, chorus, band, physical education, computer instruction. **Extracurricular:** drama, gymnastics, dance, choral and instrumental music, computers, yearbook, newspaper, service groups, Model UN. **Sports:** badminton, basketball, cheerleading, cross-country, field hockey, rugby, soccer, softball, squash, swimming, table tennis, track and field, volleyball, crew, sailing. **Tests:** PSAT, SAT, ACT, TOEFL. **Graduates attending college:** 90%. **Graduates have attended:** Harvard, Brown, Colombia, Princeton, Stanford.

Physical plant

Location: middle and high school buildings on Tai Tam Road, 5 miles from elementary campus, in residential areas on south side of Hong Kong Island (Repulse Bay). **Campuses (2):** 10 acres. **Libraries:** 60,000 volumes. **Facilities:** 4 buildings, auditorium, 2 cafeterias, covered play area, 4 gymnasiums, playing field, 2 swimming pools, tennis courts, science labs, computer labs, nurse infirmary, 2 squash courts, full facilities for the arts, air conditioning.

*Once only fee **Hong Kong dollar

International Christian School

Street address: 45 Grampian Road, Kowloon City, Hong Kong
Phone: (852)23389606 **Facsimile:** (852)23389517 **E-mail:** ics@hk.super.net
Web: http://www.hk.super.net/~ics
Mail: PO Box 89009, Kowloon City Post Office, Hong Kong
Headmaster: Frank Martens, Ed.D.
High school principal: Andrew Harnet
Elementary principal: Mary Gleason
Head of library: Karen Barnett
Head of computers: Don Zapfe
Teaching staff: full-time, 30; part-time, 4; total, 34
Nationalities of teaching staff: U.S., 20; host, 4; other, 10; total, 34
Grade levels: preK – 12
Enrollment: preK, 15; K, 35; 1 – 6, 234; 7 – 9, 95; 10 – 12, 72; total, 451
Nationalities of student body: U.S., 230; U.K., 5; host, 25; other, 191; total, 451
Teacher/student ratio: 1/15
Tuition (annual): preK – 6, $5,420; 7 – 12, $8,000
Other fees (annual): registration*, $125; books, $2,000
School year: late August to mid-June

Year founded: 1992. **Type of school:** coed, private nonprofit. **Governed and sponsored by:** Multi-Mission. **Accredited by:** Western.

Curriculum/physical plant

Type: U.S., AP. **Languages taught:** French, Chinese. **Staff specialists:** counselor. **Special programs:** correspondence. **Special curricular:** art, chorus, band, physical education, computer instruction, drama. **Extracurricular:** computers, yearbook, newspaper, literary magazine, excursions/expeditions, choral and instrumental music. **Tests:** PSAT, SAT, AP. **Graduates attending college:** 95%. **Graduates have attended:** Aoyama, Carnegie-Mellon, Boston U., North Texas, Le Touneau. **Location:** in city. **Campus:** 2 acres. **Libraries (3):** 7,000 volumes, Internet. **Facilities:** 4 buildings, 35 classrooms, auditorium, cafeteria, covered play area, gymnasium, 2 science labs, 2 computer labs, air conditioning, new school opening in West Kowloon in September 1997.

*Once only fee

Island School

Street address: 20 Borrett Road, Hong Kong
Phone: (852)25247135 **Facsimile:** (852)28401673 **E-mail:** school@is.esf.edu.hk
Academic head: Mr. D. J. James
Teaching staff: full-time, 72; part-time, 22; total, 94
Grade levels: 7 – 13
Enrollment: 7 – 9, 524; 10 – 13, 649; total, 1,173
Capacity: 7 – 9, 540; 10 – 13, 690; total, 1,230
Teacher/student ratio: 1/14
Tuition (annual): 65,000**
Other fees (annual): busing, 1,000**; uniform, 1,000
School year: September through June

Year founded: 1967. **Type of school:** coed, nonprofit, community. **Governed by:** appointed and elected school council, English Schools Foundation. **Accredited by:** London University Schools Examination Board; Southern Regions Examination Board, United Kingdom; UCAS.

Curriculum/physical plant

Type: U.K. **Special curricular:** art. **Extracurricular:** drama, yearbook, newspaper, literary magazine, all major games, orchestra, debating, Model UN, choirs, brass group, string group, theater club. **Tests:** SSAT, PSAT, SAT, ACT, TOEFL, A-level, AS-level, GCSE, GNVQ. **Graduates have attended:** Oxford, Cambridge, Harvard, MIT, Princeton. **Location:** on mountainside, overlooking Victoria Harbor, above heart of central district. **Library:** 26,000 volumes. **Facilities:** swimming pool, science labs, language lab, darkroom, Arthur Samy Studio Theater, computer centers, private study areas, careers center, 3 playgrounds, bookshop, first-aid room, pottery workshop.

**Hong Kong dollar

King George V School

Street address: 2 Tin Kwong Road, Kowloon, Hong Kong
Phone: (852)27113028 – 9 **Facsimile:** (852)27607116
Principal: Michael J. Behennah
Teaching staff: full-time, 83; part-time, 14; total, 97
Grade levels: 7 – 13
Enrollment: 7 – 9, 700; 10 – 13, 500; total, 1,200
Capacity: 7 – 9, 700; 10 – 13, 550; total, 1,250
Teacher/student ratio: 1/13
Tuition (annual): $9,100
Other fees (annual): busing, $400
School year: September through June

Year founded: 1900. **Type of school:** coed, nonprofit, community. **Governed by:** appointed and elected school council, English Schools Foundation. **Accredited by:** London University Schools Examination Board, Southern Regions Examination Board – United Kingdom, UCAS, CRCH, HMC.

Curriculum/physical plant

Type: U.K. **Special curricular:** art, drama. **Extracurricular:** yearbook, newspaper, literary magazine, flute ensemble, orchestra, choirs, pop group, jazz band, theater club, Times network, sports club. **Tests:** PSAT, SAT, ACT, TOEFL, GCSE, A-level, A/S level, Pitmans, RSA. **Graduates have attended:** Oxford, Cambridge, Princeton, Sydney, London. **Location:** on spacious 10-acre site close to Kai Tak International Airport. **Facilities:** resource center including educational video library, conference rooms, 8 computer suites, teachers' in-service training center, language labs, computer center with 240 personal computers, private study areas, student information center for U.K. and U.S. university placement, 10 science labs, medical room with qualified nurse, pottery workshop, tennis courts, swimming pool, playing field for football and rugby, athletics track, air conditioning, grades 12 and 13 center, purpose-built center completed spring 1996.

Li Po Chun United World College of Hong Kong

Street address: 10 Lok Wo Sha Lane, Sai Sha Road, Sha Tin, Hong Kong
Phone: (852)26400441 **Facsimile:** (852)26434088
E-mail: lpcnetwk@asiaonline.net
Principal: T. Blair Forster
Business manager: Y. C. Lee
Teaching staff: full-time, 22; part-time, 2; total, 24
Nationalities of teaching staff: U.S., 1; U.K., 8; host, 3; other, 12; total, 24
Grade levels: 11 – 12
Enrollment: total, 240
Capacity: total, 250
Teacher/student ratio: 1/12
Boarders: boys, 120; girls, 120 **Program:** planned 7-day
Tuition and board (annual): $18,750
School year: mid-August to late May

Year founded: 1992. **Type of school:** coed, boarding, private nonprofit. **Governed by:** board of directors.

Curriculum/physical plant

Type: IB. **Extracurricular:** drama, dance, choral music, computers, yearbook, newspaper, photography, excursions/expeditions, variety of sports, major community service commitment. **Tests:** IB. **Location:** purpose-built campus at seashore, 10 kilometers from Sha Tin. **Campus:** 6.5 hectares. **Library:** 9,000 volumes. **Facilities:** 7 buildings, cafeteria, infirmary, 4 science labs, computer lab, swimming pool, hard courts, gymnasium complex, air conditioning, full boarding facilities.

HUNGARY

Region: Europe
Size: 35,919 square miles
Population: 10,002,541
Capital: Budapest

Telephone code: 36
Currency: forint
Language: Hungarian

BUDAPEST

AMERICAN INTERNATIONAL SCHOOL OF BUDAPEST

Street address: Kakukk U. 1 – 3, Budapest 1121, Hungary
Phone: (36)(1)2754273/3952176/3952178 **Facsimile:** (36)(1)3952179
Mail: PO Box 53, 1525 Budapest, Hungary
Director: John K. Johnson
High school principal: Jeremy Lewis
Middle school principal: Mary–Ann Sullivan
Lower school principal: Bob Wenger
Teaching staff: full-time, 73; part-time, 6; total, 79
Nationalities of teaching staff: U.S., 48; U.K., 10; host, 2; other, 19; total, 79
Grade levels: preK – 13
Enrollment: preK, 17; K, 26; 1 – 6, 268; 7 – 13, 237; total, 548
Nationalities of student body: U.S., 138; U.K., 31; host, 44; other, 335; total, 548
Teacher/student ratio: 1/7
Tuition (annual): preK, $6,300; K – 5, $9,300; 6 – 8, $10,200; 9 – 11, $10,800; 12 – 13, $11,000
Other fees (annual): registration*, $250; building fee, $2,500
School year: August to June

Year founded: 1973. **Type of school:** coed, day, private nonprofit. **Governed by:** appointed board of directors. **Accredited by:** Middle States, ECIS. **Regional organizations:** AAIE, ECIS, CEESA.

Curriculum

Type: U.S., IB. **Languages taught:** French, German. **Staff specialists:** computer, art, music, physical education. **Special programs:** ESL. **Special curricular:** art, chorus, physical education, computer instruction, Hungarian studies. **Extracurricular:** drama, gymnastics, choral music, computers, excursions/expeditions, stamp collecting, board games. **Sports:** basketball, soccer, swimming. **Clubs:** computer, drama, cooking, dance, judo, film, stamp collecting, choir, art, swimming, sports. **Tests:** PSAT, SAT, IB, ERB.

Physical plant

Upper School (5 – 13): rented facilities in quaint old building situated in forest, 5 kilometers from lower school. **Library:** 10,492 volumes. **Facilities:** 7 buildings, 31 classrooms, outside sports facilities and gym. **Lower School (K – 4):** in residential area in Buda hills, 5 kilometers from Budapest. **Campus:** 3 acres. **Library:** 11,463 volumes. **Facilities:** 1 building, 20 classrooms, auditorium, cafeteria, tennis court, gymnasium, science lab, computer lab, swimming pool.

*Once only fee

International School of Budapest

Street address: Konkoly Thega utca 19/B, Hungary
Phone: (36)(1)1758258 **Facsimile:** (36)(1)1695140
Web: http://www.ett.net.hu/isb/isb.htm
Headmaster: John Paduano
Teaching staff: full-time, 18; part-time, 12; total, 30
Nationalities of teaching staff: U.S., 8; U.K., 5; host, 8; other, 9; total, 30
Grade levels: N (age 2) – grade 8
Enrollment: N – preK, 80; K, 40; 1 – 6, 120; total, 240
Teacher/student ratio: 1/8
Tuition (annual): N, $2,500; 3-year-old, $7,000; preK, $8,500; K, $9,000; 1, $8,500; 2 – 6, $10,000; 7 – 8, $10,600
Other fees: registration*, $250
School year: late August to mid-June

Year founded: 1992. **Type of school:** coed, day, private.

Curriculum/physical plant

Type: ISCP. **Languages taught:** French, Spanish, German, Hungarian. **Staff specialists:** computer, music. **Special programs:** ESL, music, dance/drama, summer school. **Special curricular:** physical education, computer. **Extracurricular:** dance. **Sports:** aerobics, gymnastics, skiing, swimming. **Location:** clean, peaceful area surrounded by forest, 5 kilometers from Budapest center, door to door bus service. **Campus:** 2 acres. **Facilities:** 1 building, 11 classrooms, covered play area, gymnasium, extensive playing field.

*Once only fee

ICELAND

Region: North Atlantic
Size: 36,699 square miles
Population: 270,292
Capital: Reykjavik
Telephone code: 354
Currency: kron
Language: Icelandic

REYKJAVIK

AMERICAN EMBASSY SCHOOL

Phone: (354)5518209/5643237 **Facsimile:** (354)5643237
Mail: c/o U.S. Embassy, Reykjavik, Iceland
U.S. mail: (no personal name) AES, c/o American Embassy, PSC 1003, Box 40, FPO AE 09728-0340
Head teacher: Barbara Sigurbjornsson
Teaching staff: full-time, 1; part-time, 2; total, 3
Nationalities of teaching staff: U.S., 3; total, 3
Grade levels: K – 6
Enrollment: K, 3; 1 – 6, 11; total, 14
Nationalities of student body: U.S., 4; host, 6; other, 4; total, 14
Capacity: K, 10; 1 – 6, 18; total, 28
Teacher/student ratio: 1/6
Tuition (annual): K, $3,050 – 3,550; 1 – 6, $4,290 – 5,000
School year: September through May

Year founded: 1959. **Type of school:** coed, day. **Governed by:** appointed school board. **Sponsored by:** American Embassy.

Curriculum/physical plant

Type: U.S. **Languages taught:** Icelandic. **Special curricular:** art, chorus, computer instruction, swimming. **Extracurricular:** literary magazine, field trips, music, sports. **Tests:** Stanford. **Location:** in city, near American, British, and Norwegian embassies. **Library:** 2,500 volumes. **Facilities:** 2 classrooms, use of local swimming pool, playground, park.

INDIA

Region: South Asia
Size: 1,222,243 square miles
Population: 952,107,694
Capital: New Delhi
Telephone code: 91
Currency: rupee
Languages: Hindi, English, others

HYDERABAD

International School of Hyderabad

Phone: (91)(40)3351110 **Facsimile:** (91)(40)241239
Cable: ICRISAT, HYDERABAD
Mail: c/o ICRISAT, Patancheru PO, Andhra Pradesh 502 324, India
Principal: Jon Jasinski
Teaching staff: full-time, 15; part-time, 4; total, 19
Nationalities of teaching staff: host, 15; other, 4; total, 19
Grade levels: N – 8
Enrollment: N – preK, 18; K, 4; 1 – 8, 41; total, 63
Nationalities of student body: U.S., 19; other, 44; total, 63
Teacher/student ratio: 1/5
Tuition (annual): $2,000
Other fees: registration*, 1,000**
School year: July to April

Year founded: 1972. **Type of school:** coed, day, company-sponsored. **Governed by:** partially elected board. **Sponsored by:** International Crops Research Institute for the Semi-Arid Tropics.

Curriculum/physical plant

Type: U.S., U.K. **Special programs:** ESL. **Special curricular:** art, physical education, computer instruction, music, French. **Extracurricular:** dance, literary magazine, field trips, judo, Hindi. **Sports:** baseball, basketball, hockey, soccer, swimming. **Tests:** Richmond, CAT. **Location:** in suburban Hyderabad. **Campus:** 5 acres. **Library:** 2,500 volumes. **Facilities:** 2 buildings, 8 classrooms, auditorium, tennis court, squash court, basketball court, access to swimming pool.

*Once only fee **Indian rupee

KODAIKANAL

Kodaikanal International School

Phone: (91)(4542)41104 – 8 **Facsimile:** (91)(4542)41109 – 10
E-mail: admissions@kis.ernet.in
Mail: PO Box 25, Kodaikanal 624101, Tamil Nadu, India
U.S. mail: c/o Jane Cummings, 159 Ralph McGill Boulevard, Room 408, Atlanta, GA 30308, U.S.A.
U.S. phone: (1)(404)5240988 **U.S. facsimile:** (1)(404)5235420
Principal: Paul Wiebe, Ph.D.
Acting vice-principal: Nancy Garrison
Admissions officer: Roxanna S. Nichol
Business manager: D. E. Chandrasekaran
Teaching staff: full-time, 76; part-time, 10; total, 86
Nationalities of teaching staff: U.S., 14; U.K., 4; host, 55; other, 13; total, 86
Grade levels: preschool – 12
Enrollment: preschool, 7; K, 13; 1 – 5, 81; 6 – 8, 116; 9 – 12, 307; total, 524
Nationalities of student body: U.S., 53; U.K., 17; host, 289; other, 165; total, 524
Teacher/student ratio: 1/7
Boarders: boys, 199; girls, 168 **Grades:** 4 – 12 **Program:** planned 7-day
Tuition and board, consolidated fee (annual): $9,500
Other fees: registration*
School year: July to May

Year founded: 1901. **Type of school:** coed, boarding, church-related, private nonprofit. **Governed by:** elected council of management. **Accredited by:** Middle States, recognized by the Association of Indian Universities. **Regional organizations:** NESA.

Curriculum/physical plant

Type: U.S., IB. **Languages taught:** French, Spanish, German, Japanese, Hindi, Tamil. **Staff specialists:** computer, counselor, nurse, chaplain, doctor. **Special programs:** ESL. **Special curricular:** art, chorus, band, physical education, computer instruction, industrial arts, home economics. **Extracurricular:** drama, gymnastics, dance, choral and instrumental music, computers, yearbook, newspaper, photography, excursions/expeditions, field trips. **Sports:** badminton, basketball, cricket, field hockey, soccer, softball, tennis, track and field, volleyball, racquetball, golf. **Clubs:** chess, computer, National Honor Society, stamp, literary, photography, sports, student government, music, astronomy, science, math, economics. **Tests:** PSAT, SAT, ACT, TOEFL, IB, ACH. **Graduates attending college:** 99%. **Graduates have attended:** Princeton, Haverford, Oxford, Reed, Indian universities. **Location:** in rural area, 120 kilometers northwest of Madurai (airport), 500 kilometers southwest of Madras (international airport). **Campuses (2):** 20 acres. **Library:** 40,000 volumes. **Facilities:** 30 buildings, 40 classrooms, auditorium, 2 cafeterias, infirmary, 3 covered play areas, 10 tennis courts, gymnasium, 3 playing fields, 5 science labs, 5 computer labs, AV facilities, 2 typing/business education labs, 13 dormitories.

*Once only fee

MUMBAI†

AMERICAN SCHOOL OF BOMBAY

Street address: 75 B. Desai Road, Mumbai 400026, India
Phone: (91)(22)3630026/3648395/3641293 **Facsimile:** (91)(22)3670035
E-mail: asb@giasbm01.vsnl.net.in
U.S. mail: c/o American Consulate General, Bombay - Dept. of State, Washington, DC 20521-6240
Superintendent: Hal Strom
Assistant superintendent: Russell Erickson
High school principal: Anne McLaughlin
Office manager: Sue Khan
Teaching staff: full-time, 42; part-time, 20; total, 62
Nationalities of teaching staff: U.S., 17; U.K., 5; host, 30; other, 10; total, 62
Grade levels: preK – 12
Enrollment: preK, 26; K, 7; 1 – 5, 95; 6 – 8, 47; 9 – 12, 41; total, 216
Nationalities of student body: U.S., 53; U.K., 39; other, 124; total, 216
Capacity: preK, 40; K, 25; 1 – 5, 110; 6 – 8, 45; 9 – 12, 60; total, 280
Teacher/student ratio: 1/4
Tuition (annual): preK, $3,000; K – 12, $6,700
Other fees (annual): registration, $4,100; surcharge, 6 – 12, $1,080; capital rent fund, $2,136 (a portion of fees payable in Indian rupees); capital fee*: preK, $2,500 non-refundable and $7,500 refundable; K – 12, $5,000 non-refundable and $15,000 refundable
School year: mid-August to early June

Year founded: 1981. **Type of school:** coed, day, private nonprofit, education trust. **Governed by:** elected board of trustees. **Accredited by:** Middle States. **Regional organizations:** NESA, SAISA, AAIE.

Curriculum/physical plant

Type: U.S., AP. **Languages taught:** French, (grades 2 – 12), Spanish (grades 3 – 5). **Staff specialists:** reading, computer, art, music. **Special programs:** ESL, remedial. **Special curricular:** art, physical education, computer instruction, music, home economics, AP calculus. **Extracurricular:** instrumental music, yearbook, literary magazine, excursions/expeditions, field trips. **Sports:** soccer, swimming, tennis, Tai Kwon Do. **Clubs:** chess, computer, Girl Scouts, arts and crafts, photography. **Tests:** PSAT, AP, MAT – 7, GOALS. **Location:** in metropolitan Mumbai. **Library:** 15,000 volumes. **Facilities:** 3 buildings, 22 classrooms, tennis court, playing field, science labs, computer labs, swimming pool, AV equipment, air conditioning.

*Once only fee †formerly Bombay

MUSSOORIE

WOODSTOCK SCHOOL

Phone: (91)(135)632610 **Facsimile:** (91)(135)632885
E-mail: admin@wdstock.globemail.com
Web: http://www.kwi.org/woodstock/
Mail: Mussoorie, UP 248 179, India
U.S. mail: c/o Jane Cummings, 159 Ralph McGill Boulevard, Room 408, Atlanta, GA 30308, U.S.A.
U.S. phone: (1)(404)5240988 **U.S. facsimile:** (1)(404)5235420
E-mail: 74301.3544@compuserve.com
Principal: R. Flaming
Vice-principal: J. Barton
Teaching staff: full-time, 60; part-time, 7; total, 67
Nationalities of teaching staff: U.S., 26; U.K., 12; host, 23; other, 6; total, 67
Grade levels: K – 12
Enrollment: K, 5; 1 – 6, 131; 7 – 9, 141; 10 – 12, 178; total, 455
Nationalities of student body: U.S., 72; U.K., 17; host, 176; other, 190; total, 455
Teacher/student ratio: 1/7
Boarders: boys, 183; girls, 183 **Grades:** 2 – 12 **Program:** planned 7-day
Tuition and board (annual): $8,950
Other fees: registration*, $40; establishment fee*, $750
School year: July to June

Year founded: 1854. **Type of school:** coed, day, boarding, church-related, private nonprofit. **Governed by:** elected board of directors. **Accredited by:** Middle States. **Regional organizations:** NESA.

Curriculum

Type: U.S., U.K., national, AP. **Languages taught:** French, German, Hindi. **Staff specialists:** math, computer, counselor, nurse, environmentalist. **Special programs:** ESL, independent study, O & A-levels. **Special curricular:** art, chorus, band, physical education, computer instruction, orchestra (junior & senior), jazz band. **Extracurricular:** drama, choral and instrumental music, computers, yearbook, newspaper, photography, excursions/expeditions, field trips, community services, environmental projects, hiking, activity week. **Sports:** badminton, basketball, cricket, soccer, track and field, volleyball. **Clubs:** National Honor Society, Amnesty International, student government, hiking. **Tests:** PSAT, SAT, ACT, AP, A-level GCE, O-level GCE, PLAN. **Graduates attending college:** 95%. **Graduates have attended:** Princeton, Harvard, Cambridge, Melbourne, Heidelberg.

Physical plant

Location: on outskirts of Mussoorie, 260 kilometers north of New Delhi, in the Himalayan foothills (altitude of 6,000 feet). **Campus:** 300 acres. **Library:** 56,000 volumes. **Facilities:** 28 classrooms, 2 auditoriums, 2 cafeterias, 2 covered play areas, 2 tennis courts, 2 gymnasiums, 3 playing fields, 4 science labs, computer lab, swimming pool, health center, 5 residential dormitories.

*Once only fee

NEW DELHI

THE AMERICAN EMBASSY SCHOOL

Street address: Chandragupta Marg, Chanakyapuri, New Delhi 110021, India
Phone: (91)(11)6117140 **Facsimile:** (91)(11)6873320
E-mail: aesindia@attmail.com **Web:** http://www.serve.com.aesndi
U.S. mail: AES-New Delhi, Dept. of State, Washington, DC 20521-9000
Director: Stephen M. Kapner
High school principal: Kevin Schafer
Middle school principal: John Zito
Elementary school principal: Sara Zito
Business manager: Robert Brown
Teaching staff: full-time, 99; part-time, 24; total, 123
Nationalities of teaching staff: U.S., 77; U.K., 11; host, 19; other, 16; total, 123
Enrollment: ECEC, 60; K, 65; 1 – 5, 390; 6 – 8, 273; 9 – 12, 279; total, 1,067
Nationalities of student body: U.S., 359; U.K., 102; other, 606; total, 1,067
Teacher/student ratio: 1/11
Tuition (annual, 1996 – 97 figures): ECEC, $2,500; K – 5, $8,300; 6 – 8, $8,650; 9 – 12, $9,500
Other fees (annual, 1996 – 97 figures): application*, $100; matriculation*, $2,500; busing, $145 – 290
School year: August through May

Year founded: 1952. **Type of school:** coed, day, private nonprofit. **Governed by:** elected board of governors. **Accredited by:** Middle States. **Regional organizations:** AAIE, NESA.

Curriculum/physical plant

Type: U.S., IB, AP. **Languages taught:** French, Spanish, Hindi. **Staff specialists:** counselor, learning disabilities, nurse, curriculum. **Special programs:** ESL, independent study, correspondence, mild learning disabilities. **Special curricular:** art, chorus, band, physical education, computer instruction, swimming, photography. **Extracurricular:** drama, choral and instrumental music, yearbook, newspaper, literary magazine, photography, many clubs. **Sports:** badminton, basketball, field hockey, soccer, softball, swimming, tennis, track and field, volleyball, water polo. **Tests:** SSAT, PSAT, SAT, ACT, IB, AP, Iowa, TAP. **Graduates attending college:** 95%. **Graduates have attended:** U. of California at Berkeley, William & Mary, Dartmouth, U. of Pennsylvania, Brigham Young U. **Location:** in the heart of diplomatic section of New Delhi. **Campus:** 12 acres. **Library:** 20,000 volumes. **Facilities:** 8 buildings, 88 classrooms, auditorium, cafeteria, infirmary, gymnasium, swimming pool, tennis courts, playing fields, science labs, computer labs.

*Once only fee

BANGALORE

Bangalore International School

Street address: No. 14, Benson Cross Road, Benson Town, Bangalore 560 046, India
Phone: (91)(812)5554007
Principal: Mrs. Meera Menon

INDONESIA

Region: Southeast Asia
Size: 741,052 square miles
Population: 206,611,600
Capital: Jakarta
Telephone code: 62
Currency: rupiah
Languages: Bahasa Indonesian, Javanese, English, Dutch

BALI

Bali International School

Street address: Banjar Taman Sari, Sanur, Bali, Indonesia
Phone: (62)(361)288467/288770 **Facsimile:** (62)(361)285103
E-mail: bis@denpasar.wasantara.net.id
Mail: PO Box 3259, Denpasar, Bali, Indonesia
Principal: Murray Vosper
Teaching staff: full-time, 14; part-time, 2; total, 16
Grade levels: preS – 10
Enrollment: preS, 20; K – 6, 115; 7 – 10, 65; total, 200
Nationalities of student body: U.S., 30; other, 170; total, 200
Capacity: preS, 20; K – 6, 140; 7 – 10, 90; total, 250
Teacher/student ratio: 1/20
Tuition (annual): preS, $3,900; K – 6, $5,500; 7 – 10, $6,100
Other fees (annual): capital levy, $600; ESL, $1,000
School year: August to June

Year founded: 1986. **Type of school:** coed, day. **Governed by:** elected seven-member school board. **Accredited by:** Western, NSW Board of Studies. **Regional organizations:** EARCOS.

Curriculum/physical plant

Type: New Zealand/Australia/International. **Languages taught:** English, Indonesian. **Staff specialists:** all curriculum areas. **Special programs:** ESL, music. **Extracurricular:** performing arts- and sports-based activities. **Location:** in beachside resort town, 10 kilometers from Denpasar. **Campus:** 3.5 acres. **Library:** 5,000 volumes. **Facilities:** 7 buildings, 10 classrooms, 2 playing fields, computers in all classrooms, air conditioning.

BALIKPAPAN

Pasir Ridge International School

Location: Balikpapan, East Kalimantan, Indonesia
Phone: (62)(542)543474 **Facsimile:** (62)(542)32993
E-mail: prschool@bpp.mega.net.id
Mail: c/o UNOCAL, Locked Bag Service No. 3, Tampines Central Post Office, Singapore 915286, Republic of Singapore
Principal: Gary Winning
Teaching staff: full-time, 14; part-time, 1; total, 15
Nationalities of teaching staff: U.S., 8; host, 2; Australia, 4; other, 1; total, 15
Grade levels: preK – 8
Enrollment: total, 154
Nationalities of student body: U.S., 65; Australia, 65; other, 24; total, 154
Teacher/student ratio: 1/10
Tuition (annual): preK, $4,000; K, $11,000; 1 – 8, $14,700
School year: late August to June

Year founded: 1972. **Type of school:** coed, day, company-sponsored. **Sponsored by:** Unocal, Ltd. **Operated by:** International Schools Services, Princeton, New Jersey. **Accredited by:** Western. **Regional organizations:** EARCOS.

Curriculum/physical plant

Type: U.S. **Languages taught:** Bahasa Indonesian. **Special curricular:** art, physical education, computer instruction, music, craft, design and technology. **Extracurricular:** drama, computers, yearbook, photography, excursions/expeditions, rain forest: care of orangutans. **Sports:** hockey, softball, squash, swimming, tennis, volleyball. **Location:** company camp overlooking Balikpapan. **Library:** 15,000 volumes. **Facilities:** 12 classrooms, auditorium, tennis court, playing field, science lab, swimming pool, computer room, preschool annex, aviary, air conditioning.

BANDUNG

Bandung Alliance International School

Street address: Jalan Gunung Agung 14, Bandung 40142, Java, Indonesia
Phone: (62)(22)231844 **Facsimile:** (62)(22)231508
E-mail: 76225.2736@compuserve.com
Principal: John Havill
Teaching staff: full-time, 10; part-time, 6; total, 16
Nationalities of teaching staff: U.S., 10; host, 3; other, 3; total, 16
Grade levels: preK – 9
Enrollment: total, 75
Nationalities of student body: U.S., 55; other, 20; total, 75
Teacher/student ratio: 1/6
Tuition (annual): preK, $1,800; K – 9, $4,675
Other fees: capital levy*, $1,000
School year: August through May

Year founded: 1956. **Type of school:** coed, day. **Governed by:** elected board of parents. **Sponsored by:** The Network of International Community Schools. **Regional organizations:** EARCOS, ACSI.

Curriculum/physical plant

Type: U.S. **Languages taught:** Indonesian. **Staff specialists:** math, computer, ESL, music, English, science. **Special programs:** ESL, remedial. **Special curricular:** art, chorus, physical education, computer instruction, ESL, Indonesian. **Extracurricular:** field trips, after-school clubs. **Sports:** basketball, soccer, softball, volleyball. **Tests:** Stanford. **Graduates attending college:** 95%. **Graduates have attended:** Canadian Bible College, Wheaton College, Westmount, Nyack Bible College. **Location:** in city. **Campus:** 2 acres. **Library:** 10,000 volumes. **Facilities:** 4 buildings, 10 classrooms, 2 playing fields, computer lab, all-purpose room, air-conditioned library.

*Once only fee

Bandung International School

Street address: Jl. Prof. Drg. Suria Sumantri No. 61, Bandung 40011, West Java, Indonesia
Phone: (62)(22)214995 **Facsimile:** (62)(22)212688
E-mail: pjoslin@melsa.net.id
Mail: PO Box 1167, Bandung, West Java, Indonesia 40011
Headmaster: Philip Joslin
Director of student services: Jane Lowery
Teaching staff: full-time, 15; part-time, 9; total, 24
Nationalities of teaching staff: U.S., 7; U.K., 8; host, Australia/New Zealand, 6; other, 3; total, 24
Grade levels: preK – 12
Enrollment: preK, 42; K – 5, 110; 6 – 12, 68; total, 220
Nationalities of student body: U.S., 52; U.K., 17; other, 151; total, 220
Teacher/student ratio: 1/10
Tuition (annual): preK, $2,500; K – 5, $6,800; 6 – 12, $7,400
Other fees: capital levy, $2,700 (depreciates over five years)
School year: August to June

Year founded: 1972. **Type of school:** coed, day. **Governed by:** elected board of parents. **Regional organizations:** EARCOS.

Curriculum/physical plant

Type: U.S. **Languages taught:** French, Dutch, Indonesian. **Staff specialists:** math, computer, art, ESL, music, science, English. **Special programs:** ESL, learning disabilities. **Special curricular:** art, physical education, computer instruction, drama, music. **Extracurricular:** drama, gymnastics, literary magazine, field trips, music band, environmental club. **Sports:** badminton, basketball, hockey, soccer, softball, swimming, volleyball. **Location:** in city. **Library:** 12,000 volumes. **Facilities:** 20 classrooms, auditorium, gymnasium, playing field, science lab, computer lab.

BOGOR

Bogor Expatriate School

Street address: Jalan Papandayan 7, Bogor, West Java, Indonesia
Phone: (62)(251)324360 **Facsimile:** (62)(251)328512 **E-mail:** bes@indo.net.id
Mail: PO Box 258, Bogor, 16151 Indonesia
Principal: Peter Ferrier
Teaching staff: full-time, 7; part-time, 2; total, 9
Nationalities of teaching staff: U.S., 1; U.K., 1; Australia/New Zealand, 5; other, 2; total, 9
Grade levels: preK – 6
Enrollment: preK, 26; K – 6, 70; total, 96
Teacher/student ratio: 1/14
Tuition (annual): K – 6, $5,975
Other fees: capital levy*, $3,000
School year: August to June

Year founded: 1974. **Type of school:** coed, day, private nonprofit. **Governed by:** elected board of directors. **Regional organizations:** EARCOS.

Curriculum/physical plant

Type: international. **Special curricular:** art, physical education, computer instruction, music. **Extracurricular:** excursions/expeditions, wide variety of after–school activities. **Sports:** athletics, badminton, gymnastics, soccer, swimming, volleyball. **Tests:** placement, diagnostic and performance as required. **Location:** in university and garden city of Bogor, 65 kilometers south of Jakarta. **Campus:** 10,000 square meters. **Library:** 4,000 volumes. **Facilities:** 2 buildings, 7 classrooms, 2 playing fields, AV equipment, computers, art/craft room, nearby swimming pool.

*Once only fee

BONTANG

Bontang International School

Location: Bontang, East Kalimantan, Indonesia
Phone: (62)(548)551176/(62)(541)42100 ext. 1176 **Facsimile:** (62)(541)43100 **E-mail:** bisbon@indo.net.id
Mail: c/o VICO, 9 Penang Road 07-09 Park Mall, Singapore 238459, Singapore
U.S. mail: c/o VICO, PO Box 1551, Houston, TX 77251-1551, U.S.A.
Principal: Barry Benger
Teaching staff: full-time, 4; total, 4
Nationalities of teaching staff: U.S., 2; other, 2; total, 4
Grade levels: preK – 8
Enrollment: total, 11
Nationalities of student body: U.S., 4; other, 7; total, 11
Teacher/student ratio: 1/3

Tuition (annual): K, $6,850; 1 – 5, $9,550; 6 – 8, $10,680
Other fees (annual): capital levy, $2,500
School year: August to June

Year founded: 1975. **Type of school:** coed, day, company-sponsored. **Sponsored by:** PT Badak NGL, Co. **Operated by:** International Schools Services, Princeton, New Jersey. **Accredited by:** Western. **Regional organizations:** EARCOS.

Curriculum/physical plant

Type: U.S. **Languages taught:** Indonesian. **Special curricular:** art, physical education, computer instruction. **Extracurricular:** drama, dance, computers, newspaper, field trips, art, cooking, Bali, dance. **Sports:** squash, swimming, tennis, sailing, racquetball, golf, water skiing, bowling. **Tests:** SSAT, Iowa. **Location:** in company camp, 30-minute flight from Balikpapan. **Library:** 7,000 volumes. **Facilities:** covered play area, tennis court, playing field, science lab, computer lab, swimming pool, ceramics room, air conditioning.

CILEGON

Cilegon International School

Street address: Jalan Raya Merak No. 49, Cilegon, West Java, Indonesia
Phone: (62)(254)396552/394460 **Facsimile:** (62)(254)394335
Principal: Robert Landau
Teaching staff: full-time, 10; part-time, 1; total, 11
Nationalities of teaching staff: U.S., 3; U.K., 4; host, 1; Australia, 3; total, 11
Grade levels: N – 9
Enrollment: N – preK, 12; K, 6; 1 – 6, 59; 7 – 9, 8; total, 85
Nationalities of student body: U.S., 7; U.K., 6; other, 72; total, 85
Capacity: N – preK, 15; K, 15; 1 – 6, 100; 7 – 9, 35; total, 165
Teacher/student ratio: 1/8
Tuition (annual): N – preK, $4,500; K – 6, $8,100; 7 – 9, $9,100
Other fees: registration*, $300; capital levy, $10,000/5 years
School year: September to mid-July

Year founded: 1994. **Type of school:** coed, day. **Governed by:** appointed school board. **Sponsored by:** Bonauli Real Estate. **Accredited by:** Board of Studies, New South Wales, Australia.

Curriculum/physical plant

Type: U.S., U.K., Australia. **Languages taught:** Bahasa Indonesian. **Special programs:** ESL. **Special curricular:** art, physical education, computer instruction, drama, music. **Extracurricular:** computers, yearbook, newspaper, after-school activities, excursions/expeditions, field trips. **Sports:** badminton, baseball, basketball, soccer, swimming, volleyball. **Tests:** basic skills testing, Australian (New South Wales) certificates. **Campus:** 10 acres. **Facilities:** 9 classrooms, covered play area, gymnasium, playing field, science lab, computer lab, air conditioning.

*Once only fee

JAKARTA

BRITISH INTERNATIONAL SCHOOL

Street address: Bintaro Jaya Sektor 9, JI Raya Jombang Ciledug, Pondok Aren, Jakarta, Indonesia
Phone: (62)(21)7451670 **Facsimile:** (62)(21)7451671 **E-mail:** bisnet@rad.net.id
Mail: PO Box 4120, Jakarta 12041, Indonesia
Headmaster: John Birchall
Head of primary school: Robert Pearson
Director of pastoral care and community activities: Paul Starkie
Director of development and admissions: Jill McLean
Business manager: Peter Sharples
Teaching staff: full-time, 104; part-time, 2; total, 106
Nationalities of teaching staff: U.K., 90; host, 3; other, 13; total, 106
Grade levels: preK – 12
Enrollment: preK – 2, 363; 3 – 6, 420; 7 – 12, 356; total, 1,139
Teacher/student ratio: 1/11
Tuition (annual): preK, $5,415; K – 2, $8,820; 3 – 6, $8,970; 7 – 12, $10,200
Other fees: registration*, $100; capital levy certificate, 24,000,000** (5-year), 6,000,000 (1-year); busing, $446/year
School year: September to July

Year founded: 1976. **Type of school:** coed, day, boarding, private nonprofit. **Governed by:** appointed and elected board of governors, board of trustees.

Curriculum/physical plant

Type: U.K., IB, GCSE. **Languages taught:** French, German, Bahasa Indonesian. **Special curricular:** art, physical education, expressive arts, technology. **Extracurricular:** drama, gymnastics, computers, ballet, music. **Sports:** basketball, football, hockey, swimming, tennis, canoeing, scuba diving, Tae Kwon Do. **Tests:** IB, GCSE. **Location:** in southwestern suburbs. **Campus:** 12.6 acres. **Libraries (3):** 20,000 volumes. **Facilities:** new, purpose-designed campus with classrooms, specialist rooms, aquatics center, playing fields, air conditioning.

*Once only fee **Indonesian rupiah

JAKARTA INTERNATIONAL SCHOOL

Street address: Jl. Terogong Raya 33, Jakarta 12430, Indonesia
Phone: (62)(21)7692555 **Facsimile:** business office, (62)(21)7657852; headmaster's office, (62)(21)7503644 **E-mail:** 76734.735@compuserve.com or jvahey@jisedu.org or jcornacc@jisedu.org
Mail: PO Box 1078 JKS, Jakarta 12010, Indonesia
Headmaster: Niall C. W. Nelson, Ed.D.
Deputy head: Jean K. Vahey
High school principal: Steven O'Brien, Ed.D.
Middle school principal: Bruce Leiper
Elementary school principals: M. Katherine Stewart, Ph.D., Susan R. Stengel, Ed.D.

Teaching staff: full-time, 288; part-time, 23; total, 311
Nationalities of teaching staff: U.S., 180; U.K., 22; host, 14; other, 95; total, 311
Grade levels: preK – 12
Enrollment: preK – K, 228; 1 – 5, 956; 6 – 8, 685; 9 – 12, 1,112; total, 2,981
Nationalities of student body: US/Canada, 1,340; other, 1,641; total, 2,981
Teacher/student ratio: 1/18
Tuition (annual): preK – K, $6,850; 1 – 5, $9,550; 6 – 8, $10,680; 9 – 12, $10,790
Other fees (annual): busing, $1,280; chaperone fee, $168 (preK – 5 only); certificate of guarantee, $10,000 (over 4 years); facilities, $500
School year: August to June

Year founded: 1951. **Type of school:** coed, day, private nonprofit. **Governed by:** elected school council. **Accredited by:** Western, ECIS. **Regional organizations:** EARCOS, NESA, ECIS. **Member of:** NAIS.

Curriculum

Type: U.S., IB, AP. **Languages taught:** French, Spanish, German, Dutch, Indonesian, Japanese, Korean. **Staff specialists:** speech/hearing, psychologist, learning disabilities, nurse, counselors, math/science, resource teachers, college adviser. **Special programs:** ESL, independent study, work study. **Special curricular:** art, chorus, band, physical education, computer instruction, vocational. **Co-curricular:** dance, choral and instrumental music, computers, yearbook, newspaper, photography, excursions/expeditions, field trips. **Sports:** basketball, rugby, soccer, softball, swimming, tennis, track and field, volleyball, intramurals. **Organizations:** National Honor Society, Model UN, jazz band, Joint Sound, Thespians, student government, chess, forensics, Tolong Anak-Anak, gamelan, stained glass, yoga, Tae Kwon Do, cricket, outdoor, peer helpers, help and information club. **Tests:** SSAT, PSAT, SAT, ACT, TOEFL, IB, AP, Iowa, ACH. **Graduates attending college:** 96%. **Graduates have attended:** major universities in the U.K., Australia, the Philippines, Japan, Korea, and the U.S.

Physical plant

Location: on three sites in suburban setting of South Jakarta. **Campuses (3):** 46 acres. **Libraries (4):** 100,000 volumes. **Facilities:** 206 classrooms, 4 auditoriums, 3 cafeterias, 3 tennis courts, 4 gymnasiums, 5 playing fields, 19 science labs, 7 computer labs, 2 swimming pools, AV equipment, fine arts building, wood shop, auto shop, photography lab, air conditioned classrooms.

North Jakarta International School

Street address: Jalan Raya Kelapa Nias, North Jakarta 14250, Indonesia
Phone: (62)(21)4500683 **Facsimile:** (62)(21)4500682 **E-mail:** njis@cbn.net.id
Mail: PO Box 6759-JKUKP, Jakarta 14250, Indonesia
Head: Michael S. Dougherty
Principal: Alexander Bien
Assistant principal: Louise Perdana
Business manager: Kristy Seng
Teaching staff: full-time, 32; total, 32
Nationalities of teaching staff: U.S., 20; U.K., 2; host, 2; other, 8; total, 32
Grade levels: preschool – 10
Enrollment: total, 380

Nationalities of student body: U.S., 60; U.K., 24; other, 296; total, 380
Capacity: total, 440
Teacher/student ratio: 1/12
Tuition (annual): preS, $5,200; K, $6,500; 1 – 5, $9,300; 6 – 10, $9,700
Other fees (annual): capital levy, $7,500 (3-year certificate); busing, $1,000 – $1,550; admission, $100
School year: August to June

Year founded: 1990. **Type of school:** coed, day, private nonprofit. **Governed by:** appointed board of governors. **Accredited by:** Western. **Regional organizations:** EARCOS, ECIS.

Curriculum/physical plant

Type: U.S. **Languages taught:** French, Bahasa Indonesian. **Staff specialists:** computer, nurse, art, music. **Special programs:** ESL. **Special curricular:** art, band, physical education, computer instruction, music, strings, climbing wall. **Extracurricular:** field trips, athletics. **Location:** in self-contained suburban village, 2 miles from central Jakarta. **Campus:** 2 hectares. **Facilities:** 7 buildings, 40 classrooms, infirmary, covered play area, gymnasium, playing field, computer labs, swimming pool, library, air conditioning.

LHOKSEUMAWE

International School of Lhokseumawe

Phone: (62)(645)43444 ext. 5209 **Facsimile:** (62)(645)43922/41312
E-mail: bxjacoby@jak.mobil.com
Mail: c/o PT Arun NGL Co.–IOSL, Tromol Pos 22, Lhokseumawe, Aceh Utara, Sumatra, Indonesia
U.S. mail: (letters only) c/o Mobil Administrative Services Co., PO Box 219023, Dallas, TX 75221-9023, U.S.A.
Principal: Bruce Jacoby
Teaching staff: full-time, 7; total, 7
Nationalities of teaching staff: U.S., 6; host, 1; total, 7
Grade levels: K – 8
Enrollment: total, 26
Teacher/student ratio: 1/6
School year: August to June

Year founded: 1972. **Type of school:** coed, day, company-sponsored. **Sponsored by:** Mobil Oil Indonesia. **Operated by:** International Schools Services, Princeton, New Jersey. **Accredited by:** Western. **Regional organizations:** EARCOS, SEATCCO.

Curriculum/physical plant

Type: U.S. **Languages taught:** Bahasa Indonesian. **Special curricular:** art, physical education, Macintosh computer lab. **Extracurricular:** field trips, swimming, mountain biking, computer club, sports clubs. **Tests:** Stanford. **Library:** 6,000 volumes. **Facilities:** 8 classrooms, covered play area, swimming pool, softball and soccer fields, tennis courts, air conditioning.

MALANG

Wesley International School

Street address: J1. Telaga Bodas 1, Badut Permai, Malang, East Java, Indonesia
Phone/facsimile: (62)(341)566560 **E-mail:** wesley@malang.wasantara.net.id
Mail: Kotak Pos 275, Malang 65101, East Java, Indonesia
Principal: Deborah Wittig
Business manager: Mr. Wasito
Teaching staff: full-time, 4; part-time, 3; total, 7
Nationalities of teaching staff: U.S., 3; U.K., 2; other, 2; total, 7
Grade levels: K – 12
Enrollment: K, 3; 1 – 6, 30; 7 – 12, 11; total, 44
Nationalities of student body: U.S., 7; other, 37; total, 44
Teacher/student ratio: 1/8
Tuition (annual): K, $2,850; 1 – 6, $3,800; 7 – 12, $4,000
Other fees (annual): registration, $50; capital fee*, $3,200
School year: August through May

Year founded: 1971. **Type of school:** coed, day, Christian. **Sponsored by:** OMS International and WEC International.

Curriculum/physical plant

Type: U.S. **Languages taught:** Indonesian. **Special curricular:** art, physical education, computer instruction, music, ESL. **Extracurricular:** yearbook. **Tests:** CAT. **Campus:** 4,800 square meters. **Library:** over 9,000 volumes. **Facilities:** 12 classrooms, covered play area, playing field, playground.

*Once only fee

MEDAN

Medan International School

Phone: (62)(61)831816 **Facsimile:** (62)(61)831894/537270
E-mail: mismedan@idola.net.id
Mail: PO Box 1190, Medan, Sumatra, Indonesia
Principal: Keith Bland
Teaching staff: full-time, 18; total, 18
Grade levels: preK – 8
Enrollment: preK, 14; K, 9; 1 – 6, 44; 7 – 9, 12; total, 79
Nationalities of student body: U.S., 4; other, 75; total, 79
Capacity: preK, 10; K, 15; 1 – 6, 90; 7 – 9, 45; total, 160
Teacher/student ratio: 1/8
Tuition (annual): preK, $4,500; K – 8, $7,000
Other fees: registration*, $1,000; development fund*, $250
School year: August through June

Year founded: 1969. **Type of school:** coed, day, private nonprofit. **Governed by:** board of governors. **Accredited by:** Western. **Regional organizations:** EARCOS.

Curriculum/physical plant

Type: U.S. **Languages taught:** French, Indonesian. **Special programs:** special French programs may be available to French nationals, ESOL. **Special curricular:** physical education, computer instruction, gamelan music. **Extracurricular:** gymnastics, instrumental music, yearbook, tennis, art, karate, cooking, athletics. **Clubs:** computer, swimming, sports, stamp. **Location:** in suburban area, 10 kilometers north of Medan. **Library:** 6,000 volumes. **Facilities:** 7 buildings, 8 classrooms, auditorium, tennis court, gymnasium, playing field, science lab, computer lab, swimming pool, air conditioning.

*Once only fee

PEKANBARU

Caltex American School

Locations: Rumbai/Minas/Duri, Sumatra, Indonesia
Phone: (62)(765)995501 (office); (62)(765)995301 (superintendent's office)
Facsimile: (62)(765)995002 **E-mail:** 72762.3416@compuserve.com (Rumbai campus); 75767.2731@compuserve.com (Duri campus)
Mail: c/o American Overseas Petroleum Ltd., PO Box 237, Orchard Post Office, Singapore 9123, Republic of Singapore
Superintendent (Duri campus): Tom C. Jenkins
Principal (Rumbai Campus): Alex Partos
Teaching staff: full-time, 35; part-time, 2; total, 37
Nationalities of teaching staff: U.S., 35; host, 2; total, 37
Grade levels: preK – 8

Enrollment: preK, 22; K, 10; 1 – 6, 120; 7 – 8, 14; total, 166
Nationalities of student body: U.S., 143; other, 23; total, 166
Capacity: preK, 30; K, 30; 1 – 6, 120; 7 – 9, 40; total, 220
Teacher/student ratio: 1/8
School year: August to June

Year founded: 1953. **Type of school:** coed, day, company-sponsored. **Sponsored by:** PT Caltex Pacific Indonesia. **Operated by:** International Schools Services, Princeton, New Jersey. **Accredited by:** Western. **Regional organizations:** EARCOS, SEATCCO.

Curriculum

Type: U.S. **Languages taught:** Bahasa Indonesian. **Staff specialists:** math, computer, art, music, physical education, counselors. **Special curricular:** art, physical education, computer instruction, music. **Extracurricular:** drama, dance, yearbook, newspaper. **Sports:** basketball, bowling, gymnastics, soccer, swimming, tennis, softball/T-ball, golf, roller skating, climbing wall. **Clubs:** Cub Scouts, Brownies, Boy Scouts, Girl Scouts. **Tests:** SSAT, ITBS.

Physical plant

Location: central Sumatra in rural jungle/oilfield setting. **Campuses (3):** 5 acres each. Rumbai, 10 kilometers from Pekanbaru; Duri, 120 kilometers from Pekanbaru; Minas, 17 kilometers from Rumbai. **Library:** 6,500 volumes (Duri); 10,000 (Rumbai) volumes. **Facilities:** Rumbai and Duri: 9 classrooms, gymnasiums, playing fields, computer labs, air conditioning. In Caltex residential camps: tennis courts, swimming pools, golf courses, bowling alleys, squash courts, softball fields, and recreation buildings are available for individual and school use.

SALATIGA

Central Java Inter-Mission School

Street address: Jl. Nakula Sadewa Raya no. 55, RT.01 RW 01 Dukah, Salatiga 50722, Jateng, Indonesia
Phone/facsimile: (62)(298)21609 **E-mail:** cjims@yogya.wasantara.net.id
Mail: PO Box 142, Salatiga 50711, Jateng, Indonesia
Headmaster: Ona L. Liles
Dormitory director: Paul Sheriff
Teaching staff: full-time, 24; part-time, 11; total, 35
Nationalities of teaching staff: U.S., 27; host, 2; other, 6; total, 35
Grade levels: K – 12
Enrollment: K – 6, 60; 7 – 9, 56; 10 – 12, 42; ESL, 22; total, 180
Nationalities of student body: U.S., 65; other, 115; total, 180
Capacity: K – 6, 80; 7 – 12, 200; total, 280
Teacher/student ratio: 1/6
Boarders: boys, 25; girls, 23 **Grades:** 4 – 12 **Program:** planned 5- and 7-day
Tuition (annual): 1 – 12, $5,000 (mission reduction available)
Other fees: capital levy*, $3,400; boarding: 5-day, $1,400/semester; 7-day, $1,950/semester
School year: August through May

Year founded: 1981. **Type of school:** coed, day, boarding, church-related, private nonprofit. **Governed by:** elected school board. **Sponsored by:** Bethany Fellowship, Christian Church, OC International, Assemblies of God, International Board.

Curriculum/physical plant

Type: U.S. **Languages taught:** Indonesian. **Staff specialists:** math, computer, ESL, chemistry, English, drama. **Special programs:** ESL (grades 7 & 8). **Special curricular:** art, chorus, band, physical education, computer instruction, English hand bells. **Extracurricular:** instrumental music, yearbook, photography, excursions/expeditions, field trips. **Sports:** basketball, tennis, karate. **Tests:** SAT, ACT, Stanford. **Graduates attending college:** 100%. **Location:** 1 kilometer from Salatiga. **Campuses (2):** 5 hectares. **Libraries (2):** 10,000 volumes. **Facilities:** 6 buildings, 20 classrooms, auditorium, science lab, computer lab, playing fields, covered basketball court, 4 dorms.

*Once only fee

SANGATA

Tanjung Bara International School

Street address: c/- PT Kaltim Prima Coal, Sangata, East Kalimantan, Indonesia
Phone: (62)(549)21800 ext. 3006 **Facsimile:** (62)(549)21800 ext. 3446 or (62)(549)22098 **E-mail:** kpcnet@bpp.mega.net.id
Mail: PO Box 101, Rosebery NSW 2018 Australia
Principal: James Anderson
Senior teacher: Dean Dunham
Teaching staff: full-time, 6; part-time, 1; total, 7
Nationalities of teaching staff: host, 1; other, 6; total, 7
Grade levels: K – 6
Enrollment: K, 15; 1 – 6, 41; total, 56
Nationalities of student body: U.S., 1; U.K., 2; other, 53; total, 56
Teacher/student ratio: 1/9
School year: January to December

Year founded: 1990. **Type of school:** coed, company-sponsored. **Governed by:** company, school board, Tasmanian government. **Sponsored by:** Tasmanian Education Department, DECCD company. **Accredited by:** Tasmanian State Department of Education, Australia. **Regional organizations:** EARCOS, SEATCCO.

Curriculum/physical plant

Type: Australia. **Languages taught:** English, Indonesian. **Staff specialists:** music. **Special curricular:** physical education. **Extracurricular:** gymnastics, instrumental music, yearbook, excursions/expeditions. **Sports:** basketball, football, soccer, swimming, volleyball, netball, T-ball. **Clubs:** Brownies, swimming. **Location:** in isolated mining community, 13 kilometers from Sangata. **Campus:** 2 acres. **Facilities:** 6 buildings, 5 classrooms, auditorium, covered play area, tennis court, 2 playing fields, swimming pool, library, air conditioning.

SEMARANG

SEMARANG INTERNATIONAL SCHOOL

Street address: Jl. Sultan Agung 132, Candi Baru, Semarang 50253, Indonesia
Phone: (62)(24)315147
Head teacher: Jacqueline Dias–Jayasinha
Board chairman: James Lavallee
Teaching staff: full-time, 9; total, 9
Nationalities of teaching staff: U.K., 2; host, 1; other, 6; total, 9
Grade levels: N – 10
Enrollment: N 11; 1 – 10, 69; total, 80
Capacity: N, 15; 1 – 10, 70; total, 85
Teacher/student ratio: 1/9
Tuition (annual): N $1,470; 1, $3,500; 2 – 10, $5,050
School year: September to mid-July

Year founded: 1982. **Type of school:** coed, day, private nonprofit. **Governed by:** elected school board. **Accredited by:** Indonesian Ministry of Education.

Curriculum/physical plant

Type: U.K., Australia, U.S., international. **Languages taught:** Indonesian. **Special programs:** ESL. **Special curricular:** art, physical education, computer instruction, instrumental music, field trips. **Extracurricular:** choral, sports, handicrafts. **Tests:** English-based assessment. **Location:** in expatriate suburb of Candi, 1 kilometer from Semarang. **Campus:** 2 acres. **Library:** 2,500 volumes. **Facilities:** 1 building, garden, air conditioning.

SENTANI

HILLCREST INTERNATIONAL SCHOOL

Street address: Jalan HIS, Sentani 99352, Irian Jaya, Indonesia
Phone: (62)(967)91460/91064 **Facsimile:** (62)(967)91673
E-mail: his.indonesia@sil.org
Mail: PO Box 249, Sentani 99352, Irian Jaya, Indonesia
Director: Kenneth J. Haugh
Elementary/middle school principal: Alex Valley
Teaching staff: full-time, 27; part-time, 8; total, 35
Nationalities of teaching staff: U.S., 26; other, 9; total, 35
Grade levels: K – 12
Enrollment: total, 160
Nationalities of student body: U.S., 75; other, 85; total, 160
Capacity: K – 6, 120; 7 – 8, 40; 9 – 12, 80; total, 240
Teacher/student ratio: 1/5
Boarders: boys, 13; girls, 13 **Grades:** 1 – 12 **Program:** planned 5- and 7-day
Tuition (annual): K – 12 (mission): $1,000 – $2,000; K – 12 (non-mission), $1,500 – 3,000

Other fees (annual): bus/gov, $2,500 – 5,000
School year: August to May

Year founded: 1958. **Type of school:** coed, day, boarding, church-related. **Governed and sponsored by:** Intermission School Board. **Accredited by:** Indonesian government, Western. **Regional organizations:** EARCOS.

Curriculum/physical plant

Type: U.S., international in development. **Languages taught:** English, Indonesian; mother tongue, studies in Dutch, German, Korean. **Staff specialists:** math, computer, physical education, science, special education, Indonesian. **Special curricular:** art, physical education, computer instruction, special education, vocal and instrumental music. **Sports:** basketball, volleyball, intramural. **Tests:** PSAT, SAT, ACT, Stanford, Iowa, Otis-Lennon. **Graduates attending college:** 90%. **Location:** in Sentani, up the hill from the Jayapura airport, about 32 kilometers from Jayapura, capital of the province. **Campus:** elementary/middle school, 10 acres; high school, 15 acres. **Library:** elementary/middle school, 5,500 volumes; high school, 5,600 volumes. **Facilities:** elementary/middle school: 6 buildings, 8 classrooms, gymnasium, playing field, science lab, computer lab, lunch room, video library, swimming pool available, air conditioning; high school: complex with classrooms, teacher study and lounge, nurse's office/clinic, gymnasium, industrial arts building, athletic field.

SURABAYA

Surabaya International School

Street address: CitraRaya International Village, Lakarsantri, Tromol Pos 2/ SBDK, Surabaya 60225, Indonesia
Phone: (62)(31)7414300; (62)(31)7414301 (business office)
Facsimile: (62)(31)7414334; (62)(31)7414313 (business office)
E-mail: sishead@rad.net.id **Web:** http://www.rad.net.id/users/personal/s/siscoord/welcome.html
U.S. mail: (no personal name) Box 1, Unit 8131, APO AP 96520-0002
Superintendent: James A. Mains
High school principal: Jim Dehner
Elementary/middle school principal: Michael Kent
Head of library: Raye Wentworth
Head of computer services: Larry Brown
Teaching staff: full-time, 47; part-time, 2; total, 49
Nationalities of teaching staff: U.S., 34; host, 5; other, 10; total, 49
Grade levels: N – 12
Enrollment: N – preK, 63; K, 32; 1 – 5, 190; 6 – 8, 110; 9 – 12, 105; total, 500
Nationalities of student body: U.S., 50; U.K., 30; other, 420; total, 500
Teacher/student ratio: 1/10
Tuition (annual): N – preK, $4,075; K, $6,125; 1 – 5, $8,040; 6 – 8, $8,140; 9 – 12, $8,355
Other fees: registration*, $800; building fund, $4,680/3 years
School year: August to June

Year founded: 1972. **Type of school:** coed, day, private nonprofit. **Governed by:** school board. **Accredited by:** Western. **Regional organizations:** SEATCCO, EARCOS.

Curriculum/physical plant

Type: U.S., AP. **Languages taught:** French, Bahasa Indonesian. **Staff specialists:** computer, counselor, nurse, art, music, physical education. **Special programs:** ESL. **Special curricular:** art, physical education, computer instruction, music, drama, photography. **Extracurricular:** drama, dance, computers, yearbook, newspaper, literary magazine, field trips, student councils. **Sports:** basketball, soccer, volleyball, swim team. **Tests:** PSAT, TOEFL, AP, Iowa. **Graduates attending college:** 100%. **Graduates have attended:** Purdue, Hawaii Pacific, Griffith U. (Austrlia), Washington U., Carnegie-Mellon. **Location:** new residential development in west Surabaya. **Campus:** 14 acres. **Library:** 12,500 volumes. **Facilities:** 4 buildings, 54 classrooms, gymnasium, playing field, computer labs, climbing wall, swimming pool, 2 infirmaries, food court, demonstration rooms, science labs, photography lab, air-conditioned classrooms, teacher housing.

*Once only fee

TANGERANG

Hope International School

Street address: 2500 Bulevar Palem Raya, Lippo Karawaci, Tangerang 15 811, Indonesia
Phone: (62)(21)5460234 Facsimile: (62)(21)5460248 **E-mail:** dvan@indo.net.id
Director: Johannes Oentoro
Teaching staff: full-time, 9; total, 9
Nationalities of teaching staff: U.S., 2; host, 2; other, 5; total, 9
Grade levels: preK – 12
Enrollment: preK, 7; K, 8; 1 – 6, 50; 7 – 9, 15; 10 – 12, 20; total, 100
Nationalities of student body: U.S., 32; U.K., 1; other, 67; total, 100
Teacher/student ratio: 1/11
Tuition (annual): preK – K, $4,000; 1 – 9, $8,000; 10 – 12, $9,000
Other fees: capital levy, $4,000/2 years
School year: mid-August through late-June

Year founded: 1996. **Type of school:** coed, day, church-related, nondenominational. **Governed by:** board. **Accredited by:** ACSI.

Curriculum/physical plant

Type: U.S. **Languages taught:** Spanish, Bahasa Indonesian. **Staff specialists:** nurse. **Special programs:** ESL. **Special curricular:** art, chorus, band, physical education. **Extracurricular:** choral music, equestrian club. **Sports:** basketball, soccer, tennis, badminton, swimming. **Tests:** SAT. **Location:** in planned community 16 miles from Jakarta. **Campus:** 25 acres. **Library:** 30,000 volumes. **Facilities:** 10 buildings, 90 classrooms, infirmary, 5 tennis courts, 2 gymnasiums, playing field, 8 science labs, 5 computer labs, 2 swimming pools, air conditioning.

*Once only fee

TEMBAGAPURA

Mt. Zaagham International Schools

Location: Tembagapura, Irian Jaya, Indonesia
Phone: (62)(901)407876 **Facsimile:** (62)(901)403170
E-mail: isstpra@fmi.com
Mail: c/o P.T. Freeport Indonesia, Timika, Irian Jaya, Indonesia 98100
U.S. mail: c/o Freeport Indonesia, Inc., PO Box 61982, New orleans, LA 7016101982
Director & principal, Tembagapura campus: Thomas Castagnola
Principal, Kuala Kencana campus: Bruce Pohlmann, Ph.D.
Teaching staff: full-time, 23; part-time, 4; total, 27
Nationalities of teaching staff: U.S., 18; other, 9; total, 27
Grade levels: preK – 9
Enrollment: preK, 32; K, 8; 1 – 6, 108; 7 – 9, 32; total, 180
Nationalities of student body: U.S., 99; Australia, 36; other, 45; total, 180
Teacher/student ratio: 1/6
Tuition (annual) Kuala Kencama only: preK – K, $6,500; 1 – 9, $10,000
School year: August to June

Year founded: 1972. **Type of school:** coed, day, company-sponsored. **Sponsored by:** Freeport Indonesia, Inc. **Operated by:** International Schools Services, Princeton, New Jersey. **Accredited by:** Western. **Regional organizations:** EARCOS, SEATCCO.

Curriculum/physical plant

Type: U.S. **Languages taught:** French, Indonesian. **Staff specialists:** computer, counselor, learning disabilities, art, French, physical education/health. **Special curricular:** art, physical education, computer instruction, music. **Extracurricular:** drama, instrumental music, computers, yearbook, photography, excursions/expeditions, baseball, soccer, tennis, basketball, student council. **Tests:** SSAT, Iowa. **Location:** Tembagapura school is in small company town in remote area; Kuala Kencana school is in a new, purpose-built community in the rainforest. **Library:** 6,000 volumes. **Facilities:** Tembagapura: 17 classrooms, 2 covered play areas, 2 tennis courts, 3 gymnasiums, playing field, science lab, computer lab, photography lab, art room, resource room, music room. Kuala Kencana: 8 classrooms, computer lab, gymnasium, playing field, swimming pool, tennis courts, squash courts, science lab.

UJUNG PANDANG

MAKASSAR INTERNATIONAL SCHOOL

Street address: Jl. Andi Mappanyukki No. 15, Ujung Pandang 90125, Sulawesi Selatan, Indonesia
Phone: (62)(411)872591/873035 **Facsimile:** (62)(411)873035
E-mail: makassar@upandang.wasantara.net.id
Mail: PO Box 1327, Ujung Pandang, Indonesia
Headmaster: Andrew E. Etheridge
Office manager: Joyce Gani
Teaching staff: full-time, 3; part-time, 8; total, 11
Nationalities of teaching staff: host, 4; other, 7; total, 11
Grade levels: preschool – 7
Enrollment: preS, 11; K – 3, 12; 4 – 7, 12; total, 35
Teacher/student ratio: 1/5
Tuition (annual): preS, $2,400; K, $4,500; 1 – 7, $6,000
Other fees (annual): registration*, $250; ESL, $170
School year: September through July

Year founded: 1981; registered international school, 1991. **Type of school:** coed, private nonprofit. **Governed by:** elected board of governors. **Regional organizations:** EARCOS.

Curriculum/physical plant

Type: U.S., U.K., Australia. **Languages taught:** Indonesian. **Staff specialists:** art, music, literacy. **Special programs:** ESL. **Special curricular:** art, physical education, computer instruction, drama, music, swimming, Indonesian studies. **Extracurricular:** excursions/expeditions, field trips, soccer, chess. **Organizations:** Friends of Makassar International School. **Location:** on a tree-lined street within city. **Facilities:** 1 building, 5 classrooms, infirmary, science lab, library, badminton court, 2 small covered play areas, nearby gymnasium, close to sports stadium and olympic-size pool with 2 smaller pools, air conditioning.

*Once only fee

YOGYAKARTA

Yogyakarta International School

Street address: Pogung Baru A-18, Jl. Kaliurang Km.5, Yogyakarta 55284, Java, Indonesia
Phone/facsimile: (62)(274)586067
Mail: PO Box 1175, Yogyakarta 55011, Indonesia
Principal: John Kenneth Stroud
Teaching staff: full-time, 6; total, 6
Nationalities of teaching staff: U.S., 2; host, 3; Australia, 1; total, 6
Grade levels: prep – 7
Enrollment: prep – K2, 18; 3 – 7, 11; total, 29
Capacity: prep, 20; 3 – 7, 10; total, 30
Teacher/student ratio: 1/5
Tuition (annual): prep, $4,000; 1 – 7, $6,000
Other fees (annual): ESL, $480
School year: August to June

Type of school: coed, private nonprofit. **Governed by:** foundation board (inter-school system). **Sponsored by:** Indonesian Yayasan. **Accredited by:** Western (in process). **Regional organizations:** EARCOS.

Curriculum/physical plant

Type: international. **Staff specialists:** reading, art. **Special programs:** ESL. **Special curricular:** art, physical education, computer instruction, music. **Location:** in suburban neighborhood. **Facilities:** 1 building, 2 classrooms, library, playground area, art room, air conditioning.

IRAQ

Region: Middle East
Size: 167,975 square miles
Population: 21,422,292
Capital: Baghdad
Telephone code: 964
Currency: dinar
Languages: Arabic, Kurdish

BAGHDAD

BAGHDAD INTERNATIONAL SCHOOL

Phone: (964)(1)5563602–3 **Facsimile:** (964)(1)5569852
UNDP fax: (964)(1)8862523/(1)(212)9633009 (U.S.)
Mail: PO Box Yarmouk 15115, Baghdad, Iraq
U.S. mail: UNDP/BIS, PO Box 5850, Grand Central Station, New York, NY 10163-5850, U.S.A.
Europe mail: UNDP/BIS, Palais des Nations, 1211 Geneva, 10 Switzerland
Acting director: Fadel El-Zubi
High school principal: Behnam Al-Soof, Ph.D.
Teaching staff: full-time, 39; part-time, 8; total, 47
Nationalities of teaching staff: U.K., 5; host, 41; other, 1; total, 47
Grade levels: preK – 12
Enrollment: preK, 3; K – 6, 111; 7 – 9, 50; 10 – 12, 59; total, 223
Nationalities of student body: U.S., 10; host, 57; other, 156; total, 223
Teacher/student ratio: 1/5
Tuition, non-host students (annual): 39,000** plus $1,000 – 1,700
Other fees: registration*, $300; application*, $500
School year: September to June

Year founded: 1967. **Type of school:** coed, private nonprofit. **Governed by:** board of trustees. **Accredited by:** Middle States (in process), ECIS (in process). **Regional organizations:** NESA, ECIS.

Curriculum/physical plant

Type: combined U.S./U.K., AP. **Languages taught:** French, Arabic. **Special programs:** ESL. **Special curricular:** art, physical education, computer instruction, music, handwriting, architectural drawing. **Extracurricular:** dance, computers, yearbook, newspaper, literary magazine, excursions/expeditions, international trips. **Tests:** GCSE, A- and O-level GCE. **Graduates attending college:** 100%. **Graduates have attended:** McGill U., Amherst, U. of Connecticut, Keel U. (U.K.). **Location:** 20 kilometers outside of Baghdad on airport road. **Library:** 25,000 volumes, over 4,350 A/V materials. **Facilities:** 2 buildings, each with 48 classrooms, auditorium, science lab, cafeteria, language lab, art room, music room, gymnasium; secondary building has physics lab, chemistry lab, biology lab; nursery in elementary building, 3 tennis courts, volleyball court, basketball court, track and field, playing area, swimming pool, infirmary, air conditioning, central heating.

*Once only fee **Iraqi dinar

IRELAND

Region: Europe
Size: 27,137 square miles
Population: 3,566,833
Capital: Dublin
Telephone code: 353
Currency: pound
Languages: English, Irish (Gaelic)

DUBLIN

St. Andrew's College

Street address: Booterstown Avenue, Blackrock, Dublin, Ireland
Phone: (353)(1)2882785 **Facsimile:** (353)(1)2831627
Headmaster: Arthur Godsil
Elementary school principal: William Mansfield
Vice-principals: Brendan McArdle, Joan Kirby, Ronnie Hay
IB coordinator: Edith Byrne
Teaching staff: full-time, 65; part-time, 30; total, 95
Nationalities of teaching staff: U.S., 2; U.K., 3; host, 90; total, 95
Grade levels: 1 – 12
Enrollment: preparatory, 250; secondary, 840; total, 1,090
Nationalities of student body: U.S., 35; U.K., 49; host, 820; other, 186; total, 1,090
Teacher/student ratio: 1/11
Tuition (annual): preparatory, $3,123; secondary, $2,621
School year: September to June

Year founded: 1894. **Type of school:** coed, day. **Governed by:** appointed board of governors. **Accredited by:** New England, ECIS. **Regional organizations:** ECIS.

Curriculum

Type: U.S., national, IB. **Languages taught:** French, Spanish, German, Irish. **Staff specialists:** math, counselor, psychologist, learning disabilities, nurse, resource. **Special programs:** ESL, honors sections. **Special curricular:** art, chorus, physical education, computer instruction. **Extracurricular:** drama, dance, choral music, computers, newspaper, excursions/expeditions, field trips. **Sports:** athletics, badminton, basketball, cricket, field hockey, rugby, soccer, swimming, tennis. **Clubs:** computer, drama, Boy Scouts, arts & crafts, debating society, book, peace. **Tests:** PSAT, SAT, ACT, TOEFL, IB, achievements. **Graduates attending college:** 85%. **Graduates have attended:** Harvard, Yale, Princeton, Middlebury, U. of California at Berkeley.

Physical plant

Location: in suburban area, 5 miles south of Dublin city center. **Campus:** 10.5 acres. **Library:** 5,000 volumes. **Facilities:** 2 buildings, 57 classrooms, auditorium, cafeteria, infirmary, tennis court, gymnasium, 3 playing fields, 5 science labs, computer lab, AV equipment, music department.

Sutton Park School

Street address: St. Fintan's Road, Sutton, Dublin 13, Ireland
Phone: (353)(1)8322940 **Facsimile:** (353)(1)8325929
Headmaster: L. J. Finnegan
Vice-principal: R. Russell
Business manager: L. Hogan Kerrigan
Teaching staff: full-time, 32; part-time, 3; total, 35
Nationalities of teaching staff: U.K., 3; host, 30; other, 2; total, 35
Grade levels: K – 13
Enrollment: K, 14; 1 – 6, 118; 7 – 9, 115; 10 – 12, 161; total, 408
Nationalities of student body: U.S., 24; U.K., 36; host, 326; other, 22; total, 408
Capacity: preK, 14; 1 – 6, 120; 7 – 9, 120; 10 – 12, 120; 13, 40; total, 414
Teacher/student ratio: 1/12
Tuition (annual): K, 1,200**; 1 – 6, 2,200; 7 – 13, 3,000
Other fees (annual): registration*, 250**; boarding, 7,500; lunch, 2/day; books, 150
School year: September to June

Year founded: 1958. **Type of school:** coed, day, boarding, private nonprofit. **Governed by:** appointed governing body. **Accredited by:** Irish Department of Education, ECIS, New England (in process).

Curriculum

Type: national, AP. **Languages taught:** French, Spanish, German, Italian, Latin, Irish (Gaelic). **Staff specialists:** reading, math, computer, counselor, nurse on call. **Special programs:** ESL, honors sections, independent study. **Special curricular:** art, chorus, band, physical education, computer instruction, woodwork. **Extracurricular:** drama, gymnastics, choral and instrumental music, computers, yearbook, newspaper, literary magazine, photography, excursions/expeditions, field trips. **Sports:** badminton, basketball, field hockey, rugby, soccer, swimming, tennis. **Clubs:** chess, computer, debating, drama, Model UN, arts & crafts, cooking, newspaper, video, European Youth Parliament. **Tests:** SSAT, PSAT, SAT, ACT, TOEFL, AP, Irish Higher Learning Certificate (A-level, AP equivalent). **Graduates attending college:** 90%. **Graduates have attended:** Trinity College, Dublin, U. College Dublin, Oxford U., Tufts U., UCLA.

Physical plant

Location: on wooded campus in Georgian house with modern classroom blocks, 10 miles from Dublin city center. **Campuses (2):** 16 acres. **Library:** 3,000 volumes. **Facilities:** 40 buildings, 30 classrooms, 2 auditoriums, cafeteria, infirmary, covered play area, 2 tennis courts, gymnasium, 2 playing fields, 2 science labs, computer lab, swimming pool, access to horse riding and sailing, boarding in large Victorian house with double rooms and family atmosphere.

*Once only fee **Irish pound

ISRAEL

Region: Middle East
Size: 7,876 square miles
Population: 5,421,995
Capital: Jerusalem
Telephone code: 972
Currency: new sheqel
Languages: Hebrew, Arabic, English

JERUSALEM

ANGLICAN INTERNATIONAL SCHOOL, JERUSALEM

Street address: 82 Prophet Street, Jerusalem 91001, Israel
Phone: (972)(2)5677200 **Facsimile:** (972)(2)5384874
Mail: PO Box 191, Jerusalem 91001, Israel
Headmaster: D. Jeffery
Business manager: Mona Ishac
Teaching staff: total, 46
Grade levels: N – 12
Enrollment: total, 331
Teacher/student ratio: 1/8
Tuition: N, $2,500; 1R/1A, $5,000; 1B – 6, $5,650; 7 – 12, $6,850
Other fees (annual): application*, $50; capital fee, first child, $1,000 (scaled); admission*, $1,500 (scaled)
School year: September through June

Year founded: 1948. **Type of school:** coed, day, church-related. **Governed by:** appointed school board. **Sponsored by:** Israel Trust of the Anglican Church. **Accredited by:** Middle States. **Regional organizations:** NESA, ECIS.

Curriculum/physical plant

Type: U.S., U.K., AP. **Languages taught:** French, Arabic, Hebrew. **Staff specialists:** reading, math, computer, counselor, music, physical education, art and ceramics, religious studies, economics, languages, physical sciences, biology, history, geography, English. **Special programs:** ESL, special needs, Jerusalem studies, music, first language schools in German and Korean. **Special curricular:** art, chorus, band, physical education, computer instruction. **Extracurricular:** drama, choral and instrumental music, computers, yearbook, photography, excursions/expeditions, field trips, Model UN. **Sports:** basketball, soccer, softball, swimming, table tennis, tennis, street hockey, physical fitness. **Clubs:** chess, Brownies, Girl Scouts, student council, yearbook, Boys Club, gymnastics, orchestra, stamp, choir, Christian fellowship. **Tests:** PSAT, SAT, ACT, TOEFL, AP, GCSE, IGCSE, Iowa, GCE. **Graduates attending college:** 75%. **Graduates have attended:** Hebrew U., Boston U., Davis, Calvin, Wheaton. **Location:** in historic buildings in center city. **Campus:** 3 acres. **Library:** 10,000 volumes. **Facilities:** 12 buildings, 22 classrooms, tennis court, playing field, 2 science labs, computer lab.

*Once only fee

RAMALLAH

Ramallah Friends School

Phone: (972)(2)9956230 **Facsimile:** (972)(2)9956231
Mail: PO Box 66, Ramallah, West Bank, via Israel
Principal: Dr. Maria C. Khoury
Head of library: Peter Kapenga
Head of computer services: Salim Zughayyar
Business manager: Diana Khoury
Teaching staff: full-time, 64; part-time, 15; total, 79
Nationalities of teaching staff: U.S., 12; host, 64; other, 3; total, 79
Grade levels: preK – 12
Enrollment: preK, 25; K, 60; 1 – 6, 350; 7 – 9, 180; 10 – 12, 190; total, 805
Capacity: preK, 25; K, 60; 1 – 6, 360; 7 – 9, 180; 10 – 12, 240; 865
Teacher/student ratio: 1/14
Tuition (annual): preK – K, $725; 1 – 6, $850; 7 – 9, $1,150; 10 – 12, $1,300
School year: September to June

Year founded: 1869. **Type of school:** coed, day, private nonprofit. **Governed by:** elected board of trustees. **Sponsored by:** Friends United Meeting. **Accredited by:** Jordanian Ministry of Education, Palestinian Ministry of Education.

Curriculum/physical plant

Type: U.S., U.K., national. **Languages taught:** English, Arabic. **Special curricular:** art, physical education, computer instruction, vocational. **Extracurricular:** drama, yearbook, folk dance. **Sports:** basketball, soccer, handball. **Tests:** SAT, TOEFL, O- & A-level GCE, Tawjihi (General Secondary Education Exams – Jordan). **Graduates attending college:** 85%. **Graduates have attended:** Earlham, Jordan U., Birzeit U., Brigham Young, Hope. **Location:** Ramallah, West Bank. **Campuses:** 4 acres. **Libraries (2):** 8,000 volumes. **Facilities:** 7 buildings, 30 classrooms, auditorium, tennis court, playing field, science labs, computer labs.

TEL AVIV

THE WALWORTH BARBOUR AMERICAN INTERNATIONAL SCHOOL IN ISRAEL

Street address: Hazorea Street, Kfar Shmaryahu, Israel
Phone: (972)(9)9584225 **Facsimile:** (972)(9)9582881
E-mail: aisisrael@american.hasharon.k12.il
Mail: PO Box 9005, Kfar Shmaryahu 46910, Israel
U.S. mail: (no personal name) American Embassy (AIS) Unit 7228, APO AE 09830
Superintendent: Richard M. Detwiler
High school principal: Kevin Haverty
Middle school principal: Norma Levkowitz
Elementary school principal: Elaine Levy
Teaching staff: full-time, 62; part-time, 18; total, 80
Nationalities of teaching staff: U.S., 54; U.K., 6; host, 11; other, 9; total, 80
Grade levels: K – 12
Enrollment: K, 30; 1 – 5, 210; 6 – 8, 130; 9 – 12, 190; total, 560
Nationalities of student body: U.S., 160; U.K., 5; host, 60; other, 335; total, 560
Capacity: K, 35; 1 – 5, 210; 6 – 8, 140; 9 – 12, 210; total, 595
Teacher/student ratio: 1/8
Tuition (annual): K – 5, $10,490; 6 – 8, $10,980; 9 – 12, $11,950
Other fees (annual): busing, $1,000 – 2,500
School year: September to June

Year founded: 1958. **Type of school:** coed, day, private nonprofit. **Governed by:** elected corporation. **Accredited by:** Middle States. **Regional organizations:** AAIE, ECIS, NESA.

Curriculum/physical plant

Type: U.S., AP. **Languages taught:** French, Spanish, Hebrew. **Staff specialists:** counselor, learning disabilities, nurse. **Special programs:** ESL, learning disabilities. **Special curricular:** art, physical education, computer instruction, music. **Extracurricular:** drama, computers, yearbook, newspaper, literary magazine, photography, excursions/expeditions, field trips, chorus, extensive after-school activities program. **Sports:** baseball, basketball, field hockey, soccer, softball, volleyball. **Tests:** PSAT, SAT, TOEFL, AP, CAT 5. **Graduates attending college:** 98%. **Graduates have attended:** Haverford, Stanford, Bryn Mawr. **Location:** in pleasant residential suburb, 10 miles north of Tel Aviv. **Campus:** 6 acres. **Library:** 22,000 volumes. **Facilities:** 40 classrooms, gymnasium, 2 playing fields, 4 science labs, 4 computer labs, 2 art rooms, fitness center, 2 viewing rooms, air conditioning.

ITALY

Region: Europe
Size: 116,336 square miles
Population: 57,460,274
Capital: Rome
Telephone code: 39
Currency: lira
Language: Italian

FLORENCE

AMERICAN INTERNATIONAL SCHOOL OF FLORENCE

Street address: Via del Carota 23/25, 50012 Bagno a Ripoli, Florence, Italy
Phone: (39)(55)640033 **Facsimile:** (39)(55)644226 **E-mail:** aisf@ats.it
Headmaster: Marc Greenside, Ed.D.
Teaching staff: full-time, 20; part-time, 3; total, 23
Nationalities of teaching staff: U.S., 13; U.K., 4; host, 3; other, 3; total, 23
Grade levels: preK – 12
Enrollment: preK – K, 32; 1 – 5, 68; 6 – 8, 40; 9 – 12, 40; total, 180
Nationalities of student body: U.S., 71; host, 57; other, 52; total, 180
Capacity: preK – K, 35; 1 – 5, 65; 6 – 8, 45; 9 – 12, 70; total, 215
Teacher/student ratio: 1/8
Tuition (annual): preK, 8,400,000**; K, 9,000,000; 1 – 5, 12,500,000; 6 – 8, 13,900,000; 9 – 12, 16,000,000
Other fees (annual): registration*, 1,200,000**; capital levy*, 1,200,000 (5% reduction after first child); application, 100,000; IB, 1,500,000; senior fee, 250,000; EFL, 1,500,000; Italian program: elementary, 500,000, middle school, 800,000
School year: September to June

Year founded: 1952. **Type of school:** coed, day, private nonprofit. **Governed by:** board of advisors. **Accredited by:** Middle States, ECIS. **Regional organizations:** ECIS.

Curriculum/physical plant

Type: U.S., IB. **Languages taught:** English, French, Italian. **Staff specialists:** computer, art, music, physical education. **Special programs:** EFL, preparation for Italian national exams. **Special curricular:** art, chorus, physical education, computer instruction. **Extracurricular:** yearbook, newspaper, field trips, student council. **Tests:** SSAT, PSAT, SAT, ACT, TOEFL, IB. **Graduates attending college:** 95%. **Location:** in Renaissance villa on hilltop in countryside, 12 kilometers from Florence. **Campus:** 18 acres. **Library:** 14,000 volumes. **Facilities:** 1 building, 18 classrooms, 3 playing fields, science lab, lunch room, Macintosh computer lab.

*Once only fee **Italian lira

GENOA

American International School in Genoa

Street address: Via Quarto 13/C, 16148 Genoa, Italy
Phone: (39)(10)386528 **Facsimile:** (39)(10)398700 **E-mail:** aisg@th.village.it
Director: Julia Alden
Teaching staff: full-time, 11; part-time, 7; total, 18
Nationalities of teaching staff: U.S., 9; U.K., 1; host, 4; other, 4; total, 18
Grade levels: preschool – 8
Enrollment: total, 142
Capacity: preS – preK, 30; K, 30; 1 – 5, 70; 6 – 8, 30; total, 160
Teacher/student ratio: 1/9
Tuition (annual): preS – preK, 7,210,000**; K, 8,450,000; 1, 10,100,000; 2, 11,330,000; 3 – 4, 12,050,000; 5 – 8, 12,875,000
Other fees: membership*, 1,000,000**
School year: September to June†

Year founded: 1966. **Type of school:** coed, day, private nonprofit. **Governed by:** elected board of directors. **Accredited by:** New England, ECIS. **Regional organizations:** AAIE, ECIS, MAIS.

Curriculum/physical plant

Type: U.S. **Languages taught:** French, Italian. **Staff specialists:** math, art, physical education, technical drawing. **Special programs:** ESL. **Special curricular:** art, physical education, computer instruction. **Extracurricular:** drama, gymnastics, computers, excursions/expeditions, field trips. **Sports:** basketball, soccer, volleyball. **Tests:** TOEFL. **Location:** 20 minutes from center city by train or bus, 100 meters from sea. **Campus:** 1 acre. **Library:** 4,000 volumes. **Facilities:** 3 buildings, 13 classrooms, cafeteria, gymnasium, playing field, science lab, computer lab.

*Once only fee **Italian lira †four-week summer school program

GROTTAFERRATA

Castelli International Bilingual School

Street address: Via degli Scozzesi 13, 00046 Grottaferrata, Rome, Italy
Phone/facsimile: (39)(6)94315779 **E-mail:** maryac@email.telpress.it
Web: http://www.pcg.it/cis
Director of studies: Marianne Palladino
Teaching staff: full-time, 5; part-time, 6; total, 11
Nationalities of teaching staff: U.S., 3; U.K., 5; host, 3; total, 11
Grade levels: 1 – 8
Enrollment: 1 – 5, 60; 6 – 8, 30; total, 90
Nationalities of student body: U.S., 20; U.K., 15; host, 28; other, 27; total, 90
Teacher/student ratio: 1/11
Tuition (annual): 1 – 5, 7,600,000 – 9,000,000**; 6 – 8, 10,200,000

Other fees (annual): registration, 400,000**; capital levy*, 500,000; busing, 1,900,000 – 2,400,000; lunch, 1,600,000
School year: September to June

Year founded: 1977. **Type of school:** coed, day, private nonprofit. **Governed by:** elected board of trustees. **Accredited by:** Italian Ministry of Education.

Curriculum/physical plant

Type: U.S., U.K., national. **Languages of instruction:** English, Italian. **Languages taught:** French, Spanish, German, Latin. **Staff specialists:** reading, math, learning disabilities. **Special programs:** ESL, independent study, remedial, IFL. **Special curricular:** art, chorus, physical education, computer instruction. **Extracurricular:** drama, gymnastics, yearbook, field trips. **Sports:** badminton, baseball, basketball, soccer, volleyball, ping-pong, track and field. **Tests:** SSAT, PSAT. **Graduates attending college:** 90%. **Graduates have attended:** U. of Rome, Columbia, Stanford, Lafayette, Vassar. **Location:** nestled amidst vineyards and olive groves, 15 kilometers from Rome. **Campus:** 13 acres. **Library:** 5,000 volumes. **Facilities:** 4 buildings, 8 classrooms, cafeteria, gymnasium, 3 playing fields, computer lab, AV equipment.

*Once only fee **Italian lira

LANCIANO

Canadian College Italy (CCI International School)

Street address: Via Cavour 13, Lanciano, Chieti, Italy
Phone: (39)(872)714969 **Facsimile:** (39)(872)45028 **E-mail:** cci@teknet.rgn.it
Web: http://www.idirect.com/~cci/
Admissions office: 59 Macamo Court, Maple, Ontario, Canada L6A 1G1
Phone: (905)5087108 **Facsimile:** (905)5085480
E-mail: marisa.cci@sympatico.ca
Director: Marisa DiCarlo D'Alessandro
Headmistress: Janette Doupe
Teaching staff: full-time, 12; part-time, 2; total, 14
Nationalities of teaching staff: host, 2; Canada, 12; total, 14
Grade levels: 10 – 13
Enrollment: 10 – 12, 35; 13, 65; total, 100
Nationalities of student body: U.S., 10; Canada, 90; total, 100
Capacity: total, 150
Teacher/student ratio: 1/7
Boarders: boys, 40; girls, 60 **Grades:** 11 – 13 **Program:** planned 7-day
Tuition (annual): 10 – 13, $13,500
Other fees (annual): boarding, $7,000; books, $450; uniforms (as needed), $350
School year: September to June

Year founded: 1994. **Type of school:** coed, day, boarding, private nonprofit. **Governed by:** appointed board of governors. **Accredited by:** Ontario Ministry of Education. **Regional organization:** ECIS.

Curriculum/physical plant

Type: Canadian, AP. **Languages taught:** French, Italian. **Staff specialists:** computer, counselor, nurse. **Special curricular:** art, science. **Extracurricular:** drama, choral music, yearbook, newspaper, excursions/expeditions, field trips. **Tests:** SAT, AP, Ontario academic credits. **Graduates have attended:** McGill U., U. of Toronto, York U. **Location:** in artistic, musical medieval town of 40,000 population. **Facilities:** 5 buildings, 8 classrooms, auditorium, cafeteria, infirmary, science lab, computer lab, library, new boarding facilities.

MILAN

American School of Milan

Street address: 20090 Noverasco di Opera, Milan, Italy
Phone: elementary, (39)(2)53000025; secondary, (39)(2)53000019
Facsimile: (39)(2)57606274 **E-mail:** directorasm@planet.it
Director: David Ottaviano
Business manager: Luisa G. Linzani
Teaching staff: full-time, 55; total, 55
Nationalities of teaching staff: U.S., 39; U.K., 6; host, 7; other, 3; total, 55
Grade levels: N – 13
Enrollment: N – preK, 31; K, 40; 1 – 6, 235; 7 – 10, 124; 11 – 13, 73; total, 503
Nationalities of student body: U.S., 160; host, 151; other, 192; total, 503
Capacity: N – preK, 30; K, 40; 1 – 6, 240; 7 – 9, 120; 10 – 13, 120; total, 550
Teacher/student ratio: 1/9
Tuition (annual): N, 8,600,000**; K, 9,600,000; 1 – 2, 12,500,000; 3 – 5, 14,500,000; 6 – 10, 16,000,000; 11 – 13, 16,500,000
Other fees (annual): registration, 1,000,000**; new student admission*, 1,000,000; senior*, 850,000; transportation (optional), 2,500,000 – 4,090,000
School year: September through June

Year founded: 1962. **Type of school:** coed, day, private nonprofit. **Governed by:** elected board of trustees. **Accredited by:** Middle States.

Curriculum/physical plant

Type: U.S., IB, AP. **Languages taught:** French, Italian. **Staff specialists:** computer, counselor, learning disabilities, nurse. **Special programs:** ESL, honors sections, pre-school Montessori (language based). **Special curricular:** art, chorus, physical education, computer instruction. **Extracurricular:** drama, gymnastics, choral music, computers, photography, excursions/expeditions, field trips, sports. **Tests:** SSAT, PSAT, SAT, ACT, TOEFL, IB, AP, Iowa, Italian national exams. **Graduates attending college:** 100%. **Graduates have attended:** U. of Pennsylvania, MIT, Yale, Georgetown, Carnegie-Mellon. **Location:** in suburban area of Milan. **Campus:** 8 acres. **Library:** 20,000 volumes. **Facilities:** 3 buildings, auditorium, cafeteria, infirmary, 3 tennis courts, gymnasium, 3 playing fields, 4 science labs, 2 computer labs, early elementary center.

*Once only fee **Italian lira

International School of Milan

Street address: Via Bezzola 6, 20153 Milano, Italy
Phone: (39)(2)40910067 – 8 **Facsimile:** (39)(2)48703644
Head, high/middle schools: Terence F. Haywood
Head, lower schools: Elizabeth Sloane
Business manager: Franco Formiga
Teaching staff: full-time, 68; part-time, 5; total, 73
Nationalities of teaching staff: U.S., 2; U.K., 59; host, 5; other, 7; total, 73
Grade levels: preK – 13
Enrollment: preK, 170; K, 45; 1 – 6, 290; 7 – 9, 135; 10 – 12, 140; 13, 30; total, 810
Teacher/student ratio: 1/11
Tuition (annual): preK, 4,750,000**; K, 6,750,000; transition, 7,600,000; 1, 8,750,000; 2 – 5, 10,600,000; 6 – 9, 11,250,000; 10 – 11, 12,600,000; 12 – 13, 13,500,000
Other fees (annual): registration*, 750,000**; capital levy, 600,000; busing, 2,000,000 (optional); lunch, 900,000 (optional); books, 250,000; new student*, 1,000,000
School year: September to June

Year founded: 1958. **Type of school:** coed, day, proprietary. **Governed by:** headteachers, sponsor, elected parents' group. **Sponsored by:** International School of Europe. **Accredited by:** Italian Ministry of Public Instruction. **Regional organizations:** ECIS.

Curriculum

Type: U.K., IB, AP. **Languages taught:** French, German, Italian. **Staff specialists:** reading, math, computer, counselor, nurse. **Special programs:** ESL, remedial. **Special curricular:** art, chorus, physical education, computer instruction, drama, dance. **Extracurricular:** drama, gymnastics, dance, choral and instrumental music, computers, yearbook, photography, excursions/expeditions, field trips, Model UN. **Sports:** athletics, basketball, hockey, rugby, soccer, swimming, tennis, volleyball. **Clubs:** chess, art. **Tests:** PSAT, IB, A-level GCE, GCSE. **Graduates attending college:** 95%. **Graduates have attended:** London School of Economics, London-University College, Oxford, Brown, Carnegie-Mellon.

Physical plant

Location: 4 main centers in city (kindergarten and elementary, middle, high schools) with 2 satellite kindergartens. **Libraries:** 20,000 volumes. **Facilities:** 2 auditoriums, 3 cafeterias, 3 infirmaries, covered play area, 3 gymnasiums, 3 playing fields, 4 science labs, 3 computer labs, 2 art studios, darkroom.

*Once only fee **Italian lira

The Sir James Henderson British School of Milan

Street address: Via Pisani Dossi 16, 20134 Milan, Italy
Phone: (39)(2)26413332/26413310 **Facsimile:** (39)(2)26413515/26413302
E-mail: sirjames@bbs.infosquare.it
Principal: Steven Anson
Head of upper school: Gregory Wright
Head of lower school: Angela Dean
Teaching staff: full-time, 38; part-time, 10; total, 48
Grade levels: N – 13
Enrollment: preschool, 80; lower school, 210; upper school, 180; total, 470
Teacher/student ratio: 1/9
Tuition (annual): N – 13, 7,000,000 – 16,000,000**
Other fees: registration, 1,000,000**; development, 1,000,000
School year: September to June

Year founded: 1969. **Type of school:** coed, day, private nonprofit. **Governed by:** elected parental body. **Accredited by:** U.K. and Italian governments. **Regional organizations:** ECIS, COBISEC, Headmasters' Conference.

Curriculum

Type: U.K. **Languages taught:** French, Spanish, German, Italian. **Staff specialists:** reading, math, computer, counselor, nurse, 15 peripatetic musicians. **Special programs:** ESL. **Special curricular:** art, chorus, physical education, computer instruction. **Extracurricular:** drama, choral and instrumental music, yearbook, excursions/expeditions, inter-house activities, including quizzes, chess, sports. **Sports:** basketball, cricket, rugby, soccer, swimming, track and field, volleyball, gym. **Clubs:** debating, drama, Brownies, Duke of Edinburgh's Award. **Tests:** A-level GCE, GCSE, IGCSE. **Graduates attending college:** 95%. **Graduates have attended:** Georgetown, Boston U., U. of California at Los Angeles, Oxford, Cambridge.

Physical plant

Location: in Northeastern Milan. **Facilities:** 2 buildings, auditorium, science labs, computer lab, library, gymnasium, playing fields, dining hall, sixth form center, music practice rooms, use of sports complex with swimming pools, athletic track, playing fields.

**Italian lira

NAPLES

The International School of Naples

Street address: HQ AFSouth Post, Building "A," Bagnoli, Naples 80125, Italy
Phone: (39)(81)7212037 **Facsimile:** (39)(81)7628429
E-mail: isn@na.cybernet.it
Principal: Josephine Sessa
Teaching staff: full-time, 21; part-time, 6; total, 27
Nationalities of teaching staff: U.S., 12; U.K., 5; host, 6; other, 4; total, 27
Grade levels: N – 12
Enrollment: N – K, 28; 1 – 6, 68; 7 – 9, 42; 10 – 12, 47; total, 185
Nationalities of student body: U.S., 23; U.K., 8; host, 47; other, 107; total, 185
Teacher/student ratio: 1/7
Tuition (annual): N, 3,150,000**; K – 3, 4,660,000; 4 – 6, 5,770,000; 7 – 12, 6,880,000
Other fees (annual): registration, 300,000**; capital levy*, 500,000; busing, 1,200,000; lunch, 400,000
School year: September to June

Year founded: 1979. **Type of school:** coed, day, private nonprofit. **Governed by:** school board. **Regional organizations:** ECIS.

Curriculum/physical plant

Type: U.S. **Languages taught:** French, Italian. **Staff specialists:** math, computer, educational and learning disabilities. **Special programs:** ESL, independent study, remedial. **Special curricular:** physical education. **Extracurricular:** drama, gymnastics, computers, yearbook, newspaper, photography, excursions/expeditions, field trips. **Sports:** basketball, soccer, volleyball. **Tests:** PSAT, SAT, ACT, ERB, SRA. **Graduates attending college:** 90%. **Graduates have attended:** U. of Maryland, Stonybrook, St. Francis College, U. of California at Los Angeles. **Location:** in Naples, on NATO base. **Facilities:** 2 buildings, auditorium, cafeteria, gymnasium, 3 playing fields, science lab, computer lab, library, AV equipment.

*Once only fee **Italian lira

ROME

Ambrit Rome International School

Street address: Via Filippo Tajani 50, Rome 00149, Italy
Phone: (39)(6)5595301–5 **Facsimile:** (39)(6)5595309
E-mail: ambrit@email.telpress.it
Headmaster: Bernard C. Mullane
Middle school principal: Robin Gilbody
Primary school principal: Veblena Finkenberg
Early childhood principal: Constance Soehnlen
Business manager: Loretta Nannini

Teaching staff: full-time, 35; part-time, 10; total, 45
Nationalities of teaching staff: U.S., 18; U.K., 15; host, 4; other, 8; total, 45
Grade levels: N – 8
Enrollment: N – preK, 40; K, 30; 1 – 6, 190; 7 – 8, 90; total, 350
Nationalities of student body: U.S., 40; U.K., 16; host, 100; other, 194; total, 350
Capacity: N – preK, 40; K, 30; 1 – 6, 190; 7 – 8, 90; total, 350
Teacher/student ratio: 1/8
Tuition (annual): N – preK, 8,150,000**; K, 11,900,000; 1 – 5, 13,700,000; 6 – 8, 14,900,000
Other fees: registration*, 1,000,000**; capital levy*, 1,600,000
School year: September to June

Year founded: 1982. **Type of school:** coed, day, nonprofit. **Governed by:** board. **Accredited by:** New England, ECIS, ISCP. **Regional organizations:** MAIS.

Curriculum/physical plant

Type: U.S., U.K., national. **Languages taught:** French, Italian. **Staff specialists:** reading, math, computer, learning disabilities. **Special programs:** ESL, remedial. **Special curricular:** art, chorus, physical education, computer instruction, dance. **Extracurricular:** drama, gymnastics, dance, choral and instrumental music, computers, yearbook, newspaper, literary magazine, photography, excursions/expeditions, field trips. **Sports:** basketball, skiing, soccer, swimming, tennis, volleyball. **Location:** on tree-lined street, 2 miles from center of Rome. **Campus:** 10 acres. **Library:** 17,000 volumes. **Facilities:** 20 classrooms, auditorium, cafeteria, infirmary, covered play area, 3 playing fields, science lab.

*Once only fee **Italian lira

American Overseas School of Rome

Street address: Via Cassia 811, 00189 Rome, Italy
Phone: (39)(6)33264841 **Facsimile:** (39)(6)33262608
E-mail: aosr.inc@agora.stm.it
U.S. mail: PSC 59, Box 68, APO AE 09624
Headmaster: Dr. Larry Dougherty
Admissions: Don Levine
Teaching staff: full-time, 43; part-time, 3; total, 46
Nationalities of teaching staff: U.S., 29; U.K., 5; host, 8; other, 4; total, 46
Grade levels: preK – 13
Enrollment: preK – K, 53; 1 – 6, 155; 7 – 9, 95; 10 – 13, 92; total, 395
Teacher/student ratio: 1/9
Tuition (annual): preK, 7,000,000**; K, 10,800,000; 1 – 2, 14,400,000; 3 – 5, 15,500,000; 6 – 8, 17,500,000; 9 – 11, 19,500,000; 12 – 13, 20,000,000
Other fees (annual): registration, 350,000**; boarding, 8 – 13, 31,500,000 capital levy*, 1,000,000; busing, 2,400,000; lunch, 1,000,000; ESL, 1,000,000
School year: September to June

Year founded: 1947. **Type of school:** coed, day, boarding, private nonprofit. **Governed by:** elected board of trustees. **Accredited by:** Middle States. **Regional organizations:** AAIE, ECIS.

Curriculum/physical plant

Type: U.S., IB, AP. **Languages taught:** French, Spanish, Italian. **Staff specialists:** reading, computer, counselor, learning disabilities, nurse. **Special programs:** ESL, honors sections, remedial. **Special curricular:** art, chorus, physical education, computer instruction, music, Model UN, ensemble. **Extracurricular:** drama, choral music, computers, yearbook, newspaper, excursions/expeditions, field trips, karate, swimming, baseball, aerobics, pottery, Latin. **Sports:** basketball, soccer, swimming, tennis, track and field, volleyball, wrestling. **Clubs:** chess, computer, drama, student council. **Tests:** PSAT, SAT, ACT, IB, AP, Iowa. **Graduates attending college:** 90%. **Graduates have attended:** Stanford, Oxford, Smith, Wellesley, Tufts. **Location:** in residential section, with easy access to center of Rome. **Campus:** 6 acres. **Libraries (2):** 22,000 volumes. **Facilities:** 5 buildings, 43 classrooms, cafeteria, infirmary, 2 tennis courts, gymnasium, 4 science labs, computer lab, grass soccer field, hillside theater; supervised, spacious boarding facility available 2 kilometers north of campus.

*Once only fee **Italian lira

Greenwood Garden School

Street address: Via Vito Sinisi 5, Rome 00189, Italy
Phone/facsimile: (39)(6)33266703
Directress: Donna Seibert Ricci
Teaching staff: full-time, 3; part-time, 1; total, 4
Nationalities of teaching staff: U.S., 1; U.K., 2; other, 1; total, 4
Grade levels: N – K (ages 2 – 6)
Enrollment: N – preK, 15; K, 15; total, 30
Nationalities of student body: U.S., 5; U.K., 4; host, 15; other, 6; total, 30
Teacher/student ratio: 1/8
Tuition (annual): 6,600,000 – 7,500,000**
Other fees (annual): registration, 350,000**; busing, 2,400,000; deposit, 500,000
School year: September to June†

Year founded: 1974. **Type of school:** coed, day, proprietary. **Accredited by:** Italian Ministry of Education, Rome International Schools Association.

Curriculum/physical plant

Type: U.S. **Languages of instruction:** English, Italian. **Staff specialists:** early childhood. **Special programs:** ESL. **Special curricular:** art, physical education, drama, music, tumbletots, cooking, mime. **Location:** 1 kilometer from Rome. **Facilities:** apartment with 700-square-meter garden/playground, 4 classrooms, cafeteria, AV equipment, library, computer.

**Italian lira †Summer school in July

The International Academy of Rome

Street address: Via di Grottarossa 295, 00189 Rome, Italy
Phone: (39)(6)33266072 **Facsimile:** (39)(6)33266071
Headmistress: Joan Bafaloukas Bulgarini
Teaching staff: full-time, 10; part-time, 5; total, 15
Nationalities of teaching staff: U.S., 5; U.K., 4; host, 3; other, 3; total, 15
Grade levels: preK – 8 (ages 2 to 14)
Enrollment: preK, 15; K, 12; 1 – 5, 56; 6 – 8, 14; total, 97
Nationalities of student body: U.S., 12; U.K., 11; host, 48; other, 26; total, 97
Capacity: preK, 30; K, 20; 1 – 5, 90; 6 – 8, 60; total, 200
Teacher/student ratio: 1/8
Tuition, (annual, 1995-96 rates): preK (half day), $4,000; preK (full day), $5,500; K, $11,400; elementary, $12,000; middle school, $14,000
Other fees (annual): registration*, $365 for first child, $260 for subsequent children; food services, $1,000; capital assessment*, $365; special education, $40/hour; sports outfit, $30
School year: September through June

Year founded: 1974. **Type of school:** coed, day, private nonprofit. **Governed by:** private professional association. **Accredited by:** Italian Ministry of Public Education.

Curriculum/physical plant

Type: U.S., U.K., national. **Languages taught:** English, Italian, French. **Staff specialists:** reading, math, counselor, learning disabilities, ESL, physical education, health assistant. **Special programs:** ESL, remedial, Optimal Match. **Special curricular:** art, chorus, computer instruction, AT&T network, summer camp. **Extracurricular:** newspaper, literary magazine, field trips, student council, sports workshops, yoga. **Sports:** baseball, cricket, soccer, swimming, volleyball, physical fitness. **Location:** renovated 18th-century farmstead in suburban Rome, near the Via Cassia. **Campus:** 9 acres. **Library:** 1,500 volumes. **Facilities:** 3 buildings, 10 classrooms, cafeteria, science lab, swimming pool, multipurpose room, indoor gymnasium, library/computer/AV resource center, health services office, sports field, volleyball court, boarding arrangements in private homes.

*Once only fee

Kendale Primary International School

Street address: Via Gradoli 86, 00189 Rome, Italy
Phone/facsimile: (39)(6)33267608
Web: http://www.mclink.it/personal/mc2205/kendale.htm
Directress: Gloria Hughes Fabriani
Principal: Veronica Tani
Teaching staff: full-time, 9; part-time, 4; total, 13
Nationalities of teaching staff: U.S., 3; U.K., 5; host, 2; other, 3; total, 13
Grade levels: preK – 5
Enrollment: preK, 24; K, 13; 1 – 5, 63; total, 100
Nationalities of student body: U.S., 13; U.K., 8; host, 68; other, 11; total, 100
Teacher/student ratio: 1/10
Tuition (annual): preK, 8,240,000**; K, 10,050,000; 1 – 5, 11,940,000

Other fees (annual): registration, 300,000**; busing, 2,300,000; books, 350,000
School year: September to June

Year founded: 1972. **Type of school:** coed, day, private nonprofit.

Curriculum/physical plant

Type: U.K. **Languages taught:** French, Italian. **Staff specialists:** reading, learning disabilities, mother-tongue Italian and French. **Special programs:** ESL. **Special curricular:** art, physical education, music. **Extracurricular:** newspaper. **Tests:** Iowa. **Location:** in city. **Library:** 3,100 volumes. **Facilities:** 1 building, 7 classrooms, playing field, computer lab, music room, AV equipment.

**Italian lira

Marymount International School

Street address: Via di Villa Lauchli 180, Via Cassia Antica, 00191 Rome, Italy
Phone: (39)(6)36301742 **Facsimile:** (39)(6)36301738
E-mail: marymount@pronet.it
Headmistress: Sr. Anne Marie Hill, RSHM
Teaching staff: full-time, 59; part-time, 8; total, 67
Nationalities of teaching staff: U.S., 33; U.K., 10; host, 5; other, 19; total, 67
Grade levels: early childhood – 12
Enrollment: EC – 5, 380; 6 – 8, 139; 9 – 12, 166; total, 685
Nationalities of student body: U.S., 182; host, 307; other, 196; total, 685
Teacher/student ratio: 1/15
Tuition (annual): early childhood, 8,100,000**; K, 10,000,000; 1 – 2, 14,500,000; 3 – 5, 15,800,000; 6 – 8, 17,100,000; 9 – 10, 18,900,000; 11, 19,400,000; 12, 19,500,000
Other fees (annual): application*, 250,000**; capital levy*, 1,000,000; lunch, 1,200,000
School year: September to June

Year founded: 1946. **Type of school:** coed, church-related. **Governed by:** Sisters of the Sacred Heart of Mary. **Accredited by:** Middle States, ECIS. **Regional organizations:** ECIS.

Curriculum/physical plant

Type: U.S., IB. **Languages taught:** French, Spanish, Italian. **Staff specialists:** counselor, learning disabilities, nurse. **Special programs:** ESL. **Special curricular:** art, chorus, physical education, computer instruction. **Extracurricular:** drama, gymnastics, dance, choral and instrumental music, yearbook, photography, excursions/expeditions, field trips, sports. **Clubs:** National Honor Society, National Junior Honor Society, student council, Model UN, intercultural, Search (religious retreat). **Tests:** PSAT, SAT, ACT, TOEFL, IB, AP, ERB. **Graduates attending college:** 96%. **Graduates have attended:** Boston College, Brown U., Georgetown U., Smith College. **Location:** 7 kilometers from Rome. **Campus:** 7 acres. **Library:** 21,000 volumes. **Facilities:** 4 buildings, auditorium, cafeteria, infirmary, 2 tennis courts, gymnasium, playing field, 3 science labs, computer lab, weight room.

*Once only fee **Italian lira

St. George's English School, Rome

Street address: Via Cassia La Storta, 00123 Rome, Italy
Phone: (39)(6)30890141 – 3 **Facsimile:** (39)(6)30892490
Principal: Brigid Gardner
Head of primary: Elizabeth Owens
Teaching staff: full-time, 60; part-time, 6; total, 66
Nationalities of teaching staff: U.K., 62; other, 4; total, 66
Grade levels: K – 13
Enrollment: K – 6, 280; 7 – 13, 320; total, 600
Teacher/student ratio: 1/11
Tuition (annual): K (half-day), 6,400,000**; K (full day), 8,400,000; reception, 9,100,000; 1 – 3, 10,700,000 – 15,000,000; 4, 15,800,000; 5, 16,500,000; 6, 17,500,000; 7, 18,000,000; 8 – 9, 18,400,000; 10 – 11, 19,000,000; 12 – 13, 19,500,000
Other fees (annual): registration*, 1,000,000**; busing, 2,420,000 (optional); refundable book deposit (secondary only), 250,000
School year: September to June

Year founded: 1958. **Type of school:** coed, day, private nonprofit. **Governed by:** appointed and elected board of governors. **Regional organizations:** ECIS.

Curriculum

Type: U.K., IB, AP. **Languages taught:** French, Spanish, German, Italian, Latin. **Staff specialists:** reading, learning disabilities, physician. **Special programs:** ESL, remedial. **Special curricular:** art, physical education, computer instruction, vocational, music. **Extracurricular:** drama, gymnastics, dance, choral and instrumental music, computers, photography, excursions/expeditions, field trips. **Sports:** athletics, badminton, basketball, field hockey, netball, soccer, swimming, tennis, volleyball. **Clubs:** computer, expeditions. **Tests:** PSAT, SAT, IB, A-level GCE, GCSE, IB. **Graduates attending college:** 95%. **Graduates have attended:** Oxford, Cambridge, Princeton, MIT, Stanford.

Physical plant

Location: in rural area, 16 kilometers from center Rome. **Campus:** 27 acres. **Library:** 20,000 volumes. **Facilities:** 3 buildings, 47 classrooms, cafeteria, infirmary, covered play area, 2 tennis courts, gymnasium, playing field, 8 science labs, computer lab, 2 swimming pools, art studios and design technology center.

*Once only fee **Italian lira

St. Stephen's School, Rome

Street address: Via Aventina 3, 00153 Rome, Italy
Phone: (39)(6)5750605 **Facsimile:** (39)(6)5741941 **E-mail:** mc0667@mclink.it **Web:** http://www.curiouspix.com/st_stephens.html
U.S. mail: 15 Gramercy Park South, New York, NY 10003, U.S.A.
Headmaster: Philip H. Allen
Teaching staff: full-time, 19; part-time, 11; total, 30
Nationalities of teaching staff: U.S., 17; U.K., 1; host, 6; other, 6; total, 30
Grade levels: 9 – 12, postgraduate year

Enrollment: 9 – 12, 149; PG, 6; total, 155
Nationalities of student body: U.S., 51; other, 104; total, 155
Teacher/student ratio: 1/6
Boarding capacity: boys, 20; girls, 20
Tuition (annual): 20,000,000**
Other fees (annual): boarding, 11,500,000**; lunch, 1,100,000 (day students only); application*, 200,000; capital levy: new student, 1,000,000, returning student, 500,000
School year: September to June

Year founded: 1962. **Type of school:** coed, day, boarding, private nonprofit, college preparatory, nondenominational. **Governed by:** elected board of trustees. **Accredited by:** New England, ECIS. **Regional organizations:** ECIS.

Curriculum/physical plant

Type: U.S., IB. **Languages taught:** French, Italian, Latin, other languages by private arrangement. **Staff specialists:** counselor, librarian. **Special curricular:** chorus, computer instruction, drama, studio art, sculpture, music appreciation, dance. **Extracurricular:** yearbook, newspaper, photography, trip program, community service, Italian cinema and theater, gardening, junior and senior math teams, recycling. **Sports:** basketball, soccer, tennis, track and field, volleyball. **Clubs:** computer, cooking, hiking, Classics-Rome. **Tests:** SSAT, PSAT, IB, AP. **Graduates attending college:** 95%. **Graduates have attended:** Wesleyan, Columbia, Boston U., U. of Michigan, Yale. **Location:** in historic center of Rome. **Campus:** 2.5 acres. **Library:** 14,000 volumes. **Facilities:** 1 building, 13 classrooms, auditorium, cafeteria, tennis court, gymnasium, 3 science labs, computer lab, basketball court, 2 art studios, AV room, 36 double and triple boarding rooms.

*Once only fee **Italian lira

TRIESTE

International School of Trieste

Street address: Villaggio del Fanciullo, Via Conconello 16 (Opicina), 34016 Trieste, Italy
Phone: (39)(40)211452 **Facsimile:** (39)(40)213122
E-mail: istrieste@interbusiness.it
Director: Peter Metzger
Teaching staff: full-time, 22; part-time, 6; total, 28
Nationalities of teaching staff: U.S., 9; U.K., 6; host, 8; other, 5; total, 28
Grade levels: N – 8
Enrollment: N – preK, 64; K, 25; 1 – 6, 114; 7 – 8, 30; total, 233
Nationalities of student body: U.S., 6; U.K., 5; host, 192; other, 30; total, 233
Teacher/student ratio: 1/9
Tuition (annual): N – preK, 6,800,000**; K, 7,900,000; 1 – 5, 8,700,000; 6 – 8, 9,200,000
Other fees (annual): registration*, 650,000**; busing, 800,000
School year: September to June

Year founded: 1964. **Type of school:** coed, day, private nonprofit. **Governed by:** appointed and elected board of directors. **Accredited by:** Middle States. **Regional organizations:** ECIS, MAIS.

Curriculum/physical plant

Type: U.S. **Languages taught:** French, German, Italian, Latin. **Staff specialists:** computer, physical education, art. **Special programs:** ESL. **Special curricular:** art, physical education, computer instruction. **Extracurricular:** computers, yearbook, excursions/expeditions, field trips. **Sports:** basketball, soccer, volleyball. **Tests:** ITBS. **Location:** in suburban area, 4 kilometers from Trieste. **Campus:** 4 acres. **Library:** 6,000 volumes. **Facilities:** 2 buildings, 18 classrooms, auditorium, cafeteria, infirmary, gymnasium, playing field, science lab, computer lab.

*Once only fee **Italian lira

TURIN

International School of Turin (ACAT)

Street address: Vicolo Tiziano 10, 10024 Moncalieri, Turin, Italy
Phone: (39)(11)645967/6407810 **Facsimile:** (39)(11)643298
Headmaster: Tomm Elliott, Ed.D.
Upper school principal: John Mores
Business manager: Maria Recrosio
Teaching staff: full-time, 25; part-time, 7; total, 32
Nationalities of teaching staff: U.S., 12; U.K., 10; host, 6; other, 4; total, 32
Grade levels: N (3 years old) – 12
Enrollment: N – preK, 20; K, 26; 1 – 6, 95; 7 – 9, 47; 10 – 12, 47; total, 235
Nationalities of student body: U.S., 31; U.K., 28; host, 121; other, 55; total, 235
Capacity: N – preK, 30; K, 20; 1 – 6, 120; 7 – 9, 60; 10 – 12, 60; total, 290
Teacher/student ratio: 1/8
Tuition (annual): N – preK, 6,000,000**; K – 1, 9,500,000; 2, 10,500,000; 3 – 5, 12,000,000; 6 – 9, 14,000,000; 10 – 12, 18,000,000
Other fees (annual): registration, 1,700,000** (new student), 1,100,000 (returning student); busing, 12,000,000; lunch, 7,000/each
School year: September to June

Year founded: 1974. **Type of school:** coed, day. **Governed by:** elected board of directors. **Accredited by:** New England, ECIS. **Regional organizations:** AAIE, ECIS.

Curriculum/physical plant

Type: U.S., national, IB. **Languages of instruction:** English, Italian. **Languages taught:** French, Italian, Latin. **Special curricular:** art, physical education, computer instruction, music. **Extracurricular:** yearbook, excursions/expeditions, field trips, student council, Model UN. **Sports:** basketball, soccer, swimming, tennis, volleyball. **Tests:** PSAT, SAT, TOEFL, IB. **Graduates attending college:** 100%. **Location:** in suburb adjacent to Turin. **Library:** 15,000 volumes. **Facilities:** cafeteria, playing field, science lab, computer lab, A/V room.

**Italian lira

VICENZA

Vicenza International School

Street address: Via Einaudi 74, 36100 Vicenza, Italy
Phone: (39)(444)240449 **Facsimile:** (39)(444)240181
Director/business manager: Dr. Antonio Baldo
IB coordinator: Dr. Antonietta Spiller
Teaching staff: part-time, 13; total, 13
Nationalities of teaching staff: U.S., 2; U.K., 1; host, 7; other, 3; total, 13
Grade levels: 11 – 12
Enrollment: total, 11
Nationalities of student body: host, 6; other, 5; total, 11
Teacher/student ratio: 1/3
Tuition (annual): $5,000
Other fees (annual): books, $300
School year: September to June

Year founded: 1987. **Type of school:** coed, private nonprofit. **Governed by:** elected board of directors.

Curriculum/physical plant

Type: IB. **Languages taught:** English, French, Italian, Russian, Albanian. **Extracurricular:** computers, excursions/expeditions. **Tests:** IB. **Graduates attending college:** 100%. **Graduates have attended:** Italian universities. **Location:** in suburban area. **Facilities:** 6 classrooms, science lab, computer lab.

TRIESTE

United World College of the Adriatic

Street address: Via Trieste 29, 34013 Duino (Trieste), Italy
Phone: (39)(40)3739111 **Facsimile:** (39)(40)3739225
E-mail: uwcad@uwc.interware.it
Headmaster: D. B. Sutcliffe

JAMAICA

Region: West Indies
Size: 4,244 square miles
Population: 2,595,275
Capital: Kingston
Telephone code: 876
Currency: Jamaican dollar
Languages: English, Jamaican Creole

KINGSTON

THE PRIORY SCHOOL

Street address: 32 Hope Road, Kingston 10, Jamaica
Phone: (1)(876)9266636 **Facsimile:** (1)(876)9267583
Director: Fay Rodgers-Jenkinson
Acting accountant: Joan Wauchope
Teaching staff: full-time, 40; part-time, 19; total, 59
Nationalities of teaching staff: host, 58; other, 1; total, 59
Grade levels: preK – 13
Enrollment: preK – 6, 157; 7 – 13, 162; total, 319
Nationalities of student body: U.S., 45; host, 230; other, 44; total, 319
Teacher/student ratio: 1/8
Tuition (annual): preK – K, $1,458; 1 – 6, $1,972; 7 – 13, $2,400
Other fees: registration*, $60; capital development*, $300 per family; PTA, $3/year; school photo/yearbook, $50
School year: September through June

Year founded: 1944. **Type of school:** coed, day, private nonprofit. **Governed by:** Priory School Trust Society, Ltd. **Accredited by:** Southern. **Recognized by:** Jamaican Ministry of Education. **Regional organizations:** ACCAS, Tri-Assoc.

Curriculum/physical plant

Type: U.S., U.K. **Languages taught:** French, Spanish. **Staff specialists:** reading, counselor, learning disabilities, nurse, enrichment/gifted. **Special programs:** ESL. **Special curricular:** art, physical education, music, computer, home economics, vocational (woodwork). **Extracurricular:** drama, gymnastics, yearbook, newspaper, excursions/expeditions, field trips, sewing, cooking. **Sports:** badminton, basketball, football, netball, soccer, swimming, tennis, track and field, volleyball, Tae Kwon Do, dance. **Clubs:** chess, student council, photography, Red Cross, prefect group. **Tests:** SSAT, PSAT, ACT, Iowa, A- and O-level GCE. **Graduates attending college:** 45%. **Graduates have attended:** Georgia Tech, Radford, Princeton, Georgetown, U. of the West Indies. **Location:** in suburb, St. Andrew. **Campus:** 15 acres. **Library:** over 12,000 volumes. **Facilities:** 20 buildings, 35 classrooms, auditorium, cafeteria, infirmary, 2 tennis courts, 2 playing fields, 3 science labs, music room, art room, AV room, home economics room, woodshop.

*Once only fee

MANDEVILLE

BELAIR SCHOOL

Street address: 43 DeCarteret Road, Mandeville, Jamaica
Phone: (1)(876)9623396/9622168/9620216 **Facsimile:** (1)(876)9623396
Cable: Belair, Mandeville
Mail: PO Box 156, Mandeville, Jamaica
Director: Burnett St. C. Burton
Elementary school principal: Sylvan Shields
Guidance counselor: Sarah Brown
Teaching staff: full-time, 46; part-time, 7; total, 53
Nationalities of teaching staff: host, 45; other, 8; total, 53
Grade levels: K – 12 and 6th form
Enrollment: K, 70; 1 – 6, 200; 7 – 12, 162; 6th form, 10; total, 442
Capacity: K, 70; 1 – 6, 225; 7 – 12, 200; 6th form, 25; total, 520
Teacher/student ratio: 1/9
Tuition (annual): K, 38,778**; 1 – 6, 68,420; 7 – 12, 88,746; 6th form, 98,460
Other fees: registration*, 150**; teaching materials (per year): K, 4,458; 1– 6, 4,974; 7 – 12, 2,178
School year: September to August

Year founded: 1967. **Type of school:** coed, day. **Governed by:** elected board of governors. **Accredited by:** Southern. **Regional organizations:** Tri-Assoc.

Curriculum/physical plant

Type: U.S., U.K., national. **Languages taught:** English, French, Spanish. **Staff specialists:** reading, math, computer, counselor, nurse. **Special programs:** honors sections, correspondence, remedial. **Special curricular:** art, physical education, computer instruction. **Extracurricular:** drama, computers, yearbook, newspaper, excursions/expeditions, field trips. **Sports:** football, hockey, netball, softball, swimming, track and field, JISA. **Clubs:** debating, Cub Scouts, Brownies, Girl Guides, ISCF, Red Cross, Key Club, Junior Achievement, science, French/Spanish. **Tests:** PSAT, SAT, ACT, TOEFL, A and O-level GCE, Caribbean Examinations Council. **Graduates attending college:** 40%. **Location:** in rural area. **Campus:** 13 acres. **Facilities:** 1 building, 31 classrooms, auditorium, cafeteria, infirmary, 2 tennis courts, 2 playing fields, 3 science labs, computer lab.

*Once only fee **Jamaican dollar

JAPAN

Region: East Asia
Size: 145,850 square miles
Population: 125,449,703
Capital: Tokyo
Telephone code: 81
Currency: yen
Language: Japanese

FUKUOKA

Fukuoka International School

Street address: Momochi 3-chome 18-50, Sawara-ku, Fukuoka-shi 814, Japan
Phone: (81)(92)8417601 **Facsimile:** (81)(92)8417602
E-mail: dclark@bamboo.paradigm.co.jp
Headmaster: Dennis Clark
Teaching staff: full-time, 16; part-time, 1; total, 17
Nationalities of teaching staff: U.S., 4; U.K., 1; host, 3; other, 9; total, 17
Grade levels: preK – 12
Enrollment: preK, 12; K, 7; 1 – 5, 51; 6 – 8, 36; 9 – 12, 38; total, 144
Nationalities of student body: U.S., 24; U.K., 5; host, 23; other, 92; total, 144
Capacity: preK – K, 20; 1 – 8, 90; 9 – 12, 90; total, 200
Teacher/student ratio: 1/10
Boarders: boys, 6; girls, 9 **Program:** Planned 5- and 7-day
Tuition (annual): K – 5, 850,000**; 6 – 12, 1,000,000
Boarding fees: room and program, 500,000**; meals, 306,000 (7-day); room deposit (refundable), 60,000
Other fees (annual): registration*, 100,000** per family; insurance, 3,000; PTA dues, 2,000
School year: August to June

Year founded: 1972. **Type of school:** coed, day, boarding, private nonprofit. **Governed by:** elected operating committee, board of directors, board of trustees. **Accredited by:** Western, Japanese Board of Education. **Regional organizations:** EARCOS.

Curriculum/physical plant

Type: U.S. **Languages taught:** Japanese. **Special programs:** ESL, remedial individualized in each classroom. **Special curricular:** art, band, physical education, computer instruction, music, yearbook/newspaper, performing arts, strings. **Extracurricular:** excursions/expeditions, field trips, U.S. homestays. **Clubs:** computer, sports. **Tests:** PSAT, SAT, College Board ATP, Wechsler (available), PLAN. **Graduates attending college:** 80%. **Graduates have attended:** universities in the U.S., U.K., and Japan. **Location:** in western part of the city near Fujisaki station and Fukuoka dome and tower. **Library:** 5,000 volumes. **Facilities:** two 2-story buildings, 20 classrooms, gymnasium, science lab, computer/language lab, art room, dispensary, kitchen, music/band room, dining area, new building with dormitory for 24 students.

*Once only fee **Japanese yen

HIROSHIMA

HIROSHIMA INTERNATIONAL SCHOOL

Street address: 3-49-1, Kurakake, Asa Kita-ku, Hiroshima 739-17, Japan
Phone: (81)(82)8434111 **Facsimile:** (81)(82)8436399
E-mail: his888@po.cisnet.or.jp
Head: Eleanor J. Jones
Teaching staff: full-time, 5; part-time, 4; total, 9
Nationalities of teaching staff: U.S., 3; host, 4; other, 2; total, 9
Grade levels: N – 12†
Enrollment: N – preK, 15; K, 6; 1 – 6, 27; 7 – 8, 9; 9 – 12, 3; total, 60
Nationalities of student body: U.S., 45; host, 2; other, 13; total, 60
Capacity: total, 150
Teacher/student ratio: 1/7
Tuition (annual): $14,000
Other fees: busing, $250/month; application*, $1,545

Year founded: 1962. **Type of school:** coed, day. **Governed by:** elected board of directors, board of trustees. **Sponsored by:** Hiroshima Prefecture Board of Education. **Accredited by:** Western. **Regional organizations:** EARCOS.

Curriculum/physical plant

Type: U.S. **Languages taught:** Japanese. **Special programs:** ESL. **Special curricular:** computer instruction, integrated topics, music, photography, Japanese culture, swimming. **Extracurricular:** instrumental music, computers, yearbook, literary magazine, photography, excursions/expeditions, martial arts. **Sports:** basketball. **Clubs:** student council, 1,000 Crane Club, music, computer. **Location:** suburban/rural setting in new area of Hiroshima. **Campus:** 2 acres. **Library:** 25,000 volumes. **Facilities:** 1 building, 9 classrooms, infirmary, gymnasium, playing field, science/craft room, dark room, ESL classrooms, air conditioning.

*Once only fee †ESL/culture programs (K – adult)

KOBE

Canadian Academy

Street address: 4–1 Koyo-cho Naka, Higashinada-ku, Kobe 658, Japan
Phone: (81)(78)8570100 **Facsimile:** (81)(78)8573250
E-mail: hdmstr@canacad.ac.jp **Web:** http://canada.canacad.ac.jp
Headmaster: Stuart J. Young, Ph.D.
High school principal: Daniel A. Hovde
Middle school principal: Robert M. Mockrish, Jr., Ph.D.
Elementary school principal: Leila Metcalf, Ed.D.
Director of admissions and new programs: Charles A. Kite, Ph.D.
Teaching staff: full-time, 68; part-time, 5; total, 73
Nationalities of teaching staff: U.S., 46; host, 10; other, 17; total, 73
Grade levels: preK – 12, postgraduate
Enrollment: preK, 28; K, 47; 1 – 5, 270; 6 – 8, 175; 9 – 12, 222; total, 742
Nationalities of student body: U.S., 256; U.K., 24; host, 154; other, 308; total, 742
Teacher/student ratio: 1/11
Boarders: boys, 11; girls, 11 **Grades:** 8 – 12 **Program:** planned 7-day
Tuition (annual): preK, 996,000**; K – 5, 1,112,000; 6 – 12, 1,336,000; PG, 976,000
Other fees (annual): registration*, 154,500**; boarding, 1,147,000
School year: late August to June

Year founded: 1913. **Type of school:** coed, day, boarding, private nonprofit. **Governed by:** appointed board of trustees. **Accredited by:** Western. **Regional organizations:** EARCOS.

Curriculum/physical plant

Type: U.S., IB. **Languages taught:** French, German, Japanese. **Staff specialists:** counselor, learning disabilities, nurse. **Special programs:** honors sections, ESOL. **Special curricular:** art, chorus, band, physical education, computer instruction. **Extracurricular:** drama, yearbook, newspaper, field trips. **Sports:** baseball, basketball, soccer, volleyball. **Tests:** PSAT, SAT, ACT, TOEFL, IB, AP, Iowa. **Graduates attending college:** 98%. **Graduates have attended:** Cornell, MIT, Princeton, Stanford, Vassar. **Location:** on Rokko Island, near Kobe. **Campus:** 9 acres. **Library:** 30,000 volumes. **Facilities:** 63 classrooms, auditorium, cafeteria, 2 tennis courts, gymnasium, 2 playing fields, 5 science labs, 3 computer labs with more than 200 computers, AV equipment, air conditioning, boarding facilities.

*Once only fee **Japanese yen

Marist Brothers International School

Street address: 2-1, 1-chome, Chimori-cho, Suma-ku, Kobe 654, Japan
Phone: (81)(78)7326266 **Facsimile:** (81)(78)7326268
Headmaster: Br. George Fontana, FMS
Upper school principal: Geraldo de Couto
Guidance: Br. John Kachinsky, FMS
Business manager: M. Sasahara
Teaching staff: full-time, 24; part-time, 3; total, 27
Nationalities of teaching staff: U.S., 13; U.K., 1; host, 5; other, 8; total, 27
Grade levels: preK – 12, ESL
Enrollment: preK, 10; K, 16; 1 – 6, 104; 7 – 9, 57; 10 – 12, 48; ESL, 12; total, 247
Capacity: preK, 20; K, 20; 1 – 6, 120; 7 – 9, 75; 10 – 12, 75; total, 310
Teacher/student ratio: 1/9
Tuition (annual): preK – K, 890,000**; 1 – 6, 1,020,000; 7 – 12, 1,100,000; ESL, 1,100,000
Other fees (annual): registration*, 200,000**; building, 100,000
School year: September to June

Year founded: 1951. **Type of school:** coed, day, church-related. **Governed by:** board of directors. **Sponsored by:** Marist Brothers. **Accredited by:** Western.

Curriculum/physical plant

Type: U.S., AP. **Staff specialists:** computer, counselor. **Special programs:** ESL, honors sections, independent study, Values, tutoring. **Special curricular:** art, chorus, band, physical education, computer instruction. **Extracurricular:** yearbook, newspaper, excursions, sports. **Tests:** PSAT, SAT, ACT, TOEFL, AP, Iowa. **Graduates attending college:** 80%. **Graduates have attended:** CalTech, U. of Pennsylvania, Lafayette College, U. of California, Georgetown. **Location:** in city. **Campus:** 2.5 acres. **Library:** 10,000 volumes. **Facilities:** 3 buildings, 22 classrooms, cafeteria, infirmary, gymnasium, playing field, chapel, IBM computer lab.

*Once only fee **Japanese yen

St. Michael's International School

Street address: 17-2 Nakayamate-dori 3-chome, Chuo-ku, Kobe 650, Japan
Phone: (81)(78)2318885 **Facsimile:** (81)(78)2318899
Principal: Sandra McGinley
Teaching staff: full-time, 10; total, 10
Nationalities of teaching staff: U.S., 1; U.K., 4; host, 4; Canada, 1; total, 10
Grade levels: preK – 6
Enrollment: preK, 33; K, 14; 1 – 6, 44; total, 91
Capacity: preK, 45; K, 25; 1 – 6, 100; total, 170
Teacher/student ratio: 1/9
Tuition (annual): preK, 760,000**; K – 6, 870,000 – 900,000
Other fees (annual): registration*, 120,000**; insurance, 3,000; maintenance, 75,000/family
School year: September to June

Year founded: 1946. **Type of school:** coed, day, church-related. **Governed by:** elected school council. **Sponsored by:** Anglican Church. **Accredited by:** Hyogo Prefecture government. **Regional organizations:** EARCOS.

Curriculum/physical plant

Type: U.K.. **Languages taught:** Japanese. **Staff specialists:** reading, math. **Special curricular:** art, band, physical education, computer instruction, typing. **Extracurricular:** instrumental music, computers, field trips, soccer, typing. **Clubs:** art, cookery, handicraft. **Location:** in city. **Library:** 50,000 volumes. **Facilities:** auditorium, gymnasium, computer lab.

*Once only fee **Japanese yen

KYOTO

KYOTO INTERNATIONAL SCHOOL

Street address: 29-1 Kami Miyanomae-cho, Shishigatani, Sakyo-ku, Kyoto 606, Japan
Phone: (81)(75)7714022 **Facsimile:** (81)(75)7521184
E-mail: hellokis@mbox.kyoto-inet.or.jp
Principal: Kurt C. Kahlenbeck
Teaching staff: full-time, 5; part-time, 8; total, 13
Nationalities of teaching staff: U.S., 3; host, 7; other, 3; total, 13
Grade levels: preschool – 8
Enrollment: total, 50
Nationalities of student body: U.S., 16; host, 10; other, 24; total, 50
Teacher/student ratio: 1/6
Tuition (annual): preschool, 585,000**; preK – 8, 1,110,000
Other fees: registration*, 100,000**
School year: September to June

Year founded: 1957. **Type of school:** coed, day, private nonprofit. **Governed by:** elected board of governors. **Accredited by:** Western. **Regional organizations:** EARCOS.

Curriculum/physical plant

Type: U.S., U.K. **Languages taught:** Japanese. **Extracurricular:** computers, newspaper, excursions/expeditions, field trips, recorder, tea ceremony, karate, chess. **Tests:** Iowa. **Location:** in northeastern Kyoto, near the Silver Pavillion. **Library:** 5,500 volumes. **Facilities:** 7 classrooms, language room, computers in all classrooms, air conditioning.

*Once only fee **Japanese yen

NAGOYA

NAGOYA INTERNATIONAL SCHOOL

Street address: 2686 Minamihara, Nakashidami, Moriyama-ku, Nagoya 463, Japan
Phone: (81)(52)7362025 **Facsimile:** (81)(52)7363883
E-mail: nisadmin@tcp-ip.or.jp
Headmaster: Charles Barton
Dean of secondary school: Eric MacDonald
Business manager: Hiroshi Sakai
Teaching staff: full-time, 33; part-time, 1; total, 34
Nationalities of teaching staff: U.S., 23; host, 6; other, 5; total, 34
Grade levels: N – 12
Enrollment: N – preK, 33; K, 36; 1 – 5, 138; 6 – 8, 54; 9 – 12, 51; total, 312
Nationalities of student body: U.S., 80; U.K., 3; host, 178; other, 51; total, 312
Teacher/student ratio: 1/10
Tuition (annual): N – preK, 400,000**; K – 5, 1,080,000; 6 – 12, 1,220,000
Other fees: registration*, 100,000**; lunch, 550/meal; application*, 20,000
School year: September to June

Year founded: 1963. **Type of school:** coed, day, private nonprofit. **Governed by:** elected board of directors. **Accredited by:** Western. **Regional organizations:** EARCOS, JCIS.

Curriculum/physical plant

Type: U.S., AP. **Languages taught:** Japanese. **Staff specialists:** reading, math, computer, art, music, physical education. **Special programs:** ESL, independent study. **Special curricular:** art, chorus, physical education, computer instruction. **Extracurricular:** drama, dance, choral and instrumental music, computers, yearbook, newspaper, literary magazine, excursions/expeditions, field trips. **Sports:** badminton, basketball, cheerleading, softball, tennis, volleyball, karate. **Clubs:** cooking, jazz dance, study session, indoor/outdoor games for K – 2 students. **Tests:** PSAT, SAT, ACT, TOEFL, Iowa, TAP. **Graduates attending college:** 90%. **Graduates have attended:** Michigan State U., Duke U., Vanderbilt, Boston U., Georgia Tech. **Location:** 40 minutes from downtown Nagoya. **Campus:** 7 acres. **Library:** 15,000 volumes. **Facilities:** 3 buildings, 28 classrooms, cafeteria, tennis court, gymnasium, playing field, 2 science labs, computer lab, media center.

*Once only fee **Japanese yen

OKINAWA

Okinawa Christian School International

Street address: Yomitan, Okinawa, Japan 904-03
Phone: (81)(989)583000 **Facsimile:** (81)(989)586279
E-mail: 102603.2026@compuserve.com
Mail: PO Box 6, Yomitan, Okinawa Japan 904-03
U.S. mail: PO Box 14250, Gainesville, FL 32604, U.S.A.
U.S. phone: (1)(352)3716012 or (1)(800)4466423
U.S. facsimile: (1)(352)3733949
Superintendent: Paul A. Gieschen
High school principal: Randy Hadley
Elementary school principal: Donna S. Russell
U.S. administrator: Dr. Bob Greninger
Teaching staff: full-time, 45; part-time, 16; total, 61
Nationalities of teaching staff: U.S., 38; host, 20; other, 3; total, 61
Grade levels: K – 12†
Enrollment: K, 52; 1 – 5, 150; 6 – 8, 58; 9 – 12, 160; ESL, 29; total, 449
Nationalities of student body: U.S., 203; host, 84; other, 162; total, 449
Capacity: K, 72; 1 – 5, 135; 6 – 8, 75; 9 – 12, 120; total, 402
Teacher/student ratio: 1/10
Tuition (annual): K – 5, 361,000**; 6 – 12, 394,250
Other fees (annual): registration*, 10,000**; book deposit (grades 6 – 12), 4,500; family*, 15,000; camp fee (grades 4 – 12), 7,000
School year: September to June

Year founded: 1957. **Type of school:** coed, day, private nonprofit. **Governed by:** elected board of directors. **Sponsored by:** Okinawa Christian School Mission. **Accredited by:** Western, ACSI.

Curriculum/physical plant

Type: U.S. **Languages taught:** Japanese. **Staff specialists:** counselor. **Special programs:** ESL. **Special curricular:** art, physical education, computer instruction. **Extracurricular:** drama, computers, yearbook, photography, field trips, student council, National Honor Society. **Sports:** basketball, soccer, volleyball. **Tests:** PSAT, Stanford. **Graduates attending college:** 60%. **Graduates have attended:** Baylor U., Grand Canyon U., DePauw, U. of Alabama, California Baptist. **Location:** in Urasoe City. **Campus:** 10,800 square meters. **Facilities:** 5 buildings, 22 classrooms, cafeteria, gymnasium, playing field, science lab, computer lab, library.

*Once only fee **Japanese yen †ESL program, K – adult

OSAKA

Osaka International School

Street address: 4-16, Onohara-Nishi 4-chome, Mino-shi, Osaka 562, Japan
Phone: (81)(727)275050 **Facsimile:** (81)(727)275055
E-mail: oia-ois@sisf.mino.osaka.jp
U.S. mail: c/o International Schools Services, PO Box 5910, Princeton, NJ 08543, U.S.A.
Headmaster: Stephen Middlebrook
High/middle school principal: Dennis L. Calkins
Elementary school principal: Julie A. Wagner
Planning/development manager: Gary W. Rust
Teaching staff: full-time, 47; part-time, 6; total, 53
Grade levels: early childhood (4 – 5 years) – 12, postgraduate
Enrollment: total, 245
Capacity: K, 30; 1 – 6, 120; 7 – 9, 60; 10 – 12, 60; 13, 5; total, 275
Teacher/student ratio: 1/5
Tuition (annual): K, 975,000 – 1,175,000**; 1 – 5, 1,200,000; 6 – 10, 1,350,000; 11 – 13, 1,480,000
Other fees (annual): registration*, 100,000**; busing, 170,000 – 290,000; lunch, 85,000; application*, 25,000
School year: September to June

Year founded: 1991. **Type of school:** coed, day, private nonprofit. **Governed by:** elected board of governors. **Accredited by:** Western. **Regional organizations:** EARCOS, JCIS.

Curriculum

Type: IB. **Languages of instruction:** English, Japanese. **Languages taught:** French, Spanish, ESL, Japanese. **Staff specialists:** computer, counselor, nurse, ESL. **Special programs:** ESL, independent study. **Special curricular:** art, chorus, band, physical education, computer instruction. **Extracurricular:** drama, dance, choral and instrumental music, computers, yearbook, newspaper, photography, field trips. **Sports:** baseball, basketball, soccer, softball, swimming, tennis, volleyball, judo, kendo. **Tests:** SSAT, PSAT, SAT, ACT, IB, Iowa, CAT, PAP.

Physical plant

Location: in new residential development, 30 minutes from central Osaka. **Facilities:** 1 building, 31 classrooms, auditorium, cafeteria, infirmary, 2 covered play areas, tennis court, 2 gymnasiums, playing field, 5 science labs, 2 computer labs, swimming pool, TV studio, 4 music practice rooms, athletic training room, bookstore, air conditioning.

*Once only fee **Japanese yen

SAPPORO

Hokkaido International School

Street address: 1-55, 5-jo, 19-chome, Hiragishi, Toyohira-ku, Sapporo 062, Japan
Phone: (81)(11)8165000 **Facsimile:** (81)(11)8162500
E-mail: hokintsc@ppp.bekkoame.or.jp
Web: http://www.bekkoame.or.jp/~hokintsc/
Headmaster: Dr. R. D. McClain
Secondary school coordinator: Keith Richardson
Elementary school coordinator: Doreen Deelstra
Early childhood coordinator: Janet McClain
Business manager: Yoko Nakamura
Teaching staff: full-time, 20; part-time, 4; total, 24
Enrollment: preK – K, 30; 1 – 6, 81; 7 – 12, 59; total, 170
Nationalities of student body: U.S., 38; host, 34; other, 98; total, 170
Teacher/student ratio: 1/8
Boarders: boys, 10; girls, 10 **Program:** planned 5- and 7-day
Tuition (annual): preK, 480,000**; K – 5, 612,000; 6 – 8, 637,000; 9 – 12, 663,000
Other fees (annual): boarding, 640,000** (5-day); 670,000 (7-day); entrance*: preK – 8, 150,000; 9 – 12, 200,000
School year: September to June

Year founded: 1958. **Type of school:** coed, day, boarding, private nonprofit. **Accredited by:** Western. **Regional organizations:** EARCOS, JCIS.

Curriculum/physical plant

Type: U.S. **Languages of instruction:** English, Spanish, Japanese. **Special curricular:** art, physical education, computer instruction, drama, music, ESL, special education. **Extracurricular:** yearbook, newspaper, excursions/expeditions, field trips. **Sports:** basketball, skiing, soccer, softball, volleyball, wrestling, ice skating. **Tests:** SSAT, SAT, ACT, TOEFL, Iowa, GRE, NM/PSAT. **Graduates attending college:** 99%. **Graduates have attended:** Cornell, Iowa State, U. of Massachusetts, Oregon, Wheaton. **Location:** 5-minute walk from Sumikawa subway station. **Campus:** 4 acres. **Library:** 6,000 volumes. **Facilities:** 2 buildings, gymnasium, playing field, science lab, computer lab, music room, art room, media room, multipurpose room, dormitory for 20 students.

*Once only fee **Japanese yen

SENDAI

Sendai American School

Street address: 4-8-1 Komatsushima, Aoba-Ku, Sendai 981, Japan
Phone: (81)(22)2348567 **Facsimile:** (81)(22)2727161
E-mail: 71651.2745@compuserve.com
Headmaster: Maynard Yutzy, Ed.D.
Teaching staff: full-time, 4; part-time, 2; total, 6

Nationalities of teaching staff: U.S., 2; host, 2; other, 2; total, 6
Grade levels: K – 12
Enrollment: K – 5, 20; 6 – 8, 11; 9 – 12, 9; total, 40
Nationalities of student body: U.S., 13; host, 9; other, 18; total, 40
Teacher/student ratio: 1/10
Tuition (annual): 600,000**
Other fees (annual): registration, 10,000**; insurance, 5,000; enrollment*, 30,000
School year: September through June

Year founded: 1989. **Type of school:** coed, day. **Governed by:** elected board comprised of 3 Japanese and 3 international members. **Sponsored by:** Tohoku-Koko. **Regional organizations:** EARCOS, JCIS.

Curriculum/physical plant

Type: U.S. **Languages taught:** Japanese. **Special programs:** ESL. **Special curricular:** art, chorus, physical education, computer instruction. **Extracurricular:** drama, dance, computers, yearbook, newspaper, photography. **Location:** in Sendai. **Campus:** .5 acre. **Library:** 2,500 volumes. **Facilities:** 1 building, 6 classrooms, cafeteria, playing field, computer lab, swimming pool.

*Once only fee **Japanese yen

TOKYO

The American School in Japan

Street address: 1-1-1, Nomizu, Chofu-shi, Tokyo 182, Japan
Phone: (81)(422)345310 **Facsimile:** (81)(422)345308 **E-mail:** info@asij.ac.jp **Web:** http://www.asij.ac.jp
Headmaster: Peter R. Cooper
High school principal: Donald J. Benes
Middle school principal: Sue O. Hale
Elementary school principal: Daniel J. Bender
Business manager: John D. Hale
Teaching staff: full-time, 137; part-time, 12; total, 149
Nationalities of teaching staff: U.S., 116; host, 19; other, 14; total, 149
Grade levels: N – 12, postgraduate
Enrollment: total, 1,348
Nationalities of student body: U.S., 783; U.K., 39; host, 200; other, 326; total, 1,348
Teacher/student ratio: 1/9
Tuition (annual): N – 12, 1,845,000**
Other fees (annual): registration*, 275,000**; busing, 300,000 (optional); building maintenance*, 275,000
School year: September to June

Year founded: 1902. **Type of school:** coed, day, private nonprofit. **Governed by:** elected board of directors. **Sponsored by:** board of trustees. **Accredited by:** Western. **Regional organizations:** AAIE EARCOS.

Curriculum

Type: U.S., AP. **Languages taught:** French, Spanish, Japanese. **Staff specialists:** computer, counselor, learning disabilities, nurse, ESL, speech. **Special programs:** honors sections, independent study. **Special curricular:** art, chorus, computer instruction, Japanese studies, outdoor education, band and strings, television production. **Extracurricular:** drama, dance, choral and instrumental music, computers, yearbook, newspaper, literary magazine, photography, excursions/ expeditions, field trips. **Sports:** 42 teams, 16 varsity sports. **Tests:** PSAT, SAT, ACT, TOEFL, AP, Iowa, ERB. **Graduates attending college:** 95%. **Graduates have attended:** Brown, Cornell, Harvard, MIT, Princeton.

Physical plant

Location: N – K, downtown Tokyo; K – 13, 45 minutes from Tokyo, in suburban area adjacent to 150-acre public park. **Library:** 41,000 volumes. **Facilities:** 9 buildings, 87 classrooms, auditorium, cafeteria, infirmary, 4 tennis courts, 3 gymnasiums, 3 playing fields, 7 science labs, 6 computer labs, swimming pool, TV-radio studio, vivarium.

*Once only fee **Japanese yen

AOBA INTERNATIONAL SCHOOL

Street address: 2-10-34 Aobadai, Meguro-ku, Tokyo, Japan 153
Phone: (81)(3)34611442 **Facsimile:** (81)(3)34639873
Headmistress/principal: Regina Doi
Chief administrator: Adam Y. Doi
Vice principal early childhood program Aoba/JIS: Benin Tolentino
Head teacher: Elizabeth de Souza
Teaching staff: full-time, 19; part-time, 5; total, 24
Nationalities of teaching staff: U.S., 5; U.K., 2; host, 11; other, 6; total, 24
Grade levels: N – pre1
Enrollment: N, 31; K – pre1, 111; total, 142
Nationalities of student body: U.S., 23; U.K., 3; host, 77; other, 39; total, 142
Teacher/student ratio: 1/8
Tuition (annual): N, 748,000** (half-day); K – pre1, 767,000 (half-day); 1,500,000 (full-day average, lunch included)
Other fees (annual): registration*, 200,000**; busing, 250,000 (optional); building fund, 50,000
School year: September to June†

Year founded: 1976. **Type of school:** coed, day, private nonprofit. **Governed by:** board of directors. **Affiliated with:** Japan International School. **Regional organizations:** JCIS, EARCOS.

Curriculum/physical plant

Type: U.S., bilingual (English and Japanese), multicultural. **Languages taught:** English, Japanese. **Special programs:** ESL, JSL, physical education, swimming, soroban (abacus). **Extracurricular:** yearbook, field trips, graduation trip, ballet, seasonal festivities (Western and Japanese). **Location:** downtown Tokyo, in residential area adjacent to beautiful public park. **Facilities:** 2 buildings, 10 classrooms, playground, air conditioning.

*Once only fee **Japanese yen †Summer school, mid-June to July

CHRISTIAN ACADEMY IN JAPAN

Street address: 1-2-14 Shinkawa-cho, Higashi Kurume shi, Tokyo 203, Japan
Phone: (81)(424)710022 **Facsimile:** (81)(424)7622002
E-mail: don.rudd@jemanet.or.jp
Headmaster: Judi Mollenkof
Secondary school principal: Jack Smith
Elementary school principal: Tom Hardeman
Business manager: Andrew Ritchie
Teaching staff: full-time, 45; part-time, 13; total, 58
Nationalities of teaching staff: U.S., 43; host, 7; other, 8; total, 58
Grade levels: K – 12
Enrollment: K, 22; 1 – 5, 135; 6 – 8, 119; 9 – 12, 139; total, 415
Nationalities of student body: U.S., 269; U.K., 4; host, 73; other, 69; total, 415
Capacity: K, 15; 1 – 5, 120; 6 – 8, 180; 9 – 12, 100; total, 415
Teacher/student ratio: 1/7
Tuition (annual): K, 870,000**; 1 – 5, 1,100,000; 6 – 8, 1,210,000; 9 – 12, 1,320,000
Other fees (annual): registration, 45,000**; application*, 15,000; entrance*, 300,000; English test*, 10,000; building fund, 20,000
School year: September to June

Year founded: 1950. **Type of school:** coed, day, church-related. **Governed by:** elected board of directors. **Sponsored by:** Christian Reformed, Conservative Baptist, TEAM, Evangelical Covenant, SEND, OMS missions. **Regional organizations:** EARCOS.

Curriculum/physical plant

Type: U.S., AP. **Languages taught:** French, Spanish, Japanese. **Staff specialists:** speech/hearing, counselor, nurse, resource. **Special programs:** ESL, independent study, correspondence. **Special curricular:** art, chorus, band, physical education, computer instruction, vocational. **Extracurricular:** drama, choral and instrumental music, computers, yearbook, newspaper, photography, excursions/expeditions, field trips. **Sports:** basketball, cross-country, hockey, soccer, tennis, track and field, volleyball, wrestling. **Tests:** PSAT, SAT, ACT, TOEFL, AP, Iowa, Lorge-Thorndike. **Graduates attending college:** 85%. **Graduates have attended:** Wheaton, Biola, Seattle Pacific, Gordon, Calvin. **Location:** in suburban area of Tokyo. **Campus:** 19,000 square meters. **Library:** 21,000 volumes. **Facilities:** 7 buildings, 20 classrooms, auditorium, cafeteria, infirmary, tennis court, gymnasium, playing field, science lab, computer lab.

*Once only fee **Japanese yen

INTERNATIONAL SCHOOL OF THE SACRED HEART

Street address: 4-3-1 Hiroo, Shibuya-ku, Tokyo 150, Japan
Phone: (81)(3)34003951 **Facsimile:** (81)(3)34003496 **E-mail:** issh@iac.co.jp
Headmistress: Sr. Masako Egawa
High school dean: Yvonne Hayes
Middle school dean: Jane Tootell
Kindergarten/junior school principal: Ellen Retelle
Director of studies: Eleanor Tobin
Teaching staff: full-time, 91; part-time, 16; total, 107

Nationalities of teaching staff: U.S., 28; U.K., 25; host, 25; other, 29; total, 107
Grade levels: K – 12
Enrollment: K, 113; 1 – 6, 236; 7 – 9, 135; 10 – 12, 116; total, 600
Nationalities of student body: U.S., 172; U.K., 63; host, 138; other, 227; total, 600
Teacher/student ratio: 1/7
Tuition (annual): K (half day), 1,020,000**; K (full day), 1,680,000; 1 – 4, 1,750,000; 5 – 8, 1,770,000; 9 – 12, 1,790,000
Other fees (annual): registration, 200,000**
School year: September to June

Year founded: 1908. **Type of school:** girls, day, church-related, coeducational kindergarten. **Governed by:** elected board of directors. **Sponsored by:** Catholic Society of the Sacred Heart. **Accredited by:** Western, ECIS. **Regional organizations:** EARCOS, ECIS.

Curriculum

Type: U.S., U.K., AP. **Languages taught:** French, Japanese. **Staff specialists:** reading, math, computer, counselor, nurse. **Special programs:** ESL, special needs, college preparatory. **Special curricular:** art, chorus, physical education, computer instruction, vocational, home economics, library, after-school activities. **Extracurricular:** drama, dance, choral and instrumental music, computers, yearbooks, newspaper, literary magazine, photography, excursions/expeditions, field trips, band, student councils. **Sports:** basketball, cross-country, tennis, track and field, volleyball. **Tests:** PSAT, SAT, TOEFL, AP, Iowa, Achievement Test. **Graduates attending college:** 100%. **Graduates have attended:** Duke, Stanford, Tufts, Oberlin, Durham.

Physical plant

Location: in heart of Tokyo. **Campus:** 5.7 acres. **Libraries (2):** 33,000 volumes. **Facilities:** 3 buildings, 49 classrooms, 4 auditoriums, cafeteria, infirmary, covered play area, 2 tennis courts, gymnasium, playing field, 4 science labs, 4 computer labs, chapel, music, art, and home economics rooms.

**Japanese yen

Japan International School

Street address: 2-10-7 Miyamae, Suginami-ku, Tokyo 168, Japan
Phone: (81)(3)33356620 **Facsimile:** (81)(3)33326967
E-mail: jised@shrine.cyber.ad.jp
Founding director: Regina M. Doi
Headmaster: Roberto L. Gomez
Deputy headmaster: Steven Parr
Principal, mainstream division: Gerald Moran
Principal, intensive English division: Aurelia Shimo
Teaching staff: full-time, 44; part-time, 12; total, 56
Nationalities of teaching staff: U.S., 13; U.K., 5; host, 20; other, 18; total, 56
Grade levels: preK – 9, postgraduate
Enrollment: total, 320
Nationalities of student body: U.S., 40; U.K., 10; host, 130; other, 140; total, 320
Capacity: preK – 6, 300; 7 – postgraduate, 200; total, 500
Teacher/student ratio: 1/6
Tuition (annual): 1,700,000** (average)

Other fees (annual): registration, 200,000**; busing, available by request
School year: September to June

Year founded: 1980. **Type of school:** coed, day. **Governed by:** board of directors. **Affiliated with:** Aoba International School. **Regional organizations:** EARCOS, ECIS.

Curriculum/physical plant

Type: U.S. **Languages of instruction:** English, Japanese. **Languages taught:** Japanese, others by request. **Staff specialists:** reading, math, resource. **Special programs:** ESL. **Special curricular:** art, chorus, physical education, computer instruction, abacus. **Extracurricular:** drama, dance, computers, newspaper, excursions/expeditions, field trips, Japanese arts and crafts, band. **Sports:** swimming, aikido, gym. **Clubs:** Japanese handicrafts, dance, model club, et al. **Tests:** Iowa. **Location:** in Tokyo. **Library:** 5,000 volumes. **Facilities:** 1 building, 25 classrooms, infirmary, tennis court, computer lab, AV equipment, playground, air conditioning.

**Japanese yen

Nishimachi International School

Street address: 2-14-7 Moto-Azabu, Minato-ku, Tokyo 106, Japan
Phone: (81)(3)34515520 **Facsimile:** (81)(3)34560197
E-mail: info@nishimachi.org
Headmaster: Saburo Matsumoto
Principal: John L. Wilson
Director of development: Phillipe Eymard
Teaching staff: full-time, 42; part-time, 10; total, 52
Nationalities of teaching staff: U.S., 25; host, 17; other, 10; total, 52
Grade levels: K – 9
Enrollment: K, 52; 1 – 6, 268; 7 – 9, 65; total, 385
Nationalities of student body: U.S., 156; U.K., 24; host, 102; other, 103; total, 385
Capacity: K, 52; 1 – 6, 289; 7 – 9, 80; total, 421
Teacher/student ratio: 1/7
Tuition (annual): K, 1,629,000**; 1 – 3, 1,683,000; 4 – 6, 1,710,000; 7 – 9, 1,731,000
Other fees (annual): registration*, 250,000**; educational enhancement*, 400,000; building, 50,000; entrance exam, 10,000
School year: late August to June

Year founded: 1949. **Type of school:** coed, day, private nonprofit. **Governed by:** elected board of trustees and board of directors. **Accredited by:** Western. **Regional organizations:** AAIE, EARCOS, ECIS.

Curriculum/physical plant

Type: U.S. **Languages of instruction:** English, Japanese. **Languages taught:** French, Japanese. **Staff specialists:** reading, math, computer, speech/hearing, counselor, nurse. **Special programs:** Japanese social studies. **Special curricular:** art, chorus, physical education, computer instruction. **Extracurricular:** drama, gymnastics, choral and instrumental music, computers, yearbook, newspaper, photography, excursions/expeditions, field trips. **Sports:** basketball, cross-country, skiing, swimming, volleyball, sumo, aikido. **Clubs:** drama, student council, Japanese. **Tests:** Iowa. **Graduates have attended:** U. of California at Berkeley, Brown, Cornell,

Harvard, Tufts. **Location:** in an upper-class residential and business center of Tokyo. **Campus:** 1 acre. **Library:** 15,000 volumes. **Facilities:** 7 buildings, 36 classrooms, auditorium, covered play area, gymnasium, 2 science labs, computer lab, 3 playgrounds, camp site (Kazuno) about 100 miles north of Tokyo, air conditioning.

*Once only fee **Japanese yen

St. Mary's International School

Street address: 1-6-19 Seta, Setagaya-ku, Tokyo 158, Japan
Phone: (81)(3)37093411 **Facsimile:** (81)(3)37071950
Headmaster: Br. Michel Jutras
High school principal: Saburo Kagei
Middle school principal: Stephen Wilson
Elementary school principal: Br. Lawrence Guy Lambert
Business manager: Unryu Haku
Teaching staff: full-time, 79; part-time, 29; total, 108
Nationalities of teaching staff: U.S., 56; U.K., 2; host, 20; other, 30; total, 108
Enrollment: K, 48; 1 – 6, 460; 7 – 9, 213; 10 – 12, 207; total, 928
Teacher/student ratio: 1/10
Tuition (annual): K – 6, 1,750,000**; 7 – 12, 1,800,000
Other fees (annual): registration*, 200,000**; busing, 300,000; lunch, 121,000; milk, 15,000
School year: late August to June

Year founded: 1954. **Type of school:** boys, day, church-related. **Governed by:** appointed and elected board of directors. **Sponsored by:** Brothers of Christian Instruction of Ploërmel. **Accredited by:** ECIS, Western. **Regional organizations:** AAIE, EARCOS, ECIS.

Curriculum

Type: U.S., IB, AP. **Languages taught:** French, Spanish, German, Latin, Japanese, Swedish, Chinese, Finnish, Danish, Korean. **Staff specialists:** counselor, nurse. **Special programs:** ESL, interactive communications simulation. **Special curricular:** art, chorus, band, physical education, computer instruction, bell choir, mechanical drawing. **Extracurricular:** drama, choral and instrumental music, computers, yearbook, newspaper, literary magazine, photography, excursions/expeditions, field trips, ski trips, musical, math contest, "artscape." **Sports:** baseball, basketball, cross-country, hockey, soccer, swimming, tennis, track and field, ice hockey, wrestling. **Clubs:** chess, debating, drama, National Honor Society, boosters, table tennis, aikido, scouts, cubs, speech, ice hockey, brain bowl, yearbook, Leo Club. **Tests:** SSAT, PSAT, SAT, TOEFL, IB, AP, Iowa. **Graduates attending college:** 98.5%. **Graduates have attended:** Princeton, Harvard, Stanford, Brown, MIT.

Physical plant

Location: in southwestern residential area of Setagaya-ku in Tokyo. **Campus:** 7 acres. **Library:** 40,000 volumes. **Facilities:** 3 buildings, 47 classrooms, auditorium, cafeteria, infirmary, covered play area, 4 tennis courts, gymnasium, 3 playing fields, 4 science labs, 2 computer labs, swimming pool, 3 art rooms, weight room, darkroom, 3 music rooms, typing room, mechanical drawing room, TV center, AV room, 2 ski lodges in Tsumagoi, Gunma Prefecture.

*Once only fee **Japanese yen

Seisen International School

Street address: 12-15, Yoga 1-chome, Setagaya-ku, Tokyo 158, Japan
Phone: (81)(3)37042661 **Facsimile:** (81)(3)37011033
E-mail: sisinfo@japan.co.jp
Headmistress: Sr. Asuncion Lecubarri
High school principal: Suzanne Kawasumi
Elementary school principal: Fiona McGrory
Kindergarten coordinator: Sheila O'Donoghue
IB coordinator: Ulrich Nikolai
Teaching staff: full-time, 53; part-time, 22; total, 75
Nationalities of teaching staff: U.S., 15; U.K., 13; host, 11; other, 36; total, 75
Grade levels: K – 12
Enrollment: K, 154; elementary, 246; high school, 204; total, 604
Nationalities of student body: U.S., 160; U.K., 49; host, 63; other, 332; total, 604
Teacher/student ratio: 1/11
Tuition (annual): K, 965,000** (half day), 1,595,000 (full day); 1 – 6, 1,700,000; 7 – 12, 1,750,000
Other fees (annual): registration*, 200,000**; busing, 280,000; lunch, 120,000; school development, 50,000; graduation*, 21,000
School year: August to June

Year founded: 1962. **Type of school:** girls, day, church-related, coeducational kindergarten. **Governed by:** Seisen Jogakuin Educational Foundation. **Sponsored by:** Handmaids of the Sacred Heart of Jesus. **Accredited by:** Western, ECIS. **Regional organizations:** AAIE, EARCOS, ECIS.

Curriculum

Type: U.S., IB, AP. **Languages taught:** French, Spanish, and Japanese IB. Languages taught on tutorial basis according to demand. **Special programs:** ESL. **Special curricular:** art, physical education, computer instruction, choir, bell choir. **Extracurricular:** drama, choral music, computers, yearbook, newspaper, photography, excursions/expeditions, field trips, math contest, "artscape," pottery. **Sports:** basketball, cross-country, soccer, swimming, tennis, track and field, volleyball. **Clubs:** debating, drama, Brownies, National Honor Society, boosters, brain bowl, Adventurers, ecology, speech, yearbook. **Tests:** SSAT, PSAT, SAT, TOEFL, IB, AP, IGCSE, Iowa, NMSQT. **Graduates attending college:** 99%. **Graduates have attended:** Harvard, MIT, London School of Economics, Brown, Cambridge.

Physical plant

Location: 30 – 40 minutes from central Tokyo. **Campus:** 6,932.86 square meters. **Library:** 22,000 volumes. **Facilities:** 3 buildings, 36 classrooms, cafeteria, infirmary, 2 covered play areas, gymnasium, playing field, 2 science labs, 2 computer labs, tennis courts, AV room, music, art, and home economics rooms.

*Once only fee **Japanese yen

Saint Maur International School

Street address: 83 Yamate-cho, Naka-ku, Yokohama, Japan 231
Phone: (81)(45)6415751 **Facsimile:** (81)(45)6416688
E-mail: creena@gol.com
Board chairperson: Sr. Carmel O'Keeffe
Headmistress: Jeanette K. Thomas
Principal, K – 12: Richard B. Rucci
Guidance counselor: Catherine O. Endo
Teaching staff: full-time, 43; part-time, 15; total, 58
Nationalities of teaching staff: U.S., 25; U.K., 8; host, 7; other, 18; total, 58
Grade levels: preK – 12
Enrollment: preK, 24; K, 74; 1 – 5, 180; 6 – 8, 94; 9 – 12, 83; total, 455
Nationalities of student body: U.S., 143; U.K., 26; host, 160; other, 126; total, 455
Capacity: preK – K, 100; 1 – 6, 180; 7 – 9, 90; 10 – 12, 90; total, 460
Teacher/student ratio: 1/8
Tuition (annual): preK, 760,000**; K, 1,115,000; 1 – 5, 1,370,000; 6 – 12, 1,548,000
Other fees: registration*, 260,000**
School year: late August to June

Year founded: 1872. **Type of school:** coed, day. **Governed by:** appointed board of directors, administrative team. **Sponsored by:** Catholic Sisters of the Infant Jesus. **Accredited by:** Western, ECIS. **Regional organizations:** EARCOS, ECIS, JCIS.

Curriculum

Type: U.S., U.K., IB, AP, IGCSE. **Languages taught:** English, French, Spanish, Japanese, other languages as independent study. **Staff specialists:** computer, counselor, ESL, special education. **Special programs:** ESL, honors sections, independent study. **Special curricular:** art, physical education, computer instruction, drama, music, home economics. **Extracurricular:** drama, choral music, yearbook, literary magazine, excursions/expeditions, field trips, elementary newspaper, junior high and high school student councils, Latin American dance, band. **Sports:** badminton, basketball, field hockey, soccer, softball, table tennis, tennis, volleyball, floor hockey. **Clubs:** drama, aerobics, band, choir, dressmaking and tailoring, Friendship Volunteers, DJ, BBC, environmental action, gymnastics, Japanese calligraphy. **Tests:** PSAT, SAT, IB, AP, Iowa, IGCSE, Otis-Lennon, Purdue. **Graduates attending college:** 95%. **Graduates have attended:** Brown, Cornell, Dartmouth, Oxford, Yale.

Physical plant

Location: in residential area of Yokohama. **Campus:** 7,810 square meters. **Library:** 14,000 volumes. **Facilities:** 3 buildings, 25 classrooms, cafeteria, infirmary, 2 covered play areas, tennis court, gymnasium, 3 science labs, computer lab, dressmaking/tailoring room, home economics room.

*Once only fee **Japanese yen

YOKOHAMA

YOKOHAMA INTERNATIONAL SCHOOL

Street address: 258 Yamate-cho, Naka-ku, Yokohama, Japan
Phone: (81)(45)6220084 **Facsimile:** (81)(45)6210379
Headmaster: Neil Richards
Deputy headmaster: Edward Bernard
Teaching staff: full-time, 41; part-time, 11; total, 52
Nationalities of teaching staff: U.S., 16; U.K., 16; host, 12; other, 8; total, 52
Grade levels: preK – 12
Enrollment: preK, 47; K, 39; 1 – 6, 250; 7 – 9, 81; 10 – 12, 75; total, 492
Capacity: preK, 45; K, 50; 1 – 6, 270; 7 – 9, 120; 10 – 12, 120; total, 605
Teacher/student ratio: 1/10
Tuition (annual): K, 752,000** (half day), 1,118,000 (full day); 1 – 6, 1,437,000; 7 – 13, 1,607,000
Other fees (annual): registration*, 155,000** (half day), 247,000 (full day); capital levy, 82,000; field studies, 60,000 – 85,000
School year: end of August to June

Year founded: 1924. **Type of school:** coed, day. **Governed by:** elected school committee. **Accredited by:** New England, ECIS. **Regional organizations:** EARCOS, ECIS.

Curriculum/physical plant

Type: U.S., U.K., IB, AP. **Languages taught:** French, German, Japanese, Dutch. **Special curricular:** art, chorus, band, physical education, computer instruction. **Extracurricular:** drama, gymnastics, dance, computers, yearbook, photography. **Sports:** basketball, cross-country, field hockey, soccer, track and field, volleyball. **Tests:** PSAT, SAT, TOEFL, IB, AP, Iowa, GCE. **Graduates attending college:** 100%. **Graduates have attended:** Harvard, Brown, Cornell, Oxford, Stanford. **Location:** in residential area of Yokohama. **Campus:** 4,896 square meters. **Library:** 30,000 volumes. **Facilities:** 5 buildings, 42 classrooms, auditorium, gymnasium, science labs, AV center, use of playing field.

*Once only fee **Japanese yen

JORDAN

Region: Middle East
Size: 34,342 square miles
Population: 4,212,15
Capital: Amman
Telephone code: 962
Currency: dinar
Language: Arabic

AMMAN

American Community School

Phone: (962)(6)813944/861997/813946 **Facsimile:** (962)(6)823357
E-mail: acsamm@go.com.jo **Telex:** 92521510 USEMB JO
Mail: c/o U.S. Embassy, Amman, Jordan
Superintendent: Gary Duckett, Ed.D.
Elementary/middle school principal: Robert Voruz
Business manager: Hamdi Hamdi
Teaching staff: full-time, 46; part-time, 6; total, 52
Nationalities of teaching staff: U.S., 39; host, 6; other, 7; total, 52
Grade levels: pre-K – 12
Enrollment: preK, 12; K, 18; 1 – 5, 129; 6 – 8, 120; 9 – 12, 163; total, 442
Nationalities of student body: U.S., 126; host, 114; other, 202; total, 442
Capacity: preK – K, 25; 1 – 5, 200; 6 – 8, 120; 9 – 12, 200; total, 545
Teacher/student ratio: 1/9
Tuition (annual): pre-K, $2,000; K, $4,785; 1 – 5, $6,483; 6 – 8, $7,426; 9 – 12, $8,725
Other fees (annual): capital levy*, $3,000; busing, $780
School year: August to June

Year founded: 1957. **Type of school:** coed, day, private nonprofit. **Governed by:** elected school board. **Accredited by:** Middle States. **Regional organizations:** ECIS, NESA.

Curriculum/physical plant

Type: U.S., AP. **Languages taught:** French, Spanish, Arabic. **Staff specialists:** reading, math, computer, counselor, nurse. **Special programs:** ESL. **Special curricular:** art, chorus, band, physical education, computer instruction. **Extracurricular:** drama, gymnastics, choral and instrumental music, computers, yearbook, newspaper, literary magazine, photography. **Sports:** baseball, basketball, cross-country, soccer, tennis, track and field, volleyball. **Organizations:** National Honor Society, student council. **Tests:** SSAT, PSAT, SAT, ACT, TOEFL, Iowa, PLAN. **Graduates attending college:** 95%. **Graduates have attended:** Georgetown, Bryn Mawr, MIT, U. of Michigan, Harvard. **Location:** in city. **Campus:** 9 acres. **Library:** 18,000 volumes. **Facilities:** 6 buildings, 39 classrooms, auditorium, gymnasium, 2 playing fields, 2 science labs, 2 computer labs, tennis courts.

*Once only fee

Amman Baccalaureate School

Phone: (962)(6)5411572/5411191 – 2 **Facsimile:** (962)(6)5412603
E-mail: abs@go.com.jo
Mail: PO Box 441, Sweileh, Amman 11910, Jordan
Principal: Samia Al Farra
Vice-principal: Dermot Keegan
Head of senior school: Mary Tadros
Head of middle school: Riham Kawar
Head of junior school: Nora Shrydeh
Teaching staff: full-time, 107; part-time, 10; total, 117
Nationalities of teaching staff: U.S., 10; U.K., 16; host, 83; other, 8; total, 117
Grade levels: K – 12
Enrollment: K, 100; 1 – 5, 269; 6 – 8, 270; 9 – 12, 372; total, 1,011
Nationalities of student body: U.S., 18; U.K., 6; host, 890; other, 97; total, 1,011
Capacity: K, 100; 1 – 5, 275; 6 – 8, 275; 9 – 12, 360; total, 1,010
Teacher/student ratio: 1/9
Tuition (annual): K, 1,150 – 1,250**; 1 – 3, 1,800 – 1,850; 4 – 5, 2,075 – 2,100; 6 – 8, 2,200 – 2,675; 9 – 12, 3,100 – 4,250
Other fees (annual): registration*, 30**; busing, 360 (optional); lunch, 325 (optional); supplies, 50 – 70; non-refundable enrollment fee, 500
School year: August to June†

Year founded: 1981. **Type of school:** coed, day, private nonprofit. **Governed by:** appointed board of trustees. **Sponsored by:** Hashemite Society for Education. **Accredited by:** Jordanian Ministry of Education. **Regional organizations:** ECIS, NESA.

Curriculum

Type: U.K., Jordanian, IB. **Languages of instruction:** English, Arabic. **Languages taught:** Arabic, English, French. **Staff specialists:** math, computer, counselor, art, librarian, music, physical education, Arabic as a Second Language, science, languages, social studies, drama, doctor, special needs. **Special curricular:** art, physical education, computer instruction, drama, music. **Extracurricular:** drama, gymnastics, dance, computers, yearbook, literary magazine, photography, excursions/expeditions, field trips, choir, music. **Sports:** basketball, soccer, swimming, table tennis, volleyball, Tae Kwon Do, horseback riding, weight lifting, fencing. **Clubs:** chess, community service, science, conservation, Thursday club, Crown Prince Award. **Tests:** SAT, ACT, TOEFL, IB, IGCSE, Jordanian Tawjihi. **Graduates attending college:** 100%. **Graduates have attended:** U. of Jordan, McGill, Harvard, Oxford, Cambridge.

Physical plant

Location: on outskirts of Amman, 15 – 20 minutes from city. **Campus:** 85,000 square meters. **Library:** 12,400 volumes. **Facilities:** 5 buildings, auditorium, cafeteria, 7 science labs, 3 computer labs, technology lab, multipurpose halls, sports complex, workshops, technical drawing office, art and ceramics rooms, AV facilities.

*Once only fee **Jordanian dinar †School week: Saturday – Wednesday

KAZAKHSTAN

Region: Central Asia
Size: 1,049,200 square miles
Population: 16,916,463
Capital: Alma-Ata
Telephone code: 7
Currency: tenge
Languages: Kazak, Russian

ALMATY

Almaty International School

Phone: (7)(3272)409412/409422 **Facsimile:** (7)(3272)409622
E-mail: general@ais.alma-ata.su
Mail: c/o American Embassy, Almaty, Dept. of State, Washington, DC 20521-7030
Director: Dr. Robert Draper
Director of instruction: Gordon Blackie
Teaching staff: full-time, 15; part-time, 4; total, 19
Nationalities of teaching staff: U.S., 13; other, 6; total, 19
Grade levels: N – 12
Enrollment: N, 8; K, 12; 1 – 6, 38; 7 – 9, 66; 10 – 12, 18; total, 142
Capacity: N, 16; K, 24; 1 – 6, 100; 7 – 9, 100; 10 – 12, 60; total, 300
Teacher/student ratio: 1/7
Tuition (annual): N – 5, $6,900; 6 – 12, $9,200
Other fees: registration*, $100; capital levy, $4,000 (deposit) or $1,600/yr (fee)
School year: September to June

Year founded: 1993. **Type of school:** coed, day, private nonprofit. **Regional organizations:** CEESA. **Governed by:** appointed board of governors. **Operated by:** Quality Schools International.

Curriculum/physical plant

Type: U.S., AP. **Special curricular:** art, physical education, computer instruction. **Extracurricular:** drama, excursions/expeditions, field trips. **Tests:** AP, IGCSE. **Location:** in residential area, 5 kilometers from center of Almaty. **Campus:** 2 hectares. **Library:** 3,500 volumes. **Facilities:** 1 building, 20 classrooms, computer lab.

*Once only fee

KENYA

Region: East Africa
Size: 224,961 square miles
Population: 28,176,686
Capital: Nairobi
Telephone code: 254
Currency: shilling
Languages: Swahili, English
Kikuyu, Luhya , Luo, Meru

KIJABE

RIFT VALLEY ACADEMY

Phone: (254)(154)64646 **Facsimile:** (254)(154)64412
Mail: PO Box 80 Kijabe, Kenya
Superintendent: Roy E. Entwistle
Principal (grades 7 – 12): Jim Long
Principal (grades 1 – 6): Don Schuit
Assistant to superintendent: Norm Dixon
Director of finance and services: Robert Christian
Teaching staff: full-time, 100; total, 100
Nationalities of teaching staff: U.S., 87; other, 13; total, 100
Grade levels: 1 – 12
Enrollment: 1 – 6, 90; 7 – 9, 171; 10 – 12, 223; total, 484
Nationalities of student body: U.S., 294; U.K., 16; host, 44; other, 130; total, 484
Capacity: 1 – 6, 120; 7 – 9, 130; 10 – 12, 239; total, 489
Teacher/student ratio: 1/5
Boarders: boys, 194; girls, 203 **Grades:** 1 – 12 **Program:** planned 7-day
Tuition (annual): Kenya citizens, $1,600; mission children, $2,550; others, $7,145
Other fees (annual): boarding, $1,700; private lessons, $24
School year: September to July (3 trimesters)

Year founded: 1906. **Type of school:** coed, day, boarding, private nonprofit, mission-sponsored. **Governed by:** elected school board. **Sponsored by:** Africa Inland Mission International. **Accredited by:** Middle States. **Regional organizations:** AISA.

Curriculum

Type: U.S., AP. **Languages taught:** French, Spanish, Swahili. **Staff specialists:** reading, math, computer, speech/hearing, counselor, learning disabilities, nurse, art, drama, band, photography. **Special programs:** ESL, independent study, remedial, speech, study skills. **Special curricular:** art, chorus, band, physical education, computer instruction, vocational. **Extracurricular:** drama, vocal and instrumental music, computers, yearbook, photography, field trips, environmental and cultural field studies. **Sports:** basketball, soccer, volleyball, rugby, track and field, field hockey. **Clubs:** Caring Community, stamps, cooking, weight training, special music groups, ensembles. **Tests:** PSAT, SAT, ACT, AP, Iowa, PLAN, TAP, GCSE. **Graduates attending college:** 95%. **Graduates have attended:** Wheaton, Messiah, John Brown, Purdue, Pepperdine.

Physical plant

Location: in rural area, 35 miles from Nairobi, within one degree of equator at 7,300-foot elevation. **Campus:** 88 acres. **Library:** 20,000 volumes. **Facilities:** 80 buildings, 31 classrooms, 2 auditoriums, cafeteria, infirmary, 6 tennis courts, gymnasium, 3 playing fields, 4 science labs, 4 computer labs, 5 racquetball courts, 2 student centers, 19 dormitories.

KISUMU

Kisumu International School

Phone: (254)(35)21678
Mail: PO Box 1276, Kisumu, Kenya
Head teacher: Nancy Rasmusson
Teaching staff: full-time, 5; total, 5
Nationalities of teaching staff: U.S., 3; other, 2; total, 5
Grade levels: preK – 7
Enrollment: preK – K, 10; 1 – 6, 28; 7, 4; total, 42
Nationalities of student body: U.K., 7; host, 15; other, 20; total, 42
Teacher/student ratio: 1/8
Tuition (annual): 93,000**
School year: September to July

Year founded: 1986. **Type of school:** day, private nonprofit. **Governed by:** board of directors.

Curriculum/physical plant

Type: U.S. **Languages taught:** French. **Staff specialists:** math, learning disabilities, classical piano instruction. **Special curricular:** art, computer instruction. **Extracurricular:** physical education, choral music, field trips. **Sports:** soccer, swimming, Tae Kwon Do. **Clubs:** newsletter, art, sports. **Location:** in city. **Campus:** 1 acre. **Facilities:** 6 classrooms, computer lab, library.

**Kenyan shilling

NAIROBI

International School of Kenya, Ltd.

Street address: Peponi Road, Nairobi, Kenya
Phone: (254)(2)582421–2/582556 **Facsimile:** (254)(2)582451
E-mail: ken@rhino140.kenya.leids.com **Telex:** 96322370 CALWANG (ISK/AISA) **Cable:** U.S. Embassy, Nairobi
Mail: PO Box 14103, Nairobi, Kenya
Superintendent: Daniel L. Scinto
High school principal: Brian Lahan
Middle school principal: Ron Dowty

Elementary school principal: Nancy Hoppe
Business manager: Kamal Rajani
Teaching staff: full-time, 63; part-time, 2; total, 65
Nationalities of teaching staff: U.S., 52; U.K., 10; host, 3; total, 65
Grade levels: preK – 13
Enrollment: preK, 13; K – 5, 210; 6 – 8, 140; 9 – 13, 219; total, 582
Nationalities of student body: U.S., 227; host, 48; other, 307; total, 582
Teacher/student ratio: 1/9
Tuition (annual): preK, $2,151; K – 5, $8,750; 6 – 13, $10,394
Other fees (annual): registration, $2,300; busing, $900; graduation*, $35
School year: August to June

Year founded: 1976. **Type of school:** coed, day, private nonprofit. **Governed by:** board of govenors/board of directors. **Sponsored by:** Canadian High Commission, American Embassy. **Accredited by:** Middle States, ECIS. **Regional organizations:** AAIE, ECIS, AISA.

Curriculum

Type: U.S., IB. **Languages taught:** French, Spanish, Kiswahili. **Staff specialists:** computer, speech/hearing, counselor, psychologist, learning disabilities, nurse. **Special programs:** ESL, remedial. **Special curricular:** art, band, physical education, computer instruction, intercultural program. **Extracurricular:** drama, gymnastics, instrumental music, computers, yearbook, newspaper, literary magazine, excursions/expeditions, field trips. **Sports:** basketball, hockey, netball, rugby, soccer, swimming, tennis, track and field, volleyball. **Clubs:** National Honor Society, social service. **Tests:** PSAT, SAT, TOEFL, IB, Iowa, ACH. **Graduates attending college:** 88%. **Graduates have attended:** Harvard, MIT, Queens, Notre Dame, Bryn Mawr.

Physical plant

Location: surrounded by a coffee plantation, 8 kilometers from Nairobi. **Campus:** 49 acres. **Library:** 13,500 volumes. **Facilities:** 20 buildings, 43 classrooms, auditorium, infirmary, 3 tennis courts, gymnasium, 4 playing fields, 4 science labs, 2 computer labs, swimming pool, darkroom, student center with snackbar and video and periodical rooms.

*Once only fee

Kenton College

Street address: Gichugu Road, Kilileshwa, Nairobi, Kenya
Phone: (254)(2)574198 **Facsimile:** (254)(2)565066
Mail: PO Box 30017, Nairobi, Kenya
Headmaster: Roger Hartley
Deputy headmistress: Maureen Cussans
Head of junior school: Lynn Savage
Teaching staff: full-time, 21; part-time, 5; total, 26
Nationalities of teaching staff: U.K., 17; host, 1; other, 8; total, 26
Grade levels: year 2 – year 8
Enrollment: total, 220
Nationalities of student body: U.S., 3; U.K., 25; host, 104; other, 88; total, 220
Teacher/student ratio: 1/10
Boarders: boys, 60 **Program:** planned 7-day

Tuition (annual): 315,000**
Other fees (annual): registration*, 1,000**; boarding, 60,000; insurance, 200/term; deposit, 10,000 (refundable), extra activities
School year: September through August

Year founded: 1924. **Type of school:** coed, day, boarding, private nonprofit. **Governed by:** elected board of governors.

Curriculum/physical plant

Type: U.K. **Languages taught:** French, Latin. **Staff specialists:** nurse, computer technician. **Extracurricular:** drama, dance, instrumental music, computers, yearbook, newspaper, literary magazine, excursions/expeditions, field trips. **Sports:** cricket, hockey, netball, rugby, rounders, others. **Clubs:** chess, drama, Cub Scouts, cookery, riding, music. **Tests:** Common Entrance Board. **Graduates have attended:** Rydal College, Strathallan College, Tonbridge, Sevenoaks, Winchester. **Location:** beautiful old building with outstanding grounds in suburban area of Nairobi. **Facilities:** 13 buildings, 14 classrooms, auditorium, infirmary, tennis court, playing field, science lab, swimming pool, library, computer design and technology center.

*Once only fee **Kenyan shilling **1996–97 listing**

Rosslyn Academy

Phone: (254)(2)520039/520702 **Facsimile:** (254)(2)521306
E-mail: rosslyn@maf.org
Mail: PO Box 14146 Nairobi, Kenya
Superintendent: Dena Brent
Secondary principal: Paul Leaman
Teaching staff: full-time, 45; part-time, 5; total, 50
Nationalities of teaching staff: U.S., 36; other, 14; total, 50
Grade levels: K – 12
Enrollment: K, 14; 1 – 5, 130; 6 – 8, 103; 9 – 12, 119; total, 366
Nationalities of student body: U.S., 290; other, 76; total, 366
Teacher/student ratio: 1/8
Tuition (annual): mission rates: K, $1,400; 1 – 5, $2,100; 6 – 12, $2,400; non-mission rates: K, $2,100; 1 – 5, $5,200; 6 – 12, $6,000
Other fees (annual): capital levy, $300; busing, $360; lunch, $1.30/day
School year: August to June

Year founded: 1967. **Type of school:** coed, day, church-related. **Governed by:** appointed board of governors. **Sponsored by:** Baptist Mission, Assemblies of God, Mennonite Mission. **Accredited by:** Middle States, ACSI. **Regional organizations:** AISA.

Curriculum/physical plant

Type: U.S., AP. **Languages taught:** French, Spanish, Swahili. **Staff specialists:** counselor, learning disabilities, campus pastor. **Special curricular:** art, chorus, physical education, computer instruction, drama, technologies, home economics, photography, yearbook, music. **Extracurricular:** field trips, Model UN. **Sports:** basketball, field hockey, rugby, soccer, track and field, volleyball. **Tests:** PSAT, SAT, AP, TAP/Iowa, PLAN. **Graduates attending college:** 95%. **Location:** 12 miles from Nairobi city center. **Campus:** 40 acres. **Library:** 20,000 volumes. **Facilities:** 17 buildings, 23 classrooms, 3 playing fields, 2 science labs, computer lab.

NAIROBI

St. Mary's School, Nairobi
Street address: Rhapta Road/James Gichuru Road, Nairobi, Kenya
Phone: (254)(2)444569 **Facsimile:** (254)(2)444754
E-mail: stmarys@arcc.permanet.org
Mail: PO Box 40580, Nairobi, Kenya
Headmaster: Fr. M. McMahon, CSSp.

KOREA

Region: East Asia
Size: 47,399 square miles
Population: 23,904,124
Capital: Pyongyang
Telephone code: 82
Currency: won
Language: Korean

PUSAN

International School of Pusan

Phone: (82)(51)6283335 **Facsimile:** (82)(51)6280349
Mail: PO Box 77 Nam Pusan Post Office, Nam Ku, Pusan, Korea
Headmaster: Peter Gotts
Teaching staff: full-time, 7; part-time, 3; total, 10
Nationalities of teaching staff: U.S., 1; U.K., 2; host, 1; other, 6; total, 10
Grade levels: preK – 8
Enrollment: preK, 12; K, 15; 1 – 6, 47; 7 – 8, 5; total, 79
Teacher/student ratio: 1/10
Tuition (annual): preK, 3,000,000**; K – 8, 6,500,000
Other fees: registration*, 50,000**; capital levy*, 4,000,000 (refundable less 10% per annum)
School year: September to June

Year founded: 1983. **Type of school:** coed, day, private nonprofit. **Governed by:** elected board of governors. **Accredited by:** ECIS. **Regional organizations:** KORCOS.

Curriculum/physical plant

Type: U.S., U.K. **Staff specialists:** computer, ESL, science. **Special programs:** ESL. **Special curricular:** physical education, computer instruction, French, Korean culture. **Extracurricular:** drama, dance, computers, yearbook, newspaper, excursions/expeditions, field trips, tennis, swimming. **Tests:** SAT. **Location:** in Pusan. **Campus:** 1 acre. **Library:** 7,000 volumes. **Facilities:** 7 classrooms, auditorium, multipurpose room.

*Once only fee **Korean won

SEOUL

International Christian School, Seoul

Street address: Yongsan Gu, Pog Wang dong 267-7, Seoul, Korea
Phone: (82)(2)7924116 – 7 **Facsimile:** (82)(2)7944729
E-mail: 76245.3525@compuserve.com
Mail: PO Box 62, SRCO Seoul, Korea 140-600
U.S. mail: (no personal name) PSC 450, Box 737, APO AP 96206
Superintendent/head administrator: Ellis Caudill
Teaching staff: full-time, 25; total, 25
Nationalities of teaching staff: U.S., 22; host, 2; other, 1; total, 25
Grade levels: preK – 10
Enrollment: total, 300
Nationalities of student body: U.S., 115; other, 185; total, 300
Capacity: total, 300
Teacher/student ratio: 1/12
Tuition (annual): preK, $2,722; K – 5, $5,737; 6 – 10, $6,300
Other fees: registration, $88; busing, $944; ESL, $833
School year: August to June

Year founded: 1990. **Type of school:** coed, day, church-related, private nonprofit. **Sponsored by:** Network of International Christian Schools. **Accredited by:** Western, ACSI. **Regional organizations:** EARCOS, KORCOS, ACSI.

Curriculum/physical plant

Type: Christian/secular. **Languages taught:** English, Spanish. **Special curricular:** art, physical education, computer, music, ESL. **Extracurricular:** after-school Bible study, tutoring, science fair, spelling bee, field day, outdoor education. **Sports:** basketball, soccer, cross-country. **Tests:** PSAT, SAT, Stanford, SLEP. **Library:** 4,500 volumes.

Seoul Academy International School

Street address: 988-5 Dae chi Dong, Seoul, Korea
Phone: (82)(2)5541690 **Facsimile:** (82)(2)5620451
Mail: Young Dong, PO Box 85, Seoul, Korea
Director: Thomas P. O'Connor
Principal: Betty Lee
Teaching staff: full-time, 25; total, 25
Grade levels: preK – 8
Enrollment: preK, 10; K, 30; 1 – 8, 175; total, 215
Capacity: total, 250
Teacher/student ratio: 1/10
Tuition (annual): K – 8, 7,300,000**
School year: August to June†

Year founded: 1983. **Type of school:** coed, day, private nonprofit.

Curriculum/physical plant

Type: U.S. **Languages taught:** Korean. **Staff specialists:** computer, nurse, art, ESL, music, science. **Special programs:** ESL, remedial, special education. **Special curricular:** computer instruction, arts. **Extracurricular:** drama, yearbook, excursions/expeditions, field trips, student council. **Clubs:** Boy Scouts, Girl Scouts, art. **Location:** in suburban area, 20 minutes from Seoul. **Library:** 9,000 volumes. **Facilities:** 1 building, air conditioning.

**Korean won †summer school/ESL school, June – August

Seoul Foreign School

Street address: 55 Yunhi-Dong, Seoul, Korea
Phone: (82)(2)3355101 – 5 **Facsimile:** (82)(2)3351857
E-mail: sfsoffice@crusader.sfs-h.ac.kr
Mail: 55 Yunhi-Dong, Sudaemun-Ku, Seoul 120-113, Korea
Headmaster: Harlan E. Lyso, Ph.D.
High school principal: Paul S. Johnston
Middle school principal: Jonathan F. Borden, Ph.D.
Elementary school principal: Kermit D. Gingerich
British school headteacher: Timothy J. Gray
Teaching staff: full-time, 116; part-time, 16; total, 132
Nationalities of teaching staff: U.S., 92; U.K., 14; host, 7; other, 19; total, 132
Grade levels: preK – 12
Enrollment: preK, 87; K, 90; 1 – 5, 431; 6 – 8, 246; 9 – 12, 342; total, 1,196
Nationalities of student body: U.S., 799; U.K., 79; other, 318; total, 1,196
Capacity: preK, 88; K, 100; 1 – 5, 465; 6 – 8, 274; 9 – 12, 352; total, 1,279
Teacher/student ratio: 1/10
Tuition (annual): preK, $4,601 (half day); K – 5, $11,845; 6 – 8, $12,675; 9 – 12, $13,902; British school, $12,550
Other fees (annual): registration, $553; busing, $1,712
School year: August to June

Year founded: 1912. **Type of school:** coed, day, private nonprofit, Christian. **Governed by:** elected school board. **Sponsored by:** community, five church groups. **Accredited by:** Western. **Regional organizations:** AAIE, EARCOS, ECIS.

Curriculum

Type: U.S., U.K., IB, AP. **Languages taught:** French, Spanish, Korean. **Staff specialists:** reading, math, computer, counselor, nurse. **Special programs:** ESL. **Special curricular:** art, chorus, band, physical education, computer instruction. **Extracurricular:** drama, choral and instrumental music, computers, yearbook, newspaper, literary magazine, photography, excursions/expeditions, field trips. **Sports:** basketball, cheerleading, cross-country, soccer, tennis, volleyball. **Clubs:** National Honor Society, student council, Fellowship of Christian Students, variety of student interest clubs. **Tests:** PSAT, SAT, ACT, TOEFL, IB, AP, CLEP, CAT. **Graduates attending college:** over 95%. **Graduates have attended:** Harvard, U. of California at Berkeley, MIT, Smith, Northwestern.

Physical plant

Location: in park-like environment within city. **Campus:** over 24 acres. **Libraries:** 41,000 volumes. **Facilities:** 6 educational buildings, 87 classrooms, 2 auditoriums, cafeteria, infirmary, 4 tennis courts, 2 gymnasiums, playing field, 4 science labs, 3 computer labs, indoor swimming pool, 11 residential buildings (72 units), partial air conditioning.

Seoul International School

Street address: Bokjung-dong, Song Nam City, Korea
Phone: (82)(2)2334551 – 2 **Facsimile:** (82)(342)7595133
Mail: Songpa P. O. Box 47, Seoul, Korea 138-600
Headmaster: Edward B. Adams
Deputy headmistress for academics: Francelle Grisham
Deputy headmaster for business: Hyung Shik Kim
Assistant headmaster for development: Robert Montoya
Teaching staff: full-time, 80; total, 80
Nationalities of teaching staff: U.S., 40; other, 40; total, 80
Grade levels: preK – 12
Enrollment: preK, 18; K, 43; 1 – 6, 290; 7 – 9, 200; 10 – 12, 250; language center, 90; total, 891
Nationalities of student body: U.S., 683; other, 208; total, 891
Teacher/student ratio: 1/10
Tuition (annual): preK, $8,600; K, $9,200; 1 – 5, $11,000; 6 – 8, $12,000; 9 – 12, $13,000
Other fees (annual): registration*, $250 – 375; busing, $1,300; books, $60 – 130 (deposit); testing*, $64; AP*, $128; senior*, $128
School year: August to June

Year founded: 1973. **Type of school:** coed, day, proprietary, private nonprofit. **Governed by:** headmaster. **Accredited by:** Western. **Regional organizations:** AAIE, EARCOS.

Curriculum/physical plant

Type: U.S., AP. **Languages taught:** French, Spanish, Korean. **Staff specialists:** reading, counselor, nurse, resource. **Special programs:** ESL, remedial. **Special curricular:** art, chorus, band, physical education, computer instruction. **Extracurricular:** drama, choral and instrumental music, computers, yearbook, newspaper, literary magazine, field trips. **Sports:** basketball, cheerleading, cross-country, soccer, tennis, volleyball. **Tests:** PSAT, SAT, AP, CTBS. **Graduates attending college:** over 90%. **Graduates have attended:** Duke, Harvard, MIT, Smith, Stanford. **Location:** in suburban area, 40 minutes from Seoul. **Campus:** 8 acres. **Library:** 20,000 volumes. **Facilities:** 3 buildings, 80 classrooms, auditorium, cafeteria, infirmary, 2 gymnasiums, playing field, 3 science labs, 3 computer labs, swimming pool.

*Once only fee

SONGTAN

INTERNATIONAL CHRISTIAN SCHOOL, SONGTAN

Street address: Jisan-dong 830-40, Songtan, Korea
Phone: (82)(333)641376 **Facsimile:** (82)(333)641377
E-mail: 75357.1402@compuserve.com
Mail: PO Box 36, Songtan, Korea 459-600
U.S. mail: Network of International Christian School, PO Box 18151, Memphis, TN 38181, U.S.A.
Superintendent: Ellis Caudill
Head administrator: Joe LeMire
Teaching staff: full-time, 20; total, 20
Nationalities of teaching staff: U.S., 18; other, 2; total, 20
Grade levels: preK – 12
Enrollment: total, 160
Nationalities of student body: U.S., 146; other, 14; total, 160
Capacity: total, 225
Teacher/student ratio: 1/8
Tuition (annual): preK, $1,822; K – 8, $3,522; 9 – 12, $4,005
Other fees (annual): registration, $88; busing, $732; ESL, $563
School year: August to June

Year founded: 1990. **Type of school:** coed, day, church-related, private nonprofit. **Sponsored by:** Network of International Christian Schools. **Accredited by:** Western, ACSI. **Regional organizations:** EARCOS, KORCOS, ACSI.

Curriculum/physical plant

Type: Christian/secular. **Languages taught:** Spanish. **Special curricular:** art, computer, music, spelling bee, field trips, outdoor education, science fair. **Extracurricular:** discipleship groups, variety of clubs. **Sports:** basketball, volleyball, soccer, cross-country. **Tests:** PSAT, SAT, Stanford, SLEP. **Library:** 6,000 volumes.

TAEJON

TAEJON CHRISTIAN INTERNATIONAL SCHOOL

Street address: 210-1 O Jung Dong, PO Box 310, Taejon, Korea 300-603
Phone: (82)(42)6333663 – 5 **Facsimile:** (82)(42)6315732
E-mail: administrator@tcis.kaist.ac.kr
Headmaster: Dr. Thomas J. Penland
Teaching staff: full-time, 30; part-time, 9; total, 39
Nationalities of teaching staff: U.S., 30; host, 5; other, 4; total, 39
Grade levels: preK – 12
Enrollment: preK – K, 26; 1 – 6, 82; 7 – 9, 70; 10 – 12, 69; total, 247
Nationalities of student body: U.S., 160; other, 87; total, 247
Teacher/student ratio: 1/6

Boarders: boys, 21; girls, 15 **Grades:** 7 – 12 **Program:** planned 7-day
Tuition (annual): preK, $2,940; K, $3,675; 1 – 6, $7,350; 7 – 12, $9,950
Other fees (annual): registration*, $290; boarding, $6,150
School year: August to June

Year founded: 1958. **Type of school:** coed, day, boarding, church-related. **Governed by:** appointed and elected board of trustees. **Sponsored by:** missions. **Accredited by:** Western. **Regional organizations:** EARCOS.

Curriculum/physical plant

Type: U.S. **Languages taught:** French, Korean. **Staff specialists:** counselor, nurse. **Special programs:** ESL, honors sections, independent study. **Special curricular:** art, chorus, band, physical education, computer instruction. **Extracurricular:** drama, gymnastics, choral and instrumental music, yearbook, newspaper, excursions/ expeditions, field trips. **Clubs:** Boy Scouts, Girl Scouts, Quill and Scroll, Youth for Christ, Tri M Music Honor Society. **Tests:** SSAT, PSAT, SAT, ACT, TOEFL, Stanford. **Graduates attending college:** 90%. **Graduates have attended:** Vanderbilt, Wheaton, U. of Illinois, Auburn, Oklahoma Baptist U. **Location:** on outskirts of Taejon. **Campus:** 9 acres. **Library:** 10,000 volumes. **Facilities:** 7 buildings, 20 classrooms, cafeteria, 4 tennis courts, gymnasium, playing field, science lab, computer lab, small auditorium, boys'/girls' dorm, limited busing system.

*Once only fee

TONGDUCHON

Indianhead School

Street address: 523-1, Saengyon 1-Dong, Tongduchon City, Korea 483-031
Phone: (82)(351)8682600–1 **Facsimile:** (82)(351)8682602
E-mail: indian@soback.kornet.nm.kr
U.S. mail: (no personal name) USAG UNIT # 15543, APO AP 96224-0453
President: Myungsin Park
Vice-president: Sung Kang, Ph.D.
Principal: Edmund Fitzgerald
Business manageer: Jeong Jin Park
Board member: Nina Kang
Teaching staff: full-time, 11; part-time, 5; total, 16
Nationalities of teaching staff: U.S., 6; host, 4; other, 6; total, 16
Grade levels: N – 12
Enrollment: total, 122
Nationalities of student body: U.S., 114; other, 8; total, 122
Teacher/student ratio: 1/9
Tuition (annual): N – preK, $1,330; K, $1,615; 1 – 6, $1,852; 7 – 12, $3,420
Other fees (annual): registration, $60; busing, $522; books, $50; computer, $30
School year: August to June

Year founded: 1979. **Type of school:** coed, day, private nonprofit. **Governed by:** school board. **Accredited by:** Western. **Regional organizations:** KORCOS, EARCOS.

Curriculum/physical plant

Type: U.S. **Languages taught:** Korean. **Special curricular:** art, chorus, physical education, computer instruction. **Extracurricular:** drama, dance, computers, yearbook, literary magazine, student council, field trips. **Sports:** basketball, soccer, volleyball. **Location:** rural setting on edge of city. **Campus:** 20 acres. **Library:** 8,000 volumes. **Facilities:** 20 buildings, 11 classrooms, auditorium, cafeteria, playing field, science lab, computer lab, language lab, air conditioning.

International Christian School, Tongduchon

Street address: Bosan dong 413-3, Tongduchon, Korea
Phone: (82)(351)628293 **Facsimile:** (82)(351)625829
E-mail: 75357.1421@compuserve.com
Mail: PO Box 13, Tongduchon, Korea 483-600
U.S. mail: (no personal name) 2nd Inf. Div. Supt. Grp. #15408, APO AP 96224-0309
Superintendent: Bonnie Roots
Head administrator: Dr. Ronald Elie
Teaching staff: full-time, 9; part-time, 1; total, 10
Nationalities of teaching staff: U.S., 10; total, 10
Grade levels: preK – 8
Enrollment: total, 120
Nationalities of student body: U.S., 120; total, 120
Capacity: total, 160
Teacher/student ratio: 1/13
Tuition (annual): preK, $1,425; K – 8, $1,852
Other fees (annual): registration, $70; busing, $525; ESL, $635
School year: August to June

Year founded: 1988. **Type of school:** coed, day, church-related, private nonprofit. **Sponsored by:** Network of International Christian Schools. **Accredited by:** Western, ACSI. **Regional organizations:** EARCOS, ACSI.

Curriculum/physical plant

Type: Christian/secular. **Languages taught:** English. **Special curricular:** art, physical education, computer, music, science fair, field day. **Extracurricular:** field trips, parent picnic, carnival, AWANA. **Tests:** PSAT, SAT, Stanford, SLEP. **Library:** 2,275 volumes.

UIJONGBU

International Christian School, Uijongbu

Street address: Kanung 1 dong, 677-14, Uijongbu, Korea
Phone: (82)(351)8723267 **Facsimile:** (82)(351)8721458
E-mail: 102232.1653@compuserve.com
Mail: PO Box 23, Uijongbu, Korea 480-600
U.S. mail: (no personal name) PSC 311, Box 44, APO AP 96258
Superintendent: Ellis Caudill
Head administrator: Phil Haliburton
Teaching staff: full-time, 19; total, 19
Nationalities of teaching staff: U.S., 17; other, 2; total, 19
Grade levels: preK – 12
Enrollment: total, 214
Nationalities of student body: U.S., 181; other, 33; total, 214
Capacity: total, 275
Teacher/student ratio: 1/11
Tuition (annual): preK, $1,675; K – 8, $3,343; 9 – 12, $3,825
Other fees (annual): registration, $87.50; busing, $1,012; ESL, $562.50
School year: August to June

Year founded: 1983. **Type of school:** coed, day, church-related, private nonprofit. **Sponsored by:** Network of International Christian Schools. **Accredited by:** Western, ACSI. **Regional organizations:** EARCOS, KORCOS, ACSI.

Curriculum/physical plant

Type: Christian/secular. **Languages taught:** Spanish. **Special curricular:** physical education, computer, music, ESL, science fair, spelling bee, outdoor education. **Extracurricular:** yearbook, tutoring. **Sports:** basketball, cross-country, soccer, girls' volleyball. **Tests:** PSAT, SAT, Stanford, SLEP. **Library:** 10,000 volumes.

KUWAIT

Region: Middle East
Size: 6,880 square miles
Population: 1,950,047
Capital: Kuwait City
Telephone code: 965
Currency: dinar
Language: Arabic

KUWAIT CITY

AL-BAYAN BILINGUAL SCHOOL

Phone: (965)5315125 **Facsimile:** (965)5332836 **E-mail:** bbs@ncc.moc.kw
Web: http://www.moc.kw/users/bbs
Mail: PO Box 24472, Safat 13105, Kuwait
Owner representative: May Al Essa
Director: Eamonn Hogan
Intermediate/high school principal: Ronald Brown
Elementary principal: Barbara Spedding
Head of library: Gordana Dimitrijevic, Ananda Padmanabhan
Teaching staff: full-time, 99; part-time, 5; total, 104
Nationalities of teaching staff: U.S., 23; U.K., 20; other, 61; total, 104
Grade levels: N – 12
Enrollment: N, 74; K1, 138; K2, 121; 1 – 4, 388; 5 – 8, 237; 9 – 12, 129; total, 1,087
Teacher/student ratio: 1/10
Tuition: N, 1,000**; K1, 1,100; K2, 1,200; 1 – 4, 1,850; 5 – 8, 1,950; 9 – 12, 2,100
School year: September to June

Year founded: 1977. **Type of school:** coed, day, private nonprofit. **Governed by:** school board. **Accredited by:** ECIS, New England, Kuwait Ministry of Education. **Regional organizations:** NESA.

Curriculum/physical plant

Type: U.S., national. **Languages of instruction:** English, Arabic. **Languages taught:** English, Arabic. **Staff specialists:** reading, computer, counselor, nurse, ESL, music. **Special curricular:** physical education, computer instruction. **Extracurricular:** drama, choral music, computers, yearbook, newspaper, excursions/expeditions. **Sports:** badminton, basketball, football, table tennis, volleyball. **Clubs:** science, pottery, cookery, painting, fabric printing. **Tests:** SAT, TOEFL, AP. **Location:** on 2 large, well-equipped sites: preschool and elementary in Jabriya, intermediate/high school in Hawalli; both suburbs of Kuwait City. **Libraries (2):** Jabriya: over 19,700 volumes; Hawalli: 12,000 volumes in Arabic and English. **Facilities:** Jabriya: 55 classrooms, infirmary, 2 gymnasiums, computer lab, canteen, air conditioning, 2 theaters, science labs, many courtyards and garden areas; Hawalli: 60 classrooms, gymnasium, theater, 6 science labs, 2 computer labs, canteen, infirmary.

**Kuwaiti dinar

The American International School – Kuwait

Street address: Block 11, Uhud Street, Salmiya, Kuwait
Phone: (965)5645083 – 7 **Facsimile:** (965)5645089
E-mail: raja@ncc.moc.kw **Web:** http://www.moc.kw/users/raja/aishom
Mail: PO Box 17464, Khaldiya 72455, Kuwait
Superintendent: Raja Abushakra
High school principal: Joanne Reykdal
Middle school principal: Noreen Hawley
Elementary principal: William Cattelle
Teaching staff: full-time, 110; total, 110
Nationalities of teaching staff: U.S., 67; U.K., 5; host, other, 38; total, 110
Grade levels: K – 12
Enrollment: K, 129; 1 – 4, 345; 5 – 8, 390; 9 – 12, 285; total, 1,149
Nationalities of student body: U.S., 71; U.K., 16; host, 618; other, 444; total, 1,149
Teacher/student ratio: 1/10
Tuition (annual): K1, $3,987; K2, $4,320; 1 – 4, $5,814; 5 – 8, $6,146; 9 – 12, $6,810
Other fees (annual): busing, $800
School year: September to June

Accredited by: Middle States. **Regional organizations:** AAIE, NESA, ECIS.

Curriculum/physical plant

Type: U.S., IB, AP. **Languages taught:** English, French, Arabic. **Extracurricular:** drama, photography, art, chess, ballet, judo, model building, music, Model UN, knowledge bowl, forensics. **Sports:** basketball, soccer, softball, table tennis, tennis, volleyball. **Graduates attending college:** 100%. **Graduates have attended:** Texas A & M, Boston U., New York U., John Hopkins U., Georgetown U. **Libraries (2):** CD-ROM, computerized card catalogs, internet facilities, AV center. **Facilities:** 90 classrooms, gymnasium, 6 science labs, 2 computer labs, photography lab, 3 music rooms, 3 art rooms, fully staffed health clinic, 800-seat multipurpose auditorium, volleyball, basketball, and tennis courts.

The American School of Kuwait

Street address: Block 7, Al-Muthanna Street and 4th Ring Road, Hawalli, Kuwait
Phone: (965)2664341/2655172 **Facsimile:** (965)2650438
E-mail: askkwt@kuwait.net
Web: http://www.kuwait.net/~ramu/index.html
Mail: PO Box 6735, Hawalli 32042, Kuwait
Superintendent: William J. Decker, Ed.D.
High school principal: John Wills, Ed.D.
Middle school principal: Andy Page-Smith
Elementary school principal: Ralph Friedly, Ed.D.
Business manager: Anwar Dhanani
Teaching staff: full-time, 116; part-time, 3; total, 119
Nationalities of teaching staff: U.S., 94; other, 25; total, 119

Grade levels: preK – 12
Enrollment: preK – 5, 550; 6 – 8, 300; 9 – 12, 420; total, 1,270
Nationalities of student body: U.S., 414; host, 496; other, 360; total, 1,270
Teacher/student ratio: 1/10
Tuition (annual): K1, $3,630; K2, $4,950; 1 – 5, $7,260; 6 – 8, $8,090; 9 – 12, $8,420
School year: late August through mid-June

Year founded: 1964. **Type of school:** coed, day, private nonprofit. **Governed by:** appointed board of directors. **Accredited by:** Middle States. **Regional organizations:** AAIE, ECIS, NESA.

Curriculum

Type: U.S., national (Arabic and Islamic studies), AP. **Languages taught:** English, French, Spanish, Arabic. **Staff specialists:** reading, computer, learning disabilities, nurse, art, ESL, physical education, guidance, science, instrumental music, vocal music, performing arts, staff development. **Special programs:** ESL, reading resource, learning disabilities, basic/remedial. **Special curricular:** art, chorus, physical education, computer instruction, yearbook, instrumental music, ASK television, journalism. **Extracurricular:** drama, computers, excursions/expeditions, field trips, choral and instrumental music, forensics, Model UN. **Sports:** badminton, basketball, gymnastics, soccer, softball, swimming, table tennis, tennis, track and field, volleyball, weight training. **Clubs:** computer, National Honor Society, photography, Spanish, student government. **Tests:** PSAT, SAT, ACT, TOEFL, AP, Iowa, TAP. **Graduates attending college:** 98%. **Graduates have attended:** Brown, U. of Chicago, Cornell, Harvard, U. of Pennsylvania.

Physical plant

Location: on large suburban campus. **Libraries (2):** 23,000 volumes, electronic data bases and card catalogs, CD-ROM, over 3,000 AV items, E-mail, internet. **Facilities:** 88 classrooms, 2 gymnasiums, 10 science labs, 4 computer labs, multimedia studio, indoor semi-olympic swimming pool, 800-seat multipurpose auditorium, outdoor performance stage, 4 music labs, 3 outdoor play areas.

Fawzia Sultan International School

Street address: Block 11, Street 3, House 107, Jabriya, Kuwait
Phone: (965)5341403–4 **Facsimile:** (965)5341405 **E-mail:** roncb123@aol.com
Mail: PO Box 719, Safat 13008, Kuwait
Director: (to be announced)
Teaching staff: full-time, 23; part-time, 2; total, 25
Nationalities of teaching staff: U.S., 9; U.K., 1; host, 3; other, 12; total, 25
Grade levels: preK – 13 (ages 3 – 15)
Enrollment: N – K, 14; 1 – 6, 18; 7 – 9, 10; 10 – 12, 4; 13, 2; total, 48
Nationalities of student body: U.S., 5; U.K., 14; host, 16; other, 13; total, 48
Teacher/student ratio: 1/3
Tuition (annual): N – K, $16,000; 1 – 13, $21,000 (U.S. Embassy and DoDDS eligible students pay no fees; many scholarships available)
School year: September to June

Year founded: 1993. **Type of school:** coed, day, private nonprofit, for children with learning disabilities. **Governed by:** private foundation. Approved for all services by the U.S. Foreign Service and DoDDS.

Curriculum

Type: U.S. **Languages taught:** English, Arabic. **Staff specialists:** reading, math, computer, psychologist, learning disabilities, speech therapists, physical therapist. **Special programs:** ESL, independent study, remedial. **Special curricular:** art, physical education, computer instruction. **Extracurricular:** computers, excursions/expeditions, field trips. **Clubs:** computer, art, martial arts. **Location:** in Kuwait City. **Facilities:** 1 building, 12 classrooms, covered play area, science lab, computer lab, access to gymnasium and library, air conditioning. The school offers an extensive range of specialized services for children of average or higher levels of intelligence with learning difficulties, including a comprehensive early intervention program for preschool children. In addition to operating a regular international school and the special education facility, it also serves as a teacher specialist training site.

The Universal American School

Street address: Area 11, Al Taween Street, Salwa, Kuwait
Phone: (965)5615857/5620297 **Facsimile:** (965)5625343
E-mail: elmo@ncc.moc.kw
Mail: PO Box 17035, 72451 Khaldiya, Kuwait
Director: Nora Al Ghanim
Assistant director/high school principal: Dr. Dale R. Koch
Middle school principal: Wayne Hopewell
Elementary principal: Mark Fox
Business manager: Mohammed Rashwan
Teaching staff: full-time, 70; total, 70
Grade levels: N – 12
Enrollment: N – K, 140; 1 – 5, 335; 6 – 7, 150; 8 – 12, 225; total, 850
Teacher/student ratio: 1/15
Tuition (annual): N, 800**; K, 1,240; 1 – 4, 1,660; 5 – 8, 1,760; 9 – 12, 1,860
Other fees (annual): registration, 150**; busing, 220
School year: August to June

Type of school: coed, day, private nonprofit. **Accredited by:** New England, ECIS. **Regional organizations:** ECIS, NESA, KFSAC, ISAC.

Curriculum/physical plant

Type: U.S., AP. **Languages taught:** English, French, Spanish, Arabic, Japanese. **Special programs:** ESL, special needs. **Extracurricular:** drama, band, Model UN, community service. **Sports:** basketball, soccer, volleyball, track and field, racquet sports. **Tests:** PSAT, ACT, TOEFL, SAT I/II, PLAN, standardized achievement tests. **Graduates attending college:** 90%. **Location:** in Salwa, a suburb of Kuwait City. **Library:** 14,000 volumes. **Facilities:** 65 classrooms, auditorium, science labs, computer labs, art suites, music suites, gymnasium, playground, administrative suites.

**Kuwaiti dinar

KYRGYZSTAN

Region: Central Asia
Size: 76,600 square miles
Population: 4,529,648
Capital: Bishkek
Telephone code: 7
Currency: som
Languages: Krygyz, Russian

BISHKEK

Bishkek International School

Phone: (7)(3312)263436 **E-mail:** admiral@qsibis.bishkek.su
U.S. mail: c/o American Embassy Bishkek, Dept. of State, Washington, DC 20521-7040
Director: Frank Laurette
Teaching staff: full-time, 2; part-time, 3; total, 5
Nationalities of teaching staff: U.S., 2; other, 3; total, 5
Grade levels: N – 10
Enrollment: N, 1; K, 3; 1 – 6, 9; 7 – 9, 2; 10 – 12, 1; total, 16
Capacity: total, 75
Teacher/student ratio: 1/8
Tuition (annual): N – 5, $7,900; 6 – 10, $10,200
Other fees: registration*, $100; capital levy, $4,000 deposit or $1,600/year fee
School year: September to June

Year founded: 1994. **Type of school:** coed, day, private nonprofit. **Governed by:** appointed board of directors. **Sponsored by:** Quality Schools International. **Regional organizations:** CEESA.

Curriculum/physical plant

Type: U.S. **Special programs:** ESL. **Special curricular:** art, physical education, computer instruction. **Extracurricular:** drama, excursions/expeditions, field trips. **Location:** in Bishkek, part of local school. **Campus:** one wing in a building shared with Kyrgyzstan kindergarten, with own separate playground area.

*Once only fee

LAOS

Region: Southeast Asia
Size: 91,429 square miles
Population: 4,975,772
Capital: Vientiane
Telephone code: 856
Currency: kip
Languages: French, English, Lao

VIENTIANE

VIENTIANE INTERNATIONAL SCHOOL

Street address: Sapanthong Tai, Vientiane, Lao People's Democratic Republic
Phone: (856)(21)312818 **Facsimile:** (856)(21)315008
E-mail: joes@loxinfo.co.th
Mail: PO Box 3180, Vientiane, Laos
Director: F. Joseph Stucker
Teaching staff: full-time, 12; total, 12
Nationalities of teaching staff: U.S., 9; Australia, 3; total, 12
Grade levels: preschool – 9
Enrollment: total, 174
Nationalities of student body: U.S., 19; host, 20; other, 135; total, 174
Capacity: preS, 20; K, 20; 1 – 9, 200; total, 240
Teacher/student ratio: 1/13
Tuition (annual): preS, $2,900; K, $3,990; 1 – 5, $5,610; 6 – 9, $5,900
Other fees (annual): capital levy*, $1,000; ESL, $1,000
School year: late August through mid-June

Year founded: 1974. **Type of school:** coed, private nonprofit. **Governed by:** elected school board. **Regional organizations:** EARCOS.

Curriculum/physical plant

Type: international. **Languages taught:** French. **Special programs:** ESL. **Special curricular:** art, physical education, music. **Extracurricular:** drama, choral music, computers, field trips, basketball, soccer. **Facilities:** 4 buildings, 12 classrooms, playing fields, library, covered eating area, air conditioning.

*Once only fee

LATVIA

Region: Eastern Europe
Size: 24,946 square miles
Population: 2,468,982
Capital: Riga
Telephone code: 371
Currency: lat
Languages: Latvian, Lithuanian, Russian

JURMALA

THE INTERNATIONAL SCHOOL OF LATVIA

Street address: Viestura iela 6A, Jurmala 2010, Latvia
Phone: (371)7892741 **Facsimile:** (371)7222709 **E-mail:** isl@com.latnet.lv
Chief school officer: Sally A. Hadden
Business manager: Astra Rozenberga
Teaching staff: full-time, 14; total, 14
Nationalities of teaching staff: U.S., 5; host, 2; other, 7; total, 14
Grade levels: preK – 12
Enrollment: preK, 20; K, 15; 1 – 6, 35; 7 – 9, 22; 10 – 12, 18; total, 110
Nationalities of student body: U.S., 15; U.K., 16; host, 7; other, 72; total, 110
Capacity: preK, 30; K, 15; 1 – 6, 90; 7 – 9, 45; 10 – 12, 45; total, 225
Tuition (annual): preK, $3,000; K – 12, $8,400
Other fees: registration*, $1,000; busing, $100/month
School year: August to June

Year founded: 1992. **Type of school:** coed, day, private nonprofit. **Governed by:** parental board of directors.

Curriculum/physical plant

Type: U.S., international. **Languages taught:** French, German. **Special programs:** ESL. **Special curricular:** art, physical education, computer instruction. **Extracurricular:** newspaper. **Facilities:** 25 classrooms, gymnasium, swimming pool, auditorium, lecture hall, outside track, fenced elementary playground. **Location:** shared facility with a Latvian college in Murmala along the Lielupe River in Bulduri, a 20-minute drive from Riga.

*Once only fee

LEBANON

Region: Middle East
Size: 3,950 square miles
Population: 3,776,317
Capital: Beirut
Telephone code: 961
Currency: pound
Languages: Arabic, French

BEIRUT

American Community School at Beirut

Street address: Rue de Paris, Beirut, Lebanon
Phone: (961)(1)367214/366137 **Facsimile:** (961)(1)366050
E-mail: acs@acs.edu.lb
Mail: PO Box 8129, Beirut, Lebanon
U.S. mail: ACS Beirut, c/o Walter Prosser, 850 Third Avenue, 18th floor, New York, NY 10022, U.S.A.
U.S. facsimile: (1)(212)5837622
Head of school: Catherine C. Bashshur
High school principal: Manahel B. Kobeissi
Middle school principal: Richard Bowden
Elementary principal: Ebba El Hage
Business manager: Jorgen Hoeven
Teaching staff: full-time, 130; part-time, 13; total, 143
Nationalities of teaching staff: U.S., 26; host, 52; other, 65; total, 143
Grade levels: N – 12
Enrollment: total, 1,002
Nationalities of student body: U.S., 223; host, 531; other, 248; total, 1002
Teacher/student ratio: 1/7
Tuition (annual): $4,226 – 5,937
Other fees (annual): registration, 750,000**; expansion, $1,000
School year: September to June

Year founded: 1905. **Type of school:** coed, day, private nonprofit. **Governed by:** self-perpetuating board of trustees. **Sponsored by:** American U. of Beirut, Presbyterian Church USA. **Licensed by:** Lebanese government. **Accredited by:** Middle States. **Regional organizations:** AAIE, NESA.

Curriculum

Type: U.S., Lebanese Baccalaureate, IB, AP. **Languages taught:** French, Arabic. **Staff specialists:** computer, counselor. **Special programs:** correspondence, remedial. **Special curricular:** art, chorus, physical education, computer instruction, band. **Extracurricular:** drama, gymnastics, computers, yearbook, newspaper, excursions/expeditions, field trips, music. **Sports:** basketball, soccer, softball, tennis, track and field, volleyball, fencing, archery. **Clubs:** social service, aerobics, student activities. **Tests:** PSAT, SAT, TOEFL, AP. **Graduates attending college:** 100%. **Graduates have attended:** American U. of Beirut, Lebanese American U., Queen's U., McGill U., Emerson College.

Physical plant

Location: in Beirut, next to American U. of Beirut, one block from the Mediterranean. **Campus:** 1,600 square meters. **Libraries (2):** 40,000 volumes. **Facilities:** 4 buildings, 65 classrooms, 2 auditoriums, cafeteria, 2 infirmaries, covered play area, 2 tennis courts, gymnasium, 3 playing fields, 4 science labs, 2 computer labs.

**Lebanese pound (lira)

INTERNATIONAL COLLEGE

Phone: (961)(1)867207/349861 **Facsimile:** (961)(1)867207/(3)647585
E-mail: proffice@cyberia.net.lb
Mail: Bliss Street, PO Box 11-0236, Beirut, Lebanon
President: Gerrit Keator
Deputy president: Edmond Tohme
VP for development, public relations, and alumni affairs: Nabil Rahhal
Directors: M. Beidas, W. Hoss, Y. Kurfali, L. Khayr, R. Khoury, M. Mourani
Teaching staff: full-time, 252; part-time, 27; total, 279
Nationalities of teaching staff: host, 265; other, 14; total, 279
Grade levels: preK – 13
Enrollment: Ras Beirut campus: preK – K, 454; 1 – 5, 779; 6 – 9, 665; 10 – 13, 686; total, 2,584
Ain Aar campus: preK – K, 220; 1 – 6, 431; 7 – 11, 196; total, 847
Teacher/student ratio: 1/12
Tuition (annual): $3,170
Other fees (annual): registration, 600,000** (deductible from fees); busing, 1,000,000; development*, $1,000
School year: late September through June

Year founded: 1891. **Type of school:** coed, day. **Governed by:** board of trustees.

Curriculum/physical plant

Type: U.S., national, French Baccalaureate. **Languages taught:** French, Arabic. **Staff specialists:** counselor, nurse. **Special programs:** remedial. **Special curricular:** art, physical education, computer instruction. **Extracurricular:** drama, gymnastics, computers, yearbook, photography. **Sports:** basketball, soccer, volleyball. **Organizations:** social service, modeling, chess, backgammon, stamp, archery, woodwork, International College Alumni Association. **Tests:** SAT, TOEFL, Scientific Quantitative. **Graduates attending college:** 100%. **Graduates have attended:** American U. of Beirut, Georgia Tech, Yale, Stanford, MIT. **Location:** in city and neighboring Ain Aar. **Campuses (2):** 38,000 square meters (Ras Beirut); 13,000 square meters (Ain Aar). **Library:** 17,000 volumes. **Facilities:** 6 buildings, 108 classrooms, 2 infirmaries, 2 playing fields, 3 science labs, computer lab, AV equipment, covered play areas.

*Once only fee **Lebanese pound (lira)

LESOTHO

Region: Africa
Size: 11,720 square miles
Population: 1,970,781
Capital: Maseru
Telephone code: 266
Currency: loti
Languages: English, Sesotho

MASERU

American International School of Lesotho

Street address: 14 United Nations Road, Old Europa, Maseru 100, Lesotho
Phone: (266)322987/311963 **Facsimile:** (266)311963
E-mail: aisl@lesoff.co.za
Mail: PO Box 333, Maseru 100, Lesotho
U.S. mail: Maseru, Dept. of State, Washington, DC 20521-2340
Director: William Vodarski
Teaching staff: full-time, 4; part-time, 3; total, 7
Nationalities of teaching staff: U.S., 4; other, 3; total, 7
Grade levels: K – 8
Enrollment: K, 4; 1 – 8, 38; total, 42
Nationalities of student body: U.S., 5; U.K., 5; host, 9; other, 23; total, 42
Teacher/student ratio: 1/15
Tuition (annual): $8,000
Other fees: registration*, $65
School year: August to June

Year founded: 1991. **Type of school:** coed, day, private nonprofit. **Governed by:** appointed and elected 7-member school board. **Regional organizations:** AISA.

Curriculum/physical plant

Type: U.S. **Staff specialists:** computer, art, music. **Special curricular:** art, physical education, computer instruction, music. **Extracurricular:** stamp club, arts & crafts. **Location:** in residential neighborhood. **Campus:** 2 acres. **Facilities:** 4 buildings, 6 classrooms, library, computer labs, art room, assembly/film room.

*Once only fee

Machabeng College/International School of Lesotho†

Street address: Tonakholo Road, Maseru, Lesotho
Phone: (266)313224 **Facsimile:** (266)316109
Mail: PO Box 1570, Maseru 100, Lesotho
Headmaster: Leif Berntsen
Deputy head: Denise Frost
Bursar: Mapulane Mahloka
Teaching staff: full-time, 33; part-time, 4; total, 37

Nationalities of teaching staff: U.K., 15; host, 6; other, 16; total, 37
Grade levels: 6 – 12
Enrollment: 6, 44; 7 – 9, 149; 10 – 12, 142; total, 335
Nationalities of student body: U.S., 1; U.K., 9; host, 228; other, 97; total, 335
Teacher/student ratio: 1/10
Boarders: boys, 20; girls, 20 **Grades:** 6 – 12 **Program:** planned 5-day
Tuition (annual): $8,550 (fee paid by a diplomatic mission, donor agency, government, etc.)
Other fees (annual): registration*, 410**; boarding, 18,000; book deposit, 480
School year: September to July

Year founded: 1977. **Type of school:** coed, day, boarding. **Governed by:** appointed and elected board of governors. **Sponsored by:** Lesotho government. **Accredited by:** Middle States, ECIS. **Regional organizations:** ECIS, AISA.

Curriculum

Type: U.K., IB. **Languages taught:** English, French, Sesotho (other languages/IB only). **Staff specialists:** math, computer, counselor, nurse, languages, history, geography, economics, business and organization, chemistry, physics, biology, English literature, physical education, art & design, performing arts, technology. **Special curricular:** art, physical education, computer instruction. **Extracurricular:** drama, gymnastics, dance, computers, yearbook, newspaper, photography, excursions/expeditions, field trips. **Sports:** athletics, basketball, football, netball, softball, swimming, table tennis, volleyball. **Clubs:** chess, debating, bird-watching, library, scripture union. **Tests:** SAT, ACT, IB, IGCSE. **Graduates attending college:** 90%. **Graduates have attended:** Cornell, London School of Economics, Imperial College London, Rhodes U., Royal College Surgeons (Dublin).

Physical plant

Location: in Maseru. **Campus:** 3 hectares. **Library:** 15,000 volumes. **Facilities:** 6 buildings, 20 classrooms, auditorium, cafeteria, infirmary, gymnasium, playing field, 4 science labs, computer lab, boarding house with kitchen and dining facilities.

*Once only fee **Lesotho maloti †formerly Machabeng High School

Maseru English Medium Preparatory School

Street address: Caldwell Road, Maseru West, Maseru, Lesotho
Phone/facsimile: (266)312276
Mail: PO Box 34, Maseru 100, Lesotho
Principal: Huw C. Price
Teaching staff: full-time, 23; part-time, 2; total, 25
Nationalities of teaching staff: U.S., 2; U.K., 4; host, 5; other, 14; total, 25
Grade levels: reception – grade 6
Enrollment: total, 280
Teacher/student ratio: 1/12
Tuition, fully aided (annual): $3,800
Other fees (annual): registration*, $50; books, $25
School year: September to July

Year founded: 1891. **Type of school:** coed, day, private nonprofit. **Governed by:** elected management committee. **Regional organizations:** AISA.

Curriculum/physical plant

Type: U.K., U.S. **Languages taught:** English, French, Sesotho. **Staff specialists:** reading, learning disabilities, art, music, physical education, French, Sesotho, science. **Special programs:** ESL, remedial. **Extracurricular:** drama, gymnastics, choral and instrumental music, excursions/expeditions. **Sports:** football, softball, tennis, track and field. **Clubs:** drama, scripture union, needlework, public speaking, choir, science. **Location:** in suburban area, 2 kilometers from Maseru. **Campus:** 3 hectares. **Library:** over 10,000 volumes. **Facilities:** 27 classrooms, auditorium, 2 tennis courts, gymnasium, playing field, science lab, computer room (IBMs).

*Once only fee

LIBYA

Region: North Africa
Size: 678,400 square miles
Population: 5,445,436
Capital: Tripoli
Telephone code: 218
Currency: dinar
Language: Arabic, Italian, English

TRIPOLI

International School of the Martyrs

Phone: (218)(21)70094 **Facsimile:** (218)(21)606800
Mail: PO Box 860, Tripoli, Libya
Superintendent: Ahmed S. Fituri, Ph.D.
Principal: Christina Nuri
Vice principal (international program): Jacqueline Al-Azawi
Financial manager: Ahmed Shabel
Teaching staff: full-time, 38; part-time, 18; total, 56
Nationalities of teaching staff: U.S., 2; U.K., 3; host, 10; other, 41; total, 56
Grade levels: preK – 12
Enrollment: total, 426
Teacher/student ratio: 1/10
Tuition (annual): preK – K, 1,140**; 1 – 12, 2,182
School year: September through June

Year founded: 1958. **Type of school:** coed, day. Sponsored by: Ministry of Education.

Curriculum/physical plant

Type: international, Irish Leaving Certificate. **Languages taught:** French, Arabic. **Staff specialists:** computer, nurse, art, music, physical education, resource. **Special programs:** remedial, EFL, Irish Leaving Certificate, counseling. **Extracurricular:** yearbook, newspaper, field trips, choir, band. **Sports:** basketball, soccer, softball, tennis, volleyball, floor hockey. **Location:** 3.5 kilometers from city center. **Campus:** 5 acres. **Library:** 14,000 volumes. **Facilities:** 11 buildings, 47 classrooms, auditorium, infirmary, 2 tennis courts, gymnasium, 2 playing fields, 3 science labs, computer lab, playground.

**Libyan dinar

LITHUANIA

Region: Europe
Size: 25,213 square miles
Population: 3,646,041
Capital: Vilnius

Telephone code: 370
Currency: litas
Languages: Lithuanian, Polish, Russian

VILNIUS

American International School of Vilnius

Street address: Subaciaus gatve 41, Darzelis 87, 2014 Vilnius, Lithuania
Phone: (370)(2)221031 **Facsimile:** (370)6706084/2221031
E-mail: aisv@post.omnitel.net **Web:** http://www.usis.lt
Mail: c/o U.S. Embassy, Akmenu g. 6, 2600 Vilnius, Lithuania
U.S. mail: c/o U.S. Embassy, PSC 78 Box V, APO AE 09723
Director: Mark Hansen
Business manager: Indre Melynyte
Teaching staff: full-time, 3; part-time, 3; total, 6
Nationalities of teaching staff: U.S., 4; host, 1; other, 1; total, 6
Grade levels: preK – 8
Enrollment: preK, 7; K, 4; 1 – 6, 19; 7 – 8, 2; total, 32
Nationalities of student body: U.S., 10; host, 4; other, 18; total, 32
Teacher/student ratio: 1/8
Tuition (annual): preK, $2,400; K – 8, $8,600
Other fees (annual): registration*, $100; capital levy, $500
School year: September to mid-June

Year founded: 1993. **Type of school:** coed, day, private nonprofit. **Governed by:** school board. **Regional organizations:** CEESA, ECIS.

Curriculum/physical plant

Type: U.S. **Languages taught:** French. **Special programs:** ESL, high school correspondence. **Special curricular:** art, physical education. **Extracurricular:** yearbook, newspaper, field trips, music, art, karate. **Location:** on a hill just outside the Old Town of Vilnius. **Facilities:** 1 building, 4 classrooms, multipurpose room, off-campus gymnasium.

*Once only fee

LUXEMBOURG

Region: Europe
Size: 999 square miles
Population: 415,870
Capital: Luxembourg
Telephone code: 352
Currency: Luxembourg franc
Languages: French, German, Luxembourgisch

LUXEMBOURG

American International School of Luxembourg

Street address: 188 ave. de la Faïencerie, L-1511 Luxembourg, Luxembourg
Phone: (352)470020 **Facsimile:** (352)460924 **E-mail:** gerald.shields@ci.educ.lu
Web: http://www.restena.lu/aisl/aisl.html
Director: Gerald Shields
Upper school principal: Nicki Crush
Lower school principal: Conal Atkins
Teaching staff: full-time, 53; part-time, 13; total, 66
Nationalities of teaching staff: U.S., 29; U.K., 16; host, 1; other, 20; total, 66
Grade levels: preschool – 12
Enrollment: preS – K, 75; 1 – 6, 201; 7 – 9, 89; 10 – 12, 60; total, 425
Nationalities of student body: U.S., 119; U.K., 52; host, 5; other, 249; total, 425
Teacher/student ratio: 1/9
Tuition (annual): preS – 6, 392,000**; 7 – 8, 515,000; 9 – 11, 525,000; 12, 541,000
Other fees: registration*, 40,000**
School year: September to June

Year founded: 1963. **Type of school:** coed, day, private nonprofit. **Governed by:** appointed and elected board of directors. **Sponsored by:** American International School Association. **Accredited by:** Middle States, ECIS. **Regional organizations:** ECIS.

Curriculum/physical plant

Type: U.S., IB. **Languages taught:** French, German. **Staff specialists:** reading, computer, speech/hearing, counselor, physical education. **Special programs:** ESL, Swedish. **Special curricular:** art, chorus, band, physical education, computer instruction. **Extracurricular:** drama, choral and instrumental music, yearbook, excursions/expeditions, field trips. **Sports:** basketball, soccer, swimming, track and field, volleyball. **Organizations:** National Honor Society, National Junior Honor Society, student council. **Tests:** PSAT, SAT, TOEFL, IB. **Graduates attending college:** 85%. **Graduates have attended:** Yale, Tufts, Dartmouth, Harvard, Smith. **Location:** on outskirts of city. **Campus:** 10 acres. **Libraries:** 15,000 volumes. **Facilities:** 3 buildings, 32 classrooms, auditorium, gymnasium, playing field, 3 science labs, 2 computer labs, AV room, band room.

*Once only fee **Luxembourg franc

MACAU

Region: East Asia
Size: 6 square miles
Population: 497,000
Capital: Macau
Telephone code: 853
Currency: Hong Kong dollar
Languages: Chinese, English, Portuguese

MACAU

School of the Nations, Macau

Street address: Rua Luis G. Gomes, 136 Edificio Lei San, 4 Andar, Macau (via Hong Kong), Macau
Phone: (853)701759 **Facsimile:** (853)701724 **E-mail:** sonmacau@macau.net
Director: Alan Fryback
Teaching staff: full-time, 40; total, 40
Nationalities of teaching staff: U.S., 4; other, 36; total, 40
Grade levels: preK – 12
Enrollment: preK, 56; K, 36; 1 – 6, 240; 7 – 12, 150; total, 482
Teacher/student ratio: 1/12
Tuition (annual): 1 – 6, 24,200**; 7 – 12, 29,600
School year: September to June

Year founded: 1988. **Type of school:** coed, day, private nonprofit. **Governed by:** Badi foundation. **Accredited by:** government of Macau.

Curriculum

Type: international. **Languages taught:** Chinese (Mandarin). **Special programs:** ESL, remedial. **Extracurricular:** drama, gymnastics, dance, instrumental music, newspaper, field trips. **Clubs:** chess, stamp. **Tests:** IGCSE.

**Hong Kong dollar

MACEDONIA

Region: Southeast Europe
Size: 9,928 square miles
Population: 2,104,035
Capital: Skopje
Telephone code: 389
Currency: denar
Languages: Macedonian, Albanian, Turkish, Serbo-Croatian

SKOPJE

AMERICAN SCHOOL, MACEDONIA

Street address: Nikola Parapunov BB, Makotex Complex, Karpos IV, Skopje 01000, FYRO Macedonia
Phone/facsimile: (389)(91)363265 **E-mail:** amschool@guest.soros.org.mk
U.S. mail: c/o Mike Bujko, 1932 Talmadge Street, Los Angeles, CA 30027, U.S.A.
Principal: Patrick Pellegrino
Superintendent: Mike Bujko
Teaching staff: full-time, 6; part-time, 10; total, 16
Nationalities of teaching staff: U.S., 4; host, 10; other, 2; total, 16
Grade levels: K – 12
Enrollment: K, 5; 1 – 6, 10; 7 – 9, 30; 10 – 12, 55; total, 100
Nationalities of student body: U.S., 10; host, 70; other, 20; total, 100
Teacher/student ratio: 1/9
Tuition (annual): K – 6, $4,500; 7 – 12, $4,000
School year: August to June

Year founded: 1994. **Type of school:** coed, day, private nonprofit. **Governed by:** school board. **Sponsored by:** parents. **Accredited by:** Northwestern.

Curriculum/physical plant

Type: U.S. **Languages taught:** French, Macedonian. **Staff specialists:** computer, counselor. **Special programs:** ESL, honors sections, independent study. **Special curricular:** art, physical education, computer instruction. **Extracurricular:** drama, dance, computers, yearbook, excursions/expeditions, field trips, basketball. **Graduates attending college:** 100%. **Graduates have attended:** U. of Malta, American College of High Studies, Greece, U. of Central Florida, U. of Florida, U. of Nice. **Location:** in controlled-access business park in Skopje. **Campus:** .5 acres. **Library:** 1,500 volumes. **Facilities:** 1 building, 7 classrooms, gymnasium, computer lab.

QSI International School of Skopje

Phone: (389)(91)361180 **Facsimile:** (389)(91)362250
E-mail: qsi.sk@lotus.mpt.com.mk
U.S. mail: c/o American Embassy—Skopje, Dept. of State, Washington, DC 20521-7121
Director: Jean Lowe
Teaching staff: full-time, 2; part-time, 2; total, 4
Nationalities of teaching staff: U.S., 2; host, 2; total, 4
Grade levels: K – 8
Enrollment: K, 1; 1 – 6, 2; 7 – 8, 1; total, 4
Capacity: K, 2; 1 – 6, 8; 7 – 8, 2; total, 12
Tuition (annual): K, $6,900; 1 – 8, $9,200
Other fees: registration, $100; capital levy, $4,000 deposit or $1,600/year fee
School year: September to June

Year founded: 1996. **Type of school:** coed, day, private nonprofit. **Governed by:** appointed board of directors. **Sponsored by:** Quality Schools International. **Regional organizations:** CEESA.

Curriculum/physical plant

Type: U.S. **Special programs:** ESL. **Location:** in a suburb of Skopje, adjacent to an elementary school. **Facilities:** 1 building, 2 classrooms, computer lab, library.

*Once only fee

MADAGASCAR

Region: Africa (Indian Ocean)
Size: 226,658 square miles
Population: 13,670,507
Capital: Antananarivo
Telephone code: 261
Currency: franc
Languages: Malagasy, French

ANTANANARIVO

American School of Antananarivo

Street address: Ivandry, Antananarivo 101, Madagascar
Phone: (261)(2)42039 **Facsimile:** (261)(2)34539 **E-mail:** asamad@dts.mg
Mail: BP 1717, Antananarivo 101, Madagascar
U.S. mail: Dept. of State–Antananarivo, Washington, DC 20521-2040
Director: Gerald Craig
Teaching staff: full-time, 11; part-time, 4; total, 15
Nationalities of teaching staff: U.S., 8; U.K., 1; host, 1; other, 5; total, 15
Grade levels: preK – 9
Enrollment: K – 4, 41; 5 – 9, 34; total, 75
Nationalities of student body: U.S., 43; host, 5; other, 27; total, 75
Capacity: preK, 14; K – 4, 50; 5 – 9, 30; total, 94
Teacher/student ratio: 1/7

Tuition (annual): preK, $3,000; K – 4, $9,200; 5 – 9, $9,900
Other fees (annual): registration, $250; capital levy*, $1,000
School year: September to June

Year founded: 1969. **Type of school:** coed, day, private nonprofit. **Governed by:** elected board of directors. **Sponsored by:** U.S. Embassy. **Accredited by:** Middle States. **Regional organizations:** AISA.

Curriculum/physical plant

Type: U.S. **Languages taught:** French. **Special programs:** ESL. **Special curricular:** art, physical education, computer instruction, music. **Extracurricular:** drama, choral music, computers, newspaper, field trips. **Sports:** baseball, basketball, swimming, track and field, volleyball. **Tests:** Iowa. **Location:** in pleasant suburban area, 5 miles from Antananarivo. **Library:** 3,250 volumes. **Facilities:** 10 buildings, 12 classrooms, playing field, computer lab, air conditioning.

*Once only fee

MALAWI

Region: Southeast Africa
Size: 45,747 square miles
Population: 9,452,84
Capital: Lilongwe
Telephone code: 265
Currency: kwacha
Languages: English, Chichewa

LILONGWE

Bishop Mackenzie International Schools

Phone: (265)744817/740412 **Facsimile:** (265)742001/744563/744674
E-mail: bmiss@unima.wn.apc.org
Mail: PO Box 102, Lilongwe, Malawi
Acting secondary head: Robert Stuart
Primary school head: Robert Tucker
Teaching staff: full-time, 50; part-time, 3; total, 53
Grade levels: K – 6 (primary); 7 – 11 (secondary)
Enrollment: total, 640
Nationalities of student body: U.S., 44; host, 190; other, 406; total, 640
Teacher/student ratio: 1/13
Tuition (annual, 1996–97 figures): K – 6, $1,500; 7 – 11, $3,000
School year: September to July

Year founded: 1944. **Type of school:** coed, day, private nonprofit, nonreligious. **Governed by:** appointed and elected board of governors. **Accredited by:** Malawi government. **Regional organizations:** ECIS.

Curriculum/physical plant

Type: U.K., GCSE in upper school. **Staff specialists:** computer, art, music, physical education. **Special programs:** ESL. **Special curricular:** art, chorus, physical education, swimming, excursions, field trips, Brownies, Scouts, Cubs. **Location:** in suburban area, 2 kilometers from Lilongwe city. **Campus:** 25 acres. **Facilities:** 20 buildings, 21 classrooms, 2 tennis courts, 3 playing fields, 3 science labs, 2 computer labs, swimming pool, home economics room.

MALAYSIA

Region: Southeast Asia
Size: 127,584 square miles
Population: 19,962,893
Capital: Kuala Lumpur
Telephone code: 60
Currency: ringgit
Languages: Malay, English, Chinese, Indian languages

KUALA LUMPUR

Garden International School

Street address: No. 16 Jalan 1/61A, off Jalan Bukit Kiara, PO Box 13056, 50798 Kuala Lumpur, Malaysia
Phone: (60)(3)6518988 **Facsimile:** (60)(3)6512468/6515688
Principal: Murray Parkes
Teaching staff: full-time, 170; total, 170
Nationalities of teaching staff: U.K., 50; host, 100; other, 20; total, 170
Grade levels: K, P1 – P6, S1 – S5
Enrollment: K, 250; P1 – P6, 690; S1 – S5, 500; total, 1,440
Teacher/student ratio: 1/13
Tuition (annual): K, $2,500; P1 – P6, $9,000 – 10,500; S1 – S5, $12,000 – 13,500
Other fees: busing, approximately $380 per term
School year: September to July

Year founded: 1951. **Type of school:** coed, day, proprietary.

Curriculum/physical plant

Type: U.K. **Languages taught:** French, Malay. **Staff specialists:** reading, math, computer, nurse. **Extracurricular:** drama, gymnastics, yearbook, newspaper, excursions/expeditions, field trips, sports. **Tests:** O-level GCE (5th form/grade 11). **Graduates attending college:** 85%. **Facilities:** cafeteria, gymnasium, playing field, science lab, hall, multi-purpose hard court, design technology lab, food technology lab, music and art room, networked computer lab, air conditioning.

The International School of Kuala Lumpur

Street address: Jalan Kerja Ayer Lama, 68000 Ampang, Malaysia
Phone: (60)(3)4560522 **Facsimile:** (60)(3)4579044 **E-mail:** iskl@iskl.po.my
Mail: PO Box 12645, 50784 Kuala Lumpur, Malaysia
Headmaster: Barry Farnham, Ed.D.
High school principal: George H. Robinson, Ed.D.
Middle school principal: Dennis Larkin, Ed.D.
Elementary School Principal: Lory Thiessen
Business manager: Dixie Wai
Teaching staff: full-time, 175; part-time, 5; total, 180
Nationalities of teaching staff: U.S., 133; U.K., 11; host, 7; other, 29; total, 180
Grade levels: preK – 12
Enrollment: preK, 25; K, 60; 1 – 5, 554; 6 – 8, 416; 9 – 12, 590; total, 1,645
Nationalities of student body: U.S., 403; U.K., 65; host, 110; other, 1,067; total, 1,645
Teacher/student ratio: 1/9
Tuition (annual): preK, $4,600; K – 5, $7,040; 6 – 8, $7,920; 9 – 12, $8,800
Other fees (annual): registration*, $4,000; busing, $277 – 510; reenrollment, $400
School year: August to June

Year founded: 1965. **Type of school:** coed, day, private nonprofit. **Governed by:** elected board of directors. **Accredited by:** Western. **Regional organizations:** AAIE, EARCOS, ECIS.

Curriculum

Type: U.S., IB, AP. **Languages taught:** French, Spanish, Chinese, Bahasa Malay. **Staff specialists:** reading, computer, speech/hearing, counselor, psychologist, learning disabilities, nurse, curriculum, enrichment. **Special programs:** ESL, summer school, university placement. **Special curricular:** art, chorus, band, physical education, computer instruction. **Extracurricular:** drama, gymnastics, dance, choral and instrumental music, computers, yearbook, photography, excursions/expeditions, field trips, debate, Model UN. **Sports:** badminton, basketball, soccer, softball, swimming, tennis, track and field, volleyball, water polo, judo, Tae Kwon Do. **Clubs:** Boy Scouts, Cub Scouts, Brownies, Little League, Girl Scouts, National Honor Society, Thespian Society. **Tests:** PSAT, SAT, ACT, TOEFL, AP, Iowa, Gates-MacGinitie. **Graduates attending college:** 95%. **Graduates have attended:** Harvard, Princeton, Yale, Brown, Stanford.

Physical plant

Campuses (2): elementary school at Melawati; middle and high schools at Ampang. **Libraries:** Melawati, 20,000 volumes; Ampang, 20,000 volumes. **Facilities:** swimming pools, air-conditioned, carpeted classrooms, canteens, gymnasiums, sports fields, theater; art, music, computer instruction rooms; air-conditioned bus service. Ampang also has 8 science labs, dance studio, 2 tennis courts, 2 basketball courts.

*Once only fee

MONT'KIARA INTERNATIONAL SCHOOL

Street address: 22 Jalan Mont'Kiara, 50480 Kuala Lumpur, Malaysia
Phone: (60)(3)2562307/2538604 **Facsimile:** (60)(3)2536045
E-mail: garymc@mkis.po.my
Headmaster: Donald R. Shoemaker
Principal: John E. Gaylord
Teaching staff: full-time, 47; part-time, 3; total, 50
Nationalities of teaching staff: U.S., 29; U.K., 5; host, 3; other, 13; total, 50
Grade levels: preK – 9
Enrollment: total, 579
Nationalities of student body: U.S., 145; U.K., 52; host, 27; other, 355; total, 579
Teacher/student ratio: 1/12
Tuition (annual): preK, $4,145; K, $4,665; 1 – 5, $7,150; 6 – 8, $7,652; 9, $8,145
Other fees (annual): registration*, $3,900; busing, $480; reenrollment, $785; uniform, $16/each
School year: August to June

Year founded: 1994. **Type of school:** coed, company-sponsored. **Governed by:** appointed board of governors. **Regional organizations:** EARCOS.

Curriculum/physical plant

Type: U.S. **Languages taught:** French, Mandarin. **Staff specialists:** nurse. **Special programs:** ESL, remedial. **Special curricular:** art, chorus, band, physical education, computer instruction. **Extracurricular:** drama, gymnastics, dance, choral music, computers, yearbook, newspaper, athletics. **Library:** 9,000 volumes. **Facilities:** 4 buildings, 50 classrooms, infirmary, gymnasium, playing field, 5 science labs, 2 computer labs, swimming pool, theater, 3 art rooms, dance room, canteen, carpeted, air conditioned rooms, 24-hour security.

*Once only fee

PENANG

DALAT SCHOOL

Street address: Tanjung Bunga, 11200 Penang, Malaysia
Phone: (60)(4)8992105 **Facsimile:** (60)(4)8902141
E-mail: office@dalat2.po.my
Director: Dwight Carlblom
Principal: Hans Fung
Head of computer services: Ed Tulloch
Teaching staff: full-time, 24; part-time, 9; total, 33
Nationalities of teaching staff: U.S., 24; other, 9; total, 33
Grade levels: K – 12
Enrollment: K – 6, 88; 7 – 9, 73; 10 – 12, 77; total, 238
Nationalities of student body: U.S., 162; host, 3; other, 73; total, 238
Teacher/student ratio: 1/8
Boarders: boys, 44; girls, 50 **Grades:** 1 – 12 **Program:** planned 7-day
Tuition (annual): K – 6, $5,830; 7 – 12, $7,315

Other fees (annual): registration, $1,000; boarding, $5,650; lunch, $135/semester; application, $10; building, $1,200
School year: August to June

Year founded: 1928. **Type of school:** coed, day, boarding, church-related. **Governed by:** appointed advisory committee of missionary field chairmen. **Sponsored by:** Christian and Missionary Alliance. **Accredited by:** Western. **Regional organizations:** EARCOS, ACSI.

Curriculum

Type: U.S., AP. **Languages taught:** French, Spanish, Malay, Mandarin. **Staff specialists:** reading, computer, counselor, psychologist, learning disabilities, nurse, chaplain. **Special programs:** honors sections, correspondence, remedial, learning lab. **Special curricular:** art, chorus, band, physical education, computer instruction, vocational, piano, yearbook, newspaper. **Extracurricular:** drama, gymnastics, choral and instrumental music, computers, yearbook, newspaper, photography, excursions/expeditions, field trips. **Sports:** basketball, soccer, tennis, track and field, volleyball. **Clubs:** chess, drama, National Honor Society, ensemble, tennis. **Tests:** PSAT, SAT, AP, Iowa. **Graduates attending college:** 90%. **Graduates have attended:** Northwestern U., Wheaton College, Stanford U., Pepperdine U., Columbia U.

Physical plant

Location: 6 miles from center of Georgetown, on north shore of Penang Island. **Campus:** 8 acres. **Library:** 16,000 volumes. **Facilities:** 17 buildings, 25 classrooms, auditorium, cafeteria, infirmary, tennis court, gymnasium, 2 playing fields, science lab, 2 computer labs, AV equipment, chapel, student center, air conditioning, 6 dormitories.

MALI

Region: West Africa
Size: 482,077 square miles
Population: 9,653,261
Capital: Bamako
Telephone code: 223
Currency: CFA franc
Languages: French, Bambara, many other African languages

BAMAKO

American International School of Bamako

Street address: Rue 111, Badalabougou Ouest, Bamako, Mali
Phone: (223)224738 **Facsimile:** (223)220853 **E-mail:** aisb@malinet.ml
Mail: BP 34, Bamako, Mali
U.S. mail: c/o U.S. Embassy—Bamako, Dept. of State, Washington, DC 20521-2050
Director: Thomas G. Hunt
Teaching staff: full-time, 11; part-time, 2; total, 13
Nationalities of teaching staff: U.S., 9; other, 4; total, 13
Grade levels: preK – 8
Enrollment: preK, 11; K, 11; 1 – 8, 77; total, 99

Nationalities of student body: U.S., 45; other, 54; total, 99
Capacity: preK, 20; K, 20; 1 – 8, 110; total, 150
Teacher/student ratio: 1/9
Tuition (annual): preK, $2,500; K – 8, $10,000
Other fees (annual): registration*, $250; busing, $950; capital development*, $2,000
School year: September to June

Year founded: 1977. **Type of school:** coed, day, private nonprofit. **Governed by:** elected board of directors. **Accredited by:** Middle States. **Regional organizations:** AISA.

Curriculum/physical plant

Type: U.S. **Languages taught:** French. **Special curricular:** art, physical education, computer instruction, music, ESL. **Extracurricular:** drama, yearbook, newspaper, field trips, art club, French club. **Sports:** basketball, soccer, swimming, volleyball, softball. **Tests:** SSAT, Iowa. **Location:** fronts south side of the Niger River, within 10 minutes of the city center. **Campus:** 2 acres. **Library:** 8,000 volumes. **Facilities:** playing field, science lab, computer lab, air conditioning.

*Once only fee

MALTA

Region: Europe
Size: 122 square miles
Population: 375,576
Capital: Valletta
Telephone code: 356
Currency: Maltese lira
Languages: Maltese, English

ST. ANDREWS

Verdala International School

Street address: Fort Pembroke, St. Andrews, Malta
Phone: (356)332361/374285 **Facsimile:** (356)372387
E-mail: vis@maltanet.net
Headmaster: J. Douglas Wolf
Teaching staff: full-time, 44; part-time, 5; total, 49
Nationalities of teaching staff: U.S., 21; U.K., 11; host, 5; other, 12; total, 49
Grade levels: preK – 12
Enrollment: preK – K, 46; 1 – 6, 100; 7 – 9, 74; 10 – 12, 65; total, 285
Nationalities of student body: U.S., 29; U.K., 34; host, 33; other, 189; total, 285
Teacher/student ratio: 1/7
Tuition (annual): playschool – 5, 1,600**; 6 – 8, 1,800; 9 – 12, 2,000
Other fees (annual): registration*, 100**; boarding, 2,300; busing, 60; boarding capitalization fee: playschool, 550; preK, 850
School year: September to June

Year founded: 1976. **Type of school:** coed, day, boarding, private nonprofit. **Governed by:** appointed and elected board of directors. **Accredited by:** Middle States. **Regional organizations:** ECIS.

Curriculum/physical plant

Type: U.S., U.K., IB, AP. **Languages taught:** English, French, Spanish, Italian. **Special programs:** ESL. **Special curricular:** art, physical education, computer instruction. **Extracurricular:** yearbook, newspaper, excursions/expeditions, field trips. **Sports:** basketball, volleyball. **Tests:** PSAT, SAT, ACT, TOEFL, IB, AP, IGCSE, Iowa. **Graduates attending college:** 90%. **Graduates have attended:** American U. in Cairo, Pennsylvania State, McGill, Colorado State, Virginia Polytechnic. **Location:** in ex-fort (with moat) in quiet residential area. **Campus:** 6 acres. **Library:** 7,500 volumes. **Facilities:** 9 buildings, 21 classrooms, auditorium, cafeteria, playing field, 3 science labs, 2 computer labs, self-contained apartments with resident and daily supervisors, access to swimming pool, tennis courts, gymnasium.

*Once only fee **Maltese lira

COTTONERA

St. Edward's College

Address: Cottonera, Malta
Phone: (356)825978 **Facsimile:** (356)681557
Headmaster: G. Briscoe

MARSHALL ISLANDS

Region: South Pacific
Size: 70 square miles
Population: 58,363
Capital: Majuro
Telephone code: 692
Currency: U.S. dollar
Languages: English, Japanese, Marshallese

KWAJALEIN

KWAJALEIN SCHOOL SYSTEM

Phone: (1)(805)3553761 **Facsimile:** (1)(805)3553584
E-mail: popejoy@aloha.net
U.S. mail: (no personal name) KSS Box 51, APO AP 96555
Superintendent/elementary principal: Karen Ammann
Junior/senior high principal: James Sebanc
Head of computer services: Carol Hockenberger
Teaching staff: full-time, 50; total, 50
Nationalities of teaching staff: U.S., 50; total, 50
Grade levels: K – 12
Enrollment: K, 44; 1 – 6, 213; 7 – 9, 81; 10 – 12, 52; total, 390
Nationalities of student body: U.S., 344; host, 46; total, 390
Teacher/student ratio: 1/8
Tuition (annual): K – 12, varies up to $6,400
School year: August to June

Year founded: 1950. **Type of school:** coed, day, company-sponsored. **Governed by:** U.S. government/Raytheon, contractor. **Accredited by:** North Central (elementary and secondary).

Curriculum/physical plant

Type: U.S., AP. **Languages taught:** French, Spanish. **Staff specialists:** psychologist, high school counselor, speech therapist, special education (2). **Special curricular:** art, chorus, band, physical education, computer instruction, typing, accounting. **Extracurricular:** choral and instrumental music, yearbook, newspaper, photography, student government. **Sports:** basketball, soccer, softball, tennis, volleyball, water skiing, water polo. **Tests:** PSAT, SAT, ACT, TOEFL, AP, Iowa, ITED, ASVAB. **Graduates have attended:** Stanford, Harvard, Brown, MIT, Baylor. **Location:** on island, 2,100 miles southwest of Honolulu. **Library:** 19,000 volumes. **Facilities:** 13 buildings, 46 classrooms, auditorium, 2 tennis courts, gymnasium, 2 playing fields, 2 science labs, 2 computer labs, 2 swimming pools, air conditioning.

MAJURO

Majuro Cooperative School

Phone: (692)(9)6253144 **Facsimile:** (692)(9)6253719
U.S. mail: PO Box 81, Majuro, Marshall Islands, MH 96960
Principal: Frank Cabral
Teaching staff: full-time, 14; total, 14
Grade levels: preK – 8
Enrollment: total, 250
Teacher/student ratio: 1/21
Tuition: $105 per month
Other fees: registration, $50
School year: August to June

Year founded: 1975. **Type of school:** elementary, nonsectarian. **Governed by:** 7-member board composed of parents. **Accredited by:** Western.

Curriculum/physical plant

Type: U.S. **Languages taught:** Marshallese. **Tests:** SATB. **Graduates have attended:** schools in Guam, Hawaii, continental U.S. **Location:** Delap, Majuro, Marshall Islands. **Facilities:** computer lab, library, AV room, playing fields with limited sports/playground equipment.

MAURITANIA

Region: West Africa
Size: 398,000 square miles
Population: 2,336,048
Capital: Nouakchott
Telephone code: 222
Currency: ouguiya
Languages: Wolof, Hasaniya Arabic, Pular, Soninke

NOUAKCHOTT

American International School of Nouakchott

Phone/facsimile: (222)252967 **Telex:** 5558 MTN
Cable: c/o American Embassy Nouakchott
Mail: c/o U.S. Embassy, BP 222, Nouakchott, Mauritania
U.S. mail: Administrative Officer (AISN), Dept. of State–Nouakchott, Washington, DC 20521-2430
Director: John Alter
Business manager: Fimelita R. Celiz
Teaching staff: full-time, 3; part-time, 3; total, 6
Nationalities of teaching staff: U.S., 5; other, 1; total, 6
Grade levels: preK – 8 (grade 9 correspondence)

Enrollment: preK, 6; K, 1; 1 – 3, 15; 4 – 7, 16; total, 38
Teacher/student ratio: 1/6
Tuition (annual): preK, $1,300; K – 8, $9,000
School year: September to June

Year founded: 1978. **Type of school:** coed, day, private nonprofit. **Governed by:** elected board of directors. **Sponsored by:** AISN Association. **Regional organizations:** AISA, AAIE.

Curriculum/physical plant

Type: U.S. **Languages taught:** French. **Staff specialists:** computer, nurse. **Special programs:** ESL. **Special curricular:** art, physical education, computer instruction, music. **Extracurricular:** computers, field trips, after-school program. **Sports:** soccer, swimming, tennis, volleyball. **Tests:** Iowa. **Location:** on U.S. Embassy compound. **Campus:** 1 acre. **Library:** 4,500 volumes. **Facilities:** 2 buildings, 8 classrooms, tennis court, science lab, computer lab, swimming pool, kitchen, air conditioning.

MAURITIUS

Region: Indian Ocean
Size: 788 square miles
Population: 1,140,256
Capital: Port Louis
Telephone code: 230
Currency: rupee
Languages: English, French, Creole, Bhojpoori, Hindi

MOKA

Le Bocage International School

Street address: Montagne Ory Moka, Mauritius
Phone: (230)4330941/4331159 **Facsimile:** (230)4334914
Headmaster: Geoffrey Darlison
Teaching staff: full-time, 46; total, 46
Nationalities of teaching staff: U.S., 1; host, 39; other, 6; total, 46
Grade levels: 7 – 13
Enrollment: total, 550
Capacity: total, 600
Teacher/student ratio: 1/11
Tuition (annual): 72,050**
Other fees (annual): capital levy, 10,000**; busing, 450/month; books, 1,200
School year: January through November

Year founded: 1990. **Type of school:** coed, day, private nonprofit. **Governed by:** board of directors. **Sponsored by:** Mauritian business sector. **Regional organizations:** AISA.

Curriculum/physical plant

Type: U.K., IB. **Languages taught:** French, Spanish. **Staff specialists:** reading, math, computer, counselor, learning disabilities, music, physical education, fine arts. **Special programs:** ESL, remedial. **Special curricular:** art, chorus, band, physical education, computer instruction. **Extracurricular:** drama, dance, choral and instrumental music, computers, newspaper, literary magazine, photography, excursions/expeditions, field trips, sports, Duke of Edinburgh Award Scheme. **Clubs:** photography, math, nature, video, cooking. **Tests:** IGCSE, Iowa, IB. **Location:** on rural mountainside, overlooking the sea. **Campus:** 8 acres. **Facilities:** 3 buildings, 30 classrooms, cafeteria, infirmary, covered play area, 2 playing fields, 3 science labs, 2 computer labs, library, home economics lab.

**Mauritian rupee

MEXICO

Region: North America
Size: 756,066 square miles
Population: 95,772,462
Capital: Mexico City
Telephone code: 52
Currency: new peso
Language: Spanish, Amerindian languages

DURANGO

Colegio Americano de Durango, A.C.

Street address: Francisco Sarabia No. 416 Pte., Durango, Mexico
Phone: (52)(181)33636 **Facsimile:** (52)(181)12839
Mail: Apartado Postal No. 495, Durango, Mexico 34000
Director general/high school principal: Dr. Jorge O. Nelson
Middle school principal: Gabriel Kaypatran
Business manager: Alberto Bustamante
Teaching staff: full-time, 46; part-time, 8; total, 54
Nationalities of teaching staff: U.S., 13; host, 40; other, 1; total, 54
Grade levels: K – 12
Enrollment: K, 87; 1 – 6, 300; 7 – 9, 120; 10 – 12, 75; total, 582
Capacity: K, 140; 1 – 6, 325; 7 – 9, 150; 10 – 12, 75; total, 690
Teacher/student ratio: 1/11
Tuition (annual): K, $1,990; 1 – 6, $2,400; 7 – 9, $3,230, 10 – 12, $3,256
Other fees: registration, K, $215; 1 – 6, $230; 7 – 12, $295; new enrollment*, $500; books, $80
School year: August to June

Year founded: 1954. **Type of school:** coed, day, private nonprofit. **Governed by:** appointed board of directors. **Accredited by:** Mexican government, Southern. **Regional organizations:** ASOMEX, Tri-Assoc.

Curriculum/physical plant

Type: U.S. **Languages taught:** English, Spanish. **Staff specialists:** computer, counselor, psychologist, art, learning differences. **Special programs:** ESL. **Special curricular:** art, chorus, band, physical education, computer instruction, vocational. **Extracurricular:** drama, gymnastics, dance, choral and instrumental music, computers, yearbook, newspaper, photography, excursions/expeditions. **Sports:** basketball, soccer, track and field, volleyball. **Tests:** PSAT, SAT, Stanford, Iowa. **Graduates attending college:** 90%. **Graduates have attended:** Stanford, UCLA, U. of Texas, Texas A&M, Technológico de Monterrey. **Location:** in the mountain-valley city of Durango. **Campus:** 2 acres. **Library:** 10,500 volumes. **Facilities:** 6 buildings, 27 classrooms, playing field, science lab, computer lab, soccer field, basketball/volleyball courts, vocational equipment. .

*Once only fee

GUADALAJARA

The American School Foundation of Guadalajara, A.C.

Street address: Colomos 2100, Guadalajara, Jalisco, Mexico
Phone: (52)(3)8173377 **Facsimile:** (52)(3)8173356
E-mail: asfg@warrior.asfg.mx
Mail: Apartado Postal 6-280, Guadalajara, Jalisco, Mexico
Director general: Robert W. Trent
High school principal: Steven Gende
Middle school principal: Brian Merrill
Primary school principal: Francisco Galicia
Early childhood coordinator: Tina Carstensen
Teaching staff: full-time, 122; total, 122
Nationalities of teaching staff: U.S., 54; host, 63; other, 5; total, 122
Grade levels: preK – 12
Enrollment: preK – 4, 775; 5 – 8, 362; 9 – 12, 284; total, 1,421
Nationalities of student body: U.S., 152; host, 1,222; other, 47; total, 1421
Teacher/student ratio: 1/12
Tuition (annual): preK – K, $1,350; 1 – 6, $1,920; 7 – 9, $2,255; 10 – 12, $2,455
Other fees (annual): registration, 9,800**
School year: late August through June

Year founded: 1956. **Type of school:** coed, day, private nonprofit. **Governed by:** board of directors. **Accredited by:** Southern. **Regional organizations:** SAIS, ASOMEX.

Curriculum

Type: U.S., AP. **Languages taught:** English, Spanish. **Staff specialists:** reading, math, computer, psychologist, nurses. **Special programs:** honors sections, independent study, correspondence, remedial. **Special curricular:** art, chorus, band, physical education, computer instruction, drama. **Extracurricular:** choral and instrumental music, computers, yearbook, literary magazine, excursions/expeditions. **Sports:** basketball, swimming, track and field, volleyball. **Clubs:** computer, chorus, art, math, science, yearbook, cheerleaders. **Tests:** PSAT, SAT, ACT, TOEFL. **Graduates attending college:** 97%. **Graduates have attended:** Wellesley, Trinity, Hofstra, Brown, Princeton.

Physical plant

Location: in city. **Campus:** 5 acres. **Libraries (2):** 28,000 volumes. **Facilities:** 72 classrooms, auditorium, infirmary, gymnasium, 2 playing fields, 3 science labs, 4 computer labs, swimming pool, technology center, weight room.

**Mexican peso

MEXICO CITY

AMERICAN SCHOOL FOUNDATION, A.C.

Street address: Bondojito 215, Colonia las Américas, 01120 Mexico DF, Mexico
Phone: (52)(5)2274900 **Facsimile:** (52)(5)2734357/2728453
Superintendent: Dr. Mary Gonzales Mend
Assistant superintendent: Janet Cruz
High school principal: Kevin Conway
Middle school principal: Bruce Yerman
Elementary principal: Sue Matus
Teaching staff: full-time, 176; part-time, 8; total, 184
Nationalities of teaching staff: U.S., 102; host, 73; other, 9; total, 184
Grade levels: early childhood center – 12
Enrollment: ECC, 343; 1 – 5, 807; 6 – 8, 568; 9 – 12, 707; total, 2,425
Teacher/student ratio: 1/14
Tuition, monthly: ECC, 1,950**; 1 – 5, $2,650; 6 – 12, $2,920
Other fees: registration (twice a year), equivalent to one month's fees; admissions*: ECC – 1, 5,000**; 2 – 12, 7,500; special education: 1 hour, 920; 2 hours, 1,840; 3 hours, 2,650
School year: mid-August through June

Year founded: 1888. **Type of school:** coed, day, private nonprofit. **Governed by:** elected board of directors. **Accredited by:** Southern, Universidad Nacional Autónoma de México, Secretaría de Educación Pública. **Regional organizations:** ASOMEX, Tri-Assoc.

Curriculum

Type: U.S., national, AP. **Languages of instruction:** English, Spanish. **Languages taught:** French, Italian. **Staff specialists:** reading, math, computer, counselor, learning disabilities, nurse, ESL, psychologists, special Spanish. **Special programs:** ESL, honors sections. **Special curricular:** art, chorus, band, physical education, computer instruction. **Extracurricular:** drama, computers, yearbook, newspaper, literary magazine, photography, excursions/expeditions, field trips, ASOMEX writing conferences, American Legion oratorical contest, art festivals and exhibitions, science fair, foreign language week, Special Olympics, Model UN, chorus, band, physical education, Boys and Girls State, National Honor Society, Math Counts, Knowledge Masters. **Sports:** baseball, basketball, football, soccer, softball, swimming, tennis, volleyball, handball. **Clubs:** drama, student council, cheerleaders, French, Italian, Project Lead, presidential classroom, community service projects, Children's Cancer Fund. **Tests:** SSAT, PSAT, SAT, ACT, TOEFL, Stanford. **Graduates attending college:** 95%. **Graduates have attended:** Stanford, Harvard, U. of Pennsylvania, Brigham Young U., Boston U.

Physical plant

Location: in Mexico City, set on extensive lawn area. **Campus:** 17 acres. **Library:** 50,000 volumes. **Facilities:** 4 buildings, 124 classrooms, auditorium, 4 tennis courts, 9 science labs, 6 computer labs, 3 gymnasiums/multipurpose facilities, dance room, weight room, covered swimming pool.

*Once only fee **Mexican new peso

COLEGIO PETERSON

Street address: (K – 12): Huizachito 80, Colonia Vista Hermosa, Mexico City;
(K – 6): Rocio 142, Colonia Pedregal San Angel, Mexico City;
(K): Montes Himalaya 615, Colonia Lomas de Chapultepe, Mexico City;
(7 – 12): Carretera Federal a Cuernavaca Km 23.8, San Andres Totoltepec, Tlalpan, Mexico City, Mexico
Phone: (52)(5)8130114/5683139/5202213/8491884
Facsimile: (52)(5)8131385 **E-mail:** kapm@mail.internet.com.mx
Mail: Apartado Postal 10-900, Mexico, DF 11000, Mexico
Chairman of the board: Marvin Peterson, Ph.D.
Superintendent: Kenneth Peterson
Business manager: Leonardo Santiago
Teaching staff: full-time, 100; part-time, 20; total, 120
Nationalities of teaching staff: host, 90; other, 30; total, 120
Grade levels: K – 12
Enrollment: K, 410; 1 – 6, 480; 7 – 9, 120; 10 – 12, 90; total, 1,100
Nationalities of student body: host, 850; other, 250; total, 1,100
Teacher/student ratio: 1/9
Tuition (annual): K, $2,450; 1 – 6, $3,200; 7 – 9, $3,700; 10 – 12, $4,100
Other fees: capital levy*, $775; registration: K, $650; 1 – 6, $590; 7 – 12, $960
School year: September to July

Year founded: 1965. **Type of school:** coed, day, private nonprofit. **Governed by:** board of directors. **Accredited by:** Mexican government (Secretary of Public Education and National University), Independent School Association of the Southwest.

Curriculum/physical plant

Type: U.S., national. **Languages of instruction:** English, Spanish. **Languages taught:** French. **Staff specialists:** reading, math, computer, counselor, psychologist, physician. **Special programs:** ESL, independent study, Apple computer pilot school. **Special curricular:** art, physical education, computer instruction, vocational. **Extracurricular:** drama, computers, yearbook, newspaper, excursions/expeditions, field trips, honor society. **Sports:** basketball, soccer, track and field, volleyball, karate, figure skating, gymnastics. **Tests:** SAT, TOEFL, Stanford. **Graduates attending college:** over 95%. **Graduates have attended:** Stanford, Rice, Instituto Tecnológico de Monterrey, U. Ibero Americano. **Location:** on quiet streets on west and south sides of Mexico City, above the smog. **Campuses (4):** 7 acres. **Libraries (2):** 14,000 volumes. **Facilities:** 7 buildings, 76 classrooms, cafeteria, infirmary, 4 science labs, 4 computer labs, 2 soccer fields, track, playing fields.

*Once only fee

Greengates School

Street address: Circumvalacion Pte. 102, Balcones de San Mateo, Naucalpan, Mexico
Phone: (52)(5)3730088/3730099 **Facsimile:** (52)(5)3604120/7370765
E-mail: gsclib@mail.internet.com.mx
Mail: Apartado Postal 41-659, 11000 Mexico DF, Mexico
Principal: Susan Mayer
Head of primary school: Jonathan Robins
Teaching staff: full-time, 80; part-time, 5; total, 85
Nationalities of teaching staff: U.S., 12; U.K., 50; host, 15; other, 8; total, 85
Grade levels: K – 12
Enrollment: K – preP, 90; 1 – 6, 430; 7 – 9, 250; 10 – 12, 200; total, 970
Nationalities of student body: U.S., 180; U.K., 90; host, 360; other, 340; total, 970
Teacher/student ratio: 1/12
Tuition (annual): $4,000 – 8,000
Other fees: busing, $75/month; books, $200/year
School year: September to June

Year founded: 1951. **Type of school:** coed, day, private nonprofit.

Curriculum/physical plant

Type: U.K., IB. **Languages taught:** French, Spanish. **Staff specialists:** reading, math, computer, counselor, psychologist, nurse. **Special curricular:** art, band, physical education, computer instruction. **Extracurricular:** drama, gymnastics, instrumental music, computers, yearbook, literary magazine, photography, excursions/expeditions, field trips. **Sports:** athletics, badminton, basketball, hockey, rugby, soccer, swimming, volleyball. **Tests:** PSAT, SAT, ACT, TOEFL, IB, GCSE. **Graduates attending college:** 100%. **Graduates have attended:** MIT, Yale, Harvard, Brandeis. **Location:** on outskirts of Mexico City. **Library:** 20,000 volumes. **Facilities:** 6 buildings, 38 classrooms, auditorium, cafeteria, infirmary, gymnasium, playing field, 6 science labs, 3 computer labs, swimming pool.

Westhill Institute

Street address: Montes Carpatos #940, Lomas de Chapultepec, Mexico DF 11000, Mexico
Phone: (52)(5)2824445/2824522/2824686 **Facsimile:** (52)(5)5202683
Director: Dr. Richard F. Ashley
High school principal: Pita Rodriguez-Pollock
Middle school principal: Bonnie Pais
Elementary principal: Babette Levy
Technical director Mexican program: Dr. Ernesto Almaraz
Teaching staff: full-time, 34; part-time, 5; total, 39
Nationalities of teaching staff: U.S., 25; U.K., 1; host, 13; total, 39
Grade levels: preK – 12
Enrollment: preK, 19; K, 19; 1 – 6, 130; 7 – 9, 60; 10 – 12, 60; total, 288
Nationalities of student body: U.S., 95; U.K., 8; host, 120; other, 65; total, 288
Tuition, (per month): preK – K, $245; 1 – 6, $330; 7 – 9, $388; 10 – 12, $395
Other fees (annual): capital levy*, $175; busing, $90 per month; books, $200; other, $150; registration*
School year: August to June

Year founded: 1992. **Type of school:** coed. **Governed by:** appointed board of directors. **Accredited by:** Southern. **Regional organizations:** ASOMEX.

Curriculum

Type: U.S., national. **Languages of instruction:** English, Spanish. **Languages taught:** English, French, Spanish. **Staff specialists:** reading, math, computer, speech/hearing, counselor, learning disabilities, nurse. **Special programs:** ESL, remedial, SSL, special education. **Special curricular:** art, chorus, computers, photography. **Extracurricular:** drama, field trips, swimming, street hockey, art, illustration, excursions. **Sports:** basketball, soccer, volleyball. **Tests:** PSAT, ITBS. **Graduates attending college:** 90%. **Graduates have attended:** Penn State, North Central Bible College, U.S. International U., ITAM and Anahuac (Mexico).

Physical plant

Location: exclusive, park-like setting. **Campuses (2):** .5 acre. **Libraries (2):** 5,000 volumes. **Facilities:** 2 buildings, 29 classrooms, auditorium, infirmary, 3 science labs, 2 computer labs, snack bar, play and sports area, 2 resource rooms; new middle and high schools under construction.

*Once only fee

MONTERREY

AMERICAN SCHOOL FOUNDATION OF MONTERREY, A.C.

Street address: Missouri 555 Ote., Col. del Valle, Garza García, Nuevo Leon, Mexico 66220
Phone: (52)(83)354850 **Facsimile:** (52)(83)782535
Mail: Apartado Postal 1762, Monterrey, NL 64000, Mexico
Superintendent: D. Jeffrey Keller, Ed.D.
Middle/high school principal: Russell Jones
Elementary school principal: Sonia Keller, Ed.D.
Teaching staff: full-time, 139; part-time, 23; total, 162
Nationalities of teaching staff: U.S., 32; host, 95; other, 35; total, 162
Grade levels: N – 12
Enrollment: N – preK, 285; K, 165; 1 – 6, 815; 7 – 9, 389; 10 – 12, 100; total, 1,754
Nationalities of student body: U.S., 208; host, 1,516; other, 30; total, 1,754
Capacity: total, 2,000
Teacher/student ratio: 1/12
Tuition (annual): N – preK, $2,895; K, $3,104; 1 – 2, $3,314; 3 – 4, $3,518; 5 – 6, $3,749; 7 – 9, $4,270; 10 – 12/Bach I – III, $4,373
Other fees (annual): registration, $400; maintenance, $475 – 890; equipment, $400; entrance contribution*, $4,200
School year: September to June

Year founded: 1928. **Type of school:** coed, day. **Governed by:** appointed board members. **Sponsored by:** 16 U.S. corporations. **Accredited by:** Southern, state educational authorities. **Regional organizations:** AAIE, ASOMEX, Tri-Assoc.

Curriculum

Type: U.S., national. **Languages of instruction:** English, Spanish. **Languages taught:** Spanish. **Staff specialists:** reading, counselor, learning disabilities, nurse, psychometrist. **Special curricular:** art, chorus, physical education, computer instruction, drama. **Extracurricular:** computers, yearbook, newspaper. **Sports:** basketball, soccer, softball, track and field, volleyball. **Clubs:** computer, drama, National Honor Society, National Junior Honor Society, senior and junior student councils, science, German, environmental. **Tests:** SSAT, PSAT, SAT, ACT, AP, ITBS. **Graduates attending college:** 98%. **Graduates have attended:** Tecnológico de Monterrey, Harvard, U. of Texas, MIT, Cornell.

Physical plant

Location: in suburban Monterrey. **Campus:** 8.5 acres. **Library:** 22,000 volumes. **Facilities:** 3 buildings, 72 classrooms, auditorium, cafeteria, infirmary, 2 tennis courts, gymnasium, 4 playing fields, 4 science labs, 5 computer labs, AV equipment, partial air conditioning. Opened state-of-the-art middle school/high school on 50-acre site in August 1996.

*Once only fee

Colegio Ingles

Street address: Real San Agustín #100, San Agustín Campestre, Garza García, Nuevo León, Mexico
Phone: (52)(8)3631717 **Facsimile:** (52)(8)3631985 **E-mail:** cingles@sdm.net
Mail: Apartado Postal 585, Col. Del Valle, Garza García, N.L. Mexico C.P. 66220
U.S. mail: 422 Rio Grande Drive, Mission, TX 78572-7420, U.S.A.
Director/principal, middle school: Norma Guerra
Principal, elementary: Alejandra Tapia
Principal, preschool: Patricia Navarro
Technology director: Gabriela Lozano
Business manager: Leticia Montemayor
Teaching staff: full-time, 91; part-time, 6; total, 97
Grade levels: K – 9
Enrollment: K, 403; 1 – 6, 735; 7 – 9, 291; total, 1,429
Teacher/student ratio: 1/14
Tuition (annual, 1996–97 figures): K, 11,100**; 1 – 6, 13,200; 7 – 9, 16,140
Other fees (annual, 1996–97 figures): registration, 2,000 – 2,450**; books, 450 – 900; new student registration*, 9,000; PTA, 50
School year: September to June

Year founded: 1971. **Type of school:** coed, day, private nonprofit. **Accredited by:** National Secretariat of Education. **Regional organizations:** ASOMEX, Tri-Assoc.

Curriculum/physical plant

Type: bilingual. **Languages of instruction:** English, Spanish. **Staff specialists:** psychologist, learning disabilities, nurse. **Special programs:** remedial. **Special curricular:** art, physical education, music. **Extracurricular:** gymnastics, computers, yearbook, excursions/expeditions, field trips. **Sports:** basketball, soccer, track and field. **Graduates attending college:** 100%. **Graduates have attended:** Instituto

Tecnológico de Monterrey, U. de Monterrey. **Location:** near foot of surrounding mountains in lush, green area, 8 kilometers from Monterrey. **Campus:** 7 acres. **Library:** 9,000 volumes, multimedia room. **Facilities:** 2 buildings, 55 classrooms, cafeteria, infirmary, covered play area, 2 science labs, 2 computer labs, 2 basketball courts, 2 soccer fields.

*Once only fee **Mexican peso

Pan American School

Street address: Downtown: Hidalgo 656 Pte., Monterrey, N.L., Mexico 64000
Campus: Casolar 200, Villas de San Agustin, San Pedro Garza Garcia, N.L. Mexico 66260
Phone: (52)(8)3420778 (downtown); (52)(8)3635200 (campus)
Facsimile: (52)(8)3402749 (downtown); (52)(8)3635602 (campus)
Mail: Apartado Postal 474, Monterrey, N.L., Mexico 64000
Directors: Robert L. Arpee, Leonor Arpee
Academic assistant: Hermelinda Coronado
Secondary school principal: Delia Gonzalez
Upper primary school principal: Nelly Granados
Lower primary/preschool principals: Patricia Himes, Amelia Landa
Teaching staff: full-time, 98; total, 98
Nationalities of teaching staff: U.S., 18; U.K., 2; host, 77; other, 1; total, 98
Grade levels: preschool (4 years) – 9; 1-year commercial
Enrollment: total, 1,321
Capacity: preK, 209; 1 – 6, 691; 7 – 9, 413; commercial, 8; total, 1,321
Teacher/student ratio: 1/14
School year: September to June

Year founded: 1952. **Type of school:** coed, day, private nonprofit. **Governed by:** board of directors. **Accredited by:** federal government.

Curriculum/physical plant

Type: U.S., national. **Languages taught:** English, Spanish. **Staff specialists:** math, counselor, psychologist, nurse. **Special curricular:** physical education, computers, science labs. **Extracurricular:** gymnastics, choral music, football, soccer, volleyball, basketball, arts. **Graduates attending college:** 100%. **Graduates have attended:** U. of Texas, U. de Nuevo Leon, Instituto Tecnológico, U. de Monterrey. **Facilities:** covered play area, science lab, computer lab, library, media center, AV equipment, partial air conditioning. Ten-acre campus under construction (first phase now operating): 30 classrooms for preschool, 80 classrooms for primary and secondary, gymnasium/auditorium, library, media center, AV equipment, cafeteria, infirmary, 2 multipurpose tennis courts, swimming pool, playing fields, 4 computer labs, 4 science labs, conference rooms, covered playground area, partial air conditioning.

PACHUCA

American School of Pachuca

Street address: Boulevard Valle de San Javier S/N, Pachuca, Hidalgo, Mexico
Phone: (52)(771)85077 **Facsimile:** (52)(771)31058/85077
General director: Joseph Flessa
Principal, grades 7 – 9: Nicéforo Ramírez
Principal, grades 1 – 6: Ricardo Espinosa de los Monteros
Principal, preschool: Ma. Elena Caballero
Business manager: Raúl Padilla
Teaching staff: full-time, 47; part-time, 11; total, 58
Nationalities of teaching staff: U.S., 14; host, 41; other, 3; total, 58
Grade levels: preK – 9
Enrollment: preschool, 155; 1 – 6, 391; 7 – 9, 158; total, 704
Teacher/student ratio: 1/12
Tuition (annual): preK, $1,164; 1 – 6, $1,320; 7 – 9, $1,923
Other fees (annual): preregistration: preK, $232; 1 – 6, $264; 7 – 9, $384; entrance fee*, $647
School year: August to July

Year founded: 1920. **Type of school:** coed, day. **Governed by:** elected board. **Regional organizations:** ASOMEX, Tri-Assoc.

Curriculum/physical plant

Type: U.S., national. **Languages of instruction:** English, Spanish. **Languages taught:** English, Spanish. **Staff specialists:** reading, art, music, physical education. **Special curricular:** physical education, computer instruction. **Extracurricular:** computers, field trips. **Sports:** basketball, soccer, track and field, volleyball. **Location:** in Pachuca. **Campus:** 20,000 square meters. **Facilities:** 9 buildings, 34 classrooms, science lab, computer lab, library, playing fields.

*Once only fee

PUERTO VALLARTA

The American School of Puerto Vallarta

Street address: Albatros S/N, Marina Vallarta, Puerto Vallarta, Jalisco 48300, Mexico
Phone: (52)(322)11525 **Facsimile:** (52)(322)11996
E-mail: camerica@pvnet.com.mx/gsel@vallarta.zonavirtual.com.mx
Mail: Apartado Postal 275-B, Puerto Vallarta, Jalisco, 48300 Mexico
Superintendent: Gerald Selitzer
Upper school coordinator: Deborah Brayton
Lower school coordinator: Donna Logan Cohen
Teaching staff: full-time, 32; part-time, 1; total, 33

Nationalities of teaching staff: U.S., 18; host, 11; other, 4; total, 33
Grade levels: preK – 12
Enrollment: preK – K, 35; 1 – 6, 134; 7 – 9, 60; 10 – 12, 60; total, 289
Nationalities of student body: U.S., 53; host, 218; other, 18; total, 289
Teacher/student ratio: 1/10
Tuition (annual): preK – K, $2,637; 1 – 6, $2,757; 7 – 9, $2,883; 10 – 12, $2,982
Other fees (annual): registration: preK, $353; K, $424; pre-1 – 12, $706; capital levy*: pre-1 – 6, $100; 7 – 12, $107
School year: September to June

Year founded: 1986. **Type of school:** coed, day, private nonprofit. **Governed by:** appointed board. **Accredited by:** Southern, Mexican Ministry of Education. **Regional organizations:** ASOMEX, Tri-Assoc.

Curriculum/physical plant

Type: U.S. **Languages of instruction:** English, Spanish. **Languages taught:** English, Spanish. **Special programs:** ESL, SSL. **Special curricular:** art, computer instruction, music. **Extracurricular:** drama, computers, yearbook, excursions/expeditions, Interact club, Internet club, student council, National Honor Society. **Sports:** baseball, soccer, tennis, volleyball, scuba diving. **Tests:** PSAT, TOEFL, CTBS. **Graduates have attended:** Monterrey Tech, U. of New Mexico, Central Washington U., Instituto de Estudios Superiores del Oriente, Savannah School of Art and Design. **Location:** in tropical beach resort, 2 kilometers from downtown Puerto Vallarta. **Campus:** 5 acres. **Facilities:** 3 buildings, science lab, computer lab, media learning center, amphitheater.

*Once only fee

QUERÉTARO

John F. Kennedy School, A.C.

Street address: Av. Sabinos 272, Jurica, Querétaro, Mexico
Phone: (52)(42)180075/180400 **Facsimile:** (52)(42)181784
E-mail: kennedy@acnet.net
Mail: Apartado Postal 93, Querétaro, Qro. 76000, Mexico
Director: Alfonso Lajud
High school principal: Paulina de la Mora
Junior high school director: Verónica Garcia
Elementary principal: Blanca Iglesias
Kindergarten director: Cristina Franco
Teaching staff: full-time, 58; part-time, 36; total, 94
Nationalities of teaching staff: U.S., 12; host, 72; other, 10; total, 94
Grade levels: K – 12
Enrollment: K – 6, 738; 7 – 9, 180; 10 – 12, 107; total, 1,025
Nationalities of student body: U.S., 86; host, 892; other, 47; total, 1,025
Teacher/student ratio: 1/28
Tuition (annual): K, $1,245; elementary, $1,440; junior high school, $1,725; high school, $2,176

Other fees (annual): new student fee*: K, $907; elementary, $718; junior high school, $673; high school, $200
School year: September to June

Year founded: 1964. **Type of school:** coed, day, private nonprofit. **Governed by:** board of directors. **Accredited by:** Southern, Mexican Ministry of Education. **Regional organizations:** ASOMEX.

Curriculum/physical plant

Type: U.S., national. **Languages of instruction:** English, Spanish. **Languages taught:** English, Spanish. **Staff specialists:** reading, computer, counselor, psychologist, nurse, photography, automotive mechanics. **Special programs:** ESL. **Special curricular:** art, physical education, computer instruction, music. **Sports:** basketball, soccer, track and field, volleyball. **Graduates have attended:** Instituto Tecnológico y de Estudios Superiores de Monterrey, U. Autónoma de Querétaro. **Location:** within a country residential area, 13 kilometers from Querétaro. **Campus:** 12 acres. **Library:** 12,000 volumes. **Facilities:** 14 buildings, 38 classrooms, cafeteria, 3 playing fields, 2 science labs, 2 computer labs, reading lab, 2 AV rooms.

*Once only fee

TAMPICO

The American School of Tampico†

Street address: Hidalgo s/n, Col. Tancol, Tampico, Tamaulipas, Mexico
Phone: (52)(12)272081 – 4 **Facsimile:** (52)(12)272080
E-mail: ast@correo.tamnet.com.mx
Mail: PO Box 407, Tampico, Tam. 89000, Mexico
Headmaster: Terrence Factor
Assistant headmaster: Emma G. de Salazar
Junior high school principal: William T. Kirschner
Elementary principal: Connie Kirkland
Technical directors: Rosa Elena Sosa (secondary); Elsa Paredes (primary)
Teaching staff: full-time, 56; part-time, 7; total, 63
Nationalities of teaching staff: U.S., 5; host, 48; other, 10; total, 63
Grade levels: N – 10
Enrollment: N, 42; preK, 79; K, 98; 1 – 6, 450; 7 – 9, 137; 10, 48; total, 854
Nationalities of student body: U.S., 35; host, 818; other, 1; total, 854
Capacity: N, 60; preK, 100; K, 100; 1 – 6, 600; 7 – 9, 160; 10, 50; total, 1,070
Teacher/student ratio: 1/11
Tuition (annual): N, $1,313; preK – K, $2,253; 1 – 7, $2,490; 8 – 10, $2,727
Other fees (annual): registration: N, $76; preK – 10, $455; books, $100; admission*, $1,894
School year: September to June

Year founded: 1917. **Type of school:** coed, day, private nonprofit. **Governed by:** appointed board of directors. **Accredited by:** Southern. **Regional organizations:** ASOMEX, Tri-Assoc.

Curriculum/physical plant

Type: U.S. **Languages taught:** English, Spanish. **Staff specialists:** counselor, psychologist, nurse, media specialist. **Special programs:** accelerated math and science. **Extracurricular:** gymnastics, yearbook, newspaper, literary magazine. **Sports:** baseball, basketball, soccer, volleyball. **Clubs:** computer, student council, art, book. **Tests:** SSAT, CTBS. **Location:** port with river, lagoons, beach, business, and agriculture, 15 minutes from downtown Tampico. **Campus:** 25 acres. **Library:** 9,000 volumes. **Facilities:** 6 buildings, 40 classrooms, infirmary, 4 playing fields, science lab, computer lab, music room, art room, air conditioning.

*Once only fee †formerly Escuela Americana de Tampico

TORREON

Colegio Americano de Torreon, A.C.

Street address: Ave. Mayran y Nogal, Col. Torreon Jardin 27200, Torreon, Coahuila, Mexico
Phone/facsimile: (52)(17)135389/173155
Director general: P. Barton Cromer
High school principal: Jeffrey P. Fraser
Assistant high school principal: Emma L. C. de Mesta
Elementary principal: James Wack
Assistant elementary principal: Ma. del Socorro F. de Obregón
Teaching staff: full-time, 92; part-time, 4; total, 96
Nationalities of teaching staff: U.S., 27; host, 55; other, 14; total, 96
Grade levels: preK – 12
Enrollment: total, 1,337
Nationalities of student body: U.S., 38; host, 1,289; other, 10; total, 1337
Teacher/student ratio: 1/14
Tuition (annual): preK, $665; K – pre-1, $995; 1 – 6, $1,541; 7 – 9, $1,850; 10 – 12, $2,130
Other fees (annual): registration, $1,250 (new student), $95 (returning student); insurance, $16.25
School year: August to June

Year founded: 1950. **Type of school:** day, private nonprofit. **Governed by:** elected board of directors. **Accredited by:** Southern. **Regional organizations:** AAIE, ASOMEX, Tri-Assoc.

Curriculum/physical plant

Type: U.S., national. **Languages of instruction:** English, Spanish. **Staff specialists:** counselor, psychologist, doctor. **Special programs:** ESL. **Special curricular:** art, chorus, physical education, computer instruction. **Extracurricular:** drama, gymnastics, dance. **Sports:** basketball, soccer, swimming, tennis, volleyball. **Tests:** PSAT, SAT, ACT, Stanford, CTBS. **Graduates attending college:** 98%. **Graduates have attended:** U. of Utah, U. of Washington, U. of Arizona, U. of Illinois, Rice. **Location:** in city. **Campus:** 5 acres. **Library:** 13,000 volumes. **Facilities:** auditorium, cafeteria, infirmary, 2 tennis courts, gymnasium, playing field, 2 science labs, 3 computer labs, swimming pool, air conditioning.

VERACRUZ

Colegio Americano de Veracruz

Street address: Progreso 52, Jardines de Mocambo, Boca del Rio, Veracruz, 94299 Mexico
Phone: (52)(29)219778 **Facsimile:** (52)(29)219777
U.S. mail: 8705 St. Thomas Court, Laredo, TX 78045, U.S.A.
Director general: Kathleen Klumb Monroy
Director of English primary: Ana Maria Camariere
Director of Spanish primary: Martha Leticia Muro Domínguez
Director of kindergarten: Veronica Espinosa Navarro
Business manager: Gloria Gomez Rodriguez
Teaching staff: full-time, 36; part-time, 6; total, 42
Nationalities of teaching staff: U.S., 4; host, 38; total, 42
Grade levels: N – 6
Enrollment: N – preK, 77; K, 69; 1 – 6, 224; total, 370
Nationalities of student body: U.S., 11; U.K., 1; host, 345; other, 13; total, 370
Capacity: N – preK, 120; K, 90; 1 – 6, 390; total, 600
Teacher/student ratio: 1/18
Tuition (annual): N – preK, $760; K, $832; 1 – 6, $1,216
Other fees (annual): registration*, $230; books, approximately $50; uniforms, approximately $80
School year: September to July

Year founded: 1992. **Type of school:** coed, day, proprietary. **Governed by:** private board of governors. **Sponsored by:** Universidad Villa Rica. **Accredited by:** Southern (in process). **Regional organizations:** ASOMEX.

Curriculum/physical plant

Type: U.S./national. **Languages of instruction:** English, Spanish. **Staff specialists:** psychologist, nurse, doctor. **Special programs:** ESL, remedial, special Spanish. **Special curricular:** art, physical education, computer instruction, music. **Extracurricular:** computers. **Sports:** basketball, soccer, volleyball, Tae Kwon Do. **Tests:** SLEP. **Location:** tropical setting, 2 miles from the Gulf of Mexico. **Library:** 6,400 volumes. **Facilities:** 23 classrooms, cafeteria, infirmary, playing field, air-conditioned computer lab, music room, soccer field.

*Once only fee

MOLDOVA

Region: Eastern Europe
Size: 13,012 square miles
Population: 4,463,847
Capital: Chisinau
Telephone code: 373
Currency: leu
Language: Moldovan, Russian

CHISINAU

QSI International School of Chisinau

Phone: (373)(2)243187 **E-mail:** qsimdu@setcom.moldnet.md
U.S. mail: c/o American Embassy Chisinau, Dept. of State, Washington, DC 20521-7080
Head teacher: Patricia Hammer
Teaching staff: full-time, 1; part-time, 2; total, 3
Nationalities of teaching staff: U.S., 3; total, 3
Grade levels: K – 8
Enrollment: 1 – 6, 2; 7 – 8, 3; total, 5
Capacity: K, 6; 1 – 6, 12; 7 – 8, 12; total, 30
Teacher/student ratio: 1/3
Tuition (annual): K – 5, $6,900; 6 – 8, $9,200
Other fees: registration*, $100; capital levy, $4,000 deposit or $1,600/year fee
School year: September to June

Year founded: 1996. **Type of school:** coed, day, private nonprofit. **Governed by:** appointed board of directors. **Sponsored by:** Quality Schools International. **Regional organizations:** CEESA.

Curriculum/physical plant

Type: U.S. **Special programs:** ESL. **Special curricular:** art, physical education, computer instruction, music. **Extracurricular:** drama, journalism, local culture, Russian, Romanian. **Location:** downtown Chisinau in large residential area near U.S. Embassy. **Facilities:** 2 large classrooms, library, music room, gymnasium, court yard.

*Once only fee

MONGOLIA

Region: Asia
Size: 604,800 square miles
Population: 2,496,617
Capital: Ulaanbaatar
Telephone code: 976
Currency: tugrik
Language: Khalka Mongolian

ULAANBAATAR

INTERNATIONAL SCHOOL OF ULAANBAATAR

Street address: DCHK, Ulaanbaatar, Mongolia
Phone: (976)(1)452959 **Facsimile:** (976)(1)358375
E-mail: inschool@magicnet.mn
Mail: PO Box 49/564, Ulaanbaatar, Mongolia
Principal and business manager: M. Thomson
Teaching staff: full-time, 11; part-time, 11; total, 22
Nationalities of teaching staff: U.S., 2; U.K., 1; host, 8; other, 11; total, 22
Grade levels: preK – 6 (grade 7+ on tutorial basis)
Enrollment: preK, 40; K, 12; 1 – 6, 60; total, 112
Nationalities of student body: U.S., 20; host, 16; other, 76; total, 112
Capacity: preK, 30; K, 15; 1 – 6, 70; total, 115
Teacher/student ratio: 1/15
Tuition (annual): $3,900
School year: September to June

Year founded: 1992. **Type of school:** coed, day, private nonprofit. **Governed by:** appointed and elected school board.

Curriculum/physical plant

Type: U.S. **Languages taught:** French, German, Mongolian. **Staff specialists:** guitar, piano. **Special programs:** ESL. **Extracurricular:** excursions/expeditions, field trips. **Tests:** Nelson Educational Research. **Location:** in Ulaanbaatar, in a cultural center within open parkland. **Library:** 500 volumes. **Facilities:** 1 building, 7 classrooms, covered play area.

MOROCCO

Region: Northwest Africa
Size: 177,117 square miles
Population: 29,779,156
Capital: Rabat
Telephone code: 212
Currency: dirham
Languages: Arabic, Berber

CASABLANCA

Casablanca American School

Street address: Route de La Mecque, Lot. Ougoug, Qtr. Californie, 20150 Casablanca, Morocco
Phone: (212)(2)214115/211416 – 7 **Facsimile:** (212)(2)212488
E-mail: 103113.1612@compuserve.com
Director: John J. Randolph
Deputy director/IB coordinator: Anne Osman
Lower school principal: Kim Aba
IB MYP supervisor: Jack F. Shepherd, Jr.
Business manager: Saad Guessous
Teaching staff: full-time, 53; part-time, 9; total, 62
Nationalities of teaching staff: U.S., 36; U.K., 3; host, 11; other, 12; total, 62
Grade levels: N – 12
Enrollment: N, 33; K, 37; pre-1, 45; 1 – 6, 209; 7 – 12, 93; total, 417
Nationalities of student body: U.S., 38; U.K., 11; host, 244; other, 124; total, 417
Teacher/student ratio: 1/7
Tuition (annual): N – K, $3,967; pre-1 – 6, $6,917; 7 – 12, $8,084
Other fees (annual): registration, $83; admission*, $1,110; application*, $63; sports, $81; building, $555
School year: September to June

Year founded: 1973. **Type of school:** coed, day, private nonprofit, college prep. **Governed by:** elected board, one member appointed by U.S. consul general. **Regional organizations:** AAIE, ECIS, MAIS.

Curriculum/physical plant

Type: U.S., IB, AP. **Languages taught:** French, Arabic, other languages available at extra cost. **Staff specialists:** computer, counselor, nurse, art, librarian, music, physical education, special education. **Special programs:** ESL. **Special curricular:** art, physical education, music, computer science. **Extracurricular:** drama, choral music, computers, yearbook. **Sports:** basketball, soccer, softball, swimming, track and field, volleyball. **Tests:** PSAT, SAT, TOEFL, IB, AP, CTB III. **Graduates have attended:** Princeton, College of William and Mary, Harvard, Duke, Boston College. **Location:** 12 kilometers from downtown Casablanca. **Libraries:** 12,000 volumes. **Facilities:** new suburban campus, cafeteria, infirmary, gymnasium, 3 science labs, 2 computer labs, art studio, dark room, music room, dance room, lower and upper school libraries.

*Once only fee

IFRANE

THE IFRANE SCHOOL

Phone: (212)(5)567407 **Facsimile:** (212)(5)567408
Mail: PO Box 104, Ifrane 53000, Morocco
Director: Emmanuel Pavlos
Teaching staff: full-time, 7; part-time, 3; total, 10
Nationalities of teaching staff: U.S., 4; host, 2; other, 4; total, 10
Grade levels: N – 10
Enrollment: N – preK, 5; K, 8; 1 – 6, 18; 7 – 10, 25; total, 56
Nationalities of student body: U.S., 9; host, 44; other, 3; total, 56
Capacity: N – preK, 18; K, 15; 1 – 6, 100; 7 – 9, 50; 10, 50; total, 233
Teacher/student ratio: 1/7
Boarders: boys, 10; girls, 10 **Grades:** 6 – 10 **Program:** planned 5-day
Tuition (annual): N – preK, $1,900; K, $3,800; 1 – 5, $4,400; 6 – 8, $5,000; 9 – 10, $5,600
Other fees (annual): registration, $60; boarding, $3,500; capital levy*, $500
School year: September to June

Year founded: 1995. **Type of school:** coed, day, boarding, private nonprofit. **Governed by:** Al Akhawayn Foundation. **Regional organizations:** MAIS.

Curriculum/physical plant

Type: modified U.S. **Languages taught:** French, Arabic. **Staff specialists:** computer, art, music. **Special programs:** ESL. **Special curricular:** computer instruction, physical education/sports. **Extracurricular:** drama, literary magazine, excursions/expeditions, field trips. **Tests:** ERB. **Location:** Alpine village in mid-Atlas mountains. **Campus:** 5 acres. **Library:** 2,500 volumes. **Facilities:** 3 buildings, 18 classrooms, playing field, science lab, computer lab, early childhood center, access to swimming pool, new dorm in 1997–98.

*Once only fee

RABAT

RABAT AMERICAN SCHOOL

Street address: 1bis, rue El Amir Abdelkader, Agdal, Rabat, Morocco
Phone: (212)(7)671476 **Facsimile:** (212)(7)670963
E-mail: info@ras.edu.ac.ma
Mail: U.S. Embassy, BP 120, Rabat, Morocco
U.S. mail: (no personal name) RAS, c/o American Embassy Rabat, PSC 74 Box 010, APO AE 09718
Director: Robert Sills, Ed.D.
Secondary principal: Robert A. Benson, Ph.D.
Elementary principal: Kathryn Morabet
Head of library: Jane Langholz
Teaching staff: full-time, 40; part-time, 16; total, 56
Nationalities of teaching staff: U.S., 30; U.K., 4; other, 22; total, 56
Grade levels: preK – 12
Enrollment: preK, 21; K, 38; 1 – 5, 180; 6 – 8, 92; 9 – 12, 92; total, 423
Nationalities of student body: U.S., 99; host, 136; other, 188; total, 423
Teacher/student ratio: 1/9
Tuition, 1996–97 rates (annual): preK, $2,500 (half-day); K, $6,600; 1 – 5, $8,100; 6 – 8, $9,175; 9 – 12, $9,325
Other fees (annual): registration*, $2,250; busing, $400 – 550
School year: September to June

Year founded: 1962. **Type of school:** coed, day, private nonprofit. **Governed by:** elected board of directors. **Accredited by:** Middle States. **Regional organizations:** AAIE, MAIS.

Curriculum

Type: U.S., IB, AP. **Languages taught:** French, Arabic. **Staff specialists:** computer, counselor, psychologist, nurse, reading enrichment, media, academic support. **Special programs:** ESL, independent study. **Special curricular:** Moroccan studies, photography, optimal match, philosophy, Harvard Model Congress. **Extra-curricular:** drama, gymnastics, yearbook, field trips, art, ballet. **Sports:** basketball, soccer, softball, swimming, volleyball. **Clubs:** chess, Cub Scouts, Brownies, Boy Scouts, Girl Scouts, teen, environmental, French, Little League T-ball and baseball. **Tests:** SSAT, PSAT, SAT, ACT, IB, AP, Iowa. **Graduates attending college:** 90%. **Graduates have attended:** MIT, McGill, Cornell, Yale, Harvard.

Physical plant

Location: 5 minutes from downtown Rabat. **Campus:** 6 acres. **Libraries:** 15,000 volumes. **Facilities:** 10 buildings, 36 classrooms, auditorium, cafeteria, infirmary, 3 playing fields, 2 science labs, 2 computer labs, sports complex/swimming pool, darkroom, gymnasium (under construction).

*Once only fee

TANGIER

The American School of Tangier

Street address: Rue Christophe Colomb, Tangier, Morocco
Phone: (212)(9)939827 – 8 **Facsimile:** (212)(9)947535
Academic head: Joseph A. McPhillips III
Teaching staff: full-time, 42; part-time, 5; total, 47
Nationalities of teaching staff: U.S., 7; U.K., 9; host, 17; other, 14; total, 47
Grade levels: preK – 12
Enrollment: total, 350
Nationalities of student body: U.S., 9; host, 251; other, 90; total, 350
Capacity: total, 400
Teacher/student ratio: 1/12
Boarders: boys, 14; girls, 5 **Grades:** 7 – 12 **Program:** planned 7-day
Tuition (annual): preK – K, $3,025; 1 – 6, $10,740; 7 – 8, $11,100; 9 – 12, $12,560
Other fees (annual): registration, $100; room and board, $4,500
School year: September to June

Year founded: 1950. **Type of school:** coed, day, boarding, private nonprofit. **Governed by:** elected board of trustees. **Regional organizations:** MAIS.

Curriculum/physical plant

Type: U.S. **Languages taught:** French, Arabic. **Staff specialists:** math. **Special curricular:** physical education. **Extracurricular:** drama, dance, literary magazine, music, karate. **Sports:** basketball, soccer, softball, track and field, volleyball. **Tests:** PSAT, TOEFL, SAT I & II. **Graduates have attended:** Bryn Mawr, MIT, Harvard, Sarah Lawrence, Stanford. **Location:** on wooded site near city. **Campus:** 6 acres. **Library:** 10,000 volumes. **Facilities:** 3 buildings, 23 classrooms, science lab, playing fields, dormitory.

MOZAMBIQUE

Region: Southeast Africa
Size: 313,661 square miles
Population: 17,877,927
Capital: Maputo
Telephone code: 258
Currency: metical
Languages: Portuguese, Makua, Malawi, Shona, Tsonga

MAPUTO

INTERNATIONAL SCHOOL OF MAPUTO

Street address: Rua de Nachingwea 389, Maputo, Mozambique
Phone: (258)(1)492131 **Facsimile:** (258)(1)492382
Mail: C.P. 4152, Maputo, Mozambique
Director: B. Cherinda
Pedagogical director: D. Hepworth
Business manager: A. Massena
Teaching staff: full-time, 38; part-time, 10; total, 48
Grade levels: preK – 13
Enrollment: preK – K, 35; 1 – 6, 149; 7 – 9, 84; 10 – 13, 45; total, 313
Capacity: preK – K, 40; 1 – 6, 300; 7 – 9, 150; 10 – 13, 50; total, 540
Teacher/student ratio: 1/8
Tuition (annual): preK – 3, $3,150; 4 – 6, $3,525; 7 – 11, $4,475; 12 – 13, $4,925
Other fees: registration*, $150

Year founded: 1975. **Type of school:** coed, day, autonomously run school under government's ownership.

Curriculum/physical plant

Type: U.K. **Languages taught:** French, Portuguese. **Staff specialists:** reading, math. **Special programs:** ESL, intensive English, computers. **Special curricular:** art, physical education. **Extracurricular:** drama, gymnastics, instrumental music, excursions/expeditions, field trips, karate, swimming, cooking, craft, needlework. **Sports:** badminton, basketball, soccer, volleyball. **Tests:** IGCSE, HIGCSE. **Location:** in city. **Library:** 5,000 volumes. **Facilities:** 2 buildings, 30 classrooms, covered play area, gymnasium, 2 science labs.

*Once only fee

MYANMAR

Region: South Asia
Size: 261,228 square miles
Population: 45,975,625
Capital: Yangon

Telephone code: 95
Currency: kyat
Languages: Burmese, Karen, Shan

YANGON

International School Yangon

Street address: 20 Shwe Taung Gyar, Yangon, Myanmar
Phone: (95)(1)512793/512795 **Facsimile:** (95)(1)525020/280409
Telex: 08321230 AMBYGN BM
U.S. mail: c/o American Embassy Rangoon, Dept. of State, Washington, DC 20521-4250
Director: Monica N. Greeley
Business manager: Wai Wai Myaing
Teaching staff: full-time, 34; part-time, 3; total, 37
Nationalities of teaching staff: U.S., 22; host, 15; total, 37
Grade levels: preK – 12
Enrollment: preK, 28; K, 27; 1 – 6, 158; 7 – 8, 51; 9 – 12, 75; total, 339
Nationalities of student body: U.S., 44; host, 74; other, 221; total, 339
Capacity: preK, 15; K, 30; 1 – 6, 186; 7 – 8, 50; 9 – 12, 120; total, 401
Teacher/student ratio: 1/9
Tuition (annual): preK, $1,680; K, $4,350; 1 – 12, $6,500
Other fees: registration*, $1,000; capital levy, $2,000 per first two semesters (new students); $500 per semester (returning students)
School year: August to June

Year founded: 1955. **Type of school:** day, private nonprofit. **Governed by:** elected board of management. **Accredited by:** Western. **Regional organizations:** AAIE, EARCOS.

Curriculum/physical plant

Type: U.S., AP. **Languages taught:** French, Spanish. **Staff specialists:** computer, guidance counselor. **Special programs:** ESL. **Special curricular:** art, physical education, music, computer. **Extracurricular:** drama, computers, yearbook, newspaper, literary magazine, excursions/expeditions. **Sports:** basketball, soccer, softball, swimming, volleyball, martial arts. **Tests:** PSAT, SAT, TOEFL, AP, ACH. **Location:** in suburban Yangon. **Campus:** 3.5 acres. **Library:** 12,000 volumes. **Facilities:** 6 buildings, 30 classrooms, 2 covered play areas, playing field, science labs, computer lab, multipurpose room, air conditioning.

*Once only fee

NAMIBIA

Region: Southern Africa
Size: 318,580 square miles
Population: 1,677,243
Capital: Windhoek
Telephone code: 264
Currency: Namibia dollar
Languages: Afrikaans, English, German, indigenous languages

WINDHOEK

WINDHOEK INTERNATIONAL SCHOOL

Street address: Sheppmann Street, Windhoek, Namibia
Phone: (264)(61)241783 **Facsimile:** (264)(61)243127
E-mail: kevin@granny.mac.alt.na
Mail: PO Box 30452, Windhoek, Namibia
Director/business manager: Kevin Bartlett
Secondary principal: Jane Cullen
Primary principal: Mark McGough
Teaching staff: full-time, 31; part-time, 2; total, 33
Nationalities of teaching staff: U.S., 4; host, 7; other, 22; total, 33
Grade levels: preK – 11
Enrollment: preK, 40; K, 32; 1 – 6, 150; 7 – 9, 51; 10, 9; 11, 5; total, 287
Nationalities of student body: U.S., 21; host, 110; other, 156; total, 287
Capacity: preK, 40; K, 25; 1 – 6, 175; 7 – 9, 75; 10, 20; 11, 20; total, 355
Teacher/student ratio: 1/9
Tuition (annual): preK, $3,000; K – 2, $5,000; 3 – 5, $5,555; 6 – 8, $6,222; 9 – 11, $6,888
Other fees: capital levy*, $1,000; family deposit* (refundable), $666
School year: August to June

Year founded: 1991. **Type of school:** coed, day, private nonprofit. **Governed by:** appointed and elected board of trustees. **Regional organizations:** AISA, ECIS.

Curriculum/physical plant

Type: U.S., U.K., ISCP, IGCSE. **Languages taught:** French, German (3 – 11). **Special programs:** ESL, special needs. **Special curricular:** art, physical education, computer instruction, music. **Extracurricular:** drama, gymnastics, instrumental music, newspaper, pottery, stamp club. **Sports:** baseball, basketball, hockey, swimming, volleyball. **Tests:** IGCSE. **Library:** 3,000 volumes. **Facilities:** 16 classrooms, gymnasium, science lab, computer lab, sports fields.

*Once only fee

NEPAL

Region: Asia
Size: 56,827 square miles
Population: 22,094,033
Capital: Kathmandu
Telephone code: 977
Currency: rupee
Languages: Nepali, others

KATHMANDU

Lincoln School

Street address: Rabi Bhawan, Kathmandu, Nepal
Phone: (977)(1)270482 **Facsimile:** (977)(1)272685
E-mail: lincoln@school.mos.com.np
Mail: GPO 2673, Kathmandu, Nepal
U.S. mail: c/o Kathmandu (LS), Dept. of State, Washington, DC 20521-6190
Director: Paul Poore
Middle/high school principal: Jim Ray
Guidance counselor: Joe LaCamera, Ed.D.
Teaching staff: full-time, 29; part-time, 3; total, 32
Nationalities of teaching staff: U.S., 24; U.K., 3; host, 1; other, 4; total, 32
Grade levels: K – 12
Enrollment: K, 14; 1 – 5, 78; 6 – 8, 70; 9 – 12, 85; total, 247
Nationalities of student body: U.S., 73; U.K., 11; host, 49; other, 114; total, 247
Teacher/student ratio: 1/8
Tuition (annual): K – 5, $8,640; 6 – 8, $9,320; 9 – 12, $10,450
Other fees (annual): busing, $650; capital development*, $2,000; admission*, $450; ESL (semester), $200
School year: August to June

Year founded: 1954. **Type of school:** coed, day, private nonprofit. **Governed by:** elected board of directors. **Sponsored by:** parents. **Accredited by:** New England, ECIS. **Regional organizations:** NESA, SAISA.

Curriculum/physical plant

Type: U.S., AP. **Languages taught:** French, Spanish. **Staff specialists:** counselor, learning disabilities, nurse. **Special programs:** ESL. **Special curricular:** art, chorus, band, physical education, computer instruction, peer counseling, community service. **Extracurricular:** drama, gymnastics, dance, choral and instrumental music, computers, yearbook, newspaper, photography, excursions/expeditions, field trips, annual 2-week trek for grades 5 – 12. **Sports:** baseball, basketball, soccer, swimming, tennis, track and field, volleyball. **Clubs:** Brownies, Boy Scouts, Girl Scouts. **Tests:** SSAT, PSAT, SAT, Iowa. **Location:** 10 minutes from downtown Kathmandu. **Campus:** 2.5 acres. **Library:** 12,000 volumes. **Facilities:** auditorium, infirmary, tennis court, gymnasium, 2 playing fields, science lab, computer lab, AV equipment, air conditioning.

*Once only fee

THE NETHERLANDS

Region: Europe
Size: 16,033 square miles
Population: 15,568,034
Capital: Amsterdam
Telephone code: 31
Currency: guilder
Language: Dutch

AMSTERDAM

INTERNATIONAL SCHOOL OF AMSTERDAM

Street address: Sportlaan 45, 1185 TB Amstelveen, The Netherlands
Phone: (31)(20)3471111 **Facsimile:** (31)(20)3471222 **E-mail:** jrich@isa.nl
Web: http://www.isa.nl
Mail: PO Box No. 920, 1180 AX Amstelveen, The Netherlands
Director: Dr. Paul Johnson
Upper school head: Trishan Stobie
Lower school head: Lesley Snowball
Admissions officer: Joanne Rich
Teaching staff: full-time, 71; part-time, 28; total, 99
Nationalities of teaching staff: U.S., 28; U.K., 19; host, 15; other, 37; total, 99
Grade levels: toddler – 13
Enrollment: toddler, 22; preS, 44; K, 7; 1 – 5, 324; 6 – 8, 113; 9 – 13, 157; total, 667
Nationalities of student body: U.S., 160; U.K., 61; other, 446; total, 667
Teacher/student ratio: 1/8
Tuition (annual): toddler, 14,385**; preS, 16,770; preK – K, 21,490; 1 – 6, 23,850; 7 – 8, 27,400; 9 – 13, 28,710
Other fees (annual): registration, 300**; enrollment*, 2,500; non-refundable deposit, 550; ESL, 1,200; IB (full diploma), 1,200; IB courses, 200; PTA, 50
School year: August to June

Year founded: 1964. **Type of school:** coed, day, private nonprofit. **Governed by:** elected board of governors. **Accredited by:** New England, ECIS. **Regional organizations:** AAIE, ECIS.

Curriculum/physical plant

Type: U.S., U.K., IB, international/U.S./U.K. **Languages taught:** French, Spanish, German, Dutch, Japanese. **Staff specialists:** reading, math, computer, counselor, learning disabilities, art, music, library, design technology, drama, Dutch, French, German, Japanese, Spanish. **Special programs:** ESL. **Special curricular:** art, chorus, band, physical education, computer instruction, drama, instrumental lessons, ensembles, library/media instruction. **Extracurricular:** drama, gymnastics, choral music, computers, yearbook, photography, excursions/expeditions, field trips, International Youth Award. **Sports:** basketball, soccer, softball, swimming, tennis, track and field, volleyball. **Clubs:** chess, computer, drama, Model UN, speech and debate, photography. **Tests:** PSAT, SAT, TOEFL, IB, IBMYP. **Graduates attending college:** more than 97%. **Graduates have attended:** Georgetown, U. of California at Berkeley, Dartmouth, McGill, Cambridge. **Location:** southwest suburb of Amsterdam. **Campus:** 15 acres. **Library:** 13,000 volumes, extensive CD-Rom collection, Internet and DIALOG access, on-line catalog. **Facilities:** 16,000 square meter building, 66 classrooms, playing field, 6 science labs, 5 computer labs, double gymnasium, theater, set design area, dance/theater studio, 4-story multimedia center, design and food technology labs.

*Once only fee **Dutch guilder

BRUNSSUM

AFCENT International School

Street address: Ferd Bolstraat 1, 6445 EE Brunssum, The Netherlands
Phone: (31)(45)5278220 **Facsimi2le:** (31)(45)5278233
U.S. mail: (no personal name) AFCENT, Unit 21606, APO AE 09703
Director: R. J. Linton
Principal, U.S. high school: K. Galloway
Principal, U.S. elementary school: R. Nance
Principal, Canadian section: G. Nijenhuis
Head, U.K. section: W. Thomas
Head, German section: W. Meissner
Teaching staff: full-time, 114; part-time, 6; total, 120
Nationalities of teaching staff: U.S., 66; U.K., 14; German, 27; other, 13; total, 120
Grade levels: preK – 13
Enrollment: preK – 1, 261; 2 – 4, 259; 5 – 8, 296; 9 – 13, 262; German section, 201; total, 1,279
Nationalities of student body: U.S., 771; U.K., 143; German, 201; other, 164; total, 1,279
Teacher/student ratio: 1/11
School year: August to June

Year founded: 1967. **Type of school:** coed, day, limited to NATO personnel. **Governed and sponsored by:** governments/defense departments of U.S., U.K., Canada, Germany.

Curriculum/physical plant

Staff specialists: reading, math, computer, speech/hearing, counselor, learning disabilities, nurse. **Special programs:** ESL, honors sections, GSL/FSL Extended German/French. **Special curricular:** art, chorus, band, physical education, computer instruction. **Extracurricular:** drama, gymnastics, dance, choral and instrumental music, computers, yearbook, newspaper, photography, excursions/expeditions, field trips, sports. **Tests:** SSAT, PSAT, SAT, ACT, AP, Stanford, Iowa, SRA, Abitur (German). **Graduates attending college:** 80%. **Graduates have attended:** U. of Maryland, Notre Dame, Florida State U., McGill, U. of Toronto. **Location:** in Brunssum. **Campus:** 12 acres. **Libraries:** 40,000 volumes. **Facilities:** 1 building, 102 classrooms, auditorium, cafeteria, infirmary, 3 gymnasiums, playing field, 10 science labs, 3 computer labs, AV equipment, track.

EINDHOVEN

INTERNATIONAL SECONDARY SCHOOL EINDHOVEN

Street address: Henegouwenlaan 2A, 5628 WK Eindhoven, The Netherlands
Phone: (31)(40)2413600 **Facsimile:** (31)(40)2424973 **E-mail:** zey@iaehv.nl
Head of school: Peter J. H. Goosens
Deputy head: Stephan Zeytountsian
Teaching staff: full-time, 17; part-time, 17; total, 34
Nationalities of teaching staff: U.S., 1; U.K., 11; host, 12; other, 10; total, 34
Grade levels: 1 – 5 (English stream); 1 – 2 (IB); ESL
Enrollment: total, 275
Teacher/student ratio: 1/12
Tuition (annual): 6,000** (including books)
Other fees (annual): company fee, 1,500**; insurance (voluntary); out-of-school activities; exams; education tax for students age 16 and over, 1,497
School year: September to mid-July

Year founded: 1974. **Type of school:** coed, day, 40% company-sponsored. **Governed by:** Eindhoven Municipality. **Sponsored by:** government and companies. **Accredited by:** IGSCE U. of Cambridge, IBO Geneva, Netherlands Ministry of Education and Sciences. **Regional organizations:** ECIS, National Association of IGO Schools.

Curriculum/physical plant

Type: IB, IGCSE. **Languages taught:** English, French, Spanish, German, Dutch. **Staff specialists:** computer, counselor, ESL, librarian, year tutors. **Special programs:** ESL. **Special curricular:** art, physical education, computer instruction. **Extracurricular:** drama, computers, yearbook, photography, excursions/expeditions, field trips, magazine, Benelux Award, musical progams, concert, Model UN. **Sports:** basketball, soccer, softball, volleyball. **Tests:** IB, IGCSE, Cambridge Preliminary English Test (ESL). **Graduates have attended:** Dutch, U.K., Canadian, American, Swedish, and Japanese universities and colleges.

Physical plant

Location: in quiet neighborhood, 10 minutes' drive from center of Eindhoven. **Library:** approximately 4,000 volumes. **Facilities:** 17 new and modern classrooms with connections to educational network in each classroom, internet and email facilities, auditorium, cafeteria, gymnasium, 2 playing fields, 4 science labs, state-of-the-art computer lab, language lab, darkroom, arts and crafts shop, covered bike shed, parking lot.

**Dutch guilder

Regionale Internationale School

Street address: Humperdincklaan 4, 5654 PA Eindhoven, The Netherlands
Phone: (31)(40)519437 **Facsimile:** (31)(40)527675
Headmaster: H. A. Schol
Deputy headmaster: J. B. Bright
Teaching staff: full-time, 24; part-time, 6
Grade levels: K – 6
Enrollment: total, 340
Nationalities of student body: U.S., 20; U.K., 50; host, 146; other, 124; total, 340
Teacher/student ratio: 1/13
Tuition (annual): 4,000**
School year: August to June

Year founded: 1965. **Type of school:** coed, day. **Regional organizations:** ECIS.

Curriculum

Type: U.K., national. **Languages of instruction:** English, Dutch.

**Dutch guilder

GRONINGEN

Maartens College International School

Street address: Rijksstraatweg 24, Haren, Groningen, The Netherlands
Phone: (31)(50)5340084 **Facsimile:** (31)(50)5340056
Mail: Postbus 6105, 9702 HC Groningen, The Netherlands
Headmistress: Jacqueline Lamoré–Meÿer
Middle school coordinator: Debbie Taylor Williams
IB coordinator: Ton Heuvelmans
Teaching staff: full-time, 3; part-time, 23; total, 26
Nationalities of teaching staff: U.S., 1; U.K., 6; host, 19; total, 26
Grade levels: 6 – 12
Enrollment: 6, 14; 7 – 9, 62; 10 – 12, 44; total, 120
Nationalities of student body: U.S., 20; U.K., 10; host, 16; other, 74; total, 120
Capacity: 6, 20; 7 – 9, 60; 10 – 12, 60; total, 140
Teacher/student ratio: 1/7
Tuition (annual): 14,500**
School year: September to July

Year founded: 1984. **Type of school:** coed, day, company-sponsored, church-related. **Governed by:** appointed board. **Sponsored by:** Dutch government.

Curriculum/physical plant

Type: national, IB, IGCSE. **Languages taught:** English, French, German, Dutch, all IB languages. **Staff specialists:** reading, math, computer, counselor. **Special programs:** ESL, remedial. **Special curricular:** art, physical education, computer instruction. **Extracurricular:** drama, yearbook, excursions/expeditions, field trips.

Tests: IB, IGCSE, Dutch state exams. **Graduates attending college:** 95%. **Graduates have attended:** University College London, U. of Leiden, Cambridge, U. of Edinburgh, U. of Groningen. **Location:** in wooded, suburban area, 3 miles from Groningen. **Facilities:** 2 campuses, 3 buildings, 3 auditoriums, 3 gymnasiums, 3 playing fields, 6 science labs, 3 computer labs.

**Dutch guilder

THE HAGUE

THE AMERICAN SCHOOL OF THE HAGUE

Street address: Rijksstraatweg 200, 2241 BX Wassenaar, The Netherlands
Phone: (31)(70)5140113 **Facsimile:** (31)(70)5112400 **E-mail:** admission@ash.nl
Web: http://www.ash.nl
Superintendent: William H. Gerritz, Ph.D.
High school principal: Clayton Lewis
Middle school principal: Bert Boonstra
Elementary school principal: Dennis Donatuti
Teaching staff: full-time, 84; part-time, 28; total, 112
Nationalities of teaching staff: U.S., 89; U.K., 10; host, 4; other, 9; total, 112
Grade levels: preK – 12
Enrollment: preK, 25; K – 4, 325; 5 – 8, 250; 9 – 12, 250; total, 850
Nationalities of student body: U.S., 445; U.K., 20; host, 50; other, 335; total, 850
Teacher/student ratio: 1/9
Tuition (annual): preK, 7,100**; K – 4, 18,160; 5 – 8, 20,740; 9 – 12, 22,000
Other fees (annual): capital levy, 3,000**; busing, 2,500 – 3,200; enrollment*, 1,000
School year: August to June

Year founded: 1953. **Type of school:** coed, day. **Governed by:** elected executive committee. **Accredited by:** Middle States, ECIS. **Regional organizations:** AAIE, ECIS.

Curriculum/physical plant

Type: U.S., IB, AP. **Languages taught:** French, Spanish, German, Dutch. **Staff specialists:** speech/hearing, counselor, learning disabilities, nurse. **Special programs:** ESL, learning skills center. **Special curricular:** art, chorus, band, physical education, computer instruction, photography, speech and debate. **Extracurricular:** drama, choral and instrumental music, computers, yearbook, newspaper, field trips, student council, Odyssey of the Mind, Close-Up. **Sports:** baseball, basketball, cross-country, soccer, softball, swimming, tennis, track and field, volleyball. **Organizations:** National Honor Society, International Political Association, Alumni Association, International Model UN held in the Hague every January. **Tests:** PSAT, SAT, ACT, TOEFL, AP, IB, Stanford. **Graduates attending college:** 92%. **Graduates have attended:** M.I.T., Brown, Harvard, Duke, Yale. **Location:** 15 minutes from downtown Den Haag by car. **Library:** 31,000 volumes. **Facilities:** 78 classrooms, cafeteria, library, arts center, 360-seat theater, sports complex, sports field.

*Once only fee **Dutch guilder

OEGSTGEEST

The Rijnlands International School†

Street address: Apollolaan 1, 2341 BA Oegstgeest, Z. H., The Netherlands
Phone: (31)(71)5177471 **Facsimile:** (31)(71)5171900
E-mail: admission@international.ros.nl
Headmaster: A. J. M. Vaessen
Head, international section: L. E. Timmermans
Teaching staff: full-time, 40; part-time, 60; total, 100
Nationalities of teaching staff: U.S., 3; U.K., 2; host, 95; total, 100
Grade levels: 6 – 12
Enrollment: 6, 15; 7 – 9, 610; 10 – 12, 700; total, 1,325
Nationalities of student body: U.S., 10; U.K., 5; host, 1,192; other, 118; total, 1,325
Capacity: total, 1,500
Teacher/student ratio: 1/21
Tuition (annual): 5,000**
Other fees (annual): book fund, 300**
School year: August to July

Year founded: 1958. **Type of school:** coed, day, boarding, private nonprofit. **Governed by:** appointed foundation board. **Sponsored by:** Dutch government. **Regional organizations:** ECIS.

Curriculum/physical plant

Type: national, IB, IBMYP. **Languages of instruction:** English, Dutch. **Languages taught:** English, French, Spanish, German, Dutch, others. **Special curricular:** art, band, physical education, computer instruction, vocational. **Extracurricular:** drama, gymnastics, dance, instrumental music, computers, yearbook, photography, excursions/expeditions, field trips. **Sports:** athletics, baseball, basketball, rugby, soccer, tennis. **Tests:** SAT, TOEFL, IB, IBMYP, ISCO, HAVO, VWO. **Graduates attending college:** 90%. **Graduates have attended:** Yale, MIT, Cambridge, Oxford, Harvard. **Location:** in suburb, 12 kilometers from The Hague. **Campus:** 200 acres. **Library:** 60,000 volumes. **Facilities:** 1 building, 65 classrooms, auditorium, tennis court, 2 gymnasiums, playing field, 5 science labs, 2 computer labs, large sports hall, 6 language labs, technology classroom, AV equipment, boarding accommodations nearby.

**Dutch guilder †formerly Het Rijnlands Lyceum Oegstgeest

ROTTERDAM

AMERICAN INTERNATIONAL SCHOOL OF ROTTERDAM (INTERNATIONAL EDUCATION CENTER)

Street address: Verhulstlaan 21, 3055 WJ Rotterdam, The Netherlands
Phone: (31)(10)4225351/4225137 **Facsimile:** (31)(10)4224075
E-mail: aisr@evronet.nl
Director: Alan Conkey
Curriculum coordinator: Earl Turko
Teaching staff: full-time, 13; part-time, 7; total, 20
Nationalities of teaching staff: U.S., 11; U.K., 1; host, 3; other, 5; total, 20
Grade levels: preK – 10
Enrollment: preK, 10; K, 10; 1 – 6, 70; 7 – 10, 40; total, 130
Nationalities of student body: U.S., 40; other, 90; total, 130
Teacher/student ratio: 1/7
Tuition (annual): preK, $7,800; K – 4, $9,300; 5 – 8, $10,500; 9 – 10, $11,100
Other fees (annual): registration*, $1,300; busing, $2,000; capital assessment, $500
School year: August to June

Year founded: 1959. **Type of school:** coed, day, private nonprofit. **Governed by:** appointed board of directors. **Accredited by:** New England, ECIS. **Regional organizations:** AAIE, ECIS.

Curriculum/physical plant

Type: U.S. **Languages taught:** French, German, Dutch. **Staff specialists:** reading, computer, art, music, physical education. **Special programs:** ESL. **Special curricular:** art, band, physical education, computer instruction. **Extracurricular:** drama, computers, yearbook. **Sports:** basketball, gymnastics, soccer, swimming, track and field, volleyball. **Tests:** ITBS. **Location:** on north side of city. **Library:** 15,000 volumes. **Facilities:** New campus shared with the Japanese School of Rotterdam, forming the International Education Center. Campus consists of 35 classrooms (entirely computer networked), 2 science labs, multiple computer centers, sports complex (with fields, double gymnasium, and rented swimming pool), cafeteria, technology and domestic science classrooms.

*Once only fee

VOORSCHOTEN

The British School in the Netherlands

Street address: senior school: Jan van Hooflaan 3, 2252 BG Voorschoten, The Netherlands
Phone: senior school: (31)(71)5602222 **Facsimile:** (31)(71)5602200
Web: http://www.britishschool.nl
Principal: M. J. Cooper
Head of senior school(11-18 years): J. Hollis
Head of junior school(3-11 years): A. Shaw
Teaching staff: full-time, 120; part-time, 6; total, 126
Nationalities of teaching staff: U.K., 120; host, 2; other, 4; total, 126
Enrollment: total, 1,200
Nationalities of student body: U.S., 28; U.K., 750; host, 30; other, 392; total, 1,200
Capacity: total, 1,400
Teacher/student ratio: 1/11
Tuition (annual): N – preK, 5,988**; 1 – 6, 14,730; 7 – 13, 20,490
Other fees (annual): registration*, 1,100**; busing, 2,000
School year: September to July

Year founded: 1935. **Type of school:** coed, day, private nonprofit. **Governed by:** appointed association. **Accredited by:** ECIS, COBISEC.

Curriculum/physical plant

Type: U.K. **Languages taught:** French, Spanish, German, Dutch. **Staff specialists:** reading, math, computer, psychologist, learning disabilities. **Special programs:** ESL, remedial. **Special curricular:** art, chorus, band, physical education, computer instruction. **Extracurricular:** drama, gymnastics, dance, choral and instrumental music, computers, newspaper, literary magazine, photography, excursions/expeditions, field trips. **Sports:** include fencing, horseback riding, trampoline. **Clubs:** chess, judo, photography. **Tests:** GCSE, A- and A/S-level GCE, MAT (ESL), ASS Board of Royal School of Music, Cambridge. **Graduates attending college:** 90%. **Graduates have attended:** universities in U.K., Japan, Switzerland, Sweden. **Campuses (2):** 1 urban, 1 rural. **Facilities:** auditorium, tennis court, gymnasium, playing field, 7 science labs, 2 computer labs, 2 music rooms, 3 art rooms.

*Once only fee **Dutch guilder

OMMEN

International School Eerde

Street address: Kasteellaan 1, 7731 PJ Ommen, The Netherlands
Phone: (31)(529)451452/456502/456529 **Facsimile:** (31)(529)456377
E-mail: eerde@dds.nl
Headmaster: A. C. Breedveld

NICARAGUA

Region: Central America
Size: 50,838 square miles
Population: 4,272,352
Capital: Managua
Telephone code: 505
Currency: gold cordoba
Language: Spanish

MANAGUA

AMERICAN-NICARAGUAN SCHOOL

Street address: UNAN Highway, Managua, Nicaragua
Phone: (505)(2)2782565/2780029 **Facsimile:** (505)(2)2673088
E-mail: anslib@ns.tmx.com.ni or hsl@ns.tmx.com.ni
Mail: PO Box 2670, Managua, Nicaragua
U.S. mail: American-Nicaraguan School, c/o American Embassy Managua, Unit 2710-Box 7, APO AA 34021
Director: Mary Ellen Normandin
High/middle school principal: Antonio Rios
High/middle school assistant principal: Tim Gardina
Primary school principal: Henningston Hammond
Business manager: Roberto Cardenal
Teaching staff: full-time, 83; part-time, 10; total, 93
Nationalities of teaching staff: U.S., 47; host, 39; other, 7; total, 93
Grade levels: preK – 12
Enrollment: preK, 38; K, 77; 1 – 4, 390; 5 – 8, 405; 9 – 12, 340; total, 1,250
Teacher/student ratio: 1/13
Tuition (annual): preK, $2,400; K – 6, $2,700; 7 – 12, $2,760
Other fees (annual): registration, $120; busing, $385 (optional); entrance*, $1,000; construction*, $750, technology fee, $100 (grades 5 – 12)
School year: August to June

Year founded: 1944. **Type of school:** coed, day, private nonprofit. **Governed by:** board of directors. **Accredited by:** Southern. **Regional organizations:** AAIE, AASCA, Tri-Assoc

Curriculum/physical plant

Type: U.S., national. **Languages taught:** French, Spanish. **Staff specialists:** reading, computer, counselor, nurses. **Special programs:** ESL. **Special curricular:** art, physical education, computer instruction, music. **Extracurricular:** drama, yearbook, newspaper, excursions/expeditions, field trips, student council. **Sports:** baseball, basketball, soccer, volleyball. **Tests:** PSAT, SAT, TOEFL, Stanford. **Graduates attending college:** 98%. **Graduates have attended:** Purdue, Boston U., Cornell, Tufts, Wellesley. **Facilities:** tennis court, gymnasium, playing field, science lab, computer lab, library.

*Once only fee

NIGER

Region: Africa
Size: 496,900 square miles
Population: 9,113,001
Capital: Niamey
Telephone code: 227
Currency: CFA franc
Languages: French, Hausa, Djerma

NIAMEY

American School of Niamey

Phone: (227)723942 **Facsimile:** (227)723457 **E-mail:** asniger@bow.intnet.ne
Mail: c/o U.S. Embassy, BP 11201, Niamey, Niger, West Africa
U.S. mail: (for urgent business) JAO Director (ASN), Dept. of State, Niamey, Washington, DC 20521-2420
Director: Andrew Schmidt
Office manager: Shelley Nunemaker
Business manager: Fidele Dassi
Teaching staff: full-time, 12; part-time, 4; total, 16
Nationalities of teaching staff: U.S., 4; host, 3; other, 9; total, 16
Grade levels: preK – 9 (10 – 12 correspondence study)
Enrollment: preK, 9; K, 2; 1 – 5, 36; 6 – 9, 22; correspondence, 4; total, 73
Nationalities of student body: U.S., 22; other, 51; total, 73
Capacity: preK, 20; K, 20; 1 – 5, 100; 6 – 9, 40; total, 180
Teacher/student ratio: 1/9
Tuition (annual): preK, $2,600; K – 5, $9,000; 6 – 9, $9,800, correspondence, $10,800
Other fees (annual): registration*, $1,500; busing, $1,500; ESL assessment, $1,500
School year: August to June

Year founded: 1982. **Type of school:** coed, day, private nonprofit. **Governed by:** elected and appointed board of directors. **Accredited by:** Middle States. **Regional organizations:** AISA.

Curriculum/physical plant

Type: U.S. **Languages taught:** French. **Staff specialists:** computer, librarian. **Special programs:** ESL, tutorial. **Special curricular:** art, physical education, computer instruction, health, performing arts, Nigerienne studies, library. **Extracurricular:** field trips, sports/social exchanges/competition, student council, Math Counts. **Sports:** basketball, soccer, softball, swimming, track and field, volleyball. **Tests:** Iowa. **Location:** on U.S. Embassy grounds at western edge of city. **Campus:** 8 acres. **Library:** 7,500 volumes. **Facilities:** 4 buildings, 12 classrooms, science lab, computer lab, swimming pool, air conditioning.

*Once only fee

NIGERIA

Region: Africa
Size: 356,669 square miles
Population: 103,912,489
Capital: Abuja
Telephone code: 234
Currency: naira
Languages: English, Hausa, Yoruba, Ibo

ABUJA

AMERICAN INTERNATIONAL SCHOOL OF ABUJA

Street address: IBB Way, Maitama, Abuja, Nigeria
Phone/facsimile: (234)(9)5235464
Mail: PO Box 5760, Maitama Abuja, Nigeria
U.S. mail: USLO Abuja (D.O.S.), U.S. Embassy Lagos, Washington, DC 20521-8300
Principal: Mrs. J. Okpanachi
Head of library: Funke Abegunde
Head of computer services: Aisha Oduwole
Teaching staff: full-time, 14; part-time, 3; total, 17
Nationalities of teaching staff: U.S., 3; U.K., 1; host, 4; other, 9; total, 17
Grade levels: preS – 8
Enrollment: preS – preK, 16; K, 12; 1 – 6, 59; 7 – 8, 11; total, 98
Nationalities of student body: U.S., 15; U.K., 6; host, 36; other, 41; total, 98
Teacher/student ratio: 1/7
Tuition (annual): preS – preK, $2,750; K, $4,455; 1 – 4, $5,985; 5 – 8, $6,270
School year: September to June

Year founded: 1993. **Type of school:** coed, day. **Governed by:** elected and appointed board of directors. **Regional organizations:** AISA.

Curriculum/physical plant

Type: U.S. **Languages taught:** French. **Staff specialists:** reading, computer, learning disabilities. **Special programs:** ESL. **Special curricular:** art, chorus, physical education, computer instruction. **Extracurricular:** drama, dance, choral music, yearbook, newspaper, sports. **Clubs:** Stitch-in-Time, Crafty Hands, French, social. **Tests:** Stanford. **Location:** in a residential area of the city. **Campus:** 1.5 acres. **Library:** 5,000 volumes. **Facilities:** 1 building, 11 classrooms, playing field, science lab, computer lab, soccer field, basketball court, volleyball court, air conditioning.

EKET

The International Foreign Residents School of Eket

Phone/facsimile: (234)(1)2621640
U.S. mail: c/o Mobil Producing Nigeria/QIT, 3225 Gallows Road, Fairfax, VA, 22031 U.S.A.
Principal: Matthew S. Whaley
Teaching staff: full-time, 2; total, 2
Nationalities of teaching staff: U.S., 2; total, 2
Grade levels: K – 8
Enrollment: total, 10

Year founded: 1997. **Type of school:** coed, day, company-sponsored. **Sponsored by:** Mobil Producing Nigeria Ltd. **Operated by:** International Schools Services, Princeton, New Jersey.

Curriculum/physical plant

Type: U.S. **Extracurricular:** excusions/expeditions, field trips. **Location:** rural company town one mile from Eket.

IKOT ABASI

Alscon International School

Phone: (871)(683)137099 ext. 2117 **Facsimile:** (871)(683)137185
U.S. mail: c/o Alscon-Nigeria, PO Box 27002, Richmond, VA 23261, U.S.A.
Headmaster: Stephen I. O'Donnell
Teaching staff: full-time, 5; total, 5
Nationalities of teaching staff: U.S., 4; host, 1; total, 5
Grade levels: K – 9
Enrollment: total, 28
Capacity: total, 40
Teacher/student ratio: 1/6
School year: late August to July

Year founded: 1996. **Type of school:** coed, day, company-sponsored. **Operated by:** International Schools Services, Princeton, New Jersey.

Curriculum/physical plant

Type: U.S. **Languages taught:** French. **Special programs:** ESL. **Extracurricular:** art, physical education, after-school activities. **Location:** rural company townsite near Calabar. **Facilities:** computer lab, library.

JOS

Hillcrest School

Street address: 13 Old Bukuru Road, Jos, Nigeria
Phone: (234)(72)465410
Mail: Box 652, Jos, Nigeria
Superintendent: Dick Seinen
High school principal: Bob Murray
Middle school principal: Sue Fine
Primary principal: Woodrow Arp
Teaching staff: full-time, 31; part-time, 4; total, 35
Nationalities of teaching staff: U.S., 26; U.K., 3; host, 1; other, 5; total, 35
Grade levels: 1 – 12
Enrollment: 1 – 5, 97; 6 – 8, 81; 9 – 12, 145; total, 323
Nationalities of student body: U.S., 100; U.K., 19; host, 116; other, 88; total, 323
Teacher/student ratio: 1/9
Tuition (annual): 1 – 5, $2,195; 6 – 8,$3,110; 9 – 12, $3,660
Other fees (annual): boarding, 1,500**
School year: August through May

Year founded: 1942. **Type of school:** coed, day, boarding, church-related. **Governed by:** appointed representatives from each of the sponsoring churches. **Sponsored by:** 11 churches. **Accredited by:** Middle States. **Regional organizations:** AISA.

Curriculum/physical plant

Type: U.S., AP. **Languages taught:** French, Spanish. **Staff specialists:** counselor, nurse. **Special programs:** remedial. **Special curricular:** art, chorus, band, physical education, computer instruction. **Extracurricular:** drama, yearbook, newspaper, field trips. **Sports:** basketball, soccer, track and field, volleyball. **Organizations:** honors society, student council. **Tests:** PSAT, SAT, ACT, TOEFL, AP, Iowa. **Graduates attending college:** 95%. **Graduates have attended:** Valparaiso, Calvin College, Carleton College, U. of Kansas, U. of Montana. **Location:** in suburb of Jos. **Campus:** 25 acres. **Library:** 12,000 volumes. **Facilities:** 7 buildings, 25 classrooms, auditorium, infirmary, 4 tennis courts, gymnasium, 2 playing fields, 3 science labs, 2 computer labs, 8 hostels.

KADUNA

Kaduna International School†

Street address: 1 Wurno Road, Badarawa GRA, Nigeria
Phone: (234)(62)214563 **Facsimile:** (234)(62)231335
Mail: PO Box 2947, Kaduna, Nigeria
U.S. mail: (letters only) c/o Administrative Officer, Dept. of State–Kaduna, Washington, DC 20521-2260

Headmaster: Joy Jibrilu
Teaching staff: full-time, 7; total, 7
Nationalities of teaching staff: U.S., 2; U.K., 2; host, 2; other, 1; total, 7
Grade levels: preK – 8
Enrollment: preK, 12; K, 8; 1 – 8, 45; total, 65
Nationalities of student body: U.S., 7; U.K., 7; host, 19; other, 32; total, 65
Capacity: preK, 15; K, 15; 1 – 8, 75; total, 105
Teacher/student ratio: 1/8
Tuition (annual): preK, $1,700; K – 8, $2,200
Other fees (annual): registration, $80; initial fee*, $900
School year: September to June

Year founded: 1985. **Type of school:** coed, day, private nonprofit. **Governed by:** appointed board of trustees. **Regional organizations:** ECIS, AISA.

Curriculum/physical plant

Type: U.S., U.K. **Languages taught:** French. **Special curricular:** art, physical education, computer instruction, music. **Extracurricular:** drama, dance, instrumental music, computers, excursions/expeditions, field trips. **Sports:** football, netball, swimming, kickball, rounders, golf. **Clubs:** stamp, wildlife. **Location:** on spacious compound, 10 minutes from Kaduna City. **Campus:** 6,000 square meters. **Library:** 6,500 volumes. **Facilities:** 4 buildings, 7 classrooms, playing field, science lab, computer lab, air conditioning.

*Once only fee †formerly Aisha Mohammed International School

LAGOS

American International School of Lagos

Street address: 1004 Federal Estates, Victoria Island, Lagos, Nigeria
Phone: (234)(1)2617793/2620775/2621544 – 5/2623829
Facsimile: (234)(1)2617794 **E-mail:** aislagos@linkserve.com.ng
Mail: PO Box 2803, Lagos, Nigeria
U.S. mail: A.I.S. c/o Dan Barkley, PO Box 1357, Tacoma, WA 98401-1357, U.S.A.
Superintendent: John Blix
Assistant superintendent: Dan Besett
Teaching staff: full-time, 46; part-time, 2; total, 48
Nationalities of teaching staff: U.S., 35; host, 9; other, 4; total, 48
Grade levels: preK – 9
Enrollment: preK, 25; K, 43; 1 – 6, 315; 7 – 9, 110; total, 493
Nationalities of student body: U.S., 187; U.K., 41; host, 85; other, 180; total, 493
Teacher/student ratio: 1/11
Tuition (annual): preK, $5,000; K – 6, $7,500; 7 – 9, $9,500
Other fees (annual): registration, $25; building assessment*: K – 9, $4,000
School year: August to June

Year founded: 1964. **Type of school:** coed, day, private nonprofit. **Governed by:** elected board of directors. **Accredited by:** Middle States. **Regional organizations:** AAIE, AISA. **School-to-school:** Tacoma Public Schools, Tacoma, WA, and Klein School District, Houston, TX.

Curriculum/physical plant

Type: U.S. **Languages taught:** French (K – 9). **Staff specialists:** counselor, nurse, librarian, optimal learning center. **Special curricular:** art, physical education, computer instruction, swimming, music. **Extracurricular:** drama, gymnastics, computers, yearbook, excursions/expeditions, field trips, choir, karate, Tae Kwon Do, table tennis. **Sports:** baseball, basketball, soccer, swimming, tennis, volleyball. **Clubs:** Boy Scouts, Girl Scouts, honor society, foreign language, student council (3 – 6), student senate (7 – 9). **Tests:** SSAT, COGAT, ITBS. **Graduates attending college:** over 90%. **Location:** within Federal Estates housing complex. **Campus:** 5 acres. **Library:** 20,000 volumes, 1,600 audio-visual resources. **Facilities:** 3-storied building, 2 tennis courts, playing field, 2 science labs, 3 computer labs, swimming pool, courtyard, auditorium/gymnasium, 4-room annex, air conditioning.

*Once only fee

WARRI

John F. Kennedy International School

Street address: Effurun, Delta State, Nigeria
Phone: (234)(53)251286
Mail: PO Box 232, Warri, Delta State, Nigeria
Administrator: V. O. M. Omonuwa
Acting head, science: Abrahim Okorode
Acting head, English: C. Dara
Business manager: Gerald Esiso
Teaching staff: full-time, 29; total, 29
Nationalities of teaching staff: U.K., 1; host, 28; total, 29
Grade levels: N – 13
Enrollment: total, 558
Nationalities of student body: U.S., 32; U.K., 15; host, 479; other, 32; total, 558
Teacher/student ratio: 1/19
Tuition (annual): N, 3,000**; K – 6, 12,000; 7 – 13, 15,000
Other fees (annual): registration*, 500**; boarding, 21,000; lunch, 500; books, 2,500
School year: September to July

Year founded: 1986. **Type of school:** coed, day, boarding, proprietary, private nonprofit. **Governed by:** elected 12-member council. **Accredited by:** Nigerian Ministry of Education.

Curriculum/physical plant

Type: U.S., national. **Languages taught:** English, French. **Staff specialists:** reading, math, computer, speech/hearing, counselor, psychologist, nurse. **Special curricular:** art, chorus, band, physical education, computer instruction. **Extracurricular:** drama, gymnastics, dance, choral and instrumental music, computer, yearbook, newspaper, literary magazine, photography, excursions/expeditions, field trips. **Sports:** basketball, lawn tennis. **Clubs:** debating, drama, science, press, current affairs. **Tests:** SAT, A-level GCE, GCSE, primary, junior, and secondary school examinations. **Location:** 1 kilometer from airport in Effurun, Warri. **Campus:** 10 acres. **Library:** 5,000 volumes. **Facilities:** 15 buildings, 30 classrooms, auditorium, cafeteria, infirmary, covered play area, 2 tennis courts, gymnasium, 2 playing fields, 3 science labs, computer lab, swimming pool.

*Once only fee **Nigerian naira **1996–97 listing**

NORWAY

Region: Europe
Size: 125,050 square miles
Population: 4,383,807
Capital: Oslo
Telephone code: 47
Currency: krone
Language: Norwegian

BERGEN

International School of Bergen

Street address: Vilhelm Bjerknesvei 15, 5030 Landas, Bergen, Norway
Phone: (47)55287716 **Facsimile:** (47)55271488
Director: June Murison
Teaching staff: full-time, 8; part-time, 9; total, 17
Nationalities of teaching staff: U.S., 5; U.K., 7; other, 5; total, 17
Grade levels: preK – 10
Enrollment: preK, 25; K – 7, 75; 8 – 10, 25; total, 125
Nationalities of student body: U.K., 10; host, 40; other, 75; total, 125
Teacher/student ratio: 1/10
Tuition (annual): company-sponsored: preK, 31,300**; K – 10, 110,000; noncompany-sponsored: K – 10, 38,000
School year: August to June

Year founded: 1975. **Type of school:** coed, day, private nonprofit. **Governed by:** elected board of trustees. **Accredited by:** New England, ECIS. **Regional organizations:** ECIS.

Curriculum/physical plant

Type: U.S., U.K., IBMYP. **Languages taught:** French, Norwegian. **Staff specialists:** computer, music, physical education. **Special programs:** ESL, IB Middle Years Program. **Special curricular:** art, physical education, computer instruction, music. **Extracurricular:** drama, computers, yearbook, field trips. **Sports:** skiing, swimming, ice skating. **Tests:** Iowa. **Location:** lakeside, surrounded by mountains, 10 kilometers from Bergen. **Campus:** 5 acres. **Library:** 4,500 volumes. **Facilities:** 3 buildings, 9 classrooms, infirmary, covered play area, 2 gymnasiums, 2 playing fields, science lab, computer lab.

**Norwegian kroner

STAVANGER

INTERNATIONAL SCHOOL OF STAVANGER

Street address: Treskeveien 3, 4042 Hafrsfjord, Norway
Phone: (47)(51)559100 **Facsimile:** (47)(51)552962
E-mail: intschol@iss.stavanger.rl.no
Web: http://www.iss.stavanger.rl.no
Director: Linda M. Duevel
Secondary principal/IB coordinator: Adrian Allan
Elementary/middle school principal: Rebecca Thompson
Teaching staff: full-time, 55; part-time, 8; total, 63
Nationalities of teaching staff: U.S., 39; U.K., 13; host, 6; other, 5; total, 63
Grade levels: preK (3 years) – 12
Enrollment: preK, 40; K, 40; 1 – 5, 200; 6 – 8, 120; 9 – 12, 120; total, 520
Nationalities of student body: U.S., 260; U.K., 70; host, 70; other, 120; total, 520
Teacher/student ratio: 1/10
Tuition (annual): private students: preK, 16,000 – 30,000**; K – 12, 38,000; company-sponsored students: K – 12, 96,000
School year: August to June

Year founded: 1966. **Type of school:** coed, day, private nonprofit. **Governed by:** board of trustees. **Accredited by:** New England, ECIS. **Regional organizations:** AAIE, ECIS.

Curriculum

Type: U.S., U.K., IB, AP, ISCP. **Languages taught:** English, French, Spanish, Norwegian. **Staff specialists:** reading, counselor, learning disabilities, nurse. **Special programs:** ESL, GCSE. **Special curricular:** art, chorus, band, physical education, computer instruction. **Extracurricular:** drama, choral and instrumental music, computers, yearbook, literary magazine, excursions/expeditions, field trips, many clubs. **Sports:** basketball, soccer, softball, track and field, volleyball. **Tests:** SSAT, PSAT, SAT, ACT, TOEFL, IB, AP, GCSE, Iowa. **Graduates attending college:** 94%. **Graduates have attended:** Harvard, Duke, Yale, London School of Economics, St. Andrews (Scotland).

Physical plant

Location: in suburb of Stavanger, a city on a fjord on the southwest coast of Norway. **Campus:** 15 acres. **Library:** 14,000 volumes. **Facilities:** 1 building, 60 classrooms, auditorium, cafeteria, infirmary, 2 covered play areas, 3 gymnasiums, 3 playing fields, 4 science labs, 3 computer labs, AV equipment, technology network.

**Norwegian kroner

OMAN

Region: Middle East
Size: 118,150 square miles
Population: 2,186,548
Capital: Muscat
Telephone code: 968
Currency: Omani rial
Language: Arabic

MUSCAT

American-British Academy

Phone: (968)603646/605287 **Facsimile:** (968)603544
Mail: PO Box 372, Madinat Al Sultan Qaboos Postal Code 115, Oman
Superintendent: David Watson, Ph.D.
High school principal: Kay Mongardi
Middle school principal: Jeff Voracek
Elementary school principal: Rod Harding
Teaching staff: full-time, 66; total, 66
Nationalities of teaching staff: U.S., 20; U.K., 27; other, 19; total, 66
Grade levels: preK – 12
Enrollment: preK, 25; K, 73; 1 – 6, 280; 7 – 9, 180; 10 – 12, 132; total, 690
Nationalities of student body: U.S., 129; U.K., 172; other, 389; total, 690
Capacity: preK, 20; K, 60; 1 – 6, 300; 7 – 9, 180; 10 – 12, 130; total, 690
Teacher/student ratio: 1/11
Tuition (annual): preK, $3,750; K2, $4,407; K3, $4,523; 1, $4,639; 2 – 3, $4,832; 4 – 5, $4,948; 6 – 7, $6,418; 8, $6,959; 9 – 10, $7,423; 11 – 12, $8,853
Other fees: capital levy*, $1,950
School year: September to June

Year founded: 1987. **Type of school:** coed, day, private nonprofit. **Governed by:** elected board of directors. **Accredited by:** Middle States. **Regional organizations:** ECIS, NESA, ISAC.

Curriculum/physical plant

Type: U.S., U.K., IB. **Languages taught:** French, Spanish, German, Arabic. **Staff specialists:** reading, nurse. **Special programs:** ESL, remedial. **Special curricular:** art, physical education, computer instruction, music. **Extracurricular:** drama, dance, computers, yearbook, music, Boy Scouts. **Sports:** basketball, soccer, softball, ice skating. **Tests:** SAT, IB, IGCSE, Royal Society of Arts. **Graduates have attended:** Princeton, MIT, Berkeley, London School of Economics, Imperial College London. **Location:** 2 kilometers from Madinat Qaboos. **Facilities:** 40 instructional areas, covered play area, use of playing field, 5 science labs, 2 computer labs, shaded drama court, gymnasium/theater, 25 meter swimming pool, air conditioning.

*Once only fee

PAKISTAN

Region: South Asia
Size: 339,697 square miles
Population: 129,275,660
Capital: Islamabad
Telephone code: 92
Currency: rupee
Languages: Urdu, English, Punjabi, Sindhi, Pashtu, Balochi,

ISLAMABAD

INTERNATIONAL SCHOOL OF ISLAMABAD

Street address: Sector H-9/1, Islamabad, Pakistan
Phone: (92)(51)252454 **Facsimile:** (92)(51)440193
E-mail: isi1@paknet1.ptc.pk
Mail: Sector H-9/1, PO Box 1124, Islamabad, Pakistan
U.S. mail: (no personal name) Administrative Officer (for ISI), American Embassy Islamabad, Dept. of State, Washington, DC 20521-8100
Superintendent: Robert E. Ambrogi, Ed.D.
Secondary school principal: Anthony Mock
Elementary school principal: Donavon K. Reinsmoen
Curriculum coordinator: Monti Hallberg
Business manager: Charles Barringer
Teaching staff: full-time, 60; part-time, 3; total, 63
Nationalities of teaching staff: U.S., 38; U.K., 7; host, 8; other, 10; total, 63
Grade levels: N – 12
Enrollment: N – preK, 20; K, 20; 1 – 5, 193; 6 – 8, 142; 9 – 12, 171; total, 546
Nationalities of student body: U.S., 179; U.K., 24; host, 76; other, 267; total, 546
Teacher/student ratio: 1/8
Tuition (annual): N, $2,638; K – 5, $8,960; 6 – 12, $9,242
Other fees: registration*, $50 (non-refundable); capital levy*, $2,000; special services, $739 per class/semester
School year: August through early June

Year founded: 1965. **Type of school:** coed, day, private nonprofit. **Governed by:** appointed and elected board of directors. **Accredited by:** Middle States. **Regional organizations:** AAIE, NESA.

Curriculum

Type: U.S., AP. **Languages taught:** French, Spanish. **Staff specialists:** math, counselor, nurse, special services. **Special programs:** ESL, honors sections, independent study, very mild disabilities. **Special curricular:** art, chorus, band, physical education, computer instruction, community service. **Extracurricular:** drama, choral and instrumental music, computers, yearbook, newspaper, literary magazine, excursions/expeditions, field trips. **Sports:** athletics, basketball, soccer, swimming, table tennis, track and field, volleyball. **Clubs:** National Honor Society, National Junior Honor Society, student council, Community Education Center, outdoor, debate and college bowl teams, French, Spanish. **Tests:** SSAT, PSAT, SAT, ACT, TOEFL, ERB. **Graduates attending college:** 98%. **Graduates have attended:** Cal Tech, MIT, Michigan, Virginia, Georgetown.

Physical plant

Location: equidistant (8 kilometers) from Islamabad and Rawalpindi, in a suburban-rural setting with several Pakistani schools. **Campus:** 23 acres. **Library:** 25,000 volumes. **Facilities:** 14 buildings, 54 classrooms, auditorium, cafeteria, infirmary, covered play area, 2 tennis courts, gymnasium, 3 playing fields, 4 science labs, 3 computer labs, swimming pool, snack bar, AV room, weight room, air conditioning.

*Once only fee

KARACHI

KARACHI AMERICAN SOCIETY SCHOOL

Street address: Amir Khusro Road, KDA Scheme No. I, Karachi 75350, Pakistan
Phone: (92)(21)4539096 – 99 **Facsimile:** (92)(21)454305
E-mail: ameschl@biruni.erum.com.pk
U.S. mail: U.S. Dept. of State – Karachi, Washington, DC 20521-6150
Superintendent: Philip Sylla
Secondary principal: Robert DeWolf
Elementary principal: Dave Weston
Business manager: Erna Faruqui
Teaching staff: full-time, 41; part-time, 2; total, 43
Nationalities of teaching staff: U.S., 32; host, 7; other, 4; total, 43
Grade levels: N – 12
Enrollment: N – preK, 15; K, 15; 1 – 6, 140; 7 – 9, 90; 10 – 12, 69; total, 329
Nationalities of student body: U.S., 99; U.K., 27; host, 118; other, 85; total, 329
Teacher/student ratio: 1/8
Tuition (annual): N, $5,500; K, $8,240; 1 – 5, $8,255; 6 – 12, $8,265
Other fees: registration*, $2,750
School year: August through May

Year founded: 1953. **Type of school:** coed, day. **Governed by:** elected board of directors. **Sponsored by:** U.S. Embassy. **Accredited by:** Middle States. **Regional organizations:** AAIE, NESA.

Curriculum

Type: U.S., AP. **Languages taught:** French, Spanish, Urdu. **Staff specialists:** computer, counselor, nurse, art, physical education, vocal music, instrumental music, drama, elementary science, ESL. **Special curricular:** art, chorus, band, physical education, computer instruction, drama, yearbook, journalism. **Extracurricular:** drama, computers, literary magazine, jazz band, chorus, student government, arts and crafts, key club. **Sports:** basketball, soccer, squash, swimming, tennis, track and field, volleyball, T-ball. **Clubs:** chess, National Honor Society, National Junior Honor Society, art, international. **Tests:** PSAT, AP, Iowa. **Graduates attending college:** 95%. **Graduates have attended:** Brown, MIT, Yale, Stanford, Harvard.

Physical plant

Location: in a well-developed residential area, 20 minutes from city center. **Campus:** 10 acres. **Facilities:** 11 buildings, 38 classrooms, auditorium, cafeteria, 2 tennis courts, gymnasium, 3 science labs, swimming pool, 2 libraries, performing arts center, clinic, 2 squash courts, athletic field, completely air conditioned.

*Once only fee

LAHORE

Lahore American Society School

Street address: 15 Upper Mall, Canal Bank, Lahore, Pakistan
Phone: (92)(42)/5762406 – 8/5762334 **Facsimile:** (92)(42)5711901
U.S. mail: c/o U.S. Consulate General Lahore, Agency, Unit 62216, APO AE 09812-2216
Superintendent: Everett P. McGlothlin
High school principal: Freeha Baqir
Elementary/middle school principal: Bruce Goforth
Teaching staff: full-time, 39; part-time, 1; total, 40
Nationalities of teaching staff: U.S., 27; host, 10; other, 3; total, 40
Grade levels: preK – 12
Enrollment: preK, 12; K, 32; 1 – 5, 159; 6 – 9, 134; 10 – 12, 107; total, 444
Nationalities of student body: U.S., 75; host, 246; other, 123; total, 444
Teacher/student ratio: 1/10
Tuition (annual): preK, $2,500; K – 5, $4,150; 6 – 12, $4,950
Other fees: registration*, $2,225
School year: August to May

Year founded: 1956. **Type of school:** coed, day, private. **Governed by:** elected board of directors. **Accredited by:** Middle States. **Regional organizations:** AAIE, NESA.

Curriculum/physical plant

Type: U.S., AP. **Languages taught:** French, German, Urdu. **Staff specialists:** counselor, ESL. **Special programs:** ESL. **Special curricular:** art, physical education, computer instruction, music. **Extracurricular:** computers, yearbook, excursions/expeditions, field trips, chorus. **Sports:** basketball, field hockey, soccer, tennis, volleyball. **Tests:** PSAT, SAT, ACT, TOEFL, AP, Iowa. **Graduates attending college:** 95%. **Graduates have attended:** Cornell, Stanford, Smith, Princeton, Harvard. **Location:** in suburban area, 2 to 3 miles from city center. **Campus:** 4.5 acres. **Library:** 20,000 volumes. **Facilities:** 6 buildings, infirmary, gymnasium, swimming pool, science labs, computer labs, soccer field, air conditioning.

*Once only fee

MURREE

Murree Christian School

Phone: (92)(593)410321/410328 **Facsimile:** (92)(593)411668
E-mail: mcs@@mcs.sdnpk.undp.org
Mail: PO Jhika Gali, Murree 47180, Pakistan
Principal: Phil Billing
Teaching staff: full-time, 20; part-time, 7; total, 27
Nationalities of teaching staff: U.S., 4; U.K., 11; host, 2; other, 10; total, 27
Grade levels: 1 – 12
Enrollment: 1 – 6, 55; 7 – 9, 40; 10 – 12, 42; total, 137
Nationalities of student body: U.S., 30; U.K., 24; host, 6; other, 77; total, 137
Teacher/student ratio: 1/7
Boarding capacity: boys, 75; girls, 75 **Grades:** 1 – 12 **Program:** planned 7-day
Tuition (annual): 1 – 12, $1,282 (mission), $4,839 (non-mission)
Other fees (annual): boarding, $900; security deposit, $1,290 (non-mission)
School year: August to July

Year founded: 1956. **Type of school:** coed, day, boarding, church-related, private nonprofit. **Governed by:** elected board of directors. **Sponsored by:** more than 20 mission groups.

Curriculum

Type: U.S., U.K. **Languages taught:** French, Urdu; German and Finnish as mother tongue. **Staff specialists:** computer, counselor, nurse. **Special curricular:** art, chorus, physical education, computer instruction. **Extracurricular:** drama, gymnastics, instrumental music, computers, yearbook, photography, excursions/ expeditions, field trips. **Sports:** basketball, football, hockey, table tennis, volleyball. **Clubs:** chess, computer, photography, gymnastics. **Tests:** PSAT, SAT, IGCSE, Iowa, Scottish Highers. **Graduates have attended:** Southern Illinois U., Trinity Western U., Sterling College, Houghton College, Heriot Watt U. (Edinburgh).

Physical plant

Location: in wooded setting in Himalayan foothills, 3 miles from Murree, 31 miles from Islamabad. **Campuses (2):** 4 acres. **Library:** 8,000 volumes. **Facilities:** 7 buildings, 17 classrooms, auditorium, 2 cafeterias, infirmary, 2 tennis courts, gymnasium, playing field, science lab, computer lab, AV equipment, 2 boarding hostels.

PESHAWAR

The International School of Peshawar

Street address: 17 Park Avenue Road, University Town, Peshawar, NWFP Pakistan
Phone: (92)(521)45352 **Facsimile:** (92)(521)840335
E-mail: principal@isp.psh.brain.net.pk
U.S. mail: c/o American Consulate-Peshawar, Dept. of State-Peshawar, Washington, DC 20521-6170

Head: Rebecca N. Qarghah
Teaching staff: full-time, 8; part-time, 7; total, 15
Nationalities of teaching staff: U.S., 8; other, 7; total, 15
Grade levels: preK – 8 and supervised correspondence
Enrollment: preK – K, 15; 1 – 8, 48; total, 63
Nationalities of student body: U.S., 10; other, 53; total, 63
Teacher/student ratio: 1/7
Tuition (annual): preK – K, $4,000; 1 – 8, $6,000
Other fees: registration*, $500
School year: September to June

Year founded: 1987. **Type of school:** coed, day, private nonprofit. **Governed by:** elected school board. **Sponsored by:** U.S. government. **Regional organizations:** NESA, ECIS.

Curriculum/physical plant

Type: U.S. **Languages taught:** English. **Staff specialists:** nurse, ESL. **Special programs:** ESL. **Special curricular:** art, physical education, music. **Extracurricular:** drawing, chess. **Sports:** basketball, soccer, tennis, Tae Kwon Do. **Clubs:** drama, French, crafts. **Location:** in suburb of Peshawar. **Library:** 6,000 volumes. **Facilities:** 2 buildings, 8 classrooms, 2 playing fields, air conditioning.

*Once only fee

PUNJAB

AES Lal Pir School

Street address: c/o AES Lal Pir Power Station, Tehsil Kot Adu, Dist. Muzaffargarh, (near Muhmud Kot) Punjab, Pakistan
Phone: (92)(661)422967 – 9 **Facsimile:** (92)(661)422993
Principal: Jacqueta Cantrell
Teaching staff: full-time, 2; total, 2
Nationalities of teaching staff: U.S., 2; total, 2
Grade levels: K – 8
Enrollment: total, 7
Nationalities of student body: U.S., 7; total, 7
Teacher/student ratio: 1/7
School year: August to June

Year founded: 1996. **Type of school:** coed, day, company-sponsored. **Operated by:** International Schools Services, Princeton, New Jersey.

Curriculum/physical plant

Type: U.S. **Special curricular:** art, physical education. **Location:** rural desert site 1-1/2 hours from Muzaffargarh. **Facilities:** 3 classrooms, playing field, swimming pool, air conditioning.

PANAMA

Region: Central America
Size: 29,157 square miles
Population: 2,655,094
Capital: Panama City
Telephone code: 507
Currency: balboa
Languages: Spanish, English

PANAMA CITY

The International School of Panama

Street address: Carretera al Nuevo Club de Golf, Cerro Viento, Panama City, Republic of Panama
Phone: (507)2667037/2669532 **Facsimile:** (507)2667808 **E-mail:** isp@pty.com
Mail: PO Box 6-7589, El Dorado, Panama, Republic of Panama
U.S. mail: (no personal name) Director, ISP, Unit 0945, APO AA 34002-0008
Director: Gary F. Kenny
Secondary school principal: James Doran
Middle school principal: Diane Guevara
Elementary school principal: Alida de Garcia de Paredes
Business manager: Laurie M. Lewter
Teaching staff: full-time, 70; total, 70
Nationalities of teaching staff: U.S., 18; U.K., 2; host, 35; other, 15; total, 70
Enrollment: JK, 26; K, 38; 1 – 5, 228; 6 – 8, 141; 9 – 12, 187; total, 620
Nationalities of student body: U.S., 176; U.K., 6; host, 185; other, 253; total, 620
Teacher/student ratio: 1/11
Tuition (annual): JK, $2,868; K, $4,836; 1 – 5, $5,044; 6 – 12, $5,616
Other fees (annual): registration, $100; capital levy*, JK – 5, $3,500 (first child), $3,000 (other children); 6 – 12, $4,000 (first child), $3,500 (other children); testing: JK, $25; K – 12, $50
School year: August to June

Year founded: 1982. **Type of school:** coed, day, private nonprofit. **Governed by:** elected board of directors. **Accredited by:** Southern. **Regional organizations:** AAIE, AASCA, Tri-Assoc.

Curriculum/physical plant

Type: U.S., IB, national. **Languages of instruction:** English, Spanish. **Languages taught:** French, Spanish. **Staff specialists:** computer, counselor, art, ESL, resource, music, physical education. **Special programs:** ESL, SSL, special education. **Special curricular:** art, physical education, computer instruction. **Extracurricular:** drama, computers, yearbook, newspaper, music, folk dancing, team sports. **Organizations:** student council, CAS program, science club. **Tests:** PSAT, SAT, TOEFL, Iowa, TAP. **Graduates attending college:** 98%. **Graduates have attended:** U. of Panama, Harvard, MIT, Notre Dame, McGill. **Location:** outer city limits. **Campus:** 16 acres. **Library:** 12,000 volumes. **Facilities:** 3 building complexes, 40 classrooms, covered play area, playing field, computer lab, prep and science labs, art room, track and field, gymnasium/multi-use facility, air conditioning.

*Once only fee

PAPUA NEW GUINEA

Region: Southeast Asia
Size: 178,704 square miles
Population: 4,394,537
Capital: Port Moresby
Telephone code: 675
Currency: kina
Languages: English, Tok Pesin, Motu

GOROKA

Goroka International School

Phone: (675)721466/721452 **Facsimile:** (675)722146
Mail: PO Box 845, Goroka, Papua New Guinea
Principal: J. K. Bastable
Teaching staff: full-time, 11; part-time, 1; total, 12
Grade levels: pre-K – 10
Enrollment: preK, 34; K – 6, 134; 7 – 10, 30; total, 198
Capacity: preK, 60; K – 6, 200; 7 – 10, 30; total, 290
Teacher/student ratio: 1/18
Tuition (annual): preK, 3,000**; K – 8, 4,000 – 5,300
School year: February to December

Year founded: 1953. **Type of school:** coed, day. **Governed by:** elected board of governors. **Accredited by:** International Education Agency (PNG) Ltd.

Curriculum/physical plant

Type: U.K., international, Australia, New Zealand. **Special curricular:** computer instruction, German (available in grades 2 – 8). **Extracurricular:** instrumental music, computers. **Sports:** athletics, cricket, cross-country, netball, soccer, softball, swimming, volleyball, Aussie sports. **Clubs:** squash, swimming, golf, tennis. **Location:** within town boundary. **Facilities:** playing fields, computer labs, libraries, outdoor education areas, science room.

**Papua New Guinea kina

LAE

The International School of Lae

Phone: (675)4723588 **Facsimile:** (675)4722394
Mail: PO Box 2130, Lae, Papua New Guinea
Principal: Bruce Gamwell
Teaching staff: full-time, 30
Grade levels: K – 12
Enrollment: K, 20; 1 – 6, 350; 7 – 9, 100; 10 – 12, 65; total, 535
Nationalities of student body: U.S., 15; U.K., 15; host, 150; other, 355; total, 535
Teacher/student ratio: 1/20
Boarders: boys, 24; girls, 2 **Grades:** 5 – 12 **Program:** planned 7-day
Tuition (annual): K – 6, 4,170**; 7 – 12, 7,100
Other fees (annual): boarding, 5,500**
School year: January to December

Type of school: coed, day, boarding, private nonprofit. **Governed by:** International Education Agency. **Accredited by:** Papua New Guinea Department of Education. **Regional organizations:** ECIS.

Curriculum/physical plant

Type: U.K., IGCSE (grade 10); Australian Capital Territories (grade 12, university entrance). **Languages taught:** French. **Staff specialists:** math, computer. **Special programs:** correspondence. **Special curricular:** art, physical education, computer instruction. **Extracurricular:** drama, gymnastics, instrumental music, computers, yearbook, literary magazine, field trips. **Sports:** hockey, rugby, soccer, softball, squash, tennis, golf. **Tests:** SAT, IGCSE, Australian Capital Territories Grade 12 Certificate. **Graduates attending college:** 80%. **Facilities:** 2 campuses, 2 cafeterias, covered play area, 3 tennis courts, 2 playing fields, 4 science labs, 2 computer labs, swimming pool, partial air-conditioning.

**Papua New Guinea kina

PORT MORESBY

PORT MORESBY INTERNATIONAL SCHOOL

Street address: Bava Street, Boroko, Port Moresby, Papua New Guinea
Phone: (675)253166 **Facsimile:** (675)254439
Mail: PO Box 276, Boroko, Papua New Guinea
Principal: Christopher J. Bowman
Head of high school: Dianne Korare
Head of middle school: Michael Cheevers
Head of primary school: Elaine Goddard-Tame
Teaching staff: full-time, 63; part-time, 2; total, 65
Nationalities of teaching staff: U.S., 2; U.K., 8; host, 4; other, 51; total, 65
Grade levels: preK (3 years) – 12
Enrollment: total, 960
Nationalities of student body: U.S., 4; U.K., 43; host, 390; Australia, 182; other, 341; total, 960
Capacity: preK – 5, 540; 6 – 8, 420; 9 – 12, 450; total, 1,410
Teacher/student ratio: 1/14
Tuition (annual): K, $2,170; preS, $3,610; prep – 3, $3,940; 4 – 5, $4,340; 6, $5,070; 7, $6,170; 8, $6,530; 9 – 10, $7,260; 11 – 12, $7,660; IB, $8,577
Other fees: registration*, $250
School year: February to December

Year founded: 1959. **Type of school:** coed, day, private nonprofit. **Governed by:** elected board of governors. **Accredited by:** International Education Agency of Papua New Guinea; Australian Capital Territory Education Department; ECIS.

Curriculum

Type: national, IB, IGCSE, AP. **Languages taught:** French, Indonesian. **Staff specialists:** reading, math, counselor, librarian. **Special programs:** ESL, remedial. **Special curricular:** art, physical education, computer instruction, drama, home economics, music, technics. **Extracurricular:** drama, gymnastics, dance, choral and instrumental music, computers, yearbook, newspaper, literary magazine, photography, excursions/expeditions, field trips, wide range of clubs. **Sports:** athletics, basketball, cricket, cross-country, netball, soccer, softball, tennis, volleyball, rugby union, etc. **Tests:** SAT, TOEFL, IB, IGCSE. **Graduates have attended:** U. of Sydney, U. of Papua New Guinea, U. of London, U. of Cambridge, Harvard.

Physical plant

Location: in Boroko, a suburb of Port Moresby. **Campus:** 35 acres. **Library:** 20,000 volumes. **Facilities:** 23 buildings, 70 classrooms, 2 tennis courts, 3 playing fields, 6 science labs, 2 computer labs, 2 libraries, auditorium/gymnasium, 2 home economics rooms, 3 art rooms, 2 music rooms, 3 technical rooms, darkroom.

*Once only fee

UKARUMPA

Ukarumpa International School - Primary

Phone: (675)6404401 ext. 498 **Facsimile:** (675)6404400
E-mail: uispc_principal_png@sil.org
Mail: PO Box 407, Ukarumpa, E.H.P. 444, Papua New Guinea
Principal: Keith Barber
Vice-principal: Jack Hauschildt
Teaching staff: full-time, 20; part-time, 6; total, 26
Nationalities of teaching staff: U.S., 17; other, 9; total, 26
Grade levels: K – 6
Enrollment: total, 300
Nationalities of student body: U.S., 154; host, 70; other, 76; total, 300
Capacity: K, 40; 1 – 6, 240; total, 280
Teacher/student ratio: 1/14
Tuition (annual): $4,000
Other fees (annual): busing, $80
School year: July to June

Year founded: 1975. **Type of school:** coed, day, church-related. **Governed by:** elected committee of sponsoring organization. **Sponsored by:** Summer Institute of Linguistics. **Accredited by:** Western. **Regional organizations:** EARCOS.

Curriculum/physical plant

Type: multinational. **Languages taught:** French, German, Japanese, Korean, Finnish (all as mother tongue studies). **Staff specialists:** learning disabilities. **Special programs:** correspondence, remedial. **Special curricular:** art, band, physical education, computer instruction, music. **Extracurricular:** choral and instrumental music, computers, field trips, outdoor education. **Sports:** baseball, basketball, hockey, soccer. **Tests:** SAT, OLMAT, diagnostic. **Location:** in rural area. **Campus:** 10 acres. **Library:** 16,000 volumes. **Facilities:** 16 buildings, 14 classrooms, auditorium, covered play area, playing field, computer lab, AV room, basketball court.

Ukarumpa International School - Secondary

Phone: (675)6404401 **Facsimile:** (675)6404400 **E-mail:** uissc.png@sil.org
Mail: PO Box 406, Ukarumpa, E.H.P. 444, Papua New Guinea
Principal: Don Fama
Assistant principals: David Glen, Steve Walker
Teaching staff: full-time, 27; part-time, 15; total, 42
Nationalities of teaching staff: U.S., 27; U.K., 3; other, 12; total, 42
Grade levels: 7 – 12
Enrollment: 7 – 9, 106; 10 – 12, 100; total, 206
Nationalities of student body: U.S., 104; host, 12; other, 90; total, 206
Capacity: 7 – 9, 120; 10 – 12, 120; total, 240
Teacher/student ratio: 1/6
Tuition (annual): $5,000
School year: July to June

Year founded: 1962. **Type of school:** coed, day, church-related. **Governed by:** appointed and elected education committee of sponsoring body. **Sponsored by:** Summer Institute of Linguistics. **Accredited by:** Western. **Regional organizations:** EARCOS.

Curriculum/physical plant

Type: U.S., U.K., Australia, AP. **Languages taught:** French, Spanish, German, Japanese. **Staff specialists:** reading, math, computer, counselor. **Special programs:** honors sections, independent study, correspondence. **Special curricular:** art, chorus, band, physical education, computer instruction, vocational. **Extracurricular:** drama, choral and instrumental music, yearbook, newspaper, photography, excursions/expeditions, field trips. **Sports:** basketball, soccer, softball, volleyball, track and field. **Tests:** PSAT, SAT, ACT, AP, GCSE, MAT, Higher School Certificate (New South Wales, Australia). **Graduates attending college:** 70%. **Graduates have attended:** Wheaton, Baylor, U. of Sydney, California Polytech, Azusa Pacific. **Location:** in rural area, 10 kilometers from Kainantu. **Campus:** 5 acres. **Library:** 13,000 volumes. **Facilities:** 8 buildings, auditorium, 7 tennis courts, playing field, 3 science labs, 2 computer labs, reading lab, AV theater.

PARAGUAY

Region: South America
Size: 157,048 square miles
Population: 5,504,146
Capital: Asunción
Telephone code: 595
Currency: guarani
Languages: Spanish, Guarani

ASUNCIÓN

THE AMERICAN SCHOOL OF ASUNCIÓN

Street address: Avenida Espana 1175, Asunción, Paraguay
Phone/facsimile: (595)(21)600479/603518/663678
E-mail: asa96@infonet.com.py
Mail: PO Box 10093, Asunción, Paraguay
U.S. mail: (no personal name) Director, ASA, American Embassy–Asunción, Unit 4750, APO AA 34036
Director: John J. Ketterer
Assistant director: Greta Gustafson
Secondary principal: Daniel Reyes-Guerra
Elementary principal: Beth Pfannl, Ph.D.
Teaching staff: full-time, 65; part-time, 8; total, 73
Nationalities of teaching staff: U.S., 37; host, 32; other, 4; total, 73
Grade levels: preK – 12
Enrollment: preK, 44; K, 45; 1 – 6, 281; 7 – 9, 123; 10 – 12, 127; total, 620
Nationalities of student body: U.S., 110; host, 426; other, 84; total, 620
Teacher/student ratio: 1/9
Tuition (annual): preK, $2,700; K – 5, $4,000; 6 – 12, $5,000
Other fees (annual): registration, $375; entrance*, $5,000
School year: August to December, February to July

Year founded: 1956. **Type of school:** coed, day, private nonprofit. **Governed by:** elected board of directors. **Accredited by:** Southern, Paraguayan Ministry of Education. **Regional organizations:** AAIE, AASSA.

Curriculum/physical plant

Type: U.S., national. **Languages of instruction:** English, Spanish for national program. **Languages taught:** French, Guarani. **Staff specialists:** counselors (elementary, middle, high). **Special programs:** ESL, SSL, learning differences, learning resource center, enrichment, host culture. **Special curricular:** art, physical education, music, computers. **Extracurricular:** drama, yearbook, excursions/expeditions, field trips, student government, journalism, Odyssey of the Mind, Knowledge Bowl, chess. **Sports:** aerobics, basketball, gymnastics, soccer, softball, volleyball, futbol de salon, handball. **Tests:** PSAT, SAT, AP, Stanford. **Graduates attending college:** 98%. **Graduates have attended:** Northwestern, Cornell, U. of California, Texas A & M, Loyola. **Location:** within city limits of Asunción. **Campus:** 14 acres. **Library:** 13,000 volumes. **Facilities:** 11 buildings, 44 classrooms, cafeteria, infirmary, gymnasium, 3 playing fields, 2 science labs, 2 computer labs, art/photo labs, air conditioning.

*Once only fee

Asunción Christian Academy

Street address: 1181 Avenida Santisimo Sacramento, Asunción, Paraguay
Phone: (595)(21)607378 **Facsimile:** (595)(21)604855
E-mail: aca@datanet.com.py
Mail: Casilla 1562, Asunción, Paraguay
U.S. mail: (no personal name) Director, American Embassy, ACA, Unit 4751, APO AA 34036
Director: Bethany Abreu
Head of library: Mirta Barreta
Teaching staff: full-time, 25; part-time, 2; total, 27
Nationalities of teaching staff: U.S., 23; host, 4; total, 27
Grade levels: preK – 12
Enrollment: preK, 13; K, 13; 1 – 6, 91; 7 – 9, 45; 10 – 12, 38; total, 200
Teacher/student ratio: 1/8
Tuition (annual): preK, $1,840; K – 6, $2,840; 7 – 12, $3,120
Other fees (annual): registration, $300; entrance*, $1,500
School year: August to December, February to June

Year founded: 1958. **Type of school:** coed, day, private nonprofit, Christian. **Governed by:** elected board of directors from evangelical missions in Paraguay. **Accredited by:** Southern, ACSI.

Curriculum/physical plant

Type: U.S. **Languages taught:** English. **Staff specialists:** counselor, learning disabilities, reading/resource. **Special curricular:** art, chorus, physical education, computer instruction. **Extracurricular:** drama, choral music, computers, yearbook, newspaper, excursions/expeditions, field trips. **Sports:** basketball, soccer, volleyball, American football. **Tests:** PSAT, SAT, ACT, MAT. **Graduates attending college:** 90%. **Graduates have attended:** U. of Pennsylvania, Georgia Tech, Evangel College, U. of California at LaJolla, Northeastern. **Location:** in suburban area. **Campus:** 5 acres. **Library:** 10,042 volumes. **Facilities:** 11 buildings, 21 classrooms, auditorium, covered play area, playing field, science lab, computer lab, AV room.

*Once only fee

Pan American International School

Street address: Loma Merlo, Calle Americano, Lugue, Paraguay
Phone/facsimile: (595)(981)422666 **E-mail:** pais@122pi.una.py
Mail: C.C. 10.0081, Asunción, Paraguay
U.S. mail: 6964 NW 50th Street, Suite No. 8435, Miami, FL 33166-5632, U.S.A.
General director: Ralph A. Davia, Ph.D.
Academic director: Beatrice M. Davia
National program director: Margarita Speratti
Business manager: Hendrik Marais
Teaching staff: full-time, 38; total, 38
Nationalities of teaching staff: U.S., 16; host, 10; other, 12; total, 38
Grade levels: preK – 12
Enrollment: preK, 42; K, 32; 1 – 6, 146; 7 – 9, 50; 10 – 12, 37; total, 307
Capacity: preK, 50; K, 50; 1 – 6, 180; 7 – 9, 60; 10 – 12, 60; total, 400
Teacher/student ratio: 1/8

Tuition (annual): preK, $2,200; K – 12, $3,700
Other fees (annual): registration, $240; books, $230; inscription fee*, $2,600
School year: August to July

Year founded: 1993. **Type of school:** coed, day, private. **Governed by:** board of directors. **Sponsored by:** foundation. **Accredited by:** Southern.

Curriculum/physical plant

Type: U.S., national, IB (in process). **Languages of instruction:** English, Spanish. **Staff specialists:** computer, counselor. **Special curricular:** art, chorus, band, physical education, computer instruction. **Extracurricular:** newspaper, excursions/expeditions, field trips. **Location:** in wooded suburban area, 5 kilometers from Asunción. **Library:** 8,000 volumes. **Facilities:** 7 buildings, 24 classrooms, auditorium, cafeteria, 2 playing fields, science lab, computer lab.

*Once only fee

PERU

Region: South America
Size: 496,225 square miles
Population: 24,523,408
Capital: Lima
Telephone code: 51
Currency: new sol
Languages: Spanish, Quechua, Aymara

ILO

Southern Peru Limited Staff Schools

Street address: Casilla 303, Tacna, Toquepala, Peru, S.A.
Phone: (51)(54)686032 (at dial tone, dial 2448) **Facsimile:** (51)(54)686031
U.S. mail: 180 Maiden Lane, New York, NY 10038, U.S.A.
Director: Tim Rawley
Principals: Mike Todd, Steve Henson, Glenn Grieshaber
Teaching staff: full-time, 21; total, 21
Nationalities of teaching staff: U.S., 18; host, 3; total, 21
Grade levels: K – 8
Enrollment: K, 7; 1 – 6, 95; 7 – 8, 13; total, 115
Nationalities of student body: U.S., 38; host, 69; other, 8; total, 115
Capacity: K, 15; 1 – 6, 90; 7 – 8, 30; total, 135
Teacher/student ratio: 1/7
School year: September to June

Year founded: 1956. **Type of school:** coed, day, company-sponsored. **Governed and sponsored by:** Southern Peru Limited. **Accredited by:** Southern.

Curriculum/physical plant

Type: U.S. **Languages taught:** Spanish. **Staff specialists:** reading. **Special curricular:** physical education, computer instruction. **Extracurricular:** newspaper, photography, field trips, hiking, fishing, camping. **Sports:** basketball, bowling, soccer, volleyball, golf, frisbee golf, racquetball, weightlifting. **Tests:** SSAT, TOEFL, Iowa. **Location:** company-owned campsites. **Campuses (3):** 5 acres. **Library:** 6,000 volumes. **Facilities:** 8 buildings, 24 classrooms, 3 infirmaries, 3 tennis courts, 3 playing fields, 3 science labs, 3 swimming pools.

LIMA

Colegio Franklin Delano Roosevelt

Street address: Avda. Las Palmeras 325, Camacho, La Molina, Lima, Peru
Phone: (51)(1)4350890 **Facsimile:** (51)(1)4360927
E-mail: fdr@amersol.edu.pe **Web:** http://www.amersol.edu.pe
Mail: Apartado 18-0977, Lima 18, Peru
U.S. mail: (official letters only) Superintendent, Colegio Franklin D. Roosevelt, Unit 3804, APO AA34031
Superintendent: David A. Randall
High school principal: Brian Weinrich
Middle school principal: David Haack
Elementary principal: Bruce Kelsh, Ph.D.
Business manager: Edwing Suni
Teaching staff: full-time, 117; part-time, 11; total, 128
Nationalities of teaching staff: U.S., 50; host, 68; other, 10; total, 128
Grade levels: preK – 12
Enrollment: preK, 95; K, 90; 1 – 6, 610; 7 – 9, 281; 10 – 12, 304; total, 1,380
Nationalities of student body: U.S., 345; host, 760; other, 275; total, 1,380
Teacher/student ratio: 1/12
Tuition (annual): preK (half day), $5,100; K, $6,800; 1 – 6, $7,400; 7 – 12, $7,500
Other fees (annual): busing, $1,000; registration*, $6,000
School year: August to July

Year founded: 1946. **Type of school:** coed, day. **Governed by:** appointed board of directors. **Sponsored by:** American companies. **Accredited by:** Southern. **Regional organizations:** AASSA.

Curriculum

Type: U.S., national, IB, AP. **Languages taught:** English, French, Spanish. **Staff specialists:** computer, counselor, learning disabilities, nurse. **Special programs:** ESL, independent study, remedial, learning differences. **Special curricular:** art, chorus, band, physical education, computer instruction. **Extracurricular:** drama, gymnastics, choral music, yearbook, newspaper, photography, excursions/expeditions, field trips, sports: baseball, basketball, field hockey, soccer, softball, volleyball. **Clubs:** computer, debating, National Honor Society, community service, varsity, Tri-M, student support group, rain forest relief. **Tests:** SAT, ACT, IB, AP, Iowa. **Graduates attending college:** 95%. **Graduates have attended:** Brown, MIT, Carnegie-Mellon, Princeton U., U. of Pennsylvania.

Physical plant

Location: attractive facilities on well-landscaped campus in Camacho, a southeast suburb 12 kilometers from Lima. **Campus:** 23 acres. **Libraries (2):** 40,000 volumes. **Facilities:** 8 buildings, 108 classrooms, infirmary, 3 tennis courts, gymnasium, 6 playing fields, 7 science labs, 5 computer labs, 6 playing fields, center stage.

*Once only fee

PHILIPPINES

Region: Southeast Asia
Size: 115,860 square miles
Population: 74,480,848
Capital: Manila
Telephone code: 63
Currency: peso
Languages: Pilipino, English, many others

BAGUIO

Brent School

Street address: Brent Road, Baguio City, Philippines
Phone: (63)(74)4424050/4422260/4423628 **Facsimile:** (63)(74)4423638
E-mail: brent@bgo.cyberspace.com.ph
Mail: PO Box 35, Baguio City 2600, Philippines
Headmaster: (to be announced)
Deputy head: Ursula B. Daoey
Financial officer: Marcial Esquejo
Teaching staff: full-time, 31; part-time, 6; total, 37
Grade levels: preK – 12
Enrollment: preK, 14; K, 11; 1 – 6, 112; 7 – 9, 75; 10 – 12, 54; total, 266
Nationalities of student body: U.S., 56; host, 64; other, 146; total, 266
Capacity: preK, 20; K, 20; 1 – 6, 150; 7 – 9, 75; 10 – 12, 75; total, 340
Teacher/student ratio: 1/8
Boarders: boys, 50; girls, 17 Grades: 4 – 12 Program: planned 7-day
Tuition (annual): preK, $1,225; K, $1,650; 1 – 3, $2,325; 4 – 6, $2,675; 7 – 8, $3,800; 9 – 12, $5,000
Other fees (annual): boarding, $5,000; capital levy, $250; lunch, $190; miscellaneous, $500 – 750, matriculation*, $650
School year: mid-August to mid-June

Year founded: 1909. **Type of school:** coed, day, boarding, church-related, private nonprofit. **Governed by:** appointed board of trustees. **Sponsored by:** Western, PAASCU. Regional organizations: EARCOS, ECIS.

Curriculum/physical plant

Type: international, IB. **Languages taught:** French, Spanish, Korean, Filipino, Chinese. **Staff specialists:** computer, nurse. **Special programs:** ESL, remedial, ability groupings in math. **Special curricular:** art, chorus, physical education, computer instruction. **Extracurricular:** drama, dance, choral music, yearbook, newspaper, field trips. **Sports:** baseball, badminton, tennis, soccer, volleyball, archery. **Clubs:** chess, squash, computer, drama, science, Pilipino. **Tests:** PSAT, SAT, ACT, IB. **Graduates have attended:** Wellesley, Syracuse U., Barnard College, Bond U. (Australia), St. Louis U. (Baguio City). **Location:** in Baguio City, nestled in mountains on island of Luzon. **Campus:** 13 hectares. **Library:** 20,206 volumes. **Facilities:** 19 buildings, 23 classrooms, 2 cafeterias, infirmary, gymnasium, playing field, 5 science labs, 2 computer labs, 2 art rooms, theater, chapel, AV room, 2 dormitories plus housing/apartments for resident staff.

*Once only fee

CAGAYAN DE ORO CITY

INTERNATIONAL SCHOOL CAGAYAN DE ORO

Street address: San Isidro Road, Kauswagan, 9000 Cagayan de Oro City, Philippines
Phone: (63)(8822)726980/727913 **Facsimile:** (63)(8822)728029
U.S. mail: 758 NE Altura Street, Port St. Lucie, FL 34952-1302, U.S.A.
President: Solona T. Canoy
Vice-president, academic affairs: Grace M. Caballero, Ph.D.
Vice-president, administrative affairs: Tabitha T. Bullecer, Ph.D.
Principal: Rhona T. Canoy
Teaching staff: full-time, 30; part-time, 2; total, 32
Nationalities of teaching staff: host, 32; total, 32
Grade levels: preK – high school
Enrollment: preK, 60; K, 46; 1 – 6, 240; high school, 162; total, 508
Nationalities of student body: U.S., 14; U.K., 4; host, 477; other, 13; total, 508
Teacher/student ratio: 1/25
Tuition (annual): preK – K, $480, 1 – 6, $560; high school, $720
Other fees (annual): registration*, $176; fourth R, $132
School year: June to March

Year founded: 1993. **Type of school:** coed, day, private nonprofit. **Governed by:** appointed board of trustees.

Curriculum/physical plant

Type: U.S., national. **Languages taught:** Filipino, Chinese. **Staff specialists:** reading, math, computer, counselor. **Special programs:** honors sections, remedial, fourth R, Chinese curriculum, economics, English. **Special curricular:** art, chorus, band, physical education, computer instruction. **Extracurricular:** drama, dance, choral and instrumental music, yearbook, newspaper, literary magazine, excusions/expeditions, field trips. **Tests:** OLMAT, ITBS. **Location:** 2 kilometers from city center. **Campus:** 4.9 acres. **Facilities:** 2 buildings, cafeteria, infirmary, gymnasium, science lab, computer lab, library, air conditioning.

*Once only fee

CAINTA

FAITH ACADEMY

Street address: Victoria Valley Subdivision, Valley Golf Road, Cainta, Rizal, Philippines
Phone: (63)(2)6580048 **Facsimile:** (63)(2)6580026
E-mail: vanguard@faith.edu.ph
Mail: PO Box 2016 MCPO, 0706 Makati, Philippines
Superintendent: Roy L. Lowrie, Ed.D.
Secondary school principal: Philip C. Parsons
Middle school principal: David Venable
Elementary school principal: Judy Severns
Teaching staff: full-time, 71; part-time, 6; total, 77
Nationalities of teaching staff: U.S., 55; U.K., 7; other, 15; total, 77
Grade levels: K – 12
Enrollment: K, 26; 1 – 6, 209; 7 – 9, 170; 10 – 12, 193; total, 598
Nationalities of student body: U.S., 430; U.K., 11; host, 12; other, 145; total, 598
Teacher/student ratio: 1/9
Boarders: boys and girls, 95 Grades: 6 – 12 Program: planned 7-day
Tuition (annual): preK, $25 (4 – 5 weeks); K – 5, $1,035; 6 – 12, $1,267; nonmissionary, $3,025
Other fees (annual): registration, $40 – 70; boarding, $3,150 – 3,450; busing, $230 – 830; capital fee: missionary, $2,140 (discounts available); nonmissionary, $3,500
School year: August to May

Year founded: 1957. **Type of school:** coed, day, boarding, private nonprofit, interdenominational, Christian. **Governed by:** appointed board of trustees. **Sponsored by:** evangelical mission boards. **Accredited by:** Western. **Regional organizations:** EARCOS.

Curriculum/physical plant

Type: U.S., U.K., AP. **Languages taught:** French, Spanish, Tagalog. **Staff specialists:** reading, computer, learning disabilities, nurse, family counselor, gifted elementary, counselors, chaplain. **Special programs:** IGCSE. **Special curricular:** art, chorus, band, physical education, computer instruction, vocational, home economics, industrial arts. **Extracurricular:** drama, choral and instrumental music, yearbook, newspaper, photography, field trips. **Sports:** cross-country, basketball, soccer, softball, tennis, volleyball, wrestling. **Clubs:** chess, Boy Scouts, French, forensics. **Tests:** PSAT, SAT, ACT, TOEFL, GCSE, Iowa, MAT, TAP, Otis-Lennon. **Graduates attending college:** 85%. **Graduates have attended:** Biola, Wheaton, West Point, Taylor, Air Force Academy. **Location:** 13 kilometers east of Manila, branch school in Davao City, Mindanao. **Campuses (2):** 12 acres. **Library:** 21,000 volumes. **Facilities:** 11 buildings, 56 classrooms, auditorium, 2 covered play areas, 2 tennis courts, gymnasium, 2 playing fields, 4 science labs, 4 computer labs, 3 boarding homes on campus and 2 off campus, air conditioning.

CEBU CITY

CEBU INTERNATIONAL SCHOOL

Phone: (63)(32)97268/70193 **Facsimile:** (63)(32)311556
Mail: Banilad, PO Box 735, Cebu City, Philippines 6000
Superintendent/high school principal: Luz V. Isobal
Registrar: Menezquieta P. Geverola
Guidance counselors: Liberty B. Vicentillo, Christofer Traxler
Chief, educational media: Jeogenes J. Biongcog
Teaching staff: full-time, 35; part-time, 15; total, 50
Nationalities of teaching staff: U.S., 2; host, 31; other, 17; total, 50
Grade levels: K – 12
Enrollment: K, 55; 1 – 5, 163; 6 – 8, 103; 9 – 12, 90; total, 411
Nationalities of student body: U.S., 86; U.K., 8; host, 156; other, 161; total, 411
Capacity: K, 50; 1 – 8, 300; 9 – 12, 100; total, 450
Teacher/student ratio: 1/12
Tuition (annual): K, $814; 1 – 5, $995; 6 – 8, $1,085; 9 – 12, $1,650
Other fees (annual): registration, $28; insurance, $2; books: K, $28; 1 – 2, $68; 3 –6, $72; 7 – 12, $88; miscellaneous, $524
School year: July to April

Year founded: 1924. **Type of school:** coed, day, private nonprofit, nonsectarian. **Governed by:** elected board of trustees. **Accredited by:** Western (in process), Philippines Department of Education. **Regional organizations:** EARCOS.

Curriculum/physical plant

Type: U.S., national. **Languages taught:** French, Spanish, German, Filipino. **Staff specialists:** reading, math, computer, counselor, nurse, science, pre-school, Filipino, performing arts, art education. **Special programs:** ESL, remedial, guidance counseling. **Special curricular:** art, drama, performance choir, photojournalism. **Extracurricular:** yearbook, field trips, scouting, journalism. **Sports:** basketball, soccer, swimming, tennis, track and field, volleyball, kickball, golf. **Organizations:** supreme student council, school newspaper. **Clubs:** drama, math, science, sports, journalism. **Tests:** SAT, National Secondary Achievement Test (NSAT), National Elementary Achievement Test (NEAT), placement, intelligence, career. **Graduates attending college:** 100%. **Graduates have attended:** Ateneo de Manila U., U. of the Philippines, Cebu Doctor's College, Communication and Research Center. **Location:** in suburban area. **Campus:** 2.2 hectares. **Library:** 12,000 volumes. **Facilities:** 7 buildings, 18 classrooms, cafeteria, playing field, science lab, computer lab, music room, AV room, covered court, clinic, guidance office.

MANILA

Brent International School Manila, Inc.

Street address: University of Life Complex, Meralco Avenue, 1603 Pasig City, Philippines
Phone: (63)(2)6311265 – 8/6338016 – 7 **Facsimile:** (63)(2)6338420
E-mail: brent@mnl.sequel.net
Mail: PO Box 12201, Ortigas Center Post Office, 1605 Pasig City, Philippines
Headmaster: Dick B. Robbins
Deputy headmaster/director for administrative services: Maria Elena C. Samson
Upper school master: Brian J. Marquand
Middle school master: Robert J. Hartleip
Lower school master: Mark Bretherton
Teaching staff: full-time, 103; total, 103
Nationalities of teaching staff: U.S., 24; U.K., 5; host, 50; other, 24; total, 103
Grade levels: N – 12
Enrollment: N – preK, 19; K, 32; 1 – 6, 357; 7 – 9, 233; 10 – 12, 270; ESL, 60; total, 971
Nationalities of student body: U.S., 94; U.K., 24; host, 396; other, 457; total, 971
Teacher/student ratio: 1/10
Tuition (annual): N – K, $3,450; 1 – 5, $4,945; 6 – 8, $6,095; 9 – 12, $7,820
Other fees (annual): capital levy, $1,500; matriculation*, $2,308; application/testing*, $85; ESL, $1,000
School year: August to May

Year founded: 1984. **Type of school:** coed, day, church-related, private non-profit. **Governed by:** elected board of trustees. **Accredited by:** Western, PAASCU. **Regional organizations:** EARCOS, NAIS, CERCOS, ECIS, NASSP.

Curriculum

Type: U.S., IB. **Languages taught:** English, French, Spanish, Filipino, Chinese. **Staff specialists:** nurse, ESL, guidance counselor. **Special programs:** ESL, remedial, computer-assisted instructor. **Special curricular:** art, chorus, band, physical education, computer instruction, musical and drama presentation. **Extracurricular:** choral and instrumental music, computers, yearbook, newspaper, field trips, academic bowl, debates, National Honor Society, student council. **Sports:** basketball, soccer, softball, swimming, tennis, track and field, volleyball. **Clubs:** computer, debating, drama, community service, crafts, glee, scouting, literary, environmental, photography, math, science. **Tests:** PSAT, SAT, ACT, TOEFL, IB, Iowa, MAT, OLMAT, DAT, CII, SLEP, CAPT. **Graduates attending college:** 100%. **Graduates have attended:** Cambridge, London School of Economics, Boston U., New York U., U. of the Philippines. **Location:** on University of Life campus, 3 minutes to Asian Development Bank, 10 minutes to Quezon City, 15 minutes to Makati. **Facilities:** 6 buildings, cafeteria, infirmary, covered play area, tennis court, 5 science labs, 3 computer labs, swimming pool, 2 libraries, chapel, amphitheater, soccer field, covered gymnasium, band room, 2 music rooms, AV rooms, air conditioning.

*Once only fee

International School, Manila

Street address: Gen. Luna Street and Kalayaan Avenue, Bel-Air, Makati City, Philippines
Phone: (63)(2)8893854 **Facsimile:** (63)(2)8893964
E-mail: isminfo@ismanila.portalinc.com
Web: http://www.portalinc.com/ismanila
Mail: PO Box 1526 MCPO, 1255 Makati City, Philippines
Superintendent: Brian L. McCauley, Ph.D.
High school principal: Jeffrey W. Hammett
Middle school principal: Allan "Buck" Forslund
Elementary school principal: Alastair Kay
Director of instructional services: Susan Rinker
Teaching staff: full-time, 221; part-time, 1; total, 222
Nationalities of teaching staff: U.S., 77; U.K., 7; host, 95; other, 43; total, 222
Grade levels: K – 12
Enrollment: K, 108; 1 – 5, 828; 6 – 8, 553; 9 – 12, 685; total, 2,174
Nationalities of student body: U.S., 603; host, 309; U.K., 76; other, 1,186; total, 2,174
Teacher/student ratio: 1/10
Tuition (annual): ECLC, $7,500; 1 – 5, $8,000; 6 – 8, $9,400; 9 – 12, $10,000
Other fees (annual): matriculation*, $2,500; capital projects, $750; assorted fees for special courses
School year: August to June

Year founded: 1920. **Type of school:** coed, day, private nonprofit. **Governed by:** elected board of trustees. **Accredited by:** Western. **Regional organizations:** AAIE, EARCOS, ECIS.

Curriculum

Type: U.S., IB, AP. **Languages taught:** French, Spanish, German, Japanese, Chinese, Filipino. **Staff specialists:** computer, counselor, nurse, dentist, doctor, library/media services. **Special programs:** ESL, optimal learning. **Extracurricular:** drama, gymnastics, dance, choral music, computers, yearbook, newspaper, literary magazine, photography, excursions/expeditions, field trips, concert band/strings/orchestral music. **Sports:** badminton, baseball, basketball, cheerleading, cross-country, soccer, softball, swimming, table tennis, tennis, track and field, volleyball, golf, water polo, wrestling. **Organizations:** student government, councils and committees, Cum Laude, Quill and Scroll, Scholia, social service. **Clubs:** chess, Model UN, Chinese, debate, environmental, Mabuhay, math, pep, Philippine culture, photography, Psi, science, social studies. **Tests:** SSAT, PSAT, SAT, ACT, TOEFL, IB, AP, Iowa. **Graduates attending college:** 95%. **Graduates have attended:** Bryn Mawr, Harvard-Radcliffe, Haverford, MIT, Stanford.

Physical plant

Location: in the city of Makati. **Campus:** 5 acres. **Library:** 60,000 volumes. **Facilities:** 16 buildings, 171 classrooms, auditorium, 3 cafeterias, infirmary, 2 covered play areas, 2 tennis courts, 3 gymnasiums, playing field, 16 science labs, 7 computer labs, 2 swimming pools, fine arts center, 2 theaters, 2 media centers, air conditioning.

*Once only fee

POLAND

Region: Europe
Size: 120,728 square miles
Population: 38,642,565
Capital: Warsaw
Telephone code: 48
Currency: zloty
Language: Polish

KRAKÓW

American International School of Kraków

Phone/facsimile: (48)(12)220774 **E-mail:** aisk@kki.krakow.pl
Web: http://www.kki.krakow.pl/aisk
Mail: c/o U.S. Consulate, ul. Stolarska 9, 31-043 Kraków, Poland
Director: Melissa Hicks
Teaching staff: full-time, 6; part-time, 2; total, 8
Nationalities of teaching staff: U.S., 7; host, 1; total, 8
Grade levels: preS – 8
Enrollment: preS, 5; K, 5; 1 – 6, 21; 7 – 8, 5; total, 36
Nationalities of student body: U.S., 11; host, 7; other, 18; total, 36
Capacity: total, 150
Teacher/student ratio: 1/12
Tuition (annual): preS, $4,000; K – 8, $10,000
Other fees: registration*, $200; building fund: new student, $2,000; returning student (annual), $1,000
School year: August to June

Year founded: 1993. **Type of school:** day, private nonprofit. **Governed by:** board of directors. **Sponsored by:** U.S. Consulate in Kraków. **Regional organizations:** CEESA.

Curriculum/physical plant

Type: U.S., U.K., ISCP. **Languages taught:** French, Polish. **Special programs:** ESL. **Special curricular:** physical education. **Extracurricular:** excursions/expeditions, field trips. **Tests:** Iowa. **Location:** near the old town of Krakow. **Library:** 1,000 volumes. **Campus:** 600 square meters.

*Once only fee

WARSAW

The American School of Warsaw

Street address: Ul. Konstancinska 13, 02–942 Warsaw, Poland
Phone: (48)(22)423952 **Facsimile:** (48)(22)6429392
U.S. mail: Dept. of State–Warsaw, Washington, DC 20521-5010
Director: Anthony Horton
High school principal: Carol Kluznik
Middle school principal: Karen Dunmire
Lower school principal: Frank Rowland
Business manager: Jolanta Wilmanska
Teaching staff: full-time, 85; part-time, 15; total, 100
Nationalities of teaching staff: U.S., 75; U.K., 5; host, 7; other, 13; total, 100
Grade levels: preK – 12
Enrollment: preK, 20; K, 60; 1 – 5, 350; 6 – 8, 175; 9 – 12, 200; total, 805
Nationalities of student body: U.S., 230; host, 80; other, 495; total, 805
Teacher/student ratio: 1/8
Tuition (annual, 1996-97 figures) preK, $2,800; K – 5, $9,800; 6 – 8, $10,600; 9 – 12, $11,200
Other fees: registration*, $200
School year: late August to mid-June

Year founded: 1953. **Type of school:** coed, day, private nonprofit. **Governed by:** elected board of directors. **Sponsored by:** parents' association. **Accredited by:** New England, ECIS. **Regional organizations:** AAIE, ECIS, CEESA.

Curriculum/physical plant

Type: U.S., IB. **Languages taught:** French, Spanish, German, Dutch, Polish. **Staff specialists:** computer, learning disabilities, nurse, counselors, speech therapist. **Special programs:** ESL, remedial. **Special curricular:** art, chorus, band, physical education, computer instruction, photography. **Extracurricular:** drama, dance, computers, yearbook, newspaper, field trips, vocal and instrumental music, sports, student council, Model UN. **Organizations:** ballet, Boy Scouts, Cub Scouts, Girl Guides, Brownies. **Tests:** SSAT, SAT, IB, AP, Iowa. **Location:** in city. **Library:** 16,000 volumes. **Facilities:** 2 sites, 3 buildings, 55 classrooms, 2 gymnasiums, playing field, 3 science labs, 3 computer labs, art and music rooms.

*Once only fee

PORTUGAL

Region: Europe
Size: 35,574 square miles
Population: 9,865,114
Capital: Lisbon
Telephone code: 351
Currency: escudo
Language: Portuguese

LISBON

American Christian International Academy

Street address: Avenida de Sintra, Lote 1, 2750 Cascais, Portugal
Phone: (351)(1)4842279/4861860 **Facsimile:** (351)(1)4842279
E-mail: orehotsky@aol.com
Director: David Orehotsky
Business manager: John Ellis
Teaching staff: full-time, 4; part-time, 1; total, 5
Nationalities of teaching staff: U.S., 4; host, 1; total, 5
Grade levels: K – 8
Enrollment: K, 10; 1 – 8, 28; total, 38
Nationalities of student body: U.S., 26; other, 12; total, 38
Capacity: K, 10; 1 – 8, 50; total, 60
Teacher/student ratio: 1/8
Tuition (annual): K, 800,000**; 1 – 6, 1,300,000; 7 – 8, 1,400,000
Other fees (annual): capital levy, 160,000**; application, 20,000; busing, 155,000 – 185,000
School year: September to June

Year founded: 1983. **Type of school:** coed, day, church-related. **Governed by:** appointed independent board. **Accredited by:** ACSI, Middle States.

Curriculum/physical plant

Type: U.S. **Languages taught:** English. **Special programs:** ESL, independent study, remedial. **Special curricular:** art, chorus, physical education, computer instruction, Portuguese. **Extracurricular:** yearbook, excursions/expeditions, field trips, student council. **Tests:** Stanford, OLSAT. **Location:** 20 kilometers from Lisbon, in quaint oceanside city on Portugal's Costa del Sol. **Campus:** 1 acre. **Library:** 4,000 volumes, CD ROM. **Facilities:** 2 buildings, 6 classrooms, auditorium, gymnasium, playground, outdoor basketball court, rented soccer field.

**Portuguese escudo

AMERICAN INTERNATIONAL SCHOOL OF LISBON

Street address: Quinta da Casa Branca, Carnaxide, Portugal
Phone: (351)(1)4171819 **Facsimile:** (351)(1)4187649
E-mail: aisl@individual. eunet.pt
Web: http://www.guilford.k12.nc.us/hp/lisbon/home.html
Mail: Apartado 10, 2795 Carnaxide, Portugal
Headmaster/upper school principal: Blannie Curtis
Elementary principal: Cindy Ataíde
Early childhood principal: Barbara Carvalho
Teaching staff: full-time, 37; part-time, 2; total, 39
Nationalities of teaching staff: U.S., 25; host, 12; other, 2; total, 39
Grade levels: early childhood (age 3) – 12
Enrollment: EC – K, 24; 1 – 5, 78; 6 – 8, 51; 9 – 12, 72; total, 225
Nationalities of student body: U.S., 78; host, 67; other, 80; total, 225
Capacity: EC – K, 45; 1 – 5, 100; 6 – 8, 60; 9 – 12, 110; total, 315
Teacher/student ratio: 1/6
Tuition (annual): EC-3, 716,400**; EC-4, 816,400; K, 916,400; 1, 1,106,800; 2 – 3, 1,160,400; 4 – 5, 1,288,400; 6 – 8, 1,434,800; 9 – 12, 1,968,400
Other fees (annual): registration*, 50,000**; busing, 226,000 (optional); lunch, 2 – 12, 750; EC-3 – 1, 500 (optional); capital fee*, 300,000 (grades 1 – 12)
School year: September through June

Year founded: 1956. **Type of school:** coed, day, community and embassy sponsored. **Governed by:** board of directors. **Accredited by:** New England, ECIS, Portuguese Ministry of Education. **Regional organizations:** MAIS, ECIS.

Curriculum

Type: U.S., AP. **Languages taught:** French, Portuguese. **Staff specialists:** reading, computer, counselor, learning disabilities, art, music. **Special programs:** ESL, computer instruction, Portuguese Equivalencia. **Extracurricular:** drama, computers, yearbook, field trips, choir, chess club, French club, student exchanges, hand bells. **Sports:** basketball, cross-country, soccer, track and field, volleyball. **Organizations:** National Honor Society, National Junior Honor Society, Model UN, student council. **Tests:** PSAT, SAT, TOEFL, AP international diploma. **Graduates attending college:** 90%. **Graduates have attended:** Brown, Vanderbilt, Pennsylvania State U., Boston U., Lafayette.

Physical plant

Location: Carnaxide campus (grades 5 – 12) on main auto route from Lisbon to Estoril; Monte Estoril campus (grades 2 – 4) in area next to Estoril; Sao Joao campus (early childhood center) in Estoril area. **Campuses (3):** 6 acres. **Library:** 15,000 volumes. **Facilities:** 14 buildings, 40 classrooms, cafeteria, infirmary, 3 playing fields, 3 science labs, 2 computer labs, AV equipment, rented gymnasium.

*Once only fee **Portuguese escudo

St. Julian's School (English Section)

Street address: Quinta Nova, Carcavelos, Portugal
Phone: (351)(1)4570140 **Facsimile:** (351)(1)4566817
E-mail: julians.@mail.telepac.pt or julians.school@ip.pt
Web: http://ourworld.compuserve.com/homepages/julians_computing
Mail: Quinta Nova, 2777 Carcavelos Codex, Portugal
Headmaster: F. D. Styan
Deputy head/head of senior school: G. Hobson
Head of primary school: L. Stagg
Teaching staff: full-time, 75; part-time, 11; total, 86
Nationalities of teaching staff: U.S., 2; U.K., 67; host, 13; other, 4; total, 86
Grade levels: N – 12
Enrollment: N – preK, 77; K, 39; 1 – 6, 306; 7 – 9, 154; 10 – 12, 127; total, 703
Nationalities of student body: U.S., 31; U.K., 258; host, 281; other, 133; total, 703
Capacity: N – preK, 76; K, 40; 1 – 6, 304; 7 – 9, 166; 10 – 12, 140; total, 726
Teacher/student ratio: 1/12
Tuition (annual): N – preK, $5,000; K, $5,653; 1 – 6, $6,853; 7 – 9, $8,546; 10 – 12, $11,453
Other fees: registration*, $233; capital levy*, $533; insurance, $27; lunch, $7/each
School year: September to July

Year founded: 1932. **Type of school:** coed, day, private nonprofit. **Governed by:** elected St. Julian's School Association. **Regional organizations:** ECIS, COBISEC, Association of English Curriculum Schools in Portugal.

Curriculum/physical plant

Type: U.K., IB. **Languages taught:** French, Portuguese. **Staff specialists:** reading, math, learning disabilities, nurse. **Special programs:** ESL. **Special curricular:** art, physical education, computer instruction, choir. **Extracurricular:** drama, gymnastics, dance, choral music, computers, literary magazine, photography, excursions/expeditions, field trips, Guides, Brownies. **Sports:** badminton, basketball, cricket, football, hockey, soccer, tennis, volleyball, weight training. **Tests:** IB, GCSE. **Location:** in suburban area, 40 minutes from center of Lisbon. **Campus:** 19 acres. **Libraries:** 9,000 volumes. **Facilities:** 5 buildings, 40 classrooms, auditorium, infirmary, 4 tennis courts, 3 gymnasiums, 3 playing fields, 6 science labs, 3 computer labs, 3 dining rooms.

*Once only fee

SÃO DOMINGOS DE RANA

St. Dominic's International School

Street address: Outeiro da Polima, Arneiro, 2775 São Domingos de Rana, Portugal
Phone: (351)(1)4444647/4440434 **Facsimile:** (351)(1)4443072
E-mail: benard@mail.telepac.pt or adm@dominic.mailpac.pt
Web: http://www.cidadevirtual.pt/dominics-n12
Principal: Maria do Rosario
Head senior school: Robert Sunderland
Head junior school: Paul Neary
Teaching staff: full-time, 64; part-time, 4; total, 68
Nationalities of teaching staff: U.S., 3; U.K., 32; host, 12; other, 21; total, 68
Grade levels: N – 13
Enrollment: N, 20; 1 – 6, 215; 7 – 11, 165; 12 – 13, 70; total, 470
Nationalities of student body: U.S., 30; U.K., 70; host, 150; other, 220; total, 470
Capacity: N – K, 45; 1 – 6, 240; 7 – 11, 200; 12 – 13, 100; total, 585
Teacher/student ratio: 1/7
Tuition (annual): N – K, 735,000**; 1 – 6, 1,000,000; 7 – 11, 1,300,000; 12 – 13, 1,900,000
Other fees: registration*, 88,000**; insurance, 1,900; busing, 50,000/term; lunch, 90,000/term; ballet, judo
School year: September to June

Year founded: 1965. **Type of school:** coed, day, church-related, private non-profit. **Accredited by:** ECIS.

Curriculum/physical plant

Type: IB, IBPYP, IBMYP. **Languages taught:** French, Spanish, German, Dutch, Swedish, Portuguese. **Staff specialists:** reading, maths, computer, speech/hearing, counselor, nurse. **Special programs:** ESL, remedial. **Special curricular:** art, band, physical education, vocational. **Co-curricular:** drama, gymnastics, dance, instrumental music, computers, yearbook, photography, excursions/expeditions, field trips. **Sports:** basketball, soccer. **Clubs:** chess, computer. **Tests:** SAT, IB. **Graduates attending college:** 80%. **Graduates have attended:** U. College London, St. Andrews, Bath, Edinburgh, Kings. **Location:** in rural area west of Lisbon. **Facilities:** 3 buildings, 31 classrooms, cafeteria, infirmary, covered play area, 2 tennis courts, 2 gymnasiums, 2 playing fields, 4 science labs, 2 computer labs, library.

*Once only fee **Portugese escudo

PUERTO RICO

Region: Caribbean
Size: 3,492 square miles
Population: 3,801,977
Capital: San Juan
Telephone code: 787
Currency: U.S. dollar
Languages: Spanish, English

BAYAMON

Baldwin School of Puerto Rico

Street address: Road 833, Km 13.1, Guaynabo, Puerto Rico 00969
Phone: (1)(787)7202421 **Facsimile:** (1)(787)7900619
E-mail: baldwinw@caribe.net
Web: http://www.gulf.net/about/webpresencebaldwin/
Mail: PO Box 1827, Bayamon, Puerto Rico, 00960-1827
Head of school: Alan P. Austen, Ed.D.
Middle/upper school principal: Sylvia Ruiz
Elementary school principal: Nancy Pagán
Business manager: Lucy Pérez
Teaching staff: full-time, 70; part-time, 2; total, 72
Nationalities of teaching staff: U.S., 14; host, 47; other, 11; total, 72
Grade levels: preK – 12
Enrollment: preK, 36; K, 60; 1 – 6, 364; 7 – 9, 151; 10 – 12, 106; total, 717
Nationalities of student body: U.S., 202; host, 442; other, 73; total, 717
Tuition (annual): preK – K, $4,750; 1 – 3, $4,975; 4 – 6, $5,350; 7 – 10, $5,700; 11 – 12, $6,200
Other fees (annual): busing, $250 – 390; initial enrollment*, $1,500; building fee, $800; technology program, $30 – 55
School year: late August through mid-June

Year founded: 1968. **Type of school:** coed, day, private nonprofit. **Governed by:** appointed board of directors and elected parents. **Accredited by:** Middle States, Department of Education of Puerto Rico.

Curriculum/physical plant

Type: U.S., AP. **Languages taught:** English, French, Spanish. **Special programs:** ESL, honors sections, independent study. **Special curricular:** art, physical education, computer instruction, music. **Extracurricular:** computers, yearbook, newspaper, photography, field trips, band, international trips. **Sports:** baseball, basketball, cross-country, soccer, softball, swimming, tennis, volleyball. **Clubs:** computer, drama, National Honor Society, National Junior Honor Society, student council, math, science, French, Close-Up, photography, forensics. **Tests:** PSAT, SAT, TOEFL, AP, Stanford, ERB. **Graduates attending college:** 100%. **Graduates have attended:** Brown, Cornell, Georgetown, Princeton, Harvard. **Location:** in suburban area of San Juan. **Campus:** 25 acres. **Facilities:** cafeteria, infirmary, covered play area, 2 tennis courts, 3 playing fields, science lab, 2 computer labs, swimming pool, multipurpose center, media center (12,000 volumes).

*Once only fee

PONCE

Caribbean School

Street address: Calle 9, La Rambla, Ponce, Puerto Rico 00731
Phone: (1)(787)8432048 **Facsimile:** (1)(787)8431174
Head: (to be announced)
Principal, upper school: Elizabeth Lago
Principal, lower school: Clarissa Moscoso
Business manager: Maramcel Rivera
Teaching staff: full-time, 52; part-time, 2; total, 54
Nationalities of teaching staff: U.S., 5; host, 49; total, 54
Grade levels: preK – 12
Enrollment: preK, 25; K, 51; 1 – 5, 262; 6 – 8, 136; 9 – 12, 153; total, 627
Nationalities of student body: host, 557; other, 70; total, 627
Teacher/student ratio: 1/13
Tuition (annual): preK, $2,400; K – 2, $2,850; 3 – 5, $3,010; 6 – 8, $3,220; 9 – 12, $3,435
Other fees (annual): registration*, $100; capital levy, $400; new family fee*, $600
School year: August through June

Year founded: 1954. **Type of school:** coed, day. **Governed by:** elected board of directors. **Accredited by:** Middle States, Consejo General de Educacion de Puerto Rico. **Regional organizations:** CAIS.

Curriculum/physical plant

Type: U.S., AP. **Languages taught:** French, Spanish. **Staff specialists:** computer. **Special programs:** ESL, independent study. **Special curricular:** art, physical education, computer instruction, music. **Extracurricular:** drama, computers, yearbook, newspaper, field trips, Close-Up, band. **Sports:** basketball, soccer, softball, tennis, track and field, volleyball. **Tests:** PSAT, SAT, ACT, Iowa. **Graduates attending college:** 100%. **Graduates have attended:** Harvard, Stanford, Yale, Princeton, U. of Virginia. **Location:** 2 miles from Ponce. **Campus:** 10 acres. **Libraries:** 19,000 volumes. **Facilities:** 3 buildings, 42 classrooms, cafeteria, infirmary, covered play area, 2 tennis courts, 3 playing fields, 4 science labs, computer lab, sports facility.

*Once only fee

SAN JUAN

Academia del Perpetuo Socorro

Street address: 704 Marti, San Juan, Puerto Rico 00907-3227
Phone: (1)(787)7214540 **Facsimile:** (1)(787)7234550
Principal: Sr. Armand Marie, SSND
Vice-principal: José M. Leavitt
Business manager: Julia Roake
Teaching staff: full-time, 55; part-time, 3; total, 58

Nationalities of teaching staff: U.S., 58; total, 58
Grade levels: 7 – 12
Enrollment: 7 – 9, 304; 10 – 12, 264; total, 568
Capacity: 7 – 9, 300; 10 – 12, 300; total, 600
Teacher/student ratio: 1/10
Tuition (annual): 7 – 8, $2,304; 9 – 12, $2,700
Other fees (annual): registration, $350; insurance, $6; books, $250 – 300; entrance*, $800; building fund, $300; other fees, $400 – 455
School year: August to May

Year founded: 1921. **Type of school:** coed, day, church-related, private non-profit. **Accredited by:** Middle States, Puerto Rican Department of Education.

Curriculum/physical plant

Type: U.S., AP. **Languages of instruction:** English, Spanish. **Languages taught:** French, German, Italian. **Staff specialists:** computer, counselor. **Special programs:** honors sections. **Special curricular:** art, physical education, computer instruction, music. **Extracurricular:** drama, computers, yearbook, newspaper, photography, excursions/expeditions, field trips, home arts. **Sports:** baseball, basketball, cross-country, softball, swimming, track and field, volleyball, golf. **Clubs:** computer, honor society, student council, Model UN, scientific research, Sign Post, camera, math, honor academy, art, aerobics, varsity, yearbook, geophysical science, English and Spanish forensics, liturgy, youth ministry, literary review, leaders for world peace. **Tests:** PSAT, SAT, ACT, AP. **Graduates attending college:** 100%. **Graduates have attended:** Harvard, Princeton, Georgetown, Cornell, Tulane. **Location:** in city. **Facilities:** auditorium, cafeteria, 2 infirmaries, covered play area, gymnasium, playing field, 2 science labs, computer lab, air conditioning.

*Once only fee

Caribbean Preparatory School

Mail: Box 70177, San Juan, Puerto Rico 00936-8177
Phone: (1)(787)7654411 **Facsimile:** (1)(787)7643809
Headmaster: F. Richard Marracino
Principal: Alfredo Torres
Middle school principal: Marybelle Colón
Lower school principal: Ivette Colezo
Admissions and development director: Lorraine Ferrer
Head of library: Magaly Sanchez
Teaching staff: full-time, 71; total, 71
Nationalities of teaching staff: U.S., 69; other, 2; total, 71
Grade levels: early development program (age 3) – 12
Enrollment: EDP, 23; preK, 43; K, 40; 1 – 6, 342; 7 – 9, 127; 10 – 12, 125; total, 700
Nationalities of student body: U.S., 665; other, 35; total, 700
Capacity: preK, 25; K, 50; 1 – 6, 400; 7 – 9, 145; 10 – 12, 135; total, 755
Teacher/student ratio: 1/10
Tuition (annual): EDP, $3,088; preK, $3,868; K, $4,250; 1 – 5, $4,940; 6 – 12, $5,036 – 5,272
Other fees (annual): registration*, $1,230; capital levy, $630; graduation*, $100 – 160
School year: August to June

Year founded: 1952. **Type of school:** coed, day, private nonprofit. **Governed by:** appointed and elected board of directors. **Accredited by:** Middle States, Puerto Rican Department of Education.

Curriculum/physical plant

Type: U.S., AP. **Languages taught:** English, Spanish. **Staff specialists:** computer, counselor, learning disabilities, psychologist. **Special programs:** ESL, honors sections. **Special curricular:** art, physical education, computer instruction, music, poetry, dance. **Extracurricular:** drama, dance, computers, yearbook, newspaper, literary magazine, photography, field trips, forensics. **Sports:** badminton, baseball, basketball, football, soccer, softball, tennis, track and field, volleyball, indoor soccer. **Organizations:** National Honor Society, National Junior Honor Society, Model UN, student council, radio, science, drama. **Tests:** PSAT, SAT, Stanford. **Graduates attending college:** 100%. **Graduates have attended:** West Point, Harvard, Georgetown, Penn State, MIT. **Location:** 6 miles from San Juan metro area, in business district at Hato Rey. **Campuses (2):** 3 acres. **Libraries (2):** 20,000 volumes. **Facilities:** 3 buildings, 43 classrooms, auditorium, 2 cafeterias, 2 playing fields, 4 science labs, 2 computer labs, air conditioning.

*Once only fee

EPISCOPAL CATHEDRAL SCHOOL

Street address: 309 Canals Street, Santurce, Puerto Rico 00907
Phone: (1)(787)7215478/7214958 **Facsimile:** (1)(787)7246668
Mail: PO Box 13305, Santurce Station, San Juan, Puerto Rico 00908
Director: Rev. Canon Gary J. DeHope
Registrar: Fr. Manuel Palacin
Teaching staff: full-time, 20; total, 20
Nationalities of teaching staff: U.S., 20; total, 20
Grade levels: K – 12
Enrollment: K, 35; 1 – 6, 165; 7 – 9, 66; 10 – 12, 63; total, 329
Nationalities of student body: U.S., 309; other, 20; total, 329
Capacity: K, 35; 1 – 6, 175; 7 – 9, 75; 10 – 12, 75; total, 360
Teacher/student ratio: 1/16
Tuition (annual): K – 6, $2,200; 7 – 12, $2,300
Other fees (annual): registration, $400; books, $100 – 175
School year: August to May

Year founded: 1946. **Type of school:** coed, day, church-related, private nonprofit. **Governed by:** Iglesia Episcopal Puertorriquena. **Accredited by:** Middle States.

Curriculum/physical plant

Type: college preparatory. **Staff specialists:** computer, counselor. **Special curricular:** computer instruction. **Extracurricular:** drama, yearbook, newspaper, excursions/expeditions, field trips. **Clubs:** computer, National Honor Society, performing arts, science, library, Club Cultural. **Tests:** PSAT, SAT, ACT, TOEFL, Iowa, Kulmann-Anderson-K. **Graduates attending college:** 100%. **Graduates have attended:** U. of Puerto Rico, George Washington U., Xavier, Harvard, MIT. **Location:** in city. **Facilities:** 1 building, 18 classrooms, auditorium, cafeteria, science lab, computer lab, library, air conditioning.

Robinson School

Street address: 5 Nairn Street, Condado, Puerto Rico 00907
Phone: (1)(787)7286767 **Facsimile:** (1)(787)7277736
Executive director: Gilberto Quintana
High school assistant: Carmen Morales
Elementary assistant: Lourdes Quintana
Learning center assistant: Ana Teresa Pavia
Business manager: Francisco Velez
Teaching staff: full-time, 50; total, 50
Grade levels: PPK – grade 12
Enrollment: PPK, 20; preK, 30; K, 22; 1 – 6, 146; 7 – 9, 61; 10 – 12, 69; learning resource center, 72; total, 420
Nationalities of student body: U.S., 387; other, 33; total, 420
Capacity: PPK, 25; preK, 25; K, 40; 1 – 6, 180; 7 – 9, 100; 10 – 12, 100; learning resource center, 80; total, 550
Teacher/student ratio: 1/10
Tuition (annual): PPK, $2,450; preK, $3,880; K, $4,300; 1 – 3, $5,063; 4 – 6, $5,171; 7 – 8, $5,340; 9 – 10, $5,600; 11 – 12, $5,710; learning resource center, $6,250
Other fees (annual): registration*, $386 – 431; new family*, $1,000; testing, $75; restoration fund, $500; books
School year: August to June

Year founded: 1902. **Type of school:** coed, day, private nonprofit. **Governed by:** appointed and elected board of directors. **Accredited by:** Middle States, Puerto Rican Department of Instruction. **Affiliated with:** United Methodist Church.

Curriculum

Type: U.S., AP. **Languages taught:** French, Spanish. **Staff specialists:** reading, math, computer, counselor, learning disabilities, speech pathologist. **Special programs:** honors sections, Spanish for continentals, English for native speakers of Spanish. **Special curricular:** art, physical education, computer instruction, music. **Extracurricular:** yearbook, newspaper, field trips. **Sports:** basketball, soccer, softball, volleyball, indoor soccer. **Clubs:** National Honor Society, National Junior Honor Society, student council, French, Spanish, science, math. **Tests:** PSAT, SAT, ACT, TOEFL, AP, NEDT, Puerto Rican College Board, Strong-Campbell. **Graduates attending college:** 100%. **Graduates have attended:** Columbia, Cornell, MIT, Georgetown, Brown.

Physical plant

Location: Condado resort section near San Juan. **Campus:** 4.5 acres. **Libraries (3):** 26,200 volumes. **Facilities:** 3 buildings, 28 classrooms, auditorium, cafeteria, gymnasium, playing field, 3 science labs, 3 computer labs, large playing field, outdoor basketball court, outdoor tennis court, air conditioning.

*Once only fee

Saint John's School

Street address: 1454-66 Ashford Avenue, San Juan, Puerto Rico 00907-1560
Phone: (1)(787)7285343 **Facsimile:** (1)(787)2681454
E-mail: sjslib@caribe.net
Headmaster: Russell Beecher, Ed.D.
Secondary school principal: Dana M. Nigaglioni
Elementary school principal: Marguerite P. Kocher
Head of computer services: Martha Ariza
Business manager: Ivan Ortiz
Teaching staff: full-time, 70; total, 70
Grade levels: preK – 12
Enrollment: preK, 27; K, 44; 1 – 5, 281; 6 – 8, 136; 9 – 12, 181; total, 669
Nationalities of student body: U.S., 622; U.K., 9; other, 38; total, 669
Capacity: preK, 30; K, 54; 1 – 5, 320; 6 – 8, 160; 9 – 12, 200; total, 764
Teacher/student ratio: 1/10
Tuition (annual): preK, $4,950; K, $5,248; 1 – 2, $5,836; 3 – 5, $5,894; 6 – 8, $6,418; 9 – 10, $6,480; 11 – 12, $6,542
Other fees (annual): registration, $500 (included in tuition); building fund, $600 per family; entrance*, $500 per family; special tuition assessment*, $1,000 per family; technology fee, $150 per family
School year: August to June

Year founded: 1915. **Type of school:** coed, day, private nonprofit. **Governed by:** appointed and elected board of trustees. **Sponsored by:** parents. **Accredited by:** Middle States, Puerto Rican Department of Instruction.

Curriculum

Type: U.S., AP. **Languages taught:** French, Spanish. **Staff specialists:** reading, computer, counselor, psychologist, art, music, math remediation. **Special programs:** independent study. **Special curricular:** art, physical education, computer instruction, music, humanities. **Extracurricular:** drama, instrumental music, computers, yearbook, newspaper, field trips, literary magazines. **Sports:** basketball, soccer, softball, tennis, track and field, volleyball, indoor soccer, golf. **Clubs:** National Honor Society, National Junior Honor Society, French, OAS, English forensics, Spanish and French oratory, fine arts, science, varsity, Natural Resources Society, science fair, Kids Care, National Art Honor Society, Interact, Cum Laude Society, International Thespian Society. **Tests:** PSAT, SAT, AP, Iowa. **Graduates attending college:** 100%. **Graduates have attended:** MIT, Harvard, U. of Pennsylvania, Yale, Princeton.

Physical plant

Location: in heart of San Juan. **Campus:** 2.05 acres. **Library:** 32,000 volumes. **Facilities:** 5 buildings, 49 classrooms, auditorium, cafeteria, covered play area, gymnasium, 5 science labs, 3 computer labs, 2 outdoor courts, photo lab, air conditioning.

*Once only fee

QATAR

Region: Middle East
Size: 4,412 square miles
Population: 547,761
Capital: Doha
Telephone code: 974
Currency: riyal
Languages: Arabic, English

DOHA

AMERICAN SCHOOL OF DOHA†

Phone: (974)806770 **Facsimile:** (974)806311 **E-mail:** aisdoha@qatar.net.qa
Mail: PO Box 22090, Doha, Qatar
Director: Robert B. Conlan
Secondary principal: Eric H. Habegger
Elementary principal: Angelyn S. Leaver
Guidance counselor: Christina J. Powers
Teaching staff: full-time, 46; part-time, 3; total, 49
Nationalities of teaching staff: U.S., 28; U.K., 2; other, 19; total, 49
Grade levels: K – 12
Enrollment: K, 18; 1 – 5, 178; 6 – 8, 126; 9 – 12, 138; total, 460
Nationalities of student body: U.S., 205; U.K., 5; host, 78; other, 172; total, 460
Capacity: K, 36; 1 – 5, 200; 6 – 8, 126; 9 – 12, 176; total, 538
Teacher/student ratio: 1/10
Tuition (annual): K, $2,990; 1 – 5, $4,485; 6 – 8, $6,305; 9 – 12, $6,646
Other fees (annual): registration*, $1,000; $685; busing, $495 – $712
School year: September to June

Year founded: 1988. **Type of school:** coed, day. **Governed by:** board of trustees, board of directors. **Sponsored by:** U.S. Embassy. **Accredited by:** New England. **Regional organizations:** NESA, AAIE.

Curriculum/physical plant

Type: U.S., AP. **Languages taught:** French, Spanish, Arabic. **Staff specialists:** nurse, guidance counselor. **Special programs:** ESL, special needs (limited program). **Special curricular:** art, chorus, physical education, drama, computer applications, excursions/expeditions. **Co-curricular:** choral music, computers, yearbook, newspaper, Model UN, after-school activities, fine arts competition, academic games. **Sports:** softball, tennis, intramural and interscholasic volleyball, basketball, soccer. **Clubs:** National Honor Society, National Junior Honor Society, student council, French, Spanish, math, science. **Tests:** SSAT, PSAT, SAT, ACT, AP, Iowa, TAP. **Location:** in central Doha. **Campus:** 10 acres. **Libraries (2):** 10,000 volumes. **Facilities:** As of December 1997, the school will relocate to its new purpose-built facility with 40 centrally air conditioned rooms, cafeteria, infirmary, shaded play areas, tennis courts, 4 science labs, 2 computer labs, 2 art rooms, drama room, music room, student center, 2 playgrounds, surfaced sports area, soccer field, basketball and volleyball courts, gymnasium, nearby swimming pools.

*Once only fee †formerly American International School

Gulf English School

Street address: Al Leqtah Street, Doha, Qatar
Phone: (974)873869/873865 **Facsimile:** (974)863947
Mail: PO Box 2440, Doha, Qatar
Vice-principal: Diana Henderson
Teaching staff: full-time, 23; part-time, 8; total, 31
Nationalities of teaching staff: U.S., 9; U.K., 11; host, 1; other, 10; total, 31
Grade levels: preK – 6
Enrollment: preK, 22; K, 44; 1 – 6, 158; total, 224
Nationalities of student body: host, 172; other, 52; total, 224
Capacity: preK, 22; K, 42; 1 – 6, 155; total, 219
Teacher/student ratio: 1/6
Tuition (annual): preK, $1,890; K – 6, $2,877; 7, $3,288
Other fees (annual): registration, $137 (preK), $274 (K – 7); busing, $63 per month
School year: September to June

Year founded: 1993. **Type of school:** coed. **Sponsored by:** Sheikh Faisal Bin Qassim Al Thani.

Curriculum/physical plant

Type: modified U.K. **Languages of instruction:** English, Arabic, French. **Staff specialists:** nurse, creative arts therapist, special education. **Special programs:** ESL. **Special curricular:** art, physical education, music. **Extracurricular:** field trips. **Location:** in a villa in Doha. **Campus:** 1 acre. **Library:** 3,500 volumes. **Facilities:** portacabins in addition to 1 building, 15 classrooms, auditorium, infirmary, covered play area, computer lab, air conditioning.

The Learning Center

Phone: (974)876294 **Facsimile:** (974)876285 **E-mail:** altamimi@qatar.net.qa
Mail: PO Box 6639, Doha, Qatar
Director: Ghadah Fakieh, Ed.D.
Teaching staff: full-time, 3; part-time, 4; total, 7
Nationalities of teaching staff: U.S., 3; host, 1; other, 3; total, 7
Grade levels: ages 3 – 17
Enrollment: N – preK, 2; K, 6; 1 – 6, 14; 7 – 9, 5; 10 – 12, 1; total, 28
Nationalities of student body: U.S., 3; U.K., 1; host, 21; other, 3; total, 28
Teacher/student ratio: 1/6
School year: September through mid-June

Year founded: 1996. **Type of school:** coed, private nonprofit. **Sponsored by:** Qatar Foundation for Education, Sciences, and Community Development.

Curriculum/physical plant

Type: U.S., U.K. **Languages of instruction:** English, Arabic. **Staff specialists:** reading, speech/hearing, psychologist, learning disabilities. **Special programs:** remedial, occupational therapist. **Location:** 2-story villa in Doha. **Facilities:** computer lab, observation room, tutoring rooms.

ROMANIA

Region: Europe
Size: 91,699 square miles
Population: 21,657,162
Capital: Bucharest
Telephone code: 40
Currency: lei
Languages: Romanian, German, Hungarian

BUCHAREST

American School of Bucharest

Phone: (40)(1)2110102 – 3 **Facsimile:** (40)(1)2110104
E-mail: director@asb.kappa.ro **Telex:** 86411416 AMEMB R
Mail: Director, Scoala Americana, American School of Bucharest, Calea Dorobantilor #39, Bucharest, Romania
Director: Frederic F. Wesson
Secondary school principal: Chris J. Muller
Elementary school principal: Gary Barr
Teaching staff: full-time, 47; total, 47
Nationalities of teaching staff: U.S., 34; host, 2; other, 11; total, 47
Grade levels: preK – 12
Enrollment: preK, 24; K, 36; 1 – 6, 195; 7 – 12, 103; total, 358
Nationalities of student body: U.S., 83; U.K., 36; host, 39; other, 200; total, 358
Capacity: preK, 32; K, 40; 1 – 6, 248; 7 – 12, 144; total, 464
Teacher/student ratio: 1/7
Tuition (annual): preK, $3,500; K – 8, $9,500; 9 – 12, $10,300
Other fees: application*, $150; capital assessment, $2,000
School year: August to June

Year founded: 1962. **Type of school:** coed, day. **Governed by:** 9-member appointed board of directors. **Sponsored by:** U.S. Embassy. **Accredited by:** New England, ECIS. **Regional organizations:** AAIE, ECIS, CEESA.

Curriculum/physical plant

Type: U.S. **Languages taught:** French, Spanish. **Staff specialists:** computer, art, ESL, music, athletics. **Special programs:** ESL. **Special curricular:** art, physical education, computer instruction, music. **Extracurricular:** drama, computers, yearbook, newspaper, excursions/expeditions, field trips, after-school activities. **Sports:** basketball, soccer, swimming, volleyball. **Clubs:** chess, drama, Model UN, arts and crafts, cooking, board games, jogging. **Tests:** Iowa. **Location:** in Bucharest. **Library:** 5,000 volumes. **Facilities:** 3 campuses, 48 classrooms, computer labs, air-dome gymnasium.

*Once only fee

RUSSIA

Region: Europe and Asia
Size: 6,592,800 square miles
Population: 148,178,487
Capital: Moscow
Telephone code: 7
Currency: ruble
Languages: Russian, others

MOSCOW

Anglo-American School of Moscow

Street address: 78 Leninsky Prospekt, Moscow, Russia
Phone: (7)(95)5648033 **Facsimile:** (7)(95)1318756/5648033
E-mail: aasoffice@glas.apc.org **Web:** http://www.glasnet.ru/~aas
U.S. mail: (no personal name) Anglo-American School of Moscow, U.S. Embassy–Moscow, PSC 77 (AAS), APO AE 09721
Director: Ellen Deitsch Stern
Principal, 8 – 12: Charles Barder, Ph.D.
Principal, 4 – 7: W. Fred Bowen
Principal, reception – 3: Judith Honor
Teaching staff: full-time, 61; part-time, 2; total, 63
Nationalities of teaching staff: U.S., 33; U.K., 9; other, 21; total, 63
Grade levels: reception – 12
Enrollment: reception, 15; K, 56; 1 – 6, 315; 7 – 12, 183; total, 569
Teacher/student ratio: 1/11
Tuition (annual): R – 6, $9,639; 7 – 8, $10,710; 9 – 10, $11,245; 11 – 12, $12,316
Other fees: application, $100
School year: August to June

Year founded: 1949. **Type of school:** coed, day. **Governed by:** appointed and elected school board. **Sponsored by:** U.S., U.K., Canada. **Accredited by:** New England, ECIS. **Regional organizations:** AAIE, ECIS, CEESA.

Curriculum/physical plant

Type: U.S., IB. **Languages taught:** French, Russian. **Staff specialists:** nurse, resource teacher. **Special programs:** honors sections. **Special curricular:** art, physical education, computer instruction, music. **Extracurricular:** drama, dance, instrumental music, computers, newspaper, photography, excursions/expeditions, field trips. **Sports:** soccer, swimming, track and field, volleyball, ice skating. **Location:** reception – 6 schools in residential area of Moscow; 7 – 12 school on grounds of U.S. Embassy. **Campuses (3):** 4 acres. **Facilities:** 3 buildings, 29 classrooms, auditorium, 2 gymnasiums, science lab, 2 computer labs, 3 libraries, playing fields, art rooms, music rooms, ice rink, AV equipment, swimming pool (U.S. Embassy).

ST. PETERSBURG

Anglo-American School of St. Petersburg

Phone: (7)(812)3256247 **Facsimile:** (7)(812)3256248
E-mail: aassp@glas.apc.org
U.S. mail: The Anglo-American School – U.S. Consulate, St. Petersburg, PSC 78, APO AE 09723
Principal: John M. "Pat" Nordquist
Teaching staff: full-time, 6; part-time, 2; total, 8
Nationalities of teaching staff: U.S., 2; U.K., 1; host, 2; Canada, 3; total, 8
Grade levels: K – 8
Enrollment: K, 10; 1 – 6, 42; 7 – 8, 4; total, 56
Nationalities of student body: U.S., 18; U.K., 13; other, 25; total, 56
Teacher/student ratio: 1/8
Tuition (annual): $11,900
Other fees: registration*, $100
School year: August to June

Year founded: 1992. **Type of school:** coed, day, private nonprofit. **Governed by:** appointed board. **Accredited by:** New England, ECIS.

Curriculum/physical plant

Languages taught: French, Russian. **Special programs:** ESL. **Location:** in the center of St. Petersburg.

*Once only fee

VLADIVOSTOK

QSI International School of Vladivostok

Phone: (7)(4232)314693 **E-mail:** qsibrady@online.ru
Mail: c/o American Consulate, Vladivostok, Russia
Director: Michael Brady
Teaching staff: full-time, 2; part-time, 2; total, 4
Nationalities of teaching staff: U.S., 2; other, 2; total, 4
Grade levels: K – 8
Enrollment: K, 2; 1– 6, 10; 7 – 8, 3; total, 15
Capacity: K, 5; 1 – 6, 25; 7 – 8, 10; total, 40
Teacher/student ratio: 1/5
Tuition (annual): K – 5, $6,900; 6 – 8, $9,200
Other fees: registration*, $100; capital levy, $4,000 deposit or $1,600/year fee
School year: September to June

Year founded: 1996. **Type of school:** coed, day, private nonprofit. **Governed by:** appointed board of directors. **Sponsored by:** Quality Schools International. **Regional organizations:** CEESA.

Curriculum/physical plant

Type: U.S. **Special programs:** ESL. **Special curricular:** physical education, computer instruction. **Extracurricular:** local culture, Russian. **Location:** north end of Vladivostok. **Campus:** part of a Russian school building.

*Once only fee

SAUDI ARABIA

Region: Middle East
Size: 865,000 square miles
Population: 19,409,058
Capital: Riyadh
Telephone code: 966
Currency: riyal
Language: Arabic

DHAHRAN

Saudi Arabian International School, Dhahran District†

Phone: (966)(3)8919555 **Facsimile:** (966)(3)8912450 (administration)/ 8916395 (purchasing) **E-mail:** leo_ruberto%sais@macexpress.org
Mail: PO Box 677, Dhahran International Airport, Dhahran 31932, Saudi Arabia
U.S. mail: (no personal name), Dhahran Academy, Unit 66804, APO AE 09858-6804
Superintendent: Leo A. Ruberto, Ph.D.
Deputy superintendent: Brent Mutsch, Ph.D.
Assistant superintendent, finance: Walter Lanz
Assistant superintendent, international division: Dan Tighe, Ph.D.
Assistant superintendent, personnel: David Bradley
Teaching staff (all SAIS schools): full-time, 318; total, 318
Nationalities of teaching staff: U.S., 166; U.K., 57; other, 95; total, 318
Grade levels: K1 (4 years) – 9 (15 years)
Enrollment (all SAIS schools): total, 3,711
Nationalities of student body: U.S., 921; U.K., 521; other, 2,269; total, 3,711
Teacher/student ratio: 1/12
Tuition (annual): Dhahran, $6,127; Jubail, $9,856; Yanbu, $7,200; Taif, $7,572; Asir, $7,700; Rahima, $2,368; Abqaiq, $3,196
Other fees: registration*, $1,865; building fee $800
School year: late August to mid-June

Year founded: 1963 (Dhahran Academy). **Type of school:** coed, day, private nonprofit. **Governed by:** appointed and elected board of directors. **Sponsored by:** Saudi Arabian Ministry of Education. **Accredited by:** Middle States.

Curriculum/physical plant (Dhahran Academy)

Type: U.S., U.K. **Languages taught:** French, Arabic. **Staff specialists:** computer, counselor, psychologist, nurse. **Special programs:** ESL. **Special curricular:** art, chorus, band, physical education, computer instruction. **Extracurricular:** drama, gymnastics, choral and instrumental music, computers, photography, excursions/expeditions, field trips. **Sports:** basketball, cross-country, soccer, softball, volleyball, track and field. **Clubs:** computer, drama, student council, photography. **Tests:** SSAT, Stanford. **Location:** close to Arabian Gulf. **Campus:** 40 acres. **Library:** 50,000 volumes. **Facilities:** infirmary, 3 covered play areas, gymnasium, 2 playing fields, 3 science labs, 5 computer labs, tennis courts, air conditioning.

*Once only fee †10 schools within Saudi Arabia

Saudi Arabian Oil Company

Saudi Aramco Schools

Phone: (966)(3)8771675 **Facsimile:** (966)(3)8720783
E-mail: harrisdo@aramco.com.sa
Mail: c/o Saudi Aramco, PO Box 73, Dhahran 31311, Saudi Arabia
U.S. mail: c/o Cynthia Hayes, MS 1099, R 10120, Aramco Services Company, Box 4534, Houston, TX 77210-4534, U.S.A.
Superintendent: Dr. Owen Harrison
Teaching staff: full-time, 203; total, 203
Nationalities of teaching staff: U.S., 194; host, 3; other, 6; total, 203
Grade levels: K – 9
Enrollment: total, 1,862
Nationalities of student body: U.S., 1,243; host, 29; other, 590; total, 1,862
Teacher/student ratio: 1/10
School year: September through July

Year founded: 1945. **Type of school:** coed, day, company-owned. **Governed by:** company management; appointed and elected school board. **Owned and operated by:** Saudi Arabian Oil Company. **Regional organizations:** NESA.

Curriculum

Type: U.S. **Languages taught:** French, Spanish, Arabic for native speakers. **Staff specialists:** reading, speech/hearing, counselor, psychologist, nurse, transition. **Special programs:** independent study, TESOL. **Special curricular:** art, chorus, band, physical education, computer instruction, industrial arts, home economics. **Extracurricular:** drama, gymnastics, choral and instrumental music, yearbook, newspaper, photography, field trips. **Sports:** basketball, bowling, tennis, track and field, volleyball. **Clubs:** computer, National Junior Honor Society, knowledge bowl, library/media, classroom newspaper, student congress. **Tests:** SSAT, ITBS, COGAT.

Physical plant

Location: 5 schools in 4 communities within Eastern Province. **Facilities:** 5 covered play areas, 6 gymnasiums, 8 science labs, 16 computer labs, swimming pools, tennis courts, bowling alleys, squash and racquetball courts, playing fields and tracks shared with the local community, air conditioning.

JEDDAH

THE CONTINENTAL SCHOOL (S.A.I.S. BRITISH SECTION) AND CAMBRIDGE PRIVATE STUDY GROUP

Phone: (966)(2)6542354 **Facsimile:** (966)(2)6542354 ext. 164
Web: http://www.prowork.com/continental
Mail: PO Box 6453, Jeddah 21442, Saudi Arabia
Director: Russ Law
Headteacher, upper school: James Walbran
Headteacher, middle school: Tony Laverick
Headteacher, lower school: Paul Guy-Byrne
Teaching staff: full-time, 102; part-time, 14; total, 116
Nationalities of teaching staff: U.S., 16; U.K., 71; other, 29; total, 116
Grade levels: preK – 11
Enrollment: preK, 60; K, 100; 1 – 6, 680; 7 – 9, 275; 10 – 11, 172; total, 1,287
Capacity: preK, 60; K, 100; 1 – 6, 680; 7 – 9, 300; 10 – 11, 180; total, 1,320
Teacher/student ratio: 1/12
Tuition (annual): preK, $3,679; K – 2, $5,359; 3 – 6, $5,479; 7 – 11, $7,038
Other fees: registration*, $53; entrance*, $800
School year: September to July

Year founded: 1977. **Type of school:** coed, day, private nonprofit. **Governed by:** elected board of governors. **Sponsored by:** British Embassy. **Accredited by:** ECIS, Cambridge. **Regional organizations:** British Schools of Middle East Heads Conference; Heads of British-style Schools in Saudi Arabia.

Curriculum

Type: U.K. **Languages taught:** French, Spanish, German, Arabic. **Staff specialists:** math, computer, counselor, nurse, art, physical education, English, geography, history, home economics, Arabic, business studies, outdoor education, music, information technology, natural economy, physics, chemistry, biology, modern languages. **Special programs:** ESL. **Special curricular:** art, physical education, computer instruction, instrumental music. **Extracurricular:** drama, gymnastics, dance, choral music, computers, photography, excursions/expeditions, field trips. **Sports:** badminton, basketball, hockey, soccer, squash, swimming, tennis, volleyball, kayaking, boardsailing, dinghysailing. **Clubs:** many different clubs, outdoor education program. **Tests:** GCSE, IGCSE, ABRSM (PSAT, SAT, and TOEFL arranged). **Graduates have attended:** Arizona State, Texas State, North Dakota.

Physical plant

Location: 20 kilometers north of downtown Jeddah, 10 minutes from Red Sea. **Campus:** 34,000 square meters. **Libraries:** more than 18,000 volumes. **Facilities:** 10 buildings, 50 classrooms, cafeteria, infirmary, 2 covered play areas, 3 tennis courts, gymnasium, 2 playing fields, 5 science labs, 5 computer labs, 2 swimming pools, sports hall/theater, staff residences, air conditioning.

*Once only fee

Dar Al Fikr School

Street address: Prince Majid Street, Jeddah, Saudi Arabia
Phone: (966)(2)6800005 (boys); (966)(2)6800004 (girls)
Facsimile: (966)(2)6800808 (boys); (966)(2)6882696 (girls)
E-mail: daralfikr@sahara.com
Mail: PO Box 14279, Jeddah, Saudi Arabia
Director general: Ghormallah A. Baradi
Principal: Mohammed Khodary
Teaching staff: full-time, 184; total, 184
Nationalities of teaching staff: U.S., 44; U.K., 8; host, 34; other, 98; total, 184
Grade levels: K – 12
Enrollment: K, 65; 1 – 6, 431; 7 – 9, 267; 10 – 12, 237; total, 1,000
Nationalities of student body: host, 910; other, 90; total, 1,000
Capacity: K, 80; 1 – 6, 440; 7 – 9, 280; 10 – 12, 250; total, 1,050
Teacher/student ratio: 1/4
Tuition (annual): K, 20,000**; 1 – 6, 21,000 – 29,000; 7 – 9, 30,000 – 32,000; 10 – 12, 33,000 – 36,000
Other fees (annual): registration*, 10,000**; lunch, 3,000
School year: September to August

Year founded: 1985. **Type of school:** coed, day, private nonprofit. **Governed by:** elected board of directors. **Sponsored by:** Hisham Alireza. **Accredited by:** Ministry of Education.

Curriculum

Type: U.S., national. **Languages of instruction:** English, Arabic. **Languages taught:** English, Arabic. **Staff specialists:** reading, math, computer, counselor, learning disabilities, nurse. **Special programs:** ESL, remedial, American curriculum (grades 9 – 12). **Special curricular:** art, physical education, computer instruction, vocational. **Extracurricular:** drama, gymnastics, computers, yearbook, literary magazine, photography, excursions/expeditions, field trips. **Sports:** soccer, tennis, karate. **Clubs:** computer, English, stamps, tennis, civic, science, arts and crafts, social relations, literary. **Tests:** SSAT, PSAT, SAT, TOEFL. **Graduates attending college:** 100%. **Graduates have attended:** UCLA, Rensselaer Polytechnic Institute, Boston U., London U., Rhode Island School of Design.

Physical plant

Location: 1 kilometer from Jeddah City. **Libraries (3):** 80,000 volumes. **Facilities:** 2 campuses, 4 buildings, 54 classrooms, 2 auditoriums, 2 cafeterias, 3 covered play areas, 2 tennis courts, 2 gymnasiums, playing field, 4 science labs, 4 computer labs, air conditioning.

*Once only fee   **Saudi riyal

SAUDIA – S.A.I.S.

Phone: (966)(2)6674513 **Facsimile:** (966)(2)6674536
E-mail: sais-saudia@tng.net
Mail: c/o Saudi Arabian Airlines, CC 404, PO Box 167, Jeddah 21231, Saudi Arabia
Superintendent: Dr. Sami J. Alam
Assistant superintendent: John K. Hazelton
Middle school principal: Paul E. Frank
Elementary school principal: Michael Gwynn
Business manager: Ahmed Taweeli
Teaching staff: full-time, 113
Grade levels: preK – 9
Enrollment: preK, 26; K, 68; 1 – 4, 370; 5 – 9, 454; total, 918
Nationalities of student body: U.S., 330; U.K., 104; other, 484; total, 918
Capacity: preK – K, 154; 1 – 4, 680; 5 – 9, 770; total, 1,604
Teacher/student ratio: 1/8
Tuition (annual): preK, $3,733; K: (full day) $4,587; 1 – 9, $6,400
Other fees: registration*, $400
School year: August to June

Year founded: 1952. **Type of school:** coed, day, company-sponsored. **Governed and sponsored by:** Saudi Arabian Airlines. **Accredited by:** Middle States, Saudi Arabian Ministry of Education. **Regional organizations:** AAIE, NESA.

Curriculum/physical plant

Type: U.S. **Languages taught:** French, Spanish, Arabic. **Staff specialists:** counselor, learning disabilities, nurse, curriculum development. **Special programs:** ESL, honors sections, remedial. **Special curricular:** art, chorus, band, physical education, computer instruction, Islamic studies, industrial arts. **Extracurricular:** drama, gymnastics, choral and instrumental music, computers, yearbook, excursions/expeditions, field trips. **Sports:** baseball, basketball, gymnastics, soccer, softball. **Clubs:** computer, science, gymnastics. **Tests:** SSAT, SAT, Stanford. **Location:** in northwest Jeddah. **Campuses (2):** 14 acres. **Library:** 50,000 volumes. **Facilities:** 5 buildings, 85 classrooms, 2 infirmaries, 4 covered play areas, 2 gymnasiums, 3 playing fields, 4 science labs, 3 computer labs, AV room, closed-circuit TV, 4-channel video network, air conditioning.

*Once only fee

RIYADH

KING FAISAL SCHOOL

Phone: (966)(1)4820802 **Facsimile:** (966)(1)4821521
Mail: PO Box 94558, Riyadh 11614, Saudi Arabia
Executive consultant: Dr. Abdullah Al–Hamdan
Director of academic affairs: Sa'd Al-Ghoraibi
Accountant: Waleed Al–Dahhan
Teaching staff: full-time, 87

Grade levels: K – 12
Enrollment: preS, 50; 1 – 6, 400; 7 – 9, 200; 10 – 12, 150; total, 800
Teacher/student ratio: 1/10
Tuition (annual): 25,000**
Other fees (annual): registration*, 5,000**; busing, 3,750
School year: September to July

Year founded: 1991. **Type of school:** boys, day. **Governed by:** board of directors. **Sponsored by:** King Faisal Foundation. **Accredited by:** Ministry of Education.

Curriculum/physical plant

Languages of instruction: English, Arabic. **Languages taught:** English, Arabic. **Staff specialists:** computer, physician. **Special programs:** ESL, honors sections, independent study. **Special curricular:** physical education, computer instruction, tutorial program, enrichment program. **Extracurricular:** gymnastics, computers, yearbook, newspaper, excursions/expeditions, field trips. **Sports:** basketball, soccer, swimming, tennis, track and field, volleyball. **Tests:** SSAT, PSAT, SAT, TOEFL. **Location:** gardenlike setting in suburban area, 10 kilometers from Riyadh. **Campus:** 22 acres. **Library:** 20,000 volumes. **Facilities:** 14 buildings, 80 classrooms, 2 auditoriums, 2 infirmaries, covered play area, 5 tennis courts, 2 gymnasiums, 4 playing fields, 4 science labs, 4 computer labs, 2 swimming pools, air conditioning.

*Once only fee **Saudi riyal

Saudi Arabian International School – Riyadh (American Section)

Phone: (966)(1)4914270 **Facsimile:** (966)(1)4917101
Mail: PO Box 990, Riyadh 11421, Saudi Arabia
Superintendent: John C. Davis, Ph.D.
Junior high school principal: Bruce McMillen
Intermediate school principal: Kenneth Parker
Primary school principal: Martha Wittnebel
Teaching staff: full-time, 215; total, 215
Nationalities of teaching staff: U.S., 195; other, 20; total, 215
Grade levels: preK – 9
Enrollment: preK, 89; K, 141; 1 – 6, 1,053; 7 – 9, 442; total, 1,725
Nationalities of student body: U.S., 865; other, 860; total, 1,725
Teacher/student ratio: 1/11
Tuition (annual): preK, $4,667; K – 9, $6,933
Other fees (annual): registration, $1,600; ESL, $800
School year: late August to early June

Year founded: 1963. **Type of school:** coed, day. **Governed by:** elected parent board. **Sponsored by:** parents' association. **Accredited by:** New England.

Curriculum/physical plant

Type: U.S. **Languages taught:** French, Spanish, Arabic. **Staff specialists:** computer, counselors, nurses. **Special programs:** ESL. **Special curricular:** art, chorus, band, physical education, orchestra, computer education. **Extracurricular:** drama, gymnastics, choral and instrumental music, computers, yearbook, study trips. **Sports:** basketball, soccer, softball, track and field, volleyball, extensive after-school activities program. **Organizations:** National Junior Honor Society, student council. **Tests:** SSAT, SAT. **Location:** southeast section of the capital city. **Campus:** 20 acres. **Library:** more than 40,000 volumes. **Facilities:** 10 buildings, 170 classrooms, 2 auditoriums, infirmary, 2 covered play areas, 6 playing fields, 6 science labs, 4-court gymnasium, 7 Macintosh computer labs, 1 DOS computer lab.

SENEGAL

Region: West Africa
Size: 75,951 square miles
Population: 9,092,749
Capital: Dakar
Telephone code: 221
Currency: CFA franc
Languages: French, others

DAKAR

Dakar Academy

Street address: Rue des Peres Maristes, 69, Hann, Dakar, Senegal
Phone: (221)320682 **Facsimile:** (221)321721
E-mail: dakar-academy-bus@maf.org or daoffice@sonatel.senet.net
Mail: B.P. 3189, Dakar, Senegal, West Africa
Director: Richard Bergen
Teaching staff: full-time, 30; part-time, 5; total, 35
Nationalities of teaching staff: U.S., 26; host, 2; other, 7; total, 35
Grade levels: K – 12
Enrollment: K, 7; 1 – 6, 59; 7 – 9, 33; 10 – 12, 51; total, 150
Nationalities of student body: U.S., 69; other, 81; total, 150
Capacity: K, 15; 1 – 6, 90; 7 – 9, 66; 10 – 12, 66; total, 237
Teacher/student ratio: 1/4
Boarders: boys, 9; girls, 9 (missionary children only) **Grades:** 1 – 12
Program: planned 7-day
Tuition (annual): K – 5, $6,000; 6 –12, $6,600
Other fees: registration*, $200; building fund, $2,500/new family
School year: August to June

Year founded: 1961. **Type of school:** coed, day, boarding, church-related. **Governed by:** Assemblies of God, Conservative Baptist International, United World Mission, Southern Baptist Convention. **Accredited by:** Middle States, Association of Christian Schools, ACSI. **Regional organizations:** AISA.

Curriculum/physical plant

Type: U.S. **Languages taught:** English, French. **Staff specialists:** computer, guidance counselor. **Special programs:** ESL. **Special curricular:** art, chorus, physical education, computer instruction, business education. **Extracurricular:** drama, yearbook, field trips. **Sports:** soccer, track and field, volleyball. **Tests:** SSAT, SAT, Stanford. **Location:** in suburban area, 8 kilometers north of Dakar. **Campus:** 2.44 hectares. **Library:** 8,000 volumes. **Facilities:** 7 buildings, 13 classrooms, auditorium, tennis court, playing field, science lab, computer lab, darkroom, fully equipped dormitory.

*Once only fee

The International School of Dakar

Street address: Fenetre Mermoz, Dakar, Senegal
Phone: (221)250871 **Facsimile:** (221)255030 **E-mail:** isd@enda.sn
Mail: PO Box 5136, Dakar, Senegal
U.S. mail: c/o Administrative Officer, Dakar - Dept. of State, Washington, DC 20521-2130
Director: Peter Todd
Teaching staff: full-time, 12; part-time, 8; total, 20
Nationalities of teaching staff: U.S., 12; other, 8; total, 20
Grade levels: preschool – 9
Enrollment: preS, 22; K, 11; 1 – 6, 78; 7 – 9, 19; total, 130
Capacity: preS, 20; K, 20; 1 – 6, 120; 7 – 9, 60; total, 220
Teacher/student ratio: 1/8
Tuition (annual): preS, $1,758; K – 9, $7,954
Other fees: registration: $50 (new students), $25 (returning students); capital development*, $2,500; ESL, $1,000
School year: September to June

Year founded: 1983. **Type of school:** coed, day, private nonprofit. **Governed by:** elected board of directors. **Accredited by:** Middle States. **Regional organizations:** AISA.

Curriculum/physical plant

Type: U.S. **Languages taught:** French. **Staff specialists:** learning disabilities. **Special programs:** ESL. **Special curricular:** art, physical education, computer instruction, music. **Extracurricular:** dance, computers, field trips, computer club, student council. **Sports:** soccer, swimming. **Location:** in residential suburb. **Library:** 8,000 volumes. **Facilities:** 3 buildings, science lab, computer lab, swimming pool, multipurpose auditorium/gymnasium, air conditioning.

*Once only fee

SEYCHELLES

Region: Africa
Size: 176 square miles
Population: 77,575
Capital: Victoria
Telephone code: 248
Currency: rupee
Languages: English, French, Creole

VICTORIA

INTERNATIONAL SCHOOL (SEYCHELLES)

Street address: Mont Fleuri, Victoria, Seychelles
Phone: (248)322641 **Facsimile:** (248)324152
Mail: PO Box 315, Victoria, Seychelles
Headmaster: Daryl Barker
Teaching staff: full-time, 18; part-time, 2; total, 20
Grade levels: N – 11
Enrollment: N, 18; R, 18; 1 – 5, 76; 6 – 11, 103; total, 215
Capacity: N – R, 38; 1 – 5, 110; 6 – 11, 130; total, 278
Teacher/student ratio: 1/12
Tuition (annual): N, 7,458**; R, 10,923; 1 – 6, 16,385; 7 – 11, 21,831
Other fees (annual): registration, 210**; enrollment deposit*, 7,500 (refundable); subscription, 75
School year: September to July

Year founded: 1969. **Type of school:** coed, day, private nonprofit. **Governed by:** elected board of governors. **Accredited by:** Seychelles and British governments. **Regional organizations:** ECIS, AISA.

Curriculum/physical plant

Type: U.K., international. **Languages taught:** English, French. **Special curricular:** physical education, computer instruction, ESL. **Extracurricular:** drama, gymnastics, photography, excursions/expeditions, field trips, ballet, craft, scouts. **Sports:** basketball, soccer, squash, swimming, volleyball, sailing, canoeing, windsurfing, scuba diving. **Tests:** IGCSE. **Location:** in suburban area, 2 kilometers from city center. **Campus:** 2 acres. **Facilities:** 4 buildings, 17 classrooms, auditorium, 2 covered canteen areas.

*Once only fee **Seychelles rupee

SIERRA LEONE

Region: West Africa
Size: 27,699 square miles
Population: 4,793,121
Capital: Freetown
Telephone code: 232
Currency: leone
Languages: English, tribal languages, Krio

FREETOWN

THE AMERICAN INTERNATIONAL SCHOOL OF FREETOWN

Street address: 24 Hillcott Brow, Hill Station, Freetown, Sierra Leone
Phone: (232)(22)232480 **Facsimile:** (232)(22)225471/241661
E-mail: aisf@sl.baobob.com
Mail: c/o U.S. Embassy, Walpole Street, Freetown, Sierra Leone
U.S. mail: c/o U.S. Embassy–Freetown, Dept. of State, Washington, DC 20521-2160
Principal: Jacqueline Leigh
Teaching staff: full-time, 6; part-time, 5; total, 11
Nationalities of teaching staff: U.S., 3; host, 6; other, 2; total, 11
Grade levels: preschool – 8
Enrollment: preS, 10; K, 6; 1 – 8, 29; total, 45
Nationalities of student body: U.S., 16; U.K., 7; other, 22; total, 45
Capacity: preS, 24; K, 15; 1 – 8, 90; total, 129
Teacher/student ratio: 1/7
Tuition (annual): preS, $2,000; K – 8, $7,000
Other fees (annual): registration, $100; capital levy: preS, $100; K – 8, $200
School year: September to June

Year founded: 1986. **Type of school:** coed, day. **Governed by:** elected board of directors. **Accredited by:** Middle States, CITA, Dept. of Defense. **Regional organizations:** AISA.

Curriculum/physical plant

Type: U.S. **Staff specialists:** computer, ESL, music, physical education. **Extracurricular:** newspaper, field trips, karate, art, tennis. **Tests:** Iowa. **Location:** hills overlooking surbarban area. **Library:** 4,000 volumes. **Facilities:** 2 buildings, 12 classrooms, playing field, preschool I and II annex, air conditioning.

SINGAPORE

Region: Southeast Asia
Size: 247 square miles
Population: 3,396,924
Capital: Singapore
Telephone code: 65
Currency: Singapore dollar
Languages: Chinese, Malay, Tamil, English

SINGAPORE

Canadian International School (Singapore)

Street address: 5 Toh Tuck Road, Singapore 596679, R.O.S.
Phone: (65)4671732 **Facsimile:** (65)4671729 **E-mail:** cis5@cdn-intl.edu.sg
Principals: Wayne MacInnis, Helen Snider
Managing director: Thomas Tang
Teaching staff: full-time, 58; part-time, 3; total, 61
Nationalities of teaching staff: U.K., 2; host, 5; Canada, 51; other, 3; total, 61
Grade levels: K – pre-university
Enrollment: K, 145; 1 – 6, 267; 7 – 9, 102; 10 – 12, 133; 13, 32; total, 679
Nationalities of student body: U.S., 75; U.K., 18; Canada, 123; other, 463; total, 679
Teacher/student ratio: 1/11
Tuition (annual): K – 3, 10,700**; 4 – 6, 13,000; 7 – 13, 15,200
Other fees: registration*, 100; refundable deposit: K – 3, 4,900; 4 – 6, 6,000; 7 – 13, 7,000
School year: September to June

Year founded: 1990. **Type of school:** coed, day, proprietary. **Governed by:** appointed board of directors. **Accredited by:** Province of Ontario.

Curriculum/physical plant

Type: Province of Ontario, AP. **Languages taught:** English, French, Mandarin. **Staff specialists:** reading, math, computer, counselor. **Special programs:** ESL, independent study, remedial. **Special curricular:** art, band, physical education, computer instruction. **Extracurricular:** drama, dance, choral and instrumental music, yearbook, photography, field trips. **Sports:** badminton, basketball, soccer, softball, tennis. **Clubs:** community outreach, culture. **Tests:** TOEFL, Ontario Secondary School Diploma. **Graduates attending college:** 90%. **Graduates have attended:** U. British Columbia, U. Toronto, Queens U., Purdue U. **Location:** in suburban area of Singapore. **Campus:** 3 hectares. **Libraries (2):** 15,000 volumes. **Facilities:** 2 buildings, 40 classrooms, auditorium, cafeteria, covered play area, playing field, science lab, computer lab, air conditioning.

*Once only fee **Singapore dollar

International Community School, Singapore

Street address: 3 Mount Faber Road, Singapore 099196, R.O.S.
Phone: (65) 270-3378/2703387 **Facsimile:** (65) 2703370
E-mail: intlcoms@pacific.net.sg
U.S. mail: PO Box 18151, Memphis, TN 38181, U.S.A.
Principal: Steve Stark
Business manager: Annetta Ikehara
Teaching staff: full-time, 14; part-time, 1; total, 15
Grade levels: K4 – 12
Enrollment: preK, 4; K, 5; 1 – 6, 60; 7 – 8, 19; 9 – 12, 14; total, 102
Teacher/student ratio: 1/7
Tuition (annual): K4, 5,500**; K, 8,500; 1 – 5, 10,000; 6 – 12, 11,500;
Other fees (annual): capital levy, 500**
School year: mid-August to June

Year founded: 1993. **Type of school:** coed, private nonprofit. **Governed by:** board of directors. **Sponsored by:** Network of International Christian Schools, Inc. **Accredited by:** Western (in process); ACSI (in process). **Regional organizations:** EARCOS.

Curriculum/physical plant

Type: U.S. **Staff specialists:** computer, art, physical education. **Special curricular:** art, physical education, computer instruction, music. **Extracurricular:** yearbook, field trips, student council, clubs, basketball, community service, secondary retreat. **Tests:** PSAT, SAT, ACT, Stanford. **Location:** at the foot of Singapore's scenic Mount Faber. **Campus:** 5 acres. **Facilities:** 3 buildings, 12 classrooms, playing field, science lab, computer lab, elementary playground, basketball court, art room, music room, air conditioning.

**Singapore dollar

International School Singapore

Street address: 21 Preston Road, Singapore 109355, R.O.S.
Phone: (65)4754188 **Facsimile:** (65)2737065 **E-mail:** intschl@pacific.net.sg
Headteacher: Margaret Alvarez
Head of upper school: Aidan Campbell
Head of lower school: Arthur Hudson
Head of library: Julie Hearnes
Business manager: Chan Ching
Teaching staff: full-time, 55; part-time, 5; total, 60
Nationalities of teaching staff: U.S., 20; U.K., 25; host, 5; other, 10; total, 60
Grade levels: preS – 12
Enrollment: preS, 30; K, 60; 1 – 6, 120; 7 – 9, 150; 10 – 12, 250; 13, 10; total, 620
Nationalities of student body: U.S., 47; U.K., 45; other, 528; total, 620
Teacher/student ratio: 1/11
Tuition: preS, 5,150**; K – 6, 11, 330 – 14,420; 7 – 13, 14,420 – 15,450
Other fees (annual): registration*, 1,545**; capital levy, 1,000
School year: late August to mid-June

Year founded: 1981. **Type of school:** coed, day proprietary, private nonprofit. **Governed by:** appointed committee of management. **Accredited by:** Western. **Regional organizations:** EARCOS, ECIS.

Curriculum

Type: U.S., U.K., AP. **Languages taught:** French, Spanish, Japanese, Mandarin. **Staff specialists:** computer, counselor, psychologist, learning disabilities, nurse. **Special programs:** ESL, independent study, remedial. **Special curricular:** art, chorus, band, physical education, computer instruction, drama. **Extracurricular:** drama, gymnastics, dance, choral and instrumental music, computers, yearbook, photography, excursions/expeditions, field trips, Mandarin, school performances. **Sports:** badminton, basketball, bowling, rugby, soccer, softball, swimming, tennis. **Clubs:** international friendship, crafts. **Tests:** PSAT, SAT, ACT, TOEFL, AP, A-level GCE, GCSE. **Graduates attending college:** 95%. **Graduates have attended:** Boston U., Michigan State, Smith, Imperial College London, Queen's University, Canada.

Physical plant

Location: on a hill in beautiful tropical surroundings. **Campuses (2):** 31,980 square meters. **Libraries (2):** 12,000 volumes. **Facilities:** 6 buildings, 42 classrooms, cafeteria, 2 infirmaries, covered play area, 2 playing fields, 6 science labs, 2 computer labs, multimedia room, air conditioning.

*Once only fee **Singapore dollar

Overseas Family School

Street address: 25F Paterson Road, Singapore 238515, R.O.S.
Phone: (65)7380211 **Facsimile:** (65)7338825
E-mail: executive_director@ofs.ac.sg **Web:** http://www.afs.ac.sg
Chairman: David A. Perry
Executive director: Irene Chee
College dean: Dr. Nancy Dowdle
High school principal: Dawn Clemens
Middle school principal: Robin Cowan
Teaching staff: full-time, 121; part-time, 22; total, 143
Nationalities of teaching staff: U.S., 35; U.K., 26; host, 10; other, 72; total, 143
Grade levels: preK – 12; college credit
Enrollment: preK, 20; K, 270; 1 – 5, 720; 6 – 8, 240; 9 – 12, 390; college, 20; total, 1,660
Nationalities of student body: U.S., 230; U.K., 170; other, 1,260; total, 1660
Capacity: preK, 20; K, 310; 1 – 5, 800; 6 – 8, 350; 9 – 12, 520; total, 2,000
Teacher/student ratio: 1/12
Tuition (annual): preK – K, 11,000**; 1 – 5, 12,000; 6 – 8, 15,000; 9 – 12, 16,000
Other fees: college registration*, 1,000**; refundable deposit* (grades 1 – 12), one semester's tuition; college, 600/credit, 900/lab credit; ESOL 1,000/semester
School year: August to June

Year founded: 1991. **Type of school:** coed, day, proprietary. **Governed by:** board of directors. **Accredited by:** Western.

Curriculum/physical plant

Type: U.S., U.K., IB, IGCSE, A-levels. **Languages taught:** English, French, Spanish, Japanese, Mandarin. **Staff specialists:** computer, counselor, nurse. **Special programs:** ESOL, international understanding, accelerated learning. **Extracurricular:** drama, dance, field trips, excursions, music, games, camps, community service. **Sports:** badminton, basketball, cricket, rugby, soccer, softball, swimming, table tennis, tennis. **Clubs:** Brownies, Guides, Scouts, Parents' Association. **Tests:** SAT, TOEFL, IB, IGCSE, A-levels. **Location:** inner city at former Singapore teacher-training campus. **Campus:** 8 acres. **Libraries (2):** 27,000 volumes. **Facilities:** 7 buildings, 110 classrooms, auditorium, tennis court, gymnasium, 8 science labs, 4 computer labs, playing fields, 2 basketball courts, health center, canteen, swimming pools, air conditioning.

*Once only fee **Singapore dollar

Singapore American School

Street address: 40 Woodlands Street 41, Singapore 738547, R.O.S.
Phone: (65)3633403 **Facsimile:** (65)3633408 **Web:** http://www.sas.edu.sg
Superintendent: Dr. Don Bergman
Assistant superintendent for business: Bill Pearson
High school principal: Harvey Alvy
Middle school principal: Joan Adams
Elementary school principal: David Hoss
Teaching staff: full-time, 209; part-time, 8; total, 217
Nationalities of teaching staff: U.S., 180; U.K., 6; host, 9; other, 22; total, 217
Grade levels: preS (age 3) – 12
Enrollment: preS – K, 314; 1 – 5, 950; 6 – 8, 527; 9 – 12, 694; total, 2,485
Nationalities of student body: U.S., 2,025; host, 25; other, 435; total, 2,485
Teacher/student ratio: 1/12
Tuition (annual): preS – preK, 7,100**; K – 2, 14,200; 3 – 5, 14,550; 6 – 8, 16,700; 9 – 12, 18,700
Other fees (annual): registration*, 3,000**; capital levy, 6,000; ESL, 2,000; tax on tuition and fees, 3%
School year: August to June

Year founded: 1956. **Type of school:** coed, day, private nonprofit. **Governed by:** elected board of governors. **Accredited by:** Western.

Curriculum

Type: U.S., AP. **Languages taught:** French, Spanish, Mandarin. **Staff specialists:** reading, math, computer, speech/hearing, counselor, learning disabilities, nurse, ESL, school psychologist. **Special programs:** ESL, honors sections, independent study, remedial, technical education, learning disabilities, resource room. **Special curricular:** art, chorus, band, physical education, computer instruction, vocational, technical education. **Extracurricular:** drama, gymnastics, dance, choral and instrumental music, computers, yearbook, newspaper, literary magazine, photography, excursions/expeditions, field trips. **Sports:** badminton, basketball, hockey, rugby, soccer, softball, swimming, tennis, track and field, volleyball. **Clubs:**

computer, Model UN, dance, humanities, social service, stamp, newspaper, Tri-M (music). **Tests:** SSAT, PSAT, SAT, ACT, TOEFL, AP, Iowa, PACT, TAP, COGAT. **Graduates attending college:** 94%. **Graduates have attended:** Dartmouth, Harvard, U. of California (Berkeley), U. of Pennsylvania, MIT.

Physical plant

Location: 30 minutes' from downtown Singapore. **Campus:** 36 acres. **Facilities:** new state-of-the-art facilities house 4 separate divisions including early childhood, intermediate elementary, middle and high schools; auditorium, 2 cafeterias, 2 covered play areas, 6 tennis courts, 4 gymnasiums, playing field, science lab, 2 swimming pools, computer facilities, language lab, 1000-seat stadium, track and field, 2 theaters, music, art rooms, air conditioning.

*Once only fee **Singapore dollar

TANGLIN TRUST SCHOOL

Street address: Portsdown Road, Singapore 139294, R.O.S.
Phone: (65)7780771 **Facsimile:** (65)7775862
Web: http://www.singnet.com.sg/~ttschool
Head of school (nursery/infant/junior departments): R. Stones
Teaching staff: full-time, 82; part-time, 6; total, 88
Grade levels: ages 3 – 16
Enrollment: ages 3 – 4, 170; 5 – 7, 550; 8 – 11, 650; 12 – 13, 80; total, 1,450
Teacher/student ratio: 1/17
Tuition (annual): ages 3 – 4, 7,650**; 5– 7, 10,500; 8 – 9, 11,100; 10 – 11, 11,250; 12 – 13, 13,950
Other fees: registration*, 1,750**
School year: September to August

Year founded: 1925. **Type of school:** coed, day, nonprofit trust. **Governed by:** appointed board of governors. **Sponsored by:** Tanglin Trust Ltd.

Curriculum/physical plant

Type: U.K. **Languages taught:** English. **Staff specialists:** reading, math, computer, psychologist, nurse. **Special programs:** remedial. **Special curricular:** art, physical education, computer instruction, music. **Extracurricular:** drama, gymnastics, computers, yearbook, field trips, recorder, arts and crafts, needlework. **Sports:** athletics, badminton, cricket, netball, rugby, soccer, rounders. **Graduates have attended:** United World College of South East Asia; schools in England and Australia. **Location:** 6 miles from center city, in parklike surroundings near National U. of Singapore. **Campus:** 4.715 hectares. **Facilities:** 3 buildings, 52 classrooms, 3 auditoriums, infirmary, 2 covered play areas, 3 gymnasiums, 2 playing fields, computer lab, 7 libraries, air conditioning.

*Once only fee **Singapore dollar

UNITED WORLD COLLEGE OF SOUTH EAST ASIA

Street address: Dover Road, Singapore 139654, R.O.S.
Phone: (65)7755344 **Facsimile:** (65)7785846
Mail: Pasir Panjang PO Box 15, Singapore 911121, R.O.S.
Head of college: Mr. A. W. Bennett
Senior deputy: Mrs. C. Solomon
Business manager: Mr. L. H. da Silva
Teaching staff: full-time, 145; total, 145
Nationalities of teaching staff: U.S., 11; U.K., 90; host, 9; other, 35; total, 145
Grade levels: 4 – 12
Enrollment: 4 – 5, 132; 6– 8, 770; 9 – 12, 1,030; total, 1,932
Nationalities of student body: U.S., 65; U.K., 501; host, 43; other, 1,323; total, 1,932
Teacher/student ratio: 1/13
Boarders: boys, 135; girls, 114 **Grades:** 7 – 12 **Program:** planned 7-day
Tuition (annual): 16,995**
Other fees (annual): registration*, 1,545**; boarding, 16,686; busing, varies with distance; development levy, 1,545
School year: August to June

Year founded: 1971. **Type of school:** coed, day, boarding, private nonprofit. **Governed by:** board of governors. **Member:** United World College Movement.

Curriculum

Type: U.K., IB. **Languages taught:** French, Spanish, German, Dutch, Japanese, Indonesian, Malay, Chinese. **Staff specialists:** reading, math, computer, counselor, nurse. **Special programs:** ESL. **Special curricular:** art, chorus, physical education, drama. **Extracurricular:** drama, gymnastics, dance, choral and instrumental music, computers, yearbook, newspaper, literary magazine, photography, excursions/expeditions, field trips, more than 100 different clubs and activities. **Sports:** aerobics, athletics, badminton, basketball, cricket, gymnastics, hockey, netball, rugby, soccer, squash, swimming, tennis, volleyball, sailing, windsurfing, canoeing, waterskiing, scuba, karate, fencing. **Tests:** PSAT, SAT, ACT, TOEFL, IB, GCSE, Oxford and Cambridge entrance, London U. scholarship exams. **Graduates attending college:** 90%. **Graduates have attended:** U. of Sydney, Australia; Oxford; Cambridge; Harvard; Utrecht, The Netherlands.

Physical plant

Location: in suburb of Singapore, next to National U. of Singapore and Singapore Polytechnic. **Campus:** 43.5 acres. **Libraries:** 25,000 volumes. **Facilities:** 12 buildings, 80 classrooms, 2 auditoriums, cafeteria, infirmary, 8 tennis courts, gymnasium, 3 playing fields, 15 science labs, 3 computer labs, swimming pool, 3 boarding houses, air conditioning.

*Once only fee **Singapore dollar

SLOVAKIA

Region: Eastern Europe
Size: 18,933 square miles
Population: 5,432,383
Capital: Bratislava
Telephone code: 421
Currency: koruna
Languages: Slovak, Hungarian

BRATISLAVA

BRATISLAVA INTERNATIONAL SCHOOL

Street address: Dolinskeho 1, Bratislava 841 02, Slovakia
Phone/facsimile: (421)(7)764784 **E-mail:** bis@computel.sk
Director: David Hurley
Teaching staff: full-time, 4; part-time, 7; total, 11
Nationalities of teaching staff: U.S., 4; host, 5; other, 2; total, 11
Grade levels: preK – 9
Enrollment: preK, 14; K, 4; 1 – 6, 16; 7 – 9, 6; total, 40
Nationalities of student body: U.S., 8; U.K., 2; Canada, 5; other, 25; total, 40
Teacher/student ratio: 1/4
Tuition (annual): preK, $3,450 – 4,750; K – 4, $5,600; 5 – 9, $6,500
Other fees (annual): registration, $450; busing (optional), $400; books, $45; swimming and/or lab, $60
School year: September to June

Year founded: 1992. **Type of school:** coed, day, private nonprofit. **Governed by:** elected school board. **Sponsored by:** foundation of parents.

Curriculum

Type: U.S. **Languages taught:** English, German, Slovak. **Special curricular:** computer instruction. **Extracurricular:** computers, newspaper, excursions/expeditions, field trips, music.

QSI INTERNATIONAL SCHOOL OF BRATISLAVA

Phone/facsimile: (421)(7)722844 **E-mail:** qsi@ba.sanet.sk
U.S. mail: American Embassy Bratislava, Dept. of State, Washington, DC 20521-7140
Director: Robert Jones
Teaching staff: full-time, 9; part-time, 8; total, 17
Nationalities of teaching staff: U.S., 7; other, 10; total, 17
Grade levels: N – 10
Enrollment: N – preK, 6; K, 14; 1 – 6, 46; 7 – 9, 24; total, 90
Capacity: N – preK, 16; K, 20; 1 – 6, 60; 7 – 9, 54; total, 150
Teacher/student ratio: 1/5
Tuition (annual): N – 5, $6,900; 6 – 10, $9,200
Other fees: registration*, $100; capital levy, $4,000 deposit or $1,600/year fee
School year: September to June

Year founded: 1994. **Type of school:** coed, day, private nonprofit. **Governed by:** appointed board of directors. **Sponsored by:** Quality Schools International. **Regional organizations:** CEESA.

Curriculum/physical plant

Type: U.S. **Languages taught:** French, German, Slovak, Dutch (for native speakers). **Special programs:** ESL. **Special curricular:** art, physical education, computer instruction. **Extracurricular:** dance, computers, newspaper, excursions/expeditions, field trips, swimming. **Location:** centrally located in Bratislava. **Library:** 1,000 volumes. **Facilities:** housed in a Ministry of Education Youth Building, which has an indoor swimming pool, drama theater, music, art and dance rooms.

*Once only fee

SLOVENIA

Region: Eastern Europe
Size: 7,821 square miles
Population: 1,951,443
Capital: Ljubljana
Telephone code: 386
Currency: tolar
Languages: Slovenia, Serbo-Croatian

LJUBLJANA

QSI International School of Ljubljana

Street address: Podlimbarskega 43, 1000 Ljubljana, Slovenia
Phone: (386)(61)558294 **Facsimile:** (386)(61)559862
E-mail: qsijmd@net.zaslon.si
Mail: c/o U.S. Embassy, Ljubljana, Dept. of State, Washington, DC 20521–7140
Director: James Doyle
Teaching staff: full-time, 2; part-time, 1; total, 3
Nationalities of teaching staff: U.S., 2; host, 1; total, 3
Grade levels: K – 8
Enrollment: K, 2; 1 – 6, 6; 7 – 8, 2; total, 10
Nationalities of student body: U.S., 4; other, 6; total, 10
Teacher/student ratio: 1/5
Tuition (annual): K, $6,900; 1 – 8, $9,200
Other fees: registration*, $100; capital levy, $4,000 deposit or $1,600 fee
School year: September to June

Year founded: 1995. **Type of school:** coed, day, private nonprofit. **Governed by:** appointed board of directors. **Sponsored by:** Quality Schools International. **Regional organizations:** CEESA.

Curriculum/physcial plant

Type: U.S. **Languages of instruction:** English. **Special programs:** ESL. **Special curricular:** art, physical education, computer instruction. **Location:** in quiet neighborhood near city center. **Facilities:** 4 instructional areas, computer lab, library.

*Once only fee

SOUTH AFRICA

Region: Africa
Size: 472,281 square miles
Population: 41,743,459
Capitals: Cape Town, Pretoria, Bloemfontein
Telephone code: 27
Currency: rand
Languages: Afrikaans, English, Sotho, Ndebele, others

JOHANNESBURG

THE AMERICAN INTERNATIONAL SCHOOL OF JOHANNESBURG

Street address: Plot 160, Diepsloot, Knoppieslaagte, Gauteng, South Africa
Phone: (27)(11)4641505 – 8 **Facsimile:** (27)(11)4641327
E-mail: pak02695@pixie.co.za
Mail: Private Bag X4, Bryanston 2021, South Africa
Director: Everett G. Gould
Teaching staff: full-time, 44; total, 44
Nationalities of teaching staff: U.S., 29; host, 4; other, 11; total, 44
Grade levels: K – 12
Enrollment: K, 23; 1 – 4, 117; 5 – 8, 111; 9 – 12, 156; total, 407
Nationalities of student body: U.S., 138; host, 27; other, 242; total, 407
Teacher/student ratio: 1/9
Boarders: boys, 30 **Grades:** 8 – 12 **Program:** planned 5- and 7-day
Tuition (annual): $8,000 – 12,800
Other fees (annual): boarding, 21,000**; capital levy*, $3,000/family; busing, 4,610 (Sandton/Bryanston), 7,526 (Pretoria); placement/registration*, 50
School year: August through June

Year founded: 1982. **Type of school:** coed, day, boarding, private nonprofit. **Governed by:** elected school board. **Accredited by:** Middle States.

Curriculum/physical plant

Type: U.S., IB, AP. **Languages taught:** French, Spanish. **Staff specialists:** counselor, learning disabilities, music. **Special programs:** ESL. **Special curricular:** art, physical education, computer instruction, drama. **Extracurricular:** yearbook, newspaper, excursions/expeditions, field trips. **Sports:** basketball, soccer, swimming, tennis, volleyball. **Tests:** PSAT, SAT, TOEFL, AP, Iowa, diagnostic testing. **Graduates attending college:** 90%. **Graduates have attended:** Carnegie-Mellon, Brigham Young, Georgetown, West Point, American College of London. **Location:** midway between Johannesburg and Pretoria. **Campus:** 60 acres. **Library:** 14,000 volumes. **Facilities:** 8 buildings, 27 classrooms, cafeteria, 2 tennis courts, 2 playing fields, 2 science labs, computer lab, swimming pool, multipurpose room, AV equipment, boarding facilities on campus for boys.

*Once only fee **South African rand

SPAIN

Region: Europe
Size: 194,898 square miles
Population: 39,181,114
Capital: Madrid
Telephone code: 34
Currency: peseta
Languages: Spanish, Catalan, Galician, Basque

BARCELONA

American School of Barcelona

Street address: Balmes 7, 08950 Esplugues de Llobregat (Barcelona), Spain
Phone: (34)(3)3714016/3715012 **Facsimile:** (34)(3)4734787
E-mail: 106046.3214@compuserve.com
Director: Elsa Lamb
Assistant director: Anna Prieto
Secondary principal: Don Reeser
Teaching staff: full-time, 42; part-time, 1; total, 43
Nationalities of teaching staff: U.S., 19; U.K., 7; host, 14; other, 3; total, 43
Grade levels: preK – 12
Enrollment: preK, 50; K, 40; 1 – 6, 185; 7 – 9, 85; 10 – 12, 70; total, 430
Capacity: preK, 70; K, 40; 1 – 6, 240; 7 – 9, 150; 10 – 12, 100; total, 600
Teacher/student ratio: 1/10
Tuition (annual): preK – K, 559,500**; 1 – 4, 746,000; 5 – 8, 855,000; 9 – 12, 945,000
Other fees (annual): registration, 74,000**; capital levy*, 198,000; busing, 150,000; lunch, 150,000
School year: September to June

Year founded: 1962. **Type of school:** coed, day, proprietary. **Governed by:** elected board of governors. **Sponsored by:** parents' association. **Accredited by:** Middle States, Spanish Ministry of Education. **Regional organizations:** ECIS, MAIS.

Curriculum/physical plant

Type: U.S., national, AP. **Languages taught:** Spanish, Catalan. **Special programs:** ESL. **Special curricular:** art, physical education, computer instruction, music. **Extracurricular:** computers, yearbook, newspaper, literary magazine, excursions/expeditions, field trips. **Sports:** basketball, soccer, swimming, volleyball. **Clubs:** chess, student council, Model UN, Close-Up. **Tests:** PSAT, SAT, ACT, Iowa. **Graduates attending college:** 90%. **Graduates have attended:** New York U., U. of Texas, Texas A&M, Boston U. **Location:** in pleasant residential suburb of Barcelona. **Library:** 9,000 volumes. **Facilities:** 3 science labs, sports court and dressing rooms, soccer field, computer room, art room, music room, dining room.

*Once only fee **Spanish peseta

The Benjamin Franklin International School

Street address: Matorell i Peña 9, 08017 Barcelona, Spain
Phone: (34)(3)4186545/4186609 **Facsimile:** (34)(3)4173633
E-mail: bfis@goliat.upc.es
Superintendent/director: Mark Klimesh
Assistant administrator: Cindy Moyer
Spanish program director: Pilar Hernando
College counselor: Mimi Geier
Computer coordinator: Tom McKenna
Teaching staff: full-time, 32; part-time, 3; total, 35
Nationalities of teaching staff: U.S., 26; host, 7; other, 2; total, 35
Grade levels: N – 12
Enrollment: N, 12; preK, 17; K, 11; 1 – 5, 92; 6 – 8, 62; 9 – 12, 82; total, 276
Nationalities of student body: U.S., 99; host, 89; other, 88; total, 276
Capacity: N, 15; preK, 15; K, 15; 1 – 5, 120; 6 – 8, 80; 9 – 12, 100; total, 345
Teacher/student ratio: 1/9
Tuition (annual): N – K, 499,000**; 1 – 5, 712,000; 6 – 8, 787,500; 9 – 12, 998,000
Other fees (annual): capital levy*, 180,000**; busing, 147,000 – 178,000 (optional); lunch, 136,500 (optional); matriculation, 82,000 (first child), 71,000 (additional children); graduation*, 15,000
School year: September through June

Year founded: 1986. **Type of school:** coed, day, private nonprofit. **Governed by:** appointed school board commission of the Benjamin Franklin Foundation. **Accredited by:** Middle States, Spanish Ministry of Education. **Regional organizations:** ECIS, MAIS.

Curriculum/physical plant

Type: U.S., AP. **Languages taught:** Spanish, Catalan. **Staff specialists:** computer, art, ESL, music, physical education, SFL. **Special programs:** ESL, independent study, SFL, Spanish, Catalan, Optimal Match, swimming. **Special curricular:** art, computer instruction, sports, yearbook, Model UN, excursions/field trips, math teams. **Extracurricular:** drama, dance, music, foreign languages, student council. **Sports:** basketball, soccer, volleyball. **Tests:** PSAT, SAT, ACT, TOEFL, AP, Iowa, TAP. **Graduates attending college:** 95%. **Graduates have attended:** U. of Pennsylvania, Bryn Mawr, Georgetown, Rice, U. of California (Irvine). **Location:** Sarriá, residential area of Barcelona. **Library:** 6,000 volumes. **Facilities:** elementary and middle schools in 2 large, converted, private residences; pre-school and high school housed in separate buildings with computer lab, music rooms, art room, science labs in separate building, cafeteria, playing courts.

*Once only fee **Spanish peseta

BILBAO

American School of Bilbao

Street address: Soparda Bidea, N. 10, 48640 Berango (Vizcaya), Spain
Phone: (34)(4)6680860 – 1 **Facsimile:** (34)(4)6680452
E-mail: amschbil@vzc.servicom.es
Director: Terry Orueta
Business manager: Begona Loizaga
Teaching staff: full-time, 27; part-time, 2; total, 29
Nationalities of teaching staff: U.S., 18; U.K., 3; host, 6; other, 2; total, 29
Grade levels: preK – 10
Enrollment: preK, 15; K, 48; 1 – 6, 145; 7 – 10, 76; total, 284
Nationalities of student body: U.S., 12; U.K., 11; host, 247; other, 14; total, 284
Capacity: preK – K, 68; 1 – 6, 144; 7 – 10, 96; total, 308
Teacher/student ratio: 1/10
Tuition (annual): preK – K, 453,075**; 1 – 6, 581,700; 7 – 10, 640,500
Other fees (annual): capital levy, 250,000**; busing, 70,000; insurance*
School year: September to June

Year founded: 1967. **Type of school:** coed, day, private nonprofit. **Governed by:** appointed and elected board of directors. **Accredited by:** New England, ECIS. **Regional organizations:** MAIS.

Curriculum/physical plant

Type: U.S. **Languages of instruction:** English, Spanish for Spanish citizens. **Languages taught:** French, Spanish, Latin, Basque. **Staff specialists:** computer, psychologist, art, music, physical education. **Extracurricular:** excursions/expeditions, field trips. **Sports:** basketball, soccer, volleyball. **Tests:** Stanford, OLSAT. **Location:** 20 kilometers from Bilbao, on hill surrounded by farms. **Campus:** 14 acres. **Library:** 7,000 volumes. **Facilities:** 8 buildings, 17 classrooms, covered play area, 2 playing fields, science lab, computer lab, art studio, music room.

*Once only fee **Spanish peseta

CARTAGENA

International School of Cartagena

Street address: La Manga Club, Los Belones, CP 30385, Cartagena (Murcia), Spain
Phone/facsimile: (34)(68)175000 ext. 2238 **E-mail:** isc@sendanet.es
Principal: Robert Risch
Teaching staff: full-time, 5; part-time, 2; total, 7
Nationalities of teaching staff: U.S., 4; host, 1; other, 2; total, 7
Grade levels: preK – 8
Enrollment: preK – K, 7; 1 – 8, 21; total, 28
Nationalities of student body: U.S., 3; host, 11; other, 14; total, 28
Teacher/student ratio: 1/6
Tuition (annual): $7,000
Other fees: registration*, 20,000**
School year: September to June

Year founded: 1989. **Type of school:** coed, day, company-sponsored, private nonprofit. **Governed by:** appointed board. **Sponsored by:** General Electric Plastics de España. **Operated by:** International Schools Services, Princeton, New Jersey. **Accredited by:** New England, Spanish Ministry of Education. **Regional organizations:** MAIS, ECIS.

Curriculum/physical plant

Type: U.S. **Languages taught:** Spanish. **Special curricular:** art, physical education, computer instruction. **Extracurricular:** yearbook, excursions, student government, German, gymnastics, art, crafts. **Sports:** soccer, swimming, tennis, volleyball, golf. **Location:** country-club setting, in suburban area near Murcia and Cartagena. **Campus:** 1 acre. **Library:** 1,000 volumes. **Facilities:** science lab, computer lab, playing fields, air conditioning.

*Once only fee **Spanish peseta

LAS PALMAS

American School of Las Palmas

Street address: Ctra. de Los Hoyos Km. 5, Tafira Alta, 35017 Las Palmas, Gran Canaria, Spain
Phone: (34)(28)430023 **Facsimile:** (34)(28)430017 **E-mail:** aslpgc@ext.step.es
Mail: Apartado 15, Tafira Alta, 35017 Las Palmas, Gran Canaria, Spain
Head of school: Celine Hammond
Business manager: Juan Carlos Alemán González
Teaching staff: full-time, 34; part-time, 6; total, 40
Nationalities of teaching staff: U.S., 14; U.K., 11; host, 8; other, 7; total, 40
Grade levels: N – 12
Enrollment: N – preK, 52; K, 32; 1 – 5, 139; 6 – 8, 79; 9 – 12, 74; total, 376

Nationalities of student body: U.S., 5; U.K., 2; host, 206; other, 163; total, 376
Teacher/student ratio: 1/11
Tuition (annual): N – 5, 44,680**; 6 – 8, 62,170; 9 – 12, 67,780
Other fees (annual): registration, 30,000**; capital levy*, N – 5, 300,000; 6 – 9, 100,000; 10 – 12, no fee; busing and lunch, at cost
School year: September to June

Year founded: 1967. **Type of school:** coed, day, private nonprofit. **Governed by:** elected board of directors. **Accredited by:** New England, Spanish Ministry of Education.

Curriculum/physical plant

Type: U.S. **Languages of instruction:** English, Spanish for national program. **Languages taught:** French, German. **Staff specialists:** computer, counselor, librarian. **Special programs:** ESL. **Special curricular:** art, physical education, computer instruction, music. **Extracurricular:** drama, computers, yearbook, newspaper, team sports, gymnastics. **Sports:** basketball, soccer, volleyball. **Tests:** SSAT, PSAT, SAT, TOEFL, AP, ERB. **Graduates attending college:** 95%. **Graduates have attended:** Boston Conservatory of Music, Boston U., Smith, Brown. **Location:** in country setting, 20 minutes from Las Palmas. **Campus:** 10 acres. **Library:** 8,000 volumes. **Facilities:** 8 buildings, 26 classrooms, cafeteria, infirmary, science lab, computer lab, soccer pitch, 2 basketball/volleyball courts, sala football court/activity sand playground.

*Once only fee **Spanish peseta

MADRID

American School of Madrid Foundation

Street address: Carretera de Aravaca-Humera, Km. 2, 28023 Madrid, Spain
Phone: (34)(1)3572154 **Facsimile:** (34)(1)3572678
E-mail: asmcc@redestb.es **Web:** http://www.netschool.com/pages/asm
Mail: Apartado 80, 28080 Madrid, Spain
Superintendent: William O'Hale
Director, upper school: Ms. B. J. Nelsen
Director, lower school: Randy Zern
Admissions head: Sholeh Farpour
Business manager: Jesus L. Hortal
Teaching staff: full-time, 71; part-time, 7; total, 78
Nationalities of teaching staff: U.S., 49; U.K., 5; host, 18; other, 6; total, 78
Grade levels: preK – 12
Enrollment: preK, 51; K, 34; 1 – 6, 234; 7 – 9, 104; 10 – 12, 142; total, 565
Nationalities of student body: U.S., 215; host, 175; other, 175; total, 565
Teacher/student ratio: 1/7
Tuition (annual): preK, $3,929; K, $5,418; 1 – 3, $7,844; 4 – 6, $8,818; 7 – 9, $10,422; 10 – 12, $10,651
Other fees (annual): registration, $78; busing (optional), $1,200; entrance*, $2,500; yearbook (optional), $55
School year: September to June

Year founded: 1961. **Type of school:** coed, day, private nonprofit. **Governed by:** appointed board of directors. **Accredited by:** Middle States, ECIS, Spanish Ministry of Education. **Regional organizations:** ECIS, MAIS.

Curriculum

Type: U.S., Spanish EGB, BUP, and COU; IB; AP. **Languages taught:** French, Spanish. **Staff specialists:** reading, computer, counselor, learning disabilities, nurse. **Special programs:** ESL, remedial, immersion English. **Special curricular:** art, chorus, physical education, computer instruction, field trips, Young Authors' Festival. **Extracurricular:** drama, gymnastics, dance, computers, yearbook, literary magazine. **Sports:** baseball, basketball, gymnastics, soccer, softball, tennis, volleyball, T-ball. **Clubs:** arts and crafts, creative dramatics, judo, scouting, bookmaking, cheerleaders. **Tests:** PSAT, SAT, TOEFL, AP, ERB, achievement tests. **Graduates attending college:** 95%. **Graduates have attended:** Boston College, Stanford, Princeton, Harvard, Georgetown U.

Physical plant

Location: 5 miles from Madrid, near suburb of Aravaca. **Campus:** 10 acres. **Library:** 40,000 volumes. **Facilities:** 3 buildings, 42 classrooms, cafeteria, infirmary, 2 tennis courts, 2 playing fields, 2 science labs, computer lab, gymnasium/auditorium, AV room, music room, track, 2 basketball courts, partial air conditioning.

*Once only fee

Evangelical Christian Academy

Street address: Calle Talia 26, 28022 Madrid, Spain
Phone: (34)(1)7412900 **Facsimile:** (34)(1)3208606
E-mail: 100430.2310@compuserve.com
Teaching staff: full-time, 10; part-time, 4; total, 14
Nationalities of teaching staff: U.S., 14; total, 14
Grade levels: 1 – 12
Enrollment: 1 – 6, 25; 7 – 9, 23; 10 – 12, 21; total, 69
Nationalities of student body: U.S., 57; other, 12; total, 69
Teacher/student ratio: 1/5
Tuition (annual): K, $1,700; 1 – 12, $3,306
Other fees (annual): registration, $50; activity, $75
School year: September through June

Year founded: 1973. **Type of school:** coed, day, church-related. **Governed by:** appointed board of directors.

Curriculum/physical plant

Type: U.S., AP. **Languages taught:** Spanish. **Staff specialists:** computer, learning disabilities, music. **Special programs:** independent study, correspondence, remedial. **Special curricular:** chorus, band, physical education, computer instruction. **Extracurricular:** choral and instrumental music, yearbook, newspaper, National Honor Society, student council. **Tests:** PSAT, SAT, AP. **Graduates attending college:** 96%. **Graduates have attended:** Wheaton College, Cedarville College, Biola U., North Carolina State U. **Location:** residential area of Madrid. **Library:** 12,000 volumes. **Facilities:** 2 buildings, 11 classrooms, science lab, computer lab.

International College Spain

Street address: Calle Vereda Norte 3, 28109 La Moraleja, Madrid, Spain
Phone: (34)(1)6502398 **Facsimile:** (34)(1)6501035
E-mail: 101373.2000@compuserve.com
Web: http://www.cuci.nl/~keulers/
Mail: Apartado 271, Alcobendas, Madrid, Spain
Director: Terry Hedger
Head of secondary: Adrian Watts
Deputy director/head of primary: Hubert Keulers
Teaching staff: full-time, 46; part-time, 11; total, 57
Nationalities of teaching staff: U.S., 10; U.K., 17; host, 7; other, 23; total, 57
Grade levels: preK – 12
Enrollment: K, 73; 1 – 6, 163; 7 – 9, 115; 10 – 12, 118; total, 469
Nationalities of student body: U.S., 85; U.K., 38; host, 112; other, 234; total, 469
Teacher/student ratio: 1/9
Boarders: boys, 5 **Grades:** 7 – 12 **Program:** planned 5-day
Tuition (annual): K, 452,000 – 763,000**; 1 – 6, 826,000 – 1,103,000; 7 – 9, 1,171,000 – 1,413,000; 10 – 12, 1,435,000 – 1,550,000
Boarding fees (annual): 810,000**; insurance*, 60,000; deposit, 50,000
Other fees (annual): registration*, 20,000**; busing, 99,000 – 150,000; lunch, 121,800 – 147,900; books, 14,500 – 42,500; refundable deposit, 80,000
School year: September through June

Year founded: 1980. **Type of school:** coed, day, boarding, private. **Governed by:** appointed independent board of trustees with advisory group. **Accredited by:** New England. **Regional organizations:** ECIS, MAIS.

Curriculum

Type: U.S., U.K., IB, IBMYP. **Languages taught:** French, Spanish, Dutch, Swedish, Hebrew, others by arrangement. **Staff specialists:** reading, math, computer, counselor, nurse. **Special programs:** ESL. **Special curricular:** art, physical education, computer instruction, drama, music. **Extracurricular:** drama, gymnastics, dance, choral and instrumental music, computers, yearbook, newspaper, excursions/expeditions, field trips, ski trips. **Sports:** athletics, basketball, football, tennis, volleyball, judo, karate. **Clubs:** chess, Brownies, community service, ecology, service credit program, guitar, ballet. **Tests:** SSAT, PSAT, SAT, ACT, TOEFL, IB, Iowa. **Graduates attending college:** 95%. **Graduates have attended:** Radcliffe, Oxford, Erasmus, Grenoble, Dublin.

Physical plant

Location: in residential area, 9 kilometers north of Madrid. **Campus:** 7.5 acres. **Library:** 15,000 volumes. **Facilities:** 2 buildings, 40 classrooms, auditorium, cafeteria, infirmary, tennis court, gymnasium, 4 science labs, 2 computer labs, track, playing fields, small boarding facility.

*Once only fee **Spanish peseta

MALLORCA

American International School of Mallorca

Street address: Calle Oratorio 4, 07015 Portals Nous, Mallorca, Spain
Phone: (34)(71)675850 – 1 **Facsimile:** (34)(71)676820
Director: James Berry
Lower school principal: Hilary Walliker
Teaching staff: full-time, 21; part-time, 2; total, 23
Nationalities of teaching staff: U.S., 8; U.K., 10; host, 5; total, 23
Grade levels: N – 12
Enrollment: N – K, 42; 1 – 6, 54; 7 – 9, 31; 10 – 12, 68; total, 195
Nationalities of student body: U.S., 30; U.K., 30; host, 83; other, 52; total, 195
Capacity: N – K, 15; 1 – 6, 80; 7 – 9, 30; 10 – 12, 85; total, 210
Teacher/student ratio: 1/9
Boarders: boys, 13; girls, 5 **Grades:** 6 – 12
Tuition (annual): N – K, 333,900**; 1 – 5, 393,750 – 485,100; 6 – 9, 513,450 – 756,000; 10 – 12, 869,400 – 989,100
Other fees (annual): registration, 36,750**; boarding, $8,745; insurance, $404; books, $525; trips, $1,418
School year: September to June

Year founded: 1969. **Type of school:** coed, day, boarding. **Governed by:** Sociedad Anonima. **Accredited by:** Middle States. **Regional organizations:** ECIS, MAIS.

Curriculum

Type: U.S., Spanish EGB, BUP, COU; IGCSE (Cambridge Syndicate), A-level U. of London, AP. **Languages taught:** French, Spanish, German, Russian. **Staff specialists:** reading, learning disabilities. **Special programs:** ESL, honors sections, independent study, remedial, dyslexia. **Special curricular:** art, physical education, computer instruction. **Extracurricular:** drama, computers, excursions/expeditions, field trips. **Sports:** basketball, soccer, tennis, track and field, volleyball, golf, horseback riding. **Clubs:** chess, computer, National Honor Society, student council, dorm council, community service projects. **Tests:** PSAT, SAT, ACT, TOEFL, AP, IGCSE, Stanford, A-level U. of London. **Graduates attending college:** 95%. **Graduates have attended:** Yale, Cornell, U. of San Antonio, London School of Economics, U. of East Anglia.

Physical plant

Location: in residential village, 9 kilometers from Palma de Mallorca. **Campus:** 8,000 square meters. **Library:** 16,000 volumes. **Facilities:** 6 buildings, 18 classrooms, cafeteria, playing field, 2 science labs, computer lab, student lounge, video lounge, boarding in double rooms with private baths and showers.

**Spanish peseta

The Baleares International School

Street address: C/Cabo Mateu Coch 17, Sant Agusti, 07015 Palma de Mallorca, Baleares, Spain
Phone: (34)(71)403161/401812 **Facsimile:** (34)(71)700319
E-mail: bispmi@ibm.net or bis@ocea.es
Web: http://www.ocea.es/bis/bis.htm
Headmaster: J. Barrie Wiggins
Business manager: Zanetta Kennedy
Teaching staff: full-time, 17; part-time, 5; total, 22
Nationalities of teaching staff: U.K., 13; host, 4; other, 5; total, 22
Grade levels: K – 13
Enrollment: total, 224
Nationalities of student body: U.S., 1; U.K., 85; host, other, 138; total, 224
Capacity: K, 20; 1 – 6, 120; 7 – 9, 60; 10 – 12, 60; 13, 10; total, 270
Teacher/student ratio: 1/11
Boarders: boys, 7; girls, 5 **Grades:** 7 – 13 **Program:** planned 5- and 7-day
Tuition (annual): K, 327,000**; 1 – 6, 393,000 – 528,000; 7 – 9, 615,000 – 798,000; 10 – 13, 864,000 – 897,000
Other fees (annual): registration, 25,000 – 50,000**; boarding, 5-day, 1,830,000
School year: September to June

Year founded: 1957. **Type of school:** coed, day, boarding, proprietary. **Accredited by:** Her Majesty's Inspectors of Schools. **Regional organizations:** ECIS, NABSS, COBISEC.

Curriculum

Type: U.K., AP. **Languages taught:** French, Spanish, German. **Staff specialists:** reading, math, computer, counselor. **Special programs:** ESL, honors sections, independent study, German language for native speakers. **Special curricular:** art, physical education, computer instruction, vocational. **Extracurricular:** drama, gymnastics, choral and instrumental music, computers, photography, excursions/expeditions, field trips. **Sports:** athletics, basketball, soccer, swimming, tennis, volleyball. **Clubs:** Cub Scouts, Brownies, Boy Scouts, Girl Scouts, mountain hiking, body building. **Tests:** PSAT, SAT, TOEFL, AP, A-level GCE, IGCSE. **Graduates attending college:** 80%. **Graduates have attended:** Harvard, Yale, London, Berlin, McGill.

Physical plant

Location: 3 miles from Palma de Mallorca. **Campus:** 3 acres. **Library:** 8,000 volumes. **Facilities:** 3 buildings, 18 classrooms, cafeteria, 2 science labs, computer lab, play area, shared 2- and 3-bedrooms, boarders' lounge.

**Spanish peseta

Bellver International College

Street address: 5, Jose Costa Ferrer, Palma de Mallorca, Baleares 07015, Spain
Phone: (34)(71)401679/404263 **Facsimile:** (34)(71)401762
Administrator: Mark Muirhead
Principals: Daphne Martin, Barbara Bauza, Anne Mollart
Registrar: Stephanie Muirhead
Teaching staff: full-time, 24; part-time, 3; total, 27
Nationalities of teaching staff: U.K., 24; host, 3; total, 27
Grade levels: N – 13
Enrollment: N – preK, 18; K, 24; 1 – 6, 142; 7 – 9, 72; 10 – 13, 38; total, 294
Nationalities of student body: U.S., 12; U.K., 98; host, 144; other, 40; total, 294
Capacity: N – preK, 22; K, 24; 1 – 6, 144; 7 – 9, 72; 10 – 13, 72; total, 334
Teacher/student ratio: 1/11
Tuition (annual): N – K, 426,000**; 1 – 6, 510,000; 7 – 9, 640,000; 10 – 13, 792,000
Other fees (annual): registration*, 75,000**; insurance, 1,600; books, 49,000
School year: September to June

Year founded: 1950. **Type of school:** coed, day, proprietary. **Governed by:** appointed administrator and shareholders. **Accredited by:** Spanish Ministry of Education, British HMI's. **Regional organizations:** ECIS, COBISEC, NABSS.

Curriculum

Type: U.K., national. **Languages taught:** French, Spanish, German, Catalan. **Staff specialists:** English, math, history, geography, languages, computer, sciences. **Special programs:** ESL. **Special curricular:** art, physical education, computer instruction, typing. **Extracurricular:** drama, dance, instrumental music, newspaper, excursions/expeditions, field trips. **Sports:** basketball, soccer, swimming, sailing, karate. **Clubs:** Boy Scouts, Girl Guides, 4 internal houses. **Tests:** A-level GCE, GCSE. **Graduates attending college:** 90%. **Graduates have attended:** Cambridge, Oxford, Michigan State, Dusseldorf, Kent.

Physical plant

Location: 3 kilometers west of Palma center, opposite king's summer palace, on cul-de-sac street in residential area. **Campus:** .5 acre. **Library:** 5,000 volumes. **Facilities:** 2 buildings, 20 classrooms, covered play area, 2 science labs, computer lab, local playing field, AV equipment, 450 square-meter hall/gymnasium.

*Once only fee **Spanish peseta

MARBELLA

THE ENGLISH INTERNATIONAL COLLEGE†

Street address: Urb. Ricmar, CN 340 Km 189.5, Marbella, 29600 Malaga Spain
Phone: (34)(52)831058 – 9 **Facsimile:** (34)(52)838992
Director/academic principal: D. G. Sutcliffe
Head of 6th form: L. Lawrence
Head of primary: M. Ritchie
Teaching staff: full-time, 27; part-time, 8; total, 35
Nationalities of teaching staff: U.K., 32; host, 3; total, 35
Grade levels: preK – 13
Enrollment: preK, 28; K, 15; 1 – 6, 99; 7 – 9, 55; 10 – 12, 78; 13, 23; total, 298
Nationalities of student body: U.S., 12; U.K., 200; host, 30; other, 56; total, 298
Capacity: preK, 28; K, 15; 1 – 6, 99; 7 – 9, 55; 10 – 12, 78; 13, 25; total, 300
Teacher/student ratio: 1/9
Tuition (annual): preK, 427,500**; K, 493,500; 1 – 2, 525,000; 3 – 6, 597,000; 7 – 9, 738,000; 10 – 11, 825,000; 12 – 13, 860,000
Other fees: registration*, 25,000**; busing, 90,000; lunch, 75,000; deposit*, 200,000 (refundable)
School year: September to June†

Year founded: 1982. **Type of school:** coed, day, private nonprofit, charitable trust.

Curriculum

Type: U.K. **Languages taught:** English, French, Spanish, German. **Staff specialists:** math, computer, learning disabilities, physics, chemistry, biology, business studies. **Special curricular:** art, physical education, computer instruction, drama, general studies. **Extracurricular:** drama, dance, choral and instrumental music, computers, yearbook, photography, excursions/expeditions, field trips. **Sports:** athletics, basketball, football, hockey, netball, softball, swimming, tennis, volleyball, trampoline. **Clubs:** art, guitar, language, typing, cookery. **Tests:** A-level GCE, GCSE. **Graduates attending college:** 95%. **Graduates have attended:** Kings College, Imperial College-London, U. of Birmingham, Edinburgh U., Oxford.

Physical plant

Location: within gardens, easy distance to the beach, 8 kilometers from Marbella. **Campus:** 3 acres. **Library:** 3,000 volumes. **Facilities:** 5 buildings, 29 classrooms, auditorium, cafeteria, gymnasium, playing field, 3 science labs, computer lab, swimming pool, outdoor play area, mini-farm; boarding arrangements can be made through parents or staff.

*Once only fee **Spanish peseta †formerly New English International College

VALENCIA

Colegio Hispano—Norteamericano American School of Valencia

Street address: Sierra Calderona 25, 46530 Puzol (Valencia), Spain
Phone: (34)(6)1405412 **Facsimile:** (34)(6)1405039
E-mail: am.school@vlc.servicom.es
Mail: Apartado de Correos no. 9, 46530 Puzol (Valencia), Spain
Director: Gillian Flaxman
High school principal: S. Price, Ph. D.
Elementary principal: Irene Conway
Business manager: Francisco Fernandez
Teaching staff: full-time, 56; part-time, 4; total, 60
Grade levels: N – 12
Enrollment: N – preK, 89; K, 50; 1 – 6, 305; 7 – 12, 276; total, 720
Capacity: N – preK, 100; K, 50; 1 – 6, 300; 7 – 9, 150; 10 – 12, 150; total, 750
Teacher/student ratio: 1/12
Tuition: 450,000 – 650,000**
Other fees (annual): registration, (refundable)*, 350,000**; insurance, 2,876 – 13,419; busing, 132,000; lunch, 103,000; materials, 21,500
School year: September to June

Year founded: 1980. **Type of school:** coed, day, private nonprofit. **Governed by:** board of directors and parents' association. **Accredited by:** Middle States, Spanish Ministry of Education. **Regional organizations:** MAIS, ECIS.

Curriculum/physical plant

Type: U.S., national. **Languages taught:** French, Spanish. **Staff specialists:** computer, art, ESL, music, physical education. **Special curricular:** art, physical education, computer instruction, music. **Extracurricular:** drama, computers, excursions/expeditions, field trips, foreign languages. **Sports:** basketball, soccer, volleyball. **Tests:** PSAT, SAT, English language exams. **Graduates attending college:** 98%. **Graduates have attended:** Spanish universities, Tufts, UMIST(UK). **Location:** on residential estate overlooking orange groves and Mediterranean Sea, 25 kilometers from Valencia. **Campus:** 33,000 square meters. **Library:** 6,000 volumes. **Facilities:** 2 buildings, 2 cafeterias, 3 science labs, 2 computer labs, art rooms, music room, technical drawing room, outside sports facilities.

*Once only fee **Spanish peseta

SRI LANKA

Region: South Asia (Indian Ocean)
Size: 25,332 square miles
Population: 18,553,074
Capital: Colombo
Telephone code: 94
Currency: rupee
Languages: Sinhalese, Tamil, English

COLOMBO

COLOMBO INTERNATIONAL SCHOOL

Street address: 28, Gregory's Road, Colombo 7, Sri Lanka
Phone: (94)(1)697587 **Facsimile:** (94)(1)699592
E-mail: cismgmnt@sri.lanka.net
Principal: David Sanders
Teaching staff: full-time, 84; part-time, 15; total, 99
Nationalities of teaching staff: U.K., 25; host, 72; other, 2; total, 99
Grade levels: N – 13
Enrollment: N – preK, 40; K, 50; 1 – 6, 320; 7 – 9, 170; 10 – 12, 225; 13, 75; total, 880
Nationalities of student body: U.S., 10; U.K., 35; host, 535; other, 300; total, 880
Capacity: N – preK, 40; K, 60; 1 – 6, 330; 7 – 9, 200; 10 – 12, 225; 13, 75; total, 930
Teacher/student ratio: 1/10
Tuition (annual): N – preK, $1,000; K – 1, $1,500; 2 – 6, $1,800; 7 – 9, $2,100; 10 – 13, $2,300
Other fees (annual): registration*, $325; capital levy*, $1,400; books, $100 – 120
School year: September to July

Year founded: 1982. **Type of school:** coed, day, private nonprofit.

Curriculum/physical plant

Type: U.K. **Languages taught:** French, German, Sinhala, Tamil. **Staff specialists:** all areas of curriculum. **Special programs:** ESL. **Special curricular:** art, band, physical education, computer instruction, vocational, music. **Extracurricular:** drama, dance, choral and instrumental music, computers, literary magazine, excursions/ expeditions, field trips. **Sports:** athletics, badminton, basketball, cricket, netball, rugby, soccer, swimming, table tennis, tennis. **Clubs:** drama, social work. **Tests:** SAT, TOEFL, A-level GCE, O-level GCE. **Graduates attending college:** 95%. **Graduates have attended:** Oxford, Cambridge, Harvard, Yale, MIT. **Location:** in a prime residential area. **Library:** 20,000 volumes. **Facilities:** 6 buildings, 48 classrooms, 4 science labs, 3 computer labs, basketball courts, 6 video rooms.

*Once only fee

The Overseas School of Colombo

Phone: (94)(1)864920 – 2 **Facsimile:** (94)(1)864999
E-mail: admin@osc.lanka.net
Web: http://www.lanka.net/directory/osc/
Mail: Pelawatte, PO Box 9, Battaramulla, Sri Lanka
Head: Moyra Hadley
Assistant head/director of administration: Sean O'Maonaigh
Assistant head/director of curriculum: Barry Clough
Teaching staff: full-time, 67; total, 67
Nationalities of teaching staff: U.S., 7; U.K., 15; host, 38; other, 7; total, 67
Grade levels: N – 12
Enrollment: N – preK, 36; K, 35; 1 – 6, 212; 7 – 9, 106; 10 – 12, 89; total, 478
Nationalities of student body: U.S., 67; U.K., 51; host, 71; other, 289; total, 478
Capacity: N – preK, 55; K, 40; 1 – 6, 390; 7 – 9, 200; 10 – 12, 150; total, 835
Teacher/student ratio: 1/7
Tuition (annual): preschool, $3,300; 1 – 5, $6,300; 6 – 8, $7,350; 9 – 10, $9,300; 11 – 12, $9,800
Other fees (annual): registration*, $2,000; capital levy, $500 per child ($1,000 maximum per family); refundable deposits: preschool – 5, 25,000**, 6 – 12, 50,000
School year: August to June

Year founded: 1957. **Type of school:** coed, day, private nonprofit. **Governed by:** elected board of directors. **Accredited by:** Middle States, ECIS.

Curriculum

Type: U.S., U.K., IB. **Languages taught:** French, Spanish, Japanese, Sinhala. **Staff specialists:** computer, counselor, learning disabilities, nurse, art, music. **Special programs:** ESL, remedial. **Special curricular:** art, chorus, physical education, computer instruction, vocational, literary magazine, social service program, yearbook. **Extracurricular:** drama, dance, choral and instrumental music, computers, yearbook, newspaper, literary magazine, photography, excursions/expeditions, field trips. **Sports:** basketball, field hockey, rugby, soccer, softball, squash, swimming, tennis, track and field, volleyball, weight training. **Clubs:** drama, student council, aerobic dancing, Kandyan dancing, home economics, woodshop, pottery/sculpture, karate. **Tests:** PSAT, SAT, TOEFL, IB, IGCSE, Iowa. **Graduates attending college:** 95%. **Graduates have attended:** MIT, U. of Pennsylvania, FIT, Lafayette, Vassar.

Physical plant

Location: 8 kilometers from center of Colombo. **Campus:** 5 acres. **Libraries:** 15,000 volumes, CD-ROM. **Facilities:** 6 buildings, 42 classrooms, cafeteria, gymnasium, 2 playing fields, 6 science labs, 3 computer labs, 2.5 meter swimming pool, 2 AV rooms, 3 art rooms, resource rooms, ESL labs, language rooms, air conditioning.

*Once only fee **Sri Lankan rupee

SUDAN

Region: Africa
Size: 966,757 square miles
Population: 31,065,229
Capitals: Khartoum
Telephone code: 249
Currency: pound
Languages: Arabic, others

KHARTOUM

Khartoum American School

Street address: Street 69 and Cemetery Road, Khartoum, Sudan
Phone: (249)(11)221386/222916 **Facsimile:** (249)(11)465965
Telex: 97022619 AMEMB SD
Mail: PO Box 699, Khartoum, Sudan
Superintendent: Richard T. Eng
Teaching staff: full-time, 15; part-time, 6; total, 21
Nationalities of teaching staff: U.S., 12; other, 9; total, 21
Grade levels: preK – 10
Enrollment: preK, 6; K – 6, 79; 7 – 10, 35; total, 120
Nationalities of student body: U.S., 10; host, 30; other, 80; total, 120
Teacher/student ratio: 1/6
Tuition (annual): preK, $3,300; K – 5, $6,900; 6 – 8, $7,300; 9 – 10, $8,500
Other fees: capital levy*, $1,500
School year: August to May

Year founded: 1956. **Type of school:** coed, day. **Governed by:** elected school board. **Accredited by:** Middle States. **Regional organizations:** AAIE, ECIS, AISA.

Curriculum/physical plant

Type: U.S. **Languages taught:** French, Arabic. **Staff specialists:** ESL, resource. **Special programs:** ESL, resource. **Special curricular:** art, physical education, computer instruction, music. **Extracurricular:** drama, computers, yearbook, intramural sports. **Tests:** SSAT, SAT, Iowa. **Location:** in new section of city near airport. **Campus:** 7 acres. **Library:** 10,000 volumes. **Facilities:** 8 buildings, 17 classrooms, covered play area, playing field, science lab, computer lab, music room, air conditioning.

*Once only fee

SURINAME

Region: South America
Size: 63,251 square miles
Population: 436,418
Capital: Paramaribo
Telephone code: 597
Currency: guilder
Languages: Dutch, Sranan Tonga, English, Hindustani

PARAMARIBO

AMERICAN COOPERATIVE SCHOOL

Street address: Lawtonlaan 20, Paramaribo, Suriname, S.A.
Phone: (597)499806/499461 **Facsimile:** (597)498853
E-mail: leo.limoges@sil.org
Principal: Leo Limoges
Teaching staff: full-time, 11; part-time, 6; total, 17
Nationalities of teaching staff: U.S., 16; host, 1; total, 17
Grade levels: 1 – 12
Enrollment: 1 – 6, 53; 7 – 8, 18; 9 – 12, 24; total, 95
Nationalities of student body: U.S., 49; other, 46; total, 95
Capacity: 1 – 6, 52; 7 – 8, 16; 9 – 12, 30, total, 98
Teacher/student ratio: 1/7
Tuition (annual): $4,000
Other fees: registration*, $50; capital levy, $500
School year: August to May

Year founded: 1966. **Type of school:** coed, day, Christian. **Governed by:** appointed cooperative mission board. **Sponsored by:** 5 mission groups.

Curriculum/physical plant

Type: U.S. **Special programs:** independent study, high school by correspondence. **Special curricular:** art, chorus, band, physical education. **Extracurricular:** choral and instrumental music, field trips. **Sports:** basketball, soccer, softball, volleyball, ping-pong. **Tests:** SAT. **Graduates attending college:** 95%. **Location:** in city. **Campus:** 1 acre. **Library:** 6,000 volumes. **Facilities:** 8 classrooms, tennis/basketball court, AV equipment, air conditioning.

*Once only fee

SWAZILAND

Region: Africa
Size: 6,704 square miles
Population: 998,730
Capital: Mbabane
Telephone code: 268
Currency: lilangeni
Languages: siSwati, English

MBABANE

SIFUNDZANI SCHOOL

Phone: (268)42465 **Facsimile:** (268)40320
Mail: Principal, Sifundzani School, PO Box A286, Swazi Plaza, Mbabane, Swaziland
Principal: Mary C. L. Fraser
Teaching staff: full-time, 24; part-time, 6; total, 30
Nationalities of teaching staff: U.S., 2; U.K., 6; host, 5; other, 17; total, 30
Grade levels: 1 – 9
Enrollment: total, 487
Capacity: 1 – 6, 360; 7 – 9, 160; total, 520
Teacher/student ratio: 1/21
Tuition (annual): nationals, 1,650**; expatriates, 4,200
Other fees (annual): registration*, 10**; building fund, 225; government levy, 60
School year: January to December

Year founded: 1981. **Type of school:** coed, day. **Governed by:** Ministry of Education. **Regional organizations:** AISA.

Curriculum/physical plant

Type: U.K. **Languages taught:** French, SiSwati. **Extracurricular:** drama, choral and instrumental music, excursions/expeditions, sports. **Tests:** Swaziland Primary Certificate. **Location:** in hillside suburban setting, 10 minutes' drive from town center. **Campus:** 5 acres. **Library:** 7,740 volumes. **Facilities:** 9 buildings, 20 classrooms, auditorium, tennis court, playing field, swimming pool.

*Once only fee **Swazi lilangeni

Waterford Kamhlaba United World College of Southern Africa

Street address: Waterford Park Estate, Mbabane, Swaziland
Phone: (268)20088 **Facsimile:** (268)20866
Mail: PO Box 52, Mbabane, Swaziland
Principal: Paul McDermott
Deputy principal: Christopher Davies
Teaching staff: full-time, 43; part-time, 5; total, 48
Nationalities of teaching staff: U.S., 2; U.K., 20; host, 1; other, 25; total, 48
Grade levels: 7 – 13
Enrollment: 7 – 9, 370; 10 – 12, 50; 13, 60; total, 480
Nationalities of student body: U.S., 20; U.K., 45; other, 415; total, 480
Capacity: total, 480
Teacher/student ratio: 1/10
Boarders: boys, 180; girls, 170 **Grades:** 7 – 13 **Program:** planned 7-day
Tuition and board (annual): 7 – 11, $8,000; 12 – 13, $11,000
Other fees (annual): registration*, 750**; O-level exam, 650; IB exam, 1,800; IB textbooks, 2,000
School year: January to December

Year founded: 1963. **Type of school:** coed, day, boarding, private nonprofit. **Governed by:** governing council. **Accredited by:** Swaziland Ministry of Education. **Regional organizations:** AISA.

Curriculum

Type: U.K., IB. **Languages taught:** English, French, Spanish, German, Portuguese, siSwati, Afrikaans. **Staff specialists:** math, computer, counselor, nurse. **Special curricular:** art, chorus, physical education, computer instruction, vocational. **Extracurricular:** drama, gymnastics, dance, choral and instrumental music, computers, yearbook, newspaper, literary magazine, photography, excursions/expeditions, field trips. **Sports:** athletics, badminton, basketball, netball, rugby, soccer, squash, swimming, tennis, volleyball, rowing. **Clubs:** chess, debating, drama, current Southern African affairs, Amnesty International, astronomy. **Tests:** SAT, IB, IGCSE, HIGCSE. **Graduates attending college:** 90%. **Graduates have attended:** Harvard, Princeton, Drew, U. of Pennsylvania, Bryn Mawr.

Physical plant

Location: on hillside, 8 kilometers from Mbabane, at elevation of 1,500 meters. **Campus:** several hundred acres. **Library:** 20,000 volumes. **Facilities:** 25 buildings, 25 classrooms, auditorium, cafeteria, infirmary, gymnasium, 3 playing fields, 7 science labs, computer lab, swimming pool, 2 tennis courts/squash court, music/languages wing, language learning center, fine art center, 4 hostels with recreation rooms and TV, theater.

*Once only fee **Swazi lilangeni

SWEDEN

Region: Europe
Size: 173,732 square miles
Population: 8,900,954
Capital: Stockholm
Telephone code: 46
Currency: krona
Language: Swedish

GÖTEBORG

HVITFELDTSKA GYMNASIET

Street address: Rektorsgatan 2, S-411 33 Göteborg, Sweden
Phone: (46)(31)7786454/7786452 **Facsimile:** (46)(31)7786501
E-mail: uhvceb@hvitfeldt.educ.goteborg.se or uhvags@hvitfeldt.educ.goteborg.se
Principal: Olof Johnard
Assistant principal: Carl-Eric Blomqvist
IB coordinator: Agneta Santesson
Head of computer services: Lars Philip
Teaching staff: full-time, 6; part-time, 20; total, 26
Nationalities of teaching staff: U.K., 2; host, 22; other, 2; total, 26
Grade levels: 9 – 12
Enrollment: total, 120
Teacher/student ratio: 1/6
Tuition (annual): 12,600**
Other fees: exam*, 4,000**
School year: August to June

Year founded: 1647. **Type of school:** coed, day. **Regional organizations:** ECIS.

Curriculum/physical plant

Type: IB. **Languages taught:** English, French, German, Russian, Swedish, Portuguese. **Staff specialists:** counselor, nurse. **Special curricular:** art, chorus, physical education. **Tests:** ACT, IB. **Location:** in city. **Facilities:** 3 buildings, auditorium, cafeteria, gymnasium, science lab, computer lab, library.

*Once only fee **Swedish krona

SIGTUNA

SIGTUNASKOLAN HUMANISTISKA LÄROVERKET

Street address: Manfred Björkquists Allé 6-8, S-193 28 Sigtuna, Sweden
Phone: (46)(8)5925700 **Facsimile:** (46)(8)59257250 **E-mail:** info@sshl.se
Web: http://www.sshl.se/
Principal: Ingrid Karlsson
Head of international section: Ake Sörman
Business manager: Jan Peter Grundström

Teaching staff: full-time, 41; part-time, 20; total, 61
Nationalities of teaching staff: US/UK, 9; host, 47; other, 5; total, 61
Grade levels: 7 – 12
Enrollment: 7 – 9, 110; 10 – 12, 470; total, 580
Teacher/student ratio: 1/10
Boarders: boys, 160; girls, 150 **Grades:** 7 – 12 **Program:** planned 7-day
Tuition and board (annual): 86,000 – 110,000**
Other fees (annual): registration, 4,000**
School year: August to June

Year founded: 1926. **Type of school:** coed, day, boarding. **Governed by:** Foundation of Sigtuna School. **Accredited by:** Swedish Ministry of Education. **Regional organizations:** ECIS.

Curriculum/physical plant

Type: national, IB. **Languages of instruction:** English, Swedish. **Languages taught:** English, French, Spanish, German, Latin, Swedish, Greek. **Staff specialists:** reading, computer, counselor, psychologist, nurse, doctor. **Special curricular:** art, chorus, computer instruction. **Extracurricular:** drama, gymnastics, dance, choral and instrumental music, computers, yearbook, newspaper, photography, excursions/expeditions, field trips, sports. **Tests:** IB. **Location:** on the banks of Lake Malaren, 45 kilometers from Stockholm. **Facilities:** 25 buildings, 40 classrooms, auditorium, cafeteria, tennis court, gymnasium, science lab, 3 computer labs, library, swimming pool, playing fields, learning studio, 11 boarding houses.

**Swedish krona

STOCKHOLM

The International School of Stockholm

Street address: Johannesgatan 18, 111 38 Stockholm, Sweden
Phone: (46)(8)249715 **Facsimile:** (46)(8)105289 **E-mail:** admin@intsch.se
Principal: Claes-Göran Widlund
Business manager: Christina McLaughlin
Teaching staff: full-time, 23; part-time, 2; total, 25
Nationalities of teaching staff: U.S., 8; U.K., 8; host, 2; other, 7; total, 25
Grade levels: K – 9
Enrollment: K, 30; 1 – 5, 147; 6 – 8, 112; 9, 37; total, 326
Nationalities of student body: U.S., 74; U.K., 20; host, 35; other, 197; total, 326
Teacher/student ratio: 1/14
Tuition (annual, 1996–97 figures): K, 42,300**; 1 – 5, 56,100; 6 – 8, 62,400; 9, 66,600
Other fees (annual, 1996–97 figures): registration*, 6,000**; lunch, 5,100
School year: August to June

Year founded: 1951. **Type of school:** coed, day. **Governed by:** appointed and elected board of directors. **Accredited by:** School Board of Stockholm, Swedish Ministry of Education, ECIS, Middle States. **Regional organizations:** ECIS.

Curriculum/physical plant

Type: U.S., U.K. **Languages taught:** French. **Staff specialists:** nurse. **Special programs:** ESL. **Special curricular:** art, physical education, computer instruction. **Extracurricular:** drama, dance, excursions/expeditions, field trips. **Sports:** basketball, volleyball. **Tests:** SSAT, Iowa. **Location:** in park, near downtown area. **Library:** 15,500 volumes. **Facilities:** 25 classrooms, auditorium, cafeteria, gymnasium, 2 science labs, computer lab, AV room.

*Once only fee **Swedish krona

Kungsholmens Gymnasium – International Section

Street address: Hantverkargatan 67 – 69, S-11292 Stockholm, Sweden
Phone: (46)(8)6935303 **Facsimile:** (46)(8)6935301
Principal: Olov Eriksson
Head, International Section: Mike Powers
Teaching staff: full-time, 20; part-time, 12; total, 32
Nationalities of teaching staff: U.S., 7; U.K., 5; host, 12; other, 8; total, 32
Grade levels: 10 – 12
Enrollment: total, 450
Teacher/student ratio: 1/14
Tuition (annual): 46,000 – 48,000** (diplomats and non-host students only)
School year: August to June

Year founded: 1973. **Type of school:** coed, day. **Regional organizations:** ECIS.

Curriculum/physical plant

Type: IB, social sciences and natural sciences programs follow the national curriculum, taught in English. **Languages taught:** French, Spanish, German, Swedish. **Staff specialists:** counselor, nurse, career adviser. **Tests:** IB. **Location:** center of Stockholm. **Facilities:** auditorium, cafeteria, gymnasium, science labs, computer labs.

**Swedish krona

SWITZERLAND

Region: Europe
Size: 15,940 square miles
Population: 7,207,060
Capitals: Bern, Lausanne
Telephone code: 41
Currency: franc
Languages: German, French, Italian

BASEL

INTERNATIONAL SCHOOL OF BASEL

Street address: Burggartenstr. 1, Bottmingen, Switzerland
Phone: (41)(61)4269626 **Facsimile:** (41)(61)4269625
E-mail: intsba@dial.eunet.ch
Mail: PO Box 316, CH – 4103 Bottmingen, Switzerland
Headmaster: Geoffrey Tomlinson
Teaching staff: full-time, 20; part-time, 20; total, 40
Nationalities of teaching staff: U.S., 10; U.K., 15; host, 4; other, 11; total, 40
Grade levels: preK – 12
Enrollment: preK, 48; K, 35; 1 – 6, 136; 7 – 9, 44; 10 – 12, 43; total, 306
Nationalities of student body: U.S., 60; U.K., 65; host, 20; other, 161; total, 306
Capacity: preK, 48; K, 36; 1 – 6, 135; 7 – 12, 108; total, 327
Teacher/student ratio: 1/7
Tuition (annual): preK, 6,000**; K – 5, 13,000; 6 – 10, 17,000; 11 – 12, 19,900
Other fees: registration*, 500**; building fee*, 500
School year: August to June

Year founded: 1979. **Type of school:** coed, day, private nonprofit. **Governed by:** elected school board. **Accredited by:** New England, ECIS. **Regional organizations:** ECIS, SGIS.

Curriculum/physical plant

Type: U.S., U.K., IB. **Languages taught:** French, German. **Staff specialists:** reading, math, art, physical education, science, English, German, French. **Special programs:** ESL. **Special curricular:** art, physical education, science. **Extracurricular:** choral and instrumental music, computers, yearbook, field trips. **Tests:** IB, AP, IGCSE, ERB. **Location:** senior school is in city, elementary school is 10 minutes by car from center city. **Library:** 20,000 volumes. **Facilities:** 2 buildings, 14 classrooms, covered play area, 2 gymnasiums, playing field, science lab, swimming pool.

*Once only fee **Swiss franc

BERNE

INTERNATIONAL SCHOOL OF BERNE

Street address: Mattenstrasse 3, 3073 Gümligen, Switzerland
Phone: (41)(31)9512358 **Facsimile:** (41)(31)9511710
E-mail: isberne@ibm.net
Director: David Gatley
High school coordinator: Peter Hedley
Upper school coordinator: Chris Warren
Middle school coordinator: Jeremy Loud
Lower school coordinator: Priscilla Schneider
Teaching staff: full-time, 26; part-time, 7; total, 33
Nationalities of teaching staff: U.S., 10; U.K., 13; other, 10; total, 33
Grade levels: preK – 12
Enrollment: preK, 14; K, 14; 1 – 6, 79; 7 – 9, 41; 10 – 12, 47; total, 195
Nationalities of student body: U.S., 45; host, 15; other, 135; total, 195
Capacity: preK, 50; K, 15; 1 – 6, 100; 7 – 9, 50; 10 – 12, 50; total, 265
Teacher/student ratio: 1/6
Tuition (annual): preK, 8,440**; K – 1, 14,500; 2 – 5, 15,000; 6 – 8, 16,600; 9 – 12, 18,600
Other fees: registration*, 2,500**
School year: August to June

Year founded: 1960. **Type of school:** coed, day, private nonprofit. **Governed by:** parent-teacher association and elected board. **Accredited by:** New England, ECIS. **Regional organizations:** SGIS.

Curriculum/physical plant

Type: IB, international. **Languages taught:** French, German, ESL. **Staff specialists:** computer, counselor, psychologist, disabilities. **Special programs:** ESL, independent study, correspondence, remedial, gifted. **Special curricular:** art, physical education, computer instruction, drama. **Extracurricular:** dance, instrumental music, computers, yearbook, newspaper, photography, excursions/expeditions, field trips, rock climbing, judo. **Sports:** soccer, swimming, track and field, volleyball, orienteering, skiing, skating. **Tests:** PSAT, SAT, IB, IGCSE, ERB. **Graduates attending college:** 95%. **Graduates have attended:** Stanford, Dartmouth, Tufts, Notre Dame, William and Mary. **Location:** in suburb, 5 miles from Bern. **Campus:** 4,800 square meters. **Library:** 12,000 volumes. **Facilities:** 3 buildings, 18 classrooms, gymnasium, playing field, 2 science labs, computer lab.

*Once only fee **Swiss franc

CHESIÈRES

AIGLON COLLEGE

Phone: (41)(24)4952721 **Facsimile:** (41)(24)4952811
E-mail: info@aiglon.ch **Web:** http://www.aiglon.ch
Mail: 1885 Chesières, Switzerland
Headmaster: Richard McDonald
Deputy headmaster: Simon Braidwood
Director of studies: David Rhodes
Teaching staff: full-time, 50; part-time, 17; total, 67
Nationalities of teaching staff: U.S., 2; U.K., 52; host, 1; other, 12; total, 67
Grade levels: 5 – 13
Enrollment: 6 – 7, 42; 8 – 10, 124; 11 – 13, 105; total, 271
Nationalities of student body: U.S., 28; U.K., 44; host, 14; other, 185; total, 271
Teacher/student ratio: 1/6
Boarders: boys, 155; girls, 125 **Grades:** 5 – 13 **Program:** planned 7-day
Tuition and board (annual): 5 – 13, 38,458 – 45, 929**
Other fees (annual): registration, 300**; enrollment*, 3,000
School year: September to July

Year founded: 1949. **Type of school:** coed, boarding, private nonprofit. **Governed by:** appointed board of governors. **Accredited by:** Swiss cantonal authorities, Head Masters' Conference (HMC). **Regional organizations:** ECIS, COBISEC.

Curriculum

Type: U.K., IB (on limited basis). **Languages taught:** French, Spanish, German. **Special programs:** ESL. **Special curricular:** art, drama, religious studies, adventure training. **Extracurricular:** gymnastics, choral and instrumental music, computers, yearbook, newspaper, literary magazine, photography, excursions/expeditions, field trips. **Sports:** athletics, basketball, cross-country, skiing, soccer, squash, swimming, tennis. **Clubs:** debating, cooking, yearbook, science, theater, choir, photography, band, astronomy, crafts. **Tests:** PSAT, SAT, TOEFL, IB, A-level GCE. **Graduates attending college:** 95%. **Graduates have attended:** Cornell, Princeton, Brown, Cambridge, Oxford.

Physical plant

Location: in rural area, 45 minutes from Lausanne and 1.5 hours from Geneva. **Library:** 15,000 volumes. **Facilities:** 12 buildings, auditorium, 2 covered play areas, 5 tennis courts, gymnasium, playing field, 4 science labs, computer lab, art school, 7 dining rooms, access to nearby swimming pools, skating rink, fitness club, extensive ski slopes within 5-minute walk, indoor sports center, 8 boarding houses.

*Once only fee **Swiss franc

CRANS-SUR-SIERRE

International School Le Chaperon Rouge

Phone: (41)(27)4812500 **Facsimile:** (41)(27)4812502
Mail: 3963 Crans-sur-Sierre, Crans/Montana, Switzerland
Directors: Mr. and Mrs. Prosper Bagnoud
Vice-director: Gabrielle Bagnoud
Teaching staff: full-time, 6; part-time, 2; total, 8
Nationalities of teaching staff: U.S., 2; other, 6; total, 8
Grade levels: 1 – 10
Enrollment: total, 60
Teacher/student ratio: 1/7
Boarders: boys, 30; girls, 30 **Program:** planned 7-day
Tuition and board (annual): 23,100**
Other fees: registration, 500**; miscellaneous, approximately 4,500
School year: September through June†

Year founded: 1955. **Type of school:** coed, day, boarding, private nonprofit.

Curriculum/physical plant

Type: U.S., U.K., national, French, German, Italian. **Languages of instruction:** English, French, German, Italian (4 different sections). **Languages taught:** English, French, German, Italian. **Special programs:** ESL (Cambridge examination). **Extracurricular:** dance, excursions/expeditions, field trips, music, picnics. **Sports:** basketball, football, gymnastics, skiing, soccer, tennis, volleyball, ice-skating, ice hockey, golf, hiking, horseback riding, minigolf, snow-surfing. **Location:** in Crans-sur-Sierre, a sunny resort in the Swiss Alps.

**Swiss franc †foreign-language/sports courses, July–August

GENEVA

Collège du Léman International School

Street address: 74, route de Sauverny, 1290 Versoix/Geneva, Switzerland
Phone: (41)(22)7552555 **Facsimile:** (41)(22)7551993 **E-mail:** info@cdl.ch; **Web:** http://www.cdl.ch
Director general: Francis A. Clivaz
Director of studies: Cyril A. Boschert
Principal: Terence B. Gale
French program: A. Cerchierini, D. Soubira
Teaching staff: full-time, 96; part-time, 10; total, 106
Nationalities of teaching staff: U.S., 11; U.K., 23; host, 40; other, 32; total, 106
Grade levels: K – 13
Enrollment: K, 130; 1 – 5, 350; 6 – 8, 158; 9 – 12, 383; 13, 35; total, 1,056
Nationalities of student body: U.S., 130; U.K., 80; host, 203; other, 643; total, 1,056
Teacher/student ratio: 1/10
Boarders: boys, 70; girls, 65 **Grades:** 3 – 13 **Program:** planned 7-day
Tuition (annual): K, 5,200 – 9,300**; 1 – 13 (day only), 12,500 – 17,500
Other fees (annual): registration*, 200**; boarding (tuition included), 35,000 – 38,000; insurance, 240; busing, 2,600 – 3,500; lunch, 2,450; books, 600; lab, 450; computer, 300; refundable deposit*: 400 (day), 5,000 (boarding)
School year: September to June

Year founded: 1960. **Type of school:** coed, day, boarding, proprietary. **Accredited by:** ECIS, New England. **Regional organizations:** AAIE, ECIS.

Curriculum

Type: U.S., U.K., Swiss Maturité, French Baccalaureate, AP. **Languages of instruction:** English, French. **Languages taught:** English, Spanish, German, Italian, Latin, Arabic. **Staff specialists:** counselor, psychologist, nurse, remedial. **Special programs:** ESL, A-level GCE . **Special curricular:** computer instruction. **Extracurricular:** drama, gymnastics, dance, instrumental music, computers, yearbook, newspaper, literary magazine, photography, excursions/expeditions, field trips. **Sports:** basketball, bowling, cross-country, rugby, skiing, soccer, softball, tennis, track and field, volleyball, weight training, judo, horseback riding, karate. **Clubs:** chess, National Honor Society, student council, Model UN, debate, math, alpine, art, aerobics, Student UN, SIMEX simulated political games. **Tests:** PSAT, SAT, TOEFL, AP, A-level GCE, IGCSE. **Graduates attending college:** 90%. **Graduates have attended:** Harvard, MIT, U. of Geneva, Wellesley, Smith.

Physical plant

Location: in suburban area about 5 miles from Geneva. **Campus:** 19 acres. **Library:** 19,000 volumes. **Facilities:** 18 buildings, 65 classrooms, auditorium, 2 cafeterias, 2 infirmaries, 2 covered play areas, 3 tennis courts, gymnasium, 2 playing fields, 4 science labs, 2 computer labs, swimming pool, language labs, AV room, 2 music rooms, 7 residences with snack bar/lounge, dining room, and 3 TV rooms.

*Once only fee **Swiss franc

THE INTERNATIONAL SCHOOL OF GENEVA

Street address: 62, route de Chêne, 1208 Geneva, Switzerland
Phone: (41)(22)7367130 **Facsimile:** (41)(22)7354128
E-mail: 1samuel@ecolint.ch **Web:** http://www.ecolint.ch
Director general: George Walker
Financial manager: Francois Collini
Coordinator: Tadea Mussard
Teaching staff: full-time, 161; part-time, 76; total, 237
Nationalities of teaching staff: U.S., 19; U.K., 95; host, 47; other, 76; total, 237
Grade levels: pre-reception – 13
Enrollment: preR – primaryR, 244; 1 – 6, 1,041; 7 – 9, 626; 10 – 12, 676; 13, 196; total, 2,783
Nationalities of student body: U.S., 386; U.K., 504; host, 415; other, 1,478; total, 2,783
Capacity: preR – primaryR, 234; 1 – 6, 1,056; 7 – 9, 696; 10 – 12, 766; 13, 211; total, 2,963
Teacher/student ratio: 1/14
Boarders: boys, 25; girls, 18 **Program:** planned 5- and 7-day
Tuition (annual): preR – primaryR, 6,350 – 8,700**; R, 13,780; 1 – 4, 14,800; 5 – 6, 15,490; 7 – 9, 17,770; 10 – 11, 18,710; 12 – 13, 19,240
Other fees (annual): registration*, 400**; insurance, 110; capital development*, 700; capital equipment, 200; boarding costs subject to review due to limited facilities; busing, lunch, books (classes 7 – 13), external exams, field trips
School year: September through June

Year founded: 1924. **Type of school:** coed, day, boarding, private nonprofit. **Governed by:** elected board. **Accredited by:** Middle States, ECIS. **Regional organizations:** ECIS.

Curriculum

Type: U.S., U.K., national, IB, French Baccalaureate, AP. **Languages of instruction:** English, French. **Languages taught:** Spanish, German, Italian. **Staff specialists:** reading, math, counselor, psychologist, learning disabilities, nurse. **Special programs:** ESL, remedial. **Special curricular:** computer instruction. **Extracurricular:** drama, gymnastics, dance, choral and instrumental music, computers, yearbook, newspaper, literary magazine, photography, excursions/expeditions, field trips. **Sports:** athletics, badminton, basketball, hockey, rugby, skiing, soccer, table tennis, volleyball, canoeing, trampoline. **Organizations:** Student Day Fair, SIMEX (political simulation exercises), ECIS, math competition, Student League of Nations. **Tests:** PSAT, SAT, TOEFL, IB, AP, IGCSE, Stanford, Iowa, SRA, GAP, Gapadol, Otis-Lennon, Raven, Salford sentence, Schonell reading and spelling. **Graduates attending college:** 95%. **Graduates have attended:** major U.S., U.K., and world universities.

Physical plant

Campuses (3): 2 suburban, 1 in rural area. **Libraries:** approximately 100,000 volumes. **Facilities:** 160 classrooms, 2 cafeterias, infirmary, 2 tennis courts, 3 gymnasiums, 3 playing fields, 18 science labs, 6 computer labs, swimming pool, AV department, 2 theater workshops, fitness center, boarding villa; extensive new buildings on rural campus.

*Once only fee **Swiss franc

GSTAAD

GSTAAD INTERNATIONAL SCHOOL

Phone: (41)(33)7442373 **Facsimile:** (41)(33)7443578 **E-mail:** gis@gstaad.ch
Web: http://www.gstaad.ch/gis/
Mail: 3780 Gstaad, Switzerland
Director: Alain Souperbiet
Teaching staff: full-time, 5; part-time, 1; total, 6
Nationalities of teaching staff: U.S., 2; U.K., 2; host, 2; total, 6
Grade levels: 8 – 12
Enrollment: total, 21
Nationalities of student body: U.S., 2; host, 16; other, 3; total, 21
Capacity: total, 22
Teacher/student ratio: 1/3
Boarders: boys, and girls, 15 **Grades:** 8 – 12 **Program:** planned 7-day
Tuition and board (annual): 53,400**
School year: September through June†

Year founded: 1962. **Type of school:** coed, boarding. **Accredited by:** Swiss Board of Education, ECIS, Swiss Federation of Private Schools.

Curriculum/physical plant

Type: U.S., U.K. **Languages taught:** French, German. **Staff specialists:** reading, math, counselor, learning disabilities. **Special curricular:** physical education. **Extracurricular:** computers, excursions/expeditions. **Sports:** basketball, skiing, squash, swimming, tennis, golf, hiking, rock climbing, ice skating. **Tests:** PSAT, SAT, ACT, TOEFL, AP, IGCSE, ACH, First Certificate in English (Cambridge). **Graduates have attended:** Sarah Lawrence, Colorado State U., Vassar College, Northeastern U., Clark. **Location:** in Gstaad in the Swiss Alps. **Facilities:** 1 building, 4 classrooms, library, off-campus gymnasium, Olympic swimming pool, tennis courts, squash courts.

**Swiss franc †summer camps in July and August

HASLIBERG/GOLDERN

ÉCOLE D'HUMANITÉ

Phone: (41)(33)9729292 **Facsimile:** (41)(33)9729211
Mail: CH-6085 Hasliberg-Goldern, Switzerland
Directors: K. Hennessy, K. C. Hill
Business manager: Hans Willi
Teaching staff: full-time, 38; part-time, 5; total, 43
Nationalities of teaching staff: U.S., 6; U.K., 2; host, 17; other, 18; total, 43
Grade levels: 1 – 13
Enrollment: 1 – 6, 21; 7 – 9, 59; 10 – 12, 61; 13, 4; total, 145

Nationalities of student body: U.S., 14; host, 84; other, 53; total, 151
Teacher/student ratio: 1/5
Boarders: boys, 80; girls, 58 **Grades:** 1 – 13 **Program:** planned 7-day
Tuition and board (annual): 27,900**
Other fees (annual): registration*, 80**; insurance, 1,620; incidentals, 1,000
School year: September through June

Year founded: 1934. **Type of school:** coed, day, boarding, private nonprofit. **Governed by:** Genossenschaft der Ecole d'Humanité. **Accredited by:** Departments of Youth and Education of the Canton of Bern. **Regional organizations:** SGIS.

Curriculum

Type: U.S., national. **Languages of instruction:** English, German. **Languages taught:** English, French, German, Italian, Latin. **Staff specialists:** counselor, psychologist, nurse, art, music, drama, sports coaches. **Special programs:** ESL, independent study, remedial. **Special curricular:** art, chorus, physical education, computer instruction, orchestra, band. **Extracurricular:** drama, gymnastics, dance, choral and instrumental music, computers, newspaper, photography, excursions/expeditions, field trips, pottery, woodwork, painting, drawing, silversmithing. **Sports:** badminton, basketball, soccer, swimming, volleyball, alpine and cross-country skiing, ski touring, hiking, kayaking, judo, folk dancing, jazz dance, ping-pong, snowboarding, rock climbing. **Clubs:** drama, student council, sports, library, social action, current events, entertainment, maintenance, gardening, film, music, student committee on discipline, etc. **Tests:** PSAT, SAT, TOEFL. **Graduates attending college:** 100%. **Graduates have attended:** Brown, American U., Wellesley, George Washington U., Middlebury.

Physical plant

Location: small alpine farming village in skiing area, an hour's drive from Lucerne and Interlaken. **Campus:** 3 acres. **Library:** 20,000 volumes. **Facilities:** 20 buildings, 32 classrooms, auditorium, cafeteria, gymnasium, 3 playing fields, 2 science labs, pottery, woodshop, swimming pool in Meiringen, 16 "family groups" in 12 buildings.

*Once only fee **Swiss franc

LAUSANNE

Brillantmont International College

Street address: Avenue Secretan 16, CH-1005 Lausanne, Switzerland
Phone: (41)(21)3124741/3129095 **Facsimile:** (41)(21)3208417
E-mail: info@brillantmont.ch
Principal: Françoise Frei-Huguenin
Teaching staff: full-time, 32; total, 32
Grade levels: 9 – 12, AP
Enrollment: total, 150
Teacher/student ratio: 1/5
Tuition and board (annual): 40,000**; personal expenses, approximately 6,000
School year: September to June

Year founded: 1882. **Type of school:** coed, day, boarding, private. **Accredited by:** New England, ECIS. **Member of:** Swiss Federation of Private Schools.

Curriculum/physical plant

Type: U.K., IGCSE and A-level; commercial diploma in French. **Languages of instruction:** English, French. **Languages taught:** English, French, Spanish, German, Italian. **Staff specialists:** special needs. **Extracurricular:** drama, instrumental music, photography, cooking, sewing, Model UN, classical and jazz ballet, art, art history; cultural activities, including excursions in Switzerland and Europe, and regular outings to plays, concerts, ballets, and operas. **Sports:** athletics, basketball, skiing, swimming, tennis, volleyball, cycling, cross-country skiing. **Tests:** PSAT, SAT, TOEFL, AP. **Graduates attending college:** 100%. **Graduates have attended:** Harvard, Georgetown, Northwestern, Franklin & Marshall, U. of Pennsylvania. **Location:** in Lausanne. **Campus:** 4 acres. **Library:** 5,000 volumes. **Facilities:** 7 buildings.

**Swiss franc

International School of Lausanne

Street address: 73, Avenue C.F. Ramuz, 1009 Pully/Lausanne, Switzerland
Phone: (41)(21)7281733 **Facsimile:** (41)(21)7287868
E-mail: 100630.322@compuserve.com
Director: Robert Landau
Teaching staff: full-time, 21; part-time, 10; total, 31
Nationalities of teaching staff: U.S., 14; U.K., 2; host, 9; other, 6; total, 31
Grade levels: reception (3 years old) – 10
Enrollment: R, 19; preK, 20; K, 16; 1 – 6, 75; 7 – 10, 70; total, 200
Nationalities of student body: U.S., 22; U.K., 40; host, 26; other, 112; total, 200
Capacity: R, 20; preK, 20; K, 18; 1 – 6, 102; 7 – 10, 80; total, 240
Teacher/student ratio: 1/9
Tuition (annual): reception, 6,950**; preK, 7,250; K – 5, 13,400; 6 – 8, 15,950; 9, 16,800; 10, 17,000
Other fees: registration*, 850**
School year: September to June

Year founded: 1962. **Type of school:** coed, day, private nonprofit. **Governed by:** appointed school council. **Accredited by:** New England, ECIS. **Regional organizations:** ECIS, SGIS.

Curriculum/physical plant

Type: U.S., U.K. **Languages taught:** French, Spanish (grades 7 – 9). **Special programs:** ESL, remedial, special needs. **Special curricular:** art, chorus, physical education, computer instruction. **Extracurricular:** computers, yearbook, newspaper, excursions/expeditions, field trips, science club. **Sports:** athletics, skiing, soccer, swimming, skating. **Tests:** ERB, Slingerland. **Location:** in suburb adjoining Lausanne. **Campus:** 1 acre. **Library:** 15,000 volumes. **Facilities:** 4 buildings, 21 classrooms, 2 science labs, computer rooms, art room.

*Once only fee **Swiss franc

LENK

The Winter Term

Street address: Chalet Hohliebi, 3775 Lenk, Switzerland
Phone: (41)(33)7331176 **Facsimile:** (41)(33)7331426
E-mail: info@hohliebi.ch
Director: John N. Curtis, Jr.
Teaching staff: full-time, 6; total, 6
Nationalities of teaching staff: U.S., 5; U.K., 1; host, total, 6
Grade levels: 7 – 8
Enrollment: total, 30
Teacher/student ratio: 1/5
Boarders: boys, 15; girls, 15 **Grades:** 7 – 8 **Program:** planned 7-day
Tuition and board (annual): 13,800**
Other fees: registration, 400**
School year: January to April

Year founded: 1988. **Type of school:** coed, boarding, proprietary.

Curriculum/physical plant

Type: U.S. **Special curricular:** physical education, computer instruction. **Extracurricular:** drama, newspaper, excursions/expeditions. **Sports:** skiing, swimming. **Location:** chalet on ski slope in Swiss Alps, overlooking village of Lenk. **Campus:** 1 acre. **Library:** 600 volumes. **Facilities:** 2 buildings, 3 classrooms.

**Swiss franc

LEYSIN

Kumon Leysin Academy of Switzerland

Street address: Avenue Secretan, 1854 Leysin, Switzerland
Phone: (41)(24)4935335 **Facsimile:** (41)(24)4955300
E-mail: 100763.555@compuserve.com
Principal: Hisashi Yoshida
Vice-principal: Alan Locke
Academic dean: Hiroshi Watanabe
Business manager: K. Otari
Teaching staff: full-time, 28; total, 28
Nationalities of teaching staff: U.S., 6; U.K., 5; Japan, 11; other, 6; total, 28
Grade levels: 10 – 12
Enrollment: total, 174
Nationalities of student body: Japan, 174; total, 174
Capacity: total, 208
Teacher/student ratio: 1/6
Boarders: boys, 88; girls, 86 **Grades:** 10 – 12 **Program:** planned 7-day
Tuition (annual): 25,080**

Other fees (annual): registration*, 4,700**; boarding, 18,920; insurance, 1,000; books, 300
School year: July to June

Year founded: 1990. **Type of school:** coed, boarding, company-sponsored, private nonprofit. **Governed by:** appointed Swiss and Japanese board. **Accredited by:** Dept. of Education, Canton de Vaud. **Regional organizations:** SGIS, ECIS.

Curriculum

Type: U.S., Japanese. **Languages of instruction:** English, Japanese. **Languages taught:** English, French, Japanese. **Staff specialists:** reading, math, computer, speech/hearing, nurse. **Special programs:** ESL. **Special curricular:** art, chorus, computer instruction, bands. **Extracurricular:** drama, dance, choral and instrumental music, computers, yearbook, photography, excursions/expeditions, field trips, social services, martial arts, cooking. **Sports:** basketball, skiing, soccer, swimming, tennis, volleyball, ice-skating, horseback-riding. **Tests:** SAT, TOEFL, Test of English Proficiency. **Graduates attending college:** 100%. **Graduates have attended:** Boston U., Carnegie-Mellon, Smith, Johns Hopkins, Japanese universities.

Physical plant

Location: in Swiss Alps, above Lake Geneva. **Campus:** 10 acres. **Library:** 10,000 volumes. **Facilities:** 3 buildings, 15 classrooms, cafeteria, infirmary, science lab, computer lab; use of local sports centers, swimming pools, playing fields, ice rink, ski facilities; girls' and boys' dorms, private bathrooms, 4 recreation rooms.

*Once only fee **Swiss franc

Leysin American School in Switzerland

Street address: The Savoy, 1854 Leysin, Switzerland
Phone: (41)(24)4933777 **Facsimile:** (41)(24)4941585
U.S. phone: (1)(603)4317654 **U.S. facsimile:** (1)(603)4311280
E-mail: 100551.734@compuserve.com
U.S. e-mail: 102105.1450@compuserve.com
Web: http://www.localnet.org/users/las
Mail: CH 1854 Leysin, Switzerland
U.S. mail: PO Box 4016, Portsmouth, NH 03802-4016, U.S.A.
Executive director: K. Steven Ott, Ph.D.
Headmaster: Grant Fiedler
Teaching staff: full-time, 42; total, 42
Nationalities of teaching staff: U.S., 32; U.K., 3; host, 3; other, 4; total, 42
Grade levels: 9 – 12, postgraduate year
Enrollment: 9 – 12, 284; PG, 2; total, 286
Capacity: total, 320
Teacher/student ratio: 1/12
Boarders: boys, 141; girls, 127 **Grades:** 9 – PG **Program:** planned 7-day
Tuition and board (annual): 9 – PG, $27,000; corporate plan, $20,340
Other fees (annual): registration, $1,125
School year: September to June

Year founded: 1961. **Type of school:** coed, boarding. **Accredited by:** Middle States, ECIS.

Curriculum

Type: U.S., AP, IB. **Languages taught:** French, Spanish, German. **Staff specialists:** nurse, college counselor. **Special programs:** ESL. **Special curricular:** art, chorus, band, drama, jazz band, string ensemble, orchestra, yearbook, Model UN, senior humanities. **Extracurricular:** literary magazine, excursions/expeditions, field trips, faculty families, private music lessons, winter ski program. **Sports:** basketball, skiing, soccer, squash, swimming, tennis, volleyball, snowboarding, rock climbing, mountain biking, weight training. **Organizations:** National Honor Society, student council, Amnesty International, OXFAM, Peace Corps. **Tests:** PSAT, SAT, ACT, TOEFL, IB, AP. **Graduates attending college:** 99%. **Graduates have attended:** West Point, Oxford, Rice, Georgetown, Yale.

Physical plant

Location: in the sunny, southern Swiss Alps above Lake Geneva. **Campus:** 10 acres. **Library:** 19,000 volumes, CD ROM programs. **Facilities:** 6 buildings, 26 classrooms, auditorium, cafeteria, gymnasium, 4 science labs, 2 computer labs, theatrical stage, darkroom, music practice rooms, health center, use of 2 sports centers and ski lifts year-round, 2 boys' residences, 2 girls' residences.

MONTAGNOLA/LUGANO

THE AMERICAN SCHOOL IN SWITZERLAND (TASIS)

Phone: (41)(91)9946471 **Facsimile:** (41)(91)9942364
E-mail: frostch@dial.eunet.ch
Web: http://www.tasis.com/tasis/tasis-lugano-html
Mail: 6926 Montagnola/Lugano, Switzerland
U.S. mail: 1640 Wisconsin Avenue NW, Washington, DC 20007, U.S.A.
Headmaster: Christopher Frost
Teaching staff: full-time, 39; part-time, 6; total, 45
Nationalities of teaching staff: U.S., 31; U.K., 5; host, 4; other, 5; total, 45
Grade levels: 7 – 12, postgraduate
Enrollment: 7 – 8, 34; 9 – 12, 223; PG, 15; total, 272
Nationalities of student body: U.S., 90; U.K., 8; host, 10; other, 164; total, 272
Teacher/student ratio: 1/7
Boarders: boys, 116; girls, 120 **Grades:** 7 – PG **Program:** planned 7-day
Tuition (annual): $25,800 (U.S. & Canadian citizens); 41,450** (international)
Other fees: one semester only supplement, 2,000**; ESL supplement, 2,000
School year: September to June

Type of school: coed, day, boarding, proprietary. **Accredited by:** New England, ECIS.

Curriculum

Type: U.S., IB, AP. **Languages taught:** French, Spanish, German, Italian. **Staff specialists:** counselor, nurse, college counselor. **Special programs:** ESL, honors sections, postgraduate year, summer programs. **Special curricular:** art, chorus, physical education. **Extracurricular:** drama, dance, choral and instrumental music, computers, yearbook, newspaper, photography, excursions/expeditions, field trips,

Model UN, MUC, environmental club, 2-week ski-term in Crans-Montana, 11 days in-program travel during year. **Sports:** aerobics, basketball, cross-country, rugby, skiing, soccer, swimming, tennis, volleyball, hiking, bicycling, water polo, track, horseback riding, climbing, golf. **Tests:** PSAT, SAT, ACT, TOEFL, IB, AP. **Graduates attending college:** 99%. **Graduates have attended:** Macalester, Cambridge, Duke, Stanford, Syracuse.

Physical plant

Location: south of the Alps, on hillside overlooking Lake Lugano, 5 kilometers from town center. **Campus:** 5 acres. **Library:** 11,000 volumes. **Facilities:** 12 buildings, 22 classrooms, infirmary, gymnasium, science lab, computer lab, swimming pool, basketball courts, dining room, AV equipment.

**Swiss franc

MONTREUX

Institut Château Beau-Cèdre

Street address: 59, Rue du Lac, 1815 Clarens/Montreux, Vaud, Switzerland
Phone: (41)(21)9643831 **Facsimile:** (41)(21)9643834
Mail: CH-1815 Clarens, Switzerland
Principal: Pierre Gay-Hörmann
Teaching staff: full-time, 7; part-time, 6; total, 13
Nationalities of teaching staff: U.S., 1; U.K., 2; other, 10; total, 13
Grade levels: 9 – 12
Enrollment: (American section) 9, 4; 10 – 12, 5; total, 9
Boarders: (Americans and general culture) girls, 30 **Program:** planned 5-day
Tuition and board (annual): 46,800**
Other fees (annual): inscription and guarantee deposit, 3,000**
School year: September to June†

Year founded: 1955. **Type of school:** girls, day, boarding, proprietary. **Governed by:** Mr. and Mrs. Pierre Gay–Hörmann, proprietors. **Member of:** Swiss Federation of Private Schools, Swiss Association of Boarding Schools.

Curriculum/physical plant

Type: U.S., languages and finishing course. **Languages of instruction:** English, French. **Languages taught:** English, French, Spanish, German, Italian. **Staff specialists:** reading, math, computer, speech/hearing. **Special curricular:** physical education, computer instruction. **Extracurricular:** gymnastics, computers, yearbook. **Sports:** aerobics, skiing, tennis, riding. **Tests:** SAT, TOEFL, Cambridge, Alliance Française. **Graduates attending college:** 80%. **Location:** castle on the banks of lake of Geneva, 2 miles from Montreux. **Facilities:** 2 buildings, cafeteria, computer lab, full board and lodging for a limited number of girls.

**Swiss franc †summer courses in French and English, July – August

St. George's School in Switzerland

Phone: (41)(21)9643411 **Facsimile:** (41)(21)9644932
Mail: 1815 Clarens/Montreux, Switzerland
Principal: L. G. Zund-Cooper
Teaching staff: full-time, 21; part-time, 7; total, 28
Nationalities of teaching staff: U.K., 23; host, 3; other, 2; total, 28
Grade levels: K – 13
Enrollment: K – 6, 52; 7 – 9, 44; 10 – 12, 52; 13, 12; total, 160
Nationalities of student body: U.S., 5; U.K., 28; host, 6; other, 121; total, 160
Teacher/student ratio: 1/5
Boarders: girls, 64 **Grades:** 7 – 13 **Program:** planned 7-day
Tuition and board (annual): K – 6, 15,300** (day only); 7 – 8, 42,810; 9 – 13, 44,510
Other fees: registration, 850**
School year: September to July†

Year founded: 1927. **Type of school:** coed, day, proprietary, girls' boarding, nondenominational. **Governed by:** board of Swiss and British governors. **Accredited by:** Educational Department of the Canton of Vaud. **Regional organizations:** ECIS, COBISEC.

Curriculum

Type: U.S., U.K. **Languages taught:** French, Spanish, German, Italian, Latin. **Staff specialists:** math, computer, music, college counselor, sciences, drama. **Special programs:** ESL. **Special curricular:** art, chorus, physical education. **Extracurricular:** drama, dance, choral and instrumental music, computers, yearbook, photography, excursions/expeditions, field trips, aerobics, golf. **Sports:** basketball, skiing, swimming, tennis, volleyball, ice skating, rounders, horseback riding, etc. **Clubs:** chess, computer, play reading, cooking, photography, handicraft. **Tests:** PSAT, SAT, TOEFL, IGCSE, ACH, A-level Cambridge and London Boards. **Graduates attending college:** 95%. **Graduates have attended:** universities worldwide.

Physical plant

Location: overlooking Lake Geneva, on the outskirts of Montreux. **Campus:** 45,000 square meters. **Library:** 15,000 volumes. **Facilities:** 3 buildings, 20 classrooms, auditorium, infirmary, 7 tennis courts, gymnasium, playing field, 2 science labs, computer lab, swimming pool, basketball court, dormitories, lounges, TV rooms, chalet for older girls.

**Swiss franc †coed summer camp in July, ages 10 – 16

ROLLE

Institut Le Rosey

Phone: (41)(21)8225500 **Facsimile:** (41)(21)8225555
E-mail: admission@rosey.ch
Web: http://www.qualischools.ch/english/rosey/htm
Mail: 1180 Rolle, Switzerland/3780 Gstaad, Switzerland (January – March)
Director: Philippe Gudin
Teaching staff: total, 82
Grade levels: 3 – 12
Enrollment: total, 320
Capacity: total, 320
Teacher/student ratio: 1/5
Boarders: boys, 160; girls, 160 **Grades:** 3 – 12 **Program:** planned 7-day
Tuition and board (annual): 51,500**
Other fees: 2,500** per term
School year: September through June

Year founded: 1880. **Type of school:** coed, boarding, proprietary. **Accredited by:** New England. **Regional organizations:** ECIS.

Curriculum

Type: U.S., U.K., national, French, AP. **Languages of instruction:** English, French. **Languages taught:** French, Spanish, German, Dutch, Italian, Arabic, Swedish, Portuguese, Persian, Greek, Turkish, others on demand. **Staff specialists:** psychologist, art, music, sports, chaplain, librarian, nurses, university counselor. **Special programs:** ESL, intensive English and French. **Special curricular:** drama, drawing, painting, computer graphics, photography, instrumental music, orchestras, choirs, Internet research, field trips, U.K. and U.S. universities trips. **Extracurricular:** yearbook, flying, karting, cultural and literary societies, cultural trips, expeditions, camping, balls, shows. **Sports:** basketball, football, gymnastics, rugby, squash, swimming, table tennis, tennis, volleyball, rowing, horseback riding, wind surfing, sailing, bicycling, skiing, judo, pistol shooting. **Clubs:** chess, debating, student council, charity. **Tests:** SSAT, PSAT, SAT, TOEFL, AP, GCSE, IGCSE, ACH, French Baccalaureat, Swiss Maturité, GCE A-levels. **Graduates attending college:** 100%. **Graduates have attended:** Harvard, Brown, Princeton, Oxbridge, London.

Physical plant

Location: 2 campuses: winter campus in Gstaad, Swiss Alps; spring/fall campus in Rolle, lake of Geneva on fully equipped, 75-acre estate. **Library:** 16,000 volumes. **Facilities:** auditorium, tennis court, gymnasium, science lab, swimming pools, library, ultra-modern science laboratories, purpose-built music rooms, computer department, theater, art rooms, school archives, ecumenical chapel, football pitches, rugby field, volleyball and basketball courts, water-sports center.

**Swiss franc

SAANEN

John F. Kennedy International School

Phone: (41)(33)7441372 **Facsimile:** (41)(33)7448982
E-mail: lovell@jfk.ch or 100125.1602@compuserve.com
Mail: CH-3792 Saanen, Switzerland
Director: William M. Lovell
Teaching staff: full-time, 15; part-time, 3; total, 18
Nationalities of teaching staff: U.S., 3; host, 1; other, 14; total, 18
Grade levels: K – 8
Enrollment: K – 6, 50; 7 – 8, 10; total, 60
Teacher/student ratio: 1/4
Boarders: boys, 14; girls, 12 **Grades:** K – 8 **Program:** planned 7-day
Tuition (annual): day student, 18,900**; boarder, 34,000
Other fees (annual): ski school, 1,300**; excursions, 1,000; school uniform, 1,000
School year: September to June

Year founded: 1949. **Type of school:** coed, day, boarding, proprietary. **Accredited by:** Canton of Bern Department of Education. **Regional organizations:** ECIS.

Curriculum

Type: U.S., Canadian. **Languages taught:** French. **Staff specialists:** reading, psychologist. **Special programs:** ESL. **Special curricular:** art, physical education, computer instruction, drama, skiing in winter. **Extracurricular:** drama, dance, computers, yearbook, excursions/expeditions, field trips. **Sports:** skiing, swimming, tennis, track and field, hiking, ice-skating, ball sports, horseback riding. **Tests:** ERB. **Graduates have attended:** Aiglon College, Le Rosey (Switzerland), Deerfield Academy, TASIS, Leysin American School.

Physical plant

Location: at mountain skiing resort, 2 miles from Gstaad. **Library:** 7,500 volumes. **Facilities:** 3 buildings, 5 classrooms, cafeteria, playing field, tennis courts, ski lifts; easy access to gymnasium, swimming pool, auditorium; large boarding chalet with bedrooms, classrooms, library, video room, computer room, staff accommodations.

**Swiss franc

ZUG

Institut Montana, American School

Street address: Zugerberg, CH 6300 Zug, Switzerland
Phone: (41)(41)7111722 **Facsimile:** (41)(41)7115465
E-mail: 706742.714@compuserve.com **Web:** http://www.montana.ch
Director: Aldo J. Haesler, Ph.D.
Principal: Daniel C. Fridez

Headmaster: V. Kevin O'Brien
Teaching staff: full-time, 15; part-time, 5; total, 20
Nationalities of teaching staff: U.S., 9; U.K., 1; host, 2; other, 8; total, 20
Grade levels: 5 – 13
Enrollment: total, 79
Nationalities of student body: U.S., 5; other, 74; total, 79
Teacher/student ratio: 1/4
Boarders: boys, 36; girls, 17 **Grades:** 5 – 13 **Program:** planned 7-day
Tuition (annual): 22,770**
Other fees (annual): boarding, 38,265 – 41,565**
School year: September to June

Year founded: 1926. **Type of school:** coed, day, boarding, private nonprofit. **Governed by:** appointed board of trustees. **Accredited by:** Swiss Federation of Private Schools. **Regional organizations:** NAIS, ECIS.

Curriculum

Type: U.S., IB, AP. **Languages taught:** French, Spanish, German, Dutch. **Special programs:** ESL. **Special curricular:** physical education, computer instruction, drawing, calligraphy. **Extracurricular:** drama, gymnastics, choral music, computers, yearbook, literary magazine, excursions/expeditions, field trips. **Sports:** basketball, skiing, soccer, tennis, volleyball. **Clubs:** chess, stamp, video, outings. **Tests:** SSAT, PSAT, SAT, ACT, TOEFL, IB, AP. **Graduates attending college:** 100%. **Graduates have attended:** Carnegie-Mellon, Cornell, New York U., Rhode Island School of Design, U. of Pennsylvania.

Physical plant

Location: in foothills of Alps, 15 minutes from Zug by public transportation. **Campus:** 65 acres. **Library:** 8,000 volumes. **Facilities:** 12 buildings, 9 classrooms, auditorium, infirmary, 4 tennis courts, gymnasium, 3 playing fields, 3 science labs, computer lab, dining room, 3 dormitories.

**Swiss franc

International School of Zug

Street address: Alte Steinhauserstrasse 15, 6330 Cham, Switzerland
Phone: (41)(41)7417874 **Facsimile:** (41)(41)7400294
Headmaster: Martin Latter
Lower school coordinator: David Winter
Teaching staff: full-time, 21; part-time, 10; total, 31
Nationalities of teaching staff: U.S., 3; U.K., 20; other, 8; total, 31
Grade levels: N – 7
Enrollment: N – preK, 60; K, 23; 1 – 6, 154; 7, 14; total, 251
Nationalities of student body: U.S., 41; U.K., 53; host, 22; other, 135; total, 251
Teacher/student ratio: 1/9
Tuition (annual): N – preK, $5,000; K, $8,800; 1 – 5, $9,400; 6 – 7, $9,900
Other fees (annual): registration*, $400; busing, $1,870
School year: September to June

Year founded: 1961. **Type of school:** coed, day, proprietary. **Regional organizations:** ECIS, SGIS.

Curriculum/physical plant

Type: international. **Languages taught:** French, German, Dutch. **Staff specialists:** reading, math, computer, speech/hearing, learning disabilities. **Special programs:** ESL, remedial. **Special curricular:** chorus, physical education, computer instruction, German, library, swimming. **Extracurricular:** drama, choral and instrumental music. **Sports:** basketball, hockey, soccer, volleyball, cross-country. **Clubs:** cooking, arts, ceramics. **Tests:** Iowa. **Location:** suburban area of Zug. **Library:** 8,000 volumes. **Facilities:** 2 campuses, 2 buildings, 19 classrooms, 2 gymnasiums, playing field, science lab, computer lab, use of skating rink and 2 swimming pools.

*Once only fee

The Riverside School

Street address: Feldstrasse 6, 6300 Zug, Switzerland
Phone: (41)(41)7245690 **Facsimile:** (41)(41)7245692
Director: David Brooks
Teaching staff: full-time, 7; part-time, 5; total, 12
Nationalities of teaching staff: U.S., 5; U.K., 4; host, 1; other, 2; total, 12
Grade levels: 7 – 13 (nongraded system)
Enrollment: total, 76
Nationalities of student body: U.S., 8; U.K., 15; host, 13; other, 40; total, 76
Teacher/student ratio: 1/6
Tuition (annual): 23,000**
Other fees (annual): capital levy*, 2,000**; books, 600
School year: August to June

Year founded: 1990. **Type of school:** coed, day, private nonprofit. **Regional organizations:** SGIS, ECIS.

Curriculum/physical plant

Type: U.S., AP. **Languages taught:** French, German. **Staff specialists:** reading, counselor, learning disabilities, EFL. **Special programs:** independent study. **Special curricular:** art, computer instruction, integrated studies. **Extracurricular:** drama, dance, yearbook, newspaper, excursions/expeditions. **Sports:** basketball, skiing, swimming, tennis, track and field, volleyball, canoeing, weight training. **Tests:** PSAT, SAT, ACT, TOEFL, AP. **Graduates attending college:** 95%. **Graduates have attended:** U. of Edinburgh, McGill, Cornell, Harvard, U. of London. **Location:** in green zone in the center of Zug, 24 kilometers from Zurich. **Library:** 3,000 volumes. **Facilities:** two-story building, 7 classrooms, 4 science labs, computer lab, music, art, and photography studios, other facilities rented from local community as needed.

*Once only fee **Swiss franc

ZURICH

The American International School of Zurich

Street address: Nidelbadstrasse 49, 8802 Kilchberg, Switzerland
Phone: (41)(1)7152795 **Facsimile:** (41)(1)7152694 **E-mail:** aisz@aisz.ch
Web: http://www.aisz.ch
Headmaster: Peter C. Mott
Teaching staff: full-time, 27; part-time, 9; total, 36
Nationalities of teaching staff: U.S., 21; U.K., 5; host, 6; other, 4; total, 36
Grade levels: 7 – 13
Enrollment: 7 – 9, 144; 10 – 13, 131; total, 275
Nationalities of student body: U.S., 75; U.K., 30; host, 24; other, 146; total, 275
Tuition (annual): 7 – 8, 20,750**; 9 – 13, 22,500
Other fees (annual): registration*, 1,000** (900 credited toward capital levy); capital levy*, 3,000; other, approximately 600
School year: late August to mid-June

Year founded: 1963. **Type of school:** coed, day, private nonprofit. **Governed by:** elected board of trustees. **Accredited by:** New England, ECIS. **Regional organizations:** ECIS, SGIS.

Curriculum/physical plant

Type: U.S., AP. **Languages taught:** French, German, Swedish. **Staff specialists:** computer, counselor, psychologist, learning specialist. **Special programs:** ESL, honors sections, independent study. **Special curricular:** art, computer instruction, theater, music. **Extracurricular:** drama, computers, yearbook, newspaper, literary magazine, photography, excursions/expeditions, field trips, Model UN, video, community service. **Sports:** basketball, rugby, skiing, soccer, softball, swimming, tennis, track and field, volleyball. **Tests:** PSAT, TOEFL, AP, SAT I & II. **Graduates attending college:** 90%. **Graduates have attended:** Yale, Cornell, Princeton, Brown, Cambridge. **Location:** in residential suburb, 8 kilometers from center Zurich, on ridge overlooking Lake Zurich and Alps. **Campus:** 3 acres. **Library:** 8,000 volumes. **Facilities:** completely renovated and expanded villa, 21 classrooms, 2 tennis courts, playing field, 4 science labs, 2 computer labs (over 50 computers with internet access), theater, music rooms, AV equipment.

*Once only fee **Swiss franc

The Inter-Community School

Street address: Strubenacher 3, 8126 Zumikon, Switzerland
Phone: (41)(1)9181656 **Facsimile:** (41)(1)9190026
E-mail: 100442.374@compuserve.com
Headmaster: John Young
Head of upper school: Nick Darlington
Head of lower school: Helen Conlon
Teaching staff: full-time, 55; part-time, 12; total, 67
Nationalities of teaching staff: U.S., 11; U.K., 27; host, 10; other, 19; total, 67
Grade levels: N – 12

Enrollment: N – preK, 103; K, 66; 1 – 6, 272; 7 – 8, 63; 9 – 12, 97; total, 601
Nationalities of student body: U.S., 105; U.K., 90; host, 56; other, 350; total, 601
Teacher/student ratio: 1/10
Tuition (annual): N, 9,600**; R – 1, 15,000; 2 – 5, 16,800; 6, 18,600; 7 – 8, 21,600; 9 – 12, 22,800
Other fees (annual): registration*, 400**; capital levy*, 1,500; busing, 2,460
School year: September through June

Year founded: 1960. **Type of school:** coed, day, private nonprofit. **Governed by:** board of trustees.

Curriculum/physical plant

Type: international, IGCSE (grades 9 and 10), IB. **Languages of instruction:** English, German. **Languages taught:** English, French, German. **Staff specialists:** computer, speech/hearing, learning disabilities, librarian, music, physical education, science, pottery, languages, swimming. **Special programs:** ESL, special needs. **Special curricular:** art, chorus, band, physical education, computer education, swimming. **Extracurricular:** drama, dance, choral and instrumental music, computers, yearbook, literary magazine, photography, excursions/expeditions, field trips. **Sports:** basketball, skiing, soccer, softball, swimming, tennis, volleyball. **Clubs:** Boy Scouts, Girl Scouts. **Location:** 5 miles from city center. **Campus:** 20 acres. **Library:** 20,000 volumes. **Facilities:** 6 buildings, 45 classrooms, auditorium, gymnasium, playing field, science lab, tennis courts, all-weather pitch, video room.

*Once only fee **Swiss franc

International Primary School of Zurich

Street address: Seestrasse 169, 8802 Kilchberg, Switzerland
Phone: (41)(1)7161040 **Facsimile:** (41)(1)7161050
Director: Paul Lieblich, Ed.D.
Teaching staff: full-time, 18; part-time, 14; total, 32
Nationalities of teaching staff: U.S., 8; U.K., 10; host, 2; other, 12; total, 32
Grade levels: playgroup – grade 6
Enrollment: total, 238
Nationalities of student body: U.S., 104; U.K., 59; host, 14; other, 61; total, 238
Teacher/student ratio: 1/7
Tuition (annual): playgroup, 9,000**; preK, 16,500; K – 6, 17,000
Other fees (annual): application*, 600**; enrollment*, 1,000; capital, 1,000
School year: late August to June

Year founded: 1970. **Type of school:** coed, day, private nonprofit. **Governed by:** elected board of trustees. **Regional organizations:** ECIS.

Curriculum/physical plant

Type: Anglo-American. **Languages taught:** German. **Special programs:** ESL, special needs. **Special curricular:** art, physical education, computer instruction, drama, music. **Extracurricular:** instrumental music, excursions/expeditions, field trips. **Sports:** gymnastics, skiing, soccer, swimming. **Clubs:** chess, cooking, music, dance, science, stamps, ceramics, choir. **Location:** 2.5 miles from center city, in private villa beside Lake of Zurich. **Library:** 10,000 volumes. **Facilities:** 1 building, 16 classrooms, auditorium, playing field.

*Once only fee **Swiss franc

SYRIA

Region: Middle East
Size: 71,498 square miles
Population: 15,608,648
Capital: Damascus
Telephone code: 963
Currency: pound
Languages: Arabic, Kurdish, Armenian

ALEPPO

INTERNATIONAL SCHOOL OF ALEPPO

Street address: Damascus Road, Aleppo, Syria
Phone: (963)(21)743104/746807/748964
Facsimile: (963)(21)744622/225105/213490
Mail: ACCAD Institute, PO Box 4101, Aleppo, Syria
Headmaster: James Bonnell
Teaching staff: full-time, 37; part-time, 20; total, 57
Nationalities of teaching staff: U.S., 8; U.K., 9; host, 30; other, 10; total, 57
Grade levels: K – 12
Enrollment: K, 39; 1 – 6, 133; 7 – 9, 72; 10 – 12, 55; total, 299
Nationalities of student body: U.S., 24; U.K., 26; host, 219; other, 30; total, 299
Teacher/student ratio: 1/8
Tuition (annual): $4,060 – 6,075
Other fees (annual): testing, activities, registration, transportation, $630
School year: September to June

Year founded: 1976. **Type of school:** coed, day, company-sponsored, private nonprofit. **Governed by:** appointed committee. **Sponsored by:** International Center for Agricultural Research in the Dry Areas. **Accredited by:** Middle States K – 8 (9 – 12 in progress). **Regional organizations:** NESA, ECIS.

Curriculum/physical plant

Type: IB, international, IGCSE. **Languages taught:** French, Arabic. **Special programs:** ESL, IGCSE, ASL. **Extracurricular:** drama, dance, choral music, computers, newspaper, excursions/expeditions, field trips, Girl Scouts, athletics, music. **Sports:** basketball, gymnastics, soccer, swimming, volleyball, running. **Tests:** IB, IGCSE. **Location:** a walled campus with gardens, play and sports areas, 2 kilometers from center of Aleppo. **Campus:** 4 hectares. **Library:** 12,000 volumes. **Facilities:** 3 buildings, 22 classrooms, infirmary, 2 tennis courts, playing field, 3 science labs, 2 computer labs, basketball court, sports club, snack bar.

DAMASCUS

DAMASCUS COMMUNITY SCHOOL

Street address: Al-Mahdi Bin Baraka Street, Damascus, Syria
Phone: (963)(11)3337737/3310331 – 2 **Facsimile:** (963)(11)3321457
Telex: 924411919 USDAMA
U.S. mail: c/o U.S. Embassy (Damascus, Syria), Dept. of State, Washington, DC 20521-6110
Director: Dr. James Liebzeit
Assistant director: Alice Dion
Business manager: Diana Yazigi
Teaching staff: full-time, 33; part-time, 3; total, 36
Nationalities of teaching staff: U.S., 26; U.K., 2; host, 4; other, 4; total, 36
Grade levels: preK – 12
Enrollment: preK, 9; K, 16; 1 – 5, 99; 6 – 8, 67; 9 – 12, 86; total, 277
Nationalities of student body: U.S., 51; U.K., 11; host, 115; other, 100; total, 277
Capacity: preK, 20; K, 18; 1 – 5, 180; 6 – 8, 108; 9 – 12, 144; total, 470
Teacher/student ratio: 1/11
Tuition (annual): preK, $3,000; K – 5, $7,550; 6 – 8, $8,400; 9 – 12, $8,900
Other fees (annual): registration, $250; building surcharge, $1,300; testing, $100; entrance fee, $500
School year: late August to early June

Year founded: 1950. **Type of school:** coed, day, private nonprofit. **Governed by:** appointed and elected board of directors. **Accredited by:** Middle States, CITA. **Regional organizations:** AAIE, NESA.

Curriculum/physical plant

Type: U.S. **Languages taught:** French, Arabic. **Staff specialists:** computer, counselor, nurse. **Special programs:** ESL, Optimal Match. **Special curricular:** art, physical education, music, computer education. **Extracurricular:** drama, yearbook, newspaper, excursions/expeditions, field trips, National Honor Society, student council. **Sports:** basketball, soccer, tennis, volleyball. **Tests:** PSAT, SAT, TOEFL, Iowa. **Location:** in center of residential district, surrounded by high wall. **Campus:** 4 acres. **Library:** 13,000 volumes, CD ROM. **Facilities:** 10 buildings, tennis court, 2 science labs, 2 computer labs, physical education building, cafeteria/theater, secondary and administration building, running track, soccer field, basketball court, baseball field, play equipment.

TAIWAN

Region: Asia
Size: 13,969 square miles
Population: 21,465,881
Capital: Taipei
Telephone code: 886
Currency: New Taiwan dollar
Languages: Mandarin Chinese, Taiwanese, Hakka dialects

HSINCHU

National Experimental High School

Street address: Science-Based Industrial Park, #101 Park Avenue 1, Hsinchu 30077, Taiwan, R.O.C.
Phone: (886)(3)5778560 **Facsimile:** (886)(3)5781813
E-mail: lmtai@mail.nehs.hc.edu.tw **Web:** http://www.nehs.hc.edu.tw
Principal: Li-Ming Tai
Dean of bilingual department: Jean Tien
Teaching staff: full-time, 45; part-time, 9; total, 54
Nationalities of teaching staff: U.S., 15; host, 38; other, 1; total, 54
Grade levels: 1 – 12
Enrollment: 1 – 6, 208; 7 – 9, 116; 10 – 12, 55; total, 379
Nationalities of student body: U.S., 305; host, 66; other, 8; total, 379
Teacher/student ratio: 1/8
Boarders: boys, 8; girls, 12 **Grades:** 10 – 12 **Program:** planned 6-day
Tuition (annual): 1 – 6, $1,215; 7 – 9, $1,430; 10 – 12, $1,525
Other fees (annual): boarding, $233; lunch, $2/each; books, $400
School year: September through June

Year founded: 1983. **Type of school:** coed, day, boarding, public nonprofit. **Governed by:** Taiwan Ministry of Education. **Sponsored by:** National Science Council. **Accredited by:** Taiwan Ministry of Education.

Curriculum/physical plant

Type: U.S., national, AP. **Languages of instruction:** English, Mandarin. **Languages taught:** English, German, Mandarin. **Staff specialists:** computer, counselor, nurse. **Special programs:** honors sections, independent study, correspondence. **Special curricular:** art, physical education, computer instruction. **Extracurricular:** instrumental music, computers, yearbook, newspaper, literary magazine, excursions/expeditions, field trips, pottery, Chinese chess, cheerleading, science fiction, media, art of living. **Sports:** badminton, basketball, table tennis. **Clubs:** student council, environment, key, Human Society, animation. **Tests:** PSAT, AP, Iowa, CTPIII. **Graduates attending college:** 100%. **Graduates have attended:** Amherst College, Stanford, Wellesley, Brown, UCLA. **Location:** in park-like, high-tech science installation, 5 kilometers from Hsinchu. **Library:** 55,000 volumes (English and Chinese). **Facilities:** 10 buildings, 20 classrooms (bilingual department), auditorium, 2 cafeterias, 3 tennis courts, gymnasium, 2 playing fields, 3 science labs, computer lab, swimming pool, air conditioning, boarding facilities.

KAOHSIUNG

KAOHSIUNG AMERICAN SCHOOL

Street address: No. 123-7 Ta-Pei Road, Niao-Sung Hsiang, Kaohsiung County 83305, Taiwan, R.O.C.
Phone: (886)(7)7315565/7313712 **Facsimile:** (886)(7)7331163
E-mail: rupert@mail.nsysu.edu.tw or rupert@ms4.hinet.net
Principal: Rupert Bale, Ph.D.
Upper school associate principal: Don Hilden
Lower school associate principal: Alida Droppert, Ph.D.
Teaching staff: full-time, 16; part-time, 10; total, 26
Nationalities of teaching staff: U.S., 10; other, 16; total, 26
Grade levels: preK – 12 (correspondence 9 – 12)
Enrollment: preK, 30; K, 15; 1 – 8, 85; 9 – 12, 10; total, 140
Nationalities of student body: U.S., 50; U.K., 10; other, 80; total, 140
Capacity: total, 160
Teacher/student ratio: 1/5
Tuition (annual): preK (5 mornings), 70,000**; K, 200,000; 1 – 3, 230,000; 4 – 8, 240,000
Other fees (annual): registration, 20,000** (preK registration, 5,000); capital levy, 35,000; busing, 30,000; activity, 4,000; ESL: elementary, 50,000; middle, 90,000
School year: August to June

Year founded: 1989. **Type of school:** coed, day, private nonprofit. **Governed by:** elected board of directors. **Sponsored by:** International Schools Services, Princeton, New Jersey. **Accredited by:** Western.

Curriculum/physical plant

Type: U.S. **Languages taught:** Chinese, French, German, Dutch. **Staff specialists:** reading, math, computer, ESL. **Special programs:** ESL. **Special curricular:** computer instruction. **Extracurricular:** computers, yearbook, newspaper, excursions/expeditions, field trips, sports. **Tests:** PSAT, SAT, Iowa. **Location:** in suburb of Kaohsiung. **Facilities:** located on hospital grounds, with swimming pool, tennis courts, rollerblade rink, adventure playgrounds, and basketball court, while new campus is being built.

**New Taiwan dollar

KAOHSIUNG/TAICHUNG/TAIPEI/YANG MEI

MORRISON ACADEMY

Street address: 136-1 Shui Nan Road, Taichung, Taiwan 406, R.O.C.
Phone: (886)(4)2921171 **Facsimile:** (886)(4)2921174
Superintendent: Greg Meeks, Ph.D.
Campus principals: Bob Walter (Kaohsiung), Ralph Bressler (Taichung), Bill MacLean (Taipei)
Teaching staff: full-time, 95; part-time, 29; total, 124
Nationalities of teaching staff: U.S., 94; host, 19; other, 11; total, 124
Grade levels: K – 12
Enrollment: K, 51; 1 – 6, 394; 7 – 9, 175; 10 – 12, 98; total, 718
Boarders: boys, 20; girls, 20 **Grades:** 9 – 12 **Program:** planned 7-day
Tuition (semester)†: K, 80,000**; 1 – 8, 112,000 – 122,000; 9 – 12, 136,000
Other fees (semester): registration, 5,000** per year; boarding: missionary, 47,500, nonmissionary, 98,000; meals, 13,500; ESL, 14,000 – 21,000; music lessons, 4,000
School year: August through June

Year founded: 1952. **Type of school:** coed, day, boarding, church-related, private nonprofit. **Governed by:** appointed board of trustees. **Sponsored by:** Morrison Christian Association. **Accredited by:** Western. **Regional organizations:** EARCOS.

Curriculum

Type: U.S. **Languages taught:** Spanish, Chinese. **Staff specialists:** counselor, nurse. **Special programs:** ESL, independent study. **Special curricular:** art, chorus, band, physical education, computer instruction. **Extracurricular:** drama, choral and instrumental music, computers, yearbook, field trips. **Sports:** basketball, soccer, tennis, track and field, volleyball. **Tests:** PSAT, SAT, ACT, AP, Stanford, Iowa, DAT. **Graduates attending college:** 95%. **Graduates have attended:** Wheaton, Goshen, Biola, Colgate, Purdue.

Physical plant

Campuses (4): Taichung, 18 acres; Taipei, .25 acre; Kaohsiung, 3 acres; Yang Mei, .1 acre. **Libraries:** 29,500 volumes. **Facilities:** cafeteria, infirmary, covered play area, swimming pool, auditoriums, tennis courts, gymnasiums, playing fields, science labs, computer labs, 3 dormitories.

**New Taiwan dollar †missionary discount available upon application

TAICHUNG

Lincoln American School

Location: #193 Sec 1, Chung Chin Road, Taya, Taichung, Taiwan, R.O.C.
Phone: (886)(4)5682387 **Facsimile:** (886)(4)5680337
E-mail: las@tc.globalnet.com.tw
Mail: PO Box 27-111, Taichung, Taiwan
Superintendent: Anna Lee
Teaching staff: full-time, 23; total, 23
Nationalities of teaching staff: U.S., 12; other, 11; total, 23
Grade levels: preK – 12
Enrollment: preK, 15; K, 15; 1 – 6, 90; 7 – 9, 45; 10 – 12, 45; total, 210
Nationalities of student body: U.S., 67; other, 143; total, 210
Tuition (annual): preK – 2, $7,709; 3 – 5, $7,855; 6 – 8, $8,436; 9 – 12, $9,236
Other fees: registration*, $909; capital levy, $1,090; insurance, $36; busing, $1,100; lunch, $655
School year: August to June

Year founded: 1989. **Type of school:** coed, boarding available in 1998, private nonprofit. **Governed by:** appointed school board. **Accredited by:** Western (in process).

Curriculum/physical plant

Type: U.S. **Languages taught:** French, Spanish. **Staff specialists:** counselor, nurse. **Special programs:** ESL. **Extracurricular:** instrumental music, yearbook. **Tests:** PSAT, SAT. **Location:** in city. **Campus:** 180,000 square feet. **Library:** 8,000 volumes. **Facilities:** 10 buildings, 14 classrooms, auditorium, cafeteria, covered play area, tennis court, gymnasium, playing field, science lab, air conditioning.

*Once only fee

TAIPEI

Dominican International School

Street address: 76 Tah Chih Street, Taipei 104, Taiwan, R.O.C.
Phone: (886)(2)5028451 **Facsimile:** (886)(2)5042914
Principal: Sr. Mary Martires, O.P.
Teaching staff: full-time, 47; total, 47
Nationalities of teaching staff: U.S., 13; host, 8; other, 26; total, 47
Grade levels: preK – 11
Enrollment: total, 495
Teacher/student ratio: 1/13
Tuition (semester): K, 47,250**; 1 – 5, 66,675; 6 – 8, 70,875; 9 – 11, 80,000
Other fees (annual): registration, 20,000**; ESL, 35,500 – 45,500; capital development, 5,000 – 12,000
School year: August to May

Year founded: 1957. **Type of school:** coed, day, church-related, private nonprofit. **Governed by:** Religious Missionaries of St. Dominic. **Regional organizations:** EARCOS.

Curriculum/physical plant

Type: U.S. **Languages taught:** French, Spanish, Chinese. **Staff specialists:** counselor, nurse, ESL. **Special curricular:** art, chorus, band, physical education, computer instruction. **Extracurricular:** drama, gymnastics, dance, choral and instrumental music, computers, yearbook, newspaper, excursions/expeditions, field trips, sports, student council, choir membership. **Tests:** Iowa, TAP. **Location:** in suburb. **Library:** 13,500 volumes. **Facilities:** 3 buildings, 24 classrooms, cafeteria, infirmary, covered play area, playing field, science lab, computer lab, AV room, gymnasium/auditorium, air conditioning.

**New Taiwan dollar

Taipei American School

Street address: 800 Chung Shan N. Road, Sec. 6, Shih Lin, Taipei 111, Taiwan, R.O.C.
Phone: (886)(2)8739900 **Facsimile:** (886)(2)8731641
E-mail: 101400.1052@compuserve.com
Superintendent: Mark Ulfers
Assistant superintendent: Ira B. Weislow
Upper school principal: Edwin Ladd
Middle school principal: Catherine Funk
Lower school principal: Gavin Allen
Teaching staff: full-time, 200; part-time, 7; total, 207
Nationalities of teaching staff: U.S., 154; host, 13; other, 40; total, 207
Grade levels: K – 12
Enrollment: K, 79; 1 – 5, 684; 6 – 8, 569; 9 – 12, 833; total, 2,165
Nationalities of student body: U.S., 1,386; Canada, 129; other, 650; total, 2,165
Capacity: total, 2,200
Teacher/student ratio: 1/11
Tuition (annual): K, 239,000**; 1 – 5, 259,600; 6 – 12, 298,600
Other fees: registration, 25,000**; insurance, 753; busing, 27,480; application, 5,000; ESL: K – 5, 75,000, 6 – 12, 89,500; activity, 2,400; lunch, 14,000
School year: August to June

Year founded: 1949. **Type of school:** coed, day, private nonprofit. **Governed by:** elected board of directors. **Accredited by:** Western. **Regional organizations:** AAIE, EARCOS, ECIS.

Curriculum

Type: U.S., AP, IB. **Languages taught:** French, Spanish, Mandarin, Japanese. **Staff specialists:** reading, computer, counselor, psychologist, nurse, ESL, resource, speech & language. **Special curricular:** chorus, physical education, band/orchestra, technology. **Extracurricular:** drama, computers, yearbook, newspaper, literary magazine, photography, music. **Sports:** badminton, basketball, soccer, softball, swimming, tennis, track and field, volleyball. **Clubs:** computer, drama, National Honor Society, Model UN, Junior Honor Society, cheerleaders, creative writing, film, key, orphanage, modern language honor societies. **Tests:** PSAT, ACT, IB, AP, ERB, SAT I & II. **Graduates attending college:** 98%. **Graduates have attended:** U. of California at Berkeley, Cornell, Boston U., Columbia, Harvard.

Physical plant

Location: Shih Lin District of Taipei City. **Campus:** 16 acres. **Libraries:** 100,000 volumes. **Facilities:** 142 classrooms, 2 auditoriums, cafeteria, 4 tennis courts, 3 gymnasiums, 3 playing fields, 12 science labs, 6 computer labs, swimming pool, nurses' office, air conditioning.

**New Taiwan dollar

TAIPEI BRITISH SCHOOL

Street address: 731 Wen Lin Road, Shih Lin, Taipei, Taiwan, R.O.C.
Phone: (886)(2)8326576 **Facsimile:** (886)(2)8326643
E-mail: tbs@ms14.hinet.net
Headmaster: Michael B. Mellor
Teaching staff: full-time, 14; part-time, 5; total, 19
Nationalities of teaching staff: U.K., 8; other, 11; total, 19
Grade levels: N (3 years) – 9 (14 years)
Enrollment: preS, 50; 1 – 6, 115; 7 – 9, 18; total, 183
Nationalities of student body: U.S., 32; U.K., 52; other, 99; total, 183
Capacity: preS, 50; 1 – 6, 115; 7 – 9, 18; total, 192
Teacher/student ratio: 1/10
Tuition (annual): N, 80,000**; reception, 170,000; 1 – 6, 250,000; 7 – 9, 312,000
Other fees (annual): registration, 20,000**; capital levy*, 250,000; busing, 36,000
School year: late August through June

Year founded: 1990. **Type of school:** coed, day, private nonprofit. **Governed by:** elected board of directors.

Curriculum/physical plant

Type: U.K., IGCSE. **Languages taught:** French, Dutch, Mandarin. **Staff specialists:** English, math, science. **Special programs:** ESL. **Special curricular:** art, computer instruction, music, drama. **Extracurricular:** drama, gymnastics, instrumental music, computers, yearbook, newspaper, excursions/expeditions, field trips, choir, Brownies. **Sports:** aerobics, badminton, baseball, basketball, cricket, gymnastics, rugby, soccer, tennis, volleyball, kung fu. **Location:** private, landscaped campus in Taipei. **Campus:** 4 acres. **Library:** 11,000 volumes. **Facilities:** 5 buildings, 15 classrooms, 2 tennis courts, 2 gymnasiums, playing field, science lab, computer lab, air conditioning.

*Once only fee **New Taiwan dollar

TANZANIA

Region: East Africa
Size: 364,017 square miles
Population: 29,058,470
Capital: Dar es Salaam
Telephone code: 255
Currency: shilling
Languages: Swahili, English, many others

DAR ES SALAAM

INTERNATIONAL SCHOOL OF TANGANYIKA LTD.

Street address: United Nations Road, Dar es Salaam, Tanzania
Phone: (255)(51)30076 – 7 **Facsimile:** (255)(51)46754/66756/67869
E-mail: ist@unidar.gn.apc.org
Mail: PO Box 2651, Dar es Salaam, Tanzania
Chief executive officer: William Powell
Secondary school headmaster: Nick Bowley
Elementary school headmaster: Walter Plotkin
Business manager: Janet Mmari
Teaching staff: full-time, 122; part-time, 3; total, 125
Nationalities of teaching staff: U.S., 40; U.K., 40; host, 10; other, 35; total, 125
Grade levels: preK – 12
Enrollment: preK, 50; K, 60; 1 – 6, 630; 7 – 9, 245; 10 – 12, 241; total, 1,226
Capacity: preK, 60; K, 60; 1 – 6, 650; 7 – 9, 300; 10 – 12, 260; total, 1,330
Teacher/student ratio: 1/10
Tuition (annual): preK – 3, $4,961; 4 – 5, $5,880; 6 – 8, $7,355; 9 – 10, $8,000; 11 – 12, $11,200
Other fees: capital levy*, $3,780; family deposit*, $500
School year: August to June

Year founded: 1963. **Type of school:** coed, day, private nonprofit. **Governed by:** elected board of directors. **Accredited by:** Middle States, ECIS. **Regional organizations:** AAIE, ECIS, AISA.

Curriculum

Type: U.S., U.K., IB. **Languages taught:** French, Spanish, Kiswahili. **Staff specialists:** computer, counselor, learning disabilities, nurse, ESL. **Special programs:** ESL, honors sections, remedial, learning disabilities. **Special curricular:** art, physical education, computer instruction. **Extracurricular:** drama, gymnastics, choral and instrumental music, computers, yearbook, photography, excursions/expeditions, field trips. **Sports:** badminton, cricket, field hockey, netball, soccer, softball, squash, swimming, volleyball, sailing, canoeing. **Clubs:** chess, Model UN, arts & crafts, Interact, student government, house sports competition, Duke of Edinburgh Awards Scheme; all students participate in social service education. **Tests:** PSAT, SAT, TOEFL, IB, IGCSE, Stanford. **Graduates attending college:** 85 – 90%. **Graduates have attended:** MIT, London School of Economics, Harvard, Cornell, Bryn Mawr.

Physical plant

Location: preK/kindergarten in city; elementary campus on edge of city; secondary campus in suburbs. **Campuses (3):** 40 acres. **Libraries:** 10,000 volumes. **Facilities:** 91 buildings, 70 classrooms, 2 auditoriums, 2 infirmaries, covered play area, 2 tennis courts, 2 gymnasiums, 2 playing fields, 8 science labs, 4 computer labs, 2 swimming pools, AV theater, photography darkroom, 3 music rooms, purpose-built studio theater.

*Once only fee

MOROGORO

Morogoro International School

Phone: (255)(56)4864
Mail: PO Box 1015, Morogoro, Tanzania
Headteacher: David Griffiths
Teaching staff: full-time, 11; total, 11
Nationalities of teaching staff: host, 4; other, 7; total, 11
Grade levels: N – 7
Enrollment: N, 13; K, 17; 1 – 7, 90; total, 120
Nationalities of student body: host, 60; other, 60; total, 120
Capacity: N, 20; K, 20; 1 – 7, 140; total, 180
Teacher/student ratio: 1/12
Tuition (annual): 1,800**
Other fees: registration, 600**
School year: September to July

Year founded: 1976. **Type of school:** coed, day, private nonprofit, nondenominational. **Governed by:** parent representatives. **Regional organizations:** AISA.

Curriculum/physical plant

Type: U.K. **Languages taught:** English, Swahili. **Special curricular:** art, physical education, swimming, music. **Extracurricular:** newspaper, field trips, music, swimming, volleyball. **Location:** on beautiful new site, 2 kilometers from Morogoro town center. **Library:** 5,000 volumes. **Facilities:** 9 classrooms, library, computer room, activity hall, 25/12-meter swimming pool.

**Pound sterling

MOSHI

International School Moshi

Street address: Lema Road, Moshi, Kilimanjaro, Tanzania
Phone: (255)(55)55004 – 5/51850 **Facsimile:** (255)(55)52877
E-mail: ismoshi@maf.org
Mail: PO Box 733, Moshi, Kilimanjaro, Tanzania
Headmaster: Geoff Lloyd
Deputy head: Keiron White
Head teacher, Arusha campus: Kevin Hawkins
Head of boarding: Terry Garbett
Business manager: Ashak Taki
Teaching staff: full-time, 45; part-time, 11; total, 56
Nationalities of teaching staff: U.S., 7; U.K., 24; host, 9; other, 16; total, 56
Grade levels: preK – 12
Enrollment: K – 6, 280; 7 – 10, 160; 11 – 12, 60; total, 500
Nationalities of student body: U.S., 15; U.K., 55; host, 130; other, 300; total, 500
Teacher/student ratio: 1/10
Boarders: boys, 40; girls, 40 **Program:** planned 7-day
Tuition (annual): K, 2,600**; 1 – 6, 2,800; 7 – 8, 3,900; 9 – 10, 4,500; 11 – 12, 5,100
Other fees (annual): registration*, 1,100**; boarding, 4,100
School year: August to June

Year founded: 1969. **Type of school:** coed, day, boarding, private nonprofit. **Governed by:** board of directors. **Accredited by:** Middle States, ECIS.

Curriculum/physical plant

Type: IB, international, IGCSE. **Languages taught:** French, Kiswahili. **Staff specialists:** computer, special needs, EFL. **Special curricular:** art, physical education. **Extracurricular:** drama, dance, choral music, literary magazine, excursions/ expeditions, field trips, sports. **Tests:** SAT, TOEFL, IB, IGCSE. **Location:** outskirts of a small town. **Campuses (2):** one in Moshi and one in Arusha.

*Once only fee **Pound sterling

MWANZA

Victoria Primary School

Mail: PO Box 1414, Mwanza, Tanzania, East Africa
Principal: Corazon C. Doolittle
Business manager: Carolyn Dunham
Teaching staff: full-time, 1; total, 1
Nationalities of teaching staff: Canada, 1; total, 1
Grade levels: K – 5
Enrollment: total, 4

Nationalities of student body: U.S., 3; host, 1; total, 4
Teacher/student ratio: 1/4
Boarders: boys, 3
Tuition and board (annual): $2,000
School year: September to July

Year founded: 1953. **Type of school:** coed, day, boarding, church-related. **Governed by:** school board. **Sponsored by:** Africa Inland Mission.

Curriculum/physical plant

Type: U.S. **Languages taught:** English. **Special curricular:** art, physical education. **Extracurricular:** instrumental music, field trips. **Sports:** soccer, softball, camping trips in Serengeti National Park, fishing in Lake Victoria, hill climbing. **Location:** on hill overlooking Lake Victoria, 60 miles from Mwanza, 700 miles from Dar es Salaam. **Campus:** 2 acres. **Facilities:** 4 buildings, 2 classrooms, covered play area, 2 playing fields, library, full boarding facilities.

TANGA

International School at Amboni

Phone: (255)(53)44383 **Facsimile:** (255)(53)43590/46875
Mail: PO Box 117, Tanga, Tanzania
Principal: Jan Hughes
Teaching staff: full-time, 2; total, 2
Grade levels: 1 – 6
Enrollment: total, 23
Teacher/student ratio: 1/16
Tuition (annual): 1,680 – 3,450** (includes registration fee, 500)
School year: August through June

Year founded: 1992. **Type of school:** coed, day, private nonprofit. **Governed by:** parents. **Regional organizations:** AISA.

Curriculum/physical plant

Type: international. **Languages taught:** English. **Special programs:** ESL. **Special curricular:** art, physical education, computer instruction, drama, dance, music, excursions/expeditions, field trips. **Sports:** badminton, basketball, football, swimming lessons at local yacht club. **Location:** on Amboni Estate with landscaped gardens, 12 kilometers from Tanga. **Campus:** 10 acres. **Facilities:** 1 building, 2 classrooms, auditorium, playing field, computer lab, library, playground equipment, air conditioning.

**Pound sterling

ZANZIBAR

International School of Zanzibar

Phone/facsimile: (255)(54)33691 **E-mail:** isz@costech.gn.apc.org
Mail: PO Box 1787, Zanzibar, Tanzania
Principal: Paul Moore
Bursar: Angelika Sepetu
Teaching staff: full-time, 8; part-time, 2; total, 10
Nationalities of teaching staff: U.K., 8; host, 1; other, 1; total, 10
Grade levels: N – 9
Enrollment: total, 85
Teacher/student ratio: 1/20
Tuition (annual): $3,000 – 5,000
Other fees: registration, busing
School year: September to July

Year founded: 1988. **Type of school:** coed, day. **Governed by:** board of governors. **Regional organizations:** AISA, ECIS.

Curriculum/physical plant

Type: U.K. **Staff specialists:** math, art, music, special needs, Montessori, English, science, humanities, physical education/swimming, technology. **Extracurricular:** drama, guitar, painting, printing, volleyball, football. **Location:** in suburban-rural area, 7 kilometers from Zanzibar. **Campus:** 15 acres. **Library:** 2,000 volumes.

THAILAND

Region: South Asia
Size: 198,115 square miles
Population: 58,851,357
Capital: Bangkok
Telephone code: 66
Currency: baht
Languages: Thai, Lao, Chinese, Malay

BANGKOK

Bangkok Patana School

Street address: 2/38 Sukhumvit 105, Soi Lasalle, Bangkok 10260, Thailand
Phone: (66)(2)3980200 **Facsimile:** (66)(2)3993179
E-mail: patanarc@info.co.th
Principal: Graham Sullivan
Head of high school: Paul Schofield
Teaching staff: full-time, 134; part-time, 4; total, 138
Nationalities of teaching staff: U.S., 1; U.K., 105; host, 7; other, 25; total, 138
Grade levels: preK – 12 (N – year 13)
Enrollment: K/first school, 475; middle school, 534; high school, 491; total, 1,500
Nationalities of student body: U.S., 146; U.K., 418; host, 197; other, 739; total, 1,500
Teacher/student ratio: 1/11
Tuition, 1995–96 (annual): preK – 6, 165,000**; 7 – 12, 250,500
Other fees: enrollment*, $80, entrance*, $3,500
School year: September to July

Year founded: 1957. **Type of school:** coed, day, private nonprofit. **Governed by:** elected board of governors. **Sponsored by:** Department of Technical and Economic Cooperation (Thai government). **Accredited by:** World-wide Education Service, U.K. OFSTED inspectors. **Regional organizations:** Federation of British International Schools in Southeast Asia.

Curriculum/physical plant

Type: U.K., IB. **Languages taught:** French, Spanish, Japanese, Thai, Mandarin. **Staff specialists:** reading, math, computer, learning disabilities, nurse, ESL, librarian. **Special programs:** ESL, remedial. **Special curricular:** chorus, band, physical education, computer instruction, dance. **Extracurricular:** drama, gymnastics, choral and instrumental music, computers, literary magazine, photography, excursions/expeditions, field trips, canoeing, chess club, Tae Kwon Do, home language instruction. **Sports:** athletics, basketball, cricket, football, squash, swimming, tennis, volleyball, rugby. **Tests:** IB, GCSE, U.K. Standard Assessment Tasks (SATs). **Location:** large suburban campus on southeast edge of city. **Campus:** 19.5 acres. **Libraries:** 35,000 volumes. **Facilities:** 15 buildings, 70 classrooms, 3 auditoriums, 2 cafeterias, 2 infirmaries, 2 covered play areas, gymnasium, 2 playing fields, 7 science labs, 3 computer labs, 3 swimming pools, full technology suite, Thai sala, air conditioning.

*Once only fee **Thai baht

International Community School

Street address: Sribhumpen Road, 72 Soi Prong Jai, Thungmahamek, Sathorn, Bangkok 10120, Thailand
Phone: (66)(2)6797175 **Facsimile:** (66)(2)2874530
E-mail: 75452.2156@compuserve.com
U.S. mail: c/o Network of International Christian Schools (NICS), PO Box 18151, Memphis, TN 38181, U.S.A.
Headmaster/director: Jim Milkins
Principal: Cindy Toland
Head of library: Jeanette Steer
Head of computer services: Grady Toland
Teaching staff: full-time, 27; part-time, 6; total, 33
Grade levels: K – 12
Enrollment: K, 20; 1 – 6, 187; 7 – 8, 38; 9 – 12, 44; total, 289
Nationalities of student body: U.S., 87; host, 87; other, 115; total, 289
Teacher/student ratio: 1/11
Tuition (annual): K – 6, 107,000**; 7 – 8, 116,000; 9 – 12, 125,000
Other fees: registration*, 50,000**
School year: August to June

Year founded: 1993. **Type of school:** coed, day, church-related, private non-profit. **Governed by:** elected school board. **Sponsored by:** Network of International Christian Schools. **Accredited by:** ACSI, Western (in process). **Regional organizations:** International School Association of Thailand.

Curriculum/physical plant

Type: U.S., AP (11th grade). **Languages taught:** Spanish, Thai. **Staff specialists:** reading, early childhood development. **Special programs:** ESL. **Special curricular:** art, chorus, physical education, computer instruction. **Extracurricular:** drama, excursions/expeditions, field trips, service projects, puppets. **Sports:** basketball, volleyball, climbing wall. **Clubs:** chess, computer, drama, science. **Tests:** SAT, ACT, TOEFL, Stanford. **Location:** central Bangkok (Sathorn area), easily accessible from all mid-city locations. **Library:** 11,000 volumes. **Facilities:** 3 buildings, 16 classrooms, cafeteria, science lab, computer lab, counseling room, chapel, nurse's station, ESL rooms.

*Once only fee **Thai baht

International School Bangkok

Street address: 39/7 Soi Nichada Thani, Samakee Road, Amphur Pakkret, Nonthaburi 11120, Thailand
Phone: (66)(2)5835401 **Facsimile:** (66)(2)5835431
Mail: PO Box 20-1015, Ha Yaek Pakkret, Nonthaburi 11120, Thailand
Superintendent: Paul DeMinico, Ed.D.
Headmistress: Dr. Absorn Meesing
High school principal: Tonya Porter
Middle school principal: Michael Connolly
Elementary school principals: Naomi Woolsey, Thomas Baker
Teaching staff: full-time, 192; part-time, 3; total, 195
Nationalities of teaching staff: U.S., 144; U.K., 10; host, 6; other, 35; total, 195

Grade levels: K – 12
Enrollment: K – 5, 729; 6 – 8, 477; 9 – 12, 751; total, 1,957
Nationalities of student body: U.S., 606; U.K., 48; host, 282; other, 1021; total, 1,957
Teacher/student ratio: 1/10
Tuition (annual): K – 5, 225,900**; 6 – 8, 245,900; 9 – 12, 251,900
Other fees: registration*, 98,000**; busing, 15,820 – 24,150/semester; assessment*, 350,000; ESL, 46,650/semester
School year: August to June

Year founded: 1951. **Type of school:** coed, day, private nonprofit. **Governed by:** elected board of directors. **Accredited by:** Western. **Regional organizations:** AAIE, EARCOS, ECIS.

Curriculum

Type: U.S., IB. **Languages taught:** French, Spanish, German, Japanese, Thai. **Staff specialists:** reading, computer, speech/hearing, counselor, psychologist, learning disabilities, nurse. **Special programs:** ESL. **Special curricular:** art, chorus, band, physical education, computer instruction. **Extracurricular:** drama, dance, choral and instrumental music, computers, yearbook, newspaper, literary magazine, photography, excursions/expeditions, field trips. **Sports:** badminton, basketball, cross-country, rugby, soccer, softball, swimming, tennis, track and field, volleyball. **Clubs:** chess, computer, National Honor Society, Model UN, Thai history and culture, Cosmopolitan, Keyettes, stagecraft, Close-Up, science, windsurfing, skateboard. **Tests:** SSAT, PSAT, SAT, ACT, IB, AP, Iowa, DAT. **Graduates attending college:** 90%. **Graduates have attended:** Harvard, Bucknell, Australian National U., Johns Hopkins, International Christian U. (Japan).

Physical plant

Location: 26 kilometers from central Bangkok in the residential area of Nonthaburi Province. **Campus:** 36 acres. **Libraries:** over 66,000 volumes. **Facilities:** over 120 classrooms, 2 cafeterias, 4 gymnasiums, 3 playing fields, 7 science labs, 5 computer labs, swimming pool, 750-seat theater, instructional media center and administration building, 400-meter track, air conditioning.

*Once only fee **Thai baht

New International School of Thailand

Street address: 36 Soi 15 (Ruamchai) Sukhumvit Road, Bangkok 10110, Thailand
Phone: (66)(2)2528600/2530109 **Facsimile:** (66)(2)2533800
E-mail: nist@ksc.au.ac.th **Web:** http://www.iteachnet.com/nist.html
Headmaster: Keith Allen
Deputy head: Keith Wecker
Secondary school principal: Rosemary Abrahms
Elementary school principal: Allan Taylor
Head of computer services: Robyn Voutier
Teaching staff: full-time, 102; part-time, 7; total, 109
Nationalities of teaching staff: U.S., 20; U.K., 28; host, 8; other, 53; total, 109
Grade levels: preK – 12
Enrollment: preK, 95; K – 5, 570; 6 – 12, 360; total, 1,025

Nationalities of student body: U.S., 135; U.K., 51; host, 253; other, 586; total, 1,025
Teacher/student ratio: 1/10
Tuition, 1996-1997 (annual): preK, 105,000**; K, 140,000; 1 – 5, 150,000; 6 – 8, 176,000; 9 – 12, 200,000
Other fees: registration*, 80,000**; ESL, 30,000 – 90,000/semester; transportation; uniform; refundable special fee, 75,000
School year: mid-August through June

Year founded: 1992. **Type of school:** coed, day, private nonprofit. **Governed by:** Foundation for International Education; elected school board. **Accredited by:** ECIS, New England (in process). **Affiliated with:** United Nations. **Regional organizations:** ECIS, EARCOS, SEATCCO.

Curriculum/physical plant

Type: IB, international, IGCSE, ISCP. **Languages taught:** French, Spanish, German, Russian, Japanese, Thai, Hindi, Korean, Mandarin (others offered by request). **Staff specialists:** computer, counselor, learning disabilities, nurse, ESL (approximately 12). **Special curricular:** art, chorus, band, physical education, drama, music, design and technology, Thai culture/traditions. **Extracurricular:** various programs and clubs (including sports) determined by faculty abilities and student interests. **Location:** in heart of Bangkok's major residential district. **Campus:** 7 acres. **Facilities:** 7 buildings, 85 classrooms, cafeteria, 3 gymnasiums, 2 playing fields, 5 science labs, 3 computer labs, libraries, dispensary, playground, air conditioning.

*Once only fee **Thai baht

Ruamrudee International School

Street address: 42 Moo 4, Ramkhamhaeng (Sukapibal 3) Road, Minburi, Bangkok 10510, Thailand
Phone: (66)(2)5180320 – 29 **Facsimile:** (66)(2)5180334
E-mail: griffith@comnet.ksc.net.th
Director: Rev. Fr. Leo J. Travis, C.Ss.R.
Headmaster: Fr. Joseph Apisit Kritsaralam, C.Ss.R.
High school principal: Glenn Chapin
Middle school principal: Samuel Phillips
Elementary school principal: Karin Caffin
Teaching staff: full-time, 170; part-time, 5; total, 175
Grade levels: preK – 12; ESL 1 – 10
Enrollment: total, 2,263
Teacher/student ratio: 1/12
Tuition (annual): preK – 5, $6,280; 6 – 8, $6,828; 9 – 12, $7,373; ESL 1 – 5, $7,546; ESL 6 – 8, $8,088; ESL 9 – 10, $8,632
Other fees: registration*, $2,800; book deposit*, $400
School year: mid-August to June

Year founded: 1957. **Type of school:** coed, day, church-related, private, international. **Sponsored by:** Thai Ministry of Foreign Affairs. **Operated by:** Redemptorist Fathers of Thailand. **Accredited by:** Western, Thai Ministry of Education, Association of Indian Universities. **Regional organizations:** EARCOS, SEATCCO, ASCD, UNESCO.

Curriculum/physical plant

Type: U.S. **Languages taught:** English, French, Spanish, German, Japanese, Thai. **Staff specialists:** psychologist, art, music, physical education, counselors, school health officer, activities coordinator. **Special programs:** ESL, special education. **Special curricular:** speech, debate, Model UN, forensics. **Extracurricular:** choral music, yearbook, newspaper, sports program. **Sports:** badminton, basketball, soccer, softball, swimming, table tennis, tennis, volleyball. **Clubs:** chess, computer, drama, Key (community service), health, math/AHSME, weight lifting, speakers' debate, photography, French, Spanish, stamp, cosmopolitan, modern dance, ecology, knowledge bowl. **Tests:** PSAT, SAT, TOEFL, Iowa, COGAT, TAP. **Graduates attending college:** 95%. **Graduates have attended:** Pepperdine U., Tufts, U. of Michigan, U. of Rochester, Oberlin College. **Location:** in residential area of Bangkok. **Campus:** 20 acres. **Library:** 24,800 volumes. **Facilities:** 6 buildings, 2 cafeterias, infirmary, tennis court, 6 science labs, swimming pool, auditorium/gymnasium, 2 covered gymnasiums, playing fields, canteen, coffee shop, high school library and arts building, teachers' flat.

*Once only fee

BANGLAMUNG

International School Eastern Seaboard

Phone: (66)(38)345556 – 9 **Facsimile:** (66)(38)345156
E-mail: ise@loxinfo.co.th
Mail: PO Box 6 Banglamung, Chonburi 20150, Thailand
U.S. mail: 6260 South Lake Drive, #117, Cudahy, WI 53110, U.S.A.
Superintendent: James Giombi, Ph.D.
Teaching staff: full-time, 30; total, 30
Nationalities of teaching staff: U.S., 22; host, 1; other, 7; total, 30
Grade levels: preK – 12
Enrollment: preK, 25; K, 20; 1 – 4, 90; 5 – 8, 80; 9 – 12, 50; total, 265
Nationalities of student body: U.S., 90; host, 35; other, 140; total, 265
Teacher/student ratio: 1/9
Tuition (annual): preK, $5,000; K – 5, $7,500; 6 – 8, $8,000; 9 – 12, $8,500
Other fees (annual): registration*, $2,000; capital levy*, $1,600 or $8,000 (refundable); busing, $1,400; lunch, $2/day; ESL, $2,000
School year: August to June

Year founded: 1994. **Type of school:** coed, day, proprietary. **Governed by:** appointed board of directors. **Sponsored by:** I.S.E. Limited. **Accredited by:** Western (in process). **Regional organizations:** EARCOS, SEATCCO.

Curriculum

Type: U.S. **Staff specialists:** math, computer, counselor, psychologist, nurse. **Special programs:** ESL. **Special curricular:** art, physical education, computer instruction, drama, Thai, French, Spanish. **Extracurricular:** drama, dance, instrumental music, computers, yearbook, literary magazine, excursions/expeditions, field trips. **Sports:** swimming, tennis, golf, sailing, horseback riding. **Tests:** Iowa.

Physical plant

Location: in rural area, 25 kilometers from Pattaya, adjacent to a planned residential community and golf course. **Campus:** 22 acres. **Libraries (2):** 8,000 volumes. **Facilities:** 11 buildings, 30 classrooms, auditorium, cafeteria, infirmary, covered play area, gymnasium, 4 science labs, 4 computer labs, access to swimming pool, tennis courts, and golf course, air conditioning.

*Once only fee

CHIANG MAI

Ake Panya International School

Street address: 158/1 Moo 3 Hangdong-Samoeng Road, Banpong, Hangdong, Chiang Mai 50230, Thailand
Phone: (66)(53)365303 **Facsimile:** (66)(53)365304
E-mail: akepanya@cm.ksc.co.th **Web:** http://www.akepanya.ac.th
Head of school: Gordon Jones
Director of studies: Emily Jones
Teaching staff: full-time, 10; total, 10
Nationalities of teaching staff: U.S., 8; host, 1; other, 1; total, 10
Grade levels: 7 – 10
Enrollment: 7 – 9, 70; 10, 10; total, 80
Nationalities of student body: host, 50; other, 30; total, 80
Teacher/student ratio: 1/8
Boarders: boys, 40; girls, 40 **Grades:** 7 – 10 **Program:** planned 7-day
Tuition (annual): 7 – 12, $15,900
School year: September through June

Year founded: 1997. **Type of school:** coed, boarding, private nonprofit. **Governed by:** appointed board of directors. **Accredited by:** Western (in process).

Curriculum/physical plant

Type: U.S., AP. **Languages taught:** English, Japanese, Mandarin, Thai (others by arrangement). **Staff specialists:** computer, nurse. **Special programs:** independent study, experiential education. **Extracurricular:** drama, dance, choral and instrumental music, computers, newspaper, literary magazine, photography, excursions/expeditions, field trips, community service. **Sports:** badminton, soccer, swimming, tennis, volleyball, outdoor leadership. **Tests:** SSAT, PSAT, SAT, TOEFL, AP. **Location:** in mountain valley on edge of national park, 28 kilometers from Chiang Mai. **Campus:** 15 acres. **Facilities:** 5 buildings, 15 classrooms, computer lab, cafeteria, infirmary, 2 tennis courts, 2 playing fields, swimming pool, library, boys' and girls' dormitories with faculty apartments, air conditioning.

Chiang Mai International School

Street address: 13 Chetupon Road, Chiang Mai, Thailand
Phone: (66)(53)242027 **Facsimile:** (66)(53)242455
E-mail: cmiskbn@loxinfo.co.th
Mail: PO Box 38, Chiang Mai, Thailand 50000
Director/principal: Kamol Boonprohm
Teaching staff: full-time, 31; part-time, 3; total, 34
Nationalities of teaching staff: U.S., 16; host, 6; other, 12; total, 34
Grade levels: K – 12
Enrollment: K, 20; 1 – 6, 199; 7 – 8, 57; 9 – 12, 81; total, 357
Nationalities of student body: U.S., 130; U.K., 20; host, 50; other, 157; total, 357
Teacher/student ratio: 1/10
Tuition (annual): K, $2,000; 1 – 6, $3,000; 7 – 8, $3,200; 9 – 12, $4,000
Other fees (annual): application, $50; registration*, $2,000; ESL, $800
School year: September to June

Year founded: 1954. **Type of school:** coed, day, private nonprofit, church-affiliated. **Governed by:** appointed administrative advisory board. **Sponsored by:** Foundation of the Church of Christ in Thailand. **Accredited by:** Western, Thai Ministry of Education, Association of Indian Universities. **Regional organizations:** EARCOS, International Schools Association in Thailand.

Curriculum/physical plant

Type: U.S. **Special programs:** ESL, Thai language and culture. **Special curricular:** art, chorus, physical education, computer instruction. **Extracurricular:** drama, computers, yearbook, newspaper, photography, field trips, sports. **Tests:** SAT, MAT. **Location:** in city. **Library:** 15,000 volumes. **Facilities:** 7 buildings, 20 classrooms, auditorium, 3 covered play areas, playing field, science lab, computer lab, AV equipment, multi-use court area.

*Once only fee

Lanna International School Thailand

Street address: 300/1 Grandview Moo 1, Chiang Mai to Hang Dong Road, Chiang Mai 50100, Thailand
Phone: (66)(53)271159/806230 – 1 **Facsimile:** (66)(53)271159
Head of school: Wayne D. Morton
Thai headmistress: Rachanee Puangwong
Business manager: Surin Demuth
Teaching staff: full-time, 15; part-time, 4; total, 19
Nationalities of teaching staff: U.S., 6; U.K., 5; host, 3; other, 5; total, 19
Grade levels: ECE – 12
Enrollment: N – preK, 4; K, 47; 1 – 6, 52; 7 – 9, 21; 10 – 12, 9; total, 133
Nationalities of student body: U.S., 15; U.K., 7; host, 40; other, 71; total, 133
Teacher/student ratio: 1/8
Tuition (annual): N – preK, 30,000** (morning); 50,000 (full day); K – 1, 70,000; 2 – 5, 87,000; 6 – 8, 95,000; 9 – 12, 103,000
Other fees (annual): registration, 5,000**; capital levy*, 5,000 – 15,000; busing, lunch
School year: late August to late June

Year founded: 1993. **Type of school:** coed, day, proprietary. **Governed by:** 6-member appointed school board. **Sponsored by:** HSIC. **Accredited by:** Thai Ministry of Education. **Regional organizations:** International Schools Association in Thailand, SEATCCO.

Curriculum/physical plant

Type: U.S., U.K., international. **Languages taught:** French, Thai. **Special programs:** ESL. **Extracurricular:** drama, computers, newspaper, field trips, Thai culture, photography, art, basketball, volleyball, swimming, soccer. **Tests:** PSAT, SAT, IGCSE. **Location:** southwest of city center, near airport. **Facilities:** 2 buildings, 17 classrooms, cafeteria, 2 play areas, science lab, computer lab, library, infirmary with full-time nurse, mini soccer field, 25-meter swimming pool, multi-purpose outside court, air conditioning.

*Once only fee **Thai baht

PHUKET

Phuket International School

Phone: (66)(76)2292634 **Facsimile:** (66)(76)288636
E-mail: info@phuketschl.com **Web:** http://www.phuketschl.com
Mail: PO Box 700, Phuket 83000, Thailand
Director: Michael Moore
Thai headmistress: Maliwan Subsakanusorn
Teaching staff: full-time, 17; total, 17
Nationalities of teaching staff: U.S., 3; host, 5; other, 9; total, 17
Grade levels: preK – 8
Enrollment: preK, 17; K, 13; 1 – 8, 92; total, 122
Nationalities of student body: U.S., 20; host, 16; other, 86; total, 122
Capacity: preK, 30; K – 8, 135; total, 165
Teacher/student ratio: 1/6
Tuition (annual): preK, 62,000**; K – 6, 85,000; 7 – 8, 105,000; ESL, 15,000
Other fees: registration*, 35,000**; capital levy, 25,000
School year: September to June

Year founded: 1989. **Type of school:** coed, day, private nonprofit. **Accredited by:** Thai government. **Regional organizations:** ECIS, EARCOS.

Curriculum/physical plant

Type: international. **Languages taught:** English, French, Thai. **Staff specialists:** art, music, physical education. **Special curricular:** computer instruction. **Extracurricular:** swimming, roller blading, soccer, basketball, computer club. **Location:** in tropical rural area, 2 miles from center of town. **Campus:** 2 acres. **Library:** 3,000 volumes. **Facilities:** 2 buildings, 14 classrooms, science lab.

*Once only fee **Thai bhat

TOGO

Region: West Africa
Size: 21,925 square miles
Population: 4,570,530
Capital: Lomé
Telephone code: 228
Currency: CFA franc
Languages: French, Ewe, Mina, Dagomba, Kabye

LOMÉ

American International School of Lomé

Street address: 35 Kayigan Lawson, Lomé, Togo
Phone: (228)213000 **Facsimile:** (228)217952
U.S. mail: c/o U.S. Embassy – Lomé, Dept. of State, Washington, D.C. 20521-2300
Director: Tom Crosby
Teaching staff: full-time, 3; part-time, 4; total, 7
Nationalities of teaching staff: U.S., 3; host, 4; total, 7
Grade levels: preK – 8 (9 – 12 correspondence)
Enrollment: preK, 17; K – 8, 34; total, 51
Capacity: preK, 18; K – 8, 60; total, 78
Teacher/student ratio: 1/6
Tuition (annual): preK, $1,750; K – 8, $5,500
Other fees: registration*, $500
School year: late August to mid-June

Year founded: 1967. **Type of school:** coed, day, private nonprofit. **Governed by:** elected board of directors. **Regional organizations:** AISA.

Curriculum/physical plant

Type: U.S. **Languages taught:** French (required daily). **Staff specialists:** computer, art, ESL, music, physical education. **Special programs:** ESL. **Special curricular:** art, physical education, French, music, computer. **Extracurricular:** field trips, basketball, soccer, swimming, ceramics. **Clubs:** chess, math. **Tests:** Iowa. **Location:** in city. **Campus:** 1 acre. **Library:** 4,000 volumes. **Facilities:** 1 building, 11 classrooms, playing field, computer lab, lunchroom, partly covered play area, air conditioning.

*Once only fee

The British School of Lomé

Street address: Residence du Benin, BP 20050 Lomé, Togo
Phone: (228)264606 **Facsimile:** (228)264989
E-mail: 103162.1615@compuserve.com
Headmaster: Mr. I. A. Sayer
Bursar: Mr. K. Richmond
Teaching staff: full-time, 25; part-time, 7; total, 32
Nationalities of teaching staff: U.K., 25; host, 4; other, 3; total, 32
Grade levels: N – 13
Enrollment: N – preK, 9; K, 10; 1 – 6, 60; 7 – 9, 65; 10 – 12, 60; 13, 16; total, 220
Nationalities of student body: U.S., 20; U.K., 27; other, 173; total, 220
Capacity: N – preK, 15; K, 30; 1 – 6, 135; 7 – 9, 90; 10 – 12, 55; 13, 30; total, 355
Teacher/student ratio: 1/8
Boarders: boys, 50; girls, 50 **Ages:** 8 – 18 **Program:** planned 7-day
Tuition (annual): N – preK, 12,000**; K –11, 28,000
Tuition and board (annual): 4 – 11, 61,000**; 12 – 13, 76,000
Other fees (annual): registration*, 1,000**; lunch, 9; boarding deposit, 10,000
School year: September to June

Year founded: 1983. **Type of school:** coed, day, boarding, proprietary. **Approved by:** London U., Cambridge U., IBO.

Curriculum/physical plant

Type: U.K., IB, ISCP. **Languages taught:** French, Spanish, German. **Staff specialists:** reading, math, computer, counselor, nurse. **Special programs:** ESL, independent study, remedial. **Special curricular:** art, chorus, band, physical education, computer instruction. **Extracurricular:** drama, choral and instrumental music, computers, newspaper, literary magazine, excursions/expeditions, field trips. **Sports:** basketball, football, netball, swimming, tennis, horseback riding. **Clubs:** cricket, brass band, violin, piano. **Tests:** SAT, TOEFL, IB, A-level GCE, GCSE, IGCSE. **Graduates attending college:** 90%. **Graduates have attended:** U.S. and U.K. universities. **Location:** spacious, modern, landscaped campus, 5 kilometers from Lomé. **Library:** 11,000 volumes. 2,000 videos. **Facilities:** 5 buildings, 21 classrooms, cafeteria, infirmary, 4 tennis courts, playing field, 5 science labs, computer lab, swimming pool, technology room, boarding in small family units, air conditioning.

*Once only fee **French franc

TRINIDAD AND TOBAGO

Region: Caribbean
Size: 1,980 square miles
Population: 1,272,385
Capital: Port of Spain
Telephone code: 809
Currency: Trinidad dollar
Language: English, Hindi, French, Spanish

MAYARO

AMOCO GALEOTA SCHOOL

Street address: 4-1/2 Mile Guayaguayare Road, Mayaro, Trinidad and Tobago
Phone: (1)(809)6308341 ext. 1157 **Facsimile:** (1)(809)6308508 ext. 1145
Mail: c/o Amoco Trinidad Oil Co., PO Box 714, Port-of-Spain, Trinidad and Tobago, West Indies
U.S. mail: Expatriate–Trinidad and Tobago, PO Box 4381, Houston, TX 77210, U.S.A.
Principal: Barbara Punch
Teaching staff: full-time, 6; total, 6
Nationalities of teaching staff: U.S., 1; host, 5; total, 6
Grade levels: preK – 8
Enrollment: preK, 9; K, 6; 1 – 8, 38; total, 47
Nationalities of student body: U.S., 19; host, 28; total, 47
Capacity: preK, 7; K, 8; 1 – 6, 65; 7 – 8, 13; total, 93
Teacher/student ratio: 1/9
School year: September to June

Year founded: 1972. **Type of school:** coed, day, company-sponsored. **Sponsored by:** Amoco Trinidad Oil Company. **Operated by:** International Schools Services, Princeton, New Jersey.

Curriculum/physical plant

Type: U.S., national. **Languages taught:** Spanish. **Staff specialists:** reading, computer, learning disabilities, music, physical education, swimming. **Special programs:** independent study, remedial, Spanish conversation. **Special curricular:** art, physical education, computer instruction, swimming. **Extracurricular:** drama, dance, choral and instrumental music, computers, yearbook, field trips, crafts, karate, drawing, Scrabble, Cub Scouts, Brownies. **Sports:** baseball, basketball, cricket, football, tennis. **Tests:** Iowa, Common Entrance Examination (national examination). **Graduates have attended:** Presentation College, St. Augustine Girls' High School, St. Stephen's College, Naparima Girls' High School, St. Joseph's Convent. **Location:** on seacoast, in the southeastern corner of the island. **Library:** 8,000 volumes. **Facilities:** 2 buildings, 6 classrooms, auditorium, covered play area, 2 tennis courts, playing field, science lab, computer lab, swimming pool, music room, air conditioning.

PORT OF SPAIN

THE INTERNATIONAL SCHOOL OF PORT OF SPAIN

Street address: 18 Victoria Avenue, Port of Spain, Trinidad, West Indies
Phone/facsimile: (1)(809)6245138/6278157 **E-mail:** ispstt@trinidad.net
U.S. mail: INTL # 1N-1369, 8340 NW 56 Street, Miami, FL 33166, U.S.A.
Headmaster: Michael D. Popinchalk
Teaching staff: full-time, 18; part-time, 4; total, 22
Nationalities of teaching staff: U.S., 3; U.K., 3; host, 10; other, 6; total, 22
Grade levels: preK – 12
Enrollment: K, 10; 1 – 6, 65; 7 – 9, 40; 10 – 12, 25; total, 140
Nationalities of student body: U.S., 85; host, 13; other, 42; total, 140
Capacity: preK – K, 20; 1 – 5, 75; 6 – 9, 55; 10 – 12, 50; total, 200
Teacher/student ratio: 1/8
Tuition (annual): K, $3,100; 1 – 12, $5,700
Other fees: registration*, $2,500
School year: August to June

Year founded: 1994. **Type of school:** coed, company-sponsored. **Governed by:** corporate and parent board. **Sponsored by:** corporations and U.S. Embassy. **Accredited by:** Southern.

Curriculum/physical plant

Type: U.S., AP. **Languages taught:** Spanish. **Staff specialists:** counselor, learning disabilities, college counselor, curriculum coordinator. **Special curricular:** art, band, physical education, computer instruction. **Extracurricular:** Model UN, inter-island sports/activities, excursions/field trips. **Sports:** basketball, soccer, softball, volleyball. **Tests:** SAT, AP, Iowa. **Location:** 2 sites during the 1997-1998 academic year: the lower school in the city center, the middle/high school in Diego Martin. A purpose-built campus will be completed by August 1, 1998. **Library:** 5,000 volumes. **Facilities:** 2 buildings, 20 classrooms, playing field, science lab, computer lab, close to large park with playing fields, air conditioning.

*Once only fee

TUNISIA

Region: North Africa
Size: 63,378 square miles
Population: 9,019,687
Capital: Tunis
Telephone code: 216
Currency: dinar
Languages: Arabic, French

SFAX

International School of Sfax

Location: British Gas, Guebiba Village, Sfax, Tunisia
Phone: (216)(4)258045 **Facsimile:** (216)(4)258046
E-mail: 106534.1121@compuserve.com
Mail: International School of Sfax, BP 66, PTT 3084, Tyna El Jadida, Sfax, Tunisia
Director: Charles Gregory
Teaching staff: full-time, 5; part-time, 2; total, 7
Nationalities of teaching staff: U.K., 3; host, 2; other, 2; total, 7
Grade levels: preK – 8
Enrollment: preK – K, 5; 1 – 8, 20; total, 25
Nationalities of student body: U.S., 1; U.K., 22; other, 2; total, 25
Capacity: preK – K, 15; 1 – 8, 60; total, 75
Teacher/student ratio: 1/7

Year founded: 1992. **Type of school:** coed, day. **Sponsored by:** British Gas Tunisia, Ltd. **Operated by:** International Schools Services, Princeton, New Jersey. **Regional organizations:** MAIS.

Curriculum/physical plant

Type: U.S., U.K. **Languages taught:** French. **Special curricular:** art, physical education, music, computer, internet communications, field trips. **Extracurricular:** drama, recorders, arts and crafts, sports, cooking, computer. **Tests:** NFER. **Library:** more than 3,000 volumes, electronic finder for periodical articles. **Facilities:** large portacabin structure located within the British Gas Tunisia residential/recreational village, with a large swimming pool, wading pool, full-size soccer pitch, tennis and squash courts, playing field, computer lab, science/art lab, extensive climbing and play apparatus.

TUNIS

AMERICAN COOPERATIVE SCHOOL OF TUNIS

Street address: Km. 10 Route de la Marsa – El Aouina, Tunis, Tunisia
Phone: (216)(1)760517/760905 **Facsimile:** (216)(1)761412
E-mail: acst@acst.intl.tn **Web:** http://www.guilford.k12.nc.us/hp/tunis/home.html
Mail: c/o American Embassy, 144 Avenue de la Liberté, Tunis,Tunisia
U.S. mail: TUNIS –A.C.S.T., Dept. of State, Washington, D.C. 20520-6360
Director: Michael Levinson
Head of library: Christine Brignoli
Head of computer services: Ruth Behrsing
Business manager: Faouzi Ben Sedrine
Accountant: Sanaa Khelif
Teaching staff: full-time, 23; part-time, 2; total, 25
Nationalities of teaching staff: U.S., 21; U.K., 1; other, 3; total, 25
Grade levels: preK – 12
Enrollment: preK, 25; K, 30; 1 – 5, 110; 6 – 8, 40; 9 – 12, 28; total, 233
Nationalities of student body: U.S., 70; U.K., 11; host, 9; other, 143; total, 233
Capacity: preK, 30; K, 38; 1 – 5, 120; 6 – 8, 45; 9 – 12, 30; total, 263
Teacher/student ratio: 1/8
Tuition (annual): preK (half day), $2,600 (other fees do not apply); K – 5, $8,000; 6 – 8, $8,500; 9 – 12, $9,000
Other fees (annual): registration*, $800; capital levy, $500; busing, $800
School year: September to June

Year founded: 1958. **Type of school:** coed, day, private nonprofit. **Governed by:** elected board of governors. **Accredited by:** Middle States. **Regional organizations:** MAIS.

Curriculum/physical plant

Type: U.S. **Languages taught:** French, Arabic. **Special programs:** ESL. **Special curricular:** art, physical education, computer instruction, music. **Extracurricular:** choral music, computers, yearbook, excursions/expeditions, field trips, Girl Scouts, Boy Scouts. **Sports:** basketball, soccer, softball, volleyball. **Tests:** PSAT, SAT, Iowa. **Location:** in suburban area, 10 kilometers from Tunis city. **Library:** 8,000 volumes. **Facilities:** 5 buildings, 21 classrooms, playing field, science lab, computer lab, multipurpose room, gymnasium/auditorium.

*Once only fee

TURKEY

Region: Europe/Middle East
Size: 300,948 square miles
Population: 62,484,478
Capital: Ankara
Telephone code: 90
Currency: lira
Languages: Turkish, Kurdish, Arabic

ANKARA

Bilkent University Preparatory School

Street address: East Campus, Bilkent, 06533 Ankara, Turkey
Phone: (90)(312)2664961 – 2 **Facsimile:** (90)(312)2664963
E-mail: school@bups.bilkent.edu.tr
Web: http://www.bups.bilkent.edu.tr
Director: Mustafa Pultar, Ph.D.
Headmaster: Jim DiSebastian
Middle school head: Jonathan Lane
Head of library: Cara Keyman
Administrative manager: Yesim Tanik
Teaching staff: full-time, 34; part-time, 4; total, 38
Nationalities of teaching staff: U.S., 8; U.K., 14; host, 9; other, 7; total, 38
Grade levels: pre-6 – 12
Enrollment: pre-6, 28; 6, 31; 7, 30; 8, 28; 9, 24; 10, 18; 11, 15; total, 174
Nationalities of student body: U.S., 9; U.K., 12; host, 135; other, 18; total, 174
Capacity: pre-6, 40; 6, 40; 7 – 8, 80; 9, 40; 10, 40; 11, 20; 12, 20; total, 280
Teacher/student ratio: 1/4
Tuition (annual): middle school, $7,800; upper school, $8,100
Other fees: busing, $250; books, $150
School year: September to June

Year founded: 1993. **Type of school:** coed, day, private nonprofit. **Governed by:** appointed executive board. **Sponsored by:** Bilkent University.

Curriculum/physical plant

Type: U.S., U.K., national, IB, IGCSE. **Languages of instruction:** English, Turkish. **Languages taught:** French, German. **Staff specialists:** computer, counselor, nurse, librarian, part-time physician. **Special programs:** ESL. **Special curricular:** art, physical education. **Extracurricular:** drama, instrumental music, computers, newspaper, photography, excursions/expeditions, field trips, THIMUN. **Sports:** badminton, basketball, soccer, volleyball. **Clubs:** chess, student council, music. **Location:** on Bilkent University campus, 16 kilometers from Ankara. **Campus:** 2 acres. **Library:** 11,000 volumes. **Facilities:** 5 buildings, 23 classrooms, 2 cafeterias, infirmary, gymnasium, 3 playing fields, 3 science labs, computer lab, music rooms, art room, ceramics lab.

ISTANBUL

ENKA OKULLARI

Street address: Sadi Gülcelik Spor Sitesi, Istinye 80860, Istanbul, Turkey
Phone: (90)(212)2768833 **Facsimile:** (90)(212)2768294
E-mail: enka@turk.net
Director: Clinton J. Vickers, Ph.D.
Assistant to director: Yuksel Osturk
Elementary head: Sule Yurcu
Pre-school head: Serpil Deniz
Business manager: Zeynep Apak
Teaching staff: full-time, 33; part-time, 2; total, 35
Nationalities of teaching staff: U.S., 17; host, 18; total, 35
Grade levels: preschool – 2
Enrollment: total, 280
Nationalities of student body: U.S., 5; U.K., 5; host, 260; other, 10; total, 280
Teacher/student ratio: 1/7
Tuition (annual): preS – K, $6,000; elementary, $6,500
School year: September to June

Year founded: 1995. **Type of school:** coed, day, private nonprofit. **Governed by:** appointed board of directors. **Sponsored by:** Enka Foundation. **Accredited by:** Turkish Ministry of Education.

Curriculum/physical plant

Type: national. **Languages of instruction:** English, Turkish. **Staff specialists:** reading, counselor, nurse, art, music, physician. **Special programs:** ESL, Summer Institute for Teachers at Enka. **Special curricular:** art, chorus, band, physical education, computer instruction. **Extracurricular:** drama, gymnastics, dance, choral and instrumental music, computers, yearbook, newspaper, literary magazine, photography, excursions/expeditions, field trips, sports. **Location:** Olympic sports site in suburban Istanbul. **Facilities:** 8 buildings, 66 classrooms, 2 auditoriums, cafeteria, 2 infirmaries, 3 covered play areas, 21 tennis courts, 2 gymnasiums, playing field, 6 science labs, 3 computer labs, 2 swimming pools, library, amphitheater, Olympic track, 3 art studios, 2 music rooms, dance studio, AV room, theater, air conditioning, middle school and high school under construction.

ISTANBUL INTERNATIONAL COMMUNITY SCHOOL

Street address: Meydan Mahallesi, Nafi Baba sokak No. 1, Rumelihisar, 80830 Istanbul, Turkey
Phone: (90)(212)2872770/2651591 **Facsimile:** (90)(212)2650580
E-mail: iics@iics.k12.tr **Web:** http://www.iics.k12.tr
Mail: P. K. 29 Bebek 80810, Istanbul, Turkey
Headmaster: Kenneth Hillmann
Secondary principal: Edward Washburn
Elementary principal: Jeffrey Degenhart
Teaching staff: full-time, 36; part-time, 3; total, 39

Nationalities of teaching staff: U.S., 27; U.K., 5; host, 2; other, 5; total, 39
Grade levels: preK – 12
Enrollment: preK – K, 30; 1 – 6, 174; 7 – 12, 116; total, 320
Nationalities of student body: U.S., 88; U.K., 33; other, 199; total, 320
Teacher/student ratio: 1/8
Tuition (annual): preK, $7,350; K– 8, $10,850; 9 – 12, $12,330
School year: September to June

Year founded: 1911. **Type of school:** coed, day, private nonprofit. **Governed by:** appointed board of governors. **Regional organizations:** ECIS, CEESA, IBO.

Curriculum/physical plant

Type: U.S., IB, IBMYP. **Languages taught:** French. **Staff specialists:** counselor. **Special programs:** ESL. **Special curricular:** art, physical education, computer instruction, drama, music. **Extracurricular:** drama, computers, yearbook, excursions/expeditions, art, International Award for Youth Math Counts, Knowledge Bowl, outdoor explore, field trips, soccer, swimming. **Sports:** basketball, volleyball. **Clubs:** Cub Scouts, Brownies, Boy Scouts, Girl Scouts. **Tests:** SSAT, PSAT, CTP. **Graduates have attended:** Philips Exeter, Williston Northampton, Andover, Northfield Mount Hermon, Avon Old Farm. **Location:** in small village overlooking the Bosphorus, 5 miles from old city. **Library:** 9,000 volumes. **Facilities:** 4 buildings, 15 pre-fabs, 25 classrooms, playing field, computer lab, science labs, AV room, physical education bubble, playground.

The Koç School

Phone: (90)(216)3041003 – 14 **Facsimile:** (90)(216)3041048
Mail: PO Box 38, Pendik-Istanbul 81481, Turkey
Headmaster: John Chandler
Academic dean: Zühal Altayli
IB coordinator: Mustafa Balkas
Business manager: Gurkan Key
Teaching staff: full-time, 87; part-time, 5; total, 92
Nationalities of teaching staff: U.S., 37; U.K., 4; host, 46; other, 5; total, 92
Grade levels: 6 – 12
Enrollment: 6 – 8, 130; 7 – 9, 390; 10 – 12, 381; total, 901
Nationalities of student body: host, 868; other, 33; total, 901
Teacher/student ratio: 1/11
Boarders: boys, 154; girls, 75 **Grades:** 6 – 12 **Program:** planned 5-day
Tuition (annual): $4,000 – 6,000
Other fees (annual): boarding, $3,000 – 6,000; busing, $570 – 950; lunch, $455; books, $285 – 380; uniform, $170
School year: September to June

Year founded: 1988. **Type of school:** coed, day, boarding, private nonprofit. **Governed by:** appointed school committee of Vehbi Koç Foundation board. **Sponsored by:** Koç Foundation. **Accredited by:** Turkish Ministry of Education. **Regional organizations:** ECIS.

Curriculum

Type: U.S., national, IB, AP. **Languages of instruction:** English, Turkish. **Languages taught:** English, French, German, Turkish. **Staff specialists:** computer, counselor, nurse, ESL, music, drama. **Special programs:** ESL, honors sections. **Special curricular:** art, chorus, physical education, computer instruction, debating, ensemble, English conversation, music. **Extracurricular:** drama, dance, choral and instrumental music, computers, yearbook, newspaper, literary magazine, photography, excursions/expeditions, field trips. **Sports:** badminton, basketball, cross-country, soccer, tennis, track and field, volleyball, handball, ping-pong, mini-football. **Clubs:** chess, student council, hiking, Turkish culture, aerobics. **Tests:** PSAT, SAT, TOEFL, IB, AP, Cambridge Language Proficiency, Turkish university entrance exams. **Graduates attending college:** 98%.

Physical plant

Location: rural setting, in rolling hills of active farm area, 5 kilometers from Kurtköy ("Wolf Village") and 35 kilometers to the east of Istanbul. **Campus:** 200 acres. **Library:** 8,000 volumes. **Facilities:** 10 buildings, 40 classrooms, 2 auditoriums, 2 cafeterias, infirmary, covered play area, 2 tennis courts, gymnasium, 2 playing fields, 4 science labs, 2 computer labs, canteen, music room, bookstore, art room, boarding facilities in 2 four-story buildings with study, recreational area, and supervisors' apartments.

Robert College of Istanbul

Phone: (90)(212)2653430; 1(212)8435550 (U.S. phone)
Facsimile: (90)(212)2575443/2572146; 1(212)8435556 (U.S. fax)
E-mail: robcol@robcol.k12.tr or robcol@kilyos.uedh.com.tr
Mail: PK 1, Arnavutkoy 80820, Istanbul, Turkey
U.S. mail: 230 Park Ave., Floor 11, New York, NY 10169-0079, U.S.A.
Headmaster: Christopher Wadsworth
Turkish assistant head: Esin Hoyi
Upper school principal: Whitman Shepard
Middle school principal: George Damon
Business manager: Umran Uras
Teaching staff: full-time, 90; part-time, 6; total, 96
Nationalities of teaching staff: U.S., 40; U.K., 12; host, 39; other, 5; total, 96
Grade levels: 7 – 12
Enrollment: 7 – 9, 514; 10 – 12, 427; total, 941
Nationalities of student body: U.S., 1; host, 940; total, 941
Teacher/student ratio: 1/11
Boarders: boys, 66; girls, 50 **Grades:** 7 – 12 **Program:** planned 5-day
Tuition (annual): 420,000,000**
Other fees (annual): boarding, 684,000,000**
School year: September to June

Year founded: 1863. **Type of school:** coed, day, boarding, private nonprofit. **Governed by:** Turkish Ministry of Education. **Sponsored by:** board of trustees. **Accredited by:** NYSAIS. **Regional organizations:** ECIS, NESA. **Member of:** NAIS.

Curriculum/physical plant

Type: U.S., national, AP. **Languages of instruction:** English, Turkish. **Languages taught:** French, German. **Staff specialists:** counselor, nurse, part-time physician. **Special programs:** ESL. **Special curricular:** art, physical education, computer instruction. **Extracurricular:** drama, instrumental music, computers, yearbook, newspaper, literary magazine, photography, excursions/expeditions, field trips. **Sports:** basketball, soccer, tennis, track and field, volleyball. **Clubs:** braille, social service, folklore. **Tests:** PSAT, SAT, ACT, TOEFL, AP. **Graduates attending college:** 100%. **Graduates have attended:** Bryn Mawr, MIT, Harvard, Stanford, Cornell. **Location:** 5 miles up the Bosphorus on wooded, hilly site near residential area, Arnavutkoy. **Campus:** 60 acres. **Library:** more than 30,000 volumes. **Facilities:** 10 buildings, 55 classrooms, auditorium, cafeteria, infirmary, covered play area, gymnasium, playing field, science lab, computer lab, tennis courts, 2 dormitories.

**Turkish lira

Üsküdar American Academy

Street address: Vakif Sok, Baglarbasi, Istanbul, Turkey
Phone: (90)(216)3106823 **Facsimile:** (90)(216)3331818
E-mail: uskudar@ibm.net
Mail: 81130 Baglarbasi, Üsküdar, Istanbul, Turkey
Director: John Heard
Turkish director: Tülin Buyukalkan
Business manager: Zehra Sunbay
Teaching staff: full-time, 55; part-time, 8; total, 63
Nationalities of teaching staff: U.S., 22; U.K., 5; host, 32; other, 4; total, 63
Grade levels: 6 – 12
Enrollment: total, 750
Teacher/student ratio: 1/12
Tuition, for Turkish students (annual): $3,800
Other fees (annual): tuition includes English textbooks and student fees; lunch, uniforms, and daily buses are extra
School year: September to June

Year founded: 1876. **Type of school:** coed, day. **Governed by:** American and Turkish board. **Sponsored by:** American Mission Board (ABH). **Accredited by:** Turkish Ministry of Education. **Regional organizations:** ECIS.

Curriculum/physical plant

Type: U.S., national. **Languages of instruction:** English, Turkish. **Languages taught:** English, French, German. **Staff specialists:** computer, counselor, nurse, librarian. **Special programs:** ESL. **Special curricular:** art, chorus, physical education, computer instruction, math contests. **Extracurricular:** drama, computers, yearbook, literary magazine, excursions/expeditions, speech/debate, social service. **Sports:** basketball, gymnastics, table tennis, track and field, volleyball, handball. **Clubs:** Model UN, art, folklore. **Tests:** PSAT, SAT, TOEFL, AP. **Graduates attending college:** 99%. **Graduates have attended:** Istanbul U., Princeton, Cornell, MIT, Brown. **Location:** in Istanbul, on Asian side of Bosphorus. **Library:** 18,000 volumes. **Facilities:** 9 buildings, 37 classrooms, auditorium, cafeteria, infirmary, gymnasium, playing field, 4 science labs, 2 computer labs, canteen, faculty housing.

IZMIR

The American Collegiate Institute

Phone: (90)(232)2853401 **Facsimile:** (90)(232)2464128
E-mail: school@aci.edu.tr **Web:** http://www.aci.edu.tr
Mail: Inonu Caddesi 476, 35290 Goztepe, Izmir, Turkey
Principal: Frederick L. Thompson, Ph.D.
Turkish first vice-principal: Hale Baran
Upper school vice-principal: Guler Erdur
Middle school vice-principal: Betsy Cakir
Prep school vice-principal: Elizabeth Orbasli
Teaching staff: full-time, 81; part-time, 10; total, 91
Nationalities of teaching staff: U.S., 19; U.K., 7; host, 60; other, 5; total, 91
Grade levels: preparatory, 7 – 12
Enrollment: prep, 144; 7 – 9, 434; 10 – 12, 407; total, 985
Nationalities of student body: U.S., 4; host, 980; other, 1; total, 985
Teacher/student ratio: 1/11
Tuition (annual): $4,400
School year: September to June

Year founded: 1878. **Type of school:** coed, day, private nonprofit. **Governed and sponsored by:** American Board Schools, Istanbul. **Accredited by:** Turkish Ministry of Education, New England, ECIS. **Regional organizations:** ECIS.

Curriculum/physical plant

Type: U.S., national, AP. **Languages of instruction:** English, Turkish. **Languages taught:** French, German. **Staff specialists:** counselor, nurse, doctor. **Special curricular:** art, chorus, band, physical education, computer instruction. **Extracurricular:** drama, dance, computers, yearbook, newspaper, photography, social service, ecology, 99 various clubs and committees. **Sports:** basketball, soccer, tennis, track and field, volleyball. **Tests:** PSAT, SAT, ACT, TOEFL, AP, CEEB. **Graduates attending college:** 90%. **Graduates have attended:** Cornell, MIT, Yale, Cal Tech, Middle East Technical U. **Location:** in suburban area, Goztepe, overlooking Izmir Bay. **Campus:** 11 acres. **Library:** 22,000 volumes. **Facilities:** 10 buildings, 45 classrooms, auditorium, cafeteria, infirmary, tennis court, gymnasium, playing field, 5 science labs, 4 computer labs, amphitheater, volleyball/basketball courts, video room, 2 art rooms, music room, lounges.

TARSUS

Tarsus American School

Street address: 64 Cengiz Topel Caddesi, Tarsus 33401, Turkey
Phone: (90)(324)6135402 – 4 **Facsimile:** (90)(324)6246347
E-mail: tarsus-f@servis2.net.tr
Mail: PK 6, Tarsus 33401, Turkey
Director: Anthony Spencer, Ph.D.
Turkish vice-principal: Dr. Esma Calik
Foreign vice-principal: Andrzej Cichy, Ph.D.
Academic dean: Jale Sever
Deans: prep, Mustafa Nacar; middle school, Wanda Etheridge; high school, Ali Karamik
Teaching staff: full-time, 59; part-time, 2; total, 61
Nationalities of teaching staff: U.S., 17; host, 33; other, 11; total, 61
Grade levels: preparatory, 6 – 12
Enrollment: prep, 120; 7 – 9, 352; 10 – 12, 336; total, 808
Nationalities of student body: host, 806; other, 2; total, 808
Teacher/student ratio: 1/13
Tuition (annual): $4,000
Other fees (annual): lunch, $350
School year: September to June

Year founded: 1888. **Type of school:** coed, day, private nonprofit. **Governed by:** appointed board of governors. **Sponsored by:** United Church Board for World Ministries. **Accredited by:** Turkish Ministry of Education. **Regional organizations:** NESA.

Curriculum

Type: U.S., national. **Languages of instruction:** English, Turkish for Turkish cultural subjects. **Languages taught:** French, German. **Staff specialists:** psychologist, counselors, tutors, doctor. **Special curricular:** art, physical education, computer instruction, music. **Extracurricular:** drama, computers, yearbook, newspaper, photography, excursions/expeditions, Model UN, speech, social service club, sports, folk dance, library club, various other clubs. **Sports:** basketball, football, soccer, tennis, track and field, volleyball. **Tests:** SAT, TOEFL, AFS. **Graduates attending college:** 95%. **Graduates have attended:** major Turkish, U.S., and European universities.

Physical plant

Location: in central Tarsus. **Campus:** 15 acres. **Library:** 34,000 volumes. **Facilities:** 11 buildings, 37 classrooms, auditorium, infirmary, 4 science labs, 2 computer labs, dining room, art room, music room, tutorial lab, counseling center, sports fields, volleyball/basketball/tennis courts, canteen, lounges, faculty living quarters.

TURKMENISTAN

Region: Central Asia
Size: 188,500 square miles
Population: 4,149,283
Capital: Ashgabat
Telephone code: 7
Currency: manat
Languages: Turkmen, Russian, Uzbek

ASHGABAT

ASHGABAT INTERNATIONAL SCHOOL

Street address: Turkmen School 48, Ashgabat, Turkmenistan
Phone: (7)(3632)445580 **Facsimile:** (7)(3632)446955
E-mail: nick@ais.ashgabad.su
U.S. mail: c/o American Embassy (ASHGABAT), Dept. of State, Washington, DC 20521-7070
Director: Nicholas Wasuck
Teaching staff: full-time, 4; part-time, 3; total, 7
Nationalities of teaching staff: U.S., 5; host, 2; total, 7
Grade levels: N – 10
Enrollment: total, 34
Capacity: total, 50
Teacher/student ratio: 1/6
Tuition (annual): N, $3,200; K – 5, $6,600; 6 – 10, $9,200
Other fees: registration*, $100; capital levy, $4,000/deposit or $1,600 yr/fee
School year: September to June

Year founded: 1994. **Type of school:** coed, day. **Governed by:** Quality Schools International. **Regional organizations:** CEESA.

Curriculum/physical plant

Type: U.S. **Special programs:** ESL. **Special curricular:** art, computer instruction, music, soccer, swimming. **Location:** near U.S. Embassy. **Facilities:** 4 classrooms, computer lab, library and office space in local school, with use of gymnasium.

*Once only fee

UGANDA

Region: Africa
Size: 93,070 square miles
Population: 20,158,176
Capital: Kampala
Telephone code: 256
Currency: shilling
Languages: English, Luganda, Swahili

KAMPALA

Kabira International School

Street address: Old Kira Road, Bukoto, Kampala, Uganda
Phone: (256)(41)530472 **Facsimile:** (256)(41)533752
E-mail: gbell@imul.com
Mail: Box 2020, Kampala, Uganda
Headmistress: Margaret Bell
Teaching staff: full-time, 20; part-time, 4; total, 24
Nationalities of teaching staff: U.S., 1; U.K., 9; host, 9; other, 5; total, 24
Grade levels: preK – 7
Enrollment: preK, 42; K, 40; 1 – 7, 118; total, 200
Nationalities of student body: U.S., 11; U.K., 80; host, 31; other, 78; total, 200
Capacity: preK, 42; K, 40; 1 – 7, 130; total, 212
Teacher/student ratio: 1/8
Tuition (annual): preK, 1,200**; K, 1,800; 1 – 7, 3,000
Other fees: registration*, 50,000†; lunch, 90,000; uniform, 50,000
School year: September to July

Year founded: 1993. **Type of school:** coed, day, proprietary. **Governed by:** three appointed directors, two elected directors, and one co-opted.

Curriculum/physical plant

Type: U.K. **Languages taught:** French. **Staff specialists:** music, physical education. **Special programs:** ESL, special education. **Special curricular:** art, chorus, physical education, computer instruction, outdoor education, personal and social education. **Extracurricular:** drama, gymnastics, dance, choral and instrumental music, computers, excursions/expeditions, field trips. **Sports:** athletics, basketball, dance, gymnastics, soccer, swimming, tennis, sailing. **Tests:** National Curriculum Tests, Common Entrance Exam on request. **Location:** wooded site on outskirts of Kampala. **Campus:** 2 acres. **Library:** 7,500 volumes. **Facilities:** 5 buildings, 12 classrooms, auditorium, cafeteria, covered play area, tennis court, swimming pool, 10 computers, library, adventure playground, small animal farm.

*Once only fee **Pound sterling †Uganda Shilling

Lincoln International School of Uganda

Street address: 41 Kira Road Close, Kampala, Uganda
Phone: (256)(41)254900 **Facsimile:** (256)(41)233121
E-mail: lincoln@starcom.co.ug
Mail: PO Box 4200, Kampala, Uganda
U.S. mail: c/o U.S. Embassy (Kampala, Uganda), Dept. of State, Washington, DC 20521-2190
Director: Ralph Hollis
Principal, secondary/college guidance: Joanne Hickey
Principal, elementary: Patricia Salleh Matta
Teaching staff: full-time, 36; total, 36
Nationalities of teaching staff: U.S., 14; U.K., 14; host, 3; other, 5; total, 36
Grade levels: preK – 12
Enrollment: preK, 37; K, 22; 1 – 6, 185; 7 – 9, 86; 10 – 12, 50; total, 380
Nationalities of student body: U.S., 75; U.K., 70; host, 15; other, 220; total, 380
Capacity: preK, 45; K, 30; 1 – 6, 150; 7 – 12, 125; total, 350
Teacher/student ratio: 1/10
Tuition (annual): preK, $2,850; K, $6,000; 1 – 5, $7,000; 6 – 10, $8,160; 11 – 12, $10,120
Other fees (annual): registration, $500; capital levy, $1,500/1st and 2nd years; $750/3rd year
School year: August to June

Year founded: 1966. **Type of school:** coed, day, private nonprofit. **Governed by:** elected board of management. **Accredited by:** Middle States, ECIS. **Regional organizations:** AAIE, ECIS, AISA.

Curriculum/physical plant

Type: U.S., U.K., IB. **Languages taught:** French. **Staff specialists:** reading, math, computer, art, music, physical education, history, geography, science, drama, local cultural studies. **Special curricular:** physical education, computer instruction, arts and crafts, music, lifeskills, community service. **Extracurricular:** drama, choral music, yearbook, field trips. **Sports:** basketball, soccer, softball, swimming, table tennis, volleyball, martial arts. **Clubs:** student council, wildlife, camping, guitar, weaving, pottery, silk-screen, dance, leather work. **Tests:** PSAT, SAT, IB, IGCSE (optional), Iowa. **Location:** in quiet, pleasant rural setting, 1 kilometer from Kampala city center. **Campus:** 35 acres. **Library:** 9,000 volumes. **Facilities:** 5 connected buildings, 23 classrooms, 2 playing fields, 2 science labs, computer lab, covered play area and multipurpose hall, tarmac basketball court, use of swimming pool.

UKRAINE

Region: Eastern Europe
Size: 233,100 square miles
Population: 50,864,009
Capital: Kiev
Telephone code: 380
Currency: Hryvna
Languages: Ukrainian, Russian

KIEV

Kiev International School

Phone/facsimile: (380)(44)2164313 **E-mail:** kis@sovam.com
U.S. mail: c/o American Embassy, Kiev, Dept. of State, Washington, DC 20521-5850
Director: Michael Tewalthomas
Director of instruction: Vernon John Zatwarnicki
Teaching staff: full-time, 16; part-time, 9; total, 25
Nationalities of teaching staff: U.S., 13; other, 12; total, 25
Grade levels: N – 12
Enrollment: N, 6; K, 19; 1 – 6, 82; 7 – 9, 28; 10 – 12, 8; total, 143
Teacher/student ratio: 1/6
Tuition (annual): N, $3,600; K – 5, $6,900; 6 – 12, $9,200
Other fees: registration*, $100; capital levy, $4,000 deposit or $1,600/yr fee
School year: September to June

Year founded: 1992. **Type of school:** coed, day, private nonprofit. **Governed by:** appointed board of directors. **Operated by:** Quality Schools International. **Regional organizations:** CEESA.

Curriculum/physical plant

Type: U.S. **Languages taught:** Ukrainian, Russian, Hindi, Dutch. **Special programs:** ESL. **Special curricular:** art, physical education, computer instruction, music. **Extracurricular:** drama, music, swimming, excursions. **Location:** building adjoining American Embassy. **Facilities:** 4-story building, 14 classrooms, library, computer center, use of gymnasium, cafeteria, and swimming pool.

*Once only fee

UNITED ARAB EMIRATES

Region: Middle East
Size: 32,228 square miles
Population: 3,057,337
Capital: Abu Dhabi
Telephone code: 971
Currency: dirham
Languages: Arabic, Persian, English, Hindi

ABU DHABI

AL AIN ENGLISH SPEAKING SCHOOL

Phone: (971)(3)678636 **Facsimile:** (971)(3)671973
Mail: PO Box 1419, Abu Dhabi, U.A.E.
Principal: James G. Crawford
Assistant principal: Sarah J. Brannon
Teaching staff: full-time, 33; total, 33
Nationalities of teaching staff: U.K., 28; other, 5; total, 33
Grade levels: N – 10
Enrollment: N, 23; reception – 2, 104; 3 – 10, 156; total, 283
Nationalities of student body: U.S., 55; U.K., 102; other, 126; total, 283
Teacher/student ratio: 1/9
Tuition: N, 10,000**; reception – 2, 13,320; 3, 13,800; 4, 14,370; 5, 14,840; 6, 15,280; 7 – 10, 15,750
School year: September to June

Year founded: 1978. **Type of school:** coed, day, private. **Governed by:** board of trustees. **Sponsored by:** D. Balfour & Sons. **Accredited by:** U.A.E. Ministry of Education.

Curriculum/physical plant

Type: U.K. **Languages taught:** French, Arabic. **Special programs:** ESL, remedial. **Extracurricular:** gymnastics, choral and instrumental music, computers, newspaper. **Sports:** athletics, football, netball, rugby, rounders. **Tests:** SAT, IGCSE, British Common Entrance Exams, Standardized Tests of Achievement. **Facilities:** 11 buildings, 5 covered play areas, science room, IT lab, air conditioning.

**U.A.E. dirham

Al-Worood School

Location: New Airport Road, facing Municipality Garage, Abu Dhabi, U.A.E.
Phone: (971)(2)447655/448990/448855 **Facsimile:** (971)(2)449732
E-mail: alworood@emirates.net.ae
Mail: PO Box 46673, Abu Dhabi, United Arab Emirates
Principal/Business manager: N. Abed
Teaching staff: full-time, 75; total, 75
Nationalities of teaching staff: U.S., 3; U.K., 8; other, 64; total, 75
Grade levels: K – 12
Enrollment: K, 134; 1 – 6, 512; 7 – 9, 202; 10 – 12, 104; total, 952
Nationalities of student body: U.S., 21; U.K., 22; host, 378; other, 531; total, 952
Capacity: total, 1,100
Teacher/student ratio: 1/13
Tuition (annual): K, $2,800; 1 – 6, $3,270; 7 – 9, $3,900; 10 – 12, $5,250
Other fees (annual): registration*, $136; busing, $650; books, $400 – 1,200; uniform, $80
School year: September to June

Year founded: 1982. **Type of school:** coed, day, proprietary. **Accredited by:** MSA, CITA, U.A.E. Ministry of Education. **Regional organizations:** ECIS, NESA.

Curriculum/physical plant

Type: international. **Languages taught:** French, Arabic. **Staff specialists:** reading, math, computer, counselor, nurse, doctor. **Special curricular:** art, chorus, band, physical education, computer instruction. **Extracurricular:** drama, dance, choral and instrumental music, computers, yearbook, newspaper, excursions/expeditions, field trips. **Sports:** basketball, soccer, table tennis, karate. **Clubs:** chess, debating, environmental, scouts. **Tests:** SAT, TOEFL, A-level GCE, IGCSE, GCE AS-level. **Graduates attending college:** 100%. **Graduates have attended:** McGill U., U. of London, U. of Manchester, Florida Institute of Technology, American U. of Beirut. **Location:** in suburban area, 15 minutes from city center. **Facilities:** 1 building, 70 classrooms, cafeteria, infirmary, 2 covered play areas, 3 science labs, 2 computer labs, gymnasium/auditorium, 2 art rooms, music room, junior science room, TV room, CCTV (K – grade 1), basketball court, air conditioning.

*Once only fee

American Community School of Abu Dhabi

Phone: (971)(2)661461/666385/660938 **Facsimile:** (971)(2)653234
E-mail: acstth@emirates.net.ae **Web:** http://www.acs-abudhabi.com
Mail: PO Box 42114, Abu Dhabi, U.A.E.
Superintendent: Tim Hansen, Ph.D.
High school principal: John Hackworth
Middle school principal: Timothy Ilse
Elementary principal: Dixie Stanton
Librarian: Carolyn Hackworth
Teaching staff: full-time, 55; part-time, 4; total, 59
Nationalities of teaching staff: U.S., 49; U.K., 2; other, 8; total, 59
Grade levels: preK – 12

Enrollment: preK, 27; K, 37; 1 – 5, 214; 6 – 8, 145; 9 – 12, 162; total, 585
Nationalities of student body: U.S., 228; U.K., 42; host, 29; other, 286; total, 585
Capacity: preK, 28; K, 40; 1 – 6, 292; 7 – 12, 253; total, 613
Teacher/student ratio: 1/11
Tuition (annual): K, $3,950; 1 – 5, $6,525; 6 – 8, $7,098; 9 – 12, $8,957
Other fees: capital levy*, $408; admission, $681
School year: September to June

Year founded: 1971. **Type of school:** coed, day, private nonprofit. **Governed by:** elected board of trustees. **Sponsored by:** U.A.E. Ministry of Education. **Accredited by:** Middle States. **Regional organizations:** NESA.

Curriculum/physical plant

Type: U.S. **Languages taught:** French, Spanish, Arabic. **Staff specialists:** computer, counselor, learning disabilities, art, ESL, music, physical education. **Special programs:** ESL, K – 6 learning disabilities. **Special curricular:** art, chorus, physical education, computer instruction, Model UN. **Extracurricular:** drama, choral music, computers, yearbook, newspaper, photography, excursions/expeditions, field trips, math league, fine arts festival, academic games. **Sports:** badminton, basketball, soccer, softball, swimming, tennis, volleyball. **Clubs:** computer, Boy Scouts, Girl Scouts, art, Arabic, service. **Tests:** SSAT, PSAT, SAT, Iowa, COGAT. **Graduates attending college:** 95%. **Graduates have attended:** U. of Texas at Austin, Tufts, Brown, Duke, Stanford. **Location:** within city. **Library:** 21,000 volumes. **Facilities:** 1 building (6 sections), 48 classrooms, cafeteria, gymnasium, playing field, swimming pool, covered play areas, tennis courts, science labs, computer rooms, media center, multipurpose room, fitness center, air conditioning.

*Once only fee

American International School in Abu Dhabi

Street address: 29th Street and Airport Road, Abu Dhabi, U.A.E.
Phone: (971)(2)444333 **Facsimile:** (971)(2)444005
E-mail: aisa@emirates.net.ae
Mail: PO Box 5992, Abu Dhabi, United Arab Emirates
Superintendent: Walid Abushakra
High school principal: Peter McMurray
Elementary school principal: Dr. Kimberly Ellis
Director of guidance/IB coordinator: Kevin Black
Teaching staff: full-time, 65; total, 65
Nationalities of teaching staff: U.S., 43; U.K., 2; other, 20; total, 65
Grade levels: preK – 12
Enrollment: preK, 57; 1 – 6, 322; 7 – 12, 334; total, 718
Teacher/student ratio: 1/11
Tuition (annual): preK – K2, $4,000; 1 – 4, $5,000; 5 – 12, $6,000
Other fees (annual): busing, $734
School year: September to June

Year founded: 1995. **Type of school:** coed. **Accredited by:** U.A.E. Ministry of Education, Middle States (in process).

Curriculum/physical plant

Type: U.S., U.K. (5 – 12 segregated), international, IB, IGSCE. **Languages taught:** French, Arabic. **Staff specialists:** computer, counselor, art, ESL, librarian, music, physical education, media center. **Special programs:** ESL, Islamic studies in English. **Special curricular:** chorus, school magazine, yearbook, math competition, field trips. **Extracurricular:** after-school program includes athletics, drama, academic club, French club, Arabic club, literary publications. **Facilities:** fully air conditioned purpose-built building, 80 classrooms, auditorium, gymnasium, 3 science labs, computer lab, library, outdoor playing courts.

The International School of Choueifat

Location: Mohammed Bin Khalifa Street, Abu Dhabi, U.A.E.
Phone: (971)(2)461444 **Facsimile:** (971)(2)461048
E-mail: iscadl@emirates.net.ae
Web: http://www.sabis.com/school-network/
Mail: PO Box 7212, Abu Dhabi, United Arab Emirates
Regional director: R. Germanos
Teaching staff: full-time, 137; total, 137
Nationalities of teaching staff: U.S., 1; U.K., 47; other, 89; total, 137
Grade levels: K – 13
Enrollment: KI, 96; KII, 157; 1 – 6, 1,103; 7 – 9, 645; 10 – 12, 451; 13, 38; total, 2,490
Nationalities of student body: U.S., 97; U.K., 225; host, 275; other, 1,893; total, 2,490
Capacity: KI, 100; KII, 175; 1 – 6, 1,152; 7 – 9, 648; 10 – 12, 540; 13, 50; total, 2,665
Tuition (annual): KI – KII, 12,300 – 13,000**; 1 – 6, 13,300 – 15,700; 7 – 9, 16,700 – 18,300; 10 – 13, 19,100 – 21,500
Other fees (annual): busing, 3,850**; lunch, 4,600; books, 500 – 1,300
School year: September to June

Year founded: 1978. **Type of school:** coed, day.

Curriculum/physical plant

Type: U.S., U.K., AP. **Languages taught:** English, French, Arabic (for native speakers). **Special programs:** honors sections, independent study. **Special curricular:** art, chorus, physical education, computer instruction. **Extracurricular:** drama, gymnastics, dance, choral music, computers, excursions/expeditions. **Sports:** badminton, basketball, cricket, football, hockey, netball, squash, tennis, volleyball. **Clubs:** drama, swimming, orchestra, gymnastics, art, trampoline, academic clubs. **Tests:** SAT, AP, A-level GCE, GCSE, IGCSE, O-level GCE. **Graduates attending college:** 100%. **Graduates have attended:** MIT, Princeton, U. of Pennsylvania, Harvard, Cornell. **Location:** purpose-built campus within city of Abu Dhabi. **Facilities:** 12 buildings, 80 classrooms, 2 cafeterias, 6 covered play areas, 3 tennis courts, gymnasium, 3 playing fields, 4 science labs, 3 computer labs, air conditioning.

**U.A.E. dirham

DUBAI

THE AMERICAN SCHOOL OF DUBAI

Phone: (971)(4)440824 **Facsimile:** (971)(4)441510
E-mail: asdadmin@emirates.net.ae **Web:** http://www.asdubai.org
Mail: PO Box 2222, Dubai, U.A.E.
Headmaster: Roger G. Hove
Principal, 9 – 12: James R. Fellabaum, Ed.D.
Principal, 6 – 8: Greg L. Von Spreecken
Principal, K – 5: Bruce W. McWilliams
Teaching staff: full-time, 65; part-time, 14; total, 79
Nationalities of teaching staff: U.S., 65; other, 14; total, 79
Grade levels: preK – 12
Enrollment: preK, 52; K, 59; 1 – 5, 344; 6 – 8, 196; 9 – 12, 195; total, 846
Nationalities of student body: U.S., 489; U.K., 22; host, 1; other, 334; total, 846
Capacity: preK, 52; K, 60; 1 – 5, 348; 6 – 8, 216; 9 – 12, 244; total, 920
Teacher/student ratio: 1/11
Tuition (annual): preK, $2,436; K, $6,844; 1 – 12, $10,272
Other fees (annual): registration*, $68; books, $27 (deposit); seat rental, $1,525 – 3,050
School year: August to June

Year founded: 1966. **Type of school:** coed, day, private nonprofit. **Governed by:** board of trustees. **Accredited by:** Middle States. **Regional organizations:** NESA.

Curriculum

Type: U.S., AP. **Languages taught:** French, Spanish. **Staff specialists:** reading, math, computer, counselor, learning disabilities. **Special programs:** ESL, remedial. **Special curricular:** art, chorus, physical education, computer instruction, instrumental music. **Extracurricular:** drama, gymnastics, choral music, computers, yearbook, literary magazine, excursions/expeditions, field trips, band, Model UN. **Sports:** badminton, basketball, cross-country, dance, soccer, softball, swimming, tennis, track and field, volleyball, T-ball, roller skating. **Organizations:** National Junior Honor Society, National Honor Society, ASPA (parents' organization). **Tests:** SSAT, SAT, ACT, TOEFL, Stanford, PLAN/PSAT, ACH, Otis-Lennon. **Graduates attending college:** 92%.

Physical plant

Location: in suburban area, 15 minutes from Dubai. **Campus:** 8 acres. **Library:** 34,500 volumes. **Facilities:** 3 buildings, 55 classrooms, cafeteria, 2 tennis courts, 2 gymnasiums, 2 playing fields, 4 science labs, 4 computer labs, swimming pool, small auditorium, first-aid station, drama room, 2 art rooms, journalism room, video production room, fitness center, elementary playground; air conditioning throughout.

*Once only fee

Emirates International School

Street address: Al Wasl Road, Dubai, U.A.E.
Phone: (971)(4)489804 **Facsimile:** (971)(4)482813
Mail: PO Box 6446, Dubai, U.A.E.
Headmaster: R. Martin Kenney
Principal/senior school: Sig Jensen
Principal/junior school: Anna Kizirian
Teaching staff: full-time, 114; total, 114
Nationalities of teaching staff: U.S., 10; U.K., 38; host, 1; other, 65; total, 114
Grade levels: K – 12
Enrollment: K, 228; 1 – 5, 642; 6 – 12, 615; total, 1,485
Teacher/student ratio: 1/13
Tuition (annual): K, 11,500**; 1 – 12, 12,500 – 28,500
School year: September through June

Year founded: 1991. **Type of school:** coed, day, private. **Regional organizations:** ECIS, NESA, MEIBA, BSME, ISCP.

Curriculum/physical plant

Type: IB, IGCSE. **Languages taught:** French, Arabic. **Staff specialists:** nurse, ESL, physician, special needs, all subjects. **Special curricular:** art, physical education, computer instruction, music. **Extracurricular:** drama, gymnastics, dance, choral and instrumental music, yearbook, excursions/expeditions, field trips, sports. **Location:** in suburban area, 20 kilometers from center of Dubai, 5 kilometers from Jumairah. **Campus:** 10 acres. **Facilities:** 6 buildings, 83 classrooms, 2 auditoriums, infirmary, 7 science labs, library/media center, covered/open play area, theater, sports hall, dining hall, specialist art/craft/CDT workshops, music rooms, swimming pool, air conditioning.

**U.A.E. dirham

Jumeirah English Speaking School

Phone: (971)(4)381515 **Facsimile:** (971)(4)381531
Mail: PO Box 24942, Jumeirah, Dubai, U.A.E.
Headmaster: C. A. Branson
Teaching staff: full-time, 40; part-time, 12; total, 52
Nationalities of teaching staff: U.K., 46; other, 6; total, 52
Grade levels: K – 6
Enrollment: K, 84; 1 – 6, 504; total, 588
Nationalities of student body: U.K., 520; host, 2; other, 66; total, 588
Teacher/student ratio: 1/12
Tuition (annual): 17,100**
Other fees: entrance/registration/capital levy* (refundable), 10,350**
School year: September to June

Year founded: 1975. **Type of school:** coed, day, private nonprofit. **Governed by:** board of governors. **Accredited by:** HMI (U.K.). **Member of:** Incorporated Association of Preparatory Schools. **Regional organizations:** ECIS.

Curriculum/physical plant

Type: U.K. **Languages taught:** French, Arabic. **Staff specialists:** nurse, librarian, music, physical education, dance, languages, language support. **Special programs:** remedial. **Special curricular:** orchestra, choir, computers. **Extracurricular:** drama, gymnastics, dance, choral and instrumental music, computers, newspaper, excursions/expeditions, field trips, pottery, chess. **Sports:** athletics, cricket, football, gymnastics, netball, swimming, tennis, mini-rugby, rounders. **Tests:** Key Stage 1 and 2 SAT's. **Location:** 10 kilometers from Dubai City. **Library:** 6,000 volumes. **Facilities:** 29 classrooms, tennis court, gymnasium, 2 playing fields, swimming pool, music room, activity room, air conditioning.

*Once only fee **U.A.E. dirham

SHARJAH

International School of Choueifat

Phone: (971)(6)582211 **Facsimile:** (971)(6)582865
E-mail: iscshj@emirates.net.ae
Mail: PO Box 2077, Sharjah, U.A.E.
Deputy director: J. Hazbun
Business director: E. Sawaya
Teaching staff: full-time, 80; total, 80
Nationalities of teaching staff: U.S., 2; U.K., 21; other, 57; total, 80
Grade levels: N – 13, EFL department
Enrollment: N – preK, 72; K, 123; 1 – 6, 711; 7 – 9, 410; 10 – 12, 298; 13, 27; EFL, 27; total, 1,668
Nationalities of student body: U.S., 64; U.K., 82; host, 300; other, 1,222; total, 1,668
Teacher/student ratio: 1/19
Tuition (annual): N – K, 12,000**; 1 – 6, 12,300 – 14,500; 7 – 9, 15,500 – 17,100; 10 – 12, 18,100 – 19,400; 13, 20,400
Other fees (annual): busing, 2,000 – 3,000**; lunch, 4,200; books, 200 – 1,000
School year: September to June†

Year founded: 1886. **Type of school:** coed, day. **Governed by:** Sabis Foundation. **Accredited by:** London University/IBO/Cambridge, College Board (AP).

Curriculum

Type: U.K., IB. **Languages taught:** English, French, Arabic. **Staff specialists:** reading, math, computer, counselor, nurse. **Special programs:** ESL. **Special curricular:** art, band, physical education, computer instruction, vocational, choirs. **Extracurricular:** gymnastics, dance, choral and instrumental music, computers, photography, excursions/expeditions, field trips, pottery. **Sports:** badminton, basketball, cricket, hockey, netball, soccer, squash, swimming, table tennis. **Clubs:** chess, computer, student council, video, aerobics, gymnastics, trampoline, photography, music, art, business. **Tests:** SAT, TOEFL, IB, LAPs, AP, GCSE, IGCSE, ACH, A-, AS- and O-levels, STEP. **Graduates attending college:** 99%. **Graduates have attended:** MIT, Princeton, Cambridge, London School of Economics, Oxford.

Physical plant

Location: in suburbs, 3 miles from center of Sharjah. **Campus:** 76 acres. **Library:** 12,000 volumes. **Facilities:** 21 buildings, 60 classrooms, auditorium, cafeteria, infirmary, tennis court, gymnasium, 3 science labs, 2 computer labs, swimming pool, covered play areas, AV equipment, squash court, cricket pitch, air conditioning.

**U.A.E. dirham †summer school: July to mid-August

ABU DHABI

Al Sanawbar School

Phone: (971)(3)679889 **Facsimile:** (971)(3)679885
Mail: PO Box 1781, Al Ain, U.A.E.

UNITED KINGDOM

Region: Europe
Size: 94,251 square miles
Population: 58,489,975
Capital: London
Telephone code: 44
Currency: pound
Languages: English, Welsh, Scottish, Gaelic

ENGLAND/LONDON

THE AMERICAN SCHOOL IN LONDON

Street address: 2-8 Loudoun Road, London NW8 0NP, England
Phone: (44)(171)4491200 **Facsimile:** (44)(171)4491350
E-mail: admissions@asl.org **Web:** http://www.asl.org
Head of school: Judith R. Glickman, Ph.D.
High school principal: Mimi Flood
Middle school principal: Veronica McCaffrey
Lower school principal: Julie Ryan
Head of library: Joan Dyer-Westacott
Teaching staff: full-time, 138; part-time, 8; total, 146
Nationalities of teaching staff: U.S., 116; U.K., 23; other, 7; total, 146
Grade levels: preK – 12 (grade 13 available)
Enrollment: preK, 35; K, 60; 1 – 5, 415; 6 – 8, 306; 9 – 12, 452; total, 1,268
Nationalities of student body: U.S., 915; U.K., 59; other, 294; total, 1,268
Capacity: preK, 40; K, 60; 1 – 5, 420; 6 – 8, 320; 9 – 12, 460; total, 1,300
Teacher/student ratio: 1/9
Tuition (annual): preK – 3, 9,400**; 4 – 5, 9,600; 6 – 8, 10,850; 9 – 13, 11,100
Other fees (annual): registration*, 75**; busing, at cost; lunch, at cost; tuition deposit, 500
School year: September to June

Year founded: 1951. **Type of school:** coed, day, independent nonprofit. **Governed by:** The American School in London Educational Trust Ltd. **Accredited by:** Middle States, ECIS. **Regional organizations:** AAIE, ECIS.

Curriculum

Type: U.S., AP. **Languages taught:** French, Spanish, German. **Staff specialists:** reading, math, computer, speech/hearing, counselor, psychologist, learning disabilities, nurse, language pathologist. **Special programs:** independent study, lower and middle school ESL, learning disabilities, senior apprenticeships. **Special curricular:** art, chorus, band, physical education, computer instruction, drama, strings, photography, yearbook, newspaper, excursions/expeditions. **Extracurricular:** drama, gymnastics, dance, choral and instrumental music, computers, literary magazine, Model UN, student council, ISTA. **Sports:** baseball, basketball, cross-country, field hockey, gymnastics, rugby, soccer, softball, swimming, tennis, track and field, volleyball, wrestling. **Clubs:** computer, juggling, Amnesty International, film, theater, debate, fencing, weight training, table tennis, hiking. **Tests:** PSAT, SAT, ACT, AP, Stanford, Iowa, ERB. **Graduates attending college:** 98%. **Graduates have attended:** Columbia U., Brown, Stanford, Georgetown, Oxford.

Physical plant

Location: in pleasant residential area of central London. **Campus:** 3.5 acres. **Library:** 50,000 volumes. **Facilities:** 1 building, 80 classrooms, auditorium, cafeteria, infirmary, 3 tennis courts, 2 gymnasiums, 8 science labs, 7 computer labs, 5 music rooms, 5 art studios, AV equipment, 21-acre playing fields nearby.

*Once only fee **Pound sterling

International Community School

Street address: 4 York Terrace East, London NW1 4PT, England
Phone: (44)(171)9351206 **Facsimile:** (44)(171)9357915
Principal: Philip Hurd
Teaching staff: full-time, 13; part-time, 6; total, 19
Nationalities of teaching staff: U.S., 1; U.K., 16; other, 2; total, 19
Grade levels: K – 13
Enrollment: K, 8; 1 – 6, 32; 7 – 9, 75; 10 – 12, 20; 13, 5; total, 140
Nationalities of student body: U.S., 2; U.K., 21; other, 117; total, 140
Teacher/student ratio: 1/9
Tuition (annual): $8,680
Other fees: registration*, $115; busing, $100/week
School year: September to June (also vacation courses)

Year founded: 1979. **Type of school:** coed, day, private nonprofit, some boarding with host families. **Governed by:** N. P. Toettcher. **Accredited by:** British Council.

Curriculum/physical plant

Type: U.K. **Languages taught:** English, French, Spanish, German, Italian, Russian, Arabic. **Staff specialists:** reading, math, computer, special needs. **Special programs:** ESL, independent study. **Special curricular:** art, physical education. **Extracurricular:** drama, dance, computers, yearbook. **Sports:** aerobics, badminton, basketball, football, swimming, tennis, volleyball. **Clubs:** Model UN, after-school Discover London. **Tests:** A-level GCE, GCSE, Cambridge First Certificate. **Location:** in central London, on outskirts of Regents Park. **Libraries (2):** 20,000 volumes. **Facilities:** 2 buildings, 30 classrooms, cafeteria, gymnasium, 3 science labs, 2 computer labs.

*Once only fee

International School of London

Street address: 139 Gunnersbury Avenue, London W3 8LG, England
Phone: (44)(181)9925823 **Facsimile:** (44)(181)9937012
E-mail: 101635.175@compuserve.com
Headmaster: R. Hermon
Business manager: S. Costandi
Teaching staff: full-time, 20; part-time, 21; total, 41
Nationalities of teaching staff: U.K., 12; other, 29; total, 41
Grade levels: reception – 13
Enrollment: total, 200
Nationalities of student body: U.K., 25; other, 175; total, 200
Tuition, (annual 1996 - 97 figures): R – 6, 5,550**; forms 1 – 5, 7,200 – 8,370;

form 6, 8,760
Other fees (annual 1996 - 97 figures): busing, 1,170**; lunch, 600; application*, 50**; school development*, 500; refundable deposit*, 500
School year: September through June

Year founded: 1972. **Type of school:** coed. **Accredited by:** ECIS. **Regional organizations:** London International Schools Association.

Curriculum/physical plant

Type: U.K., IB. **Languages taught:** English, French, Spanish, German, Dutch, Italian, Arabic, Japanese, Danish, Korean, Mandarin, Turkish, Finnish, any other on request. **Staff specialists:** math. **Special programs:** ESL. **Special curricular:** art, chorus, physical education, computer instruction. **Extracurricular:** drama, dance, computers, yearbook, photography, excursions/expeditions, ballet. **Sports:** basketball, soccer, swimming, volleyball, karate. **Tests:** IB, GCSE, IGCSE. **Graduates attending college:** 100%. **Location:** in city. **Facilities:** 2 buildings, 30 classrooms, cafeteria, gymnasium, science lab, computer lab, library.

*Once only fee **Pound sterling

Southbank International School

Street address: 36/38 Kensington Park Road, London W11 3BU, England
Phone: (44)(171)2298230 **Facsimile:** (44)(171)2293784
Headmaster: Milton E. Toubkin
High school coordinator: Nigel Hughes
Teaching staff: full-time, 21; part-time, 56; total, 77
Nationalities of teaching staff: U.S., 13; U.K., 28; other, 36; total, 77
Grade levels: early childhood education – 12
Enrollment: ECE – 5, 46; 6 – 9, 67; 10 – 12, 130; total, 243
Nationalities of student body: U.S., 37; U.K., 31; other, 175; total, 243
Teacher/student ratio: 1/5
Tuition (annual): ECE – 5, 7,680**; 6 – 8, 8,340; 9 – 10, 9,030; 11 – 12, 9,480
Other fees: registration*, 50**; capital levy*, 500
School year: September to June

Year founded: 1979. **Type of school:** coed, day, private nonprofit. **Governed by:** board of directors. **Accredited by:** ISJC. **Regional organizations:** ECIS.

Curriculum/physical plant

Type: U.S., IB. **Languages taught:** French, Spanish, German, Italian, Japanese, Swedish, plus 12 others on request. **Special programs:** ESL. **Special curricular:** art, physical education, computer instruction, drama, music. **Extracurricular:** drama, dance, instrumental music, computers, yearbook, newspaper, photography, excursions/expeditions, field trips, Model UN, ISTA. **Sports:** basketball, soccer, swimming, tennis, volleyball, ice skating. **Tests:** PSAT, SAT, ACT, TOEFL, IB. **Graduates attending college:** 97%. **Graduates have attended:** London, Oxford, Harvard, Columbia, MIT. **Location:** in central London, near Notting Hill Gate; new branch in Hampstead in North London. **Facilities:** 4 buildings, 32 classrooms, auditorium, 5 science labs, canteen, computer centers, music and art rooms.

*Once only fee **Pound sterling

HILLINGDON, MIDDLESEX

AMERICAN COMMUNITY SCHOOL

Street address: 108 Vine Lane, Hillingdon, Uxbridge, Middlesex UB10 OBE, England
Phone: (44)(1895)813734 **Facsimile:** (44)(1895)810634
E-mail: hmulkey@acs-england.co.uk
Headmaster: Paul Berg
Middle school principal: Alex Hendry
Lower school principal: Tony Pearson
Teaching staff: full-time, 73; part-time, 2; total, 75
Grade levels: preK – 13
Enrollment: preK – 4, 197; 5 – 8, 185; 9 – 13, 214; total, 596
Nationalities of student body: U.S., 285; other, 311; total, 596
Capacity: preK – 4, 236; 5 – 8, 156; 9 – 13, 224; total, 616
Teacher/student ratio: 1/8
Tuition (annual): preK, 4,980**; K – 4, 7,970; 5 – 8, 8,700; 9 – 13, 9,260
Other fees (annual): registration*, 75**; busing, 1,320; debenture subscription*, 500
School year: August to June

Year founded: 1967. **Type of school:** coed, day. **Governed by:** board of directors. **Accredited by:** New England, ISJC. **Regional organizations:** ECIS.

Curriculum

Type: U.S., IB. **Languages taught:** French, Spanish, German. **Staff specialists:** nurse, speech therapist (lower school), study skills (middle school), counselors (high school). **Special programs:** ESL. **Special curricular:** art, band, physical education, computer instruction, choir. **Extracurricular:** drama, gymnastics, instrumental music, computers, yearbook, newspaper, photography, excursions/expeditions, field trips, cheerleading. **Sports:** basketball, cross-country, rugby, soccer, softball, swimming, tennis, track and field, volleyball. **Clubs:** Boy Scouts, Girl Scouts, National Honor Society, student council, Model UN, art. **Tests:** PSAT, SAT, ACT, TOEFL, IB, ACH. **Graduates attending college:** 95%. **Graduates have attended:** Georgetown, Duke, Purdue, Harvard, Princeton.

Physical plant

Location: in suburbs, 15 miles northwest of London. **Campus:** 11 acres. **Libraries:** 22,600 volumes. **Facilities:** 4 buildings, 53 classrooms, cafeteria, infirmary, 2 tennis courts, 5 science labs, auditorium/gymnasium, playing fields, computer labs, art and music rooms.

*Once only fee **Pound sterling

COBHAM, SURREY

American Community School

Street address: "Heywood," Portsmouth Road, Cobham, Surrey KT11 1BL, England
Phone: (44)(1932)867251 **Facsimile:** (44)(1932)869790
Web: http://www.pncl.co.uk/am-com-schools
Headmaster: Thomas Lehman
High school principal: Paul MacKaill
Middle school principal: Ann Haynes
Lower school principal: Lacy Chapman
Teaching staff: full-time, 118; part-time, 16; total, 134
Nationalities of teaching staff: U.S., 76; U.K., 42; other, 16; total, 134
Grade levels: preK – 12 (grade 13 available)
Enrollment: preK, 87; K – 4, 402; 5 – 8, 374; 9 – 13, 425; total, 1,288
Nationalities of student body: U.S., 804; other, 484; total, 1,288
Teacher/student ratio: 1/10
Boarders: boys, 48; girls, 48 **Grades:** 7 – 13 **Program:** planned 5- & 7-day
Tuition (annual): scramblers, 3,400** (half day); preK, 3,650 (half day), 4,980 (full day); K – 4, 7,970; 5 – 8, 8,700; 9 – 13, 9,260
Tuition and board: 13,040 – 13,540** (5-day), 14,650 – 15,210 (7-day)
Other fees (annual): registration, 75**; busing, 1,320; debenture, 500
School year: August to June

Year founded: 1967. **Type of school:** coed, day, boarding, proprietary. **Governed by:** appointed board of directors. **Accredited by:** New England, ISJC. **Regional organizations:** ECIS.

Curriculum/physical plant

Type: U.S., IB. **Languages taught:** French, Spanish, German, (IB only: Danish, Japanese, Swedish, Norwegian, and others by demand). **Special curricular:** art, chorus, physical education, computer instruction. **Extracurricular:** drama, instrumental music, computers, yearbook, newspaper, photography, excursions/expeditions, field trips, community service. **Sports:** baseball, basketball, cross-country, rugby, soccer, softball, tennis, track and field, volleyball. **Clubs:** Boy Scouts, Girl Scouts, National Honor Society, student council, Model UN, public speaking, math competition teams. **Tests:** PSAT, SAT, IB, AP, ACH, ERB. **Graduates attending college:** 95%. **Graduates have attended:** U. of Pennsylvania, Duke, U. of California, Boston College. **Location:** 25 miles southwest of London. **Campus:** 128 acres. **Libraries:** 21,094 volumes. **Facilities:** 35 buildings, 83 classrooms, 2 auditoriums, cafeteria, infirmary, 7 tennis courts, gymnasium, 6 playing fields, 8 science labs, 4 computer labs, AV equipment, outdoor Olympic-standard track, 7-hole golf course, art and music rooms, purpose-built boarding facility.

**Pound sterling

EGHAM, SURREY

American Community School

Street address: "Woodlee," London Road (A30), Egham, Surrey TW20 OHS, England
Phone: (44)(1784)430800 **Facsimile:** (44)(1784)430153
Principal: Kay Alderdice
Chief accountant: R. P. Gossain
Teaching staff: full-time, 31; part-time, 6; total, 37
Nationalities of teaching staff: U.S., 27; U.K., 8; other, 2; total, 37
Grade levels: N – 8
Enrollment: N – preK, 51; K, 30; 1 – 6, 169; 7 – 8, 13; total, 263
Nationalities of student body: U.S., 201; other, 62; total, 263
Capacity: N – preK, 30; K, 30; 1 – 6, 150; 7 – 8, 30; total, 240
Teacher/student ratio: 1/7
Tuition (annual): N – preK, 5,318**; K – 4, 7,970; 5 – 8, 8,700
Other fees (annual): registration*, 75**; capital levy*, 500; busing, 1,250
School year: August to June

Year founded: 1995. **Type of school:** coed, day, proprietary. **Governed by:** appointed board of directors. **Regional organizations:** ECIS.

Curriculum/physical plant

Type: U.S. **Languages taught:** French, Spanish. **Staff specialists:** reading, math, computer, speech/hearing, counselor, learning disabilities, nurse, gifted. **Special programs:** ESL, remedial, gifted. **Special curricular:** art, physical education, computer instruction. **Extracurricular:** drama, instrumental music, computers, yearbook, field trips. **Sports:** baseball, basketball, cross-country, soccer, softball, tennis, volleyball. **Clubs:** Boy Scouts, Girl Scouts, student council. **Tests:** ERB. **Location:** in suburban area, 25 miles from London. **Campus:** 17 acres. **Facilities:** cafeteria, infirmary, 2 tennis courts, gymnasium, science lab, computer lab.

*Once only fee **Pound sterling

KINGSTON UPON THAMES, SURREY

Marymount International School

Street address: George Road, Kingston upon Thames, Surrey KT2 7PE, England
Phone: (44)(181)9490571 **Facsimile:** (44)(181)3362485
Principal: Sr. Rosaleen Sheridan, RSHM
Business manager: Mr. W. D. B. Lord
Teaching staff: full-time, 23; part-time, 6; total, 29
Nationalities of teaching staff: U.S., 5; U.K., 9; other, 15; total, 29
Grade levels: 6 – 12
Enrollment: total, 219

Nationalities of student body: U.S., 15; U.K., 25; other, 179; total, 219
Capacity: 6 – 9, 80; 10 – 12, 150; total, 230
Teacher/student ratio: 1/10
Boarders: girls, 119 **Grades:** 6 – 12 **Program:** planned 5- and 7-day
Tuition (annual): middle school, 7,700**; high school, 8,600
Other fees (annual): registration*, 100**; boarding: middle school, 13,700 – 13,900; high school, 13,900 – 14,800; busing, variable; books, 125; initial enrollment*, 500
School year: September to June

Year founded: 1955. **Type of school:** girls, day, boarding, church-related. **Governed by:** appointed board of trustees and board of regents. **Accredited by:** Middle States, ECIS, GSA.

Curriculum/physical plant

Type: U.S., IB. **Staff specialists:** computer, counselor, psychologist, nurse, learning resources specialist. **Special programs:** ESL. **Special curricular:** art, chorus, physical education, computer instruction. **Extracurricular:** drama, gymnastics, dance, instrumental music, yearbook, photography, excursions/expeditions, field trips, National Honor Society. **Tests:** PSAT, SAT, ACT, IB, AP. **Graduates attending college:** 98%. **Graduates have attended:** Cambridge, Oxford, Smith, Wellesley, Sophia U. in Japan. **Location:** in suburban area, 12 miles from central London. **Campus:** 7 acres. **Library:** 10,000 volumes. **Facilities:** 9 buildings, 27 classrooms, auditorium, cafeteria, infirmary, 2 tennis courts, gymnasium, playing field, 3 science labs, computer lab, AV equipment, art studio/music center, language lab, bedrooms, lounges, TV rooms, kitchenette.

*Once only fee **Pound sterling

THORPE, SURREY

TASIS England American School

Street address: Coldharbour Lane, Thorpe, Surrey TW20 8TE, England
Phone: (44)(1932)565252 **Facsimile:** (44)(1932)564644
E-mail: ukadmissions@tasis.com
Web: http://www.tasis.com/tasis/tasis-england.html
U.S. mail: 1640 Wisconsin Avenue, NW, Washington, DC 20007, U.S.A.
Headmaster: Lyle D. Rigg
Upper school head: Diana E. Dearth
Middle school head: Paul Geise
Lower school head: Deborah Cross
Teaching staff: full-time, 75; part-time, 25; total, 100
Nationalities of teaching staff: U.S., 69; U.K., 25; other, 6; total, 100
Grade levels: preK – 12
Enrollment: preK, 20; K, 30; 1 – 6, 230; 7 – 9, 170; 10 – 12, 250; total, 700
Nationalities of student body: U.S., 460; U.K., 35; other, 205; total, 700
Teacher/student ratio: 1/7
Tuition (annual): preK, 4,150**; K – 3, 8,100; 4 – 8, 8,850; 9 – 12, 9,500

Other fees (annual): registration, 50**; boarding, 5,500; capital levy*, 500; busing, 850; lunch, 330; books, 205; in-program travel, 750
School year: September to June

Year founded: 1976. **Type of school:** coed, day, boarding, proprietary. **Governed by:** appointed governing board. **Accredited by:** New England, ECIS. **Regional organizations:** ECIS.

Curriculum

Type: U.S., AP. **Languages taught:** French, Spanish, German, Latin. **Special programs:** ESL, honors sections, independent study, summer school. **Special curricular:** art, chorus, physical education, computer instruction, drama. **Extracurricular:** drama, dance, choral and instrumental music, computers, yearbook, newspaper, photography, excursions/expeditions, field trips, film, theater, community service, in-program European travel. **Sports:** aerobics, baseball, basketball, cheerleading, cross-country, rugby, soccer, softball, squash, tennis, volleyball, horseback riding. **Clubs:** chess, computer, Cub Scouts, Brownies, student council, Model UN, Webelos, Junior Girl Scouts, Cum Laude Society, International Club, parents' council. **Tests:** PSAT, SAT, ACT, TOEFL, AP, Stanford, ERB. **Graduates attending college:** 98%. **Graduates have attended:** Boston U., Dartmouth, Cornell, William and Mary, Northwestern.

Physical plant

Location: a Georgian country estate in the Surrey countryside near Windsor, 18 miles southwest of London. **Campus:** 35 acres. **Library:** 15,000 volumes. **Facilities:** 10 buildings, 50 classrooms, infirmary, 4 tennis courts, gymnasium, 4 playing fields, 6 science labs, 2 computer labs, 2 dining rooms, AV equipment, study hall, art and music rooms, theater, snack bar, lounge, 12 supervised residential cottages/dormitories.

*Once only fee **Pound sterling

SCOTLAND/ABERDEEN

International School of Aberdeen Educational Trust Ltd.†

Street address: Fairgirth, 296 North Deeside Road, Milltimber, Aberdeen AB13 OAB, Scotland
Phone: (44)(1224)732267 **Facsimile:** (44)(1224)734879
E-mail: admin@isa.abdn.sch.uk **Web:** http://www.isa.abdn.sch.uk
Director: John D. Osbo
Business manager: Cyria Scott
Teaching staff: full-time, 34; part-time, 7; total, 41
Nationalities of teaching staff: U.S., 14; U.K., 24; other, 3; total, 41
Grade levels: preK – 12
Enrollment: preK, 29; K, 22; 1 – 6, 152; 7 – 9, 60; 10 – 12, 35; total, 298
Nationalities of student body: U.S., 230; other, 68; total, 298
Teacher/student ratio: 1/7
Tuition (annual): K – 6, 8,650**; 7 – 12, 9,300
School year: August to June

Year founded: 1972. **Type of school:** coed, day, company-sponsored. **Governed by:** elected and appointed board of directors. **Sponsored by:** oil/service companies. **Accredited by:** Middle States, ECIS. **Regional organizations:** AAIE, ECIS.

Curriculum/physical plant

Type: U.S., IB, AP. **Staff specialists:** reading, math, counselor, resource. **Special programs:** honors sections, independent study. **Special curricular:** art, physical education, computer instruction, drama, school musical. **Extracurricular:** drama, gymnastics, instrumental music, computers, yearbook, newspaper, photography, excursions/expeditions, field trips. **Sports:** basketball, soccer, volleyball. **Clubs:** Model UN, AV/disco, Helping Hands. **Graduates attending college:** 85%. **Graduates have attended:** Texas A&M, U. of Texas, Rice, Oklahoma State, U. of Washington. **Location:** in rural setting, 5 miles west of Aberdeen. **Library:** 25,000 volumes. **Facilities:** gymnasium, playing field, 3 science labs, 2 computer labs.

**Pound sterling †formerly American School in Aberdeen Educational Trust Ltd.

EDINBURGH

Edinburgh Tutorial College†

Street address: 29 Chester Street, Edinburgh EH3 7EN, Scotland
Phone: (44)(131)2259888 **Facsimile:** (44)(131)2252133
E-mail: 100667.3226@compuserve.com
Principal: A. W. Morris
Teaching staff: full-time, 5; part-time, 15; total, 20
Nationalities of teaching staff: U.K., 20; total, 20
Grade levels: 10 – 12

Enrollment: 10, 10; 11, 10; 12, 10; total, 30
Nationalities of student body: U.K., 20; other, 10; total, 30
Teacher/student ratio: 1/3
Boarders: boys, 5; girls, 5 **Grades:** 10 – 12 **Program:** planned 5- and 7-day
Tuition (annual): 5,000**
Other fees (annual): boarding, 3,000**
School year: September to June

Year founded: 1976. **Type of school:** coed, day, boarding. **Accredited by:** Scottish Education Department.

Curriculum/physical plant

Type: U.S., U.K., AP. **Languages taught:** French, Spanish, Italian. **Staff specialists:** reading, math. **Special programs:** ESL. **Special curricular:** art, computer instruction. **Extracurricular:** computers, self-access and social program. **Tests:** PSAT, SAT, ACT, TOEFL, A-level GCE, GCSE, Scottish Examination Board. **Graduates attending college:** 70%. **Graduates have attended:** Edinburgh U., St. Andrews U. **Location:** in city. **Library:** 6,000 volumes. **Facilities:** 1 building, 11 classrooms, cafeteria, science lab, computer lab, AV equipment, boarding at Douglas House (2 minutes' walk from school).

**Pound sterling †formerly Edinburgh Tutorial College & American School

WALES/GLAMORGAN

United World College of the Atlantic

Street address: St. Donat's Castle, Llantwit Major, South Glamorgan CF61 1WF, Wales
Phone: (44)(1446)792530 **Facsimile:** (44)(1446)794163
Principal: C. D. O. Jenkins
Director of studies: J. R. Fletcher
Teaching staff: full-time, 40; part-time, 4; total, 44
Grade levels: 12 – 13
Enrollment: total, 348
Nationalities of student body: U.S., 10; U.K., 80; other, 258; total, 348
Teacher/student ratio: 1/8
Boarders: boys, 174; girls, 174 **Program:** planned 7-day
Tuition and board (annual): 11,900** (most students on scholarship through National Committees)
School year: September through May

Year founded: 1962. **Type of school:** coed, boarding. **Governed by:** appointed governing body. **Sponsored by:** United World Colleges. **Accredited by:** U.K. Dept. of Education and Employment.

Curriculum/physical plant

Type: IB. **Languages taught:** English, French, Spanish, German, Dutch, Russian, Arabic, Japanese, Services: (at least one is compulsory) life boat, coast guard, environmental monitoring, beach rescue, social service, arts center service, extramural service, estate service. **Sports:** sports, wide range of activities. **Tests:** SAT, IB. **Graduates have attended:** Cambridge, Oxford, Harvard, Princeton, Sorbonne. **Location:** 2 miles from small town, 20 miles from Cardiff. **Campus:** 200 acres. **Library:** 30,000 volumes. **Facilities:** auditorium, cafeteria, gymnasium, AV room, science labs, computer rooms, tennis courts, swimming pools, playing fields, social center, gardens, sea/coast.

**Pound sterling

UNITED STATES OF AMERICA

Region: North America
Size: 3,536,278 square miles
Population: 265,562,845
Capital: Washington, DC
Telephone code: 1
Currency: U.S. dollar
Language: English

SAN FRANCISCO, CALIFORNIA

CHINESE AMERICAN INTERNATIONAL SCHOOL

Street address: 150 Oak Street, San Francisco, CA 94129, U.S.A.
Phone: (415)7511381/3796730 **Facsimile:** (415)3796725
E-mail: caishead@aol.com
Mail: PO Box 29484, San Francisco, CA, 94129, U.S.A.
Head: Shirley Lee
Assistant head: Natalie Sundberg, Ed.D.
Director of development: Evelyn Woo
Director of admissions: Joana Fong
Business manager: Anne Averill
Teaching staff: full-time, 30; total, 30
Nationalities of teaching staff: U.S., 13; U.K., 1; other, 16; total, 30
Grade levels: preK – 8
Enrollment: preK, 50; K, 50; 1 – 6, 126; 7 – 8, 24; total, 250
Nationalities of student body: U.S., 240; other, 10; total, 250
Teacher/student ratio: 1/8
Tuition (annual): preK, $7,900; K – 5, $8,350; 6 – 8, $8,450
Other fees: registration*, $50; activity fee, $150 – 300
School year: September to June

Year founded: 1981. **Type of school:** coed, day, private nonprofit. **Governed by:** appointed board of trustees. **Accredited by:** California Association of Independent Schools.

Curriculum/physical plant

Type: U.S., IB. **Languages of instruction:** English, Mandarin. **Languages taught:** Spanish. **Staff specialists:** reading, math, computer, counselor, psychologist, learning disabilities, nurse, music, art, Chinese curriculum. **Special programs:** ESL, correspondence, CSL, CFL. **Special curricular:** art, chorus, physical education, computer instruction, student council, ensemble. **Extracurricular:** drama, dance, choral and instrumental music, computers, yearbook, newspaper, excursions/ expeditions, field trips. **Sports:** basketball, soccer, volleyball. **Clubs:** chess, computer, Boy Scouts, Girl Scouts. **Tests:** SSAT. **Location:** in the heart of the cultural Civic Center district. **Library:** 50,000 volumes. **Facilities:** 3 buildings, 25 classrooms, auditorium, infirmary, 4 covered play areas, gymnasium, science lab, computer lab, art studio, music room, theater.

*Once only fee

French–American International School

Street address: 220 Buchanan Street, San Francisco, CA 94102-6124, U.S.A.
Phone: (1)(415)6268564 **Facsimile:** (1)(415)6268551
E-mail: faiswexler@aol.com **Web:** http://www.fais-ihs.org
Head of school: Jane Camblin
Middle school principal: Joan Dimancescu
Lower school principal: Claude Farrugia
Admissions director: Edie Wexler
Teaching staff: full-time, 79; part-time, 10; total, 89
Nationalities of teaching staff: U.S., 33; U.K., 2; other, 54; total, 89
Grade levels: preK – 12
Enrollment: preK, 30; K, 60; 1 – 6, 315; 7 – 9, 120; 10 – 12, 110; total, 635
Nationalities of student body: U.S., 418; U.K., 10; other, 207; total, 635
Teacher/student ratio: 1/10
Tuition (annual): preK – K, $8,540; 1 – 5, $8,990 (average); 6 – 8, $9,850 (average); 9 – 12, $12,135 (average)
Other fees: enrollment*, $300; deposit, $200; incidentals, $200
School year: September to June

Year founded: 1962. **Type of school:** coed, day, international, nondenominational. **Governed by:** elected board of directors. **Accredited by:** Western, French Ministry of National Education, California Association of Independent Schools. **Regional organizations:** ECIS, NAIS, AFSA.

Curriculum/physical plant

Type: U.S., French Baccalaureate, IB, AP. **Languages of instruction:** English, French. **Languages taught:** Spanish, German, Mandarin. **Staff specialists:** math, computer, counselor, art, music, physical education, drama. **Special programs:** ESL, remedial, FSL. **Special curricular:** art, chorus, physical education, computer instruction, theater. **Extracurricular:** drama, dance, instrumental music, computers, yearbook, photography, field trips, film, Tae Kwon Do. **Sports:** basketball, soccer, swimming, volleyball. **Clubs:** drama, photography, student government. **Tests:** PSAT, SAT, IB, AP, ERB, CTBS, French Baccalaureate. **Graduates attending college:** 100%. **Graduates have attended:** Yale, Stanford, Oxford, U. of California campuses, Georgetown. **Location:** central San Francisco. **Campus:** 50,000 square feet. **Library:** 14,000 volumes. **Facilities:** 2 buildings, 30 classrooms, auditorium, gymnasium, 2 science labs, computer labs, play area, art room, music room, theater, 3 recreational areas, moving to new facility in late fall of 1997.

*Once only fee

WASHINGTON, DC

WASHINGTON INTERNATIONAL SCHOOL

Street address: 3100 Macomb Street, NW, Washington, DC, 20008, U.S.A.
Phone: (1)(202)3641815 **Facsimile:** (1)(202)3640080
Head of school: Anne-Marie Pierce
Upper school principal: David Merkel
Middle school principal: Sandy Bourne
Intermediate school principal: Sonja Cowie
Lower school principal: Stephen Dare
Teaching staff: full-time, 92; part-time, 20; total, 112
Grade levels: N – 12
Enrollment: N – preK, 44; K, 44; 1 – 6, 298; 7 – 9, 149; 10 – 12, 145; total, 680
Nationalities of student body: U.S., 311; U.K., 78; other, 291; total, 680
Teacher/student ratio: 1/6
Tuition (annual): N – preK, $6,600 (half-day), $9,850 (full-day); K – 5, $11,900; 6 – 12, $13,350
Other fees (annual): capital levy, $750/500; busing, $300 – 500; books, $200 – 400; application*, $40; IB*, $775 (average)
School year: September to June

Year founded: 1966. **Type of school:** coed, day, private nonprofit. **Governed by:** appointed board of trustees. **Accredited by:** Middle States, ECIS. **Regional organizations:** ECIS.

Curriculum/physical plant

Type: IB, international, AP (languages). **Languages of instruction:** English, French, Spanish. **Languages taught:** French, Spanish, Japanese, Dutch (K – 12). **Special programs:** ESL. **Special curricular:** art, chorus, physical education, computer instruction, debating, music, public speaking. **Extracurricular:** drama, choral and instrumental music, yearbook, newspaper, literary magazine, excursions/expeditions, field trips, Model OAS. **Sports:** basketball, soccer, softball, tennis, track and field, volleyball. **Tests:** PSAT, SAT, TOEFL, IB, AP (languages), ERB. **Graduates attending college:** 99%. **Graduates have attended:** universities in the U.S., U.K., Canada, The Netherlands, Norway. **Campuses (2):** Cleveland Park, 6 acres; Georgetown, 1.5 acres. **Libraries:** 17,000 volumes. **Facilities:** 8 buildings, 80 classrooms, playing field, 7 science labs, 2 computer labs, basketball court, assembly hall, partial air conditioning.

*Once only fee

ATLANTA, GEORGIA

Atlanta International School

Street address: 2890 North Fulton Drive, Atlanta, GA, 30305 U.S.A.
Phone: (1)(404)8161006 **Facsimile:** (1)(404)8163060
Director: Dr. David Hawley
Head, upper school: Donna Dunson
Head, middle school: Virginia Ferandel
Head, lower school: Bill Moon
Business manager: Charlotte Bizzell
Teaching staff: full-time, 92; part-time, 6; total, 98
Nationalities of teaching staff: U.S., 43; U.K., 17; other, 38; total, 98
Grade levels: preK – 12
Enrollment: preK, 35; K, 50; 1 – 6, 230; 7 – 12, 335; total, 650
Teacher/student ratio: 1/7
Tuition (annual): preK – K, $7,900; 1 – 5, $8,100; 6 – 8, $8,950; 9 – 10, $9,500; 11 – 12, $9,950
Other fees (annual): registration*, $100; books, $380 (middle/upper school)
School year: August to June

Year founded: 1984. **Type of school:** coed, day. **Governed by:** elected board of trustees. **Accredited by:** Southern, ECIS, French Ministry of Education.

Curriculum/physical plant

Type: U.S., IB, French, German. **Languages of instruction:** English, French, Spanish, German. **Languages taught:** Latin, Japanese, Hebrew. **Special programs:** ESL. **Special curricular:** art, chorus, band, physical education, computer instruction. **Extracurricular:** drama, instrumental music, yearbook, newspaper, field trips. **Sports:** baseball, basketball, soccer, softball, tennis, track and field, volleyball. **Tests:** PSAT, SAT, IB, ERB. **Graduates have attended:** Bryn Mawr, Stanford, Harvard, U. of Rome, U. of London. **Location:** in residential area, 6 miles from downtown Atlanta. **Campus:** 10 acres. **Library:** 12,000 volumes. **Facilities:** 65 classrooms, auditorium, gymnasium, playing field, 6 science labs, computer lab, air conditioning.

*Once only fee

EDEN PRAIRIE, MINNESOTA

THE INTERNATIONAL SCHOOL OF MINNESOTA

Street address: 6385 Beach Road, Eden Prairie, MN, 55344 U.S.A.
Phone: (1)(612)9413500 **Facsimile:** (1)(612)9414015
E-mail: ism@spacestar.com
Head of school: Nadia Reda
Assistant head of school: Anne Rennick
Upper school coordinator: Janet Mahr
Lower school coordinator: Sue Berg
Teaching staff: full-time, 40; part-time, 4; total, 44
Nationalities of teaching staff: U.S., 34; other, 10; total, 44
Grade levels: preschool – 12
Enrollment: preS, 30; preK, 43; K, 58; 1 – 6, 210; 7 – 9, 70; 10 – 12, 40; total, 451
Nationalities of student body: U.S., 330; other, 121; total, 451
Teacher/student ratio: 1/9
Tuition (annual): preS – preK, $5,030 (half day); preS – 12, $8,400
Other fees (annual): registration, $400; insurance, $129.50; busing, $890 – $1,280; lunch, preS – K, $745, 1 – 12, $830; books, $200 – 300 (average); uniform; field trips; monthly payment plan processing, $200
School year: September to mid-June

Year founded: 1985. **Type of school:** coed, day, proprietary. **Governed by:** SABIS School Network. **Accredited by:** North Central.

Curriculum

Type: U.S., AP. **Languages taught:** French, Spanish. **Staff specialists:** computer, counselor. **Special programs:** ESL. **Special curricular:** art, chorus, physical education, computer instruction, orchestra. **Extracurricular:** instrumental music, computers, yearbook, literary magazine, excursions/expeditions, field trips. **Sports:** basketball, soccer, swimming, tennis, track and field, volleyball, karate, golf. **Clubs:** chess, drama, yearbook, math league, Math Counts, student life, international festival. **Tests:** SAT, ACT, AP, ERB. **Graduates attending college:** 100%. **Graduates have attended:** Carleton, Duke, Wellesley, Cal Tech, MIT.

Physical plant

Location: wooded lakefront, 15 miles from Minneapolis. **Campus:** 55 acres. **Library:** 12,000 volumes. **Facilities:** 3 buildings, 32 classrooms, cafeteria, 2 tennis courts, gymnasium, playing field, science lab, computer lab, swimming pool, beach, 2 playgrounds, air conditioning.

MONTEZUMA, NEW MEXICO

THE ARMAND HAMMER UNITED WORLD COLLEGE OF THE AMERICAN WEST

Phone: (1)(505)4544201 **Facsimile:** (1)(505)4544274
U.S. mail: PO Box 248, Montezuma, NM 87731, U.S.A.
President: Philip O. Geier, Ph.D.
Vice-president: Barbara Johnson
Teaching staff: full-time, 24; part-time, 4; total, 28
Nationalities of teaching staff: U.S., 16; other, 12; total, 28
Grade levels: 12 – 13
Enrollment: total, 200
Nationalities of student body: U.S., 50; other, 150; total, 200
Teacher/student ratio: 1/8
Boarding capacity: boys, 100; girls, 100
Tuition and board (annual): $19,500
School year: August to May

Year founded: 1981. **Type of school:** coed, boarding, private nonprofit. **Governed by:** board of directors. **Accredited by:** North Central.

Curriculum/physical plant

Type: IB. **Languages taught:** French, Spanish, German. **Special programs:** ESL. **Special curricular:** art, computer instruction. **Extracurricular:** drama, choral and instrumental music, computers, yearbook, newspaper, photography, excursions/expeditions, field trips. **Sports:** basketball, skiing, soccer, softball, swimming, tennis, volleyball, skating. **Tests:** PSAT, SAT, ACT, TOEFL, IB. **Graduates attending college:** 98%. **Graduates have attended:** Oxford, Harvard, Yale, MIT, Princeton. **Location:** 5 miles from Las Vegas, New Mexico; 60 miles east of Santa Fe; 60 miles southeast of Taos. **Campus:** 110 acres. **Facilities:** 11 buildings, 20 classrooms, cafeteria, infirmary, covered play area, 3 tennis courts, 3 playing fields, 9 science labs, computer lab, 4 dormitories.

NEW YORK, NEW YORK

THE DWIGHT SCHOOL

Street address: 291 Central Park West, New York, NY 10024, U.S.A.
Phone: (1)(212)7242146 **Facsimile:** (1)(212)7242539
Web: http://starbase.ingress.com/~dwight
Chancellor: Stephen H. Spahn
Head of school: Dr. Joyce M. Robinson
Assistant headmaster: Anthony Foster
Dean of admissions: Elizabeth Callaway
Director of admissions: Kristina McCoobery
Teaching staff: full-time, 60; part-time, 3; total, 63
Nationalities of teaching staff: U.S., 53; U.K., 2; other, 8; total, 63
Grade levels: K – 12
Enrollment: K – 4, 48; 5 – 8, 85; 9 – 12, 237; total, 370
Nationalities of student body: U.S., 259; other, 111; total, 370
Teacher/student ratio: 1/7
Tuition (annual): K – 4, $14,800; 5 – 8, $16,000; 9 – 10, $16,800; 11 – 12, $17,000
Other fees (annual): registration*, $500; application, $40; books/activities, $375; optional programs are available
School year: September to June

Year founded: 1880. **Type of school:** coed, day, private, international. **Governed by:** board of trustees. **Accredited by:** Middle States, New York State, ECIS.

Curriculum/physical plant

Type: U.S., U.K., IB. **Languages taught:** French, Spanish, Italian, Latin, Japanese, Chinese, Hebrew. **Staff specialists:** reading, math, computer, ESL, learning specialist, remedial reading. **Special curricular:** art, computer instruction, music, theater, student exchange, sports teams. **Extracurricular:** drama, computers, yearbook, newspaper, literary magazine, photography, excursions/expeditions, field trips, chess. **Sports:** baseball, basketball, cross-country, soccer, softball, tennis, volleyball, wrestling, weight training. **Clubs:** National Honor Society, Model UN, Blue Key Society. **Tests:** PSAT, SAT, TOEFL, IB, GCSE, Stanford, AP Achievement. **Graduates attending college:** 100%. **Graduates have attended:** Princeton, U. of Pennsylvania, Columbia, Dartmouth, London School of Economics. **Location:** on Upper West Side of Manhattan. **Facilities:** 34 classrooms, 2 gymnasiums, 4 science labs, computer lab, multi-media resource center with internet, intranet, and videoconferencing capabilities, language lab, photography dark room, visual and performing arts center, lunch room.

*Once only fee

United Nations International School

Street address: 24-50 Franklin D. Roosevelt Drive, New York, NY 10010-4046, U.S.A; 173-53 Croydon Road, Jamaica Estates, Queens, NY 11432, U.S.A.
Phone: (1)(212)5843001; (1)(718)6586166
Facsimile: (1)(212)6841382; (1)(718)6585742
E-mail: adminmail@unis.org **Web:** http://www.unis.org
Director: Joseph J. Blaney, Ed.D.
Principal, Tutorial House: Raymond Taylor, Ed.D.
Principal, Middle House: Radha Rajan, Ph.D.
Principal, Junior House: Lea Rangel-Ribeiro
Principal, Queens campus: Mary Blake
Teaching staff: full-time, 152; part-time, 19; total, 171
Nationalities of teaching staff: U.S., 70; U.K., 15; other, 86; total, 171
Grade levels: K – 12
Enrollment: total, 1,505
Nationalities of student body: U.S., 804; other, 701; total, 1,505
Teacher/student ratio: 1/9
Tuition (annual): K – 4, $10,500; 5 – 9, $11,500; 10 – 12, $12,500
Other fees (annual): registration*, $150; insurance, $20; books, $65; endowment fund*, $1,000; yearbook, $29; camps, $165; graduation*, $75; UNIS Parents Association, $25; IB dues, $15
School year: September to June

Year founded: 1947. **Type of school:** coed, day, independent nonprofit. **Governed by:** appointed and elected board of trustees. **Sponsored by:** United Nations. **Accredited by:** New York State Board of Regents, ECIS. **Regional organizations:** ECIS.

Curriculum

Type: IB. **Languages taught:** French, Spanish, German, Italian, Russian, Latin, Arabic, Japanese, Chinese, Greek. **Staff specialists:** psychologist, nurse, counselors, technologist. **Special programs:** ESL. **Special curricular:** art, chorus, band, drama, sports teams, computer, UNIS/UN conference, nuclear issues. **Extracurricular:** drama, gymnastics, dance, choral and instrumental music, computers, yearbook, newspaper, literary magazine, photography, excursions/expeditions, field trips, drivers' education, extended-day program. **Sports:** basketball, soccer, softball, tennis, track and field, volleyball, judo. **Clubs:** chess, French, German, Spanish, Amnesty International. **Tests:** IB, SAT II. **Graduates attending college:** 98%. **Graduates have attended:** Cambridge, MIT, Yale, Princeton, Williams.

Physical plant

Campuses (2): Manhattan, 3 acres; Queens, 1.5 acres. **Library:** 48,000 volumes. **Facilities:** 2 buildings, 112 classrooms, 3 auditoriums, 2 cafeterias, infirmary, covered play area, tennis court, 3 gymnasiums, playing field, 10 science labs, 4 computer labs, AV equipment, garden, 3 art studios, performing arts center, air conditioning.

*Once only fee

DALLAS, TEXAS

Dallas International School

Street address: 6039 Churchill Way, Dallas, TX 75230, U.S.A.,
Phone: (1)(972)9916379 **Facsimile:** (1)(972)9916608
E-mail: jjdis@metronet.com
Director: Jeanne Jeannin
Teaching staff: full-time, 17; part-time, 3; total, 20
Nationalities of teaching staff: U.S., 6; other, 14; total, 20
Grade levels: preK – 12
Enrollment: preK, 60; K, 30; 1 – 6, 100; 7 – 9, 5; 10 – 12, 5; total, 200
Capacity: preK, 60; K, 30; 1 – 6, 120; 7 – 9, 45; 10 – 12, 45; total, 300
Teacher/student ratio: 1/11
Tuition (annual): preK – K, $4,870; 1 – 6, $5,450; 7 – 12, $7,800
Other fees (annual): registration, $225; lunch, $50/month; books, $110
School year: August to June

Year founded: 1987. **Type of school:** coed, day, private nonprofit. **Governed by:** French Ministry of Education. **Sponsored by:** Mission Laique Francaise. **Accredited by:** French Ministry of Education.

Curriculum/physical plant

Type: French Baccalaureate. **Languages of instruction:** English, French. **Languages taught:** French, Spanish, German. **Staff specialists:** ESL/FLE. **Special programs:** ESL. **Special curricular:** language. **Extracurricular:** drama, dance, computers, field trips, Tae Kwon Do, music, ceramics, painting. **Sports:** soccer, tennis. **Graduates attending college:** 100%. **Facilities:** 5 buildings, 16 classrooms, 2 cafeterias, tennis court, playing field, science lab, computer lab, library, air conditioning.

HOUSTON, TEXAS

The Awty International School

Street address: 7455 Awty School Lane, Houston, TX 77055-7222, U.S.A.
Phone: (1)(713)6864850 **Facsimile:** (1)(713)6864956
Web: http://www.awty.org
Headmaster: Jarek E. Garlinski
Upper school head: Samuel Waugh
Middle school head: Tom Beuscher
Lower school head: Chantal Vessali
Business manager: Alan Woodbury
Teaching staff: full-time, 84; part-time, 17; total, 101
Nationalities of teaching staff: U.S., 63; other, 38; total, 101
Grade levels: preK – 12
Enrollment: preK, 101; K, 56; 1 – 5, 307; 6 – 8, 159; 9 – 12, 200; total, 823
Capacity: preK, 105; K, 72; 1 – 5, 360; 6 – 8, 208; 9 – 12, 250; total, 995

Teacher/student ratio: 1/9
Tuition (annual): preK, $6,550; K, $7,100; 1 – 5, $7,500; 6 – 8, $8,350; 9 – 12, $9,075
Other fees (annual): registration, $250; tuition payment plan fee, $100; new-family fee*, $500; testing*, $40; senior*, $300; capital building, $500/child; application fee, $50
School year: August to June

Year founded: 1956. **Type of school:** coed, day, private nonprofit. **Governed by:** board of trustees (self-perpetuating). **Accredited by:** ISAS, ECIS, French Ministry of Education. **Regional organizations:** ECIS.

Curriculum

Type: U.S., IB, French Baccalaureate. **Languages taught:** French, Spanish, German, ESL, Italian, Arabic. **Staff specialists:** computer, nurse. **Special programs:** ESL, independent study. **Special curricular:** art, physical education, computer instruction, choral and instrumental music. **Extracurricular:** drama, dance, computers, yearbook, newspaper, literary magazine, photography, excursions/expeditions, field trips. **Sports:** basketball, soccer, swimming, tennis, track and field, volleyball. **Clubs:** Model UN, French, Spanish. **Tests:** PSAT, SAT, ACT, TOEFL, IB, ERB. **Graduates attending college:** 99%. **Graduates have attended:** Yale, Oxford, Columbia, Johns Hopkins, Harvard.

Physical plant

Location: in central Houston, with easy access to downtown and residential areas. **Campus:** 12.5 acres. **Library:** 17,000 volumes. **Facilities:** 13 buildings, 64 classrooms, cafeteria, 2 covered play areas, 2 playing fields, 2 science labs, 5 computer labs, 2 language labs, 2 playgrounds, soccer field.

*Once only fee

U.S. VIRGIN ISLANDS

Region: Caribbean
Size: 171 square miles
Population: 97,564
Capital: Charlotte Amalie, St. Thomas
Telephone code: 809
Currency: U.S. dollar
Languages: English, Spanish, Creole

ST. CROIX

The Good Hope School

Phone: (1)(809)7720022 **Facsimile:** (1)(809)7724626
Mail: Frederiksted, St. Croix, U.S. Virgin Islands 00840
Head of school: Tanya L. Nichols
Director, upper school: Mary Jane Provost
Director, middle school: Luther Renee
Director, lower school: Sarah Otis
Business manager: Brian Romine
Teaching staff: full-time, 40; total, 40
Nationalities of teaching staff: U.S., 39; other, 1; total, 40
Grade levels: preK – 12
Enrollment: preK, 23; K, 9; 1 – 6, 192; 7 – 9, 113; 10 – 12, 94; total, 431 (East Campus: preK, 7; K, 4; total, 11)
Teacher/student ratio: 1/11
Tuition (annual): preK, $3,250 (half-day); K, $4,150; 1, $4,300; 2 – 3, $4,610; 4 – 6, $4,935; 7 – 12, $5,245
Other fees (annual): registration, $100; books, $75 – 150
School year: September to June

Year founded: 1967. **Type of school:** coed, day, private nonprofit. **Governed by:** elected board of trustees. **Accredited by:** Middle States.

Curriculum

Type: U.S., AP. **Languages taught:** French, Spanish. **Staff specialists:** computer, counselor, nurse, librarian, resource teacher. **Special programs:** honors sections. **Special curricular:** art, chorus, band, physical education, computer instruction, Spanish (K – 12). **Extracurricular:** drama, gymnastics, computers, yearbook, literary magazine, photography, field trips, sports. **Tests:** PSAT, SAT, ACT, AP, Stanford, NEDT. **Graduates attending college:** 98%. **Graduates have attended:** Tulane, Columbia, Harvard, U. of Pennsylvania, American U.

Physical plant

Location: in small town near the Caribbean Sea, amidst a grove of mahogany trees. East campus located east of Christiansted, St. Croix. **Campuses (2):** 34 acres. **Library:** 17,000 volumes. **Facilities:** 11 buildings, 23 classrooms, covered play area, gymnasium, 3 playing fields, 3 science labs, computer lab, swimming pool, library media center, amphitheater, weight training room.

St. Croix Country Day School

Phone/facsimile: (1)(809)7781974
Mail: Rt. 1, Box 6199, Kingshill, St. Croix, U.S. Virgin Islands 00850
Head: James C. Sadler
Dean, upper school: Patricia Bessette
Dean, lower and middle schools: Charles S. Adams
Business manager: Francine Winfrey
Teaching staff: full-time, 70; total, 70
Nationalities of teaching staff: U.S., 64; other, 6; total, 70
Grade levels: N – 12
Enrollment: N – 8, 330; 9 – 12, 124; total, 454
Capacity: total, 500
Teacher/student ratio: 1/6
Tuition (annual): $4,200 – 5,450
Other fees (annual): registration, $150; testing (admission)*, $25
School year: September to June

Year founded: 1964. **Type of school:** coed, day, private nonprofit. **Governed by:** appointed board of trustees. **Accredited by:** Middle States.

Curriculum/physical plant

Type: U.S., AP. **Languages taught:** French, Spanish. **Staff specialists:** counselor, nurse, technology coordinator. **Special curricular:** art, chorus, physical education, computer instruction, swimming. **Extracurricular:** drama, gymnastics, dance, choral and instrumental music, computers, yearbook, newspaper, literary magazine, photography, excursions/expeditions. **Sports:** baseball, basketball, soccer, softball, swimming, volleyball. **Tests:** PSAT, SAT, ACT, Stanford. **Graduates attending college:** 100%. **Graduates have attended:** Georgetown, Tulane, U.S. Naval Academy, Princeton, Tufts. **Location:** on outskirts of Christiansted. **Campus:** 25 acres. **Library:** 16,000 volumes. **Facilities:** gymnasium, 2 playing fields, 2 science labs, computer lab, Olympic swimming pool, fine arts center, art studio and gallery.

*Once only fee

ST. THOMAS

Antilles School

Street address: 7280 Frenchman's Bay 16-1, St. Thomas,
U.S. Virgin Islands 00802
Phone: (1)(809)7761600 **Facsimile:** (1)(809)7761019
Headmaster: Mark C. Marin
Head, upper and middle schools: Kaye Knoepfel
Head, lower school: Polly Watts
Academic dean: Alan Eberhart
Dean of faculty: Kathy Streibich
Teaching staff: full-time, 38; part-time, 10; total, 48
Nationalities of teaching staff: U.S., 37; other, 11; total, 48
Grade levels: early learning center – 12

Enrollment: ELC, 49; 1 – 5, 145; 6 – 8, 110; 9 – 12, 116; total, 420
Capacity: ELC, 73; 1 – 5, 157; 6 – 8, 120; 9 – 12, 160; total, 510
Teacher/student ratio: 1/10
Tuition (annual): ELC, $7,430; 1 – 5, $7,520; 6 – 8, $7,670; 9 – 11, $7,970; 12, $8,120
Other fees (annual): registration, $40; refundable deposit*, $500
School year: September to June

Year founded: 1950. **Type of school:** coed, day, private nonprofit. **Governed by:** elected board of trustees. **Accredited by:** Middle States.

Curriculum/physical plant

Type: U.S., AP. **Staff specialists:** reading, computer, counselor, learning disabilities, gifted and talented, 2 fine arts, choral music, 2 librarians, 2 physical education. **Special programs:** honors sections. **Special curricular:** art, chorus, physical education, computer instruction, elementary Spanish. **Extracurricular:** drama, choral music, computers, yearbook, newspaper, literary magazine, photography, excursions/expeditions, field trips. **Sports:** flag football, volleyball, basketball, soccer, tennis, softball. **Clubs:** National Honor Society, student council, ecology, French, scouting, science, SADD, intramural sports. **Tests:** PSAT, SAT, Stanford, MAT. **Graduates attending college:** 100%. **Graduates have attended:** Georgetown, Amherst, Swarthmore, Johns Hopkins, Harvard. **Location:** 2.5 miles from Charlotte Amalie. **Campus:** 27 acres. **Library:** 13,000 volumes. 100 periodicals. **Facilities:** 8 buildings, 33 classrooms, auditorium, covered play area, tennis court, 2 playing fields, 3 science labs, computer lab, 2 art studios, physical education facilities with showers and weight room.

*Once only fee

URUGUAY

Region: South America
Size: 68,037 square miles
Population: 3,238,952
Capital: Montevideo
Telephone code: 598
Currency: peso
Language: Spanish

MONTEVIDEO

URUGUAYAN AMERICAN SCHOOL

Street address: Dublin 1785, CP 11500, Montevideo, Uruguay
Phone: (598)(2)607681 **Facsimile:** (598)(2)606316
E-mail: amschool@chasque.apc.org
Web: http://www.chasque.apc.org/amschool
U.S. mail: Administrative Officer (UAS), U.S. Embassy – Montevideo, APO AA 34035
Director: Ginger Apple
Assistant director: Michael Baldwin
Business manager: Jorge Rivero

Teaching staff: full-time, 28; part-time, 16; total, 44
Nationalities of teaching staff: U.S., 14; host, 25; other, 5; total, 44
Grade levels: N – 12
Enrollment: N – preK, 20; K, 16; 1 – 6, 92; 7 – 9, 36; 10 – 12, 36; total, 200
Nationalities of student body: U.S., 98; host, 28; other, 74; total, 200
Capacity: N – preK, 36; K, 20; 1 – 6, 108; 7 – 9, 54; 10 – 12, 54; total, 272
Teacher/student ratio: 1/5
Tuition (annual): N – preK, $2,500; K, $6,000; 1 – 5, $7,900; 6 – 12, $11,900
Other fees: registration*, $2,000
School year: August to June

Year founded: 1958. **Type of school:** coed, day, private nonprofit. **Governed by:** elected board of directors. **Accredited by:** Southern. **Regional organizations:** AAIE, AASSA.

Curriculum/physical plant

Type: U.S., AP. **Languages taught:** French, Spanish. **Staff specialists:** reading, math, computer, counselor, learning disabilities, science. **Special programs:** ESL, full-day kindergarten. **Special curricular:** art, physical education, computer, music. **Extracurricular:** drama, gymnastics, computers, yearbook, photography, field trips, karate. **Sports:** basketball, soccer, volleyball, team handball. **Tests:** SSAT, PSAT, SAT, ACT, AP, Stanford. **Graduates attending college:** 90 – 100%. **Graduates have attended:** George Washington U., Fresno Pacific, Yale, Amherst, U. of Texas. **Location:** in suburban area, Carrasco, 20 kilometers east of Montevideo. **Campus:** 2.5 acres. **Library:** 10,000 volumes. **Facilities:** 3 buildings, 28 classrooms, auditorium, cafeteria, gymnasium, 2 science labs, computer lab, play area, art room, photo lab, AV equipment.

*Once only fee

UZBEKISTAN

Region: Central Asia
Size: 172,700 square miles
Population: 23,418,381
Capital: Tashkent
Telephone code: 7
Currency: sum
Languages: Uzbek, Russian

TASHKENT

Tashkent International School

Street address: 23 Chekhov Street, Tashkent, Uzbekistan
Phone: (7)(3712)339572 **Facsimile:** (7)(3712)406621
U.S. mail: (no individual or school name) U.S. Embassy-Tashkent, ADM-2, Dept. of State, Washington, DC 20521-7110
Director: Ron Halsey
Teaching staff: full-time, 19; part-time, 9; total, 28
Nationalities of teaching staff: U.S., 7; U.K., 3; host, 12; other, 6; total, 28
Grade levels: K – 12

Enrollment: K, 11; 1 – 6, 86; 7 – 12, 43; total, 140
Nationalities of student body: U.S., 9; host, 34; other, 97; total, 140
Capacity: K, 15; 1 – 6, 108; 7 – 12, 75; total, 198
Teacher/student ratio: 1/8
Tuition (annual): K, $4,000; 1 – 6, $8,000; 7 – 12, $9,000
School year: August to June

Year founded: 1994. **Type of school:** coed, day, private nonprofit. **Governed by:** elected board of directors. **Regional organizations:** ECIS (prospective member).

Curriculum/physical plant

Type: U.S. **Languages taught:** Russian. **Special programs:** ESL. **Extracurricular:** dance, yearbook, field trips, Model UN, school newspaper. **Location:** in Tashkent. **Library:** 1,500 volumes. **Facilities:** 1 building, 10 classrooms, playing field, multipurpose room.

The Tashkent Ulugbek International School

Street address: 17 Usman Nasir Street, 700070 Tashkent, Uzbekistan
Phone: (7)(3712)562586/567306 **Facsimile:** (7)(3712)562586
E-mail: ulugbek@tuis.edu.uz
Principal: Selim Özdemir
First deputy: Sabir Khalikov
Deputy (primary): Murat Erguvan
Deputy (secondary): Alettin Duman
Business manager: Elena Lavrinenko
Teaching staff: full-time, 22; part-time, 1; total, 23
Nationalities of teaching staff: U.S., 1; U.K., 4; host, 5; other, 13; total, 23
Enrollment: 1 – 6, 50; 7 – 9, 40; 10 – 12, 15; 13, 22; total, 127
Teacher/student ratio: 1/5
Tuition (annual): 1 – 6, $5,000; 7 – 13, $6,000
Other fees: registration*, $200; books, $250
School year: September to June

Year founded: 1995. **Type of school:** coed, day, private nonprofit. **Governed by:** Ministry of Foreign Affairs of Uzbekistan. **Accredited by:** ECIS.

Curriculum/physical plant

Type: U.K., IB. **Languages taught:** French, Russian, Uzbek. **Staff specialists:** math, computer, counselor, nurse. **Special programs:** ESL. **Special curricular:** art, chorus, physical education, computer instruction. **Extracurricular:** dance, computers, newspaper, excursions/expeditions. **Clubs:** computer, English, music, dance. **Tests:** IB, A-level GCE, GCSE, national. **Library:** 1,500 volumes. **Location:** in refurbished building with large garden in city. **Facilities:** 12 classrooms, auditorium, cafeteria, infirmary, covered play area, gymnasium, 2 playing fields, 2 science labs, computer lab, swimming pool.

*Once only fee

VENEZUELA

Region: South America
Size: 352,144 square miles
Population: 21,983,188
Capital: Caracas
Telephone code: 58
Currency: bolivar
Language: Spanish

ANACO

Escuela Anaco Internacional

Street address: Detras de National Oil Well, Av. Jose Anzoategui 98, Anaco, Venezuela
Phone/facsimile: (58)(82)22683
Mail: Apartado 31, Anaco, Venezuela
U.S. mail: c/o Jet Cargo, PO Box 020010, M-42, Miami, FL 33102, U.S.A.
Superintendent: Warren Ortloff, Ed.D.
Assistant superintendent: Luz Marina Escobar
Teaching staff: full-time, 15; part-time, 3; total, 18
Nationalities of teaching staff: U.S., 12; host, 1; Canada, 2; other, 3; total, 18
Grade levels: preK – 12
Enrollment: preK, 15; K, 15; 1 – 6, 68; 7 – 9, 11; 10 – 12, 11; total, 120
Nationalities of student body: U.S., 40; U.K., 5; host, 30; other, 45; total, 120
Capacity: preK, 15; K, 15; 1 – 6, 120; 7 – 9, 30; 10 – 12, 45; total, 225
Teacher/student ratio: 1/7
Tuition (annual): preK, $2,100; K, $5,400; 1 – 12, $8,300
Other fees: registration*, $1,500
School year: August to June

Year founded: 1956. **Type of school:** coed, day, private nonprofit. **Governed by:** elected board of directors. **Accredited by:** Southern (in process). **Regional organizations:** ACCAS, Tri-Assoc.

Curriculum/physical plant

Type: U.S. **Languages taught:** Spanish. **Staff specialists:** counselor, art, librarian, music, physical education. **Special programs:** ESL, SSL. **Special curricular:** art, physical education, computer instruction, music. **Extracurricular:** computers, yearbook, newspaper, field trips. **Tests:** PSAT, SAT, ACT, Iowa. **Location:** rural campus, 2 kilometers from Anaco. **Campus:** 20 acres. **Facilities:** 12 buildings, 14 classrooms, auditorium, cafeteria, gymnasium, 2 playing fields, science lab, computer lab, library, air conditioning.

*Once only fee

CARACAS

COLEGIO INTERNACIONAL DE CARACAS

Street address: Calle Colegio, Las Minas de Baruta, Caracas, Venezuela
Phone: (58)(2)930444/930508 **Facsimile:** (58)(2)930533/9414161
E-mail: cic@cic-caracas.org
U.S. mail: PO Box 025323, Miami, FL 33102-5323, U.S.A.
Superintendent: Winthrop Sargent
High school principal: Michael Saffarewich
Elementary school principal: Carmen Sweeting
Registrar: Teresa Smith
Head of library: Diane Austin
Teaching staff: full-time, 59; part-time, 4; total, 63
Nationalities of teaching staff: U.S., 31; U.K., 3; host, 26; other, 3; total, 63
Grade levels: N – 12
Enrollment: N – preK, 21; K, 25; 1 – 6, 158; 7 – 9, 83; 10 – 12, 113; total, 400
Nationalities of student body: U.S., 100; U.K., 7; host, 120; other, 173; total, 400
Capacity: N – preK, 30; K, 15; 1 – 6, 150; 7 – 9, 150; 10 – 12, 370; total, 715
Teacher/student ratio: 1/7
Tuition (annual): N – preK, $2,750; K – 6, $5,800; 7 – 10, $6,550; 11 – 12, $7,200
Other fees (annual): registration, $484; busing, $300; share per student*, $24 (refundable); capital assessment*, $2,000
School year: August to June

Year founded: 1971. **Type of school:** coed, day, private nonprofit. **Governed by:** elected board of directors. **Sponsored by:** parents. **Accredited by:** Southern. **Regional organizations:** AASSA, Tri-Assoc.

Curriculum/physical plant

Type: U.S., IB, AP. **Languages taught:** French, Spanish, Japanese. **Staff specialists:** computer, counselor, psychologist, learning disabilities, nurse, gifted and talented, resource. **Special programs:** ESL, honors sections, independent study, correspondence, remedial. **Special curricular:** art, chorus, physical education, computer instruction, Japanese. **Extracurricular:** drama, yearbook, newspaper, photography, excursions/expeditions, field trips. **Sports:** basketball, soccer, softball, volleyball, futbolito. **Clubs:** chess, student council, scuba, photography, French, Ayuda y Amistad, adventure, debate. **Tests:** PSAT, SAT, ACT, TOEFL, IB, AP, Iowa. **Graduates attending college:** 98%. **Graduates have attended:** Notre Dame, Yale, Cornell, MIT, Georgetown. **Location:** on hilltop overlooking Caracas. **Campus:** 15 acres. **Library:** 30,000 volumes. **Facilities:** 6 buildings, 51 classrooms, auditorium, cafeteria, infirmary, gymnasium, playing field, science lab, computer lab, air conditioning.

*Once only fee

Escuela Campo Alegre

Street address: Final Calle La Cinta, Las Mercedes, Caracas D.F., Venezuela
Phone: (58)(2)9937135/9938907/9935446/9936606
Facsimile: (58)(2)9930219 **E-mail:** pgreben@internet.ve
Mail: Apartado del Este 60382, Caracas 1060-A, Venezuela
U.S. mail: M – 314 Jet Cargo Int'l, PO Box 020010, Miami, FL 33102-0010, U.S.A.
Superintendent: Paul Greben
Principal, upper school: Gary Crippin
Principal, middle school: Jill Sperandio
Co-principals, elementary school: Jane Shartzer, Patricia Handly-Johnson
Teaching staff: full-time, 117; part-time, 2; total, 119
Grade levels: preK – 12
Enrollment: preK, 32; K, 63; 1 – 5, 387; 6 – 8, 256; 9 – 12, 225; total, 963
Nationalities of student body: U.S., 351; U.K., 32; host, 232; other, 348; total, 963
Teacher/student ratio: 1/8
Tuition (annual): preK, $5,180; K – 5, $10,035; 6 – 11, $12,195; 12, $12,690
Other fees: matriculation, $600; capital fund*, $5,000
School year: August to June

Year founded: 1937. **Type of school:** coed, day, company-sponsored, private nonprofit. **Governed by:** appointed board of directors. **Sponsored by:** multinational companies, parents. **Accredited by:** Southern, ECIS. **Regional organizations:** ACCAS, AASSA, NAIS, ECIS.

Curriculum/physical plant

Type: U.S., IB, AP. **Languages taught:** French, Spanish. **Staff specialists:** computer, speech/hearing, learning disabilities, nurse, ESL, language arts, math/science, counselors. **Special programs:** honors sections, remedial, child study team, Model UN. **Special curricular:** art, physical education, computer instruction, drama, music, academically talented. **Extracurricular:** gymnastics, dance, choral music, computers, yearbook, newspaper, literary magazine, field trips, community service, after-school activities program (bus transportation). **Sports:** basketball, soccer, softball, volleyball, interscholastic league (grades 5 – 12). **Organizations:** National Honor Society, National Junior Honor Society, student council, Boy Scouts, Cub Scouts, Girl Scouts, Brownies. **Tests:** SSAT, PSAT, SAT, AP, IB, CTP, Achievement. **Location:** in city. **Campus:** 11 acres. **Library:** 25,000 volumes. **Facilities:** 9 buildings, 77 classrooms, cafeteria, infirmary, covered play area, gymnasium, playing field, 8 science labs, 3 computer labs, theater-auditorium, AV equipment, weight room.

*Once only fee

OJEDA

Escuela Las Morochas

Street address: Avenida Intercomunal – Sector Las Morochas, Ojeda, Zulia, Venezuela
Phone/facsimile: (58)(65)25539
Mail: Apartado Postal #235, Ojeda, Venezuela
U.S. mail: BAMCO-MAR 01900, PO Box 522237, Miami, FL 33152-2237, U.S.A.
Director: Stephen Sibley
Teaching staff: full-time, 11; part-time, 3; total, 14
Nationalities of teaching staff: U.S., 11; host, 2; other, 1; total, 14
Grade levels: K – 10
Enrollment: K, 16; 1 – 6, 54; 7 – 9, 23; total, 93
Nationalities of student body: U.S., 55; other, 38; total, 93
Teacher/student ratio: 1/8
Tuition (annual): K – 10, $9,000
School year: late August to early June

Type of school: coed, private nonprofit. **Governed by:** appointed board of directors. **Accredited by:** Southern (in process).

Curriculum/physical plant

Type: U.S. **Languages taught:** Spanish. **Staff specialists:** computer, ESL, music, physical education. **Special programs:** ESL. **Special curricular:** art, physical education, computer instruction, music. **Extracurricular:** drama, computers, excursions/expeditions, intramural sports. **Clubs:** chess, arts. **Tests:** Iowa. **Location:** in city, 90-minute drive from Maracaibo. **Campus:** 3 acres. **Facilities:** 1 building, 20 classrooms, auditorium, covered play area, tennis court, playing field, science lab, computer lab, library, air conditioning.

PUERTO ORDAZ

Morrocoy Tutorial Services

Street address: Unare II, Urb. Río Caura, Calle Yuruani, Manz 131-01, Frente al Polideportivo Venalum, Puerto Ordaz 8016, Edo. Bolivar, Venezuela
Phone: (58)(86)520016 **Facsimile:** (58)(86)521861
E-mail: john_mitchell@placerdome.com
U.S. mail: c/o Placer Dome de Venezuela, CA-M114 Jet Cargo Int'l, PO Box 020010, Miami, FL 33103-0013, U.S.A.
Headmaster: John C. Mitchell
Teaching staff: full-time, 7; part-time, 2; total, 9
Nationalities of teaching staff: U.S., 5; host 2, other, 2; total, 9
Grade levels: K – 9
Enrollment: total, 29

Nationalities of student body: U.S., 7; other, 22; total, 29
Capacity: total, 65
Teacher/student ratio: 1/4
Tuition (annual): $16,000
School year: August to June

Year founded: 1990. **Type of school:** coed, day, company-sponsored, non-profit, tutorial. **Governed by:** appointed and elected board of directors. **Sponsored by:** Minera Las Cristinas, C.A. **Operated by:** International Schools Services, Princeton, New Jersey.

Curriculum/physical plant

Type: U.S. **Languages taught:** Spanish. **Special curricular:** art, ESL, music, physical education including swimming, computer, field trips. **Extracurricular:** computers, drama, arts/crafts, sports. **Library:** 5,000 volumes. **Facilities:** 8 classrooms, covered outdoor gymnasium, shower/changing rooms, large playing fields, playground equipment, bus service available, air conditioning.

VALENCIA

Colegio Internacional de Carabobo

Street address: Calle Zuloaga Cruce Con Calle El Colegio, El Trigal Centro, Valencia, Venezuela
Phone: (58)(41)421807/426551 **Facsimile:** (58)(41)426510
U.S. mail: VLN 1010, PO Box 025685, Miami, FL 33102-5685, U.S.A.
Superintendent: Frank Anderson
High school principal: Lauren Wilson
Elementary school principal: Judith Tostenrud
Business manager: Virginia Campi
Teaching staff: full-time, 36; part-time, 10; total, 46
Nationalities of teaching staff: U.S., 26; host, 13; other, 7; total, 46
Grade levels: JK – 12
Enrollment: JK, 26; K, 36; 1 – 6, 176; 7 – 9, 68; 10 – 12, 44; total, 350
Nationalities of student body: U.S., 68; host, 170; other, 112; total, 350
Capacity: total, 450
Teacher/student ratio: 1/9
Tuition (annual): JK – K, $7,500; 1 – 8, $10,800; 9 – 12, $11,500
Other fees (annual): registration, $600 (new student), $300 (returning student); capital levy, $3,000; busing, $1,200; entrance*, $3,000; special projects, $2,000
School year: August to June

Year founded: 1955. **Type of school:** coed, day, company-sponsored. **Governed by:** elected board of education. **Sponsored by:** corporate/private sectors. **Accredited by:** Southern. **Regional organizations:** AASSA.

Curriculum/physical plant

Type: U.S. **Languages taught:** French, Spanish. **Staff specialists:** math, computer, counselor, nurse, music. **Special programs:** ESL. **Special curricular:** art, chorus, physical education, computer instruction. **Extracurricular:** drama, dance, choral music, computers, yearbook, literary magazine, field trips. **Sports:** basketball, soccer, softball, volleyball, frequent student-parent/faculty sports competition. **Clubs:** very extensive secondary school and elementary activities programs, intramurals, mothers' service club. **Tests:** PSAT, SAT, TOEFL, AP, Iowa. **Graduates attending college:** 100%. **Graduates have attended:** prestigious U.S. and other international universities. **Location:** on picturesque, sprawling campus in suburb of El Trigal, 5 minutes from central Valencia, 90 miles from Caracas. **Campus:** 15 acres. **Libraries (2):** 16,200 volumes. **Facilities:** 10 buildings, 43 classrooms, auditorium, cafeteria, 3 computer labs, covered recreational area, 2 athletic fields, science labs.

*Once only fee

VIETNAM

Region: South Asia
Size: 127,816 square miles
Population: 73,976,973
Capital: Hanoi
Telephone code: 84
Currency: dong
Languages: Vietnamese, Chinese, French

HANOI

Hanoi International School

Street address: Lieu Giai Street, Ba Dinh District, Hanoi, Vietnam
Phone: (94)(4)8327379 **Facsimile:** (94)(4)8327535
U.S. mail: PO Box 2876, Reston, VA 20195, U.S.A.
Principal: Bruce Gilbert, Ed.D.
Director of studies: Sue Pears
Teaching staff: full-time, 15; part-time, 5; total, 20
Nationalities of teaching staff: U.S., 3; U.K., 6; host, 3; other, 8; total, 20
Grade levels: preK – 12
Enrollment: preK, 5; K, 5; 1 – 6, 40; 7 – 9, 30; 10 – 12, 20; total, 100
Teacher/student ratio: 1/6
Tuition (annual): preK, $6,400; K, $7,200; 1 – 6, $8,400; 7 – 9, $9,300; 10 – 12, $11,500
Other fees: registration*, $1,000; capital levy, $1,250 (3 yearly payments)
School year: August to June

Year founded: 1996. **Type of school:** coed, day, private. **Governed by:** appointed board of directors. **Sponsored by:** Vietnamese Ministry of Education.

Curriculum/physical plant

Type: IB, international. **Languages taught:** English, French, Vietnamese. **Special programs:** ESL. **Special curricular:** art, chorus, physical education, computer instruction. **Extracurricular:** drama, dance, choral music, computers, yearbook, newspaper, excursions/expeditions, field trips. **Tests:** IB. **Location:** in city.

*Once only fee

United Nations International School Hanoi

Phone: (84)(4)8235782/8234910 **Facsimile:** (84)(4)8463635
E-mail: unis@netnam.org.vn
Mail: c/o UNDP-Hanoi, PO Box 618, Bangkok 10501, Thailand
U.S. mail: c/o UNDP–Vietnam, Box 1608, Grand Central Station Center, New York, NY 10163-1608, U.S.A.
Director: Dr. Frances Rhodes
High school principal: Peter Ostrom
Elementary principal: Ron Auckland
Teaching staff: full-time, 39; part-time, 17; total, 56
Nationalities of teaching staff: U.S., 11; U.K., 6; host, 5; other, 34; total, 56
Grade levels: preK – 11
Enrollment: preK, 16; K, 34; 1 – 6, 215; 7 – 11, 85; total, 350
Nationalities of student body: U.S., 30; U.K., 7; host, 4; other, 309; total, 350
Capacity: preK, 16; K, 32; 1 – 6, 270; 7 – 11, 108; total, 426
Teacher/student ratio: 1/8
Tuition (annual): preK – K, $6,400; 1 – 6, $7,400; 7 – 8, $7,600; 9 – 11, $8,500
Other fees (annual): busing, $300; enrollment, $1,500; development, $1,500
School year: August to June

Year founded: 1988. **Type of school:** coed, day, private nonprofit. **Governed by:** board of trustees.

Curriculum/physical plant

Type: international. **Languages taught:** French, Swedish, Vietnamese. **Staff specialists:** computer, art, music, resource, physical education, resource. **Special programs:** ESL. **Special curricular:** art, chorus, physical education, computer instruction. **Extracurricular:** drama, choral music, excursions/expeditions, field trips, youth club. **Sports:** basketball, softball, Tae Kwon Do. **Location:** in Van Phuc area, 3 kilometers from central Hanoi. **Library:** 8,000 volumes. **Facilities:** Hanoi-Amsterdam: space rented from and shared with a Vietnamese school for grades 4 – 10. Van Phuc: rented ground floor of apartment building, 1 kilometer from main campus for preK – 3.

*Once only fee

HO CHI MINH CITY

International Grammar School

Street address: 236 Nam Ky Khoi Nghia Street, District 3, Ho Chi Minh City, Vietnam
Phone: (84)(88)293237 **Facsimile:** (84)(88)230000
Principal: Neil McWilliam
Business manager: Martin Snell
Teaching staff: full-time, 63; part-time, 2; total, 65
Nationalities of teaching staff: host, 4; other, 61; total, 65
Grade levels: preschool – 10
Enrollment: preS – 1, 170; 2 – 5, 280; 6 – 10, 150; total, 600

Teacher/student ratio: 1/10
Tuition (annual): preS, $6,300; K – 5, $9,100; 6 – 8, $10,000; 9 – 10, $10,700
Other fees: capital levy*, $6,500
School year: August to June

Year founded: 1993. **Type of school:** coed, day, proprietary. **Governed by:** appointed board of management. **Accredited by:** Australian NSW Department of Education.

Curriculum/physical plant

Type: modified Australian, IGCSE (grades 9 & 10). **Languages taught:** French, Japanese, Korean, Vietnamese. **Staff specialists:** math, computer. **Special programs:** ESL. **Special curricular:** art, chorus, physical education, computer instruction. **Extracurricular:** drama, choral music, computers, excursions/expeditions. **Sports:** badminton, soccer, volleyball. **Tests:** Iowa. **Location:** junior campus in city, senior campus in suburb. **Library:** 20,000 volumes. **Facilities:** science labs, computer labs, swimming pool, sports field, air conditioning.

*Once only fee

YEMEN

Region: Middle East
Size: 205,356 square miles
Population: 13,483,178
Capitals: Sanaa, Aden
Telephone code: 967
Currency: rial
Language: Arabic

ADEN

Aden International School

Phone/facsimile: (967)(2)231897 **E-mail:** ais.h@netqsi.com
Mail: Box 6227, Khormaksar, Aden, Yemen
Head teacher: Kevin Hall
Teaching staff: full-time, 2; total, 2
Nationalities of teaching staff: Canada, 2; total, 2
Grade levels: K – 8
Enrollment: total, 4
Capacity: K, 7; 1 – 6, 7; 7 – 8, 7; total, 21
Tuition (annual): K – 5, $6,900; 6 – 8, $9,200
Other fees: registration*, $100; capital levy: $4,000 deposit or $1,600/year fee
School year: September to June

Year founded: 1991. **Type of school:** coed, day, private nonprofit. **Governed by:** appointed board of directors. **Sponsored by:** Quality Schools International. **Regional organizations:** CEESA.

Curriculum/physical plant

Type: U.S. **Languages taught:** French. **Special programs:** ESL, independent study. **Special curricular:** art, physical education, computer instruction, music. **Extracurricular:** excursions/expeditions. **Sports:** swimming, ping-pong, field games. **Location:** quiet residential area, 1 kilometer from Aden International Airport. **Facilities:** 2-story building, 3 classroooms, resource center, air conditioning.

*Once only fee

SANAA

Sanaa International School

Phone: (967)(1)234437–8 **Facsimile:** (967)(1)234438
E-mail: jim.g@netqsi.com
Mail: Box 2002, Sanaa, Yemen
Director: James E. Gilson
Director of instruction: Frank Underhill
Teaching staff: full-time, 16; part-time, 7; total, 23
Nationalities of teaching staff: U.S., 14; other, 9; total, 23
Grade levels: N – 12
Enrollment: N, 14; K, 9; 1 – 6, 84; 7 – 9, 34; 10 – 12, 25; total, 166
Capacity: N, 20; K, 20; 1 – 6, 150; 7 – 9, 75; 10 – 12, 75; total, 340
Teacher/student ratio: 1/6
Tuition (annual): N, $2,000; K – 5, $6,900; 6 – 12, $9,200
Other fees: registration*, $100; busing, $600; capital levy: $4,000 deposit or $1,600/year fee
School year: September to June

Year founded: 1971. **Type of school:** coed, day, private nonprofit. **Governed by:** appointed board of directors. **Accredited by:** Middle States. **Regional organizations:** NESA, CEESA.

Curriculum/physical plant

Type: U.S., AP. **Languages taught:** Arabic and French as foreign languages; Arabic and Dutch as native languages. **Staff specialists:** nurse, resource. **Special programs:** ESL, independent study. **Special curricular:** art, physical education, computer instruction, instrumental music. **Extracurricular:** drama, excursions/expeditions, field trips. **Sports:** basketball, field hockey, soccer, track and field, volleyball, roller hockey. **Tests:** AP, IGCSE. **Graduates have attended:** Georgetown, American U., John Hopkins, Columbia, American U. of Cairo. **Location:** agricultural area in hills, 5 kilometers from Sanaa. **Campus:** 34 acres. **Facilities:** 3 buildings, 21 classrooms, 3 playing fields, 2 science labs, 2 computer labs, library, auditorium.

*Once only fee

TAIZ

Mohamed Ali Othman School

Phone: (967)(4)223671 – 2 **Facsimile:** (967)(4)211495
Mail: PO Box 5713, Taiz, Yemen
Head of trustees: Dr. Abdul Qadir Algunied
Principal: Dr. Ezzat Mahmoud Ali
Teaching staff: full-time, 131; total, 131
Grade levels: K – 12
Capacity: K, 160; 1 – 6, 550; 7 – 9, 180; 10 – 12, 120; total, 1,010
Tuition (annual): $1,200
School year: September to June

Year founded: 1972. **Type of school:** coed, day. **Governed by:** elected board of trustees. **Accredited by:** ECIS.

Curriculum/physical plant

Type: U.S., U.K. **Staff specialists:** computer, librarian, music. **Special curricular:** educational trips, debates, science exhibitions, activity programs. **Tests:** SAT, TOEFL, A- and O-level GCE. **Facilities:** 7 buildings, auditorium, playing field, science lab, computer lab, library, AV room.

YUGOSLAVIA

Region: Europe
Size: 39,449 square miles
Population: 10,614,558
Capital: Belgrade
Telephone code: 381
Currency: dinar
Languages: Serbo-Croatian, Albanian

BELGRADE

International School of Belgrade

Street address: Temisvarska 19, Belgrade, 11040 Serbia, Yugoslavia
Phone: (381)(11)651832 **Facsimile:** (381)(11)652619 **E-mail:** isb@eunet.yu
U.S. mail: Dept. of State, Washington, DC 20521-5070
Director/business manager: Nikola Kodzas, Ph.D.
Teaching staff: full-time, 12; total, 12
Nationalities of teaching staff: U.S., 4; U.K., 4; other, 4; total, 12
Grade levels: K – 8
Enrollment: K, 3; 1 – 6, 41; 7 – 8, 14; total, 58
Nationalities of student body: U.S., 3; host, 9; other, 46; total, 58
Capacity: K, 36; 1 – 6, 124; 7 – 8, 36; total, 196
Teacher/student ratio: 1/5
Tuition (annual): $10,720
School year: September to June

Year founded: 1948. **Type of school:** coed, day. **Governed by:** international school board. **Accredited by:** New England, ECIS. **Regional organizations:** AAIE, ECIS, CEESA.

Curriculum/physical plant

Type: U.S. **Languages taught:** French. **Staff specialists:** computer, nurse, librarian, music. **Special programs:** ESL. **Special curricular:** chorus, physical education, computer instruction, swimming. **Extracurricular:** computers, yearbook, field trips, after-school enrichment/activity program. **Tests:** Iowa, CAT, DAT. **Location:** in suburban area. **Campus:** 1.5 acres. **Library:** 8,000 volumes. **Facilities:** 5 buildings, 15 classrooms, playing field, science lab, computer lab, AV room.

ZAMBIA

Region: Southern Africa
Size: 290,586 square miles
Population: 9,159,072
Capital: Lusaka
Telephone code: 260
Currency: kwacha
Languages: English, Bantu dialects

LUSAKA

American International School†

Street address: Leopards Hill Road, Lusaka, Zambia
Phone: (260)(1)260509 – 10/260543 **Facsimile:** (260)(1)252225
E-mail: aesl@zamnet.zm
Mail: PO Box 31617, Lusaka, Zambia
U.S. mail: c/o Dept. of State – Lusaka, Washington, DC 20521-2310
Director: John Ritter
Library media specialist: Lori Lawrenz
Teaching staff: full-time, 21; part-time, 6; total, 27
Nationalities of teaching staff: U.S., 10; U.K., 9; other, 8; total, 27
Grade levels: preK – 9
Enrollment: preK, 77, K, 23; 1 – 6, 113; 7 – 9, 18; total 231
Nationalities of student body: U.S., 51; U.K., 39; other, 141; total, 231
Teacher/student ratio: 1/9
Tuition (annual): preS, $2,200; preK, $5,400; K – 6, $7,200; 7 – 9, $7,800
Other fees (annual): admission*, $2,000; busing, $1,000; special services, $10/hour
School year: August to June

Year founded: 1986. **Type of school:** coed, day. **Governed by:** American Embassy and elected board of directors. **Sponsored by:** American Embassy. **Accredited by:** Middle States, ECIS.

Curriculum/physical plant

Type: U.S., international. **Languages taught:** French. **Special programs:** ESL, special needs. **Special curricular:** art, physical education, drama, field studies, computers, music. **Extracurricular:** drama, computers, art, music, conservation club. **Sports:** basketball, field hockey, soccer, softball, swimming, tennis, volleyball. **Tests:** SSAT, Iowa. **Location:** in suburban area of Lusaka. **Campus:** 15 acres. **Library:** more than 6,000 volumes. **Facilities:** 8 buildings, 20 classrooms, 6 tutoring rooms, library media center, music room, art studio; physical education complex, including covered courts for basketball, volleyball, and badminton, soccer/softball field, running track, swimming pool, tennis courts.

*Once only fee †formerly AESL International School

Lusaka International Community School

Street address: 242 B Kakola Road, Roma, Lusaka, Zambia
Phone/facsimile: (260)(1)292447 **E-mail:** lics@zamnet.zm
Web: http://www.zamnet.zm/zamnet/education/lics/lics.html
Headmaster: Hugh Younger
Deputy head: Maria Plant
Teaching staff: full-time, 21; part-time, 5; total, 26
Nationalities of teaching staff: U.S., 3; U.K., 8; host, 2; other, 13; total, 26
Grade levels: N – 9
Enrollment: N, 56; K, 30; 1 – 6, 134; 7 – 9, 40; total, 260
Nationalities of student body: U.S., 15; U.K., 65; host, 55; other, 125; total, 260
Teacher/student ratio: 1/10
Tuition (annual): N, $1,950; K – 9, $5,400
Other fees: registration*, $200; capital levy*, $2,000; books, $500
School year: August to June

Year founded: 1993. **Type of school:** coed, day, private nonprofit. **Governed by:** board of directors.

Curriculum/physical plant

Type: international. **Languages taught:** French, German. **Staff specialists:** reading, computer, art, ESL, music, physical education, academic support, French. **Special programs:** ESL. **Special curricular:** physical education, computer instruction. **Extracurricular:** drama, computers, newspaper, literary magazine, excursions/expeditions, field trips. **Sports:** field hockey, soccer, swimming, volleyball. **Clubs:** chess, embroidery, papercraft, nature, aerobics. **Location:** garden setting, 3 miles from city center. **Campus:** 4 acres. **Library:** 5,000 volumes. **Facilities:** 8 buildings, 19 classrooms, 2 covered play areas, 2 tennis courts, playing field, computer lab, 2 swimming pools.

*Once only fee

The International School of Lusaka - Zambia

Street address: Nangwenya Road, Lusaka, Zambia
Phone: (260)(1)252291/253959 **Facsimile:** (260)(1)252865
E-mail: isl@zamnet.zm or isladmin@zamnet.zm
Mail: PO Box 50121, Ridgeway, Lusaka, Zambia
Superintendent: Helge H. Gallinger
Secondary school principal: Kent Kildahl
Primary school principal: Earl J. Ballard
Teaching staff: full-time, 73; part-time, 1; total, 74
Nationalities of teaching staff: U.S., 6; U.K., 15; host, 18; other, 35; total, 74
Grade levels: N – 12 (reception – IB)
Enrollment: N – 6, 462; forms 1 – 6, 385; total, 847
Nationalities of student body: U.S., 15; U.K., 120; host, 280; other, 432; total, 847
Capacity: N – 6, 580; forms 1 – 6, 470; total, 1,050
Teacher/student ratio: 1/11
Tuition (annual): N – 6, $3,000; forms 1 – 3, $4,350; forms 4 – 5, $4,500; form 6, $6,000
Other fees: registration*, $200; enrollment*, $1,500
School year: August to June

Year founded: 1963. **Type of school:** coed, day, private nonprofit. **Governed by:** board of governors. **Accredited by:** ECIS, New England (in process). **Regional organizations:** ECIS, AISA.

Curriculum/physical plant

Type: U.K., IB, IGCSE. **Languages taught:** English, French, Spanish, German. **Staff specialists:** counselor, nurse, resource, diagnostician. **Special programs:** ESL, remedial. **Special curricular:** art, physical education, computer instruction, drama, music, field trips. **Extracurricular:** gymnastics, dance, computers, yearbook, newspaper. **Sports:** badminton, basketball, rugby, soccer, swimming, tennis, volleyball. **Tests:** SSAT, PSAT, SAT, ACT, TOEFL, IB, GCSE. **Graduates attending college:** 80%. **Location:** 5 kilometers from city center. **Campus:** 33 acres. **Library:** 10,000 volumes. **Facilities:** 12 buildings, 62 classrooms, auditorium, infirmary, covered play area, computer labs, tennis courts, playing fields, science labs, new olympic-size swimming pool, 400-meter track.

*Once only fee

ZIMBABWE

Region: Southern Africa
Size: 150,872 square miles
Population: 11,271,314
Capital: Harare
Telephone code: 263
Currency: dollar (Zimbabwe)
Languages: English, Shona, Sindebele

HARARE

Harare International School

Street address: 66 Pendennis Road, Mt. Pleasant, Harare, Zimbabwe
Phone: (263)(4)883336 **Facsimile:** (263)(4)883371
Director: Cynthia A. Gray
Teaching staff: full-time, 21; part-time, 6; total, 27
Nationalities of teaching staff: U.S., 13; U.K., 2; other, 12; total, 27
Grade levels: preK – 10
Enrollment: total, 265
Nationalities of student body: U.S., 43; U.K., 35; other, 187; total, 265
Teacher/student ratio: 1/11
Tuition (annual): preK, $2,000; K – 5, $7,900; 6, $8,900; 7 – 8, $9,150; 9 – 10, $11,700
Other fees: registration*, K – 5, $3,000; 6 – 8, $3,500; 9 – 10, $4,500
School year: late August through June

Year founded: 1992. **Type of school:** coed, day, private nonprofit. **Governed by:** appointed and elected board of trustees.

Curriculum/physical plant

Type: U.S. **Languages taught:** English, French. **Staff specialists:** art, music, physical education. **Sports:** basketball, soccer, volleyball. **Location:** prime residential neighborhood in northern Harare. **Campus:** 20 acres. **Library:** 8,500 volumes. **Facilities:** 3 buildings, 14 classrooms, playing field, art room, music room.

*Once only fee

MAPS

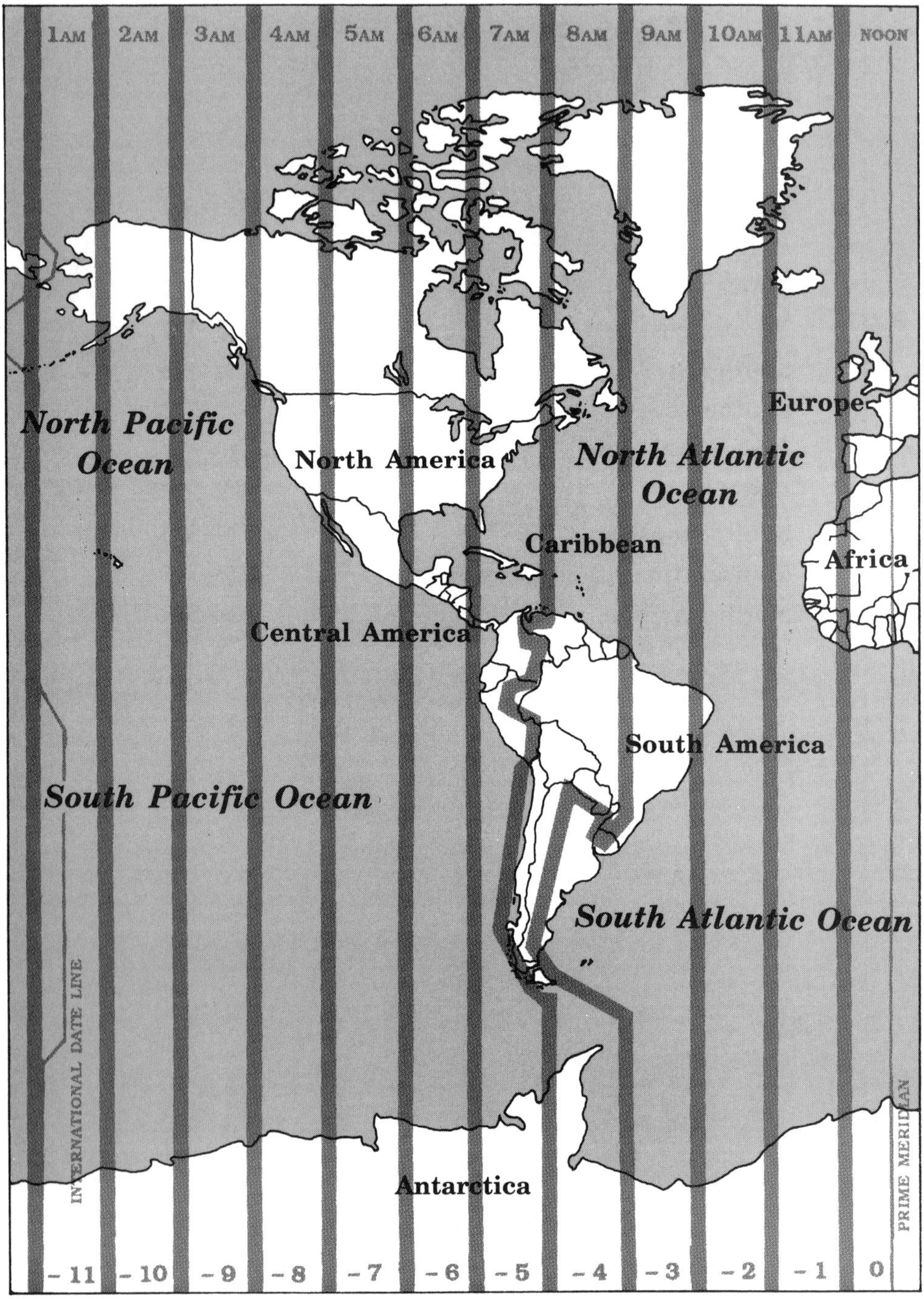
1AM
2AM
3AM
4AM
5AM
6AM
7AM
8AM
9AM
10AM
11AM
NOON
North Pacific Ocean
North America
North Atlantic Ocean
Europe
Caribbean
Africa
Central America
South America
South Pacific Ocean
South Atlantic Ocean
Antarctica
INTERNATIONAL DATE LINE
PRIME MERIDIAN
− 11
− 10
− 9
− 8
− 7
− 6
− 5
− 4
− 3
− 2
− 1
0

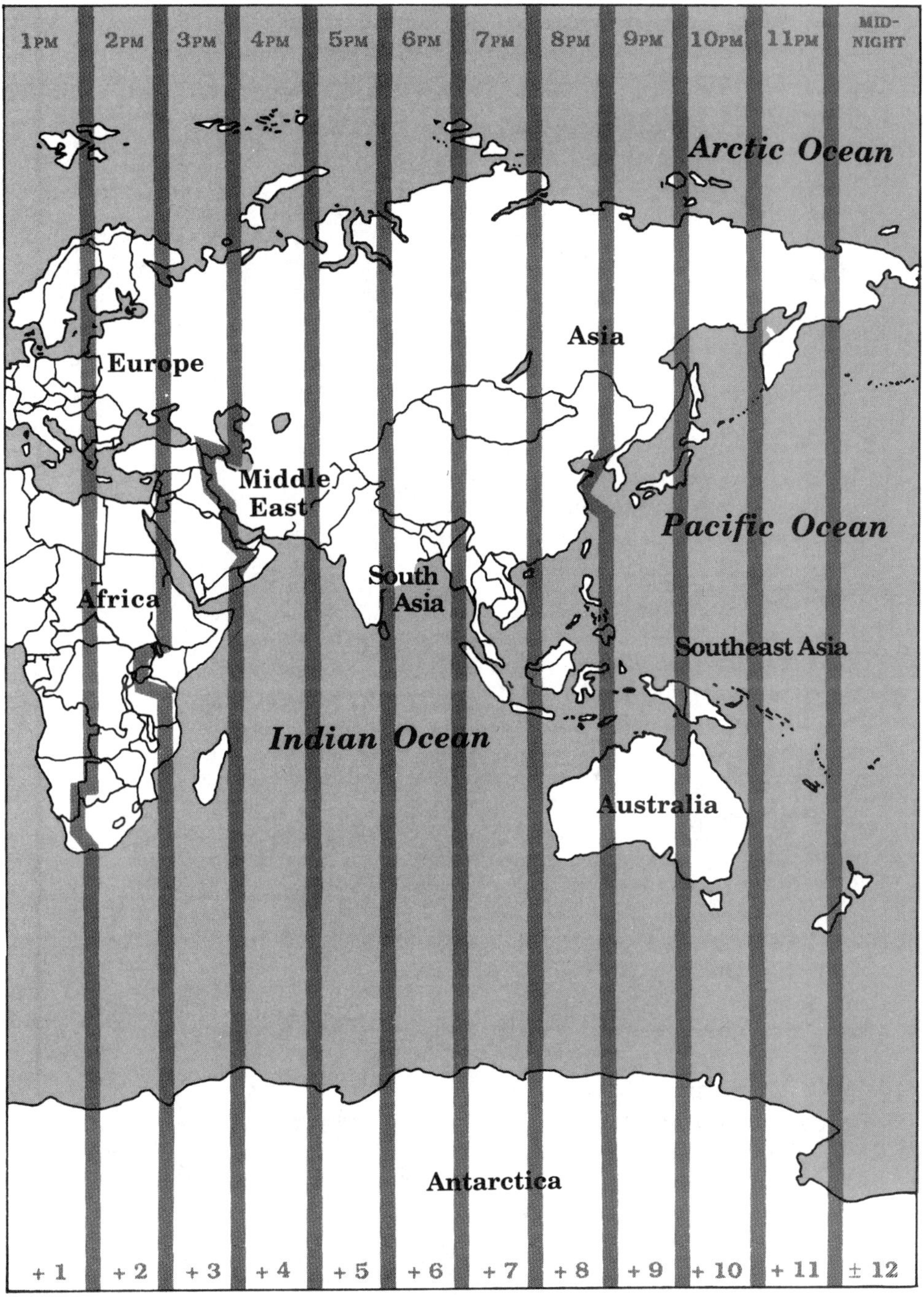
1PM
2PM
3PM
4PM
5PM
6PM
7PM
8PM
9PM
10PM
11PM
MID-NIGHT
Arctic Ocean
Asia
Europe
Middle East
Pacific Ocean
South Asia
Africa
Southeast Asia
Indian Ocean
Australia
Antarctica
+1
+2
+3
+4
+5
+6
+7
+8
+9
+10
+11
±12

Atlantic Ocean
Reykjavik
Iceland
1 **Portugal**, Lisbon
2 **Luxembourg**, Luxembourg
3 **Belgium**, Brussels
4 **The Netherlands**, Amsterdam
5 **Germany, Federal Republic of**, Berlin
6 **Switzerland**, Bern
7 **Czech Republic**, Prague
8 **Slovakia**, Bratislava
9 **Austria**, Vienna
10 **Hungary**, Budapest
11 **Albania**, Tirana
12 **Romania**, Bucharest
13 **Greece**, Athens
14 **Yugoslavia**, Belgrade
15 **Croatia**, Zagreb
16 **Denmark**, Copenhagen
17 **Bulgaria**, Sofia
18 **Estonia**, Tallinn
19 **Latvia**, Riga
20 **Lithuania**, Vilnius
21 **Belarus**, Minsk
22 **Moldova**, Chisinau
23 **Georgia**, Tbilisi
24 **Armenia**, Yerevan
25 **Azerbaijan**, Baku
26 **Uzbekistan**, Tashkent
(not shown) **Kyrgyzstan**, Bishkek (east of Uzbekistan)
27 **Turkmenistan**, Ashgabat
28 **Slovenia**, Ljubljana
29 **Macedonia**, Skopje
30 **Bosnia Herzegovina**, Sarajevo
Norway
Oslo
North Sea
Ireland
Dublin
16
London
United Kingdom
4
5
3
Paris
2
7
France
6
28
Italy
Madrid
1
Spain
Rome

Arctic Ocean
Sweden
Finland
Helsinki
Stockholm
Baltic Sea
Russian Federation
Moscow
18
19
20
21
Poland
Warsaw
Kiev
Ukraine
8
9
10
15
30
14
12
22
17
29
11
13
Black Sea
Kazakhstan
Caspian Sea
23
24
25
26
27
Mediterranean Sea

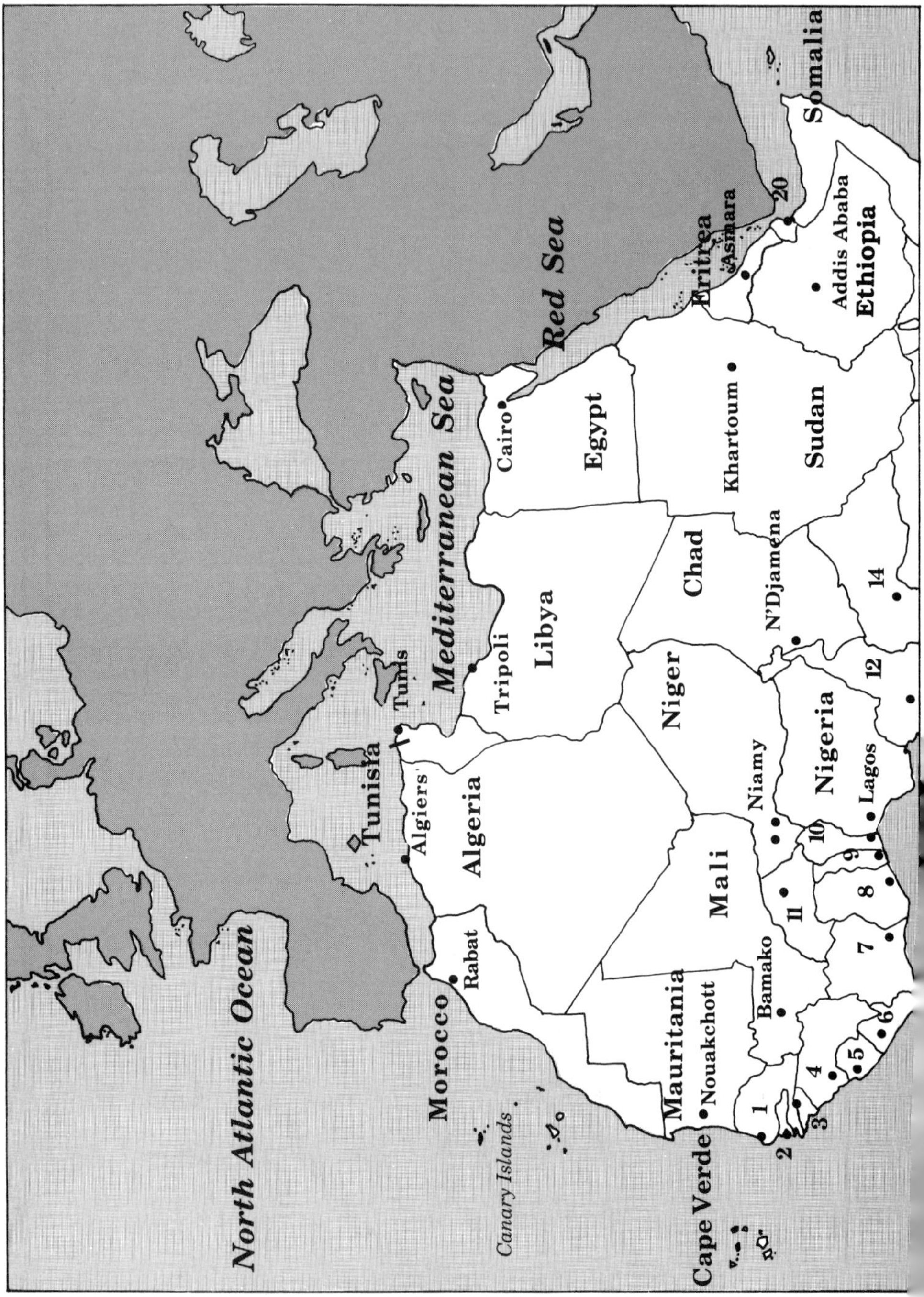
North Atlantic Ocean
Mediterranean Sea
Red Sea
Canary Islands
Cape Verde
Morocco
Rabat
Algeria
Algiers
Tunisia
Tunis
Tripoli
Libya
Cairo
Egypt
Sudan
Khartoum
Eritrea
Asmara
Addis Ababa
Ethiopia
Somalia
Chad
N'Djamena
Niger
Niamey
Nigeria
Lagos
Mali
Bamako
Mauritania
Nouakchott
1
2
3
4
5
6
7
8
9
10
11
12
14
20

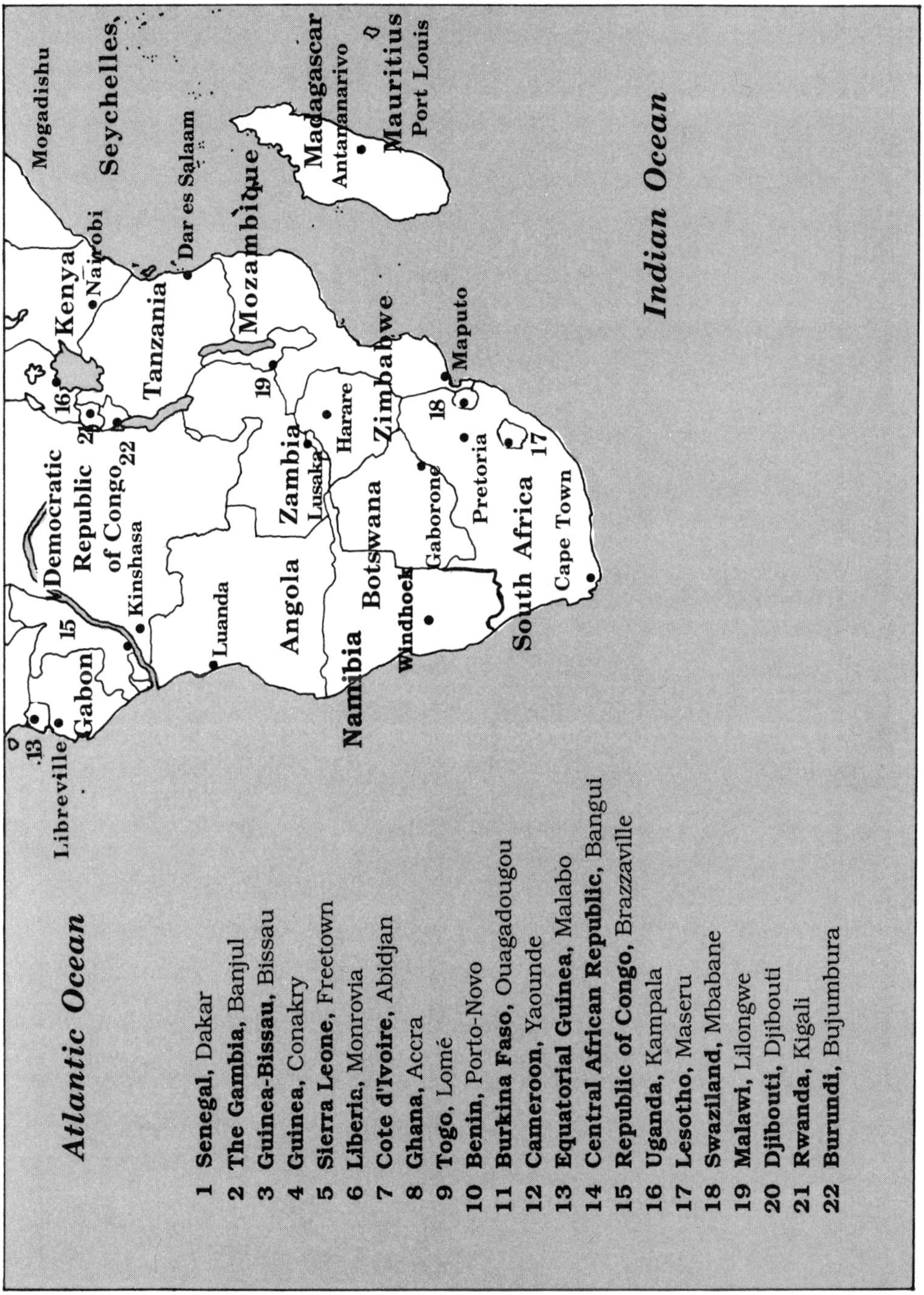
Atlantic Ocean
Indian Ocean
Libreville
Gabon
13
15
Kinshasa
Luanda
Democratic Republic of Congo
22
21
16
Angola
Namibia
Windhoek
Botswana
Gaborone
Zambia
Lusaka
19
Zimbabwe
Harare
18
Pretoria
17
South Africa
Cape Town
Maputo
Mozambique
Tanzania
Dar es Salaam
Kenya
Nairobi
Mogadishu
Seychelles
Madagascar
Antananarivo
Mauritius
Port Louis
1 Senegal, Dakar
2 The Gambia, Banjul
3 Guinea-Bissau, Bissau
4 Guinea, Conakry
5 Sierra Leone, Freetown
6 Liberia, Monrovia
7 Cote d'Ivoire, Abidjan
8 Ghana, Accra
9 Togo, Lomé
10 Benin, Porto-Novo
11 Burkina Faso, Ouagadougou
12 Cameroon, Yaounde
13 Equatorial Guinea, Malabo
14 Central African Republic, Bangui
15 Republic of Congo, Brazzaville
16 Uganda, Kampala
17 Lesotho, Maseru
18 Swaziland, Mbabane
19 Malawi, Lilongwe
20 Djibouti, Djibouti
21 Rwanda, Kigali
22 Burundi, Bujumbura

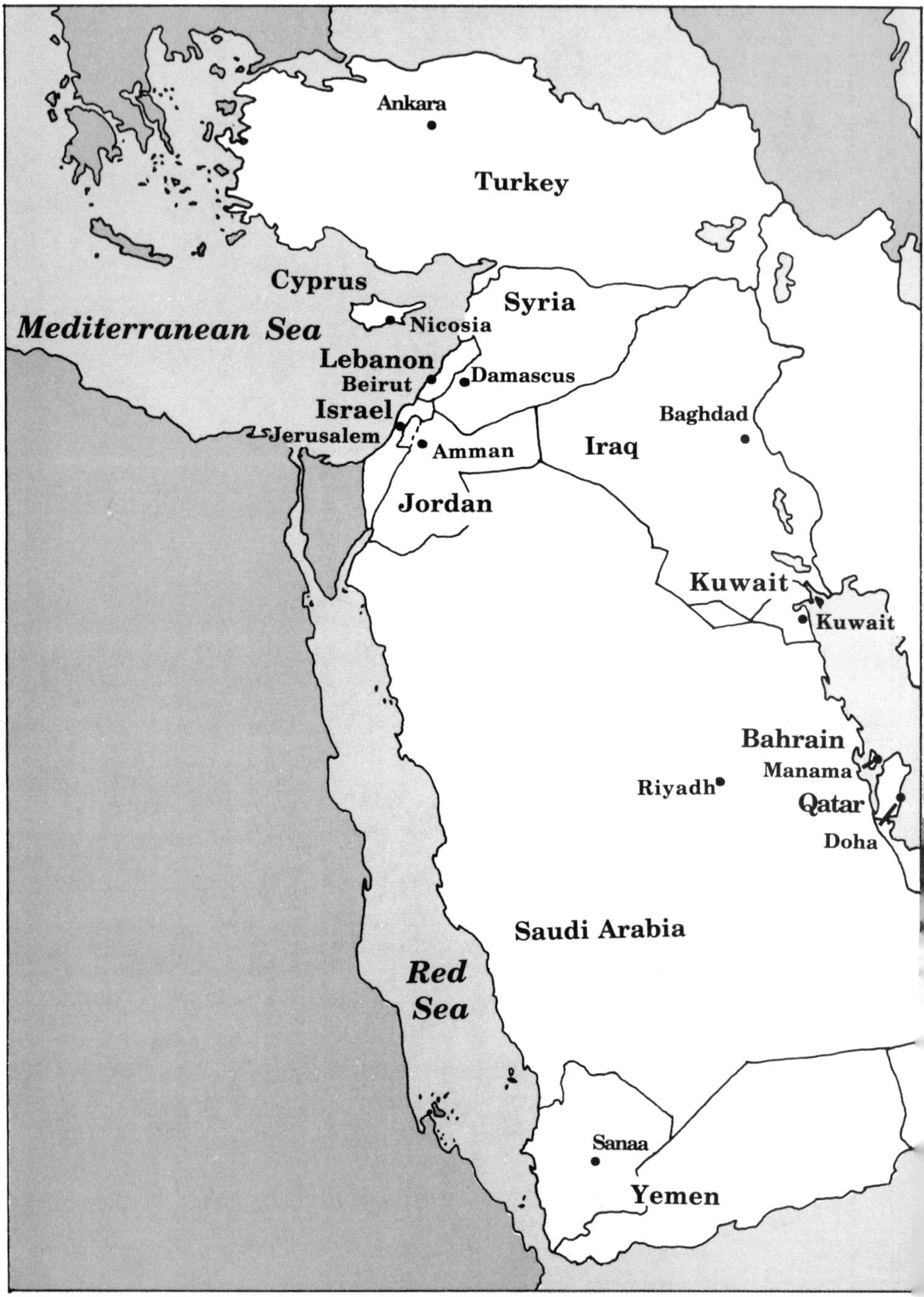
Ankara
Turkey
Cyprus
Syria
Mediterranean Sea
Nicosia
Lebanon
Beirut
Damascus
Israel
Jerusalem
Amman
Iraq
Baghdad
Jordan
Kuwait
Kuwait
Bahrain
Manama
Riyadh
Qatar
Doha
Saudi Arabia
Red Sea
Sanaa
Yemen

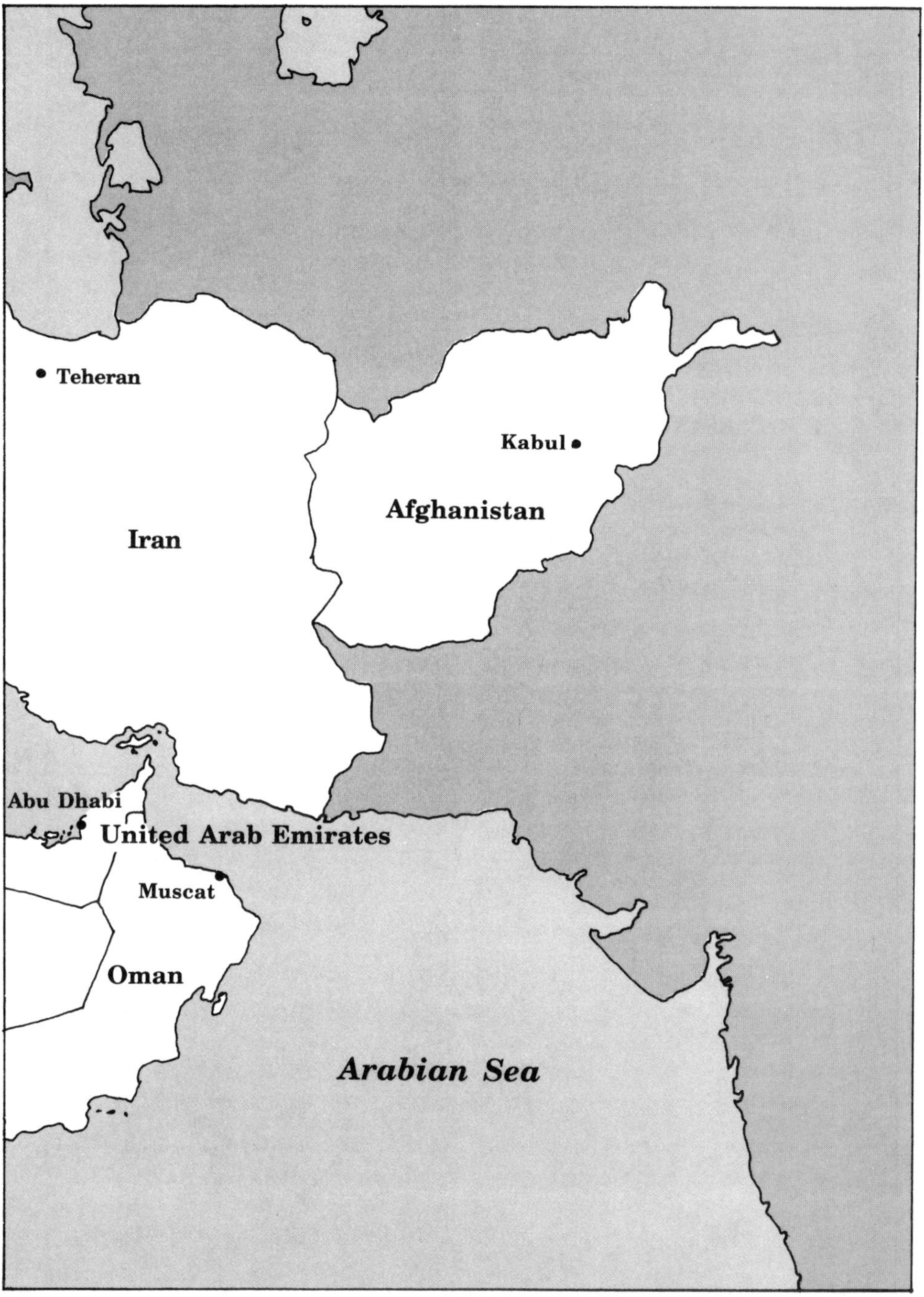
Teheran
Kabul
Afghanistan
Iran
Abu Dhabi
United Arab Emirates
Muscat
Oman
Arabian Sea

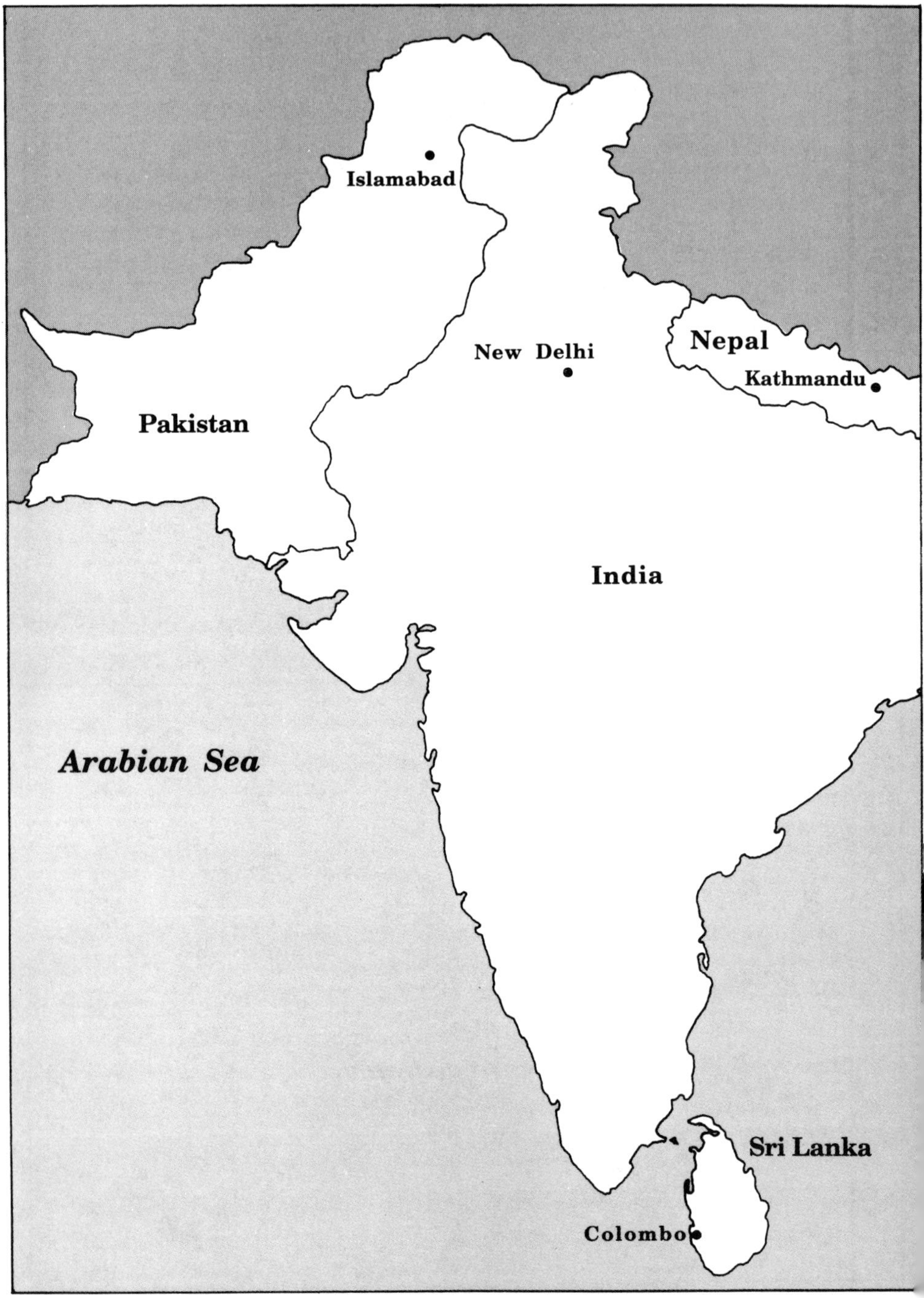
Islamabad
Nepal
New Delhi
Kathmandu
Pakistan
India
Arabian Sea
Sri Lanka
Colombo

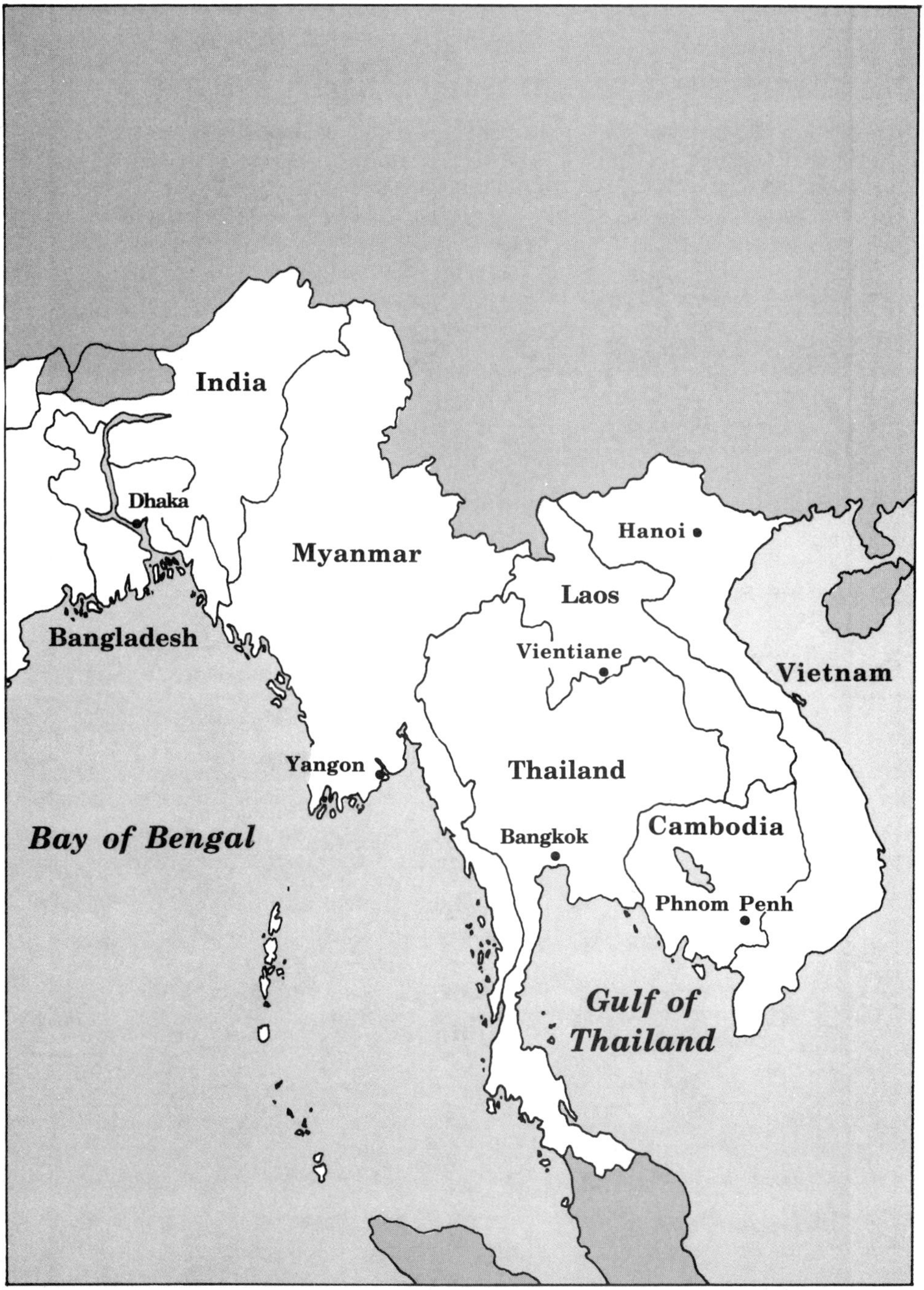
India
Dhaka
Myanmar
Hanoi
Laos
Bangladesh
Vientiane
Vietnam
Yangon
Thailand
Cambodia
Bay of Bengal
Bangkok
Phnom Penh
Gulf of Thailand

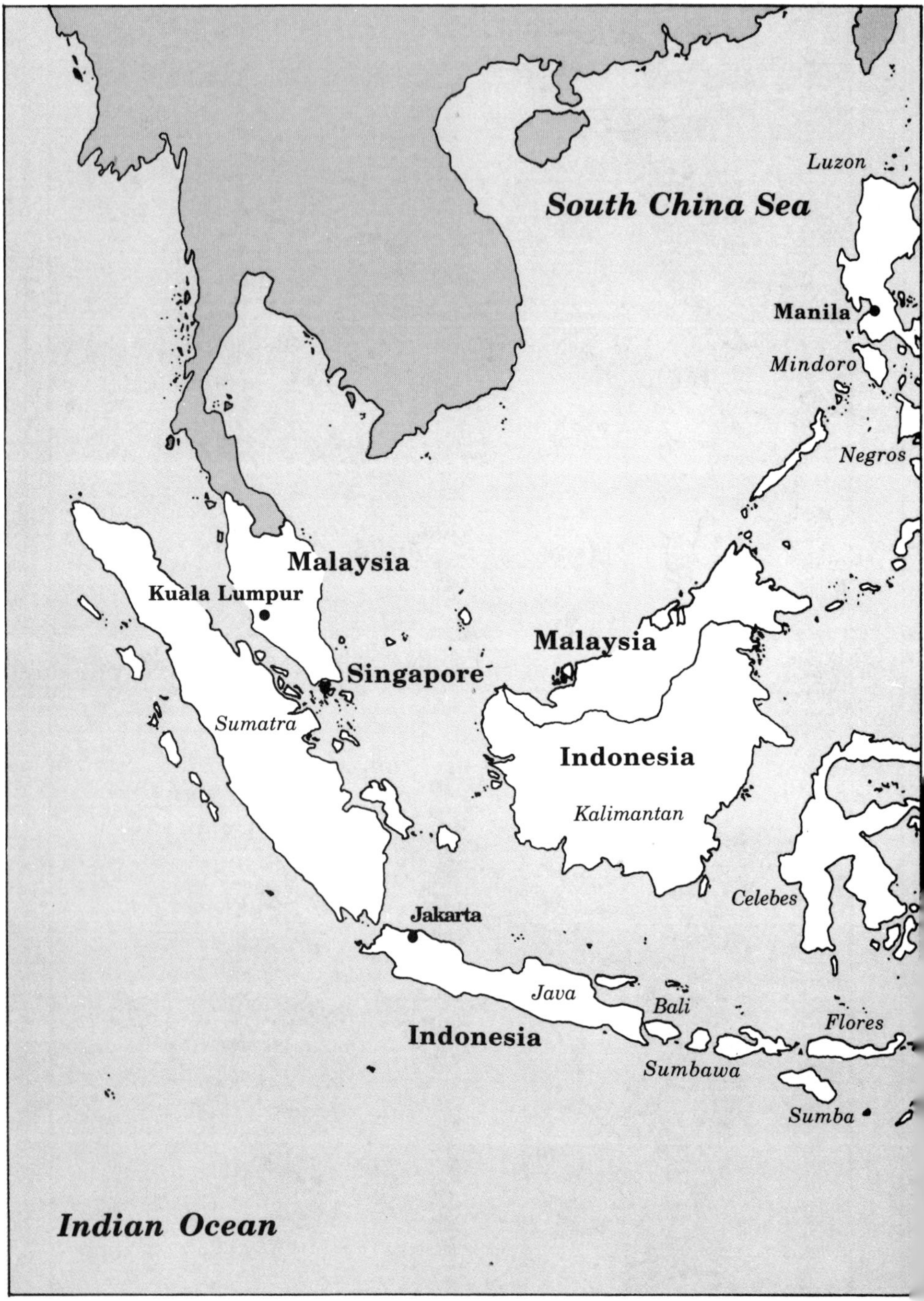
Luzon
South China Sea
Manila
Mindoro
Negros
Malaysia
Kuala Lumpur
Malaysia
Singapore
Sumatra
Indonesia
Kalimantan
Celebes
Jakarta
Java
Bali
Flores
Indonesia
Sumbawa
Sumba
Indian Ocean

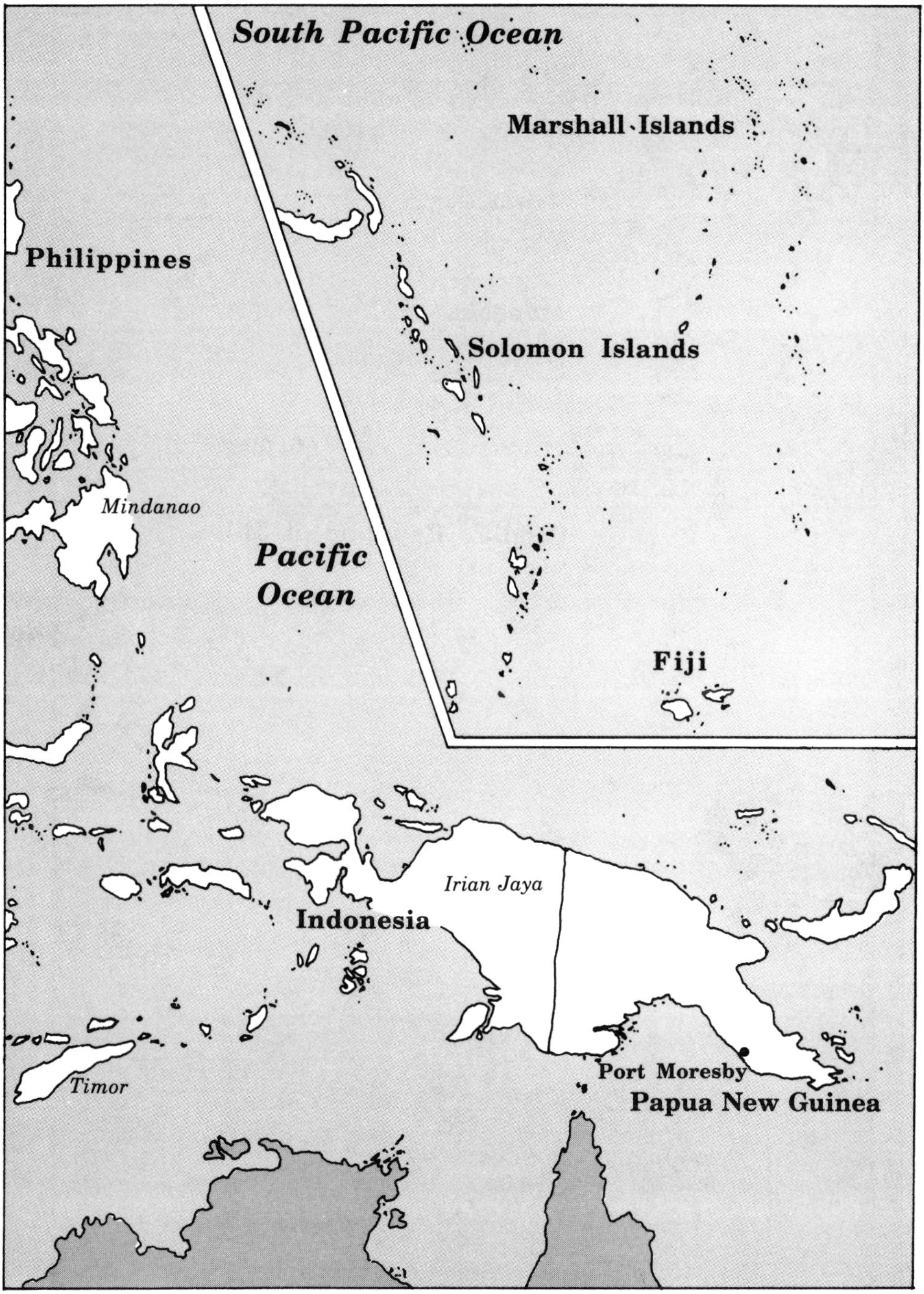
South Pacific Ocean
Marshall Islands
Philippines
Solomon Islands
Mindanao
Pacific
Ocean
Fiji
Irian Jaya
Indonesia
Port Moresby
Papua New Guinea
Timor

Ulaanbaatar
Mongolia
Beijing
People's Republic of China
Yellow Sea
Taipei
Hong Kong
Taiwan
South China Sea

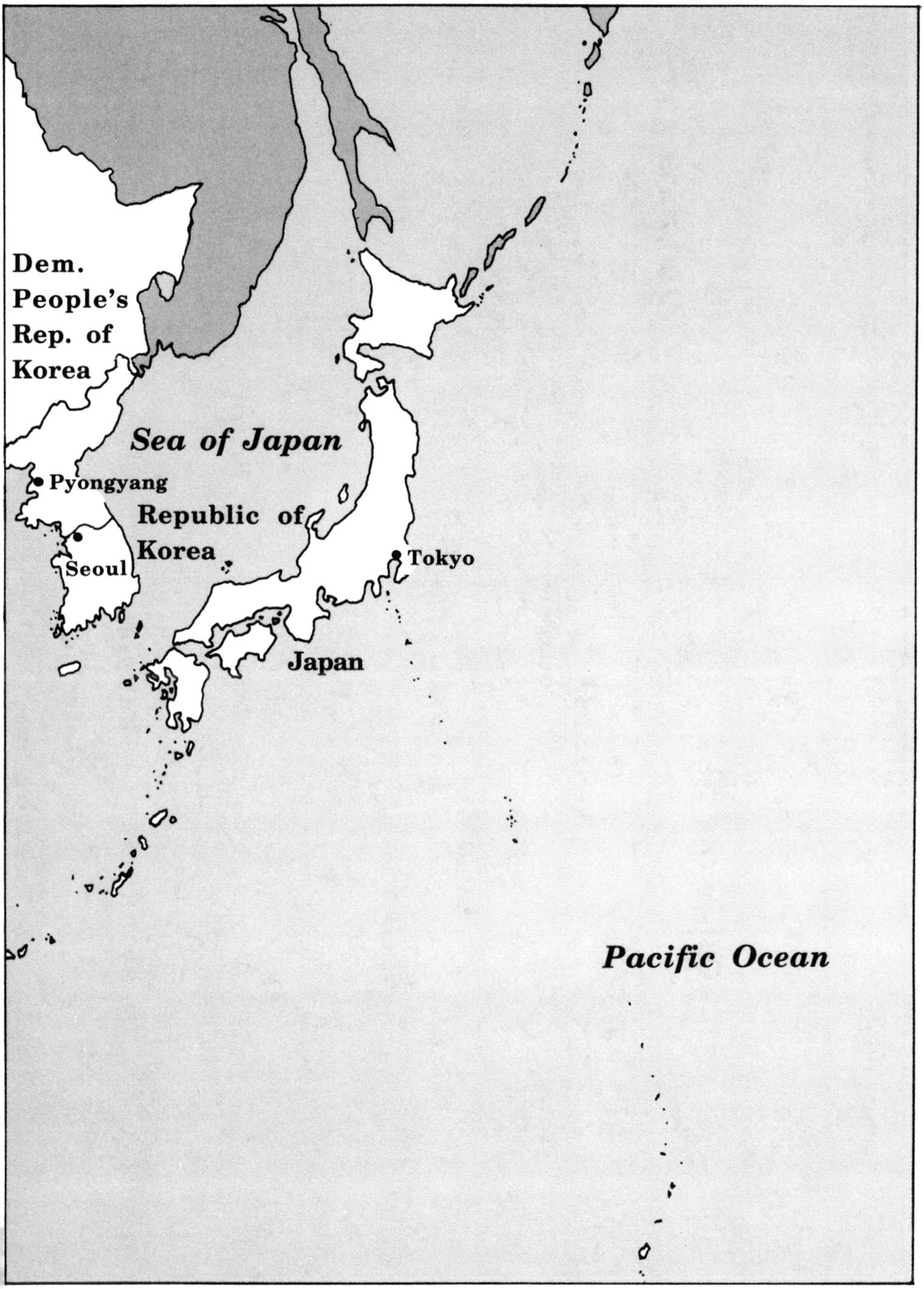
Dem.
People's
Rep. of
Korea
Sea of Japan
Pyongyang
Republic of
Korea
Seoul
Tokyo
Japan
Pacific Ocean

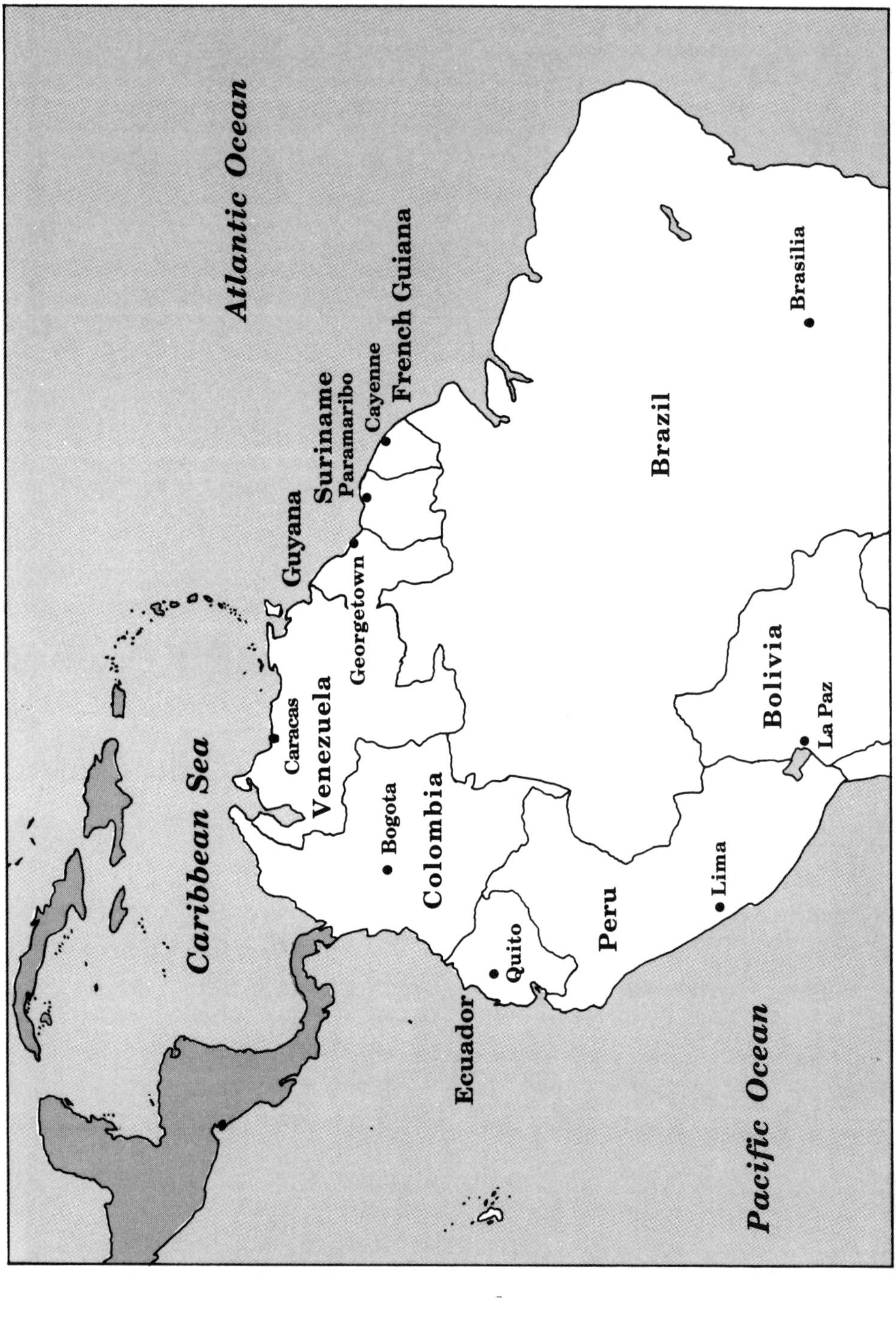
Atlantic Ocean
Caribbean Sea
Pacific Ocean
Guyana
Georgetown
Suriname
Paramaribo
French Guiana
Cayenne
Venezuela
Caracas
Colombia
Bogota
Ecuador
Quito
Peru
Lima
Brazil
Brasilia
Bolivia
La Paz

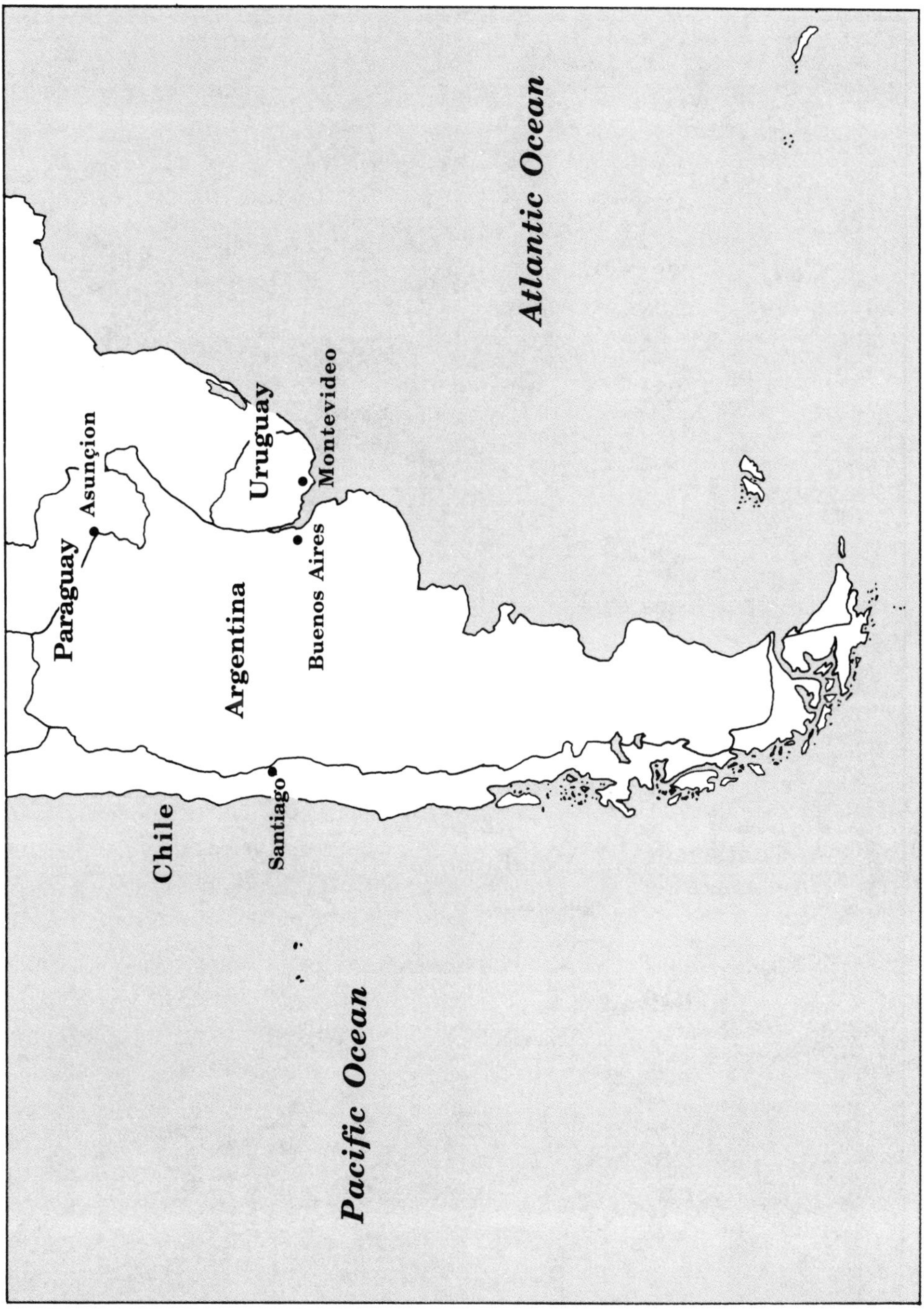
Atlantic Ocean
Paraguay
Asunçion
Uruguay
Montevideo
Argentina
Buenos Aires
Chile
Santiago
Pacific Ocean

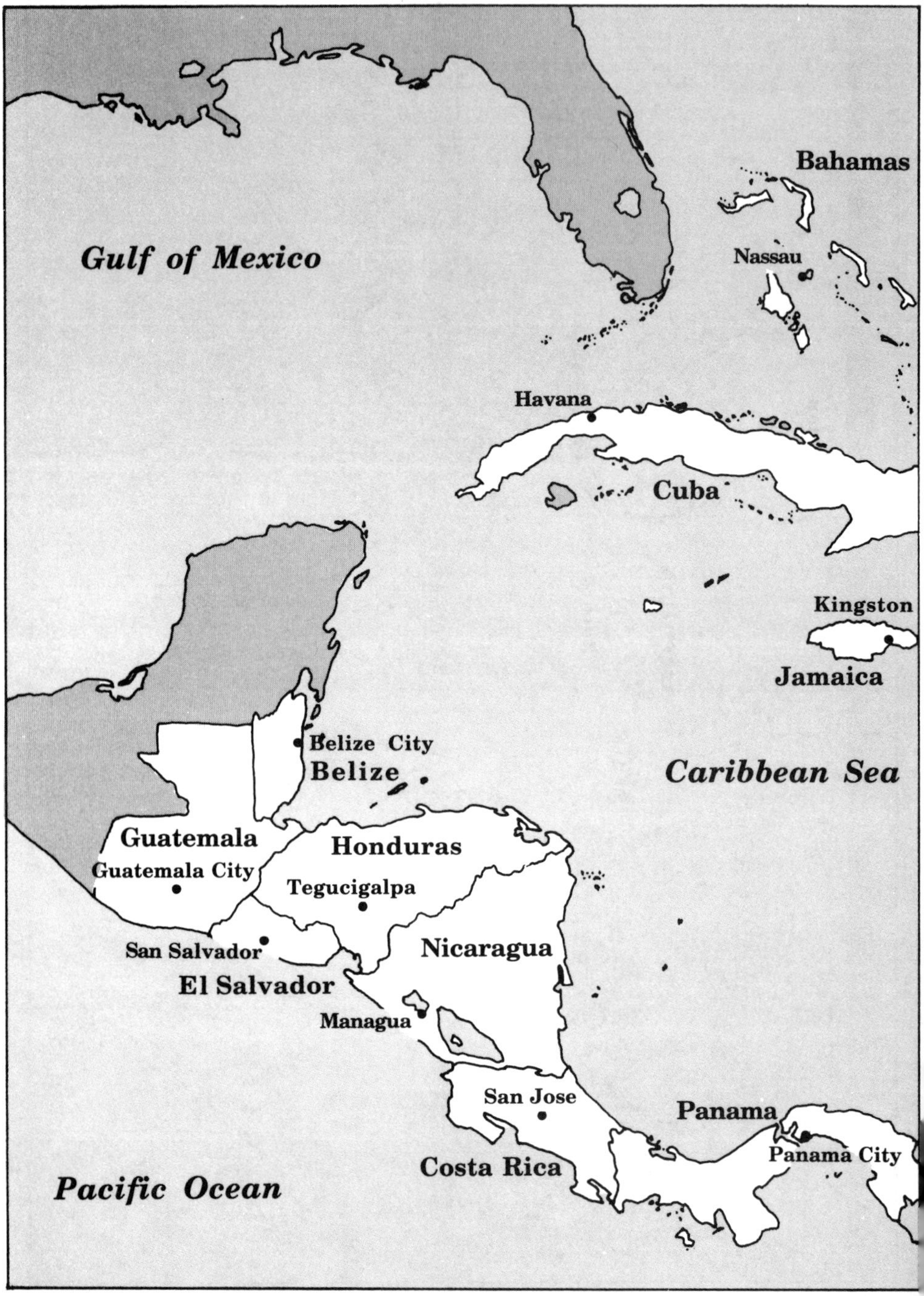
Gulf of Mexico
Bahamas
Nassau
Havana
Cuba
Kingston
Jamaica
Belize City
Belize
Caribbean Sea
Guatemala
Honduras
Guatemala City
Tegucigalpa
Nicaragua
San Salvador
El Salvador
Managua
San Jose
Panama
Panama City
Costa Rica
Pacific Ocean

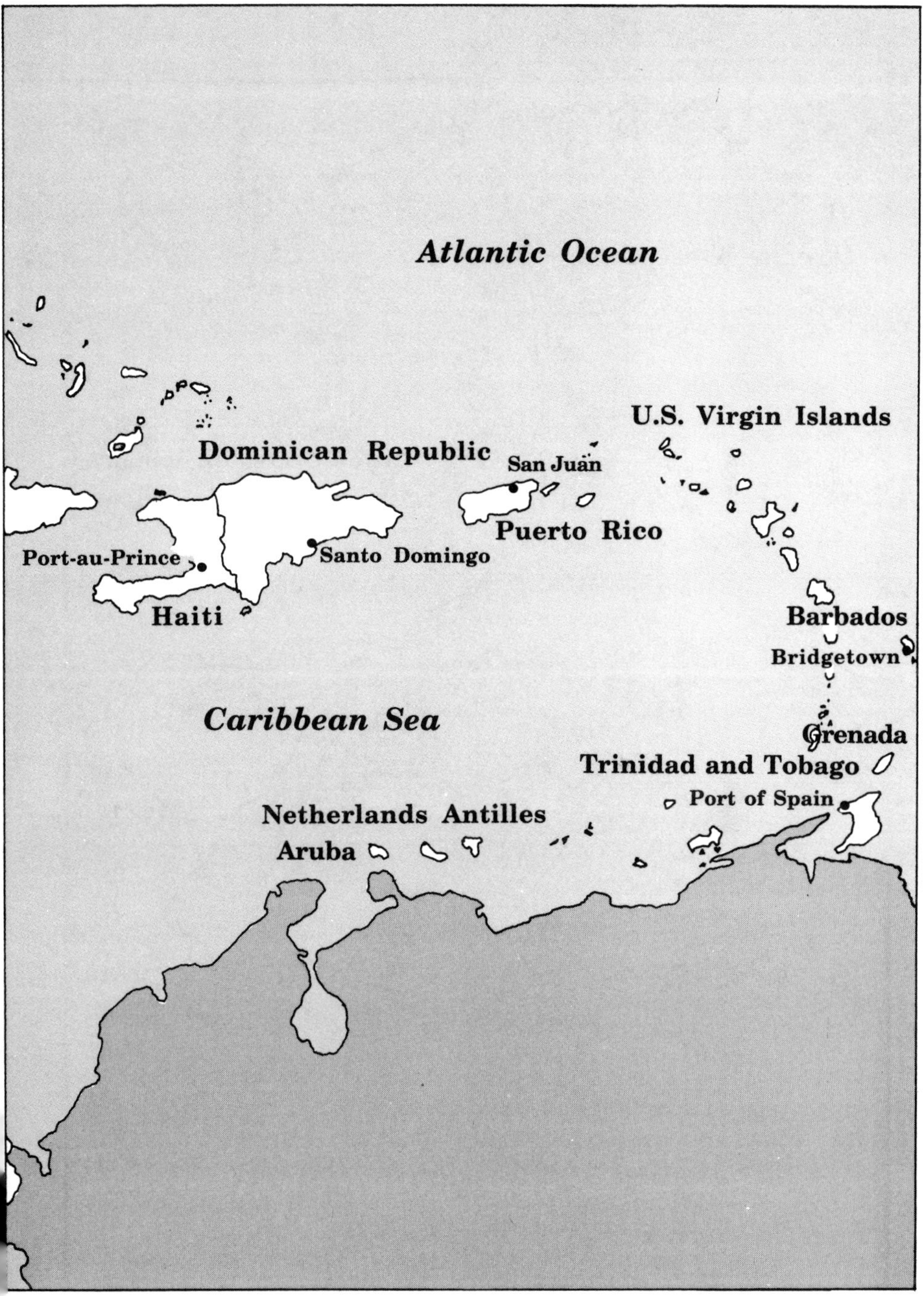
Atlantic Ocean
U.S. Virgin Islands
Dominican Republic
San Juan
Puerto Rico
Port-au-Prince
Santo Domingo
Haiti
Barbados
Bridgetown
Caribbean Sea
Grenada
Trinidad and Tobago
Port of Spain
Netherlands Antilles
Aruba

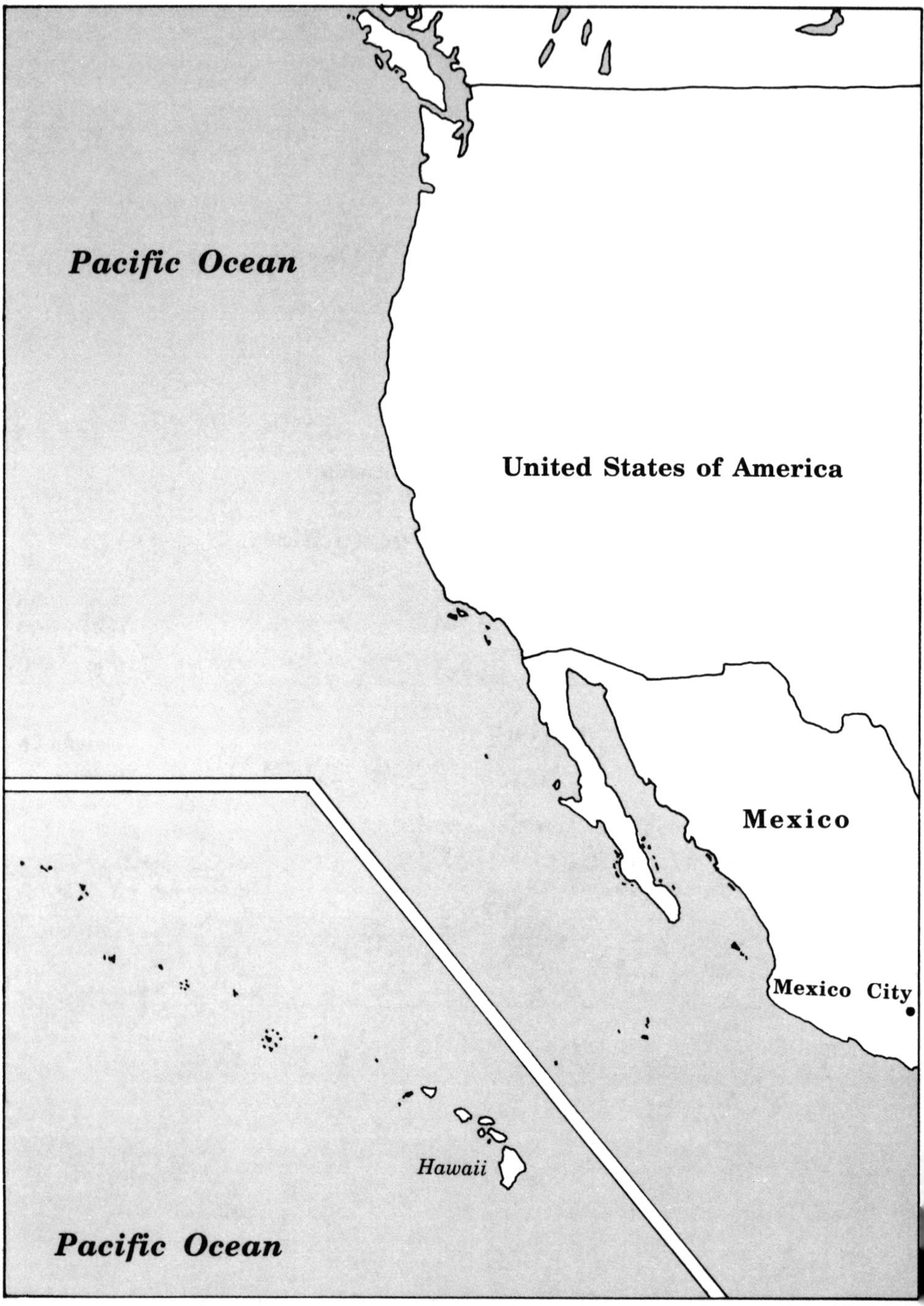
Pacific Ocean
United States of America
Mexico
Mexico City
Hawaii
Pacific Ocean

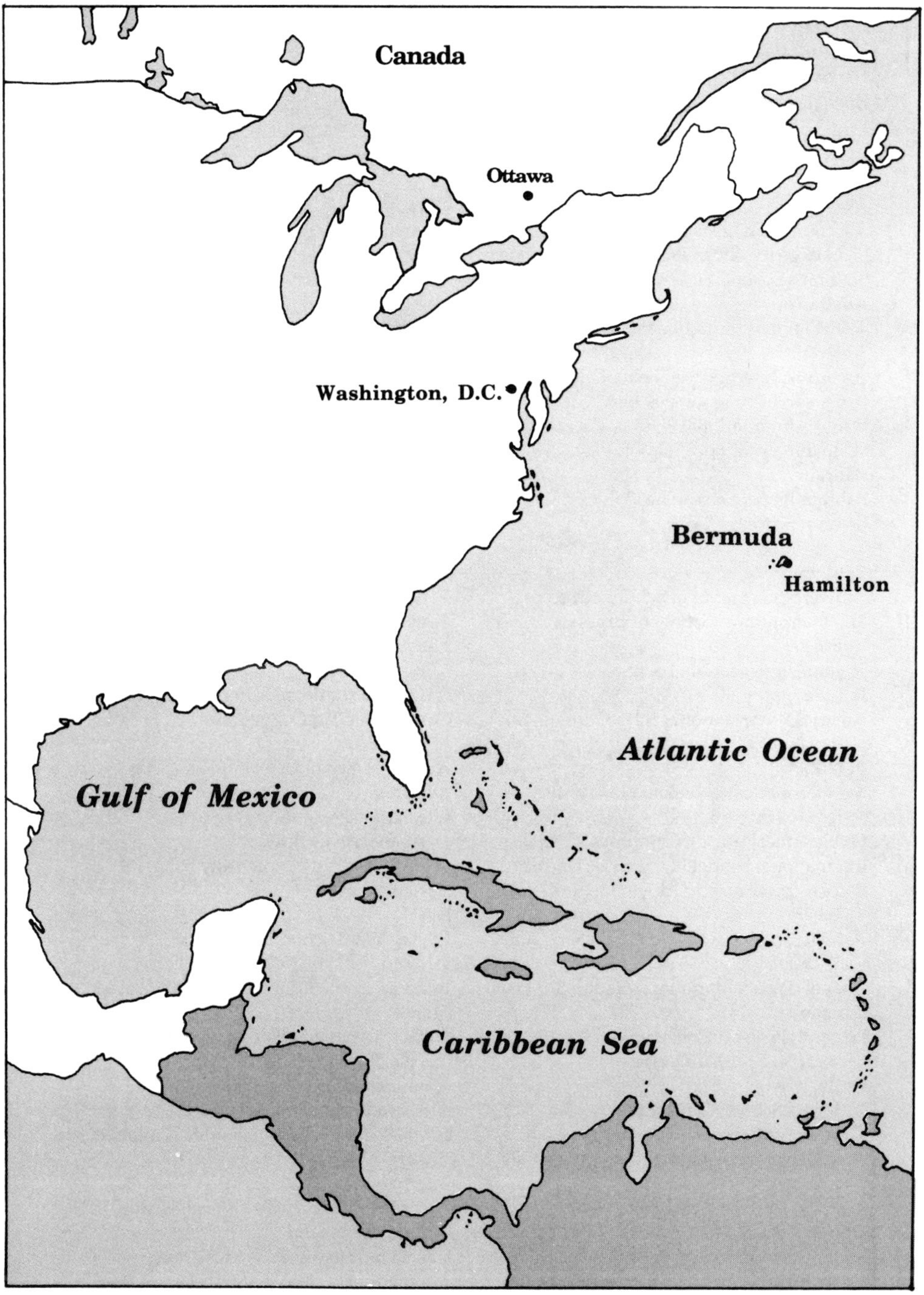
Canada
Ottawa
Washington, D.C.
Bermuda
Hamilton
Atlantic Ocean
Gulf of Mexico
Caribbean Sea

International Baccalaureate Schools

Schools which list the International Baccalaureate offer specialized intensive curriculum during the final two years of high school. The program culminates with the IB Examination, which is comparable to the British GCE A-level, the French Baccalaureate, and other national examinations. The IB Diploma is recognized by most universities throughout the world and enables students to gain advanced placement in university courses.

Argentina
Asociacion Escuelas Lincoln, *Buenos Aires*
St. George's College, *Buenos Aires*
St. John's School, *Buenos Aires*
Australia
The Kilmore International School, *Kilmore*
Austria
American International School, *Salzburg*
American International School, *Vienna*
Danube International School, *Vienna*
Vienna International School, *Vienna*
Bahrain
Bahrain Bayan School, *Isa Town*
Bahrain School, *Manama*
Ibn Khuldoon National School, *Manama*
Belgium
Antwerp International School, *Antwerp*
The International School of Brussels, *Brussels*
St. John's International School, *Waterloo*
Bolivia
American International School of Bolivia, *Cochabamba*
Brazil
Escola Americana de Belo Horizonte, *Belo Horizonte*
Escola Americana de Campinas, *Campinas*
International School of Curitiba, *Curitiba*
Escola Americana do Rio de Janeiro, *Rio de Janeiro*
Associacao Escola Graduada de Sao Paulo, *Sao Paulo*
Chapel (Escola Maria Imaculada), *Sao Paulo*
Canada
Lester B. Pearson College of the Pacific, *Victoria, British Columbia*
Chile
St. John's School, *Concepcion*
The Grange School S.A., *Santiago*
The International School Nido de Aguilas, *Santiago*
Santiago College, *Santiago*
China, People's Republic of
The International School of Beijing, *Beijing*
Costa Rica
Lincoln School, *San José*
Curaçao
International School of Curaçao, *Curaçao*
Cyprus
American International School of Cyprus, *Nicosia*
Czech Republic
International School of Prague, *Prague*
Denmark
Copenhagen International School, *Copenhagen*
Ecuador
Colegio Americano de Guayaquil, *Guayaquil*
Inter-American Academy, *Guayaquil*
American School of Quito, *Quito*
Cotopaxi Academy, American International School, *Quito*
Egypt
The American International School in Egypt, *Cairo*
British International School, Cairo, *Cairo*
Cairo American College, *Cairo*
El Salvador
Academia Britanica Cuscatleca, *Santa Tecla*
Ethiopia
International Community School/Addis Ababa, *Addis Ababa*
Sanford English Community School, *Addis Ababa*
Fiji
International School, Suva, *Suva*
Finland
International School of Helsinki, *Helsinki*
France
Ecole Internationale de Lille Metropole, *Lille*
American International School, *Nice*
American School of Paris, *Paris*
Ecole Active Bilingue Jeannine Manuel, *Paris*
International School of Paris, *Paris*
Lycee International, American Section, *St. Germain-en-Laye*
Centre International de Valbonne,
International School of Sophia Antipolis, *Valbonne*

Germany, Federal Republic of
International School Berlin—Potsdam, *Berlin*
Bonn American High School, *Bonn*
International School of Düsseldorf e.V., *Düsseldorf*
The Frankfurt International School e.V. & Int'l School Wiesbaden, *Frankfurt*
International School Hamburg, *Hamburg*
Bavarian International School, *Munich*
Munich International School, *Munich*
Greece
American Community Schools of Athens, *Athens*
Guam
St. John's School, *Tumon Bay*
Hong Kong
Chinese International School, *Hong Kong*
French International School "Victor Segalen," *Hong Kong*
Li Po Chun United World College of Hong Kong, *Hong Kong*
Hungary
American International School of Budapest, *Budapest*
India
Kodaikanal International School, *Kodaikanal*
The American Embassy School, *New Delhi*
Indonesia
British International School, *Jakarta*
Jakarta International School, *Jakarta*
Ireland
St. Andrew's College, *Dublin*
Italy
American International School of Florence, *Florence*
American School of Milan, *Milan*
International School of Milan, *Milan*
American Overseas School of Rome, *Rome*
Marymount International School, *Rome*
St. George's English School, *Rome*
St. Stephen's School, Rome, *Rome*
International School of Turin (ACAT), *Turin*
Vicenza International School, *Vicenza*
Japan
Canadian Academy, *Kobe*
Osaka International School, *Osaka*
St. Mary's International School, *Tokyo*
Seisen International School, *Tokyo*
Saint Maur International School, *Yokohama*
Yokohama International School, *Yokohama*
Jordan
Amman Baccalaureate School, *Amman*
Kenya
International School of Kenya, Ltd., *Nairobi*
Korea, Republic of
Seoul Foreign School, *Seoul*
Kuwait
The American International School—Kuwait, *Kuwait City*
Lebanon
American Community School at Beirut, *Beirut*
Lesotho
Machabeng College/International School of Lesotho, *Maseru*
Luxembourg
American International School of Luxem bourg, *Luxembourg*
Malaysia
The International School of Kuala Lumpur, *Kuala Lumpur*
Malta
Verdala International School, *St. Andrew's*
Mauritius
Le Bocage International School, *Moka*
Mexico
Greengates School, *Mexico City*
Morocco
Casablanca American School, *Casablanca*
Rabat American School, *Rabat*
The Netherlands
International School of Amsterdam, *Amsterdam*
International Secondary School Eindhoven, *Eindhoven*
Maartens College International School, *Groningen*
The American School of The Hague, *The Hague*
The Rijnlands International School, *Oegstgeest*
Norway
International School of Stavanger, *Stavanger*
Oman
American-British Academy, *Muscat*
Panama
The International School of Panama, *Panama City*
Papua New Guinea
Port Moresby International School, *Port Moresby*
Peru
Colegio Franklin D. Roosevelt, *Lima*
Philippines
Brent School, *Baguio*
Brent International School Manila, Inc., *Manila*
International School, Manila, *Manila*
Poland
The American School of Warsaw, *Warsaw*
Portugal
St. Julian's School (English Section), *Lisbon*
St. Dominic's International School, *Parede*

Russia
Anglo-American School of Moscow, *Moscow*
Singapore
Overseas Family School, *Singapore*
United World College of South East Asia, *Singapore*
South Africa
The American International School of Johannesburg, *Johannesburg*
Spain
American School of Madrid Foundation, *Madrid*
International College Spain, *Madrid*
Sri Lanka
The Overseas School of Columbo, *Colombo*
Swaziland
Waterford Kamhlaba UWC of Southern Africa, *Mbabane*
Sweden
Hvitfeldtska Gymnasiet, *Göteborg*
Sigtunaskolan Humanistiska Laroverket, *Sigtuna*
Kungsholmen's Gymnasium – International Section, *Stockholm*
Switzerland
International School of Basel, *Basel*
International School of Berne, *Berne*
Aiglon College, *Chesieres* (limited basis)
The International School of Geneva, *Geneva*
Leysin American School in Switzerland, *Leysin*
Institut Montana, American School, *Zug*
The Inter-Community School, *Zurich*
Syria
International School of Aleppo, *Aleppo*
Tanzania
International School of Tanganyika Ltd., *Dar es Salaam*
International School Moshi, *Moshi*
Thailand
Bangkok Patana School, *Bangkok*
International School Bangkok, *Bangkok*
The New International School of Thailand, *Bangkok*
Togo
The British School of Lomé, *Lomé*
Turkey
Istanbul International Community School, *Istanbul*
Bilkent University Preparatory School, *Ankara*
The Koç School, *Istanbul*
Uganda
Lincoln International School of Uganda, *Kampala*
United Arab Emirates
American International School in Abu Dhabi, *Abu Dhabi*
Emirates International School, *Dubai*
United Kingdom
International School of London, *London*
Southbank International School, *London*
American Community School, *Middlesex*
American Community School, *Cobham, Surrey*
Marymount International School, *Surrey*
International School of Aberdeen Educational Trust Ltd., *Aberdeen, Scotland*
United World College of the Atlantic, *Glamorgan, Wales*
United States
Chinese American International School, *San Francisco, California*
French–American International School, *San Francisco, California*
Washington International School, *Washington, D.C.*
Atlanta International School, *Atlanta, Georgia*
The Armand Hammer United World College of the American West, *Montezuma, New Mexico*
The Dwight School, *New York, New York*
United Nations International School, *New York, New York*
The Awty International School, *Houston, Texas*
Uzbekistan
The Tashkent Ulugbek International School, *Tashkent*
Venezuela
Colegio Internacional de Caracas, *Caracas*
Escuela Campo Alegre, *Caracas*
Vietnam
Hanoi Internation School, *Hanoi*
Zambia
International School of Lusaka, *Lusaka*

Schools Offering Boarding Facilities

Argentina
St. George's College, *Buenos Aires*
Australia
Geelong Grammar School, *Corio*
The Kilmore International School, *Kilmore*
Austria
American International School Salzburg, *Salzburg*
Bahrain
Bahrain School, *Manama*
Belgium
EEC International School, *Antwerp*
Bolivia
American International School of Bolivia, *Cochabamba*
Botswana
Maru a Pula School, *Gaborone*
Canada
Lester B. Pearson College of the Pacific, *Victoria, British Columbia*
China
Clifford School, *Panyu*
Cyprus
Logos School of English Education, *Limassol*
American International School of Cyprus, *Nicosia*
The International School of Paphos, *Paphos*
Dominican Republic
Escuela Caribe (Caribe – Vista School), *Jarabacoa*
Ecuador
Alliance Academy, *Quito*
Ethiopia
Bingham Academy, *Addis Ababa*
France
Bordeaux International School, *Bordeaux*
College Lycee Cevenol International, *Le Chambon-sur-Lignon*
Ecole Active Bilingue Jeannine Manuel, *Lille*
Centre International de Valbonne:
International School of Sophia Antipolis, *Valbonne*
Greece
TASIS HELLENIC International School in Athens, *Athens*
Anatolia College, *Thessaloniki*
Pinewood Schools of Thessaloniki, Greece, *Thessaloniki*
Hong Kong
Li Po Chun United World College of Hong Kong, *Hong Kong*
India
Kodaikanal International School, *Kodaikanal*
Woodstock School, *Mussoorie*
Indonesia
British International School, *Jakarta*
Central Java Inter-mission School, *Salatiga*
Hillcrest International School, *Sentani*
Ireland
Sutton Park School, *Dublin*
Italy
Canadian College Italy, *Lanciano*
American Overseas School of Rome, *Rome*
St. Stephen's School, Rome, *Rome*
Japan
Fukuoka International School, *Fukuoka*
Canadian Academy, *Kobe*
Hokkaido International School, *Sapporo*
Kenya
Rift Valley Academy, *Kijabe*
Kenton College, *Nairobi*
Korea, Republic of
Taejon Christian International School, *Taejon*
Lesotho
Machabeng College/Intl. School of Lesotho, *Maseru*
Malaysia
Dalat School, *Penang*
Malta
Verdala International School, *St. Andrews*
Morocco
The Ifrane School, *Ifrane*
The American School of Tangier, *Tangier*
The Netherlands
The Rijnlands International School, *Oegstgeest*
Nigeria
Hillcrest School, *Jos*
John F. Kennedy International School Nigeria, *Warri*
Pakistan
Murree Christian School, *Murree*
Papua New Guinea
The International School of Lae, *Lae*
Philippines
Brent School, *Baguio*
Faith Academy, *Cainta*
Senegal
Dakar Academy, *Dakar*
Singapore, Republic of
United World College of South East Asia, *Singapore*
South Africa, Republic of
The American International School of Johannesburg, *Johannesburg*
Spain
International College Spain, *Madrid*

American International School of Mallorca, *Mallorca*
The Baleares International School, *Mallorca*

Swaziland

Waterford Kamhlaba UWC of Southern Africa, *Mbabane*

Sweden

Sigtunaskolan Humanistiska Laroverket, *Sigtuna*

Switzerland

Aiglon College, *Chesieres*
International School Le Chaperon Rouge, *Crans-sur-Sierre*
Collège du Léman International School, *Geneva*
The International School of Geneva, *Geneva*
Gstaad International School, *Gstaad*
Ecole d'Humanité, *Hasliberg/Goldern*
Brillantmont International College, *Lausanne*
The Winter Term, *Lenk*
Kumon Leysin Academy in Switzerland, *Leysin*
Leysin American School in Switzerland, *Leysin*
The American School in Switzerland (TASIS), *Montagnola/Lugano*
Institut Château Beau-Cèdre, *Montreux*
St. George's School in Switzerland, *Montreux* (girls only)
Institut Le Rosey, *Rolle*
John F. Kennedy International School, *Saanen*
Institut Montana, American School, *Zug*

Thailand

Ake Panya International School, *Chang Mai*

Taiwan

National Experimental High School, *Hsin-Chu*
Morrison Academy, *Kaohsiung*

Tanzania

International School Moshi, *Moshi*
Victoria Primary School, *Mwanza*

Togo

The British School of Lomé, *Lomé*

Turkey

The Koç School, *Istanbul*
Robert College of Istanbul, *Istanbul*

United Kingdom

American Community School, *Cobham, Surrey*
Marymount International School, *Surrey* (girls only)
TASIS England American School, *Surrey*
Edinburgh Tutorial College, *Edinburgh, Scotland*
United World College of the Atlantic, *Glamorgan, Wales*

United States

The Armand Hammer United World College of the American West, *Montezuma, New Mexico*

Accrediting Associations

ACSI: Association of Christian Schools International
Contact: David K. Wilcox, Ph.D., Assistant to the Vice President
Address: PO Box 35097, Colorado Springs, CO 80935-3509, U.S.A.
Telephone: (1)(719)5944612 **Facsimile:** (1)(719)5310631
E-mail: 102256.2544@compuserve.com **Web:** http://www.acsi.org

ECIS: European Council of International Schools
Director of Accreditation Services: Peter Stokes
Address: ECIS, PO Box 6066, 28080 Madrid, Spain
Telephone: (34)(1)5626722 **Facsimile:** (34)(1)5636854
E-mail: psecis@ctv.es or 106500.3325@compuserve.com
Web: http://www.ecis.org

ISJC: Independent Schools Joint Council
General Secretary: Dr. Alistair Cooke, OBE
Address: Grosvenor Gardens House, 35–37 Grosvenor Gardens, London SW1W OBS, England
Telephone: (44)(171)6300144 **Facsimile:** (44)(171)9310036

Middle States: Middle States Association of Colleges and Schools
Executive Director: Dr. Joseph J. DeLucia, Commission on Secondary Schools
Address: 3624 Market Street, Philadelphia, PA 19104, U.S.A.
Telephone: (1)(215)6625603 **Facsimile:** (1)(215)6620957
E-mail: msacss@aol.com Web: http://www.business-edge.com/msa-css

Executive Director: Dr. John A. Stoops, Commission on Elementary Schools
Address: GSB Bldg., Ste. 618, 1 Belmont Avenue, Bala Cynwyd, PA 19004, U.S.A.
Telephone: (1)(610)6171100 **Facsimile:** (1)(610)6171106 **E-mail:** ces@gim.net

New England: New England Association of Schools and Colleges
Executive Director: Dr. Vincent L. Ferrandino
Address: 209 Burlington Road, Bedford, MA 01730-1433, U.S.A.
Telephone: (1)(617)2710022 **Facsimile:** (1)(617)2710950
E-mail: vferrandino@neasc.org **Web:** http://www.neasc.org

North Central: North Central Association of Colleges and Schools
Executive Director: Dr. Kenneth F. Gose
Address: Commission on Schools, Arizona State University, Box 873011, Tempe, AZ 85287-3011, U.S.A.
Telephone: (1)(602)9658700, (1)(800)5259517 **Facsimile:** (1)(602)9659423

Northwestern: Northwestern Association of Schools and Colleges
Executive Director: David Steadman
Address: Boise State University, 1910 University Drive, Boise, ID 83725-1060 U.S.A.
Telephone: (1)(208)3343210 **Facsimile:** (1)(208)3343228
E-mail: sclemens@varney.idbsu.edu **Web:** http://www.idbsu.edu/nasc

Southern: Southern Association of Colleges and Schools
Chief Administrative Officer: Dr. Stephen Baker
Address: 1866 Southern Lane, Decatur, GA 30033-4097, U.S.A.
Telephone: (1)(404)6794500 **Facsimile:** (1)(404)6794556

Texas Education Agency

Commissioner of Education: Dr. Mike Moses
Address: 1701 North Congress Avenue, Austin, TX 78701-1494, U.S.A.
Telephone: (1)(512)4638985 **Facsimile:** (1)(512)4639008
Web: http://www.tea.texas.gov

Western: Western Association of Schools and Colleges Accrediting Commission for Schools
Executive Director: Dr. Donald Haught
Address: 533 Airport Boulevard, Suite 200, Burlingame, CA 94010, U.S.A.
Telephone: (1)(415)6961060 **Facsimile:** (1)(415)3757790
E-mail: wasc@ed.co.sanmateo.ca.us

Regional and International Organizations

AAIE: Association for the Advancement of International Education
Executive Director: Dr. Lewis A. Grell
Address: Thompson House, Westminster College, New Wilmington, PA 16172, U.S.A.
Telephone: (1)(412)9467192 **Facsimile:** (1)(412)9467194
E-mail: grellla@westminster.edu **Web:** http://www.aaie.org

AASB: Association of American Schools in Brazil
President: Charles Lyndaker
Address: c/o Our Lady of Mercy School, Rua Visconde de Caravelas, 48, 22271-030 Rio de Janeiro, Brazil
Telephone: (55)(21)2468060/2468068 **Facsimile:** (55)(21)2665495
E-mail: olmrio@ibm.br

AASCA: Association of American Schools in Central America
President: Mr. Jack Delman
Address: Lincoln School 565-20, PO Box 025216, Miami, FL 33102-5216, U.S.A.
Telephone: (506)2357733/2972080 **Facsimile:** (506)2361706
E-mail: director@ns.lincoln.ed.cr

AASSA: Association of American Schools in South America
Executive Director: James Morris
Address: 14750 NW 77th Court, #210, Miami Lakes, FL 33016-1507, U.S.A.
Telephone: (1)(305)8210345 **Facsimile:** (1)(305)8214244 **E-mail**: aassa@gate.net

ACCAS: Association of Colombian-Caribbean American Schools
Director: Brian Lewallen
Address: Colegio Albania, A.A. 52499, Barranquilla, Colombia
Telephone: (57)(5)3505086 **Facsimile:** (57)(1)2113720

ACSI: Association of Christian Schools International
President: Ken Smitherman
Overseas schools contact: Dr. David K. Wilcox, International Ministries
Mail: PO Box 35097, Colorado Springs, CO 80935-3509, U.S.A.
Telephone: (1)(719)5944612 **Facsimile:** (1)(719)5310631
E-mail: ken_smitherman@acsi.org **Web:** http://www.ecis.org

AISA: Association of International Schools in Africa
Executive Director: Mary (Miffie) Greer
Address: c/o International School of Kenya, PO Box 14103,
Nairobi, Kenya
Telephone: (254)(2)582578/582421/582422
Facsimile: (254)(2)580596/582451 **E-mail:** aisa@isk.ac.ke

AASA: American Association of School Administrators
Executive director: Dr. Paul Houston
Address: 1801 North Moore St., Arlington, VA 22209-1813
Telephone: (1)(703)5280700 **Facsimile:** (1)(703)8411543
Web: http://www.aasa.org

A/OS: Office of Overseas Schools
Director: Dr. Keith D. Miller
Address: Room 245, SA-29, U.S. Department of State, Washington, D.C. 20522-2902
Telephone: (1)(703)8757800 **Facsimile:** (1)(703)8757979
Web: http://www.state.gov/www/about_state/schools

ASOMEX: Association of American Schools in Mexico
President: Dr. Mary Mend
Address: c/o The American School of Mexico City, Bondojito 215, Col. Las Americas, Mexico, D.F., 01120
Telephone: (52)(5)2274900 **Facsimile:** (52)(5)2734357/2728453
E-mail: azenteno@servidor.unam.mx

CAIS: Canadian Association of Independent Schools
President: Janet M. Lewis
Address: Box 1502, St. Catharines, ON L2R 7C3 Canada
Telephone: (1)(905)6884866 **Facsimile:** (1)(905)6885778 **E-mail:** cais@ridley.on.ca

CEESA: Central and Eastern European Schools Association
Executive Director: David M. Cobb
Address: Dept. of State–Warsaw, Washington, D.C. 20521-5010
Tel/Fax: (48)(22)409380 **E-mail:** ceesa@it.com.pl

COBISEC: Council of British Independent Schools in the European Communities
Honorary President: Sir Dick Pantlin, C.B.E.
Chairman: Roger Fry OBE
Secretariat: c/o Lucy's, Lucy's Hill, Hythe, Kent CT21 5ES, U.K.
Telephone/facsimile: (44)(1)303260857

EARCOS, SEATCCO, CERCOS, KORCOS, JCIS: East Asia Regional Council of Overseas Schools
Executive Director: Dr. Richard T. Krajczar
Board President: Monica Greeley
Address: PO Box 10359, 50712 Kuala Lumpur, Malaysia
Telephone: (60)(3)4069306 **Facsimile:** (60)(3)4069304
E-mail: earcos@iskl.po.my

ECIS: European Council of International Schools
Executive Secretary: T. Michael Maybury
Address: 21 Lavant Street, Petersfield, Hampshire, GU32 3EL, U.K.
Telephone: (44)(1730)268244 **Facsimile:** (44)(1730)267914
E-mail: ecis@ecis.org **Web:** http://www.ecis.org

European Council of International Schools (Madrid Office)
Regional Representative: Peter Stokes
Address: ECIS, PO Box 6066, 28080 Madrid, Spain
Telephone: (34)(1)5626722 **Facsimile:** (34)(1)5636854
E-mail: psecis@ctv.es or 106500.3325@compuserve.com

European Council of International Schools (Australian Office)
Regional Representative: Allan Wilcox
Address: "Cumburri" I.E.C., PO Box 367, Kilmore 3764, Victoria, Australia
Telephone: (61)(3)57811351 **Facsimile:** (61)(3)57811151

European Council of International Schools (North American Office)
Regional Officer: Nancy Maly
Address: 105 Tuxford Terrace, Basking Ridge, New Jersey 07920, U.S.A.
Telephone: (1)(908)9030552 Facsimile: (1)(908)5809381
E-mail: malyecisna@aol.com

IBNA: International Baccalaureate North America
Regional Director: Bradley Richardson
Address: 200 Madison Avenue. Suite 2007, New York, NY 10016, U.S.A.
Telephone: (1)(212)6964464 **Facsimile:** (1)(212)8899242 **E-mail:** ibna@ibo.org

IBO: International Baccalaureate Organization
Director General: Roger M. Peel
Address: Route des Morillons 15, 1218 Grand-Saconnex, Geneva, Switzerland
Telephone: (41)(22)7910274 **Facsimile:** (41)(22)7910277 **E-mail:** ibhq@ibo.org
Web: http://www.ibo.org

IRC: Inter-Regional Center for Curriculum and Materials Development
Director: Dr. Burton Fox
Address: Apartado Aereo 3250, Barranquilla, Colombia
Telephone: (57)(53)598589/598988
U.S. office: PO Box 020470, Tuscaloosa, AL 35402, U.S.A.
Telephone: (1)(205)3910727 **Facsimile:** (1)(205)3910927

ISS: International Schools Services
President: Dr. John M. Nicklas
Address: 15 Roszel Road, PO Box 5910, Princeton, NJ 08543-5910, U.S.A.
Telephone: (1)(609)4520990 **Facsimile:** (1)(609)4522690
E-mail: iss@iss.edu **Web:** http://www.iss.edu

Latin American Tri-Association: American Schools Association of Central America, Colombia-Caribbean and Mexico
Executive Director: Mary Virginia Sanchez
Address: (no personal name) Executive Director (ASQ), c/o U.S. Embassy Quito, Unit 5372 Box 004, APO AA 34039-3420
Telephone: (593)(2)472974/477534/472975
Facsimile: (593)(2)434985/472972 **E-mail:** marysanc@uio.satnet.net

MAIS: Mediterranean Association of International Schools
Executive Director: Reina O'Hale
Address: c/o American School of Madrid, Apartado 80, 28080 Madrid, Spain
Telephone: (34)(1)3572154/3527795 **Facsimile:** (34)(1)3572678
E-mail: 100553.162@compuserve.com **Web:** http://www.mais-web.org

NABSS: National Association of British Schools in Spain
Chair: Anne Farre
Address: c/o Anglo-American School, Paseo de Garbi 152, 08860 Castelldefels, Barcelona, Spain
Telephone: (34)(3)6651584 **Facsimile:** (34)(3)6641444

NAESP: National Association of Elementary School Principals
Executive Director: Dr. Samuel Sava
Address: 1615 Duke St., Alexandria, VA 22314-3483 U.S.A.
Telephone: (1)(703)6843345 **Facsimile:** (1)(703)5186281
E-mail: naesp@naesp.org

NAIS: National Association of Independent Schools
President: Peter D. Relic
Address: 1620 L Street, N.W., 11th Floor, Washington, D.C. 20036, U.S.A.
Facsimile: (1)(202)9739790

NASSP: National Association of Secondary School Principals
Executive director: Dr. Timothy Dyer
Address: 1904 Association Drive, Reston, VA 22091-1537 U.S.A.
Telephone: (1)(703)8600200 **Facsimile:** (1)(703)4765432

NESA: Near East South Asia Council of Overseas Schools
Executive Director: David Chojnacki
Address: c/o The American College of Greece, PO Box 60018, GR153 42 Aghia Paraskevi, Attikis, Greece
Telephone: (30)(1)6009821 **Facsimile:** (30)(1)6009928
E-mail: nesa@ath.forthnet.gr

SAISA: South Asia International Schools Association
Executive Director: Hal Strom
Address: c/o American School of Bombay, 75 B. Desai Road, Mumbai 400-026, India
Telephone: (91)(22)3630026/3636292 **Facsimile:** (91)(22)3670035/3630350
E-mail: admin@osc.lanka.net

SGIS: Swiss Group of International Schools
Chairman: Grant Fiedler
Address: c/o Leysin American School, CH 1854 Leysin, Switzerland
Telephone: (41)(24)4943704 **Facsimile:** (41)(24)4943790
Secretary: George Krasker
Address: PO Box 10, CH 1279 Chavannes de Bogis, Switzerland
Telephone: (41)(22)7762703 **Facsimile:** (41)(22)7766536

Key To Examinations

A-level GCE: Advanced-level General Certificate of Education
ACER: Australian Council for Educational Research Tests
ACH: National Achievement Tests
ACT: American College Testing
AP: Advanced Placement
AS-level GCE: Advanced Supplementary-level General Certificate of Education
BAT: Bristol Achievement Test
Botel: Reading Inventory
Brigance: Test of Basic Skills
Cambridge: First Certificate
CAT: California Achievement Test
CEEB: College Entrance Examination Board
CELT: Comprehensive English Language Test for Speakers of English as a Second Language; Listening
CLEP: College-Level Examination Program
COGAT: Cognitive Abilities Test
CSA: Career Skills Assessment
CSE: Certification of Secondary Education
CTBS: California Test of Basic Skills
CTP: Comprehensive Testing Program
DAT: Differential Aptitude Test
DTA: Diagnostic Achievement Test for Adolescents
Durrell: Reading Test
ERB: Education Records Bureau Comprehensive Testing Program
GAP: Reading Comprehension Test
Gates-MacGinitie: Reading Test
GCSE: General Certificate of Secondary Education
GMAT: General Mental Ability Test
Gray Oral and Comprehension: Reading Test
GRE: Graduate Record Examinations
Holborn: Reading Scale
IB: International Baccalaureate
IGCSE: International General Certificate of Secondary Education
Iowa: Iowa Tests of Basic Skills
ITBS: Iowa Tests of Basic Skills
ITED: Iowa Test of Educational Development
Kuder: Vocational Preference Test
LAB: Language Assessment Battery
MAT: Metropolitan Achievement Test
McGraw-Hill: Basic Skills Systems
Michigan: Tests for Emotional Adjustment
Monroe: Diagnostic Reading Test
MTBS: Metropolitan Test of Basic Skills
NCEE: National Council of Engineering Examiners; Principles and Practice of Engineering
NEDT: National Educational Development Test
Nelson-Denny: Reading Test
NFER: Neale Analysis of Reading Ability
NMSQT: National Merit Scholarship Qualifying Test
NZCER: New Zealand Council for Educational Research Tests
O-level GCE: Ordinary-level General Certificate of Education
OLMAT: Otis-Lennon Mental Ability Test
Otis-Lennon: Mental Ability Test
OVIS: Ohio Vocational Interest Survey
PIAT: Peabody Individual Achievement Test
PLAN: Preliminary American College Testing
PSAT: Preliminary Scholastic Aptitude Test
Purdue: Multipurpose Vocational Test
Richmond: Test of Basic Skills
SAT: Scholastic Achievement Test
SAT I: Scholastic Assessment Tests I: Reasoning Test
SAT II: Scholastic Assessment Tests II: Subject Tests
SCAT: School and College Ability Test
SLEP: Secondary-Level English Proficiency Test
SRA: Science Research Associates, Primary Mental Abilities
SSAT: Secondary School Admission Test
Stanford: Achievement Test
STEP: Sequential Test of Educational Progress
Strong-Campbell: Interest Inventory
TAP: Tests of Achievement and Proficiency
TASK: Stanford Test of Academic Skills
TOEFL: Test of English as a Foreign Language
TSE: Test of Spoken English
U.K. SAT: U.K. Standard Assessment Tasks
Wechsler: Intelligence Scale for Children
WRAT: Wide Range Achievement Test

E-MAIL ADDRESSES

The following is a list of the e-mail addresses that were reported by schools in this edition. All of the addresses are formatted for the Internet. Overseas e-mail addresses change often, so if you cannot get through, please verify address with school.

Albania
Tirana Intl. School, glenn_mosher@tis.tirana.al
Argentina
Asociacion Escuelas Lincoln, doll_g@lincoln.edu.ar
St. Catherine's Moorlands,
104767.1611@compuserve.com
St. George's College, info@stgeorge.com.ar
Armenia
QSI Intl. Sch. of Yerevan, qsi@arminco.com
Aruba
Intl. School of Aruba, intschool@setarnet.aw
Australia
Geelong Grammar Sch, simonl@ggscorio.vic.edu.au
Kilmore Intl. Sch, kilmorei@hyperlink.net.au
Austria
American Intl. Sch., director@ais.at
Vienna Christian Sch., 100337.1501@compuserve.com
Vienna Intl. Sch., info@vis.ac.at
Azerbaijan
Baku Intl. Sch., qsi@bis.baku.az
Bahrain
Bahrain Bayan Sch., bayan@batelco.com.bh
Ibn Khuldoon National Sch., iknsnet@batelco.com.bh
Bangladesh
American Intl. Sch./Dhaka,
admin@aisd.pradeshta.net
Belarus
Minsk Intl. Sch., mis@brc.minsk.by
Belgium
Antwerp Intl. Sch., 101352.1676@compuserve.com
B.E.P.S. 2-Limal Intl. Sch, info@beps.com
Brussels' English Primary School, info@beps.com
EEC Intl. Sch., eurunia@eunet.be
The Intl. Sch. of Brussels, admissions@isb.be
St. John's Intl. Sch., 72233.3322@compuserve.com
Bermuda
Bermuda Inst. of Seventh-Day Adventists,
svholder@ibl.bm
Mount Saint Agnes Academy, msa@ibl.bm
Bolivia
American Cooperative Sch., acs@megalink.com
Amer. Intl. Sch. of Bolivia, aisb@llajta.nrc.bolnet.bo
Santa Cruz Christian Learning Center,
learning.center@mail.scbbs-bo
Santa Cruz Coop. Sch., students@datacom-bo.net
Botswana
Maru a Pula Sch., pua@aztec.co.za
Brazil
Amazon Valley Academy, miceb@amazon.com.br
American School of Brasilia, rwerner@bus.eabdf.br
American School of Recife, ear@elogica.com.br
Associacao Escola Graduada de Sao Paulo,
graded@eagle.aegsp.br
Escola Americana de Belo Horizonte,
amschool.eabh@metalink.com
Escola Americana de Campinas, 2146993@mcimail.com
Escola Americana do Rio de Janeiro,
dennis@uninet.com.br
Intl. Sch. of Curitiba, isc@eic.arauc.br
Pan Amer. Christian Academy, paca@opus.com.br
Pan Amer. Sch. of Bahia, epaba@svn.com.br
Pan Amer. Sch. of Porto Alegre,
paspoa@portoweb.com.br
Bulgaria
American College of Sofia, acs@sf.cit.bg
Cambodia
Intl. Sch. of Phnom Penh, ispp@uni.fi
Cameroon
Amer. Sch. of Yaounde, asoy@camfido.gn.apc.org
Chile
The Antofagasta Intl. Sch., ais@reuna.cl
The Grange Sch. S.A., sinclair@grange.cl
The Intl. Preparatory Sch., inschool@inet.macland.cl
The Intl. Sch. Nido de Aguilas, mail@nido.cl
Santiago College, admiss@scollege.cl
St. John's Sch., stjohns@arauco.reuna.cl
China
American Intl. Sch. of Guangzhou,
asg@gitie.guangzhou.gd.cn
Intl. Sch. of Beijing, isb-info@isb.bj.edu.cn
Shanghai American Sch., shaamsch@public.sta.net.cn
Teda Intl. Sch., Tianjin Branch, tist@public.tpt.tj.cn
Tianjin Intl. Sch., tmis@public.tpt.tj.cn
Western Academy of Beijing, ian@wab.hk.net
Yew Chung Shanghai Intl. Sch.,
ycsis@public.sta.net.cn
Colombia
Colegio Granadino, granadino@amtelsa.com.co
Colegio Karl C. Parrish, kcparrish@rnd.net.co
Colegio Nueva Granada, sngrana@col.telecom.com.co
Columbus Sch., columbus@inter.net.co
Costa Rica
Lincoln Sch., director@ns.lincoln.ed.cr
Marian Baker Sch., mbschool@sol.racsa.co.cr
Côte d'Ivoire
Intl. Community Sch. of Abidjan, 75204.1313@
compuserve.com
Cyprus
American Intl. Sch. in Cyprus, aisc@aisc.ac.cy
Logos Sch. of English Education, pr@logos.ac.cy
Czech Republic
Intl. Sch. of Prague, ispmail@isprague.anet.cz
Dominican Republic
Escuela Caribe, e.caribe@codetel.net.do
Carol Morgan School of Santo Domingo,

headmaster@cms.edu.do
Santiago Christian School, c.school@codetel.net.do
Ecuador
Alliance Academy, alliance@hcjb.org.ec
American Sch. of Quito, pponce@uio.satnet.net
Colegio Americano de Guayaquil, amschool@telconet.net
Cotopaxi Academy, director@cotopaxi.k12.ec
Inter-American Academy, admin@acig.k12.ec
Egypt
Amer. Intl. Sch. in Egypt, ais@powermail.intouch.com
Cairo American College, bhetzel@tc.cac.edu.eg
Schutz Amer. Sch., 103375.1022@compuserve.com
El Salvador
Academia Britanica Cuscatleca, rbraund@es.com.sv
American Sch. of El Salvador, wscotti@trojans.edu.sv
Estonia
Intl. Elementary Sch. of Estonia, iese@online.ee
Ethiopia
Bingham Academy, bingham@telecom.net.et
Intl. Comm. Sch./Addis Ababa, ics@telecom.net.et
Finland
Intl. Sch. of Helsinki, mainoffice@ish.edu.hel.fi
France
American Intl. Sch., 101644.1546@compuserve.com
Intl. Sch. of Paris, isp@compuserve.com
Intl. Sch. of Sophia Antipolis, aseica@riviera.fr
Mougins School, mouginsschool@riviera.fr
Georgia
QSI Intl. Sch. of Tbilisi, bev@access.sanet.ge
Germany
Bavarian Intl. Sch., admissions@bis-school.com
Frankfurt Intl. Sch. e.V., 100430.2764@compuserve.com
Intl. Sch. Hamburg, 100272.410@compuserve.com
Internationale Schule Frankfurt-Rhein-Main, isfrm@ipf.de
Ghana
Ghana Intl. Sch., gis@ncs.com.gh
Lincoln Community Sch., lincoln@ncs.com.gh
Greece
Amer. Comm. Schs. of Athens, acsi@ath.forthnet.gr
Athens College, acpresoff@hol.gr
TASIS HELLENIC Intl. Sch. in Athens, bhani@hol.gr
Grenada
Intl. Sch. of Grenada, isog@caribsurf.com
Guatemala
American Sch. of Guatemala, cagadm@cag.edu.gt
Colegio Maya, colmaya@pronet.net.gt
Haiti
Ecole Flamboyant, has-pap@acn.com
Honduras
Academia Los Pinares, apinares@ns.gbm.hn
Escuela Internacional Sampedrana, seis@netsys.hn
Mazapan Sch., mazapan@ns.gbm.hn
Hong Kong
Carmel Sch., carmelhk@netvigator.com
Chinese Intl. Sch., cis_info@cis.edu.hk
Christian Alliance P.C. Lau Memorial Intl. Sch., cais@netvigator.com
Hong Kong Intl. Sch., cdull@admin.hkis.edu.hk
Intl. Christian Sch., ics@hk.super.net
Island Sch., school@is.esf.edu.hk
Li Po Chun UWC of Hong Kong, lpenetwk@asiaonline.net
India
Amer. Embassy Sch., aesindia@attmail.com
Amer. Sch. of Bombay, asb@giasbm01.vsnl.net.in
Kodaikanal Intl. Sch., admissions@kis.ernet.in
Woodstock Sch., admin@wdstock.globemail.com
Indonesia
Bali Intl. Sch., bis@denpasar.wasantara.net.id
Bandung Alliance Sch., 76225.2736@compuserve.com
Bandung Intl. Sch., pjoslin@melsa.net.id
Bogor Expatriate Sch., bes@indo.net.id
Bontang Intl. Sch., bisbon@indo.net.id
British Intl. Sch., bisnet@rad.net.id
Caltex Amer. Sch., 72762.3416@compuserve.com
Central Java Inter-Mission Sch., cjims@yoga.wasantara.net.id
Hillcrest Intl. Sch., his.indonesia@sil.org
Hope Intl. Sch., dvan@indo.net.id
Intl. Sch. of Lhokseumawe, bxjacoby@jak.mobil.com
Jakarta Intl. Sch., jvahey@jisedu.org
Makassar Intl. Sch., makassar@upandang.wasantar
Medan Intl. Sch., mismedan@idola.net.id
Mt. Zaagham Intl. Sch., isstpra@fmi.com
North Jakarta Intl. Sch., njis@cbn.net.id
Pasir Ridge Intl. Sch., prschool@bpp.mega.net.id
Surabaya Intl. Sch., sishead@rad.net.id
Tanjung Bara Intl. Sch., kpcnet@bpp.mega.net.id
Wesley Intl. Sch., wesley@malang.wasantara.net.id
Israel
Walworth Barbour Amer. Intl. Sch., aisisrael@american.hasharon.k12.il
Italy
Ambrit Rome Intl. Sch., ambrit@email.telpress.it
Amer. Intl. Sch. of Florence, aisf@ats.it
Amer. Intl. Sch. in Genoa, aisg@thvillage.it
American Overseas Sch. of Rome, aosr.inc@agora.stm.it
American Sch. of Milan, directorasm@planet.it
Canadian College Italy, cci@teknet.rgn.it
Castelli Intl. Bilingual Sch., maryac@email.telpress.it
Intl. Sch. of Naples, isn@na.cybernet.it
Intl. Sch. of Trieste, istrieste@interbusiness.it
Marymount Intl. Sch., marymount@pronet.it
Sir James Henderson British Sch. of Milan, sirjames@bbs.infosquare.it
St. Stephen's Sch., Rome, mc0667@mclink.it
United World College of the Adriatic, uwcad@uwc.interware.it
Japan
Amer. Sch. in Japan, info@asij.ac.jp
Canadian Academy, hdmstr@canacad.ac.jp
Christian Academy in Japan, don.rudd@jemanet.or.jp
Fukuoka Intl. Sch., dclark@bamboo.paradigm.co.jp
Hiroshima Intl. Sch., his888@po.cisnet.or.jp
Hokkaido Intl. Sch., hokintsc@ppp.bekkoame.or.jp
Intl. Sch. of the Sacred Heart, issh@iac.co.jp
Japan Intl. Sch., jised@shrine.cyber.ad.jp
Kyoto Intl. Sch., hellokis@mbox.kyoto-inet.or.jp

Nagoya Intl. Sch., nisadmin@tcp-ip.or.jp
Nishimachi Intl. Sch., info@nishimachi.org
Okinawa Christian Sch. Intl., 102603.2026@compuserve.com
Osaka Intl. Sch., oia-ois@sisf.mino.osaka.jp
Saint Maur Intl. Sch., creena@gol.com
Seisen Intl. Sch., sisinfo@japan.co.jp
Sendai American Sch., 71651.2745@compuserve.com

Jordan
American Community Sch., acsamm@go.com.jo
Amman Baccalaureate Sch., abs@go.com.jo

Kazakhstan
Almaty Intl. Sch., general@ais.alma-ata.su

Kenya
Intl. Sch. of Kenya, Ltd., ken@rhino140.kenya.leids.com
Rosslyn Academy, rosslyn@maf.org
St. Mary's Sch., stmarys@arcc.permanet.org

Korea
Indianhead Sch., indian@soback.kornet.nm.kr
Intl. Christian Sch., Seoul, 76245.3525@compuserve.com
Intl. Christian Sch., Songtan, 75357.1402@compuserve.com
Intl. Christian Sch., Tongduchon, 75357.1421@compuserve.com
Intl. Christian Sch., Uijongbu, 102232.1653@compuserve.com
Seoul Foreign Sch., sfsoffice@crusader.sfs-h.ac.kr
Taejon Christian Intl. Sch., administrator@tcis.kaist.ac.kr

Kuwait
Al-Bayan Bilingual Sch., bbs@ncc.moc.kw
American Intl. Sch.–Kuwait, raja@ncc.moc.kw
American Sch. of Kuwait, askkwt@kuwait.net
Fawzia Sultan Intl. Sch., roncb123@aol.com
The Universal American Sch., elmo@ncc.moc.kw

Kyrgyzstan
Bishkek Intl. Sch., admiral@qsibis.bishkek.su

Laos
Vientiane Intl. Sch., joes@loxinfo.co.th

Lebanon
Amer. Comm. Sch. at Beirut, acs@acs.edu.lb
International College, proffice@cyberia.net.lb

Lesotho
Amer. Intl. Sch. of Lesotho, aisl@lesoff.co.za

Lithuania
American Intl. Sch. of Vilnius, aisv@post.omnitel.net

Luxembourg
American Intl. Sch. of Luxembourg, gerald.shields@ci.educ.lu

Macau
School of the Nations, sonmacau@macau.net

Macedonia
American School, amschool@guest.soros.org.mk

Madagascar
Amer. Sch. of Antananarivo, asamad@dts.mg

Malawi
Bishop Mackenzie Intl. Sch., bmiss@unima.wn.apc.org

Malaysia
Dalat School, office@dalat2.po.my
Intl. Sch. of Kuala Lumpur, iskl@iskl.po.my
Mont'Kiara Intl. Sch., garymc@mkis.po.my

Mali
Amer. Intl. Sch. of Bamako, aisb@malinet.ml

Malta
Verdala Intl. Sch., vis@maltanet.net

Marshall
Kwajalein Sch. System, popejoy@aloha.net

Mexico
Amer. Sch. Ftn. of Guadalajara, asfg@warrior.asfg.mx
Amer. Sch. of Puerto Vallarta, camerica@pvnet.com.mx
Colegio Ingles, cingles@sdm.net
Colegio Peterson, kapm@mail.internet.com.mx
Escuela Americana de Tampico, A.C., ast@correo.tamnet.com.mx
Greengates School, gsclib@mail.internet.com.mx
John F. Kennedy Sch., kennedy@acnet.net

Moldava
QSI INtl. Sch. of Chisinau, qsimdu@setcom.moldnet.md

Mongolia
Intl. Sch. of Ulaanbaatar, inschool@magicnet.mn

Morocco
Casablanca Amer. Sch., 103113.1612@compuserve.com
Rabat American Sch., info@ras.edu.ac.ma

Namibia
Windhoek Intl. Sch., kevin@granny.mac.alt.na

Nepal
Lincoln Sch., lincoln@school.mos.com.np

Netherlands
Intl. Sch. of Amsterdam, jrich@isa.nl

Nicaragua
American-Nicaraguan Sch., anslib@ns.tmx.com.ni

Niger
Amer. Sch. of Niamey, asniger@bow.intnet.ne

Nigeria
Amer. Intl. Sch. of Lagos, aislagos@linkserve.com.ng

Norway
Intl. Sch. of Stavanger, intschol@iss.stavanger.rl.no

Pakistan
Intl. Sch. of Islamabad, admin%isipak@sdnpk.undp.org
Intl. Sch. of Peshawar, principal@isp.psh.brain.net.pk
Karachi Amer. Society Sch., ameschl@biruni.erum.com.pk
Murree Christian Sch., mcs@mcs-sdnpk.undp.org

Panama
Intl. Sch. of Panama, isp@pty.com

Papua New Guinea
Ukarumpa Intl. Sch., Primary, uispc_principal_png@sil.org
Ukarumpa Intl. Sch., Secondary, uissc.png@sil.org

Paraguay
American Sch. of Asunción, asa96@infonet.com.py
Asunción Christian Academy, aca@datanet.com.py
Pan American Intl. Sch., pais@122pi.una.py

Peru
Colegio Franklin D. Roosevelt, fdr@amersol.edu.pe

Philippines
Brent Intl. Sch. Manila, brent@mnl.sequel.net
Brent Sch, brent@bgo.cyberspace.com.ph
Faith Academy, vanguard@faith.edu.ph

Intl. School, Manila, isminfo@ismanila.portalinc.com
Poland
Amer. Intl. Sch. of Kraków, aisk@kki.krakow.pl
Portugal
American Christian Intl. Academy, orehotsky@aol.com
Amer. Intl. Sch. of Lisbon, aisl@individual.eunet.pt
St. Dominic's Intl. Sch., benard@mail.telepac.pt
St. Julian's Sch., julians@mail.telepac.pt
Puerto Rico
Baldwin Sch. of Puerto Rico, baldwinw@caribe.net
Saint John's Sch., sjslib@caribe.net
Qatar
Amer. Sch. of Doha, aisdoha@qatar.net.qa
Learning Center, altamimi@qatar.net.qa
Romania
American Sch. of Bucharest, director@asb.kappa.ro
Russia
Anglo Amer. Sch. of Moscow, aasoffice@glas.apc.org
Anglo-Amer. Sch. of St. Petersburg, aassp@glas.apc.org
QSI Intl. Sch. of Vladivostock, qsibrady@online.ru
Saudi Arabia
Dar Al Fikr Sch., daralfikr@sahara.com
Saudi Arabian Intl. Sch., Dhahran District, leo-ruberto%sais@macexpress
Saudi Arabian Oil Co., Saudi Aramco Schs., harrisdo@aramco.com.sa
Saudi—S.A.I.S., sais-saudia@tng.net
Senegal
Dakar Academy, dakar-academy-bus@maf.org
The Intl. Sch. of Dakar, isd@enda.sn
Sierra Leone
Amer. Intl. Sch. of Freetown, aisf@sl.baobob.com
Singapore
Canadian Intl. Sch., cis5@cdn-intl.edu.sg
Intl. Community Sch., Singapore, intlcoms@pacific.net.sg
Overseas Family Sch., executive_director@ofs.ac.sg
Slovakia
Bratislava Intl. Sch., bis@computel.sk
QSI Intl. Sch. of Bratislava, qsi@ba.sanet.sk
Slovenia
QSI Intl. Sch. of Ljubljana, qsijmd@net.zaslon.si
South Africa
Amer. Intl. Sch. of Johannesburg, pak02695@pixie.co.za
Spain
Amer. Sch. of Barcelona, 106046.3214@compuserve.com
American Sch. of Bilbao, amschbil@vzc.servicom.es
American Sch. of Las Palmas, aslpgc@ext.step.es
American Sch. of Madrid Foundation, asmcc@redestb.es
Baleares Intl. Sch., bispmi@ibm.net
Benjamin Franklin Intl. Sch., bfis@goliat.upc.es
Colegio Hispano-Norteamericano, am.school@vic.servicom.es
*Evangelical Christian Academy,*100430.2310@compuserve.com
Intl. College Spain, 101373.2000@compuserve.com
Intl. Sch. of Cartagena, isc@sendanet.es
Sri Lanka
Colombo Intl. Sch., cismgmnt@sri.lanka.net
Overseas Sch. of Colombo, admin@osc.lanka.net
Suriname
American Cooperative Sch., leo.limoges@sil.org
Sweden
Hvitfeldtska Gymnasiet, uhvceb@hvitfeldt.educ.goteborg.se
Intl. Sch. of Stockholm, admin@intsch.se
Sigtunaskolan Humanistiska Laroverket, info@sshl.se
Switzerland
Aiglon College, info@aiglon.ch
American Intl. Sch. of Zurich, aisz@aisz.ch
Brillantmont Intl. College, info@brillantmont.ch
Collège du Léman Intl. Sch., info@cdl.ch
Gstaad Intl. Sch., gis@gstaad.ch
Institut Le Rosey, admission@rosey.ch
Institut Montana, 706742.714@compuserve.com
Inter-Comm. Sch., 100442.374@compuserve.com
Intl. Sch. of Basel, intsba@dial.eunet.ch
Intl. Sch. of Berne, isberne@ibm.net
Intl. Sch. of Geneva, isamuel@ecolint.ch
Intl. Sch. of Lausanne, 100630.322@compuserve.com
John F. Kennedy Intl. Sch., lovell@jfk.ch
Kumon Leysin Academy of Switzerland, 100763.555@compuserve.com
Leysin American Sch. in Switzerland, 100551.734@compuserve.com
Winter Term, info@hohliebi.ch
Taiwan
Kaohsiung American Sch., rupert@mail.nsysu.edu.tw
Lincoln American Sch., las@tc.globalnet.com.tw
National Exper. High Sch., lmtai@mail.nehs.hc.edu.tw
Taipei Amer. Sch., 101400.1052@compuserve.com
Taipei British Sch., tbs@ms14.hinet.net
Tanzania
Intl. Sch. Moshi, ismoshi@maf.org
Intl. Sch. of Tanganyika Ltd., ist@unidar.gn.apc.org
Thailand
Ake Panya Intl. Sch., akepanya@cm.ksc.co.th
Bangkok Patana Sch., patanarc@info.co.th
Chiang Mai Intl. Sch., cmiskbn@loxinfo.co.th
Intl. Comm. Sch., 75452.2156@compuserve.com
Intl. Sch. Eastern Seaboard, ise@loxinfo.co.th
New Intl. Sch. of Thailand, nist@ksc.au.ac.th
Phuket Intl. Sch., info@phuketschl.com
Ruamrudee Intl. Sch., griffith@comnet.ksc.net.th
Togo
The British Sch. of Lomé, 103162.1615@compuserve.com
Trinidad
Intl. Sch. of Port of Spain, ispstt@trinidad.net
Tunisia
Amer. Cooperative Sch. of Tunis, acst@acst.intl.tn
Intl. Sch. of Sfax, 106534.1121@compuserve.com
Turkey
American Collegiate Institute, school@aci.edu.tr
Bilkent University Prep. Sch., school@bups.bilkent.edu.tr

Enka Okullari, enka@turk.net
Robert College of Istanbul, robcol@robcol.k12.tr
Tarsus American Sch., tarsus-f@servis2.net.tr
Üsküdar American Academy, uskudar@ibm.net

Turkmenistan

Ashgabat Intl. Sch., nick@ais.ashgabad.su

U.A.E.

Al-Worood School, alworood@emirates.net.ae
Amer. Comm. Sch. of Abu Dhabi, asdadmin@emirates.net.ae
Amer. Intl. Sch. in Abu Dhabi, aisa@emirates.net.ae
Amer. Sch. of Dubai, asdlmc1@emirates.net.ae
Intl. Sch. of Choueifat, Sharjah, iscshj@emirates.net.ae
Intl. Sch. of Choueifat, iscadl@emirates.net.ae

Uganda

Kabira Intl. Sch., gbell@imul.com
Lincoln Intl. Sch. of Uganda, lincoln@starcom.co.ug

Ukraine

Kiev Intl. Sch., kis@sovam.com

United Kingdom

American Community Sch., hmulkey@acs-england.co.uk
American School in London, admissions@asl.org
Edinburgh Tutorial College, 100667.3226@compuserve.com
International Sch. of Aberdeen, admin@isa.abdn.sch.uk
TASIS England Amer. Sch., ukadmissions@tasis.com

United States of America

Chinese American Intl. Sch., caishead@aol.com
Dallas Intl. Sch., udis@metronet.com
French–American Intl. Sch., faiswexler@aol.com
The Intl. Sch. of Minnesota, ism@spacestar.com
United Nations Intl. Sch., adminmail@unis.org

Uruguay

Uruguayan Amer. Sch., amschool@chasque.apc.org

Uzbekistan

Tashkent Ulugbek Intl. Sch., ulugbek@tuis.edu.uz

Venezuela

Colegio Internacional de Caracas, cic@cic-caracas.org
Escuela Campo Alegre, pgreben@internet.ve
Morrocoy Tutorial Services, john_mitchell@placerdome.com

Vietnam

United Nations Intl. Sch.–Hanoi, unis@netnam.org.vn

Yemen

Aden Intl. Sch., ais.h@netqsi.com
Sanaa Intl. Sch., jim.g@netqsi.com

Yugoslavia

Intl. Sch. of Belgrade, isb@eunet.yu

Zaire

The American Sch. of Kinshasa (TASOK), tasok-teachers@maf.org

Zambia

Amer. Intl. Sch., aesl@zamnet.zm
Intl. Sch. of Lusaka, isl@zamnet.zm
Lusaka Intl. Community Sch., lics@zamnet.zm

Chief School Officers

The following is a list of the chief school officers of each school alphabetized by last name. Due to space constraints, we could not include the city and country of each school. After you find the name of the school, use the index in the back of the book to find the page number on which the school is located.

Abed, N., *Principal/Business manager, Al-Worood Sch.*
Abel, Priscilla, *Director, Pan Amer. Sch. of Porto Alegre*
Abreu, Bethany, *Director, Asunción Christian Academy*
Abushakra, Raja, *Superintendent, The Amer. Intl. Sch.—Kuwait*
Abushakra, Walid, *Superintendent, Amer. Intl. Schools in Abu Dhabi and Egypt*
Adams, Edward B., *Headmaster, Seoul Intl. Sch.*
Al-Hamdan, Abdullah, *Executive Consultant, King Faisal School*
Al Essa, May, *Owner, Al-Bayan Bilingual Sch.*
Al Farra, Samia, *Principal, Amman Bacc. Sch.*
Al Ghanim, Nora, *Director, The Universal Amer. Sch.*
Alam, Sami J., *Superintendent, Saudia – S.A.I.S.*
Albrecht, Carl, *Principal, Bahrain Sch.*
Alden, Julia, *Director, Amer. Intl. Sch. in Genoa*
Alderdice, Kay, *Principal, Amer. Comm. Sch., Egham, Surrey*
Algunied, Dr. Abdul Qadir, *Head of trustees, Mohamed Ali Othman Sch.*
Allen, Keith, *Headmaster, New Intl. Sch. of Thailand*
Allen, Philip H., *Headmaster, St. Stephen's Sch., Rome*
Alter, John, *Director, Amer. Intl. Sch. of Nouakchott*
Ambrogi, Robert E., *Superintendent, Intl. Sch. of Islamabad*
Amman, Karen, *Superintendent, Kwajalein Sch. System*
Anderson, Frank, *Superintendent, Colegio Internacional de Carabobo*
Anderson, James, *Principal, Tanjung Bara Intl. Sch.*
Anson, Steven, *Principal, The Sir James Henderson British Sch. of Milan*
Apple, Ginger, *Director, Uruguayan Amer. Sch.*
Arango, Gonzalo, *Director, Colegio Granadino*
Arpee, Leonor, *Director, Pan Amer. Sch.*
Arpee, Robert L., *Director, Pan Amer. Sch.*
Ashley, Richard F., *Director, Westhill Institute*
Asp-Schusshe, Steven, *Director, Intl. Sch. of Ouagadougou*
Aspden, Valerie, *Head teacher, Berlin British Sch.*
Ater, Robert L., *Director, Intl. Sch. of Dusseldorf, e.V.*
Austen, Alan P., *Head, Baldwin Sch. of Puerto Rico*
Austin, Helen, *Superintendent, Mazapan School*
Bagnoud, Mr. and Mrs., *Directors, Intl. Sch. Le Chaperon Rouge*
Bailey, John S., *President, The Amer. Coll. of Greece*
Baiter, Pete, B., *Director, Pinewood Schs. of Thessaloniki*
Baker Barillas, Barbara, *Director, The Amer. Sch. of Guatemala*
Baldo, Dr. Antonio, *Director, Vicenza Intl. Sch.*
Bale, Rupert, *Principal, Kaohsiung Amer. Sch.*
Baradi, Ghormallah A., *Director general, Dar Al Fikr Sch.*
Barber, Keith, *Principal, Ukarumpa Intl. Sch.–Primary*
Barker, Daryl, *Director, Intl. Sch. (Seychelles)*
Bartlett, Kevin, *Director, Windhoek Intl. Sch.*
Barton, Charles, *Headmaster, Nagoya Intl. Sch.*
Bashshur, Catherine C., *Head, Amer. Comm. Sch. at Beirut*
Bastable, J. K., *Principal, Goroka Intl. Sch.*
Bavinton, Peter, D., *President, Lester B. Pearson College of the Pacific*
Beecher, Russell, *Headmaster, Saint John's Sch.*
Behennah, Michael J., *Principal, King George V Sch.*
Bell, M., *Headmistress, Kabira Intl. Sch.*
Benger, Barry, *Principal, Bontang Intl. Sch.*
Bennett, Mr. A. W., *Head, United World College of South East Asia*
Bergen, Richard, *Director, Dakar Academy*
Bergman, Don, *Superintendent, Singapore Amer. Sch.*
Berntsen, Leif, *Head teacher, Machabeng College*
Berrisford, Christopher, *Headmaster, Chinese Intl. Sch.*
Berry, James, *Director, Amer. Intl. Sch. of Mallorca*
Billing, Phil, *Principal, Murree Christian Sch.*
Billings, James, T., *Head, QSI Intl. Sch. of Yerevan*
Billingsley, Donald, *Head, Amer. Sch. of Paris*
Birchall, John, *Headmaster, British Intl. Sch., Jakarta*
Bland, Keith, *Principal, Medan Intl. Sch.*
Blaney, Joseph J., *Director, United Nations Intl. Sch.*
Blix, John, *Superintendent, Amer. Intl. Sch. of Lagos*
Boonprohm, Kamol, *Director, Chiang Mai Intl. Sch.*
Bowman, Christopher J., *Principal, Port Moresby Intl. Sch.*
Brady, Michael, *Director, QSI Intl. Sch. of Vladivostok*
Brandt, Günther, *Director, The Country Day Sch.*
Branson, C. A., *Head, Jumeirah English Speaking Sch.*
Braund, Ralph, *Head, Academia Britanica Cuscatleca*
Bray, Jennifer, *Principal (senior section), The British Sch. of Brussels*
Breedveld, A. C., *Headmaster, Intl. Sch. Eerde*
Brent, Dena, *Superintendent, Rosslyn Academy*
Briscoe, G., *Headmaster, St. Edward's College*
Brooks, David, *Director, The Riverside School*
Brown, Ronald C., *Director, Amer. Sch. of Kinshasa*
Buck, David W., *Director, Intl. Sch. of Prague*
Buckheit, James E., *Headmaster, The Frankfurt Intl. Sch., e.V.*
Burton, Burnett St. C., *Director, Belair Sch.*
Byers, John, *Director, Cochabamba Cooperative Sch.*
Cabral, Frank, *Principal, Majuro Cooperative Sch.*

Camblin, Jane, *Head, French–Amer. Intl. Sch.*
Cannon, Jonathan, *Executive Director, Carmel School*
Canoy, Solona T., *President, Intl. Sch. Cagayan de Oro*
Cantrell, Jacqueta, *Principal, AES Lal Pir School*
Cardenas, David E., *Superintendent, Escola Americana de Campinas*
Carlblom, Dwight, *Director, Dalat School*
Caroca, Verónica, *Director, Lincoln Intl. Academy*
Castagnola, Tom, *Superintendent, Mt. Zaagham Intl. Schools*
Caudill, Ellis, *Superintendent, Intl. Christian Sch., Seoul, Songtan, Uijongbu*
Chammaa, Samir J., *President, Ibn Khuldoon National Sch.*
Chandler, John, *Headmaster, The Koç School*
Cherinda, B., *Director, Intl. Sch. of Maputo*
Clark, Dennis, *Head, Fukuoka Intl. Sch.*
Clark, Geoffrey, *Headmaster, Intl. Sch. Hamburg*
Clivaz, Francis A., *Director general, Collège du Léman Intl. Sch.*
Conkey, Alan, *Director, Amer. Intl. Sch. of Rotterdam*
Conlan, Robert B., *Director, Amer. Sch. of Doha*
Cooper, Alun, *Principal, British Intl. Sch., Cairo*
Cooper, M. J., *Principal, The British Sch. in the Netherlands*
Cooper, Peter R., *Head, The Amer. Sch. in Japan*
Costello, Keith, *Director, Escola Americana de Belo Horizonte*
Craig, Gerald, *Director, Amer. Sch. of Antananarivo*
Cramer, David, *Superintendent, Amer. Intl. Sch./ Dhaka*
Crawford, James G., *Principal, Al Ain English Speaking Sch.*
Cromer, Bart P., *Director general, Colegio Americano de Torreon, A.C.*
Crosby, Tom, *Director, Amer. Intl. Sch. of Lomé*
Curtis, Blannie, *Headmaster, Amer. Intl. Sch. of Lisbon*
Curtis, Jr., John N., *Director, The Winter Term*
Cussac, Christine, *Director, Bordeaux Intl. Sch*
D'Alessandro, Marisa Di Carlo, *Director, Canadian College Italy*
Darlison, Jeff J., *Headmaster, Le Bocage Intl. Sch.*
Davia, Ralph A., *General director, Pan Amer. Intl. Sch.*
Davis, John C., *Superintendent, Saudi Arabian Intl. Sch. – Riyadh*
Davis, Margaret, *Director, Baku Intl. Sch.*
Decker, William J., *Superintendent, The Amer. Sch. of Kuwait*
DeHope, Rev. Canon J., *Director, Episcopal Cathedral Sch.*
Deitsch Stern, Ellen, *Director, Anglo Amer. Sch. of Moscow*
Delbarre, Ivan, *Headmaster, Cite Scolaire Internationale de Lyon Gerland*
Delman, Jack, *Director, Lincoln Sch., San José*
DeMinico, Paul, *Superintendent, Intl. Sch. Bangkok*
Detwiler, Richard M., *Superintendent, The Walworth Barbour Amer. Intl. Sch. in Israel*
Deuel, David, *Director, Santa Cruz Cooperative Sch.*
Dias-Jayasinh, Jacqueline, *Head teacher, Semarang Intl. Sch.*
Dixon-Warren, Margaret, *Head, Northside Primary*
Doi, Regina, *Headmistress/principal, Aoba Intl. Sch. and founding director, Japan Intl. Sch.*
Doll, Gloria J., *Superintendent, Asociacion Escuelas Lincoln*
Doolittle, Corazon C., *Principal, Victoria Primary Sch.*
Dougherty, Michael S., *Head, North Jakarta Intl. Sch.*
Dougherty, Larry, *Head, Amer. Overseas Sch. of Rome*
Doyle, James, *Director, QSI Intl. Sch. of Ljubljana*
Draper, Robert, *Director, Almaty Intl Sch.*
Duckett, Gary, *Superintendent, Amer. Comm. Sch., Amman*
Duevel, Linda M., *Director, Intl. Sch. of Stavanger*
Dull, Charles W., *Headmaster, Hong Kong Intl Sch.*
Easton Allen, Lesley, *Headmistress, The Intl. Preparatory Sch.*
Eaton, David E., *Superintendent, Intl. Sch. Cambodia*
Egawa, Sr. Masako, *Headmistress, Intl. Sch. of the Sacred Heart*
Egeler, Daniel J., *Director, Alliance Academy*
Elliott, Tomm, *Headmaster, Intl. Sch. of Turin (ACAT)*
Empis, Maria R., *Principal, St. Dominic's Intl. Sch.*
Eng, Richard T., *Superintendent, Khartoum Amer. Sch.*
Entwistle, Roy E., *Superintendent, Rift Valley Academy*
Epp, Michael, Director, *Pan Amer. Christian Academy*
Eriksson, Olov, *Principal, Kungsholmens Gymnasium – Intl. Section*
Etheridge, Andrew E., *Headmaster, Makassar Intl. Sch.*
El-Zubi, Fadel, *Acting director, Baghdad Intl., Sch.*
Fabriani, Gloria Hughes, *Directress, Kendale Primary Intl. Sch.*
Factor, Terence, *Headmaster, Escuela Americana de Tampico, A.C.*
Fakieh, Ghadah, *Director, The Learning Center*
Fama, Don, *Principal, Ukarumpa Intl. Sch.—Secondary*
Farnham, Barry, *Head, Intl. Sch. of Kuala Lumpur*
Farr, Michael, *Director, Colegio Karl C. Parrish*
Feltham, David, *Principal, Intl. Sch. Kaprun*
Felton, Martin, *Director, Colegio Bolivar*
Ferrier, Peter, *Principal, Bogor Expatriate Sch.*
Fiedler, Grant, *Headmaster, Leysin Amer. Sch. in Switzerland*
Finn, Stewart, *Principal, The Kilmore Intl. Sch.*
Finnegan, L. J., *Headmaster, Sutton Park Sch.*
Fisher, A. G. F., *Headmaster, St. Andrew's Scots Sch.*
Fisher, James, *Director, The Intl. Sch. of Conakry*
Fituri, Ahmed S., *Superintendent, Intl. Sch. of the Martyrs*
Flaming, R., *Principal, Woodstock Sch.*
Flaxman, Gillian, *Director, Colegio Hispano—Norteamericano*
Flessa, Joseph, *General director, Amer. Sch. of Pachuca*
Fontana, Br. George, *Headmaster, Marist Brothers Intl. Sch.*

Forster, S., *Acting headteacher, Marina Intl. School*
Forster, T. Blair, *Principal, Li Po Chun United World College of Hong Kong*
Fox, Elisabeth, *Headmistress, Santiago College*
Francis, Michael, *Director, Intl. Sch. of Phnom Penh*
Frei-Huguenin, Françoise, *Principal, Brillantmont Intl. College*
Frnka, Ron, *Director, Minsk Intl. School*
Frost, Christopher, *Headmaster, The Amer. Sch. in Switzerland (TASIS)*
Fryback, Alan, *Director, Sch. of the Nations, Macau*
Gallinger, Helge H., *Superintendent, Intl. Sch., of Lusaka—Zambia*
Gamwell, Bruce, *Principal, The Intl. Sch. of Lae*
Gardner, Brigid, *Principal, St. George's English Sch.*
Garlinski, Jarek E., *Headmaster, The Awty Intl. Sch.*
Garton, Brian, *Director, Anglo-American School, Sofia*
Gates, Gerald C., *Superintendent, Chapel (Escola Maria Imaculada)*
Gatley, David, *Director, Intl. Sch. of Berne*
Gay-Hörmann, Pierre, *Principal, Institut Château Beau-Cèdre*
Geier, Philip O., *President, The Armand Hammer UWC of the American West*
Gellar, Charles A., *Director, Brussels' English Primary Sch. and B.E.P.S. 2 – Limal Intl. Sch.*
Germanos, R., *Regional director, The Intl. Sch. of Choueifat*
Gerritz, William H., *Director, The Amer. Sch. of The Hague*
Gieschen, Paul A., *Superintendent, Okinawa Christian Sch. Intl.*
Gilbert, Bruce, *Principal, Hanoi Intl. School*
Gilson, James E., *Director, Sanaa Intl. Sch.*
Giombi, James, *Superintendent, Intl. Sch. Eastern Seaboard*
Glickman, Judith R., *Head of Sch., The Amer. Sch. in London*
Godsil, Arthur, *Headmaster, St. Andrew's College*
Gonzales Mend, Mary, *Superintendent, Amer. Sch. Foundation, A.C.*
Goosens, Peter J. H., *Head of Sch., Intl. Secondary Sch. Eindhoven*
Gotts, Peter, *Headmaster, Intl. Sch. of Pusan*
Gould, Everett G., *Director, The Amer. Intl. Sch. of Johannesburg*
Gray, Cynthia A., *Director, Harare Intl. Sch.*
Greben, Paul, *Superintendent, Escuela Campo Alegre*
Greeley, Monica N., *Director, Intl. Sch. Yangon*
Green, N. P. O., *Headmaster, St. George's College*
Greenside, Marc, *Headmaster, Amer. Intl. Sch. of Florence*
Gregoriou, Akis, *Director general, The Grammar Sch.*
Gregory, Charles, *Director, Intl. Sch. of Sfax*
Griffiths, David, *Head teacher, Morogoro Intl. Sch.*
Grisdale, W. S., *Principal, Legae Academy*
Groves, Don, *Superintendent, The Amer. Sch. of Tegucigalpa*
Gudin, Philippe, *Director, Institut Le Rosey*
Guerra, Norma, *Director, Colegio Ingles*
Hadden, Sally A., *Chief sch. officer, Intl. Sch. of Latvia*
Hadley, Moyra, *Head, Overseas School of Colombo*
Haesler, Aldo J., *Director, Institut Montana*
Hall, Kevin, *Head teacher, Aden Intl. Sch.*
Hall, Richard P., *Director, The Intl. Sch. of Brussels*
Halsey, Ron, *Director, Tashkent Intl. Sch.*
Hammer, Patrcia, *Head teacher, QSI Intl. Sch. of Chisinau*
Hammond, Celine, *Head of school, Amer. Sch. of Las Palmas*
Hanna, Charles C., *Managing principal, John F. Kennedy Sch., Berlin*
Hannah, Lister, *Principal, Geelong Grammar School*
Hansen, Mark, *Headmaster, Amer. Intl. Sch. of Vilnius*
Hansen, Tim, *Superintendent, Amer. Comm. Sch. of Abu Dhabi*
Harding, Peter, *Director, Danube Intl. School*
Harrison, John, *Headmaster, St. John's Sch., Acassuso*
Harrison, Owen, *Superintendent, Saudi Arabian Oil Company, Saudi Aramco Schools*
Hartley, Roger, *Headmaster, Kenton College*
Haugh, Kenneth J., *Director, Hillcrest Intl. School*
Havill, John, *Principal, Bandung Alliance Sch.*
Hawley, David, *Director, Atlanta Intl. Sch.*
Haywood, Terence F., *Head, Intl. Sch. of Milan*
Heard, John, *Director, Üsküdar Amer. Academy*
Heatherington, Mary Jo, *Superintendent, Pan Amer. Sch. of Bahia*
Hedger, Terry, *Director, Intl. College Spain*
Henderson, Diana, *Vice-principal, Gulf English School*
Hennessy, K., *Director, École d'Humanité*
Hermon, R., *Headmaster, Intl. Sch. of London*
Hetzel, Robert J., *Superintendent, Cairo Amer. College*
Hickmore, Brian, *Principal, Mougins Sch.*
Hicks, Melissa, *Director, Amer. Intl. Sch. of Kraków*
Hilgeman, Thomas, *Director, Santa Cruz Christian Learning Center*
Hill, David, *Director, Intl. School, Suva*
Hill, K. C., *Director, École d'Humanité*
Hill, RSHM, Sr. Anne Marie, *Headmistress, Marymount Intl. Sch.*
Hillmann, Kenneth, *Headmaster, Istanbul Intl. Comm. Sch.*
Holder, Sheila, *Principal, Bermuda Institute of Seventh-day Adventists*
Hollis, Ralph, *Director, Lincoln Intl. Sch. of Uganda*
Horsley, Alex, *Director, The Intl. Sch. of Beijing*
Horton, Anthony, *Director, The Amer. School of Warsaw*
Hove, Roger G., *Headmaster, The Amer. Sch. of Dubai*
Hughes, Sr. Barbara, *Superintendent, St. John's Intl. Sch.*
Hughes, Jan, *principal, Intl. Sch. at Amboni*
Hull, Kevan, *principal, Ecole Flamboyant*
Hunt, Thomas G., *Director, Amer. Intl. Sch. of Bamako*
Hunter, Adrienne, *Principal, Intl. Sch. of Havana*

Hurd, Philip, *Principal, Intl. Community Sch., London*
Hurley, David, *Director, Bratislava Intl. School*
Isobal, Luz V., *Superintendent, Cebu Intl. Sch.*
Jacoby, Bruce, *Principal, Intl. Sch. of Lhokseumawe*
Jahr, Ralph, *Headmaster, The Carol Morgan Sch. of Santo Domingo*
James, D. J., *Academic head, Island Sch.*
Jarman, Ken C., *Administrator, Amer. Sch. of Douala*
Jasinski, Jon, *Principal, Intl. Sch. of Hyderabad*
Jeannin, Jeanne, *Director, Dallas Intl. Sch.*
Jeffery, D., *Headmaster, Anglican Intl. Sch., Jerusalem*
Jenkins, C. D. O., *Principal, United World College of the Atlantic*
Jenkins, Tom C., *Superintendent, Caltex Amer. Sch.*
Jibrilu, Joy, *Headmaster, Kaduna Intl. School*
Johnard, Olof, *Principal, Hvitfeldtska Gymnasiet*
Johnson, John K., *Director, Amer. Intl. Sch. of Budapest*
Johnson, Paul, *Director, Intl. Sch. of Amsterdam*
Jones, Eleanor J., *Head, Hiroshima Intl. Sch.*
Jones, Gareth, *Headmaster, Intl. Sch. of Paris*
Jones, Gordon, *Head of school, Ake Panya Intl. Sch.*
Jones, Larry, *Director, Intl. Community Sch. of Abidjan*
Jones, Robert, *Director, QSI Intl. Sch. of Bratislava*
Joslin, Philip, *Principal, Bandung Intl. Sch.*
Jutras, Br. Michel, *Headmaster, St. Mary's Intl. Sch.*
Kahlenbeck, Kurt C., *Principal, Kyoto Intl. Sch.*
Kapner, Stephen M., *Director, The Amer. Embassy Sch., New Delhi*
Karlsson, Ingrid, *Head, Sigtunaskolan Humanistiska Laroverket*
Keator, Gerrit, *President, Intl. College, Beirut*
Keller, D. Jeffrey, *Superintendent, Amer. Sch. Foundation of Monterrey, A.C.*
Kenney, R. Martin, *Headmaster, Emirates Intl. Sch.*
Kenny, Gary F., *Director, The Intl. Sch. of Panama*
Ketterer, John J., *Director, The Amer. Sch. of Asunción*
Khoury, Maria C., *Principal, Ramallah Friends School*
Kingsbury, Eleanor, *Principal, The Bermuda High Sch. for Girls*
Klimesh, Mark, *Superintendent, The Benjamin Franklin Intl. Sch.*
Klumb Monroy, Kathleen, *Director general, Colegio Americano de Veracruz*
Klumpp, Dennis, *Headmaster, Escola Americana do Rio de Janeiro*
Kodzas, Nikola, *Director/business manager, Intl. Sch. of Belgrade*
Lagriffoul, Paul, *Headmaster, French Intl. School "Victor Segalen"*
Lajud, Alfonso, *Director, John F. Kennedy School*
Lamb, Elsa, *Director, Amer. Sch. of Barcelona*
Lamoré-Meÿer, Jacqueline, *Headmistress, Maartens College Intl. Sch.*
Landau, Robert, *Principal, Cilegon Intl. School*
Langley, Mary, *Director, Intl. Sch. of Stuttgart*
Larson, Eric, *Principal, Teda Intl. Sch.*
Latter, Martin, *Headmaster, Intl. Sch. of Zug*
Laurette, Frank, *Director, Bishkek Intl. School*
Law, Russ, *Director, The Continental Sch.*
Lecubarri, Sr. Asuncion, *Headmistress, Seisen Intl. Sch.*
Leddy, John P., *Principal, Escuela Bilingue Santa Barbara*
Lee, Anna, *Superintendent, Lincoln Amer. School*
Lee, Shirley, *Head, Chinese Amer. Intl. School*
Leigh, Jacqueline, *Principal, The Amer. Intl. Sch. of Freetown*
Levinson, Michael, *Director, American Cooperative School of Tunis*
Lewallen, Bryan K., *Director, Colegio Albania*
Lieblich, Paul, *Director, Intl. Primary Sch. of Zurich*
Liebzeit, James, *Director, Damascus Community School*
Liles, O. L., *Headmaster, Central Java Inter-mission Sch.*
Limoges, Leo, *Principal, Amer. Cooperative Sch., Paramaribo*
Linton, R. J., *Director, AFCENT Intl. Sch.*
Lloyd, Geoff, *Headmaster, Intl. Sch. Moshi*
Long, Richard, D., *Director, Internationale Schule Frankfurt-Rhein-Main*
Loosle, Lyle J., *General director, Colegio Interamericano*
Lovell, William M., *Director, John F. Kennedy Intl. Sch., Switzerland*
Lowe, Jean, *Head, QSI Intl. School of Skopje*
Lowrie, Roy L., *Superintendent, Faith Academy*
Lux, Mrs., *Headmistress, Ecole Active Bilingue Jeannine Manuel*
Lyons, Lawrence D., *Director, Amer. Intl. Sch. of Costa Rica*
Lyso, Harlan, E., *Headmaster, Seoul Foreign Sch.*
MacInnis, Wayne, *Principal, Canadian Intl. Sch.*
Mackenzie, John, *Headmaster, The Grange School*
Magee, Harry, *Headmaster, Abraham Lincoln Sch.*
Mains, James A., *Superintendent, Surabaya Intl. Sch.*
Malpass, Derek, *Bavarian Intl. School*
Mandrell, Ed, *Superintendent, Amer. Intl. Sch. Cyprus*
Marie, Sr. Armand, *Principal, Academia del Perpetuo Socorro*
Marin, Mark C., *Headmaster, Antilles Sch.*
Markland, Barbara, *Co-principal, Yew Chung Shanghai Intl. School*
Markland, Roy, *Co-principal, Yew Chung Shanghai Intl. School*
Marracino, F. Richard, *Headmaster, Caribbean Preparatory Sch.*
Marshall, Raymond, *Executive director, Inter-Amer. Academy*
Martens, Frank, *Headmaster, Intl. Christian Sch.*
Martires, O. P., Sr. Mary, *Principal, Dominican Intl. Sch.*
Maselli-Boucicaut, Rita, *Director, Union Sch.*
Matsumoto, Saburo, *Headmaster, Nishimachi Intl. Sch.*
Mayer, Susan, *Principal, Greengates Sch.*
Mazzini, Mabel, *Principal, St. Catherine's Moorlands*
McAloon, Beverly, *Director, QSI Intl. Sch. of Tbilisi*

McCarthy, Hannah, *Director, Asmara Intl. Comm. Sch.*
McCauley, Brian L., *Superintendent, Intl. Sch., Manila*
McClain, R. D., *Headmaster, Hokkaido Intl. Sch.*
McCombs, Barry, *Director, Colegio Nueva Granada*
McDermott, Paul, *Principal, Waterford Kamhlaba*
McDonald, Richard, *Headmaster, Aiglon College*
McGee, Jerry C., *Headmaster, Intl. Sch. of Aruba*
McGinley, Sandra, *Principal, St. Michael's Intl. Sch.*
McGlothlin, Everett P., *Superintendent, Lahore Amer. Society Sch.*
McGrew, William W., *President, Anatolia College*
McKenzie, Malcolm H., *Principal, Maru a Pula Sch.*
McLean, Paul, *Principal, Amer. Intl. Sch. Salzburg*
McMahon, Fr. M., *Headmaster, St. Mary's Sch.*
McPhillips III, Joseph A., *Academic Head, The Amer. Sch. of Tangier*
McWilliam, Neil, *Principal, Intl. Grammar Sch.*
Meeks, Greg, *Superintendent, Morrison Academy*
Meirans, Biruta, *Principal, The English Sch.*
Mellor, Michael B., *Headmaster, Taipei British School*
Menon, Meera, *Principal, Bangalore Intl. Sch.*
Merchant, Livingston, *Director, Intl. Sch. of Curaçao*
Metzger, Peter, *Director, Intl. Sch. of Trieste*
Middlebrook, Stephen, *Headmaster, Osaka Intl. Sch.*
Mitchell, John C., *Director, Morrocoy Tutorial Services*
Mollenkof, Judi, *Headmaster, Christian Academy in Japan*
Mongiat, Laura, *Head, Intl. Sch. of Sophia Antipolis*
Montgomery, Ronald I., *Superintendent, Shanghai Amer. Sch.*
Moore, Michael, *Director, Phuket Intl. Sch.*
Moore, Paul, *Principal, Intl. Sch. of Zanzibar*
Morris, A. W., *Principal, Edinburgh Tutorial College*
Morrison, Robert, *Director, Amer. Sch. of Zagreb*
Morton, Wayne D., *Head, Lanna Intl. Sch. Thailand*
Mosher, Glenn H., *Director, Tirana Intl. Sch.*
Mott, Peter C., *Headmaster, The Amer. Intl. Sch. of Zurich*
Moyaert, Blanch, *Director, Brillant Stars Intl. Sch.*
Muirhead, Mark, *Administrator, Bellver Intl. College*
Mullane, Bernard C., *Headmaster, Ambrit Rome Intl. School*
Murison, June, *Director, Intl. Sch. of Bergen*
Murphy, RSHM, Sr. Genevieve, *Headmistress, Marymount Sch.*
Nanos, Peter J., *Superintendent, Amer. Comm. Sch. of Athens*
Neil, Judy, *Principal, Bingham Academy*
Nelson, Jorge O., *Director general, Colegio Americano de Durango, A.C.*
Nelson, Niall C. W., *Headmaster, Jakarta Intl. Sch.*
Nessler, Juergen, *Principal, Goethe Gymnasium*
Ng, Rose, *Headmistress, Hong Kong Amer. Intl. Sch.*
Nichols, Tanya L., *Head of Sch., The Good Hope Sch.*
Nieberding, F. X., *Director, EEC Intl. Sch. and The City Int'l Sch., Brussels*
Niehaus, Linda A., *Director, Marian Baker Sch.*
Nordquist, John Pat, *Principal, Anglo-Amer. Sch. of St. Petersburg*
Normandin, Mary Ellen, *Director, American-Nicaraguan Sch.*
O'Connor, Thomas P., *Director, Seoul Academy Intl. Sch.*
O'Donnell, Stephen I., *Headmaster, Alscon Intl. Sch.*
O'Hale, William, *Superintendent, Amer. Sch. of Madrid Foundation*
O'Keefe, Sr. Carmel, *Board chairperson, Saint Maur Intl. Sch.*
Oentoro, Johannes, *Director, Hope Intl. School*
Okpanachi, J., *Principal, Amer. Intl. Sch. of Abuja*
Olynpiou, L., *Headmaster, Intl. Sch. of Paphos*
Omonuwa, V. O. M., *Administrator, John F. Kennedy Intl. Sch. Nigeria*
Orehotsky, David, *Director, Amer. Christian Intl. Academy*
Ortloff, Warren, *Superintendent, Escuela Anaco Internacional*
Orueta, Terry, *Director, Amer. Sch. of Bilbao*
Osbo, John D., *Director, Intl. Sch. of Aberdeen*
Ott, K. Steven, *Executive director, Leysin Amer. Sch. in Switzerland*
Ottaviano, David, *Director, Amer. Sch. of Milan*
Özdemir, Selim, *Principal, Tashkent Ulugbek Intl. Sch.*
Paden, Phillip, *Director, Vienna Christian School*
Paduano, John, *Headmaster, Intl. Sch. of Budapest*
Palladino, Marianne, *Director of studies, Castelli Intl. Bilingual Sch.*
Park, Myungsin, *President, Indianhead School*
Parks, Murray, *Principal, Garden Intl. School*
Pasquale, Fred, *Director, Colegio Maya, The Amer. Intl. Sch.*
Pattee, Lawrence, *Headmaster, Schutz Amer. Sch.*
Pavlos, Emmanuel, *Director, The Ifrane Sch.*
Pellegrino, Patrick, *Principal, American School, Macedonia*
Penland, Thomas J., *Superintendent, Taejon Christian Intl. School*
Pérez, Góngora Elsa, *Principal, Anglo American Sch.*
Perry, David A., *Chairman, Overseas Family Sch.*
Perske, Louis J., *Director, Amer. College of Sophia*
Peterson, Laurel A., *Principal, The Antofagasta Intl. Sch.*
Peterson, Marvin, *Chairman, Colegio Peterson*
Pholar, Conrad, *Director, Colegio Jorge Washington*
Pierce, Anne-Marie, *Head, Washington Intl. Sch.*
Ponce, Pilar, *Director, Amer. Sch. of Quito*
Poore, Paul, *Director, Lincoln School, Kathmandu*
Popinchalk, Michael D., *Headmaster, Intl. Sch. of Port of Spain*
Porter, Brian W., *Headmaster, Munich Intl. Sch.*
Poteat, Patricia L., *President, Athens College*
Powell, William, *Chief executive officer, Intl. Sch. of Tanganyika Ltd.*
Price, Huw C., *Principal, Maseru English Medium Preparatory Sch.*

Psiloinis, Christo, *Principal, The Amer. Academy Nicosia*
Pugh, Christopher, *Headmaster, St. John's Sch., Concepcion*
Pultar, Mustafa, *Director, Bilkent University Preparatory Sch.*
Punch, Barbara, *Principal, Amoco Galeota Sch.*
Qarghah, Rebecca N., *Head, The Intl. Sch. of Peshawar*
Quintana, Gilberto, *Executive director, Robinson School*
Raffo, Susana R., *Headmistress, Colegio San Marcos*
Randall, David, *Superintendent, Colegio Franklin D. Roosevelt*
Randolph, John J., *Director, Casablanca Amer. Sch.*
Rawley, Tim, *Director, Southern Peru Limited Staff Schools*
Reda, Nadia, *Head of Sch., The Intl. Sch. of Minnesota*
Rhodes, Francis J., *Superintendent, UN Intl. School—Hanoi*
Richards, Neil, *Headmaster, Yokohama Intl. Sch.*
Riehl, Thurston, *Director, Georgetown Amer. Intl. Sch.*
Rigg, Lyle, *D., Headmaster, TASIS England Amer. Sch.*
Risch, Robert, *Principal, ISS Intl. Sch. of Cartagena*
Ritter, John, *Director, American Intl. Sch.*
Robbins, Dick B., *Headmaster, Brent Intl. Sch. Manila*
Robinson, Ernestine Rochelle, *Director, The Caribbean-Amer. Sch.*
Rodgers-Jenki, Fay, *Director, The Priory School*
Rollo, Sr. Judith Marie, *High school principal, Mount Saint Agnes Academy*
Roots, Bonnie, *Superintendent, Int'l Christian School, Tongduchon*
Rose, William D., *Headmaster, Intl. Sch. of Helsinki*
Ross, Peter, *Principal, Logos Sch. of English Education*
Rowell, Trevor, *Headmaster, Saltus Grammar Sch.*
Ruberto, Leo A., *Superintendent, Saudi Arabian Intl. Sch., Dhahran District*
Rubi, Martha, *Director, Discovery School*
Rysdale, Ian, *Director, Western Academy of Beijing*
Sadler, James C., *Head, St. Croix Country Day Sch.*
Salimbene, George B., *Director/headmaster, TASIS HELLENIC Intl. Sch. in Athens*
Sanders, David, *Principal, Colombo Intl. Sch.*
Sanders, Lionel, *Principal, Christian Alliance P. C. Lau Memorial Intl. School*
Sargent, Winthrop, *Superintendent, Colegio Internacional de Caracas*
Satchell, Gloria, *Principal, Escuela Caribe*
Sawyer Jr., Frank N., *Director, Amer. Intl. Sch. of Libreville*
Sawyerr, Judith S., *Principal, Ghana Intl. Sch.*
Sayer, I. A., *Headmaster, The British Sch. of Lomé*
Sbeiti, M. A., *Director, Green Hill Intl. Sch.*
Schaecher, Robert F., *Headmaster, Antwerp Intl. Sch.*
Schmidt, Andrew, *Director, Amer. Sch. of Niamey*
Schober, John K., *Superintendent, The Columbus Sch.*
Schol, H. A., *Headmaster, Regionale Internationale Sch.*
Schultz, Ronald H., *Director, Intl. Comm. Sch./ Addis Ababa*
Scinto, Daniel L., *Superintendent, Intl. Sch. of Kenya, Ltd.*
Seibert Ricci, Donna, *Directress, Greenwood Garden Sch.*
Seinen, Dick, *Superintendent, Hillcrest School*
Selig, Mike S., *Acting principal, International School of Aleppo*
Selitzer, Gerald, *Superintendent, The Amer. Sch. of Puerto Vallarta*
Sessa, Josephine, *Principal, The Intl. Sch. of Naples*
Sheehan, Dennis, *Superintendent, Amer. Coop. Sch.*
Sheridan, Sr. Rosaleen, *Principal, Marymount Intl. Sch., Surrey*
Shields, Gerald, *Director, Amer. Intl. Sch. of Luxembourg*
Shoemaker, Donald R., *Headmaster, Mont'Kiara Intl. Sch.*
Sibley, Stephen, *Director, Escuela Las Morochas*
Sigurbjornsson, Barbara, *Head teacher, Amer. Embassy Sch., Reykjavik*
Sills, Robert, *Director, Rabat Amer. Sch.*
Silvetz, Robert M., *Headmaster, The Amer. Intl. Sch., Nice*
Slovenz, Stephen L., *Principal, International School of Grenada*
Smith, Dennis, *Superintendent, Amer. Intl. Sch. of Bolivia*
Smith, Gene, *Superintendent, Academia Los Pinares*
Snider, Helen, *Principal, Canadian Intl. School*
Souperbiet, Alain, *Director, Gstaad Intl. Sch.*
Spahn, Stephen H., *Chancellor, The Dwight Sch.*
Spencer, Anthony, *Tarsus Amer. Sch.*
Spradling, Richard L., *Director, Amer. Intl. School*
Stark, Steve, *Principal, Intl. Community Sch., Singapore*
Stemp, Chester, *Principal, Colegio Internacional de San Salvador*
Stephan, Nancy, *Director, Amer. Sch. of Guangzhou*
Stones, R., *Head, Tanglin Trust School*
Strom, Hal, *Director, Amer. Sch. of Bombay*
Strommen, Clifford H., *Headmaster, The Intl. Sch. Nido de Aguilas*
Stroud, John K., *Principal, Yogyakarta Intl. Sch.*
Stuart, Robert, *Acting secondary school head, Bishop Mackenzie Intl. Schs.*
Stucker, F. Joseph C., *Director, Vientiane Intl. Sch.*
Styan, F. D., *Head, St. Julian's Sch. (English Section)*
Sukhun, Nabil, *Director general, Bahrain Bayan Sch.*
Sullivan, Graham, *Principal, Bangkok Patana Sch.*
Sutcliffe, D. B., *Head, United World College of the Adriatic*
Sutcliffe, D. G., *Director, The English Intl. College*
Swall, Dale, *Director, Colegio Panamericano*
Swetz, James, *Director, Banjul Amer. Embassy Sch.*
Sylla, Philip, *Superintendent, Karachi Amer. Society Sch.*
Sylvester, Robert F., *Principal, Westwood Sch.*

Tai, Li-Ming, *Principal, National Experimental High Sch.*
Tarlet, Lionel, *Head, College Lycee Cevenol Intl.*
Tawney, Lavonne K., *Principal, Bonn Amer. High Sch.*
Tewalthomas, Michael, *Director, Kiev Intl Sch.*
Thompson, Frederick L., *Principal, The Amer. Collegiate Institute*
Thompson, Michael J., *Headmaster, Sandford English Comm. Sch.*
Thompson, Robert E., *Director general, Colegio Americano de Guayaquil*
Thomson, M., *Principal, Intl. Sch. of Ulaanbaatar*
Todd, Peter, *Director, The Intl. Sch. of Dakar*
Toland, Cindy, *Principal, Intl. Comm. School*
Tomlinson, Geoffrey, *Headmaster, Intl. Sch. of Basel*
Tooman, A. Ronald, *Headmaster, St. John's Sch., Tumon Bay*
Toubkin, Milton E., *Headmaster, Southbank Intl. Sch.*
Toze, David, *Director, Vienna Intl. Sch.*
Travis, Rev. Fr. Leo J., *Director, Ruamrudee Intl Sch.*
Trent, Robert W., *Director general, American Sch. Ftn. of Guadalajara*
Trough, Ken F., *Principal, Amazon Valley Academy*
Trüper, Matthias, *Headmaster, Intl. Sch. Berlin—Potsdam*
Tully, David, *Superintendent, Associacao Escola Graduada de Sao Paulo*
Ulfers, Mark, *Superintendent, Taipei Amer. Sch.*
Vaessen, A. J. M., *Headmaster, The Rijnlands International School*
VanDerVeer Gueiros, Helen Ruth, *Superintendent, Amer. Sch. of Recife*
Veitch, D. Michael, *Director, Lycee Intl., Amer. Section*
Veitch, James E., *Director, Clifford School*
Vickers, Clinton J., *Director, Enka Okullari*
Vodarski, William, *Director, Amer. Intl. Sch. of Lesotho*
Vosper, Murray, *Principal, Bali Intl. Sch.*
Vossler, Gregg A., *Principal, Tianjin Intl. Sch.*
Wade, Merry, *Superintendent, Lincoln Community Sch.*
Wadsworth, Christopher, *Headmaster, Robert College of Istanbul*
Walker, George, *Director general, The Intl. Sch. of Geneva*
Walker, Joe, *Director, Intl. Sch. of Curitiba*
Ward, P. A., *Head, Independent Bonn Intl. Sch., e.V.*
Wasuck, Nicholas, *Director, Ashgabat Intl. Sch.*
Watson, Graham, *Principal, Amer. Aademy Larnaca, Cyprus*
Weill, Brigitte, *Directrice, United Nations Nursery Sch. Association, Paris*
Werber, Bruce, *Director, Shekou Intl. Sch.*
Werner, Gregory E., *Superintendent, Escuela Internacional Sampedrana*
Werner, Robert, *Headmaster, Amer. Sch. of Brasilia*
Wesson, Frederic F., *Director, Amer. Sch. of Bucharest*
Widlund, Claes-Göran, *Principal, Intl. Sch. of Stockholm*
Wiebe, Paul, *Principal, Kodaikanal Intl. School*
Wiggins, J. Barrie, *Headmaster, The Baleares Intl. Sch.*
Williams, Areta, *Director, Amer. Sch. of Yaounde*
Winning, Gary, *Principal, Pasir Ridge Intl. Sch.*
Wise, Don, *Superintendent, Cotopaxi Academy*
Wittig, Deborah, *Principal, Wesley Intl. School*
Wolf, J. Douglas, *Headmaster, Verdala Intl. Sch.*
Wrye, Kenneth J., *Director, Copenhagen Intl. Sch.*
York, Richard, *Director, Santiago, Christian Sch.*
Yoshida, Hisashi, *Principal, Kumon Leysin Academy of Switzerland*
Young, John, *Headmaster, The Inter-Comm. Sch.*
Young, Stuart J., *Headmaster, Canadian Academy*
Younger, Hugh, *Headmaster, Lusaka Intl. Comm. Sch.*
Yutzy, Maynard, *Headmaster, Sendai Amer. Sch.*
Zeboulon, Madame, *Headmistress, Ecole Active Bilingue Jeannine Manuel*
Zein, Kamal, *Administrator, Intl. Sch. of Brazzaville*
Zund-Cooper, L. G., *Principal, St. George's Sch. in Switzerland*

Web Site Addresses: (http:// precedes each address)

Austria
Vienna International School, www.vis.ac.at
Belgium
B.E.P.S.2 - Limal Int'l School, www.beps.com
Brussels' English Primary School S.P.R.L, www.beps.com
Bolivia
Santa Cruz Christian Learning Center, www.scclc.org/
Brazil
American School of Brasilia, www.eabdf.br
Associacao Escola Graduada de Sao Paulo, www.aegsp.br
International School of Curitiba, www.eic.arauc.br
Pan American Christian Academy, www.opus.com.br/~paca/
Chile
The Grange School, www.grange.cl
China
Shanghai American School, www.sasch.org
Costa Rica
Lincoln School, www.lincoln.ed.cr
Cyprus
Logos School of English Education, www.logos.ac.cy
Dominican Republic
The Carol Morgan School of Santo Domingo, www.cms.edu.do
Ecuador
Inter-American Academy, www.acig.k12.ec
Finland
International School of Helsinki, www.ish.edu.hel.fi
France
International School of Paris, sunsite.unc.edu:80/isp/index.html
International School of Sophia Antipolis, www.ibo.org/schools/civ/civ.htm
Germany
Bavarian International School, www.bis-school.com
Int'l Schule Frankfurt-Rhein-Main, www.sabis.com/school-network/isf.htm
The Frankfurt International School e.V., cocos.cocos.de/fis
Greece
Athens College, www.hol.gr/hosted/athens_college/gr.html
TASIS Hellenic Int'l School in Athens, www.tasis.com
Honduras
Escuela Internacional Sampedrana, www.netsys.hn/~seis
Mazapan School, www.mazapan.stdfruit.hn
Hong Kong
Chinese International School, www.hk.super.net/~cis
International Christian School, www.hk.super.net/~ics
Hungary
International School of Budapest, www.ett.net.hu/isb/isb.htm
India
The American Embassy School, www.serve.com.aesndi
Woodstock School, www.kwi.org/woodstock/
Indonesia
Surabaya International School, www.rad.net.id/users/personal/s/siscoord/welcome.html
Italy
Canadian College Italy, www.idirect.com/~cci/
Castelli International Bilingual School, www.pcg.it/cis
Kendale Primary Int'l School, www.mclink.it/personal/mc2205/kendale.htm
St. Stephen's School, Rome, www.curiouspix.com/st_stephens.html
Japan
Canadian Academy, canada.canacad.ac.jp
Hokkaido International School, www.bekkoame.or.jp/~hokintsc/
The American School in Japan, www.asij.ac.jp
Kuwait
Al-Bayan Bilingual School, www.moc.kw/users/bbs
The American International School-Kuwait, www.moc.kw/users/raja/aishom
The American School of Kuwait, www.kuwait.net/~ramu/index.html
Lithuania
American International School of Vilnius, www.usis.lt
Luxembourg
American Int'l School of Luxembourg, www.restena.lu/aisl/aisl.html
Netherlands
International School of Amsterdam, www.isa.nl
The American School of The Hague, www.ash.nl
The British School in the Netherlands, www.britishschool.nl

Norway
International School of Stavanger, www.iss.stavanger.rl.no
Peru
Colegio Franklin D. Roosevelt, www.amersol.edu.pe
Philippines
International School Manila, www.portalinc.com/ismanila
Poland
American International School of Kraków, www.kki.krakow.pl/aisk
Portugal
American Int'l School of Lisbon, www.guilford.k12.nc.us/hp/lisbon/home.html
St. Dominic's International School, www.cidadevirtual.pt/dominics-n12
St. Julian's School, ourworld.compuserve.com/homepages/julians_computing
Puerto Rico
Baldwin School of Puerto Rico, www.gulf.net/about/webpresence baldwin/
Russia
Anglo American School of Moscow, www.glasnet.ru/~aas
Saudi Arabia
The Continental School S.A.I.S., www.prowork.com/continental
Singapore
Overseas Family School, www.afs.ac.sg
Singapore American School, www.sas.edu.sg
Tanglin Trust School, www.singnet.com.sg/~ttschool
Spain
American School of Madrid Foundation, www.netschool.com/pages/asm
International College of Spain, www.cuci.nl/~keulers/
The Baleares International School, www.ocea.es/bis/bis/htm
Sri Lanka
The Overseas School of Columbo, www.lanka.net/directory/osc/
Sweden
Sigtunaskolan Humanistiska Laroverket, www.sshl.se/
Switzerland
Aiglon College, www.aiglon.ch
Institut Le Rosey, www.qualischools.ch/english/rosey/htm
Institut Montana, Zugerberg, www.montana.ch
Leysin American School in Switzerland, www.localnet.org/users/las
The American Int'l School of Zurich, www.aisz.ch
The International School of Geneva, www.ecolint.ch
Taiwan
National Experimental High School, www.nehs.hc.edu.tw
Thailand
Ake Panya International School, www.akepanya.ac.th
New International School of Thailand, www.iteachnet.com/nist.html
Phuket International School, www.phuketschl.com
Tunisia
American Cooperative School of Tunisia, www.guilford.k12.nc.us/hp/tunis/home.html
Turkey
Istanbul International Community School, www.iics.k12.tr
The American Collegiate Institute, www.aci.edu.tr
U.A.E.
American Community School of Abu Dhabi, www.acs-abudhabi.com
The American School of Dubai, www.asdubai.org
The International School of Choueifat, www.sabis.com/school-network/
United Kingdom
American Community School, www.pncl.co.uk/am-com-schools
American School in London, www.asl.org
Int'l School of Aberdeen, www.isa.abdn.sch.uk
TASIS England American School, www.tasis.com/tasis/tasis-england.html
United States
French American International School, www.fais-ihs.org
The Awty International School, www.awty.org
United Nations International School, www.unis.org
Uruguay
Uruguayan American School, www.chasque.apc.org/amschool
Zambia
Lusaka International Community School, www.zamnet.zm/zamnet/education/lics/lics.html

INDEX